Some Sort of Epic Grandeur
THE LIFE OF F. SCOTT FITZGERALD

ALSO BY MATTHEW J. BRUCCOLI

Some Sort of Epic Grandeur
THE LIFE OF F. SCOTT FITZGERALD

MATTHEW J. BRUCCOLI

With a Genealogical Afterword by
Scottie Fitzgerald Smith

A Revised Edition

Carroll & Graf Publishers, Inc.
New York

First Carroll & Graf edition 1993

Carroll & Graf Publishers, Inc.
260 Fifth Avenue
New York, NY 1001

Library of Congress Cataloging-in-Publication Data is available.

ISBN: 0-88184-907-3

Cover photograph of F. Scott Fitgerald courtesy of Charles Scribner's Sons, an imprint of Macmillan Publishing Company.

Manufactured in the United States of America.

I am not a great man, but sometimes I think the impersonal and objective quality of my talent, and the sacrifices of it, in pieces, to preserve its essential value has some sort of epic grandeur.

—F. Scott Fitzgerald

To Scottie
For 9 October 1964

I am the last of the novelists for a long time now.

.   .   .   .

Show me a hero and I will write you a tragedy.

.   .   .   .

There never was a good biography of a good novelist. There couldn't be. He is too many people if he's any good.

.   .   .   .

Biography is the falsest of the arts. That is because there were no Keatzians before Keats, no Lincolnians before Lincoln.

.   .   .   .

I left my capacity for hoping on the little roads that led to Zelda's sanitarium.

.   .   .   .

The voices fainter and fainter – How is Zelda, how is Zelda – tell us – how is Zelda.

.   .   .   .

Genius is the ability to put into effect what is in your mind. There's no other definition of it.

.   .   .   .

I look out at it– and I think it is the most beautiful history in the world. It is the history of me and of my people. And if I came here yesterday like Sheilah I should still think so. It is the history of all aspiration – not just the American dream but the human dream and if I came at the end of it that too is a place in the line of pioneers.

.   .   .   .

Then I was drunk for many years, and then I died.

—From the *Notebooks*

CONTENTS

Contents

Contents

Contents

ILLUSTRATIONS

Illustrations

PREFACE
TO THE REVISED EDITION

When this biography was first published in 1981, my prefatory claim that its publication was justified by 'More facts' did not pass unnoticed. One practicing biographer protested that biography should not be limited by facts. A one-book biographer declared that too much evidence interferes with the free play of the biographer's insights. It is free because it has not been paid for by research; it may indeed become a form of play or game.

Facts are the only things a biographer can trust – and only after they have been verified. Insights are as good as the evidence that supports them. This second edition of *Some Sort of Epic Grandeur* provides still more facts.

Fitzgerald's work continues to attract buffs and serious readers. During the decade since the publication of the first edition of this biography, there have been three other biographies; two volumes of personal recollections; and a dozen books of literary criticism and collections of critical articles. The Cambridge University Press critical edition of Fitzgerald's collected works commenced publication in 1991. The eighteen facsimile volumes of Fitzgerald's manuscripts published in 1990-1991 provide the best evidence for literary study: the writer revising and rewriting in the process of attempting to express what is in his mind.

Scottie Fitzgerald died 18 June 1986. This is the truth: I could not and would not have done my Fitzgerald work without her. She provided material and connections, of course. And she made it all so much fun. The party is over.

M.J.B.
18 June 1991

PREFACE
TO THE FIRST EDITION

Many of us share Samuel Johnson's admission that 'the biographical part of literature . . . is what I love most,' because great writers perform the world's most precious and enduring work. But the popularization of the Fitzgerald myth has diminished his stature and cheapened his work. He is regarded by a certain kind of Twenties buff as having scribbled his masterpieces during the course of a lifelong bender. Given the kind of writer he was, it is proper to identify Fitzgerald with his material; but it is a distortion of the record to portray him as an uncritical reveler. There was always a judging process operating in him – combined, in his finest work, with a quality of aspiration. Zelda Fitzgerald observed after her husband's death: 'I do not know that a personality *can* be divorced from the times which evoke it . . . I feel that Scott's greatest contribution was the dramatization of a heart-broken + despairing era, giving it a new raison-d'etre in the sense of tragic courage with which he endowed it.'[1]

F. Scott Fitzgerald created his own legends. His life overshadows his work as he has become an archetypal figure – or a cluster of overlapping archetypes: the drunken writer, the ruined novelist, the spoiled genius, the personification of the Jazz Age, the sacrificial victim of the Depression. These

1. Notes are on pages 675-702

images were largely his own fault because he dramatized his success and failure. Loving attention, he embraced his symbolic roles. The glamour, the triumph, the euphoria, the heartbreak, and the tragedy of his life were genuine; but the most important thing is what he wrote. Everything else matters only to the extent that it explicates his work or clarifies his career. But it is impossible to dissociate a great writer from his work, and Fitzgerald was one of the most personal authors.

This volume is the third biography of Fitzgerald in English, in addition to shelves of reminiscences and critical studies. Its justification is that research has provided new evidence in the twenty years since the publication of Andrew Turnbull's *Scott Fitzgerald* (1962). I have corrected and augmented the record. When asked what is new in this biography, I reply, 'More facts.' My intention was to focus on Fitzgerald as writer by tracing the ontogeny of his major work while providing a detailed account of his career as a professional author.

My understanding of the responsibility of a biographer is that he should assemble a great many details in a usable way, relying heavily on the subject's own words. Even when Fitzgerald's testimony is less than totally reliable, it is his testimony and reveals how he saw himself or wanted to be regarded. His exaggerations have been corrected here, but mostly he was a truthful man – exceptionally so for a writer. Quotations from letters and manuscripts have been transcribed from the original documents. There are no silent emendations.

A biographer's first duty is to get things right. Accordingly, I have tried to rescue events from the myth-making process that encapsulates Fitzgerald. Readers who are familiar with the writings about Fitzgerald – which occasionally degenerate into the underworld of literary gossip – will find that well-known anecdotes are repeated here. The repetition is necessary because Fitzgerald has become the subject of what might be called defining anecdotes that seem to epitomize certain aspects of his character. Moreover, some of these standard vignettes require clarification or correction. The most widely repeated Fitzgerald anecdote is untrue: Ernest Hemingway did not tell him that the rich have more money when Fitzgerald remarked, 'The very rich are different from you and me.' Yet this apocryphal piece of lore has acquired the force of literary history.

I do not practice psychiatry. No doubt André Maurois was correct in decreeing that 'the need to express oneself in writing springs from a maladjustment to life, or from an inner conflict, which the adolescent (or grown man) cannot resolve in action.'[2] The maladjustment may account for the compulsion to write, but not for genius. There is no way to explain why the son of an unsuccessful manufacturer of wicker furniture wrote the best American prose.

Inevitably a Fitzgerald biography becomes a joint biography of F. Scott and Zelda Fitzgerald. She was the strongest influence on his life after 1919, and the conditions of their marriage shaped his career. Without Zelda he might or might not have been a better caretaker of his genius; but it is folly to assign blame to either partner. They conspired in a dangerous game for which only they knew the rules.

As its title indicates, this biography has a theme or bias: F. Scott Fitzgerald's life had 'some sort of epic grandeur.' He was a hero with many flaws, but a hero. His life was a quest for heroism. In a professional career of twenty years he wrote three of the best American novels (one of them unfinished) and a score of brilliant stories while afflicted with a host of troubles – many of his own making. He was honorable and generous. His words endure.

ACKNOWLEDGMENTS

My wife, Arlyn, has accepted her subordination to Fitzgerald for thirty-three years; she vetted two drafts of this biography and made many discouraging recommendations. I have neglected my children, who retaliated by taking my pencils.

Sometimes the clichés of acknowledgment rhetoric are accurate: William Jovanovich made it possible for me to undertake this work. Frazer Clark, my partner, provided support and many books. This volume was completed after the death of Vernon Sternberg, who would have improved it – as he improved my work-in-progress. Julian Muller of Harcourt Brace Jovanovich has many times proved himself my friend – as well as a shrewd editor. Alexander Clark, curator emeritus of the Princeton University Library Manuscript Department, has helped me in every possible way for twenty-six years. This biography could not have been written without the generous collaboration of the excellent people at the Princeton University Library: Richard M. Ludwig, Jean F. Preston, Ann Van Arsdale, Margarethe Fitzell, Charles E. Greene, Barbara Taylor, Mardel Pacheco, Wanda Randall, Agnes Sherman.

I am grateful to my colleagues and masters at the University of South Carolina, who have allowed me to do my work. George Geckle, chairman of the Department of English during the time I wrote the last drafts, provided me with all the help I dared ask for.

Meredith Walker not only typed three drafts of this book but improved it each time she touched it. I have relied on her editorial skills and sound judgment. Miss Walker's forbearance commands my admiration.

Judith S. Baughman assisted mightily in the preparation of this revised edition.

Lynn Strong is the best copy editor I have ever worked with.

These research assistants helped me: Jennifer Atkinson, Heather Barker, Linda Berry, John Clewis, Margaret Duggan, Glenda Fedricci, Cara White Irvin, Carol Johnston, Inge Kutt, Richard Layman, Karen Rood, Katherine Wade, Susan Walker.

These are some of the institutions that provided material: the Bodleian Library, Oxford University; the British Library; the John F. Kennedy Library; the Library of Congress; the Lilly Library, Indiana University; the New York Public Library; the Enoch Pratt Free Library; the United States Copyright Office; the University of Virginia Library; Yale University Library. The interlibrary loan and reference staff at the Thomas E. Cooper Library, University of South Carolina, is a marvel of patience and efficiency: Lori Finger, Harriet B. Oglesbee, Joyce C. Werner. Through the permission of Frances Scott Fitzgerald Smith access was granted to me by the Alan Mason Chesney Medical Archives of the Johns Hopkins Medical Institutions to study the medical records of her late parents which are on deposit at the Johns Hopkins Hospital. Nancy McCall, Assistant Archivist, provided crucial assistance. Dr William Ober, scholar-physician, spent hours studying Fitzgerald's medical records and explaining them to me.

The following are only some of the people who helped me during the years I have worked on Fitzgerald: Sally Taylor Abeles, Jo August, Dr. Benjamin Baker, Carlos Baker, Jeanne Bennett, Judge John Biggs, Jr., John Biggs III, Fredson Bowers, Mario Braggiotti, Joseph Bryan, Anthony Buttitta, William Cagle, Lawton Campbell, André Chamson, Duncan Chaplin, Theodore Chanler, James Charters, Robert Clark, Morrill Cody, Malcolm Cowley, James Dickey, Honoria

Acknowledgments

Murphy Donnelly, John Dos Passos, Charles Fenton, George Frazier, Donald Gallup, Arnold Gingrich, Sheilah Graham, Joseph L. Greenberg, John Guilds, Albert Hackett, Frances Goodrich Hackett, Marise Hamilton, Muriel Hamilton, Laura Guthrie Hearne, Mary Welsh Hemingway, Jay B. Hubbell, Norris Jackson, William Johnson, John S. Van E. Kohn, James Laughlin, Roger Lewis, Elizabeth Taylor Little, Harold Loeb, A.E. LeVot, Helen Hayes MacArthur, Margaret Finney MacPherson, Dr. Paul McHugh, Paul McLendon, Charles Mann, Elizabeth Manning, Alan Margolies, Alice Lee Meyers, Frances Mitchell, Dr. Harold Morgan, Gerald Murphy, Anne Ober, Isabelle Palmer, Ginevra King Pirie, Landon T. Raymond, Joan Redington, Frances Kroll Ring, Anthony Rota, Dr. Thomas Rowland, Waldo Salt, R.L. Samsell, Budd Schulberg, Charles Scribner III, Peter Shepherd, Dr. D. Loren Southern, Annabel Fitzgerald Sprague, Dr. Michael Sribnick, Donald Ogden Stewart, Robert Stocking, Allen Tate, Cecilia Taylor, Virginia Taylor, Willard Thorp, Courtney Vaughan, Henry Wenning, Alden Whitman, Edmund Wilson, John Cook Wyllie, Lois Moran Young.

My concern with F. Scott Fitzgerald began on 27 March 1949 when I heard a radio dramatization of 'The Diamond as Big as the Ritz.' Then I read *The Great Gatsby*, and my work was determined. My mother and father – who were certain that literature was a waste of time – extravagantly supported what they regarded as their only child's cruel derangement.

CHRONOLOGY

1853 Birth of Edward Fitzgerald at 'Glenmary' farm near Rockville in Montgomery County, Maryland.

1858 Birth of Anthony D. Sayre in Tuskegee, Alabama.

1860 Birth of Mary ('Mollie') McQuillan in St. Paul, Minnesota. Birth of Minnie Buckner Machen in Eddyville, Kentucky.

June 1884 Marriage of Anthony Sayre and Minnie Machen at 'Mineral Mount', near Eddyville, Kentucky.

13 February 1890 Marriage of Edward Fitzgerald and Mollie McQuillan in Washington, D.C.

24 September 1896 Birth of Francis Scott Key Fitzgerald at 481 Laurel Avenue, St. Paul.

April 1898 After failure of his St. Paul furniture factory, Edward Fitzgerald takes job as salesman with Procter & Gamble in Buffalo, New York.

24 July 1900 Birth of Zelda Sayre at South Street, Montgomery, Alabama.

January 1901 Fitzgerald family moves to Syracuse, New York.

July 1901 Birth of Annabel Fitzgerald.

September 1903 Fitzgerald family moves back to Buffalo.

1907 Sayre family moves to 6 Pleasant Avenue, Zelda's home until her marriage.

July 1908 Edward Fitzgerald loses his job and the Fitzgerald family returns to St. Paul. FSF enters St. Paul Academy in September.

1909 Judge Sayre of the City Court is appointed Associate Justice of the Supreme Court of Alabama.

October 1909 Publication of 'The Mystery of the Raymond Mortgage' in *St. Paul Academy Now & Then* – FSF's first appearance in print.

August 1911 FSF writes his first play, *The Girl from Lazy J*, in St. Paul.

September 1911 FSF enters Newman School, Hackensack, New Jersey.

August 1912 Production of *The Captured Shadow* in St. Paul.

November 1912 FSF meets Father Sigourney Fay and Shane Leslie.

August 1913 Production of *'Coward'* in St. Paul.

September 1913 FSF enters Princeton University with Class of 1917; meets Edmund Wilson '16 and John Peale Bishop '17.

August 1914 Production of *Assorted Spirits* in St. Paul.

Fall 1914 FSF contributes to *Princeton Tiger*.
Zelda enters Sidney Lanier High School.

December 1914 Production of *Fie! Fie! Fi-Fi!*, FSF's first Princeton Triangle Club show.

Christmas 1914 FSF meets Ginevra King in St. Paul.

April 1915 'Shadow Laurels,' FSF's first publication in *Nassau Literary Magazine*.

December 1915 FSF drops out of Princeton for remainder of junior year.
Production of *The Evil Eye* by Triangle Club.

September 1916 FSF returns to Princeton as member of Class of 1918.

December 1916 Production of *Safety First* by Triangle Club.

26 October 1917 FSF receives commission as infantry 2nd lieutenant.

20 November 1917 FSF reports to Fort Leavenworth, Kansas; begins novel 'The Romantic Egotist.'

February 1918 FSF reports to Camp Taylor, Louisville, Kentucky.

March 1918 FSF completes first draft of 'The Romantic Egotist' while on leave at Princeton; submits novel to Scribners.

April 1918 FSF transferred to Camp Gordon, Georgia.

May 1918 Zelda graduates from Sidney Lanier High School.

June 1918 FSF reports to Camp Sheridan near Montgomery, Alabama.

July 1918 FSF and Zelda meet at country club dance in Montgomery.

August 1918 Scribners declines 'The Romantic Egotist'; revised typescript rejected in October.

November 1918 FSF reports to Camp Mills, Long Island, to await embarkation; war ends before unit sent overseas.

December 1918 FSF returns to Camp Sheridan; becomes aide-de-camp to General J.A. Ryan.

February 1919 FSF discharged from army. Planning to marry Zelda, he goes to New York and works for the Barron Collier advertising agency; lives in room at 200 Claremont Avenue.

Spring 1919 FSF visits Montgomery in April, May and June as Zelda remains reluctant to commit herself to marriage. *The Smart Set* takes 'Babes in the Woods' – his first commercial story sale.

June 1919 Zelda breaks engagement.

July–August 1919 FSF quits advertising job and returns to St. Paul; rewrites novel while living with parents at 599 Summit Avenue.

16 September 1919 Maxwell Perkins of Scribners accepts *This Side of Paradise*.

November 1919 FSF becomes client of Harold Ober at Reynolds agency. First sale to *The Saturday Evening Post*: 'Head and Shoulders.'
FSF visits Zelda in Montgomery.

November 1919–February 1920 *The Smart Set* publishes 'The Debutante,' 'Porcelain and Pink,' 'Benediction,' and 'Dalyrimple Goes Wrong.'

Mid-January 1920 FSF lives in boarding house at 2900 Prytania Street in New Orleans, where he stays less than a month. Engagement to Zelda resumes during his visits to Montgomery.

March–May 1920 'Myra Meets His Family,' 'The Camel's Back,' 'Bernice Bobs Her Hair,' 'The Ice Palace,' and 'The Offshore Pirate' appear in *The Saturday Evening Post*.

26 March 1920 Publication of *This Side of Paradise*.

3 April 1920 Marriage of FSF and Zelda at rectory of St. Patrick's Cathedral in New York. Honeymoon at Biltmore Hotel.

May–September 1920 Fitzgeralds rent house at Westport, Connecticut.

July 1920 Publication of 'May Day' in *The Smart Set*.

Summer 1920 Fitzgeralds drive to Montgomery; return to Westport by mid-August.

10 September 1920 Publication of *Flappers and Philosophers*: FSF's first short-story collection.

October 1920–April 1921 Fitzgeralds take apartment at 38 West 59th Street, New York City.

May–July 1921 Fitzgeralds make first trip to Europe; sail to England then visit France and Italy. Return home and visit Montgomery.

August 1921 Fitzgeralds travel to St. Paul; rent house at Dellwood, White Bear Lake.

September 1921–March 1922 *The Beautiful and Damned* serialized in *Metropolitan Magazine*.

26 October 1921 Birth of daughter Scottie.

November 1921–June 1922 Fitzgeralds rent house at 646 Goodrich Avenue, St. Paul.

Summer 1922 Fitzgeralds move to White Bear Yacht Club.

4 March 1922 Publication of *The Beautiful and Damned*.

June 1922 Publication of 'The Diamond as Big as the Ritz' in *The Smart Set*

22 September 1922 Publication of *Tales of the Jazz Age*: FSF's second collection of short stories.

Mid-October 1922–April 1924 Fitzgeralds rent house at 6 Gateway Drive in Great Neck, Long Island. Friendship with Ring Lardner.

December 1922 Publication of 'Winter Dreams' in *Metropolitan Magazine*.

27 April 1923 Publication of *The Vegetable*.

November 1923 *The Vegetable* fails at tryout in Atlantic City, New Jersey.

Mid-April 1924 Fitzgeralds sail for France.

May 1924 Fitzgeralds visit Paris, then leave for Riviera; stop at Grimm's Park Hotel in Hyères and settle in June at Villa Marie, Valescure, St. Raphaël.

June 1924 Publication of 'Absolution' in *The American Mercury*.

Summer–Fall 1924 FSF writes *The Great Gatsby*. ZF's involvement with French aviator Edouard Jozan in July.

July 1924 Publication of " 'The Sensible Thing' " in *Liberty*.

Summer 1924 Fitzgeralds meet Gerald and Sara Murphy at Cap d'Antibes.

Winter 1924-25 Fitzgeralds stay at Hôtel des Princes, Rome, where FSF revises *The Great Gatsby*.

February 1925 Fitzgeralds travel to Capri; stay at Hotel Tiberio.

10 April 1925 Publication of *The Great Gatsby*.

Late April 1925 Fitzgeralds move to Paris; rent apartment at 14 rue de Tilsitt.

May 1925 FSF meets Ernest Hemingway in Dingo bar.

August 1925 Fitzgeralds leave Paris for month at Antibes.

January 1926 ZF takes 'cure' at Salies-de-Béarn.

January and February 1926 Publication of 'The Rich Boy' in *Redbook Magazine*.

February 1926 Play version of *The Great Gatsby*, by Owen Davis, produced on Broadway.

26 February 1926 Publication of *All the Sad Young Men:* FSF's third short-story collection.

Early March 1926 Fitzgeralds return to Riviera and rent Villa Paquita at Juan-les-Pins.

May 1926 Hemingways join Murphys and Fitzgeralds on Riviera. Fitzgeralds move to Villa St. Louis, Juan-les-Pins where they remain until end of 1926.

December 1926 Fitzgeralds return to America.

January 1927 Fitzgeralds go to Hollywood, to work on 'Lipstick' (unproduced) for United Artists. Meet Lois Moran.

March 1927–March 1928 Fitzgeralds rent 'Ellerslie,' near Wilmington, Delaware. ZF begins ballet lessons.

April 1928 Fitzgeralds return to Europe.

April–August 1928 Fitzgeralds rent apartment at 58 rue de Vaugirard, Paris.

April 1928 Publication of 'The Scandal Detectives' in *The Saturday Evening Post*: first of eight-story Basil Duke Lee series.

Mid-summer 1928 ZF begins ballet training with Lubov Egorova in Paris.

September 1928 Fitzgeralds return to America.

September 1928–March 1929 Fitzgeralds at 'Ellerslie.'

Winter 1928–March 1929 ZF begins writing series of short stories for *College Humor*.

March 1929 Publication of 'The Last of the Belles' in *The Saturday Evening Post*.

March 1929 Fitzgeralds return to Europe; travel from Genoa along Riviera, then to Paris.

June 1929 Fitzgeralds leave Paris for Riviera; rent Villa Fleur des Bois, Cannes.

October 1929 Fitzgeralds return by car to Paris by way of Provence; take apartment at 10 rue Pergolese.

February 1930 FSF and ZF travel to North Africa.

April 1930 ZF has first breakdown in Paris, enters Malmaison clinic outside Paris on 23 April, then Valmont clinic in Switzerland on 22 May.

Publication of 'First Blood' in *The Saturday Evening Post*: first of five-story Josephine Perry series.

5 June 1930 ZF enters Prangins clinic at Nyon, Switzerland.

Summer and Fall 1930 FSF lives in Switzerland.

Late January 1931 Death of Edward Fitzgerald, FSF returns alone to America to attend burial; reports to Sayres about ZF.

February 1931 Publication of 'Babylon Revisited' in *The Saturday Evening Post*.

July 1931 Fitzgeralds spend two weeks at Lake Annecy, France.

15 September 1931 ZF released from Prangins. Fitzgeralds return to America.

September 1931–Spring 1932 Fitzgeralds rent house at 819 Felder Avenue in Montgomery. FSF goes to Hollywood alone to work on *Red-Headed Woman* for Metro-Goldwyn-Mayer.

17 November 1931 Death of Judge Sayre.

February 1932 ZF suffers second breakdown; enters Phipps Psychiatric Clinic of Johns Hopkins Hospital in Baltimore.

March 1932 ZF completes first draft of her novel, *Save Me the Waltz*, while at Phipps Clinic.

20 May 1932–November 1933 FSF rents 'La Paix' at Towson outside Baltimore.

26 June 1932 ZF discharged from Phipps; joins family at 'La Paix.'

7 October 1932 Publication of *Save Me the Waltz*

26 June–1 July 1933 ZF's play, *Scandalabra*, produced by Vagabond Junior Players in Baltimore.

December 1933 FSF rents house at 1307 Park Avenue, Baltimore.

January–April 1934 Serialization of *Tender Is the Night* in *Scribner's Magazine*.

January 1934 ZF's third breakdown; enters Sheppard-Pratt Hospital outside Baltimore.

March 1934 ZF transferred to Craig House, Beacon, New York.

29 March–30 April 1934 ZF's art exhibition in New York.

12 April 1934 Publication of *Tender Is the Night*.

19 May 1934 ZF transferred back to Sheppard-Pratt Hospital.

February 1935 FSF at Oak Hall Hotel in Tryon, North Carolina.

20 March 1935 Publication of *Taps at Reveille*.

May 1935 FSF spends summer at Grove Park Inn, Asheville, North Carolina.

September 1935 FSF takes apartment at Cambridge Arms, Charles Street, Baltimore.

November 1935 FSF at Skyland Hotel in Hendersonville, North Carolina; begins writing 'The Crack-Up' essays.

8 April 1936 ZF enters Highland Hospital in Asheville.

July–December 1936 FSF returns to Grove Park Inn.

September 1936 Death of Mollie McQuillan Fitzgerald in Washington. Scottie enters Ethel Walker School in Connecticut.

January–June 1937 FSF at Oak Hall Hotel in Tryon.

July 1937 Deeply in debt, FSF goes to Hollywood for third time with six-month M-G-M contract at $1,000 a week. Lives at Garden of Allah on Sunset Boulevard; meets Sheilah Graham 14 July.

First week of September 1937 FSF visits ZF in Asheville; they spend four days in Charleston and Myrtle Beach, South Carolina.

September 1937–January 1938 FSF works on *Three Comrades* script, his only screen credit.

December 1937 M-G-M contract renewed for one year at $1,250 a week; FSF works on scripts for 'Infidelity,' *Marie Antoinette, The Women,* and *Madame Curie.*

End of March 1938 Fitzgeralds spend Easter at Virginia Beach, Virginia.

April 1938 FSF rents bungalow at Malibu Beach, California.

September 1938 Scottie enters Vassar College.

October 1938 FSF moves to cottage at 'Belly Acres,' Encino.

December 1938 M-G-M contract not renewed.

January 1939 FSF works briefly on *Gone with the Wind.*

February 1939 FSF travels to Dartmouth College with Budd Schulberg to work on *Winter Carnival;* fired for drinking.

March 1939–October 1940 FSF takes free-lance jobs at Paramount, Universal, Twentieth Century-Fox, Goldwyn and Columbia studios.

April 1939 Fitzgeralds travel to Cuba. FSF goes on bender; is hospitalized on return to New York.

July 1939 FSF breaks with Harold Ober.

October 1939 FSF begins work on *The Last Tycoon;* attempts to sell serial rights to *Collier's.*

January 1940 Publication of 'Pat Hobby's Christmas Wish' in *Esquire*, first of seventeen-story series.

c. 15 April 1940 ZF discharged from Highland Hospital; lives with her mother at 322 Sayre Street in Montgomery.

May 1940 FSF moves to 1403 North Laurel Avenue, Hollywood.

May–August 1940 FSF works on 'Cosmopolitan' ('Babylon Revisited') script.

21 December 1940 FSF dies of heart attack at Sheilah Graham's apartment, 1443 North Hayworth Avenue, Hollywood.

27 December 1940 FSF buried in Rockville Union Cemetery, Rockville, Maryland.

27 October 1941 Publication of *The Last Tycoon*.

August 1945 Publication of *The Crack-Up*.

September 1945 Publication of *The Portable F.Scott Fitzgerald*.

November 1947 ZF returns to Highland Hospital from Montgomery.

10 March 1948 ZF dies in fire at Highland Hospital, Asheville, N.C.

17 March 1948 ZF buried with FSF.

TAPS
AT
REVEILLE

[21 December 1940]

▓▓ *F. Scott Fitzgerald*, an unemployed screenwriter, spent
21 December 1940 with his companion, Hollywood
columnist Sheilah Graham, at 1443 North Hayworth Avenue
in Hollywood. After a heart attack some six weeks earlier he
had moved to her apartment from his apartment a block away
at 1403 North Laurel Avenue.

Fitzgerald slept late that Saturday morning. When Sheilah
brought him coffee, he sat up in bed and made notes for *The
Last Tycoon*, his novel-in-progress. Then he dressed in slacks
and a sweater and loafed while waiting for Dr. Clarence H.
Nelson, who was due in the afternoon with a portable
electrocardiograph.

Sheilah was sending Fitzgerald's nineteen-year-old daughter Scottie, a Vassar junior, her silver fox fur jacket and the
dress she had worn to the première of *The Westerner*.
Concerned about offending Scottie with hand-me-downs,
Sheilah asked Fitzgerald to help phrase the letter. He dictated
a joking message about the mortality rate of Scottie's
wardrobe, with the postscript: 'Your father has not been well,
but he's getting better now. He hasn't had a drink in over a
year.'[1]

Frances Kroll, Fitzgerald's secretary, brought the mail,
which included the 9 December issue of *The Princeton Alumni
Weekly*. Fitzgerald ate a late sandwich lunch and read the
newspapers, predicting that the German-Italian pact would
force America into the war. He said he'd like to cover the war
from Europe after his novel was completed, adding, 'Ernest
won't have that field all to himself, then.'[2] After three and a
half years in Hollywood, Fitzgerald felt a rueful desire to
reestablish himself as Hemingway's equal.

Fitzgerald wanted to go to nearby Schwab's drugstore on

3

Sunset Boulevard for ice cream. As a dried-out alcoholic, he craved sweets. Sheilah reminded him that he might miss the doctor and gave him a chocolate bar, which he ate in the living room while making notes in *The Princeton Alumni Weekly* on the 1941 football prospects. Sheilah listened to Beethoven's *Eroica* symphony on the phonograph while reading a book on the history of music Fitzgerald had assigned in his program for educating her. She saw him start out of his chair, clutch the mantelpiece, and fall to the floor. After trying to force brandy through his clenched teeth, she ran for the manager of the building, Harry Culver, who said when he saw Fitzgerald, 'I'm afraid he's dead.' Sheilah phoned the fire department and the police to bring oxygen equipment.

F. Scott Fitzgerald was pronounced dead of a coronary occlusion at 5:15 P.M. by Dr. Nelson. He had lived forty-four years, two months, and twenty-seven days. The body was removed to the Pierce Brothers Mortuary, 720 West Washington Boulevard, in Los Angeles.

Sheilah phoned Harold Ober, Fitzgerald's former agent in Scarsdale, New York, where Scottie Fitzgerald was spending part of her Christmas vacation. Ober called Fitzgerald's wife, Zelda, in Montgomery, Alabama. During their courtship she had written Fitzgerald, 'We will die together – I know –'[3] F. Scott Fitzgerald died in the apartment of his last love while Zelda Sayre Fitzgerald was a discharged mental patient 3,000 miles away in the Southern city where their love story had begun in 1918. Their love was one of a century, he had said.[4]

The newspapers gave Fitzgerald's death prominent treatment. His obituaries combined nostalgia with a patronizing tone, as in *The New York Times*.

> F. Scott Fitzgerald, novelist, short story writer and scenarist, died at his Hollywood home yesterday. His age was 44. He suffered a heart attack three weeks ago.

———

[21 December 1940]

Epitomized 'Sad Young Men'

Mr. Fitzgerald in his life and writings epitomized 'all the sad young men' of the post-war generation. With the skill of a reporter and ability of an artist he captured the essence of a period when flappers and gin and 'the beautiful and the damned' were the symbols of the carefree madness of an age.

Roughly, his own career began and ended with the Nineteen Twenties. 'This Side of Paradise,' his first book, was published in the first year of that decade of skyscrapers and short skirts. Only six others came between it and his last, which, not without irony, he called 'Taps at Reveille.' That was published in 1935. Since then a few short stories, the script of a moving picture or two, were all that came from his typewriter. The promise of his brilliant career was never fulfilled.

The best of his books, the critics said, was 'The Great Gatsby.' When it was published in 1925 this ironic tale of life on Long Island at a time when gin was the national drink and sex the national obsession (according to the exponents of Mr. Fitzgerald's school of writers), it received critical acclaim. In it Mr. Fitzgerald was at his best, which was, according to John Chamberlain, his 'ability to catch * * * the flavor of a period, the fragrance of a night, a snatch of old song, in a phrase.'

Symbol of 'Jazz Era'

This same ability was shown in his first book and its hero, Amory Blaine, became as much a symbol of Mr. Fitzgerald's own generation as, two years later, Sinclair Lewis's Babbitt was to become a symbol of another facet of American culture. All his other books and many of his short stories (notably 'The Beautiful and the Damned') had this same quality.

Francis Scott Key Fitzgerald (he was named after the author of the National Anthem, a distant relative of his mother's) was a stocky, good-looking young man with blond hair and blue eyes who might have stepped from the gay pages of one of his own novels. He was born Sept. 24, 1896 at St. Paul, Minn., the son of Edward and Mary McQuillan Fitzgerald.

At the Newman School, in Lakewood, N.J., where he was sent, young Fitzgerald paid more attention to extra-curricular activities than to his studies. When he entered Princeton in 1913 he had already decided upon a career as a writer of musical comedies. He spent most of his first year writing an operetta for

5

the Triangle Club and consequently 'flunked' in several subjects. He had to spend the Summer studying. In his sophomore year he was a 'chorus girl' in his own show.

War came along in 1917 and Fitzgerald quit Princeton to join the Army. He served as a second lieutenant and then as a first lieutenant in the Forty-fifth and Sixty-seventh Infantry Regiments and then as aide de camp to Brig. Gen. J.A. Ryan.

Wrote Novel in Club

Every Saturday he would hurry over to the Officers' Club and there 'in a room full of smoke, conversation and rattling newspapers' he wrote a 120,000-word novel on the consecutive week-ends of three months. He called it 'The Romantic Egotist.' The publisher to whom he submitted it said it was the most original manuscript he had seen for years – but he wouldn't publish it.

After the war he begged the seven city editors of the seven newspapers in New York to give him a job. Each turned him down. He went to work for the Barron Collier advertising agency, where he penned the slogan for a Muscatine, Iowa, laundry:

'We keep you clean in Muscatine.'

This got him a raise, but his heart was not in writing cards for street cars. He spent all his spare time writing satires, only one of which he sold – for $30. He then abandoned New York in disgust and went back to St. Paul, where he wrote 'This Side of Paradise.' Its flash and tempo and its characters, who, in the estimation of Gertrude Stein, created for the general public 'the new generation,' made it an immediate success.

At the same time he married Miss Zelda Sayre of Montgomery, Ala., who has been called more than once 'the brilliant counterpart of the heroines of his novels.' Their only child, Frances Scott Fitzgerald, was born in 1921.

His next two books were collections of short stories: 'Flappers and Philosophers' (1920) and 'Tales of the Jazz Age' (1922). In 1923 he published a satirical play, 'The Vegetable; or, From President to Postman,' and then for the next two years he worked on 'The Great Gatsby.' He had gathered material for it while living on Long Island after the war, and all its characters were taken compositely from life. He wrote most of it in Rome or on the Riviera, where he also wrote his most successful short stories. These, in 1926, were gathered under the title 'All the Sad Young Men.'

Only two other books were to follow: 'Tender Is The Night' (1934) and 'Taps at Reveille' (1935). After that, for several years, he lived near Baltimore, Md., where he suffered a depression of spirit which kept him from writing. He made several efforts to write but failed, and in an autobiographical article in Esquire likened himself to a 'cracked plate.'

'Sometimes, though,' he wrote, 'the cracked plate has to be retained in the pantry, has to be kept in service as a household necessity. It can never be warmed on the stove nor shuffled with the other plates in the dishpan; it will not be brought out for company but it will do to hold crackers late at night or to go into the ice-box with the left overs.'*5

The *Times* and the *New York Herald Tribune* accompanied their obituaries with editorials that assessed Fitzgerald as a failed writer. Both papers identified him with the alcoholic 'lost generation,' and the *Times* offered the diagnosis that he had been unable to adjust to the changes after the Twenties. *The New Yorker* protested the condescending obituaries in the 4 January 1941 issue; but even this tribute regarded Fitzgerald as a ruined man: 'The desperate knowledge that it was much too late, that there was nothing to come that would be more than a parody of what had gone before, must have been continually in his mind the last few years.' Referring to the last sentence of *Tender Is the Night*, the eulogy ended with the admission that at forty-four Fitzgerald had outlived his fame: 'In a way, we are glad he died when he did and that he was spared so many smaller towns, much further from Geneva.'6

There was agreement that F. Scott Fitzgerald was an exemplary and monitory figure – that he epitomized his generation, that he had not fulfilled his promise, that his

---

* There are errors in this obituary: the Francis Scott Key connection was on his father's side; *The Beautiful and Damned* was a novel, not a short story; the Newman School was in Hackensack, New Jersey, when Fitzgerald was a student there.

Taps at Reveille*

history provided a warning. It would have seemed absurd in 1940 to suggest that his elegy had been written in 1821 when Shelley mourned Keats – Fitzgerald's favorite poet – in *Adonaïs:*

> . . . till the Future dares
> Forget the Past, his fate and fame shall be
> An echo and a light unto eternity!

None of the obituaries anticipated that Fitzgerald would be resurrected like Adonis, the beautiful youth adored by the goddess of love.

THE
ROMANTIC
EGOTIST

[1896–1913]

1

Backgrounds and Childhood

[1896–1908]

Philip F. McQuillan was an exemplar of the American Dream that his grandson F. Scott Fitzgerald would respond to so complexly in his fiction. Born in County Fermanagh, Ireland, he moved in 1857 from Illinois to St. Paul, Minnesota, where he worked as a bookkeeper. Two years later, at twenty-five, he opened his own small business 'in the general line.' In 1860 he married Louisa Allen, the daughter of an Irish immigrant carpenter. By 1862 he was a grocery wholesaler. Prospering with the post-Civil War expansion of the territory, McQuillan became one of the most substantial businessmen in St. Paul and a benefactor of the Catholic Church as McQuillan, Beaupre & Co. grew to two million dollars a year in billings. His home was an impressive three-story Victorian structure with a cupola, and he owned the building at Third and Wabash streets known as the McQuillan Block. When he died in 1877 at forty-three of Bright's disease complicated by tuberculosis, McQuillan left the then-considerable estate of $266,289.49.[1] There were five surviving children; the eldest was Mary (Mollie), born in 1860. Her father's success provided Mollie with an education at the Visitation Convent in St. Paul and Manhattanville in

11

New York; and she went to Europe four times.

Almost nothing is known about Scott's paternal grandfather, Michael Fitzgerald, who may have kept a general store in Maryland. He married Cecilia Ashton Scott of 'Glenmary,' Rockville, Maryland, and died in 1855 when their son Edward was two years old. Cecilia's family could be traced back to the seventeenth century in Maryland – to the first Scotts, Keys, Ridgelys, and Dorseys. The Scotts' sympathies were Southern: Mary Surratt, Edward's first cousin, was hanged for conspiracy in Lincoln's assassination, and as a boy Edward guided Confederate spies during the Civil War. Edward attended Georgetown College* and then went west to seek his fortune.

Mollie McQuillan Fitzgerald and her son

*Edward Fitzgerald was enrolled at Georgetown in 1871 as a member of the Class of 1875 but did not graduate.

Edward Fitzgerald and Mollie McQuillan probably met in St. Paul. They were married on 12 February 1890 in Washington, D.C., where Mollie's mother had a house at 1815 N Street.[2] That Mollie was married in Washington may indicate something about the McQuillans' uncertain social position in St. Paul. Her father had been a respected figure in the city, and there was little anti-Catholic bias since the local aristocrats were descended from the early French Catholic settlers; but the Irish were regarded as common, a step above the Swedes. However, Governor Merriam of Minnesota attended the wedding reception.

At twenty-nine Mollie was approaching spinsterhood. The only one of the three McQuillan daughters to marry, she was not beautiful and seems to have been considered a bit eccentric. Thirty-seven-year-old Edward was a handsome, dapper man with excellent Southern manners but without much force of character; he was uncomfortable among the ambitious men of the Midwest. The couple honeymooned in France and Italy. On their first day in Paris, when Edward tried to hurry his bride out of the hotel so they could see the city, Mollie said, 'But I've already seen Paris.' This remark became a family anecdote relished by her son Scott.

By 1893 Edward Fitzgerald was listed in the St. Paul directories as president of the American Rattan and Willow Works, furniture manufacturers at 55 and 57 East Third Street. The business did not prosper. In 1894 he was in financial trouble, explaining to his brother John that he was 'not in a position' to send him a Christmas remembrance.[3]

Edward and Mollie had two daughters who died in 1896 at the ages of one and three. Their only son was born at 3:30 P.M. on 24 September 1896 at 481 Laurel Avenue in a building known as the San Mateo Flats in the Summit Avenue neighborhood of St. Paul. Forty years later Fitzgerald wrote: 'Well, three months before I was born my mother lost her other two children and I think that came first of all though I don't know how it worked exactly. I think I started then to be a writer.'[4]

13

Victoria was on the throne of the British Empire. Grover Cleveland was in the White House, and William McKinley and William Jennings Bryan were campaigning for the Presidency. The year 1896 was the birth date of Benny Leonard, Legs

The birthplace of F. Scott Fitzgerald: 481 Laurel Avenue, St. Paul, Minnesota

Diamond, James Doolittle, Rogers Hornsby, Lillian Gish, Buster Keaton, Philip Barry, John Dos Passos, and Robert E. Sherwood. The first edition of Sarah Orne Jewett's *The Country of the Pointed Firs* was published that year, as was the first trade edition of Stephen Crane's *Maggie: A Girl of the*

Fitzgerald in Buffalo, New York, c. 1899

Streets. The week of Fitzgerald's birth Joseph Conrad's *Outcast of the Islands* was published in America; Princeton University announced plans for its sesquicentennial celebration; Baltimore philanthropist Enoch Pratt left most of his fortune to the Sheppard-Pratt hospital for the insane.

The boy was named Francis Scott Key Fitzgerald, a choice that indicates something about his parents' ambitions for their son. In hard fact, the name was something of an imposture, implying a closer connection than existed: Scott Fitzgerald – he was never called Francis or Frank – and Francis Scott Key were second cousins, three times removed. Philip Key, founder of the Maryland family and Francis Scott Key's great-grandfather, was Scott's great-great-great-great-grandfather. Scott was baptized on 6 October by Father John T. Harrison at the Cathedral of St. Paul. His first credited word was 'up' at ten months. Despite his hefty size at birth – ten pounds, six ounces – the baby was subject to colds and chest problems, which caused his mother to worry whether she would lose him, too.

Fitzgerald later described his mother as 'half insane with pathological nervous worry.'[5] One of the causes for her anxiety was her husband's business career. His son later became convinced that Edward Fitzgerald had never recovered from the Civil War and that its disappointments had sapped his ambition. The American Rattan and Willow Works failed in 1898, and Edward took a job as a wholesale grocery salesman with Procter & Gamble in Buffalo, New York. The Fitzgerald household moved regularly. In Buffalo they first lived at the Lennox, an apartment hotel, then in 1899 rented a flat at Summer Street and Elmwood Avenue. The family's standard of living was not limited to Edward's earnings; Mollie's money supplemented his salary and provided her son with the advantages of the upper middle class. Scott was treated to frequent trips with his mother.

Mollie spoiled Scott. Sent to nursery school in Buffalo in 1900, he cried so vociferously that he was withdrawn after the first morning. Edward tried to compensate for Mollie's

Edward Fitzgerald with his son Scott

indulgence by teaching his son standards of conduct from his Southern background. Scott grew up listening to his father's stories of the war and the lost South: ' . . . so many legends of my family went west with father, memories of names that go back before Braddock's disaster, such as Caleb Godwin of Hockley-in-ye-Hole, or Philip Key of Tudor Hall, or Pleasance Ridgeley . . .'[6]

A third daughter, born in 1900, lived only an hour. In 1901 Edward was transferred by Procter & Gamble to Syracuse, New York, where Scott's sister Annabel was born in July. Fitzgerald later noted in his *Ledger* that his 'first certain memory is the sight of her howling on a bed.'* The family moved in Syracuse to apartments on James Street and on East Willow Street. In September 1902 Scott was enrolled in Miss Goodyear's School, where he made an impression by working out the spelling C-A-T with a girl pupil. Syracuse playmates recalled that Scott's histrionic instincts found an outlet in declaiming, 'Friends, Romans, and countrymen . . . ' from the back of a grocery wagon.

A memorable event of 1903 was the trip to 'Randolph,' the home of Edward's sister Eliza Delihant in Montgomery County, Maryland, where Scott was a ribbon-holder at the wedding of her daughter Cecilia. He much preferred his Maryland relatives to those in Minnesota and retained a lifelong affection for his Cousin Ceci, who was some

---

* At the beginning of his writing career, Fitzgerald acquired a 9½" × 14½" business ledger in which he methodically recorded his professional and personal activities. He maintained this record through 1936, when he moved to California. The *Ledger* is the best source for the biographical and bibliographical facts about Fitzgerald, and there is nothing like it for any other American author. It is divided into five sections: 'Record of Published Fiction' [16 columns giving the publication history of each work], 'Money earned by Writing Since Leaving Army,' 'Published Miscelani (including movies) for which I was Paid,' 'Zelda's Earnings,' 'Outline Chart of my Life' [a month-by-month chronology beginning with the day of his birth, partly in the third person]. Fitzgerald probably began keeping his *Ledger* late in 1919 or early in 1920, but he may have started it in 1922 when he wrote his agent that he was 'getting up a record of all my work.' A facsimile of *F. Scott Fitzgerald's Ledger* has been published (Washington: Bruccoli Clark/NCR Microcard Books, 1972).

seventeen years older than he. Scott respected his Aunt Eliza for trying to provide him with discipline; and Ceci's brother Thomas Delihant, a Jesuit, was for a time one of his heroes.

Fitzgerald in Syracuse, New York, 1902

Both Edward and Mollie were practicing Catholics, though Mollie was more devout than her husband. Scott was raised in the Church and experienced fluctuating periods of piety when a particular religious figure or an aspect of ritual appealed to his imagination. But literature was a stronger influence. He acquired his first taste for poetry from his

19

father, who read Poe and Byron to him. Scott became an eclectic reader and would try to imitate the stories that impressed him. He was a loyal subscriber to the *St. Nicholas*, a popular children's magazine published by Charles Scribner's Sons, which he preferred to the competing *Youth's Companion*.

Fitzgerald later wrote in 'The Romantic Egotist,' his unpublished first novel, about the impression his reading made on him at this time:

> First there was a book that was I think one of the big sensations of my life. It was nothing but a nursery book, but it filled me with the saddest and most yearning emotion. I have never been able to trace it since. It was about a fight that the large animals, like the elephant, had with the small animals, like the fox. The small animals won the first battle; but the elephants and lions and tigers finally overcame them. The author was prejudiced in favor of the large animals, but my sentiment was all with the small ones. I wonder if even then I had a sense of the wearing-down power of big, respectable people. I can almost weep now when I think of that poor fox, the leader – the fox has somehow typified innocence to me ever since.[7]

This story provided Scott with a personal mythology that he would try to apply to his childhood activities. Although he was a small boy, he competed for athletic recognition because sports were a way to distinction or even power among his friends.

In 1903 Edward was transferred back to Buffalo, where the family took an apartment at 29 Irving Place. Scott attended school at Holy Angels Convent – 'under the arrangement that he need go only half a day and was allowed to choose which half '[8] – and 'fell under the spell' of Father Michael Fallon, a prominent local preacher.

Samuel Johnson is supposed to have been loved by his schoolmates for his proficiency in Latin, but intelligence and cleverness could not inspire the admiration Scott craved from his contemporaries. More than popularity, he wanted leadership – which made him boastful and bossy. Like many boys with exceptional minds, he found it difficult to tolerate the circumstance that others were not ready to acknowledge his superiority. In 1905 his desire for leadership was complicated by his interest in girls when he entered Mr. Van Arnum's dancing class at the Century Club in Buffalo. Scott was a handsome boy, with blond hair and eyes that were variously described as green, blue, or gray. He projected an intensity that made people notice him, and he catches the eye in boyhood group photos. He was clothes-conscious and something of a dandy – at seven he carried a cane when he went with his father to have their shoes shined on Sunday mornings. Yet with girls, too, he found that boys he considered to be his obvious inferiors were more popular than he was.

In the fall of 1905 the family moved to 71 Highland Avenue and Scott transferred from Holy Angels to Miss Narden's, a private Catholic school in Buffalo. A suspicion that he was not the son of his parents, that he was a foundling of royal lineage, developed when he was nine. He imagined that he had been placed on the Fitzgerald doorstep wrapped in a blanket with the Stuart coat of arms – a fantasy that may have been fueled by a growing recognition of his father's shortcomings. In his *Ledger* Fitzgerald noted for August 1905: 'His father used to drink too much and then play baseball in the back yard.' There is no hard evidence that Edward Fitzgerald was an alcoholic, though he is known to have gone on an occasional 'spree.' Whether his drinking contributed to his unprosperous business career cannot be determined.

Scott's interest in history was initiated by his father's Civil War stories, which made him a strong Confederate sympathizer. As soon as he could, he read *Scottish Chiefs*, *Ivanhoe*, and the Henty books, from which he developed his historical biases. He acquired his Henty library by earning twenty-five cents a day from his Aunt Clara McQuillan for eating a raw egg every day during a vacation in the Catskill Mountains.

At the age of ten Scott achieved his first recognition as a writer with a school essay on George Washington and Ignatius

21

Loyola. He also began writing a history of America and attempted a detective story about a necklace hidden under a trapdoor. None of these was preserved. Like most successful authors, Scott found as a boy that writing came more easily to him than to his friends. It provided a road to the admiration he wanted as well as a substitute for action since he could make life behave on paper. His interests became increasingly literary; he made up plays based on the American Revolution, read works of historical fiction for boys – *The Young Kentuckian* series, *Washington in the West, Riding wih Morgan* – and attended the theater where he was delighted by E.H. Sothern's performance as Lord Dundreary in *Our American Cousin*. He was also becoming a precocious social observer and began keeping a 'character book' in which he recorded his impressions of his playmates. His ability with language impressed his Highland Avenue friend, Edwin Benson. Fitzgerald responded to the watch Benson received for Christmas 1906: 'That's great, Ed. It's steam wind, fourteen carots, and Swiss cheese movement.'[9]

One piece of writer's equipment he was polishing was his memory for detail. Most ten-year-olds observe little and remember less. The born writer is a born retainer. Some twelve years later Fitzgerald recalled his 1907 summer camp experience in his *Ledger*:

> He went to Camp Chatham at Orillea Ontario, where he swam and fished and cleaned and ate fish and canoed and rowed and caught behind the bat and was desperately unpopular and went in paper chases and running contests and was always just edged out by Tom Penny. He remembers boys named Whitehouse, Alden, Penny, Block, Blair and one awful baby. He remembers 'Pa' Upham singing 'The Cat Came Back,' and a sawdust road and a camera and making blueprints and the camp library and 'Blow ye winds hiegh-oh' and tournaments with padded spears in canoes and Pa Upham's Cornell stroke.

One of his earliest surviving letters was written from Orillia:

> Dear Mother, I received your letter this morning and though I would like very much to have you up here I dont think you

would like it as you know no one hear except Mrs. Upton and she is busy most of the time I dont think you would like the accomadations as it is only a small town and no good hotels. There are some very nise boarding houses but about the only fare is lamb and beef. Please send me a dollar becaus there are a lot of little odds and ends i need. I will spend it causialy. All the other boys have pocket money besides their regular allowence.

Your loving son
Scott Fitzgerald[10]

About this time he told a lie in confession, 'saying in a shocked voice to the priest "Oh *no*, I *never* tell a lie." '[11] The dramatic opportunity was too good to waste. Fitzgerald wrote in 'Absolution' (1924) about a boy who also lies in confession that God 'must have understood that Rudolph had done it to make things finer in the confessional, brightening up the dinginess of his admissions by saying a thing radiant and proud. At the moment when he had affirmed immaculate honor a silver pennon had flapped out into the breeze somewhere and there had been the crunch of leather and the shine of silver spurs and a troop of horsemen waiting for dawn on a low green hill.'[12]

The most dramatic family crisis in young Scott's life came in March 1908 when his father lost his job with Procter & Gamble. Eleven-year-old Scott overheard his mother talk about it on the phone and returned the quarter she had given him to go swimming, because he was sure the family would have to go to the poorhouse. When his father came home that day, Scott tried to make him feel important by asking him who would be the next president.

Edward Fitzgerald was fifty-five when he lost his salesman's job. His son remarked twenty-eight years later: 'That morning he had gone out a comparatively young man, a man full of strength, full of confidence. He came home that evening, an old man, a completely broken man. He had lost his essential drive, his immaculateness of purpose. He was a failure the rest of his days.'[13]

2

A Summit Avenue Boyhood

[1908–1911]

The Fitzgeralds returned to St. Paul in the summer of 1908, when Scott was almost twelve. Scott and Annabel moved in with their Grandmother McQuillan at 294 Laurel Avenue; their parents lived with a friend, Dr. John Fulton, a few blocks away on Summit Avenue. When Louisa McQuillan went abroad in April 1909, the family was reunited at her apartment until they took a house at 514 Holly Avenue in September. Thereafter the Fitzgeralds moved almost annually, in the Summit Avenue section.

The temporary separation of the Fitzgerald family may have been dictated by financial problems. In St. Paul, Edward unprosperously operated as a grocery salesman from his McQuillan brother-in-law's real-estate office. At this time Scott became familiar with his mother's refrain: 'If it weren't for your Grandfather McQuillan, where would we be now?' Mollie was not a domineering personality, however, and there does not seem to have been unusual discord in the Fitzgerald household. As she became reconciled to her husband's lack of business acumen, her hopes for her bright and handsome son increased. Although she was not strong or

24

ambitious enough to direct Scott's life, she spoiled him and contributed to his sense of uniqueness. But she did not encourage his literary ambitions, hoping that he would become a successful businessman. Her opposition to Scott's literary ambitions may have prompted her destruction of his juvenilia: '. . . my mother did me the disservice of throwing away all but two of my very young efforts – way back at twelve and thirteen, and later I found that the surviving fragments had more quality than some of the stuff written in the tightened-up days of seven or eight years later.'[14] As a young man Edward Fitzgerald had collaborated on an unpublished novel, and he praised Scott's literary efforts; but he seems to have wanted his son to become an army officer. There is little documentation for young Scott's relationship with his parents. Nearly all of their correspondence has been lost, and Scott rarely spoke about them. His sister Annabel had no vivid memories of them, either; it is as if they scarcely existed.

The amount of Mollie's capital is unknown, but there were increments as pieces of family property were sold. After the death of Louisa McQuillan in 1913, Mollie's income of five or six thousand dollars a year afforded the Fitzgeralds a comfortable life in the Summit Avenue area.* Summit Avenue – now regarded as the best-preserved Victorian residential boulevard in America – runs west from the Cathedral of St. Paul four and a half miles to the Mississippi River. The most impressive residence on the street was the mansion of

---

* It is impossible to convert the purchasing power of pre-World War I dollars to 1991 dollars. The usual computation is that the dollar's buying power was six or seven times what it is now – in which case Mollie Fitzgerald's income would be worth between about $30,000 and $42,000. But no conversion factor can accommodate the availability of cheap servants and low taxes. In 1913 the income tax on $100,000 was $2,390.

There is a great deal about finances in this biography. Fitzgerald struggled with debts during his twenty years as a professional author, although he was one of the highest-paid magazine writers of his time. The $4,000 per story that *The Saturday Evening Post* paid him in 1929 was perhaps the equivalent of $20,000 now. Fitzgerald's admission that he could not live on $36,000 a year seemed almost incredible in 1924, when two-thirds of Americans earned less than $1,500 a year.

railroad tycoon James J. Hill at No. 240, which provided an icon for the American success story. Summit was the best street in St. Paul, while 'Summit Avenue' designated the twelve-square-block neighborhood at the eastern end of Summit above downtown St. Paul. Here the Fitzgeralds lived in apartments or rented houses, a source of chagrin for Scott.

In a neighborhood of imposing houses known by their owners' names, Scott was keenly aware of his father's failure. He was Mollie McQuillan's boy, not Edward Fitzgerald's son. He played with the children of the well-to-do – E. L. Hersey the lumberman and Charles W. Ames of the West Publishing Company and C. Milton Griggs the wholesaler – but he felt that he was an outsider. Moreover, he was embarrassed by his mother, who dressed carelessly and sometimes seemed mildly confused. When Mollie died in 1936, Fitzgerald told his sister Annabel, 'Mother and I never had anything in common except a relentless stubborn quality, but when I saw all this it turned me inside out realizing how unhappy her temperament made her. . . .'[15] Indifferent to society, Mollie spent much of her time reading sentimental and religious books. (Poets Alice and Phoebe Cary were among her favorite authors.) There were few Catholics among Scott's playmates; he later remarked that his friends thought Catholics secretly drilled in their churches to overthrow the government.

His sense of differentness in St. Paul sharpened his skills as a social observer and shaped his lifelong self-consciousness. In 1933 he analyzed his social insecurity in a letter to John O'Hara, attributing it to the clash between his McQuillan and his Key-Scott blood:

> I am half black Irish and half old American stock with the usual exaggerated ancestral pretensions. The black Irish half of the family had the money and looked down upon the Maryland side of the family who had, and really had, that certain series of reticences and obligations that go under the poor old shattered word 'breeding' (modern form 'inhibitions') So being born in that atmosphere of crack, wise crack and countercrack I developed a two cylinder inferiority complex.

So if I were elected King of Scotland tomorrow after graduating from Eton, Magdelene the Guards with an embryonic history which tied me to the Plantagonets, I would still be a *parvenue.* I spent my youth in alternately crawling in front of the kitchen maids and insulting the great.

I suppose this is just a confession of being a Gael though I have known many Irish who have not been afflicted by this intense social self consciousness. If you are interested in colleges, a typical gesture on my part would have been, for being at Princeton and belonging to one of its snootiest clubs, I would be capable of going to Podunk on a visit and being absolutely booed and overawed by its social system, not from timidity but simply because of an inner necessity of starting my life and my self justification over again at scratch in whatever new environment I may be thrown.[16]

In September 1908 Scott entered the St. Paul Academy, a nonsectarian private school for boys at 25 North Dale Street, ten blocks from his grandmother's apartment. Here he resumed his struggle for recognition, playing end for the football second team and pitching for second and third-team baseball. (He was left-handed in everything except writing.) He was also enrolled in Professor Baker's dancing class at Ramaley Hall on Grand Avenue, the proper meeting place for the children of good families. Quickly labeled a showoff, he endured the humiliation of seeing the school paper, the *St. Paul Academy Now and Then*, print in 1909: 'If anybody can poison Scotty or stop his mouth in some way, the school at large and myself will be obliged.'[17]

The outsider was not a loner who withdrew into his sense of uniqueness. Scott's drive for recognition required an audience and admiring companions. Despite his boasting and officiousness, he made friends he treasured all his life – including Richard (Tubby) Washington, Norris Jackson, Gustave (Bobby) Schurmeier, Reuben Warner, Benjamin Griggs, Cecil Read, Ted and Betty Ames, Sidney Stronge, Marie Hersey, Katherine Ordway, Katherine Tighe, Elisabeth Dean, Margaret Armstrong, Ardietta Ford, Paul

27

Ballion, Bob Clark and Alida Bigelow. (Some of these Summit Avenue friends later provided models for the characters in the Basil Duke Lee stories about his adolescence: Margaret Armstrong became Imogene Bissell; Marie Hersey became Margaret Torrence; Cecil Read became Ripley Buckner; Paul Ballion became Bill Kemp.) His playmates' mothers were favorably impressed by his good manners. The Read house at 449 Portland Avenue was a favorite meeting place, and Scott organized secret clubs in its attic ballroom; he also visited the Reads' summer home at White Bear Lake outside St. Paul. The Ames's yard at 501 Grand Hill, with its three-story tree house, was the neighborhood rendezvous. Twenty years later Fitzgerald recalled the Ames's yard in 'The Scandal Detectives' (1928) as 'one of those predestined places where young people gather in the afternoon':

> It had many advantages. It was large, open to other yards on both sides, and it could be entered upon skates or bicycles from the street. It contained an old seesaw, a swing and a pair of flying rings; but it had been a rendezvous before these were put up, for it had a child's quality – the thing that makes young people huddle inextricably on uncomfortable steps and desert the houses of their friends to herd on the obscure premises of 'people nobody knows.' The Whartons' yard had long been a happy compromise; there were deep shadows there all day long and ever something vague in bloom, and patient dogs around, and brown spots worn bare by countless circling wheels and dragging feet.[18]

The Summit neighborhood children had an active but supervised social life. A regular winter entertainment was the bob party, when children were taken by horse-drawn wagons or sleds to the Town and Country Club for dancing. Scott avoided winter sports as much as possible; he didn't like the cold, and his ankles did not support him on ice skates. He played football as back or end – the inglorious line was not for him – on school and neighborhood teams, and was usually 'scared silly.' It was a matter of pride for him when he cracked a rib playing football. Scott's heroes at this time included Yale football star Ted Coy, Richard Harding Davis 'in default of someone better,' and Theodore Roosevelt.[19]

Mollie decided to take twelve-year-old Scott abroad in the summer of 1909. Their trip was canceled when he developed appendicitis, but surgery was not required. Scott was sent to camp at Frontenac, Minnesota, instead. An indication of Edward Fitzgerald's relationship with his son – as well as his feeling for words – is provided by a letter he sent Scott at camp, that summer:

> My dear Scott:
> Yours of July 29th received. Am glad you are having a good time. Mother and Annabelle are very well and enjoying Duluth. I enclose $1.00. Spend it liberally, generously, carefully, judiciously, sensibly. Get from it pleasure, wisdom, health and experience.[20]

Scott's first distinction at the St. Paul Academy came with his first appearance in print, 'The Mystery of the Raymond Mortgage,' published in the October 1909 issue of the *Now and Then*. He never forgot the excitement of the day the magazine was distributed: 'I read my story through at least sic times, and all day I loitered in the corridors and counted the number of men who were reading it, and tried to ask people casually, "If they had read it"?'[21] Like most juvenile attempts, 'The Mystery of the Raymond Mortgage' is imitative and overplotted, and has a high quota of absurdities. Nonetheless, the story is competently presented through the device of an obtuse narrator, the police chief, who relates the activities of a brilliant amateur detective. Here is the thirteen-year-old writer wrapping up the loose ends of his story:

> 'Up the stairs,' shouted Syrel, and we followed him, taking two steps at a bound. As we reached the top landing we were met by a young man.
> 'What right have you to enter this house?' he demanded.
> 'The right of the law,' replied Syrel.

'I didn't do it' broke out the young man. 'It was this way. Agnes Raymond loved me – she did not love Standish – he shot her; and God did not let her murder go unrevenged. It was well Mrs. Raymond killed him, for his blood would have been on my hands. I went back to see Agnes before she was buried. A man came in. I knocked him down. I didn't know until a moment ago that Mrs. Raymond had killed him.'

'I forgot Mrs. Raymond,' screamed Syrel, 'where is she?'

'She is out of your power forever,' said the young man.

Syrel brushed past him and, with Smidy and I following, burst open the door of the room at the head of the stairs. We rushed in.

On the floor lay a woman, and as soon as I touched her heart I knew she was beyond the doctor's skill.

'She has taken poison,' I said. Syrel looked around, the young man had gone. And we stood there aghast in the presence of death.[22]

Scott's second story, which appeared in the February 1910 *Now and Then*, is a perfect example of fiction as wish-fulfillment. In 'Reade, Substitute Right Half,' a small boy comes off the bench to lead his football team to victory. Scott was learning to use writing as a substitute for action. His third story, 'A Debt of Honor' (March 1910), is a Civil War tale about a Confederate soldier who is pardoned by General Lee for falling asleep on sentry duty and redeems himself by an act of heroism. Scott participated in other school activities that required verbal ability and became a debater, taking the negative on 'Resolved: The Mexican War was Justified' in April 1910.

Despite his intelligence and a store of information gleaned from books, Scott was a poor student. He preferred reading and writing to the dull school assignments: '. . . I wrote all through every class in school in the back of my geography book and the first year Latin and in the margins of themes and declensions and mathematics problems.'[23] Only one of his teachers, headmaster C. N. B. Wheeler, encouraged him to write. Scott's major unpublished projects were an imitation of *Ivanhoe* called 'Elavo' (which he may have started in Buffalo) and another story about knights. There is no evidence to indicate that at thirteen or fourteen Fitzgerald recognized his literary destiny and deliberately pursued a program of self-apprenticeship to the neglect of his schoolwork. His literary apprenticeship was a mixture of self-indulgence and aptitude. Writing gave him pleasure. Yet there was a surprising capacity for discipline in the boy who had developed no sound work habits; he was able to complete literary projects – usually in bursts of effort. His reading taste improved, and he claimed that he had read his way through Thackeray by the time he was sixteen. Scott also developed a temporary interest in photography, and in October 1910 his name appeared in the *St. Nicholas Magazine* roll of honor for a photo he had submitted. His name has not been found on any of the magazine's honor rolls for writing.

Fitzgerald at age fifteen

Beginning with September 1910–August 1911 Fitzgerald made a summary in his *Ledger* at the head of each year of his 'Outline Chart of my Life,' judging it in terms of his development or achievement. For his fourteenth year he noted: 'A year of Much Activity but dangerous.'

In his third year at the St. Paul Academy he became 'an inveterate author and a successful, not to say brilliant debater and writer' and distinguished himself at track.[24] That year he started smoking. Scott's fourth and final story for the *Now and Then* appeared in the June 1911 issue after a fifteen-month interval. 'The Room with the Green Blinds' offers another version of the fate of John Wilkes Booth. That two of Scott's first four stories deal with the Civil War indicates the influence of Edward Fitzgerald's reminiscences. No distinction can be claimed for any of these stories beyond a structural competence. The boy author knew how to tell a story – he had narrative sense – but the writing does not foreshadow the style that would distinguish his prose.

In 1910 and 1911 Scott kept a *Thoughtbook of Francis Scott Key Fitzgerald* – of which twenty-six pages survive – where he chronicled his romantic adventures and logged his campaigns for popularity. Violet Stockton was a Southern girl visiting the Finches on Summit Avenue in the summer of 1910:

> She had some sort of a book called flirting by sighns and Jack and I got it away from Violet and showed it to all the boys. Violet got very mad and went into the house. I got very mad and therefor *I* went home. Imediatly Violet repented and called me up on the phone to see if I was mad. However I did not want to make up just then and so I slammed down the receiver. The next morning I went down to Jacks to find that Violet had said that she was not coming out that day. It was now my turn to repent and I did so and she came out that evening befor however I had heard several things and, as I found afterwards so had Violet that I wanted to have justified. Violet and I sat down on the hill back of Schultze's a little away from the others.
>
> 'Violet,' I began, 'Did you call me a brat.'

32

'No'.
'Did you say that you wanted your ring and your picture and your hair back.'
'No'
'Did you say that you hated me'
'Of course not, is that what you went home for'.
'No, but Archie Mudge told me those things yesterday evening.'
'He's a little scamp,' said Violet Indignantly At this juncture Elanor Michell almost went into histerics because Jack was teasing her, and Violet had to go home with her. That afternoon I spanked Archie Mudge and finished making up with Violet.[25]

The *Thoughtbook* reveals a self-historiographer, someone for whom things were not fully experienced until he had written about them. It also shows the beginnings of Fitzgerald's list-making compulsion. All his life he would compile lists and charts of people and events. His concentration on himself may have been poor preparation for a well-adjusted personality; but it was valuable training for a writer.

Scott's inventive capacity and his need to be a leader of any activity he participated in found an outlet in the organization of secret clubs – the White Handkerchief Club (he was secretary), the Boys' Secret Service of St. Paul (he was chief scout), the Cruelty to Animals Society, the Gooserah Club, and the Scandal Detectives. The greatest escapade of the Scandal Detectives was an attack on Reuben Warner, whose popularity with girls they resented – an adventure that provided Fitzgerald with his first Basil story in 1928. The club was also reputed to keep a book of scandal in which damaging information about neighborhood people was recorded.

This period of social activity was accompanied by one of Scott's religious revivals in which he 'became desparately Holy'[26] and by literary effort. He wrote an unpublished, lost poem on 'Paris, the night + the Lure of the Dark,' for *The Smart Set*[27] and commenced writing plays with a theatrical group organized by Elizabeth Magoffin, a Summit Avenue drama buff. After acting in *A Regular Fix*, Scott wrote his first play in August 1911 for the Elizabethan Dramatic Club, as it was called in honor of its founder. *The Girl from Lazy J*, a one-acter, was performed at the Magoffin home with the playwright acting the lead. Absurdly plotted and freighted with stagy speech, the play does not show particular promise. Why the thief sends this message to his victim in advance of the robbery remains unexplained and unexplainable: 'Mr. Kendall, I warn you that on the night of August 12 I will relieve you of the five thouand dollars that you received last week in payment for the yearling steers. Yours very sincerely – D.S.H.'[28]

By the time he was fifteen Scott was accustomed to hearing the drums of destiny beating for him. He knew that he was different from his friends, that he had larger – if inchoate – ambitions, and that some rare fate was reserved for him. As he wrote of his autobiographical hero, Amory Blaine, in *This Side of Paradise*, 'Always, after he was in bed, there were voices – indefinite, fading, enchanting – just outside his window, and before he fell asleep he would dream one of his favorite waking dreams, the one about becoming a great half-back, or the one about the Japanese invasion, when he was rewarded by being made the youngest general in the world. It was always the becoming he dreamed of, never the being.'[29]

3

The Newman School

[1911–1913]

The summer of 1911 was filled with the anticipation of going away to an Eastern school. A family conference had decided that Scott's poor academic record at the St. Paul Academy indicated a need for the discipline of a boarding school, and the Newman School in Hackensack, New Jersey, was selected because it was trying to develop a reputation as the Catholic equivalent of the prestigious New England prep schools. Situated forty minutes from New York City, Newman had sixty students 'drawn from the Roman Catholic families of wealth in all parts of the United States'[30] and was unusual among Catholic schools in having a lay faculty and lay board of trustees. The basic fee was $850 a year.

With his head full of Owen Johnson's prep school and college stories, Scott arrived at Newman in September and promptly established himself as the most unpopular boy at school. He was bossy and boastful; he irritated the teachers and students; he was regarded as a coward and a bully; he humiliated himself by running from a tackle in a football scrimmage. He was rebuffed when he tried to join groups of boys and criticized when he kept to himself. He accumulated

conduct demerits and did poorly in his studies. His courses at
Newman included English, history, mathematics, Latin,
French, and a science. None of Scott's teachers made an
impression on him.

Again Scott sought distinction and self-justification
through writing. His first known contribution to the school
magazine, the *Newman News,** was a thirty-six-line poem,
'Football,' in the Christmas 1911 issue, written after he had
disgraced himself on the football field.

> Now they're ready, now they're waiting,
> Now he's going to place the ball,
> There, you hear the referee's whistle,
> As of old the baton's fall.[31]

He later wrote about the circumstances behind the poem:

> I remember the desolate ride in the bus back to the train and
> the desolate ride back to school with everybody thinking I had
> been yellow on the occasion, when actually I was just distracted
> and sorry for that opposing end. That's the truth. I've been
> afraid plenty of times but that wasn't one of the times. The
> point is it inspired me to write a poem for the school paper
> which made me as big a hit with my father as if I had become a
> football hero. So when I went home that Christmas vacation it
> was in my mind that if you weren't able to function in action
> you might at least be able to tell about it, because you felt the
> same intensity – it was a back door way out of facing reality.[32]

At Newman, Scott felt the lure of Princeton. He preserved
the ticket stub for the 4 November 1911 Princeton-Harvard
game in his scrapbook with the caption 'Sam White decides
me for Princeton.'[33] End White starred in Princeton's 8–6
victory with a 95-yard touchdown run after a blocked kick.
Because it came in the first Princeton–Harvard game since
1896, the upset was regarded as one of Princeton's great
athletic triumphs. Another factor in Princeton's attraction

* There is no file of the *Newman News*. Fitzgerald's contributions are known
from the clippings in his scrapbooks.

was the Triangle Club, founded by Booth Tarkington '93; every year the club produced an original musical comedy, which it took on tour during the Christmas vacation. When Scott saw the printed libretto for *His Honor the Sultan*, he began trying to imitate it, leaning heavily on Gilbert and Sullivan. During his period of unpopularity and unhappiness at Newman, Scott was infected by the enticement of New York. His trips to the Broadway theater excited his craving for metropolitan glamour and reinforced his theatrical ambitions: 'There was first the ferry boat moving softly from the Jersey shore at dawn – the moment crystallized into my first symbol of New York. Five years later when I was fifteen I went into the city from school to see Ina Claire in *The Quaker Girl* and Gertrude Bryan in *Little Boy Blue*. Confused by my helpless and melancholy love for them both, I was unable to choose between them – so they blurred into one lovely entity, the girl. She was my second symbol of New York. The ferry boat stood for triumph, the girl for romance.'[34]

In his *Ledger* Fitzgerald summarized 1911–12, his first year at Newman, as 'A year of real unhappiness excepting the feverish joys of Xmas.' He tried to redeem himself when he returned to school in January, but it was difficult. Academic problems placed him on bounds – limited to the school grounds. At Easter he visited his cousins Ceci Taylor at Norfolk, Virginia, and Tom Delihant at the Woodstock, Maryland, Jesuit seminary. He won the junior field meet in May, but managed to pass only four of his final exams – getting his only A in ancient history and probably failing algebra and physics.*

On the train back to St. Paul for the summer of 1912 vacation he drafted a full-length play for the Elizabethan Dramatic Club. An imitation of the popular crook-comedies such as *Alias Jimmy Valentine*, *The Captured Shadow* is a much more accomplished play than *The Girl from Lazy J*, with well-plotted action and clever dialogue. Scott played the lead,

---

* Fitzgerald's Newman School transcript at Princeton University is not divided into terms.

37

Thornton Hart Dudley, the gentleman crook who is not really a thief. The play was presented on 23 August 1912 at Mrs. Backus's School for Girls in Oak Hall. Assessing this achievement sixteen years later in a Basil Duke Lee story, 'The Captured Shadow' (1928), Fitzgerald commented on his young playwright: 'It might all have been very bad and demoralizing for Basil, but it was already behind him. Even as the crowd melted away and the last few people spoke to him and went out, he felt a great vacancy come into his heart. It was over, it was done and gone – all that work, and interest and absorption. It was a hollowness like fear.'[35]

Scott started his second year at Newman in the fall of 1912 determined to expiate his first-year sins, and to a large extent he succeeded – except academically. He starred as substitute left halfback in Newman's 7–0 victory over the Kingsley School, and the *Newman News* commended him for his 'fine running with the ball' that set up the touchdown by Charles W. (Sap) Donahoe,[36] who became a lifelong friend.

Newman was not entirely populated with athletes. Among Scott's fellow students were Herbert Agar, who won the Pulitzer Prize for history in 1934, and future novelists Cyril Hume (*The Wife of the Centaur*) and Edward Hope (*She Loves Me Not*). Quarterback Sap Donahoe was editor of the *Newman News*. A reserved boy from the Northwest, Donahoe went to Princeton with Fitzgerald and became one of his permanent heroes: '. . . another man represented my sense of the "good life," though I saw him once a decade. . . .But in difficult situations I had tried to think what *he* would have thought, how *he* would have acted.'[37] By this time Scott was a confirmed hero worshiper. He later admitted in his *Notebooks*: 'When I like men I want to be like them – I want to lose the outer qualities that give me my individuality and be like them. I don't want the man. I want to absorb into myself all the qualities that make him attractive and leave him out. I cling to my own inards. When I like women I want to own them, to dominate them, to have them admire me.'[38]

During the 1912–13 school year Scott published three

stories in the *Newman News*: 'A Luckless Santa Claus,' 'Pain and the Scientist,' and 'The Trail of the Duke.' The second of these stories is a negligible spoof of Christian Science; but the other two mark the earliest appearances of a subject that runs through Fitzgerald's work – the servitude of a man to a woman. In 'A Luckless Santa Claus' the young man accepts, with disastrous results, his fiancée's challenge to give away $25. In 'The Trail of the Duke' the lover gets into difficulties searching for a lost duke who improbably turns out to be his sweetheart's poodle. Although these plots are trivial, both stories foreshadow Fitzgerald's mature treatment of the young man who performs a grand deed for the sake of his beloved and who sometimes breaks against her selfishness.

Scott's Newman short stories demonstrate his rapid progress toward a distinctive style and a controlling tone of his own:

> It was a hot July night. Inside, through screen, window and door fled the bugs and gathered around the lights like so many humans at a carnival, buzzing, thugging, whirring. From out the night into the houses came the sweltering late summer heat, over-powering and enervating, bursting against the walls and enveloping all mankind like a huge smothering blanket. In the drug stores, the clerks, tired and grumbling handed out ice cream to hundreds of thirsty but misled civilians, while in the corners buzzed the electric fans in a whirring mockery of coolness. In the flats that line upper New York, pianos (sweating ebony perspiration) ground out rag-time tunes of last winter and here and there a wan woman sang the air in a hot soprano. In the tenements, shirt-sleeves gleamed like beacon lights in steady rows along the streets in tiers of from four to eight according to the number of stories in the house. In a word, it was a typical, hot New York summer night.
>
> –'The Trail of the Duke'[39]

The image 'sweating ebony perspiration' bears the Fitzgerald mark.

The great event of Scott's second year at Newman was meeting Father Cyril Sigourney Webster Fay in November

1912. Fay was Fitzgerald's ideal priest – a romantic, intellectual figure who made the Church seem glamorous. Formerly an Episcopalian minister, Fay had converted to Catholicism and was ordained in 1910. He was a popular preacher and as a Church statesman was the confidential adviser to Cardinal Gibbons of Baltimore. A portly man, so fair that he was sometimes described as an albino, Fay had a private income that permitted him to live well and be at home in the highest Catholic society. He had a wide range of enthusiasms. A lover of ritual, he sometimes recited the Mass in Gaelic. In addition to his sermons, which were admired for their scholarship, Fay wrote conventional religious poems.

> Clothed with the Sun, the Moon beneath,
> The Stars above thy brow,
> The Darling of the Trinity,
> O Queen of Heaven, art Thou.

'The Queen of Heaven'[40]

The thirty-seven-year-old priest and the sixteen-year-old student responded to the egotistical qualities they shared and enjoyed their self-analytical conversations. Fay soon became Scott's surrogate father. Fitzgerald provided a portrait of him as Monsignor Darcy in *This Side of Paradise:*

> He was intensely ritualistic, startlingly dramatic, loved the idea of God enough to be a celibate, and rather liked his neighbor.
> Children adored him because he was like a child; youth revelled in his company because he was still a youth, and couldn't be shocked. In the proper land and century he might have been a Richelieu – at present he was a very moral, very religious (if not particularly pious) clergyman, making a great mystery about pulling rusty wires, and appreciating life to the fullest, if not entirely enjoying it.[41]

Fay later served as headmaster at Newman, but at the time of their meeting he was living in Washington. Scott visited him there and was introduced to Henry Adams and Shane

Monsignor Cyril Sigourney Webster Fay

Leslie. In *This Side of Paradise* Fitzgerald described Amory's
first luncheon with Darcy as 'one of the memorable events in
Amory's early life. He was quite radiant and gave off a
peculiar brightness and charm. Monsignor called out the best
that he had thought by question and suggestion, and Amory
talked with an ingenious brilliance of a thousand impulses
and desires and repulsions and faiths and fears.'[42] Fay was the
first important person who responded to Scott and
encouraged his aspirations.

Shane Leslie (later Sir Shane) was an Anglo-Irish Catholic
convert and a successful writer and lecturer. Educated at
Eton and King's College, Cambridge, he was the son of one of
the American Jerome sisters and the first cousin of Winston
Churchill. Fitzgerald later recorded the impression Leslie
made on him as a schoolboy:

> He first came into my life as the most romantic figure I had
> ever known. He had sat at the feet of Tolstoy, he had gone
> swimming with Rupert Brooke, he had been a young
> Englishman of the governing classes when the sense of being
> one must have been, as Compton McKenzie says, like the sense
> of being a Roman citizen.
>
> Also, he was a convert to the church of my youth, and he
> and another, since dead, made of that church a dazzling,
> golden thing, dispelling its oppressive mugginess and giving
> the succession of days upon gray days, passing under its
> plaintive ritual, the romantic glamour of an adolescent
> dream.[43]

Fay and Leslie encouraged Scott to think of himself as one
of the brilliant young men who would make American
Catholicism socially and intellectually respectable; and under
their influence Scott sporadically talked about entering the
priesthood to become an American equivalent of the English
priest-novelist Robert Hugh Benson. Fay and Leslie also tried
to win him to Irish independence as a romantic cause, but it
did not seize his imagination as the lost South had – probably
because Scott had no sense of his Irish past. His Irish roots

were mercantile and unglamorous. A younger Newman student, Stephan Parrott, shared Fay's attention. Peevie Parrott was the son of a wealthy San Francisco family, and for a few years he and Scott were close on the basis of their brotherhood as Fay's spiritual sons.

Despite the heady events of 1912–13, Fitzgerald summarized that year in his *Ledger* with 'Reward in fall for work of previous summer. A better year but not happy.' The cause of his unhappiness is unknown. Perhaps it was a feeling that he was marking time at Newman and that his destiny required a larger setting.

Scott and his friends had experimented with drugstore sherry in St. Paul. In 1913 he began to try stronger liquors at Newman. He had his first whiskey in March, and an April *Ledger* entry notes that he was 'Tight at Susquehanna.' His academic situation remained shaky; his Newman School record shows that he failed four courses in two years:

English A	C
English B	B
Ancient History	A
English History	C
Algebra I	E
Algebra II	C
Plane Geometry	B
Solid Geometry	B
Latin Grammar	D
Latin Composition	B
Caesar	E
Cicero	C
Vergil	D
French A	B
French B	E
Physics	E

It is normal – almost obligatory – for literary geniuses to get poor grades in math and science; but Scott did not distinguish himself in his English courses, either.

At the end of the term he took the examinations for

Princeton, on which he did a little 'cribbing.'[44] The entrance exams included French, three exams in Latin, two exams in English, three exams in algebra and plane geometry, and other exams in history, mathematics, and science. He left Newman with medals for elocution and track, and returned to St. Paul to await word of his acceptance by Princeton.

During the summer of 1913 Scott wrote his third play for the Elizabethan Dramatic Club, *Coward*, a Civil War melodrama about a reluctant Southern soldier who proves his courage. He played one of the leads and enjoyed the whole business of rehearsals and backstage crises because he always liked being in charge. *Coward* was warmly received by the local press at its performance at the St. Paul Y.W.C.A. for the benefit of the Baby Welfare Association on 29 August 1913, and a second performance was given 'upon urgent demand' at the White Bear Yacht Club on 2 September. Fitzgerald captioned the reviews in his scrapbook: THE GREAT EVENT and ENTER SUCCESS![45]

The death of Grandmother McQuillan that summer solved the problem of Scott's college tuition. When she received her share of her mother's estate, Mollie may have had as much as $125,000 in capital. The idea that he might be sent to the University of Minnesota to save money had filled Scott with dismay, and he was not attracted by the offer of his maiden aunt, Annabel McQuillan, to underwrite his education at Catholic Georgetown University. It was Princeton or nothing. The other Big Three universities failed to exert the same pull on his emotions: 'I don't know why, but I think of all Harvard men as sissies, like I used to be, and all Yale men as wearing big blue sweaters and smoking pipes. . . .I think of Princeton as being lazy and good-looking and aristocratic – you know, like a spring day.'[46] Princeton was the Southerner's Ivy League college, and Fitzgerald thought of himself as a courtesy Southerner by virtue of his father's pedigree.

SPIRES

AND

GARGOYLES

[1913–1917]

4

A Princeton Freshman

[1913–1914]

The *news from* Princeton was that Fitzgerald's performance on the entrance exams was not good enough to
warrant admission. Make-up exams and a personal interview
were required. Fitzgerald traveled to Princeton and
persuaded the admissions committee to accept him by
pleading that it would be too cruel to deny him a place in the
Class of 1917 on his birthday. On 24 September 1913 he
wired home: ADMITTED SEND FOOTBALL PADS AND SHOES
IMMEDIATELY PLEASE WAIT TRUNK.[1] It was a near thing; he
was admitted with conditions in algebra, Latin, French, and
physics – which had to be made up by passing exams in
December. (Of the 430 freshmen, 66 percent were admitted
with conditions.)

Fitzgerald described pre-World War I Princeton as 'the
pleasantest country club in America,'[2] where he planned to
succeed according to the guidelines set forth in Owen
Johnson's *Stover at Yale*. The town was not yet a bedroom
community for New York commuters; 'the loveliest riot of
Gothic architecture in America'[3] was an academic town
surrounded by country estates. 'Horsing,' a mild form of

47

hazing, was practiced, and freshmen were forbidden to wear soft shirts or cuffed trousers. Presbyterian Princeton was still a strait-laced university. Although there were undergraduates who frequented the fleshpots of New York, organized Christianity was a strong force on campus. The Philadelphian Society was an influential campus religious organization, and daily chapel attendance was compulsory until September 1915. In the 1917 class survey, only 182 out of 333 seniors claimed to have kissed a girl, and 41 stated that they regarded kissing as morally wrong. Only 117 admitted that they drank, and 61 regarded drinking as morally wrong. The campus tennis nets were taken down on Sunday.

The Big Man on Campus at certain Eastern universities was a figure of almost national prominence among the prep school and Ivy League population. Social success was regarded with intense seriousness. The quickest way to campus recognition was on the football field, and Fitzgerald reported for freshman practice at five foot seven and 138 pounds. In those days 140- or 150-pounders played first-string football, but it required physical toughness and ability which Fitzgerald did not have. Hobey Baker '14, captain of the football team during Fitzgerald's freshman year, was the greatest athlete in Princeton's history. At five foot nine and 167 pounds, playing without a helmet, the star halfback seemed like a Galahad figure on and off the field and was the most exciting ball carrier of his time. Baker was precisely the sort of hero Fitzgerald could identify with, and he was one of the players who made Big Three football glamorous in the days when it was regarded as a gentleman's sport.

According to one report, Fitzgerald wrenched his knee in practice and had to withdraw; another report is that he was cut from the squad on the first day of practice. In either case, within a week the road to gridiron glory was closed – leaving him with a 'dream of a defeated dream' that he used to induce sleep for the next twenty years:

'Once upon a time' (I tell myself) 'they needed a quarterback at Princeton, and they had nobody and were in despair. The head coach noticed me kicking and passing on the side of the field, and he cried: "Who is *that* man – why haven't we noticed *him* before?" The under coach answered, "He hasn't been out," and the response was: "Bring him to me!" '

'. . . we go to the day of the Yale game. I weigh only one hundred and thirty-five, so they save me until the third quarter, with the score—'⁴

Again Fitzgerald turned to his pencil for compensatory recognition, going out for the Triangle Club and the *Princeton Tiger*, the humor magazine. College humor magazines were then approaching the peak of reputation they would occupy in the Twenties when the *Tiger*, the *Yale Record*, and the *Harvard Lampoon* had national readerships and were training schools for writers. The first fall 1913 issue of the *Tiger* had an unidentified Fitzgerald contribution. He almost certainly contributed to the *Tiger* throughout his freshman year, but none of his contributions before 1915 has been identified because there were few bylines. Most of his *Tiger* work is known only by the clippings he saved.⁵ Fitzgerald entered Princeton with no clear career plans beyond the determination to earn his living by writing, probably as a newspaperman. Students preparing for journalism usually worked on *The Daily Princetonian*, but Fitzgerald did not heel the *Prince*.

Although Princeton was regarded as a college for the sons of the rich, and most of its students came from prep schools, the fees were not higher than at other colleges of its class. Tuition was $160 per year; room, board, and other fees averaged $350. Fitzgerald never lacked for money at Princeton, and his expenses may have run as high as $2,000 a year – roughly a third of his family's income.

During his first year Fitzgerald roomed alone off campus at 15 University Place because there was not enough dormitory space for freshmen. Two of his Newman classmates, Sap Donahoe and Paul Nelson, also roomed there. Norris Jackson from the St. Paul Academy was in the Class of '17, and another St. Paul friend, Joe McKibbin, was a popular and prominent member of the Class of 1915. Through his work with the Triangle Club, Fitzgerald met two wealthy freshmen, Townsend Martin and Ludlow Fowler, who were roommates. Alexander McKaig '17, a new friend with literary ambitions, was active on the *Prince* and *The Nassau Literary Magazine*. Although Fitzgerald was not friendless, he was up against the most complex system of social stratification he had yet encountered. The delegations from the Princeton feeder schools – Lawrenceville, Hill, Hotchkiss, Exeter, Andover – arrived with inside knowledge about Princeton and provided each other with support. The boy from an obscure Catholic prep school felt that he was a member of the lower class. He did not resent the existence of an exclusive system, but he wanted to be at the top of the Princeton social ladder.

On 15 November 1913 Fitzgerald went to New Haven to watch Princeton and Yale play a 3–3 tie as Hobey Baker drop-kicked a 43-yard field goal. The lasting impression of the game for Fitzgerald was Princeton's Buzz Law kicking from behind his own goal line with a bandage around his head.

There were classes. As a candidate for a Litt. B. or a B.S. degree (the A.B. required Greek), Fitzgerald was assigned six compulsory courses: Latin 103 (historical literature of Rome – Livy, Sallust, Cicero), Mathematics 101 (plane trigonometry), English 101 (readings in English literature – composition and rhetoric), Physics 101 (general physics), French 203 (survey of French literature), and Hygiene 101 (personal hygiene). In addition there was physical education as well as a seventh academic course in Mathematics 105 (algebra) to prepare him to clear his entrance conditions in math.

The method of instruction was the preceptorial system, a modification of the Oxford-Cambridge tutorial system, introduced by Woodrow Wilson when he was president of Princeton. The lectures in each course were supplemented by weekly one-hour meetings with preceptors on the assignments; three to six students attended each preceptorial session. The Princeton grading system was by groups: First group, highest standing; Second group, high standing; Third Group, satisfactory; Fourth group, below average; Fifth group, poor; Sixth group, unsatisfactory. Seventh group, very unsatisfactory. Fitzgerald's record for the first term of his freshman year shows 5 in Latin; failed/failed/passed in trigonometry (he took the exam three times); 4 in English; 5 in physics; 5 in French; failed/passed in hygiene; failed/failed/ passed in algebra. His average of 5.17 for the term was barely passing. Since failed courses had to be made up, in addition to his entrance conditions, Fitzgerald established a pattern of having to make up for past failures while failing current courses. It was a predicament that would get worse every term.

The Princeton English department – though by no means a great department – included Henry Van Dyke, George MacLean Harper, Thomas Marc Parrott, J. Duncan Spaeth, Charles G. Osgood, and Gordon Hall Gerould. The English poet Alfred Noyes, author of 'The Highwayman,' joined the department in 1914. Fitzgerald found most of his teachers disappointing and characterized them as having 'an uncanny knack of making literature distasteful to young men.'[6] The only one of his English teachers he acknowledged a debt to was Courtland Van Winkle, who taught him in freshman year: '. . . he gave us the book of *Job* to read and I don't think any of our preceptorial group ever quite recovered from it.'[7] Fitzgerald gave Professor Spaeth credit for arousing 'interest and even enthusiasm for the romantic poets, an interest later killed in the preceptorial rooms where mildly poetic gentlemen resented any warmth of discussion and called the prominent men of the class by their first names.'[8]

Fitzgerald managed to remain in college by luck and by all-night cramming sessions with wet towels and pots of coffee. He regarded the Princeton honor system as a 'sacred tradition.' 'I can think of a dozen times when a page of notes glanced at in a wash room would have made the difference between failure and success for me, but I can't recall any moral struggles in the matter.'[9] The attrition rate was fairly high: 10 percent of the Class of 1917 did not survive freshman year. The removal of prep school or parental supervision enabled some students to do no work at all, and the easy commute to Broadway terminated other undergraduate careers.

Christmas vacation was splendid. As a Princeton man Fitzgerald was invited to so many parties and dances in St. Paul that he had to keep an engagement book. This may have been the holiday when, having gotten tight on Christmas Eve, he felt the need to hear hymns and went to St. John Evangelist Episcopal Church. With clinking overshoes he walked the aisles searching the congregation for a friend, remarking to the minister, 'Don't mind me, go on with the sermon.'[10]

Once he was away at school, Fitzgerald gradually stopped thinking of himself as a Midwesterner. The McQuillan connection became increasingly remote. The family roots that mattered to him were in Maryland, and he felt an immediate affinity with New York City. Yet his memories of Minnesota could exert an emotional pull on him. He evoked his sense of the Midwest as a place of exciting vacation returns in *The Great Gatsby*:

> One of my most vivid memories is of coming back West from prep school and later from college at Christmas time. Those of us who went farther than Chicago would gather in the old dim Union Station at six o'clock of a December evening, with a few Chicago friends, already caught up into their own holiday gayeties, to bid them a hasty good-by. I remember the fur coats of the girls returning from Miss This-or-That's and the chatter of frozen breath and the hands waving overhead as we caught sight of old acquaintances, and the matchings for invitations: 'Are you going to the Ordways'? the Herseys'? the Schultzes'?' and the long green tickets clasped tight in our gloved hands. And last the murky yellow cars of the Chicago, Milwaukee & St. Paul railroad looking cheerful as Christmas itself on the tracks beside the gate.[11]

He returned to Princeton in January 1914 to take his midyear exams and begin hard work on the competition for the 1914–15 Triangle Club show. His book and lyrics for *Fie! Fie! Fi-Fi!* won the competition over the submission of Lawton Campbell '16 from Montgomery, Alabama. The selection of the script was up to Walker Ellis '15, the Triangle Club president, who may – as Campbell believed – have picked *Fie! Fie! Fi-Fi!* because it had a good part for him. Ellis, whom Edmund Wilson charged with 'brazen duplicities,'[12] revised it with the author until he decided to award himself credit for the dialogue and characters. The published libretto credits Fitzgerald with only the plot and lyrics. It is impossible to determine from the acting script how much of the produced play Ellis changed. The plot deals with an American con man, who has become prime minister of Monaco, and his abandoned wife, the manicurist in a Monte Carlo hotel; a love subplot involves an Englishman and an American dancer. Ellis cast himself in the female lead as the manicurist, and the role of the dancer Celeste was reserved for Fitzgerald. The dialogue shows the influence of Oscar Wilde as the characters epigrammatize between song cues. Fitzgerald's seventeen song lyrics were impressive work for a freshman who had never written a musical.

> A Slave to Modern Improvements
> A victim to modern improvements am I,
> I've a silver chest and a crystal eye;
> A platinum lung and a grafted nose,
> Aluminum fingers,
> Asbestos toes.
> And when I walk I clank and clash,
> And rust when damp you see:
> And the wildest lot of anonymous trash
> That ever crossed the sea.[13]

In April 1914 Fitzgerald began his friendship with a Princetonian who would shape his college education, most of which was acquired outside of classrooms. John Peale Bishop '17 was three and a half years older than Fitzgerald, having started college late because of boyhood illness. Their meeting probably occurred very much as the meeting between Amory

Blaine (Fitzgerald) and Thomas Park D'Invilliers (Bishop) is reported in *This Side of Paradise*. Amory strikes up a conversation with a Princetonian at the Peacock Inn and discovers that the student is D'Invilliers, the author of highbrow poetry in the *Lit*:

> So he found 'Dorian Gray' and the 'Mystic and Sombre Dolores' and the 'Belle Dame sans Merci'; for a month was keen on naught else. The world became pale and interesting, and he tried hard to look at Princeton through the satiated eyes of Oscar Wilde and Swinburne – or 'Fingal O'Flaherty' and 'Algernon Charles,' as he called them in précieuse jest. He read enormously every night – Shaw, Chesterton, Barrie, Pinero, Yeats, Synge, Ernest Dowson, Arthur Symons, Keats, Sudermann, Robert Hugh Benson, the Savoy Operas – just a heterogeneous mixture, for he suddenly discovered that he had read nothing for years.[14]

Bishop provided Fitzgerald with intensive tutoring in poetry. Writing to his daughter when she was in college, Fitzgerald acknowledged Bishop's influence on his understanding of poetry:

> It isn't something easy to get started on by yourself. You need at the beginning, some enthusiast who also knows his way around – John Peale Bishop performed that office for me at Princeton. I had always dabbled in 'verse' but he made me see, in the course of a couple of months, the difference between poetry and non-poetry. After that one of my first discoveries was that some of the professors who were teaching poetry really hated it and didn't know what it was about. I got in a series of endless scraps with them so that finally I dropped English altogether.[15]

Bishop was the first friend who fully shared Fitzgerald's commitment to writing, and under his influence Fitzgerald began to develop more serious literary ambitions. For his part, Fitzgerald considered it his obligation to bring Bishop out – to direct him toward Princeton success. Since Bishop was from Charles Town, West Virginia, Fitzgerald regarded him as socially deprived. In point of fact, Bishop had attended Mercersburg, a better-known school than Newman.

It is not known when Fitzgerald met another member of the *Lit* staff, Edmund Wilson '16, who became a more enduring influence on him; but Bishop probably provided the connection. A graduate of the Hill School, Bunny Wilson had an imposing campus reputation as a scholar and literary critic. Fitzgerald's friendship with Wilson was close but not intense at Princeton; the reserved Wilson was put off by

John Peale Bishop

Fitzgerald's antics. An indication of Fitzgerald's position at the university is Wilson's admission that Fitzgerald was the only Catholic he knew at Princeton. Fitzgerald subsequently delegated his intellectual responsibilities to him, admitting at the time of 'The Crack-Up' in 1936: ' . . . I had done very little thinking, save within the problems of my craft. For twenty years a certain man had been my intellectual conscience. That was Edmund Wilson.'[16]

While not overwhelmingly literary, the Class of 1917 included – in addition to Fitzgerald and Bishop – other men

Edmund Wilson

who would become writers. Elliott White Springs used his experiences as a World War I ace to write aviation fiction (*War Birds, Nocturne Militaire, Leave Me with a Smile*) but later became better known for his Spring Maid sheet ads. George R. Stewart became a professor of English who wrote scholarly and popular books (*Storm*). Townsend Martin wrote for the movies and had a Broadway success, *A Most Immoral Lady*.

In June 1914 Fitzgerald took his second-term exams and managed to pass everything but coordinate geometry, in which his grade was 'a-' indicating that he was absent from the exam and that his term grade was unsatisfactory. His best grade was a 3 in English; his other grades were 4's and 5's. Fitzgerald's *Ledger* summary for his freshman year at Princeton was 'A year of work and vivid experience.'

While compiling a poor academic record, Fitzgerald was nonetheless acquiring an education through wide reading. The lessons he needed were not to be found in coordinate geometry or qualitative analysis classes. The strongest influences on him were the novels he called 'quest' books:

> In the 'quest' book the hero sets off in life armed with the best weapons and avowedly intending to use them as such weapons are usually used, to push their possessors ahead as selfishly and blindly as possible, but the heroes of the 'quest' books discover that there might be a more magnificent use for them. 'None Other Gods' [Robert Hugh Benson], 'Sinister Street' [Compton Mackenzie], and 'The Research Magnificent' [H.G. Wells] were examples of such books. . . .[17]

The son of the Archbishop of Canterbury, Monsignor Robert Hugh Benson was a Catholic convert who wrote religious novels. In *None Other Gods* (1910) a young English aristocrat forsakes his heritage when he converts to Catholicism and becomes a tramp, seeking spiritual fulfillment on the road. Benson, who had been at Cambridge with Shane Leslie, spoke at Princeton in March 1914. The social reform literature of Wells and George Bernard Shaw made a strong impression on Fitzgerald and his friends. Although

Fitzgerald admired Wells for the power of his intelligence, and in 1917 cited *The New Machiavelli* to Wilson as 'the greatest English novel of the century,'[18] it was Compton Mackenzie's *Sinister Street* that most clearly influenced him.* In 1922 Fitzgerald admitted that Mackenzie and Booth Tarkington 'together taught me all I know about the English language.'[19] *Sinister Street* traces Michael Fane's history at school and Oxford, until he ends his quest in the arms of Rome as a priest. In the Oxford chapters the young gentlemen analyze and intellectualize with little interference from the university. No doubt this was Fitzgerald's notion of how a university should be run. When he came to write his own quest novel, Fitzgerald imitated Mackenzie and to a lesser extent Wells. What Fitzgerald took from *Sinister Street* was an aristocratic egotism combined with a sense of noblesse oblige. Michael Fane and Amory Blaine (there is a name echo) share a concept of duty to their unique abilities. Both characters require goals that will employ their talents to serve some higher purpose – as did Fitzgerald.

It was probably later on at Princeton that Fitzgerald discovered the American realists. Two novels that made a strong impression on him were Stephen French Whitman's *Predestined* (1910) and Charles G. Norris's *Salt* (1917) – both deterministic novels of character deterioration. Charles Norris's work led Fitzgerald to the naturalistic novels of his brother, Frank Norris.

Father Fay kept in touch with his protégé, inviting him to his mother's home at Deal Beach, New Jersey, and introducing him to prominent figures in Catholic society. Fitzgerald remained a practicing – but not devout – Catholic at Princeton. He told Wilson, 'Why I can go up to New York on a terrible party and then come back into the church and *pray* – and mean every word of it, too!'[20] He retained a strong sense of evil and sexual corruption. In *This Side of Paradise* Fitzgerald summarized: 'The problem of evil had solidified for Amory into the problem of sex . . . Inseparably linked

---

* *Sinister Street* was published in two volumes in London, 1913–14; it was published in America as *Youth's Encounter* (1913) and *Sinister Street* (1914).

with evil was beauty . . . Amory knew that every time he had reached toward it longingly it had leered out at him with the grotesque face of evil.'[21] Though a connoisseur of kisses, Fitzgerald retained the capacity to be shocked by blatant sexuality. When Bishop and McKaig went off with two pick-ups, he primly announced to Wilson, 'That's one thing that Fitzgerald's never done!'[22]

In the summer of 1914 Fitzgerald wrote his fourth and last play for the St. Paul Elizabethan Drama Club, *Assorted Spirits*, a complicated ghost comedy in which he took a leading role and served as stage manager. It was performed at the Y.W.C.A. on 8 September and the next night at the White Bear Yacht Club – raising $500 for the Baby Welfare Association. There was the possibility of panic when a fuse blew at the yacht club performance. According to a local paper, 'Fitzgerald proved equal to the situation, however, and leaping to the edge of the stage quieted the audience with an improvised monologue.'[23]

5

Sophomore Year

[1914–1915]

Fitzgerald *was tutored* in August 1914 and probably returned to Princeton early in September to attend cram school for the make-up exam in coordinate geometry. He failed the exam and was ruled ineligible for extracurricular activities – which did not prevent him from devoting most of the fall term to the Triangle Club, although he was not permitted to appear in *Fie! Fie! Fi-Fi!* He roomed alone at 71 Patton Hall. His program for the first term of his sophomore year required five courses: philosophy (logic); Latin (Roman comedy, Plautus and Terence); chemistry (inorganic); English (survey of English literature); French (seventeenth-century literature). In addition, Fitzgerald was assigned a sixth course in Latin to make up for an entrance deficiency.

When the European war broke out in the summer of 1914 Fitzgerald was not particularly excited or strongly partisan, although he was moved by the death of Johnny Poe '95 with the Black Watch – the first Princetonian to die in the war. Like most of his friends he expected America to remain neutral, which was the policy of Princeton's Woodrow Wilson.

The chief concern of Fitzgerald's sophomore year – apart

from the Triangle show – was the club elections in the spring. There were eighteen eating clubs, most of which occupied impressive buildings on Prospect Street. In the absence of fraternities and secret societies, the eating clubs marked an undergraduate's social standing; and there was an elaborate stratification among them. Each club took in about twenty-five sophomores. Only 75 percent of the class received bids. Some of the clubs were firmly established at the top of the system: Ivy, Cottage, Tiger Inn, Cap and Gown. Others were places where the obscure banded together for mutual comfort. Failure to make a club or making a weak club meant that a sophomore had failed at Princeton and that his life would be clouded by this rejection – or so it seemed. The snobbery of the system did not bother Fitzgerald; he simply wanted to make one of the top clubs. During that year Fitzgerald and his classmates had the sense of being scrutinized by the upperclassmen. He had decided that he wanted the University Cottage Club, which he regarded as the most powerful as well as the most social. Walker Ellis, his collaborator on *Fie! Fie! Fi-Fi!*, was president of the club.

Fie! Fie! Fi-Fi! premiered at Princeton on 19 December 1914 and went on a 3,500-mile Christmas tour, from which Fitzgerald was excluded by the Committee on Non-Athletic Eligibility. The *Princetonian* reviews gave most of the credit to Walker Ellis, but the *Baltimore Sun* singled out Fitzgerald: 'The lyrics of the songs were written by F. S. Fitzgerald, who could take his place right now with the brightest writers of witty lyrics in America.'[24]

Fitzgerald went home for Christmas a celebrity – the local boy who had made good at Princeton and was on his way to becoming one of the gods of his class. On January 4 he capped a splendid term by meeting Ginevra King. Marie Hersey of St. Paul was attending Westover, a Connecticut girls' school, and had invited her schoolmate for a Christmas visit. A sixteen-year-old beauty from Lake Forest, Illinois, Ginevra King already had a string of conquests among Ivy Leaguers. Fitzgerald met her at a party in her honor at the

Ginevra King

Town and Country Club, followed by supper at the McDavitt home. He secured a movie date for the next afternoon before his departure for Princeton and promptly fell in love with Ginevra, who matched his dreams of the perfect girl: beautiful, rich, socially secure, and sought after. The last qualification was important. His ideal girl was one pursued by many men; there had to be an element of competition. As he wrote of Jay Gatsby, 'It excited him too that many men had already loved Daisy – it increased her value in his eyes.'[25] Ginevra later remarked that Fitzgerald thought she knew the way up. He recorded in his *Notebooks*: 'I didn't have the two top things – great animal magnetism or money. I had the two second things, tho', good looks and intelligence. So I always got the top girl.'[26]

His style with girls involved an elaborate line ('Please fall in love with me'), and they responded to him because he gave them the impression that he was concentrating wholly on them. He made them feel interesting as well as attractive. There was a touch of exhibitionism in almost everything Fitzgerald did, and with the right sort of girl he had a stimulating audience.

Fitzgerald managed to pass five out of his six courses in January 1915, cutting the chemistry exam. He received Third groups in English and logic, and Fifths in his other courses. In the second term of his sophomore year he took seven courses – the five required courses plus a repeat of coordinate geometry and a seventh course as a penalty for exceeding the fifty-cut limit while working on the Triangle production. His spring 1915 program was psychology, Latin (Horace and Catullus), chemistry (qualitative analysis), English (survey of English literature), French (seventeenth-century literature), coordinate geometry, and an unidentified history course for exceeding the cut limit.

Upon returning to Princeton after Christmas, Fitzgerald began writing Ginevra King almost daily letters – some so long that they had to be mailed in two envelopes. None of these letters survives. (At the same time he was also corresponding with several St. Paul girls.) Ginevra tried to keep up her end of the correspondence, but she was clearly outclassed. What was easy for him became a chore for her. In February Fitzgerald visited her at Westover.

On 26 February 1915 Fitzgerald was elected secretary of the Triangle Club for 1915–16; this meant that he would almost certainly be president in his senior year – if he could remain in college and be eligible for extracurricular activities. His social success at Princeton was satisfactorily established in March when he received bids from Cap and Gown, Quadrangle, Cannon, and Cottage. The night of the club elections he romped in the snow with Sap Donahoe and passed out at the club dinner. Donahoe was Fitzgerald's only close friend to join Cottage with him; his other friends – Alexander McKaig, Townsend Martin, Ludlow Fowler, and John Bishop – went to Quadrangle, the club for literary types.

Although he got drunk at the Cottage election dinner, Fitzgerald was not regarded as a heavy drinker. He would take Bronxes and daiquiris during trips to New York, but in Princeton he confined himself to beer. When he got tight, his friends suspected him of pretending to be drunker than he really was – that it was a way of getting attention. All his life he would play the clown when he found himself in a social situation that he felt he could not handle.

While he was emerging as a campus figure, Fitzgerald devoted thought to achieving personal perfection. He analyzed his classmates and cataloged the qualities of the most prominent undergraduates. Observing that a tenor voice seemed to be one of the hallmarks, he tried to develop one. A February 1915 *Ledger* entry reads: 'If I couldn't be perfect I wouldn't be anything.' This acute self-consciousness was poor training for an exemplary citizen 'but good material for those who do much of the world's rarest work,' as he later wrote.[27]

Fitzgerald continued to contribute unsigned jokes, parodies, and poems to the *Tiger* and was elected to the editorial board in 1915. He began appearing in the *Lit* in 1915, commencing his serious literary apprenticeship as he worked with more difficult material and refined his technique. Under the editorships of Wilson and Bishop, the *Lit* was then at the peak of its prominence and was regarded respectfully on and off campus. Fitzgerald's first *Lit* appearance came in spring 1915 with 'Shadow Laurels' – a one-act play about an American who goes to Paris to find out about his dead father, a drunken failure, and discovers that the father was loved by his friends because he gave expression to their lives. At the end the American offers this toast: 'I drink to one who might have been all, who was nothing – who might have sung; who only listened – who might have seen the sun; but who watched a dying ember – who drank of gall and wore a wreath of shadow laurels –'[28] 'Shadow Laurels' was the first story in which Fitzgerald explored his feelings about his father; a series of weak fathers would appear in his work. The second Fitzgerald *Lit* appearance that spring was 'The Ordeal' (later rewritten as 'Benediction'), a symbolic piece about a Jesuit novice's waverings before taking his vows. The story reveals Fitzgerald's awareness of evil – not just sin – and his sense of the supernatural. 'The Ordeal' probably expresses his concern about his own destiny. Whether or not Fitzgerald seriously considered entering the priesthood, he was searching for some ideal, a concept of perfection, to which he could dedicate himself.

As a *Lit* contributor, Fitzgerald developed a closer friendship with Bunny Wilson, its chairman in 1915–16. They decided to collaborate on a Triangle show – one that would be different and have a real plot. Wilson wrote the book and Fitzgerald provided the lyrics for *The Evil Eye*, the club's 1915 production. Set in a Normandy fishing village, the plot dealt with an amnesiac shipwreck survivor and her rescuer, who is reputed to have the evil eye. As the *Princetonian* put it: 'The taking of the girl by Boileau and the arrest of Jacques on the instigation of the peasants form a tangle from which the hero and heroine are able to extricate themselves only in time for the last curtain'[29] – which indicates that *The Evil Eye* was not so very different from

other Triangle shows, although it was regarded as rather
literary. Fitzgerald's lyrics again attracted favorable notice:

> The Girl of the Golden West
> Ride your horse right to my heart
> (*All a-whirl, all a-whirl, for my little girl.*)
> Tied am I by cowgirl art
> (*To a tree, to a tree, hanging over me*)
> We await the hour
> When we can round 'em up again
> In that operatic style.
> I'm happy while Caruso twirls his rope
> (*While the hills, while the hills, ring with tenor trills*)
> You could swear he had the dope
> (*On the names, on the names, such as Jesse James,*)
> Don't know whether to bide or go
> To the borders of Idaho
> Oh – Puccini, do it some more.[30]

Fitzgerald's showing on his June 1915 exams was his worst
yet. Of his seven courses he managed to pass only four on the
first try: psychology (4), English (3), French (4), history (5).
He failed the Latin exam twice before passing it and failed
coordinate geometry again before passing a make-up exam.
He failed qualitative analysis three times. Fitzgerald
summarized his sophomore year in his *Ledger* as 'A year of
tremendous rewards that toward the end overreached itself
and ruined me. Ginevra-Triangle year.'

In June, Ginevra came to the Princeton prom chaperoned
by her mother. Fitzgerald took her to New York, where they
dined at the Ritz, saw *Nobody Home*, and attended the
Midnight Frolic cabaret. He then visited her at Lake Forest on
his way back to St. Paul. His stay at home was short; he had
been invited to the Donahoe ranch in Montana, where he
thoroughly enjoyed himself – getting drunk with the
cowhands and winning $50 in a poker game. The trip
provided the setting for 'The Diamond as Big as the Ritz' in
1922.

6

Junior Year

[1915–1916]

Fitzgerald's junior year, 1915–16, was a disaster. He began the college year by failing the make-up exam in qualitative analysis, thereby again becoming ineligible for campus offices – and in particular for the presidency of the Triangle Club, which went to Paul Nelson. Twenty years later Fitzgerald analyzed the permanent results of that disappointment:

> To me college would never be the same. There were to be no badges of pride, no medals, after all. It seemed on one March afternoon that I had lost every single thing I wanted – and that night was the first time that I hunted down the spectre of womanhood that, for a little while, makes everything else seem unimportant.
>
> Years later I realized that my failure as a big shot was all right – instead of serving on committees, I took a beating in English poetry; when I got the idea of what it was all about, I set about learning how to write. On Shaw's principle that 'If you don't get what you like, you better like what you get,' it was a lucky break – at the moment, it was a harsh and bitter business to know that my career as a leader of men was over.

Since that day I have not been able to fire a bad servant, and I am astonished and impressed by people who can. Some old desire for personal dominance was broken and gone. Life around me was a solemn dream, and I lived on the letters I wrote to a girl in another city. A man does not recover from such jolts – he becomes a different person and, eventually, the new person finds new things to care about.[31]

Fitzgerald's expression for sexual intercourse with a whore – 'I hunted down the spectre of womanhood' – is noteworthy. As late as 1936 fornication would still carry connotations of supernatural corruption in his fiction.

That Fitzgerald's reaction to the deprivation of a college honor was so extreme as to cripple his whole life may seem incredible; but his analysis of the loss provides a gauge of the intensity of his commitment to the prizes of life – not just the prizes of Princeton. For Fitzgerald the prizes of life were more than badges of position or even fame. He measured himself against personal standards of character and will, believing that 'life was something you dominated if you were any good.'[32] His Princeton failure provoked another seizure of self-assessment in which he tried to develop new ways to realize his aspirations. If *This Side of Paradise* can be trusted as autobiography, Father Fay helped him to reach the concept of the 'personage,' the man who is known by his achievements. Monsignor Darcy – the Fay figure – counsels Amory Blaine in the novel:

'A personality is what you thought you were . . . Personality is a physical matter almost entirely; it lowers the people it acts on – I've seen it vanish in a long sickness. But while a personality is active, it overrides "the next thing." Now a personage, on the other hand, gathers. He is never thought of apart from what he's done. He's a bar on which a thousand things have been hung – glittering things sometimes, as ours are; but he uses those things with a cold mentality back of them.'[33]

Fitzgerald would always display a perplexing ability to do 'the next thing' and then disregard it. He wanted to be both a personality and a personage, a magnetic individual and an achiever.

In the fall of 1915 Fitzgerald roomed alone at 32 Little Hall. He scribbled wake-up notes on the dorm wall, and Dale Warren, a freshman who roomed across the hall, became his alarm clock. Warren remembered that manuscripts were piled all around Fitzgerald's room. The first term of his junior year Fitzgerald's courses included English (the Renaissance – Spenser, Marlowe, Sidney), English (Chaucer), Italian (grammar, composition, and reading), French (the Romantic Movement from Rousseau to France), philosophy (history of philosophy), and a sixth course in ancient art for exceeding the fifty-cut limit.

The French literature course was taught by Christian Gauss, the only Princeton professor with whom Fitzgerald maintained a friendship after college. Gauss later observed that at Princeton Fitzgerald reminded him of all of the Karamazov brothers at once.[34] Fitzgerald acknowledged this mixture of unreconciled qualities in his character in a letter to Wilson: 'I don't think you ever realized at Princeton the childish simplicity that lay behind all my petty sophistication and my lack of a real sense of honor.'[35] The need for values or codes was much on Fitzgerald's mind at college, and he told Norris Jackson and Joe McKibbin that he wanted five good principles to live up to.

Although still ineligible to hold office or perform in the Triangle Club show, Fitzgerald became involved in the production of *The Evil Eye*, impressing the cast with his ability to write new lyrics on demand during rehearsals. Perhaps as compensation for his ineligibility, the Triangle Club used a publicity photo of Fitzgerald costumed as a showgirl. It appeared in several newspapers, including *The New York Times*, and brought him fan letters from men who wanted to meet him and from an agent who offered to book him for a vaudeville tour as a female impersonator – a popular act at the time. There is no evidence that Fitzgerald especially delighted in dressing as a woman. All the female roles in the Triangle Club shows were played by male undergraduates, which was regarded as part of the fun. It was conventional collegiate humor and elicited no ominous comment.

Fitzgerald continued to write steadily for the *Tiger* in his junior year. In October 1915 there was a competition for a new Princeton football song, which Fitzgerald won with 'A Cheer for Princeton':

> Glory, Glory to the Black and Orange,
> It's the Tiger's turn to-day.
> Glory, glory it's the same old story
> Soon as Princeton starts to play.
> Eli, Eli, all your hopes are dead
> For the Tiger's growling in his lair.
> Don't you hear him?
> You'll learn to fear him,
> Try to face him if you dare.
>
> *Chorus*
> Princeton, cheer for Princeton,
> Raise your voices loud and free
> Strong and steady
> Ever ready
> For defeat or victory.
> Princeton cheer for Princeton,
> Always sure to win renown,
> So we'll raise our praise to Nassau
> To the pride of the Tiger town.[36]

'A Cheer for Princeton' seems unique in its genre for anticipating defeat – which may be why it never caught on.

Fitzgerald went to the Yale game at New Haven in October, perhaps to hear 'A Cheer for Princeton,' and had dinner with Ginevra in Waterbury, Connecticut. His epistolary courtship continued unabated, some of his letters running to thirty pages. He paid less attention than ever to his classes, for the loss of the 'badges of pride' made the effort of studying seem worthless. His dissipations took the form of conversation, unrequired reading, and writing. He found his English

n Talking
Spain.

SCOTT FITZGERALD.
Considered the Most Beautiful "Show Girl" in the Princeton Triangle Club's New
Musical Play, "The Evil Eye," Coming to the Waldorf on Next Tuesday.
He Is Also the Author of the Lyrics of the Play.   (Photo by White.

professors lacking in real enthusiasm for literature, as shown
by two of the poems he incorporated into *This Side of Paradise*:

> Good-morning, Fool . . .
>   Three times a week
> You hold us helpless while you speak,
> Teasing our thirsty souls with the
> Sleek 'yeas' of your philosophy . . .
> . . . .
> The hour's up . . . and raised from rest
> One hundred children of the blest
> Cheat you a word or two with feet
> That down the noisy aisle-ways beat . . .
> Forget on *narrow-minded earth*
> The Mighty Yawn that gave you birth.
>   —'In a Lecture Room'[37]

Fitzgerald wrote a four-stanza poem during a lecture on
Tennyson's 'A Song in the Time of Order' and handed it to
the teacher, Alfred Noyes:

> Songs in the time of order
>   You left for us to sing,
>   Proofs with excluded middles,
>   Answers to life in rhyme . . .[38]

Fitzgerald was in the infirmary twice in November with
what was diagnosed as malaria, but which may have been a
mild case of tuberculosis. On 28 November he attended his
last class and went home early for Christmas vacation. The
Triangle Club's tour with *The Evil Eye* was a great success. In
Chicago 300 girls occupied the front rows; after the final
curtain they gave the Princeton locomotive cheer and tossed
bouquets at the cast. In St. Paul and Minneapolis the shop
windows and trolleys were decorated with Princeton colors;
but Fitzgerald was in the audience and not on the stage.

He dropped out of college for the rest of the year to
recuperate, a decision dictated by his academic situation. His
Princeton transcript notes that 'Mr Fitzgerald was required to
withdraw from the University January 3, 1916 for scholastic
deficiencies'; but in May he persuaded Dean Howard

McClennan to provide him with a To-Whom-It-May-Concern letter stating that he had voluntarily withdrawn 'because of ill health and that he was fully at liberty, at that time, to go on with his class.'[39] The dean sent this letter with a note saying, 'This is for your sensitive feelings. I hope you will find it soothing.'[40] For the rest of his life Fitzgerald remained touchy about remarks that he had flunked out of Princeton, insisting that he had left on a stretcher. The *Ledger* judgment for 1915–16 is: 'A year of terrible disappointments + the end of all college dreams. Everything bad in it was my own fault.'

In February, Fitzgerald cooked up a locally famous hoax when, with Gus Schurmeier, he attended a Psi U dance at the University of Minnesota dressed as a girl and shocked his dancing partners with a racy line. (The joke supposedly ended when Fitzgerald tried to use the men's room.) He spent the spring of 1916 in St. Paul ostensibly studying, but mostly loafing and writing. His book for a Triangle Club show was declined, and he continued to send contributions to the *Tiger* and the *Lit*. Fitzgerald's only *Lit* appearance in the spring was 'To My Unused Greek Book,' an imitation of Keats's 'Ode on a Grecian Urn.'

Fitzgerald was never close to his sister Annabel, who did not share his intense self-awareness. Five years younger than he, Annabel did not interest him during his boyhood, and while he was at Newman and Princeton she was at convent schools. When she was a teenager, Fitzgerald turned his attention to refining her social skills – he always wanted to educate or improve the women he knew. He provided detailed written instructions on how to improve her image and make herself more popular with boys.

(2)

(C)   I'll line up your good points against your bad physically.

Good	Bad
Hair	Teeth only fair
Good general size	Pale complexion
Good features	Only fair figure
	Large hands and feet

73

Now you see of the bad points only the last cannot be remedied. Now while slimness is a fashion you can cultivate it by exercise – Find out now from some girl. Exercise would give you a healthier skin. You should never rub cold cream into your face because you have a slight tendency to grow hairs on it. I'd find out about this from some Dr. who'd tell you what you could use in place of a skin cream.

(D) A girl should always be careful about such things as underskirt showing, long drawers showing under stocking, bad breath, mussy eyebrows (with such splendid eyebrows as yours you should brush them or wet them and train them every morning and night as I advised you to do long ago. They oughtn't to have a hair out of place.)

(E) Walk and general physical grace. The point about this is that you'll be up against situations when ever you go out which will call for you to be graceful – not to be physically clumsy. Now you can only attain this by practise because it no more comes naturally to you than it does to me. Take some stylish walk you like and imitate it. A girl should have a little class. Look what a stylish walk Eleanor and Grace and Betty have and what a homely walk Marie and Alice have. Just because the first three deliberately practised every where until now its so natural to them that they can't be ungraceful – This is true about every gesture. I noticed last Saturday that your gestures are awkward and so unnatural as to seem affected. Notice the way graceful girls hold their hands and feet. How they stoop, wave, run and then try because you can't practise those things when men are around. It's two late then. They ought to be incentive then.

(F) General summing up.
(1) Dress scrupulously neatly and then forget your personal appearance. Every stocking should be pulled up to the last wrinkle.
(2) Don't wear things like that fussy hat that aren't becoming to you – At least buy no more. Take someone who knows with you – some one who really knows.
(3) Conform to your type no matter what looks well in the store

(4) Cultivate deliberate physical grace. You'll never have it if you don't. I'll discuss dancing in a latter letter.*[41]

Fitzgerald's remote relationship with his sister can be seen in the comment of the hero of 'The Romantic Egotist' on his younger brother: 'I was intensely critical about him and tried desperately to keep him from falling into a severe self-complacency. I succeeded only too well and finally forced him into a state of self-defence where he leaned almost wholly on mother. All through the next ten years, close as we were thrown together, we never really understood each other.'[42]

In March 1916 Ginevra was dismissed from Westover. Fitzgerald regarded it as a calamity and later incongruously paired it with his wife's insanity in one of his admonishing letters to his daughter when she was at school: 'It was in the cards that Ginevra King should get fired from Westover – also that your mother should wear out young.'[43] He visited Ginevra at Lake Forest in August 1916, but the meeting was unsatisfactory. Fitzgerald was no longer her number one suitor, and the competition included sons of wealth. It was pointedly remarked in Fitzgerald's hearing that poor boys shouldn't think of marrying rich girls.

* Fitzgerald later noted on this ten-page document: 'Written by me at 19 or so Basis of Bernice.' But Annabel would have been thirteen or fourteen then, and his instructions seem to apply to an older girl. In 'Bernice Bobs Her Hair,' written in 1919, the heroine is given popularity lessons.

7

Another Junior Year

[1916–1917]

When *Fitzgerald returned* to Princeton in September 1916 to repeat his junior year, he was officially a member of the Class of 1918 but continued to regard himself as Princeton '17. He roomed with Paul Dickey, who wrote the music for his Triangle songs, at 185 Little Hall. Although his Triangle book had been rejected, he provided the lyrics for the 1916–17 show, *Safety First*, which was written by John Biggs, Jr. '18 and J. F. Bohmfalk '17.

Fitzgerald repeated four of the courses he had taken the year before – the English Renaissance, Chaucer, the French Romantic Movement, and history of philosophy – and also took European history and qualitative analysis (which he had failed as a sophomore.) The English Renaissance literature preceptor was Nathaniel Griffin, whom Fitzgerald resented for dissecting the language of poetry. In his textbook edition of Sidney's *Defense of Poesy* Fitzgerald recorded this protest:

> Gee but this man Griffin is terrible. I sit here bored to death and hear him pick English poetry to pieces. Small man, small mind. Snotty, disagreeable Damn him. 'Neat' is his favorite

word. Imagine Shakespeare being neat. Yesterday I counted and found that he used the expression, 'Isn't that so' fifty four times. Oh what a disagreeable silly ass he is. He's going to get married. God help his wife. Poor girl. Shes in for a bad time. They say Griffin has made more men leave the English department than any other praeceptor in College. The slovenly old fool! *I have the most terrible praeceptors.*[44]

Ginevra came to the Yale game in November 1916, but their relationship was clearly wearing out. The final break would occur in January.

Fitzgerald worked on the December *Lit* 'Chaopolitan' issue, a burlesque of *Cosmopolitan* magazine, supplying unsigned parodies of popular writers John Fox, Jr., and Robert W. Chambers: 'Jemima A Story of the Blue Ridge Mountains by John Phlox, Jr.' and 'The Usual Thing by Robert W. Shameless.' He liked the Fox parody so much that he later reprinted it in *Vanity Fair* and collected it in *Tales of the Jazz Age* (1922). Fox, the author of the best-selling *Trail of the Lonesome Pine*, wrote sentimental novels about Southern mountaineers. Fitzgerald's burlesque is routine: 'Her feet were bare. Her hands, large and powerful, hung down below her knees. Her face showed the ravages of work. Although but sixteen, she had for over a dozen years been supporting her aged pappy and mappy by brewing mountain whiskey.'[45]

Fitzgerald was again ineligible for the Christmas Triangle tour. *Safety First*, a satire set in 'a Futurist art community,' had some of Fitzgerald's most admired lyrics.

It Is Art
Art, Art, the period is o'er
When your standards stand apart;
Mister Comstock's indignation
Gives a picture reputation
And doubles its sale as Art.
Art, Art, you're getting rather deep,
Common sense and you must part;
For a complex cubist dimple
Makes the 'Mona Lisa' simple,
There's no 'Safety First' in Art.[46]

77

The January 1917 *Lit* published Fitzgerald's 'The Debutante,' a play inspired by Ginevra King in which he admiringly delineates the selfishness of a society belle. Helen Halcyon's admission of her enjoyment in playing the love game anticipates the attitude of a string of Fitzgerald's heroines: 'I like the feeling of going after them, I like the thrill when you meet them and notice that they've got black hair that's wavey, but awfully neat, or have dark lines under their eyes, and look charmingly dissipated, or have funny smiles that come and go and leave you wondering whether they smiled at all. Then I like the way they begin to follow you with their eyes. They're interested. Good! Then I begin to place him. Try to get his type, find what he likes; right then the romance begins to lessen for me and increase for him.'[47] 'The Debutante' was reprinted by *The Smart Set* in 1919 and rewritten into *This Side of Paradise* for Amory Blaine's first meeting with the heroine, Rosalind.

Fitzgerald came close to flunking out in January 1917 when he failed three of his six courses: English Renaissance (2), Chaucer (3), history (F), French (2), philosophy (absent), chemistry (F). The two second groups (the equivalent of B's) were the highest grades he received at Princeton; one came in Louis Miles's English Renaissance poetry course and the other in Christian Gauss's French romantic literature course. Despite his strong interest in history, Fitzgerald failed Walter Hall's European history course. This failure still rankled in 1938 when he wrote his daughter: 'It has been so ironic to me in after life to buy books to master subjects in which I took courses at college which made no impression on me whatsoever. I once flunked a course on the Napoleonic era, and now I have over 300 books in my library on the subject + the other A scholars wouldn't even remember it now.'[48]

Like many undergraduates who are not training for a profession, Fitzgerald brooded over the problem of what to do after college, and his problem was intensified by the conviction that a high destiny awaited him. He wanted to be a great man, if not a leader of men. When he spoke about his writing ambitions, he astonished Edmund Wilson by announcing: 'I want to be one of the greatest writers who ever lived, don't you?' He meant it. Wilson later observed: 'I had not myself really quite entertained this fantasy because I had been reading Plato and Dante. Scott had been reading Booth Tarkington, Compton Mackenzie, H. G. Wells and Swinburne; but when he later got to better writers, his standards and his achievement went sharply up, and he would always have pitted himself against the best in his own line that he knew. I thought this remark rather foolish at the time, yet it was one of the things that made me respect him; and I am sure that his intoxicated ardor represented the healthy way for a young man of talent to feel.'[49]

Before America entered the war, Princetonians were joining the Allies or the American-sponsored ambulance units serving with the Allies, and Fitzgerald considered going to war – not for patriotic reasons but as a way to end what had become a pointless college career. In the spring of 1917, during what should have been his graduating term, he took only five courses, indicating that he (or Princeton) had abandoned trying to make up his failed courses. His courses were Shakespeare, history of the English language, French (the second term of the Romantic Movement), history of philosophy (Descartes to Kant), and again qualitative analysis. His poor scholastic record does not betray indifference to Princeton. He loved it and became almost a caricature of the loyal alumnus. For the rest of his life he returned to Princeton as though looking for some irrecoverable part of himself.

That spring Fitzgerald concentrated on the *Lit* instead of the Triangle Club and appeared thirteen times, with a play, four stories, three poems, and five reviews of books by Shane Leslie, E.F. Benson. H. G. Wells, and Booth Tarkington. 'The Spire and the Gargoyle' (February 1917), which he regarded as his first mature writing, is a story into which he put his feelings about Princeton – his love for the physical place itself and his sense of having failed to take advantage of all that the university offered. The story is built around three encounters between an undergraduate who flunks out and a preceptor who is compelled for financial reasons to resign his position and teach at a Brooklyn, New York, high school. Both regret their exile from Princeton, but the ex-student's feeling of loss is greater because for him the campus symbolizes blocked aspiration. 'Tarquin of Cheapside' (April 1917), which Fitzgerald later collected in *Tales of the Jazz Age*, relates how Shakespeare wrote 'The Rape of Lucrece' after committing the same offense. 'Babes in the Woods' (May 1917), a companion story to 'The Debutante,' was incorporated into *This Side of Paradise* for the first encounter between Amory and Isabelle. Based on Fitzgerald's meeting with Ginevra King in St. Paul, it describes how a pair of well-matched young veterans play the love game. The most ambitious of the four *Lit* stories in terms of Fitzgerald's development as a social historian – that is, as a moralist – is 'Sentiment – and the Use of Rouge' (June 1917), which examines the change in sexual conduct among the upper-class English during the war and a dying young officer's longing for meanings in a meaningless slaughter: 'Well, he'd find out the whole muddled business in about three minutes, and a lot of good it'd do anybody else left in the muddle. Damned muddle – everything a muddle, everybody offside, and the referee gotten rid of – everybody trying to say that if the referee were there he'd have been on their side. He was going to go and find that old referee – find him – get hold of him, get a good hold – cling to him – cling to him – ask him –.'[50]

The three poems – 'Rain Before Dawn' (February), 'Princeton – The Last Day' (May), and 'On a Play Twice Seen' (June) – are mood pieces that show Fitzgerald's heavy reliance on poetic diction. He had developed a prose style, but his poetry was derivative and self-conscious.

> Princeton – The Last Day
> The last light wanes and drifts across the land,
> The low, long land, the sunny land of spires.
> The ghosts of evening tune again their lyres
> And wander singing, in a plaintive band
> Down the long corridors of trees. Pale fires

Echo the night from tower top to tower.
Oh sleep that dreams and dream that never tires,
Press from the petals of the lotus-flower
Something of this to keep, the essence of an hour!

No more to wait the twilight of the moon
In this sequestrated vale of star and spire;
For one, eternal morning of desire
Passes to time and earthy afternoon.
Here, Heracletus, did you build of fire
And changing stuffs your prophecy far hurled
Down the dead years; this midnight I aspire
To see, mirrored among the embers, curled
In flame, the splendor and the sadness of the world.[51]

'Princeton – The Last Day' was included in *This Side of Paradise*, but in prose format. Although Wilson praised the poem for its 'depth and dignity of which I didn't suppose you capable,'[52] Fitzgerald's ear for the cadence and color of language would be put to better use in prose. He admitted that he could never become a great poet because he was 'not enough of a sensualist' and noticed only the obvious in beauty. Nonetheless, his apprenticeship to poetry helped to form his prose style: '. . . I don't think anyone can write succinct prose unless they have at least tried to write a good iambic pentameter sonnet, and read Browning's short dramatic poems, etc. – but that was my personal approach to prose.'[53] Fitzgerald reveled in the alliterative rhythms of Swinburne, but the rich imagery of Keats became his standard for great poetry.

When his daughter was in college, Fitzgerald tried to imbue her with his love of Keats:

Poetry is either something that lives like fire inside you – like music to the musician or Marxism to the communist – or else it is nothing, an empty, formalized bore around which pedants can endlessly drone their notes and explanations. *The Grecian Urn* is unbearably beautiful with every syllable as inevitable as the notes in Beethoven's Ninth Symphony or it's just something you don't understand. It is what it is because an extraordinary genius paused at that point in history and touched it. I suppose I've read it a hundred times. About the tenth time I began to know what it was about, and caught the chime in it and the exquisite inner mechanics. Likewise with *The Nightingale* which I can never read through without tears in my eyes; likewise the *Pot of Basil* with its great stanzas about the two brothers. 'Why were they proud, etc.'; and *The Eve of St. Agnes* which has the richest, most sensuous imagery in English, not excepting Shakespeare. And finally his three or four great sonnets, *Bright Star* and the others.

Knowing those things very young and granted an ear, one could scarcely ever afterwards be unable to distinguish between the gold and dross in what one read. In themselves those eight poems are a scale of workmanship for anybody who wants to know truly about words, their most utter value for evocation, persuasion or charm. For awhile after you quit Keats all other poetry seems to be only whistling or humming.[54]

Fitzgerald would presently try to become a prose Keats, imitating the poet's rhythms and enriching his own style with lush Keatsian imagery. He later observed that 'all fine prose is based on the verbs carrying the sentences. Probably the finest technical poem in English is Keats's *Eve of St. Agnes*. A line like: The hare limped trembling through the frozen grass,* is so alive that you race through it, scarcely noticing it, yet it has colored the whole poem with its movement – the limping, trembling and freezing is going on before your own eyes.'[55]

Keats became an enduring presence in Fitzgerald's life, providing him with a model of creative sensibility. Like Keats, Fitzgerald was painfully responsive to the mutability of beauty and the evanescence of youth. Both yearned for immortality through art, and Keats's early death imbued Fitzgerald with a sense of urgency. Above all, Fitzgerald identified with the Keatsian archetype – the handsome youth

---

* He imitated this line in 'The limousine crawled crackling down the pebbled drive' ('Love in the Night').

acclaimed for his genius. Literature was a glamorous thing for Fitzgerald. He aspired to early triumph and the fame that went with it. Grub Street and la vie bohème were not for him. He was not prepared to starve for art or to endure neglect. Fitzgerald's commitment to the dream of the literary life that has entertained many undergraduates was ingenuously immaculate. He knew he had talent; he wondered whether he had the genius to match his ambitions.

Despite his concern that he was marking time at Princeton, the spring 1917 term was stimulating. A visit to Wilson – now a literary journalist living in Greenwich Village – provided him with a possible model for his own career, strengthening New York's pull on him. The great event at Princeton that term was the anti-club movement led by sophomores Henry H. Strater, Carl Mickey, David K. E. Bruce (the son of a U.S. senator), and Richard F. Cleveland (the son of Grover Cleveland), which brought about resignations from the eating clubs on the grounds that they were not only snobbish but inimical to the ideals of Princeton. Fitzgerald did not become involved in the controversy, but he was friendly with Bruce and Strater – and was impressed by the latter's Whitmanesque-Tolstoyan principles.

On 6 April 1917 America entered the war, rather to Fitzgerald's relief, for it solved the problem of his future. He did not volunteer immediately, although the aviation service attracted him as the romantic equivalent of the Civil War cavalry. Instead, he signed up in May for three weeks of intensive military training under a plan by which students were given full credit for their dropped academic courses. Fitzgerald thereby passed all his courses with straight Third group grades.

Fay and Leslie maintained their interest in their protégé, and Fitzgerald saw them in Washington and New York. Leslie took him to visit his brother-in-law, Congressman Bourke Cockran, on Long Island, where Fitzgerald delivered a late-night oration to the Cockrans' Pekingese, climaxing with the declaration that 'A man only wants to know for certain that his children are his own!'[56]

Fitzgerald was included in the *Nassau Herald Class of 1917*, the graduating class yearbook, in which his statement of future plans reads: 'He will pursue graduate work in English at Harvard, then he will engage in newspaper work.'[57] In the class poll he received two votes for Most Brilliant (Bishop received fifty), two for Handsomest, five for Prettiest, seven for Wittiest, fifteen for Thinks He Is Wittiest, two for Thinks He Is Best Dressed, eight for Thinks He Is Biggest Politician, and six as the class's Favorite Dramatist. At the Princeton '17 graduation John Peale Bishop carried off most of the literary honors: he was class poet, collaborated on the class ode, and won English prizes. Fitzgerald's *Ledger* summary of what should have been his senior year at Princeton was 'pregnant year of endeavor. Outwardly failure, with moments of anger but the foundation of my literary life.'

Fitzgerald spent July with Bishop at Charles Town, West Virginia, writing poetry and discussing literature and religion. Then he went home to St. Paul, where he took the exam for an infantry commission at Fort Snelling. Father Fay, who had been engaged in a scheme for securing Ireland's independence in return for American Catholic support of the Allies, was slated for a secret mission to Russia aimed at unifying the Catholic Church, using the cover of a Red Cross mission. Proposing to take Fitzgerald along as his aide, Fay instructed him to apply for a passport and wait until plans were firm. The priest's letters to Fitzgerald show his relish in playing the role of secret agent:

> Deal Beach, New Jersey
> August 22nd, 1917.

> Dear Fitz:—
> I cannot tell you how delighted I am to have gotten your letter.
> First of all as to money. Your $3600 will cover everything except your uniforms. There is no salary for any of us; they expect us to take it out in glory, and really there will be glory enough if we manage to do what I hope we will.

Now, in the eyes of the world, we are a Red Cross Commission sent out to report on the work of the Red Cross, and especially on the State of the civil population, and that is all I can say. But I will tell you this, the State Department is writing to our ambassador in Russia and Japan, the British Foreign Office is writing to their ambassador in Japan and Russia, and I have other letters to our ambassador in Japan and Russia, and to everybody else in fact who can be of the slightest assistance to us. Moreover I am taking letters from Eminence to the Catholic Bishops.

The conversion of Russia has already begun. Several millions of Russians have already come over to the Catholic Church from the schism in the last month. Whether you look at it from the spiritual or temporal point of view it is an immense opportunity and will be a help to you all the rest of your life.

You will be a Red Cross Lieutenant, and I will let you know as soon as I get your commission what your uniform will be.

Will you come on and join me in New York and get your uniforms there at the regular Red Cross place, where you can get them in 24 hours. You are measured at dawn, fitted at noon and fitted out at sunset. Or will you join me in Chicago and we can go thence to San Francisco and bid affectionate farewell to Peevie, and get to Vancouver in time for the 27th. Or shall I come to St. Paul, and will we go by the C.P.R. But what will Peevie do then, poor fellow. It is hard enough on him in any case.

I think the best thing you and I can do is to write a book while we are away. I am going to take a Corona typewriter. I am so glad you know how to work one.

We shall have to work very hard going over on your French. Get a Rosenthal method at once and go right through it.

You will have to take plenty of warm clothes as we shall be in a very cold climate most of the time. You will be in Russia three months, not away only three months. Your money ought to be in this form: It costs $1600 for our traveling over and back, and $2000 in a letter of credit while we are living in Russia, as we shall have to keep at least some state.

Now, do be discreet about what you say to anybody. If anybody asks you say you are going as secretary to a Red Cross Commission. Do not say anything more than that, and if you show this letter to anybody, show it only in the strictest confidence. I would not show it to anybody but your mother, father and aunt.

To my mind the most extraordinary thing about it is that we may play a part in the restoration of Russia to Catholic unity. The schismatic church is crumbling to pieces; it has now no State to lean on.

I am tremendously glad you are going to have this experience. It really will change your whole life. Poor Peevie could not go. I was hoping that he might and I would have taken you both in that case.

Leslie cannot go as he is not an American citizen, and the Red Cross is now the Government, so they cannot send anybody who is not an American. Besides he could not leave the Dublin; we cannot all be away.

I think the Dublin Review will be jolly glad to get anything we send them, signed with any initials we care to put to it. But I think we had better save our efforts for a book which we will write together, and to which we will put both our names.

Though we get no salary we all have to work hard, and you will have to help me with an enormous amount of correspondence. As you would elegantly express it, 'the whole thing is a knock-out.' I sincerely hope the war will be over long before you take to flying.

Now, last of all, whatever you surmise about the commission, keep your brilliant guesses to yourself. You guess far too well. Above all be careful what you say about religion. It is for that very reason that the attaches are Protestant. There will be no Catholics except yourself, myself and my servant. Whatever is done A.M.D.G. will be done by you and me. For this reason I shall arrange for you to share my cabin, and we can take a room together when we get to Russia, as it will save some money at least and give us a chance to talk the things over which must be strictly confidential between us.

About your commission – give it up now, and say that as you have heard nothing you have decided to wait until you are of age and then go in for aviation. But I hope to goodness, as I said before that the war will be over before you take to that.

As soon as you have read this letter and shown it at home, burn it.

With best love,

S. W. Fay[58]

86

After Fitzgerald obtained his passport for 'secretarial work' in Russia, Fay's mission was canceled. Fay went to Rome as a Red Cross major ('Followed by the Secret Service of three nations,' according to Leslie), but was unable to take Fitzgerald.[59] After reporting to the Pope on a discussion with President Wilson about Vatican participation in the post-war peace conference, he was elevated to monsignor.

That summer Fitzgerald tried to tutor himself in philosophy, reporting to Wilson that he was reading James, Schopenhauer, and Bergson, as well as drinking gin.[60] He returned to Princeton in September 1917 and roomed in Campbell Hall with John Biggs, Jr., the editor of the *Tiger*, while waiting for his commission. Although he must have registered for classes, his Princeton transcript has no courses listed for that term. He wrote for the *Tiger* and the *Lit* and had his first professional acceptance when *Poet Lore* magazine took 'The Way of Purgation,' which it did not publish. When the *Tiger* was short of copy that fall, Biggs and Fitzgerald wrote the whole issue overnight. Fitzgerald claimed that his 'Intercollegiate Petting-Cues' – 'You really don't look comfortable there'[61] – in the *Tiger* attracted wide collegiate attention. Only seven of the Fitzgerald *Tiger* contributions are signed; twenty-seven others have been attributed to him on the basis of clippings in his scrapbooks. The contributions include parodies, jokes, cartoon ideas, and verse.

Robert Frost
A rugged young rhymer named Frost,
Once tried to be strong at all cost
   The mote in his eye
   May be barley or rye,
But his right in that beauty is lost.

Though the meek shall inherit the land,
He prefers a tough bird in the hand,
   He puts him in inns,
   And feeds him on gins,
And the high brows say, 'Isn't he grand?'[62]
      F.S.F.

Fitzgerald appeared in the October issue of the *Lit* with a long poem, 'The Cameo Frame,' and a story, 'The Pierian Springs and the Last Straw.' The story develops a major theme in Fitzgerald's fiction: the gifted man ruined by a selfish woman. The hero is a scandalous middle-aged novelist who lost his Ginevra as a young man and never got over it. When he marries her after she is widowed, he stops writing. Much of Fitzgerald's fiction would take the form of self-warnings or self-judgments, and this story is the first in which he analyzed the conflicting pulls of love and literature. The girl is the writer's inspiration, but only when she is

The 1917 Tiger *board, Princeton. Fitzgerald is standing in the center behind John Biggs, Jr.*

unattained. The satisfied artist is unproductive. Yet Fitzgerald was determined to pursue both love and literature because his idealized girl was an integral part of his ambitions.

It is impossible to determine the extent to which Fitzgerald's attitudes toward women were shaped by Irish-Catholic Jansenism. Cornelis Jansen (1585–1638) maintained the doctrine of total human depravity. His followers were notable for their rigidly puritanical sexual views and misogyny, and Jansenist priests were influential in Ireland. Fitzgerald created a procession of female destroyers of men, but his judgment was not misogynistic. His women – even at their most destructive – are warmly attractive. If his men become their victims, it is the fault of the men for being weak. Given the romantic temperament of his male characters, it is clear they seek destruction – or at least welcome its potentiality. The romantic pattern of behavior expresses itself in defeat as well as triumph; and the noble failure who throws himself away for a gesture is a familiar romantic figure. Fitzgerald made a distinction which clearly pleased him since he used it twice in *This Side of Paradise*: 'the sentimental person thinks things will last – the romantic person has a desperate confidence that they won't.'[63]

Fitzgerald's attitude toward women as agents of destruction has little to do with sexual corruption, although he remained puritanical about sex. His women do have strong sexual appeal, of course; but that does not account for the conduct of his men who come to the battlefield of love hampered by a romantic disposition usually associated in fiction with the feminine nature. The women are realistic about love and marriage. His men – not his women – render allegiance to the notion of the world well lost for love.

The literary traditions for Fitzgerald's male lovers may be traced to the code of courtly love and to Keats's 'La Belle Dame Sans Merci.' His heroes, like Shakespeare's Troilus, are betrayed or destroyed by women who lack the capacity for total romantic commitment. Thus Gatsby idealizes Daisy, who is unworthy of his devotion. Indeed, a strain of masochism

89

can be detected in some of Fitzgerald's men – almost as though they deliberately choose destructive women. Yet his condemnation of feminine selfishness is often mixed with respect for female strength of character.

THE LAST
OF THE
BELLES

[1917–1920]

8

The Army and
'The Romantic Egotist'

[1917–1918]

Fitzgerald's commission as a second lieutenant in the infantry is dated 26 October 1917. Before leaving Princeton, he attitudinized for his mother: 'If you want to pray, pray for my soul and not that I won't be killed – the last doesn't seem to matter particularly and if you are a good Catholic the first ought to.'[1] Having outfitted himself at Brooks Brothers, he reported in November for training at Fort Leavenworth, Kansas.

Fay sent a keen on 10 December, which Fitzgerald later incorporated into *This Side of Paradise*:

> *A Lament for a Foster Son, and He going to the War*
> *Against the King of Foreign*

Ochone
He is gone from me the son of my mind
   And he in his golden youth like Angus Oge
Angus of the bright birds
   And his mind strong and subtle like the mind of Cuchulin
    on
     Muirtheme.

93

. . . .
Jia du Vaha Alanav
May the Son of God be above him and beneath him, before
him and behind him
May the King of the elements cast a mist over the eyes of the
King of Foreign,
May the Queen of the Graces lead him by the hand the way he
can go through the midst of his enemies and they not seeing
him
May Patrick of the Gael and Collumb of the Churches and the
five thousand Saints of Erin be better than a shield to him
And he go into the fight.
Och Ochone.[2]

Like all infantry lieutenants at the time, Fitzgerald
expected to be killed in battle. He began writing a novel in
training camp, hoping to leave evidence of his genius:* 'Every
evening, concealing my pad behind Small Problems for
Infantry, I wrote paragraph after paragraph on a somewhat
edited history of me and my imagination. The outline of
twenty-two chapters, four of them in verse, was made, two
chapters were completed; and then I was detected and the
game was up. I could write no more during study period.'[4]
Working in the officers' club from 1 P.M. to midnight on
Saturdays and 6 A.M. to 6 P.M. on Sundays, he completed a
120,000-word novel in about three months.

Fitzgerald wrote into his manuscript an explanation of his
sense of urgency, indicating his conception of himself as a
spokesman for his generation:

A week has gone here in the aviation school just hurried by

---

* Christian Gauss later recalled that Fitzgerald showed him the manuscript
for a novel before leaving Princeton, which Gauss dissuaded him from
publishing. Gauss's memory was almost certainly inaccurate on this point.
There is no evidence that Fitzgerald had written any substantial portion of
his novel before reporting to Leavenworth. Fitzgerald probably showed Dean
Gauss 'The Romantic Egotist' when he was working on it at the Cottage Club
in March 1918. In a 1934 letter Fitzgerald thanked Gauss for putting in a
good word 'for my first book, then bound for Scribners.'[3]

with early rising by the November moon, and here I am with not one chapter finished – scrawled pages with no form or style – just full of detail and petty history. I intended so much when I started, and I'm realizing how impossible it all is. I can't re-write and all I do is form the vague notes for chapters that I have here beside me and the uncertain channels of an uneven memory. I don't seem to be able to trace the skeins of development as I ought. I'm trying to set down the story part of my generation in America and put myself in the middle as a sort of observer and conscious factor.

But I've got to write now, for when the war's over I won't be able to see these things as important – even now they are fading out against the back-ground of the map of Europe. I'll never be able to do it again; well done or poorly. So I'm writing almost desperately – and so futily.[5]

On 22 December 1917 he informed Leslie:

– My novel isn't a novel in verse – it merely shifts rapidly from verse to prose – but it's mostly in prose.

The reason I've abandoned my idea of a book of poems is that I've only about twenty poems and cant write any more in this atmosphere – while I can write prose so I'm sandwitching the poems between rheams of autobiography and fiction.

It makes a pot-pouri especially as there are pages in dialogue and in verse libre but it reads as logically for the times as most public utterances of the prim and prominent. It is a tremendously conceited affair.[6]

On 10 January 1918 he reported to Edmund Wilson:

There are twenty-three chapters, all but five are written and it is poetry, prose, verse libre and every mood of a temperamental temperature. It purports to be the picaresque ramble of one Stephen Palms from the San Francisco fire, thru school, Princeton to the end where at twenty one he writes his autobiography at the Princeton aviation school. It shows traces of Tarkington, Chesterton, Chambers Wells, Benson (Robert Hugh), Rupert Brooke and includes Compton-McKenzie like love affairs and three psychic adventures including an encounter with the devil in a harlots apartment.

It rather damns much of Princeton but its nothing to what it thinks of man and human nature in general. I can most nearly describe it by calling it a prose, modernistic Childe Harold and really if Scribner takes it I know I'll wake some morning and find that the debutantes have made me famous over night. I really believe that no one else could have written so searchingly the story of the youth of our generation. . . .'[7]

The manuscript for 'The Romantic Egotist' does not survive. There are only the five carbon-copy typescript chapters at Princeton that Fitzgerald sent to Sap Donahoe in October 1918.*

CHAPTER I. The Egotist Up [Stephen's boyhood in San Francisco and Minneapolis]
CHAPTER II. The Egotist Down [Stephen at prep school]
CHAPTER V. Spires and Gargoyles [Stephen at Princeton]
CHAPTER XII. Eleanor [Stephen's poetic interlude in Maryland]
CHAPTER XIV. The Devil [Stephen's supernatural experience in the chorus girl's apartment]

These first-person chapters show that 'The Romantic Egotist' was so close to *This Side of Paradise* as to be a working draft for the novel Fitzgerald published in 1920. Every major episode in these five chapters was salvaged – except for Stephen and Eleanor's unconvincing supernatural encounter with her levitating fur coat in Chapter XII, based on an experience that Fay had related to Fitzgerald.

Fitzgerald was a poor soldier, for he regarded the army as an impediment to his writing. The captain in charge of Fitzgerald's training platoon at Fort Leavenworth was Dwight D. Eisenhower, but neither man made an impression on the other. When he received leave at the end of February 1918, Fitzgerald went to Princeton, where he finished his novel at the Cottage Club. (In 1936 he presented a page of the

* Since Fitzgerald's cover note to Donahoe says, 'Book is back at Scribner's,' it is impossible to determine whether these carbon copies represent the revised or the original version. One of the drafts of the novel was typed in the law office of John Biggs's father.

manuscript to the Cottage Club library.) He sent the typescript to Shane Leslie, who had offered to recommend it to his publisher, Charles Scribner's Sons. Fitzgerald hoped his novel would receive favorable attention because the Scribners were Princetonians and the house maintained close relations with the university. After correcting grammar and spelling, Leslie sent 'The Romantic Egotist' to Charles Scribner on 6 May with a cover letter describing the author as an American prose Rupert Brooke: 'Though Scott Fitzgerald is still alive it has a literary value. Of course when he is killed, it will also have a commercial value.'[8] Fitzgerald circulated chapters to Fay and Bishop as well.

On 15 March, Fitzgerald reported to the 45th Infantry Regiment at Camp Zachary Taylor, near Louisville, Kentucky. He was scheduled to be given a platoon; but his superior officers felt he couldn't be entrusted with a command, and for several weeks he served as assistant to the regimental school officer. In April the 45th was transferred to Camp Gordon, Georgia, and in June it was combined with the 67th Infantry Regiment of the Ninth Division at Camp Sheridan near Montgomery, Alabama, to be built up for overseas service. Fitzgerald was promoted to first lieutenant at Camp Sheridan, but his brother officers declined to take him seriously and made him the victim of pranks. On their advice he forced a conscientious objector in his platoon to drill at gunpoint – unaware that he was committing a prison offense. As a leader of enlisted men, he was an arbitrary disciplinarian: when his platoon complained about the food, he ordered a punishment march.[9]

With his novel out of the way, Fitzgerald was able to pay more attention to soldiering and social activities. He was still unreliable in the field. There was a near disaster when his mortar group was practicing, and a live shell jammed in a Stokes mortar; another officer picked up the mortar and threw it away from the soldiers. Fitzgerald did distinguish himself by preventing men from drowning when a barge sank during an exercise crossing the Talapoosa River.

The Montgomery girls welcomed the Yankee officers, who were more sophisticated than the local swains. Two of the top girls were May Steiner and Zelda Sayre, and Fitzgerald dated both of them. He met eighteen-year-old Zelda at the Country Club of Montgomery in July 1918, where she performed the 'Dance of the Hours.' During their later years of bitter

Zelda Sayre in dancing costume
COURTESY OF WILDA WILLIAMS

recriminations Fitzgerald insisted that Zelda was reeling drunk the first time he saw her. Zelda recorded her early impression of Fitzgerald in her autobiographical novel, *Save Me the Waltz.* 'There seemed to be some heavenly support beneath his shoulder blades that lifted his feet from the ground in ecstatic suspension, as if he secretly enjoyed the ability to fly but was walking as a compromise to convention.'[10] It was not love at first sight for Fitzgerald. He stipulated in his September 1918 *Ledger* entry: 'Fell in love on the 7th' – two months after their first encounter.

On 19 August 1918 Scribners rejected 'The Romantic Egotist.' The long letter – not a form rejection – signed 'Charles Scribner's Sons' was almost certainly written by Maxwell Perkins, who had moved from the advertising department to the editorial staff. Perkins was inclined to publish the novel but was overruled by the senior editors, Edward L. Burlingame and William C. Brownell. After stating that 'no ms. novel has come to us for a long time that seemed to display so much originality,' the letter made suggestions for revisions and invited Fitzgerald to resubmit the novel:

> . . . the story does not seem to us to work up to a conclusion: – neither the hero's career nor his character are shown to be brought to any stage which justifies an ending. This may be intentional on your part for it is certainly not untrue to life; but it leaves the reader distinctly disappointed and dissatisfied since he has expected him to arrive somewhere either in an actual sense by his response to the war perhaps, or in a psychological one by 'finding himself' as for instance Pendennis is brought to do. He does go to war, but in almost the same spirit that he went to college and school, – because it is simply the thing to do. It seems to us in short that the story does not culminate in anything as it must to justify the reader's interest as he follows it; and that it might be made to do so quite consistently with the characters and with its earlier stages.
>
> It seems to us too that not enough significance is given to

some of those salient incidents and scenes, such as the affairs with girls. We do not suggest that you should resort to artificiality by giving a significance inconsistent with that of the life of boys and girls of the age of the hero, but that it would be well if the high points were heightened so far as justifiable; and perhaps this effect could partly be gained by pruning detail you might find could be spared elsewhere. Quite possibly all that we have said is covered by your own criticism of the ms. as at present a little 'crude' and that the revision you contemplate will itself remove the basis of our criticism, and if when you make this you allow us a second reading we shall gladly give it. We do not want anything we have said to make you think we failed to get your idea in the book, – we certainly do not wish to 'conventionalize' it by any means in either form or manner, but only to do those things which it seems to us important to intensify its effect and so satisfy a reader that he will recommend it, – which is the great thing to accomplish toward a success.[11]

Fitzgerald undertook a rapid revision. In a 1919 preface written for *This Side of Paradise* he explained how he tried to provide the conclusion that Scribners wanted:*

At length I took a tip from Schopenhauer, Hugh Walpole, and even the early Wells – begged the question by plunging boldly into obscurity; astounded myself with an impenetrable chapter where I left the hero alone with rhapsodic winds and hyper-significant stars: gemmed the paragraphs with neo-symbolic bits culled from my own dismantled poems – such awe-inspiring half-lines as***the dark celibacy of greatness ***Youth, the Queen Anne clavichord from which age wrings the symphony of art***the tired pitying beauty of monotony that hung like summer air over the gate of his soul***
And finding that I had dragged the hero from a logical muddle into an illogical one, I dispatched him to the war and callously slew him several thousand feet in the air, whence he fell 'not like a dead, but a splendid life-bound swallow ****down****down****'[12]

* This preface, not used in the novel, was published separately in 1975.

100

Ginevra King married Ensign William Hamilton Mitchell in September. Fitzgerald saved the wedding invitation and a piece of her handkerchief in his scrapbook with the note 'THE END OF A ONCE POIGNANT STORY.' His summary for 1917–18, his twenty-first year, read: 'A year of enormous importance. Work and Zelda. Last year as a Catholic.'

Perkins rejected the revised novel in October, and in his scrapbook Fitzgerald captioned the telegram 'The end of a dream.' Fitzgerald believed that the unfavorable decision had been partly based on the circumstance that his material was too strong for a conservative publisher and asked Perkins to send it to another publisher, who also declined it.

9

Zelda Sayre

[1918]

Zelda Sayre, born 24 July 1900, was three years and ten months younger than Fitzgerald. She had been named for a gypsy heroine in a novel (probably Jane Howard's *Zelda*, 1866). The daughter of Minnie Machen Sayre and Judge Anthony D. Sayre of the Alabama Supreme Court, Zelda knew exactly who she was and what she could get away with – which was almost anything. She later observed: 'When I was a little girl I had great confidence in myself, even to the extent of walking by myself against life as it was then. I did not have a single feeling of inferiority, or shyness, or doubt, and no moral principles.'[13] At eighteen she was a celebrated belle with a domain that extended over Alabama and Georgia. She was like nobody else and practiced a don't-give-a-damn code. Even more dramatically than Ginevra, Zelda possessed the qualities that Fitzgerald required in a girl. She was beautiful, independent, socially secure (but not wealthy), and responsive to his ambitions. More than any girl he had ever known, Zelda shared his romantic egotism. She and Fitzgerald wanted the same things – metropolitan glamour, success, fame. It is surprising that her ambitions so closely matched his, because she had no background for them. At eighteen she had never been out of the South, and her formal education had terminated at

102

Sidney Lanier High School. She was not well-read, but her mind had a brilliant quality in its ability to make unlikely connections and express itself in fresh or startling ways. One of her attractions for Fitzgerald was her conversational stamina. Both were talkers for whom nothing was entirely meaningful until they had analyzed it. Although Fitzgerald later claimed that she was sexually reckless when he met her, Zelda's Montgomery friends deny the charge: 'No one to my knowledge ever questioned her good reputation as to morals.'[14] She was unconventional and even wild, but she maintained her reputation within the boundaries of Southern feminine conduct. Later Zelda wrote of the heroine of *Save Me the Waltz*: ' "She's the wildest of the Beggs, but she's a thoroughbred," people said. . . "Thoroughbred!" she thought, "meaning that I never let them down on the dramatic possibilities of a scene – I give a damned good show." '[15]

Zelda's beauty does not emerge in her photographs. Indeed, she had a chameleon quality; it is sometimes hard to be certain that two photos of her are really of the same person. Part of her impact was what she projected. Her hair was a dark-blond honey color – like a chow's, as Fitzgerald described it. She had blue eyes, thin lips, and a straight nose that gave her an almost hawklike profile. Though Zelda was two or three inches shorter than Fitzgerald's five feet seven, her erect posture made her seem taller than she was, and she moved with a dancer's grace. She had taken ballet lessons and was the star of local dance recitals.

Minnie Machen Sayre, the daughter of Kentucky Senator Willis B. Machen, had been musical and literary as a girl. She had once been offered a stage role by Georgia Drew, but her father – who was being considered as a dark-horse Presidential candidate – refused to countenance his daughter's entering what he regarded as the demimonde. It is not clear that Minnie Sayre tried to compensate for her frustrated career hopes through Zelda, but she did indulge her daughter. Minnie's fifth surviving child, born when she was forty, Zelda was breastfed until she was three. She was not close to her siblings. Her three sisters, Marjorie, Rosalind,

103

and Clothilde, were eighteen, eleven, and nine when she was born; her brother, Anthony, was six. Rosalind (Tootsie) and Clothilde (Tilde) were beautiful and popular; but Marjorie, who had been a delicate child, was subject to nervous illness most of her life. Though Zelda had girlfriends, she preferred the company of boys because they were less bound by convention. Indifferent to Montgomery society, Minnie allowed Zelda considerable freedom and abetted her daughter's defiance of the Judge.

Zelda was one of the most popular girls in town because she was known as a good sport who would do anything for the fun of it. She once phoned the fire department that there was a child trapped on the roof of the Sayre house, then climbed up to await her rescuers. She mounted the driver's seat of Judge Mayfield's carriage and took it for a short, wild ride. By the age of eighteen Zelda had started a legend that extended to the campuses of the University of Alabama, Auburn University, and Georgia Tech. When the chaperones at a Christmas party reprimanded her for dancing too affectionately, she pinned mistletoe to her dress over her backside. As Camp Sheridan and Camp Taylor filled up with young officers, the Sayre residence at 6 Pleasant Avenue became an obligatory calling-place. The commander at the Camp Taylor airfield is supposed to have issued an order against stunting planes over her house.

Like Fitzgerald, Zelda had an exhibitionistic streak. But there was a difference: Fitzgerald wanted admiration or at least attention; Zelda did not care what people thought. His behavior indicated insecurity; hers seemed to display defiance. Nonetheless, she clung to the securities of the Southern establishment. As she wrote in her novel, ' . . . it's very difficult to be two simple people at once, one who wants to have a law to itself and the other who wants to keep all the nice old things and be loved and safe and protected.'[16] She was, after all, Judge Sayre's daughter.

Anthony Dickinson Sayre was remote from his family. Zelda described him as a 'living fortress.'[17] His devotion to the

104

law excluded all other interests, and he was regarded as a
pillar of rectitude. Judge Sayre was the son of Daniel Sayre,
editor of the *Montgomery Post* and an influential figure in
Masonic politics, and Musidora Morgan Sayre, the sister of
Alabama Senator John Tyler Morgan. It was in part due to
Senator Machen's friendship with Senator Morgan that
Minnie Machen was sent to school in Montgomery. There she
met Morgan's nephew, the studious Anthony Sayre, whom
she married in 1884. After a career in the Alabama legislature
– he was president of the State Senate for a term – and as
judge of the City Court of Montgomery, Sayre was appointed
to the Alabama Supreme Court in 1909. He was elected to the
court in 1910 and reelected for the rest of his life, although
he refused to campaign because he regarded electioneering
as beneath the dignity of the bench. An austere figure, Judge
Sayre read Homer, Hesiod, Sallust, and Juvenal in the
original for pleasure. The Judge, who was sixty in 1918, was
upset by his youngest daughter's conduct. Because he retired
at 8 P.M., he was unaware of most of Zelda's nocturnal
activities. When he forbade her to do something, she would
ignore his prohibitions.

Providing for his large family (at one time the household
included the Judge's brother and Minnie's sister and mother)
on his $6,000-a-year salary caused Judge Sayre severe
worry. Since he abhorred any form of debt, the Sayres lived
in rented houses. He suffered a nervous breakdown that was
rarely mentioned.[18] Nor was the suicide of Minnie's mother
ever referred to.

During the summer of 1918 Fitzgerald worked his way up
to the position of Zelda's number-one suitor, but she
continued to date other men. Fitzgerald's jealousy did not
deter her, and he suspected that she enjoyed his distress.
From Fitzgerald's later remarks it seems clear that he and
Zelda consummated their romance before he left Camp
Sheridan for presumed battle in France. His response was
probably the same as Jay Gatsby's after taking Daisy: 'He felt
married to her, that was all.'[19] A sheet with his 1934 Philippe

stories has this note: 'After yielding she holds Philippe at bay like Zelda + me in summer 1917.'[20] (The year was 1918; Fitzgerald was not in Alabama in 1917.)

On 26 October the 67th Infantry was shipped north for embarkation to France. As supply officer, Fitzgerald was supposed to supervise the unloading of equipment at Hoboken, New Jersey, but he got off the train to visit Princeton. His unit went to Camp Mills on Long Island preparatory to embarkation. Fitzgerald claimed that he boarded a train for a Canadian port before his orders were canceled, but he also claimed that he was on a troop ship when the war ended.[21] He was disappointed because he wanted to test himself in battle, and he saw the war as a great romantic experience from which he was being excluded. In 'The Offshore Pirate' (1920) Fitzgerald wrote of a young man who also misses out on action: 'It was not so bad – except that when the infantry came limping back from the trenches he wanted to be one of them. The sweat and mud they wore seemed only one of those ineffable symbols of aristocracy that were forever eluding him.'[22] For the rest of Fitzgerald's life 'I didn't get over' was an expression of regret. The dream of war became another wish fulfillment that he used to seek sleep during his years of insomnia: ' – my division is cut to rags and stands on the defensive in a part of Minnesota where I know every bit of the ground. The headquarters staff and the regimental battalion commanders who were in conference with them at the time have been killed by one shell. The command devolved upon Captain Fitzgerald. With superb presence. . . .'[23]

Camp Mills officers had leave in New York City, where Fitzgerald engaged in alcoholic escapades that may have been a response to his disappointment at missing the war. On one occasion he was caught by the Hotel Astor house detective with a naked girl. Fitzgerald was confined to Camp Mills to keep him out of trouble; but when the 67th was ordered back to Montgomery in November, he was AWOL in New York and was left behind. When the troop train arrived in

Washington, Fitzgerald was waiting at trackside with a bottle and two girls. He explained that he had commandeered an engine at Pennsylvania Station by claiming that he had a message for President Wilson.[24]

At Camp Sheridan he was made aide to General J.A. Ryan. Again he was the target of a prank when his fellow officers instructed him that he should sleep late to rest up for the late-night socializing required by his new position. The general was not amused when he found his aide in bed during an inspection tour. Fitzgerald also fell off his horse at parade and was ordered to take riding lessons.

While he was awaiting discharge, Fitzgerald had ample time to devote to Zelda. At first he resisted the idea of early marriage because it would interfere with his literary ambitions. On 4 December 1918 he wrote to his friend Ruth Sturtevant: '. . . my mind is firmly made up that I will not, shall not, can not, should not, must not marry – still she *is* remarkable. I'm trying desperately *exire armis* – '[25] Despite his resolves, it was not long before Fitzgerald regarded himself as engaged; then he wanted Zelda to marry him as soon as possible. Zelda's friends did not believe she would marry him, and her family did not encourage the match. Although there was strong anti-Catholic prejudice in the South, the Episcopalian Sayres were not opposed to Fitzgerald because he was Catholic and a Yankee. They felt that he lacked stability and would not be able to take proper care of their daughter.

Reckless and impulsive about many things, Zelda was cautious about marriage to an unpublished writer with no money. His $141-a-month army pay went far in Montgomery, but he had no other income and no financial expectations. She was ready to marry Fitzgerald when he was a success in New York – it was understood they would live there – but she knew that love on a budget would be impossible for them. Fitzgerald was hurt by her lack of faith in his destiny; yet at the same time he recognized that her stand was consistent with her refusal to compromise on what she required from life.

They quarreled about her refusal to gamble on his future and her insistence that she had every right to date other men – going to a dance or party with someone else, she said, had nothing to do with her love for him. Fitzgerald responded to their quarrels by getting drunk, the worst tactic he could have chosen. Zelda admired confidence, and Fitzgerald's displays of weakness eroded her belief that he would really be able to achieve all the great things he promised.

10

New York:
Failure and Heartbreak

[Spring 1919]

Monsignor Fay died of pneumonia in New York on 10 January 1919. On that day, before he learned the news, Fitzgerald had a seizure of trembling. The element of the supernatural in Fitzgerald's experience apparently ended with Fay's death; but it found continuing expression in his fiction. Fitzgerald could not attend the funeral. In late January he wrote Leslie from the base hospital, where he was being treated for influenza.

> Your letter seemed to start a new flow of sorrows in me. I've never wanted so much to die in my life – Father Fay always thought that if one of us died the others would and now how I've hoped so.
>
> Oh it all seemed so easy, life I mean – with people who understood and satisfied needs. Even the philistines seemed very good and quiet always ready to be duped or influenced or something and now my little world made to order has been shattered by the death of one man.
>
> I'm beginning to have a horror of *people*; I can quite sympathize with your desire to be a Carthusian.

This has made me nearly sure that I will become a priest – I feel as if his mantle had descended apon me – a desire, or more, to some day recreate the atmosphere of him – I think he was the sort of man St. Peter was, so damned human.

Think of the number of people who in a way looked to him and depended on him – His faith shining thru all the versatility and intellect.

I think I did feel him but cant tell you of it in a letter. It was rather ghastly — [26]

This letter was mostly a pose for Leslie's benefit. Fitzgerald's priestly vocation had never been strong, and his talk about the priesthood was a way of getting attention. Despite the generalization that no Irishman ever really leaves Holy Mother Church, Fitzgerald left without a backward glance or lingering guilt. His spells of devoutness had come when his imagination was stimulated by some religious role or some priest. Fitzgerald's Catholicism died with Fay. Zelda replaced the influence of Fay and the Church.

Fitzgerald was discharged early from the army because he was expendable. On his way to seek rapid success in New York he wired Zelda from Charlotte, North Carolina, on 21 February 1919: YOU KNOW I DO NOT YOU DARLING.[27] The message was probably a reference to their quarrel about her insistence on attending a party at Auburn as the date of a football player. The next day he wired from New York: DARLING HEART AMBITION ENTHUSIASM AND CONFIDENCE I DECLARE EVERYTHING GLORIOUS THIS WORLD IS A GAME AND WHILE I FEEL SURE OF YOU LOVE EVERYTHING IS POSSIBLE I AM IN THE LAND OF AMBITION AND SUCCESS AND MY ONLY HOPE AND FAITH IS THAT MY DARLING HEART WILL BE WITH ME SOON.[28]

His plan was to succeed at a job that would allow them to marry as soon as possible. That was what poor young men did in novels, and, as Fitzgerald once remarked, he could always do what people did in books. After applying unsuccessfully for newspaper work, he took a job with the Barron Collier advertising agency composing trolley-car cards at a salary he variously reported as $90 a month and $35 a week. He spent most of his nights writing stories, verse, jokes – anything that might sell – until the walls of his room at 200 Claremont Avenue, near Columbia University, were covered with rejection slips. During the spring of 1919 he wrote 19 stories and accumulated 122 rejections. His only sale was a revision of the 1917 *Lit* story 'Babes in the Woods,' which *The Smart Set* took for $30. The check was used to buy a pair of white flannels and a present for Zelda.* On 24 March he sent her his mother's engagement ring; she wore it to a dance and enjoyed the attention it attracted, but still no one in Montgomery believed she would marry her Yankee.

They had promised to write each other every day, and Fitzgerald had no trouble keeping his part of the bargain.† Zelda's first letters were loving and longing, but she soon began skipping days and expressing irritation with his epistolary requirements. She was not prepared for a long engagement and apparently assumed that it would be a matter of a month or two before Fitzgerald could provide for her. By April she was showing strain:

> Scott, you've been so sweet about writing – but I'm so damned tired of being told that you 'used to wonder why they kept princesses in towers' – you've written that verbatim, in your last six letters! It's dreadfully hard to write so very much – and so many of your letters sound forced – I know you love me, Darling, and I love you more than anything in the world,

---

* In her letters Zelda thanked Fitzgerald for pajamas ('They're the most adorably moon-shiney things on earth – I feel like a Vogue cover in 'em – I do wish yours were touching – ') and a feather fan ('Those feathers – those wonderful, wonderful feathers are the most beautiful things on earth – '). 'Early Success' states that the $30 Fitzgerald earned from *The Smart Set* for 'Babes in the Woods' in spring 1919 was spent 'on a magenta feather fan for a girl in Alabama.' But 'Auction – Model 1934' notes that the *Smart Set* money was used to buy Fitzgerald's flannels and that the fan was 'paid for out of a first *Saturday Evening Post* story' – which was 'Head and Shoulders,' written in the fall of 1919.

† Zelda did not preserve Fitzgerald's letters. He saved hers, but they are difficult to place in a chronology because she rarely dated letters.

but if its going to be so much longer, we just *can't* keep up this
frantic writing. It's like the last week we were to-gether – and
I'd like to feel that you know I am thinking of you and loving
you always – I hate writing when I haven't time, and I just have
to scribble a few lines – I'm saying all this so you'll understand
– Hectic affairs of any kind are rather trying, so please let's
write calmly and whenever you feel like it.[29]

When Zelda sent him her photograph inscribed for another
man Fitzgerald was not sure whether it was a mistake.

Wild with disappointment and jealousy, Fitzgerald made
three weekend trips to Montgomery in April, May, and June
to try to persuade Zelda to marry him immediately. After one
of his visits, Zelda wrote:

Scott, my darling lover – everything seems so smooth and
restful, like this yellow dusk. Knowing that I'll always be yours
– that you really own me – that nothing can keep us apart – is
such a relief after the strain and nervous excitement of the last
month. I'm so glad you came – Like Summer, just when I
needed you most – and took me back with you. Waiting doesn't
seem so hard now. The vague despondency has gone – I love
you Sweetheart.

Why did you buy the 'best at the Exchange'? – I'd rather have
had 10¢ a quart variety – I wanted it just to know you loved the
sweetness – To breathe and know you loved the smell – I think
I like breathing twilit gardens and moths more than beautiful
pictures or good books – It seems the most sensual of all the
sences – Something in me vibrates in a dusky, dreamy smell – a
smell of dying moons and shadows –

I've spent to-day in the grave-yard – It really isn't a
cemetery, you know – trying to unlock a rusty iron vault built
in the side of the hill. It's all washed and covered with weepy,
watery blue flowers that might have grown from dead eyes –
sticky to touch with a sickening odor – The boys wanted to get
in to test my nerve – to-night – I wanted to *feel* 'William
Wreford, 1864.' Why should graves make people feel in vain?
I've heard that so much, and Grey is so convincing, but
somehow I can't find anything hopeless in having lived – All
the broken columnes and clasped hands and doves and angels

112

mean romances and in an hundred years I think I shall like
having young people speculate on whether my eyes were
brown or blue – of cource, they are neither – I hope my grave
has an air of many, many years about it – Isn't it funny how,
out of a row of Confederate soldiers, two or three will make
you think of dead lovers and dead loves – when they're exactly
like the others, even to the yellowish moss? Old death is so
beautiful – so very beautiful – We will die together – I know —
Sweetheart – [30]

Zelda's letters were remarkable for a nineteen-year-old with
only a high school education. Her epistolary technique was
based on free association in response to a mood, and she was
keenly sensitive to place.

Fitzgerald went apartment hunting in April: ZELDA FOUND
KNOCK-OUT LITTLE APARTMENT REASONABLE RATES I HAVE
TAKEN IT FROM TWENTY SIXTH SHE MOVES INTO SAME
BUILDING EARLY IN MAY BETTER GIVE LETTER TO YOUR
FATHER IM SORRY YOURE NERVOUS DONT WRITE UNLESS YOU
WANT TO I LOVE YOU DEAR EVERYTHING WILL BE MIGHT FINE
ALL MY LOVE.[31] He had written to Judge Sayre, formally
requesting Zelda's hand in marriage. Although he was bitterly
hurt by her inconstancy, he understood that 'the girl really
worth having won't wait for anybody.'[32]

New York was full of Princeton friends who were not
committed to an increasingly hopeless pursuit of love and
money. Princeton was sharing the Yale Club on Vanderbilt
Avenue across from Grand Central Station, and Fitzgerald
spent time there discoursing on his tragic love affair. When
he climbed out on a window ledge and threatened to jump,
no one tried to stop him. In May he went on an alcoholic
party during which he and Yale undergraduate Porter
Gillespie rolled empty champagne bottles along Fifth Avenue
on Sunday morning. It was a time of discouragement in
everything. He was losing his girl. He disliked his work, which
he couldn't take seriously. His writing wasn't selling. The next
year he would put his feelings about that spring into one of

his most brilliant stories: Gordon Sterret, the failed artist in 'May Day' (1920), is an obvious projection of Fitzgerald's despair during the days when New York was celebrating the birth of the Jazz Age. Fitzgerald called this unhappy time 'the four most impressionable months of my life.'[33] In 'My Lost City' (1936), a chronicle of his responses to New York, he recalled the anxiety of 1919:

> As I hovered ghost-like in the Plaza Red Room of a Saturday afternoon, or went to lush and liquid garden parties in the East Sixties or tippled with Princetonians in the Biltmore Bar I was haunted always by my other life – my drab room in the Bronx,* my square foot of the subway, my fixation upon the day's letter from Alabama – would it come and what would it say? – my shabby suits, my poverty, and love. While my friends were launching decently into life I had muscled my inadequate bark into mid-stream. The gilded youth circling around young Constance Bennett in the Club de Vingt, the classmates in the Yale-Princeton Club whooping up our first after-the-war reunion, the atmosphere of the millionaires' houses that I sometimes frequented – these things were empty for me, though I recognized them as impressive scenery and regretted that I was committed to other romance. The most hilarious luncheon table or the most moony cabaret – it was all the same; from them I returned eagerly to my home on Claremont Avenue – home because there might be a letter waiting outside the door. . . .I was a failure – mediocre at advertising work and unable to get started as a writer.[34]

Fitzgerald did not work on a novel during this time because he was seeking quick money from magazine fiction. He almost certainly consulted Maxwell Perkins at Scribners, but the meeting has not been documented. Perkins is supposed to have recommended that Fitzgerald rewrite his novel in the third person to achieve more control over the material.†

---

* There is no evidence that Fitzgerald lived in the Bronx. Claremont Avenue is on Manhattan's West Side.
† In *The Making of Many Books* (New York: Scribners, 1946), a history of Scribners, Roger Burlingame notes that during the summer of 1918 Perkins suggested that Fitzgerald shift to the third person.

In June, Fitzgerald made his third trip to Montgomery and tried to compel Zelda to marry him by threats and pleading. She broke off the engagement, and he returned to New York, where he went on a lachrymose bender that took him to see Stephan Parrott in Boston and ended when the country went dry on 1 July. During this attempt at alcoholic convalescence, he quit his job and decided to return to St. Paul. He had probably already determined to stake everything on his novel, though he claimed that reading Hugh Walpole convinced him he could write a better novel: 'After that I dug in and wrote my first book.'[35]

11

Return to St. Paul

[Summer 1919]

◥◤ *Back in St. Paul,* Fitzgerald holed up on the top floor of
◣◢ his parents' house at 599 Summit Avenue and wrote
steadily. Although they disapproved, his parents left him
alone and brought meals to his room. Since they refused to
provide an allowance, he was forced to borrow small sums
from his friends for cigarettes and Cokes. Fitzgerald
eschewed alcohol and parties during this period of intense
work. His main relaxation was conversation with Father
Joseph Barron, dean of students at St. Paul Seminary, and
Donald Ogden Stewart, a Yale graduate who was working for
the American Telephone and Telegraph Company and living
at a nearby boarding house. Fitzgerald recited poetry to
Stewart, including his favorite line from John Masefield: 'Be
with me, Beauty, for the fire is dying.' Another boarder, John
De-Quedville Briggs, headmaster of the St. Paul Academy,
sometimes joined their discussions. Stewart had embarked on
a business career, but he had literary leanings and would
become – with a boost from Fitzgerald – one of the most
popular humorists of the Twenties. Fitzgerald shared his
work-in progress with his friend Katharine Tighe, whose
editorial advice he found helpful. His parents were upset
when Fitzgerald declined an impressive salary as advertising

116

manager at Griggs Cooper & Co., a St. Paul wholesaler. He didn't want to write ad copy and was not attracted by the cycle of wholesaler to wholesaler in two generations.

Although he was not corresponding with Zelda, Fitzgerald had the lingering hope that publication of his novel might win her back. About this time he told Wilson, 'I wouldn't care if she died, but I couldn't stand to have anybody else marry her.'[36] Fitzgerald remembered the summer of 1919 as a time when certain of his attitudes were permanently fixed:

> During a long summer of despair I wrote a novel instead of letters, so it came out all right, but it came out all right for a different person. The man with the jingle of money in his pocket who married the girl a year later would always cherish an abiding distrust, an animosity toward the leisure class – not the conviction of a revolutionist but the smoldering hatred of a peasant. In the years since then I have never been able to stop wondering where my friends' money came from, nor to stop thinking that one time a sort of *droit de seigneur* might have been exercised to give one of them my girl.[37]

That summer Fitzgerald achieved his first appearance in a book when *Princeton Verse II* was published. His three contributions – 'Marching Streets,' 'The Pope at Confession,' and 'My First Love' – were reprinted from the *Nassau Lit*. The pleasure of publication may have been diminished by the circumstance that all of his poems were signed 'T. Scott Fitzgerald.'

By 26 July, Fitzgerald reported to Maxwell Perkins that he had finished the first draft of a novel called 'The Education of a Personage,' which he inaccurately stated was 'in no sense a revision of the ill-fated *Romantic Egotist* but it contains some of the former material improved and worked over and bears a strong family resemblance besides.'[38] Characteristically, he wanted to know if his novel could be published in October if he sent the final draft by 20 August. Perkins expressed interest in seeing the novel but explained that, if accepted, it would have to be put on the spring 1920 list. On 16 August, Fitzgerald informed Perkins that the title was now *This Side of Paradise*.* The *Ledger* summary for Fitzgerald's twenty-second year is: 'The most important year of my life. Every emotion and my life work decided. Miserable and exstatic but a great success.'

On 4 September the typescript of *This Side of Paradise* was entrusted to a friend, Thomas Daniels, for delivery to New York. That day Fitzgerald sent Perkins a letter detailing the extent to which the novel had been salvaged from 'The Romantic Egotist':

> (1) Chapter II Bk I of the present book contains material from 'Spires + Gargoyles, Ha-Ha Hortense, Babes in the Wood + Crescendo' – rewritten in third person, cut down + re-edited
> (2) Chapter III Bk I contains material from 'Second descent of the Egotist and the Devil.' rewritten ect.
> (3) Chapter IV Bk I contains material from 'The two Mystics, Clara + the End of Many Things'
> (4) Chapter III Bk II is a revision of Eleanor in 3rd person – with that fur incident left out.

> Chap I Bk I, + Chaps I, II, IV + V of Bk II are entirely new.[39]

Fitzgerald was therefore able to claim that five chapters out of nine represented fresh material. Eighty pages of typescript were transferred into *This Side of Paradise* from 'The Romantic Egotist.' While waiting for Scribners' decision, the novelist took a laborer's job at the Northern Pacific Railroad car barns, where he had his new overalls stolen and was reprimanded for sitting while hammering.

When *This Side of Paradise* came up at the Scribners editorial meeting, only Perkins supported it. After Charles Scribner said he could not put his name on a book without literary merit and Brownell dismissed the material as

---

* The title was taken from Rupert Brooke's 'Tiare Tahiti,' the last lines of which appeared on the title page of the novel: 'Well this side of Paradise! . . . /There's little comfort in the wise.' The second epigraph was adapted from Oscar Wilde's *The Picture of Dorian Gray*: 'Experience is the name so many people give to their mistakes.'

frivolous, Perkins in effect offered his resignation: 'My feeling is that a publisher's first allegiance is to talent. And if we aren't going to publish a talent like this, it is a very serious thing. . . . If we're going to turn down the likes of Fitzgerald, I will lose all interest in publishing books.'[40] Scribner said he would reconsider. On 16 September, eight days before Fitzgerald's twenty-third birthday, Perkins accepted the novel:

> I am very glad, personally, to be able to write you that we are all for publishing your book, 'This Side of Paradise'. Viewing it as the same book that was here before, which in a sense it is, though translated into somewhat different terms and extended further, I think that you have improved it enormously. As the first manuscript did, it abounds in energy and life and it seems to be to be in much better proportion. I was afraid that, when we declined the first manuscript, you might be done with us conservatives. I am glad you are not. The book is so different that it is hard to prophesy how it will sell but we are all for taking a chance and supporting it with vigor.[41]

Fitzgerald had found the editor who would back him for the rest of his life, and Perkins had made his first great find and was launched on his career as America's legendary literary editor.

Fitzgerald's 18 September response to Perkins repeated his plea for early publication: 'I have so many things dependent on its success – including of course a girl – not that I expect it to make me a fortune but it will have a psychological effect on me and all my surroundings and besides open up new fields. I'm in that stage where every month counts frantically and seems a cudgel in a fight for happiness against time.'[42] Seventeen years later Fitzgerald described his euphoria in 'Early Success':

> Then the postman rang, and that day I quit work and ran along the streets, stopping automobiles to tell friends and acquaintances about it – my novel *This Side of Paradise* was

Maxwell E. Perkins

accepted for publication. That week the postman rang and rang, and I paid off my terrible small debts, bought a suit, and woke up every morning with a world of ineffable toploftiness and promise.

While I waited for the novel to appear, the metamorphosis of amateur into professional began to take place – a sort of stitching together of your whole life into a pattern of work, so that the end of one job is automatically the beginning of another.

The essay draws the conclusion: 'The compensation of a very early success is a conviction that life is a romantic matter.'[43]

In November, Wilson read *This Side of Paradise* in typescript, pronouncing it 'an exquisite burlesque of Compton Mackenzie with a pastiche of Wells thrown in at the end.' Always magisterial, he warned Fitzgerald against becoming a 'very popular trashy novelist.'[44]

12

The Emergence of a Professional

[Fall 1919]

That fall Fitzgerald had two connected ambitions: to get his girl back and to make money on the strength of his novel. It appears that he had not corresponded with Zelda since June, but now he wrote her the news about *This Side of Paradise* and asked if he could visit her. She replied: ' 'S funny, Scott, I don't feel a bit shaky and "do-don't'ish like I used to when you came – I really want to see you – that's all—'45 Fitzgerald did not rush to Montgomery because he had not yet earned any money (there was no advance from Scribners for the novel) and possibly because his parents discouraged a resumption of the engagement.

Another concern that fall was finding material for a second novel; Fitzgerald had used up most of his personal experiences in *This Side of Paradise*. Hoping for quick financial returns, he revised his rejected stories and salvaged stories from the *Nassau Lit*. At first he submitted stories to *The Smart Set*, which took 'The Debutante' (published November 1919), 'Porcelain and Pink' (January 1920), 'Benediction' (February 1920), and 'Dalyrimple Goes Wrong' (February 1920). 'The

Debutante' and 'Benediction' ('The Ordeal') were both revised *Nassau Lit* pieces. 'Dalyrimple,' in which a war hero rises to the state senate after a career of burglary, was Fitzgerald's earliest ironic treatment of the Horatio Alger success story. These acceptances were encouraging because the magazine had an influential position under the editorship of H.L. Mencken and George Jean Nathan, although its circulation was not large. Surprisingly, Fitzgerald does not seem to have been aware of Mencken's position as the most powerful critic in America.*

The Smart Set paid only $35 or $40 for a story, so Fitzgerald began trying to crack more lucrative markets. At the same time that he was sending 'sophisticated' or realistic stories to *The Smart Set*, he exploited his connection with the house of Scribner by offering another kind of story to *Scribner's Magazine*. Robert Bridges, the editor of *Scribner's*, preferred didactic stories and took 'The Cut Glass Bowl' and 'The Four Fists' at $150 each. In 'The Four Fists' a young man is cured of his bad qualities by four punches. But Fitzgerald needed more money than *Scribner's* paid. As a monthly it could not accept much fiction, and Bridges declined most of the stories Fitzgerald submitted. *This Side of Paradise* would not be published until March, and the income from the novel was uncertain – although Fitzgerald had great expectations for it. He believed his writing should bring a good deal of money as well as celebrity.

Through St. Paul writer Grace Flandrau, Fitzgerald was

---

* When Fitzgerald sent Mencken a copy of *This Side of Paradise* in March 1920, he explained in the inscription: 'As a matter of fact Mr. Menken, I stuck your name in on Page 224 in the last proof – partly I suppose as a vague bootlick and partly because I have since adapted a great many of your views. But the other literary opinions, especially the disparagment of Cobb, were written when you were little more than a name to me—

'This is a bad book full of good things, a novel about flappers written for Philosophers, an exquisite burlesque of Compton McKenzie with a pastiche of Wells at the end—'[46]

The final phrase about Mackenzie and Wells was lifted from Wilson's comment on the novel.

introduced in October to the New York literary agency of Paul Revere Reynolds. A leading agent who specialized in placing fiction with the popular magazines, Reynolds sold 'Head and Shoulders' to *The Saturday Evening Post* for $400. The publication of this story in the 21 February 1920 issue marked Fitzgerald's first appearance in a mass-circulation magazine. In 'Head and Shoulders' the marriage of a brilliant scholar to

Harold Ober

a chorus girl results in a role reversal: the scholar becomes a vaudeville acrobat and the girl becomes a celebrated writer. The story was intended as pure entertainment, but it has an ominous note – as though Fitzgerald were speculating on the consequences of his renewed hope of marrying Zelda.

By the end of 1919 Fitzgerald had earned $879 from six stories, three plays, and a poem. At the Reynolds agency he was the special client of Harold Ober, a partner in the firm. His connection with the agency strongly influenced the shape of Fitzgerald's career. Because of his early sales to the high-circulation magazines, he developed the pattern of regarding his career as double or divided – separated into commercial short stories and serious novels. The problem would be to keep his two careers separated.

The Saturday Evening Post became the basic market for Fitzgerald's short stories. Under the editorship of George Horace Lorimer, the *Post* dominated the slick magazines* with a combination of fiction and general-information articles. The issues frequently offered more than 200 pages for five cents. As circulation climbed to 2,750,000 copies a week in the Twenties, advertising revenues permitted the *Post* to pay top prices and thereby attract the best commercial literary talent. In addition to its stable of crowd-pleasers (Ben Ames Williams and Octavus Roy Cohen, for example), in the Twenties and Thirties the magazine published Joseph Hergesheimer, John P. Marquand, William Faulkner, Ring Lardner, and Thomas Wolfe.†

* The slicks were the high-paying magazines printed on coated paper. The pulps were printed on cheap paper and paid a penny a word. The only pulp magazine Fitzgerald wrote for was *The Smart Set*, which had literary stature.
† The 226-page *Post* issue for 8 October 1927 included the first part of a serial by Sir Arthur Conan Doyle, an historical article by Joseph Hergesheimer, Fitzgerald's 'The Love Boat,' an article on the *Uncle Tom* plays, a story by Ben Ames Williams, a travel article by Cornelius Vanderbilt, Jr., a story by Nunnally Johnson, a story by Horatio Winslow, an article on foreign policy by Henry L. Stimson, an animal story by Hal G. Evarts, a story by Thomas Beer, an article about Caruso, a story by Octavus Roy Cohen, an article about German recovery by Isaac Marcosson, the continuation of a serial by Donn Byrne, the continuation of a serial by Frances Noyes Hart, an

In 1919 Fitzgerald equated cynicism or pessimism with realism and asked his agent whether realistic stories could be sold to the slicks, but Lorimer did not restrict Fitzgerald to flapper stories. He appreciated good writing and bought Fitzgerald stories that had unhappy endings if they were not too iconoclastic for a family readership. Over the next seventeen years some of Fitzgerald's best stories appeared in the *Post*, although three of his masterpieces – 'May Day,' 'The Diamond as Big as the Ritz,' and 'The Rich Boy' – were rejected. While competing magazines such as *Cosmopolitan*, *Collier's*, and *Redbook* also published his work, the *Post* was his most dependable story market. Fitzgerald came to regard himself as a *Post* author, as did his readers.

Fitzgerald delayed his trip to Montgomery until late November 1919 and stopped off in New York for four days to meet with Maxwell Perkins and Harold Ober, the two men who would manage his literary and financial affairs for the next twenty years. At thirty-five, Perkins was twelve years older than Fitzgerald. He had grown up in New Jersey, but came from Vermont stock and had graduated from Harvard in the Class of 1907. Conservative in everything except his literary judgments, Perkins was an unlikely sponsor for the ebullient young novelist. As was almost inevitable with Fitzgerald, their professional relationship became a warm personal friendship. Ober, Harvard '05, was another conservative New Englander. Again, despite their differences in temperament, business became friendship. These two Yankees shared Fitzgerald's heady success in the Twenties and assumed responsibility for him in the desperate Thirties.*

---

article on international affairs by Alonzo E. Taylor, a story by F. Britten Austin, and an article on crime by Kenneth Roberts. Magazine readers of that time had a large appetite for fiction: this issue included eight short stories, three serial installments, and eight articles.

* James R. Mellow has written: 'It was quite possibly the case that during his expedition to New York in late November and early December that he became briefly involved in a wild sexual affair with a young English actress...'[47] Mellow provides evidence that Fitzgerald had an affair with Rosalinde Fuller, but the time is uncertain.

The reunion with Zelda, which Fitzgerald may have concealed from his parents, went well. They did not renew the engagement, but their intimate correspondence resumed. Fitzgerald was confident that he could win back his girl. The best of the stories he wrote after returning to St. Paul in December is 'The Ice Palace' (*Post*, May 1920), in which he drew upon his trip to Montgomery. He was functioning as a professional writer, regarding everything that happened to him as material. 'The Ice Palace' tells about a belle who wants to leave the somnolent South. She visits her fiancé in Minnesota and nearly dies when she gets lost in a castle built from blocks of ice – convincing her that she belongs in the South. Though the character was based on Zelda, the story was written before she saw the North. Always sensitive to the moods of place, Fitzgerald examined the Deep South in several stories: 'It is a grotesquely pictorial country as I found out long ago, and as Mr. Faulkner has since abundantly demonstrated.'[48] Fitzgerald's Southern stories drew on Zelda and the responses to her world that were generated by his love for her.

13

Zelda Recaptured

[Winter 1919–1920]

While Fitzgerald was writing commercial stories, he was planning more ambitious projects and seeking models for the management of his career. In the 18 September 1919 letter that acknowledged Perkins's acceptance of *This Side of Paradise*, Fitzgerald mentioned that he was beginning 'a very ambitious novel called "The Demon Lover" '[49] and reading Samuel Butler's *Notebooks* – 'the most interesting human document ever written,'[50] he wrote on the endpaper of his copy the next day. Fitzgerald soon abandoned 'The Demon Lover'; nothing is known about its plot. At this time he was forsaking the English quest novelists for American realists and naturalists, and studying the technique of Joseph Conrad. His new literary enthusiasms were shaped partly by Mencken. Fitzgerald admitted to Perkins in February 1920: 'Another of my discoveries is H.L. Menken who is certainly a factor in present day literature. In fact I'm not so cocksure about things as I was last summer – this fellow Conrad seems to be pretty good after all.'[51]

In October 1919 Fitzgerald had asked Robert Bridges if *Scribner's* would consider serializing 'a literary forgery purporting to be selections from the note-books of a man who is a complete literary radical. ... It will be in turns cynical, ingenious, life saturated, critical and bitter. It will be racy and startling with opinions and personalities. I have a journal I have kept for 3½ yrs. which my book didn't begin to exhaust. . . .'[52] Nothing survives from 'The Diary of a Literary Failure'; if it existed, Fitzgerald's journal has been lost. It is not known whether another abandoned novel from this time, 'The Drunkard's Holiday,' developed beyond the planning stage.

Fitzgerald returned to St. Paul from his trip east 'in a thoroughly nervous alcoholic state.'[53] He was anxious to build on *This Side of Paradise* with a second novel and in January 1920 asked Perkins: 'Do you think a book on the type of my first one would have any chance of being accepted for serial publication by any magazine? I want to start it but I don't want to get broke in the middle + start in and have to write short stories again – because I don't enjoy it + just do it for money.'[54] This complaint about story work initiated a refrain that echoed during the rest of Fitzgerald's life. Even before his first novel was published, the financial connection between his short stories and novels was established in Fitzgerald's career plans: he regarded stories as a way to support novels.

Between November 1919 and February 1920, Fitzgerald wrote 'Head and Shoulders,' 'Myra Meets His Family,' 'The Camel's Back,' 'Bernice Bobs Her Hair,' 'The Ice Palace,' and 'The Offshore Pirate' – all of which were sold to the *Post*. After the rejection slips of spring 1919 it was exciting for Fitzgerald to find that his stories were now welcome at the best markets. At first he enjoyed writing the commercial stories that were making him famous. Clever stories about young love, written with facility, they established the tone of Fitzgerald's early popular fiction. He wrote plot stories but created fresh characters who were not magazine types. What differentiated his stories from those of other writers mining the same lode was that Fitzgerald treated the concerns of youth seriously. In 'Bernice Bobs Her Hair' the game of popularity is played in earnest, and the reader understands that the characters – especially the girls – are playing for high stakes. Typical of his early commercial stories, 'Bernice' examines the tutelage of a stodgy girl in the art of attracting boys. For Fitzgerald's girls marriage is the only future, and they are determined to make the best matches because their lives depend on whom they marry. As one of Fitzgerald's heroines explains to the man she loves in 'New Leaf' (1931), 'Remember, I'm also deciding for my children.'[55] The early stories often introduce an element of fantasy or heightened imagination. In 'The Offshore Pirate' a young man devises an elaborate plot, pretending to be a pirate, in order to win an imperious girl he has never seen. When the *Post* complained about the weakness of the original ending, which explained that the story was just a dream, Fitzgerald obliged with a new ending that accepts the whole thing as real while wittily reminding the reader that the story is really just a story: 'reaching up on her tiptoes she kissed him softly in the illustration.'[56]

Worried that he was risking tuberculosis in the Minnesota winter, he decided to go to New Orleans to write. The proximity of New Orleans to Montgomery no doubt influenced the move. By 21 January 1920 he was living in a rooming house at 2900 Prytania Street, where he corrected proofs for *This Side of Paradise*, wrote stories, and started a seduction novel called 'Darling Heart,' of which nothing survives. Perkins is regarded as a collaborative editor because of his subsequent labors with Thomas Wolfe, but the nature of his contributions to *This Side of Paradise* is impossible to determine. The final setting typescript and proofs do not survive,* and the correspondence between author and editor gives no indication that anything beyond routine editing was required; however, they may have worked on the novel together during Fitzgerald's November visit to New York.

---

* The only extant typescript of *This Side of Paradise* comprises forty-eight pages of carbon copy for Chapter I and part of Chapter II that Fitzgerald sent to Stephan Parrott, probably in the fall of 1919 (Bruccoli Collection). Every page was revised before book publication, but the alterations are not major.

Fitzgerald made two trips from New Orleans to Mont-gomery in January, bringing Zelda sazarac cocktails, her first orchids, and a $600 platinum-and-diamond wristwatch paid for by writing 'The Camel's Back' in one day. He told Perkins that he started at 8 A.M. and finished at 7 P.M., then recopied the manuscript by 4:30 A.M. and mailed it a half-hour later. Fitzgerald was not proud of this trick story about a masquerade party; but it brought his first inclusion in the *O. Henry Prize Stories* series and was later bought by the movies. The young author must have thought he could write a popular story anytime he needed to. His best story ideas came to him as complete structures, and by writing them in concentrated bursts of effort he was able to preserve the spontaneity of the narrative. He later explained, 'Stories are best written in either one jump or three, according to the length. The three-jump story should be done in three successive days, then a day or so for revise and off she goes. This is of course the ideal – In many stories one strikes a snag that must be hacked at but on the whole, stories that drag along or are terribly difficult (I mean a difficulty that comes from a poor conception and consequent faulty construction) never flow quite as well in the reading.'[57]

An understanding developed that Zelda would marry him when *This Side of Paradise* was published, but the engagement announcement did not appear in the *Montgomery Journal* until 28 March – six days before the wedding. Her reconsideration was not entirely a mercenary matter: she was not committing herself to a famous and wealthy author. The reception of his novel was uncertain, and neither of them had any idea what Fitzgerald's income would be. Zelda responded to his regained confidence, to his ability to fulfill his ambitions. As she later wrote, he made life 'promisory.'[58]

During his visits to Montgomery they slept together. (For years Fitzgerald would annoy friends and new acquaintances by asking whether they had slept with their wives before they were married.) When Zelda suspected she was pregnant, he sent her pills that were supposed to induce menstruation. Her response was characteristic of her attitude toward consequences:

> I wanted to for your sake, because I know what a mess I'm making and how inconvenient it's all going to be – but I simply *can't* and *won't* take those awful pills – so I've thrown them away. I'd rather take carbolic acid. You see, as long as I feel that I had the right, I don't much mind what happens – and besides, I'd rather have a whole *family* than sacrifice my self-respect. They just seem to place everything on the wrong basis – and I'd feel like a damned whore if I took even one, so you'll try to understand, please Scott – and do what you think best – but don't do ANYTHING till we *know* because God – or something – has always made things right, and maybe this will be.[59]

Zelda was not pregnant.

Despite the geographical advantages of New Orleans, Fitzgerald was bored there and in February 1920 moved to New York, where he stayed at the Murray Hill Hotel and then the Allerton. He was in New York when 'Head and Shoulders' appeared in the 21 February *Post* issue and Metro Films bought it for $2,500. His first movie sale encouraged him to expect that such windfalls would continue. New York was the right place to be a winner, and Fitzgerald fueled the intoxication of success with bootleg liquor. He flashed large bills and spent them carelessly, establishing a pattern for his treatment of money. Having suffered because his happiness was nearly destroyed by the lack of money and having grown up with the spectacle of his father's failure, Fitzgerald responded to money by showing contempt for it – much like a man in a dangerous occupation deliberately taking unnecessary risks. He became a big tipper, admitting that it was an expression of his need to be loved. In the early months of 1920 his income doubled every month, and it seemed to him during his first success that more money would always be forthcoming.

Fitzgerald and Zelda corresponded about their impending marriage, although characteristically no firm date was set until just before the ceremony. In February she wrote him:

132

Darling Heart, our fairy tale is almost ended, and we're going to marry and live happily ever afterward just like the princess in her tower who worried you so much – and made me so very cross by her constant recurrence – I'm so sorry for all the times I've been mean and hateful – for all the miserable minutes I've caused you when we could have been so happy. You deserve so much – so very much–

I think our life together will be like these last four days – and I *do* want to marry you – even if you do think I 'dread' it – I wish you hadn't said that – I'm not afraid of anything – To be afraid a person has either to be a coward or very great and big. I am neither. Besides, I know you can take much better care of me than I can, and I'll always be very, very happy with you – except sometimes when we engage in our weekly debates – and even then I rather enjoy myself. I like being very calm and masterful, while you become emotional and sulky. I don't care whether you think so or not – I do.

There are 3 more pictures I unearthed from a heap of débris under my bed – Our honored mother had disposed of 'em for reasons of her own, but personally I like the attitude of my emaciated limbs, so I solict your approval. Only I waxed artistic, and ruined one–

Sweetheart – I miss you so – I love you so – and next time I'm going back with you – I'm absolutely nothing without you – Just the doll that I should have been born – You're a necessity and a luxury and a darling, precious lover – and you're going to be a husband to your wife–[60]

At the end of February, Fitzgerald moved to the Cottage Club because he wanted to be in Princeton when *This Side of Paradise* was published. On the twenty-sixth he wrote Isabelle Amorous, the sister of a Newman friend, who had congratulated him when he broke off with Zelda:

No personality as strong as Zelda's could go without getting criticisms and as you say she is not above reproach. I've always known that. Any girl who gets stewed in public, who frankly enjoys and tells shocking stories, who smokes constantly and makes the remark that she has 'kissed thousands of men and intends to kiss thousands more,' cannot be considered beyond reproach even if above it. But Isabelle I fell in love with her courage, her sincerity and her flaming self respect and its these things I'd believe in even if the whole world indulged in wild suspicions that she wasn't all that she should be.

But of course the real reason, Isabelle, is that I love her and that's the beginning and end of everything. You're still a catholic but Zelda's the only God I have left now.[61]

This letter indicates, possibly, that the puritanical side of Fitzgerald – the part of his mind that retained the capacity to be shocked by departures from rectitude – had reservations about the wisdom of his marriage. Any doubts were overruled by the circumstance that Zelda was an integral element in his dream of success. Fitzgerald was determined to wipe out the humiliations and failures of spring 1919, and for him everything had to be the way he had wanted it to be then. He wanted to repeat the past and would settle for nothing less than complete restoration. Any missing element would mar the perfection of his triumph.

EARLY
SUCCESS

[1920–1925]

14

A Famous First Novel

[April 1920]

On 26 March 1920 Scribners published *This Side of Paradise* in a first printing of 3,000 copies at $1.75. The first ads featured the slogan A NOVEL ABOUT FLAPPERS WRITTEN FOR PHILOSOPHERS, which was the author's contribution. Scribners would have been satisfied to sell out the first printing, and 5,000 was regarded as more than respectable for a first novel. The first 3,000 copies were sold within three days. Fitzgerald was not surprised. As he had predicted, he was famous almost overnight. The twenty-three-year-old novelist became a newspaper celebrity and began to keep scrapbooks of his clippings, memorabilia, and correspondence with prominent writers.* Fitzgerald's appearance accelerated his elevation to celebrity status. His striking good looks combined with his youth and brilliance to complete the image of the novelist as a romantic figure. He

---

* Fitzgerald eventually filled five large scrapbooks: for the years before his marriage ('A Scrap book record compiled from many sources of interest to and concerning one F. Scott Fitzgerald'); for *This Side of Paradise* and *Flappers and Philosophers*; for *The Beautiful and Damned*, *The Vegetable*, and *Tales of the Jazz Age*; for *The Great Gatsby* and *All the Sad Young Men*; and for *Tender Is the Night* and *Taps at Reveille*. In addition, there are Zelda's scrapbook and family photo albums. The scrapbooks and photo albums at the Princeton University Library provided the basis for *The Romantic Egoists*.

photographed handsomely, especially in profile; and, though never a dandy, he dressed well in Brooks Brothers collegiate style. During the Twenties he often carried a cane, as did many young men. It was frequently remarked that Fitzgerald looked like a figure in a collar ad.

Most of the reviewers were warmly receptive, and the few unfriendly reviews helped sell the book because they generated interest. Harry Hansen of the *Chicago Daily News* sent Scribners a fan letter that began, 'My, how that boy Fitzgerald can write!'[1] The *Chicago Tribune* review by Burton Rascoe announced, ' "This Side of Paradise" gives him, I think, a fair claim to membership in that small squad of contemporary American fictionists who are producing literature. . . . it bears the impress, it seems to me, of genius. It is the only adequate study that we have had of the contemporary American in adolescence and young man-hood.'[2] In *The Smart Set* H. L. Mencken called it 'The best American novel that I have seen of late.'[3] The most prominent disparaging review was by Heywood Broun in the *New York Tribune*, which ridiculed the novel as callow and self-consciously overwritten.[4]

When Frances Newman called *This Side of Paradise* a 'desecration' of Mackenzie's *Sinister Street* in the *Atlanta Constitution* in February 1921, Fitzgerald defended himself in a letter to the critic. While acknowledging the influence of *Sinister Street*, he denied that he had borrowed details or imitated characters. 'But I was also hindered by a series of resemblances between my life and that of Michael Fane which, had I been a more conscientious man, might have precluded my ever attempting an autobiographical novel. . . . When I was twenty-one and began *This Side of Paradise* my literary taste was so unformed that *Youth's Encounter* was still my "perfect book." My book quite naturally shows the influence to a marked degree. . . . You seem to be unconscious that even Mackenzie had his sources such as *Dorian Gray* and *None Other Gods* and that occasionally we may have drunk at the same springs.'[5]

A *Famous First Novel* [April 1920]

Although *This Side of Paradise* now seems naïve after seventy years, it was received in 1920 as an iconoclastic social document – even as a testament of revolt. Surprisingly, it was regarded as an experimental or innovative narrative because of the mixture of styles and the inclusion of plays and verse. The variety of techniques includes Amory's stream-of-consciousness passage near the end of the novel:

> Wonder where Jill was – Jill Bayne, Fayne, Sayne – what the devil – neck hurts, darned uncomfortable seat. No desire to sleep with Jill, what could Alec see in her? Alec had a coarse taste in women. Own taste the best; Isabelle, Clara, Rosalind, Eleanor were all-American. Eleanor would pitch, probably southpaw. Rosalind was outfield, wonderful hitter, Clara first base, maybe. Wonder what Humbird's body looked like now. If he himself hadn't been bayonet instructor he'd have gone up to line three months sooner, probably been killed. Where's the darned bell—[6]

The loose form of *This Side of Paradise* resulted from Fitzgerald's inexperience with structuring a novel. The *New Republic* review made a valid point in describing the novel as 'the collected works of F. Scott Fitzgerald.'[7] Drawing on his undergraduate writings as well as his reading, Fitzgerald assembled a montage of scenes and poses. Along with structure his main technical problem in writing *This Side of Paradise* was controlling the point of view – the relation of the narrative voice to the story, or how the story is told by the novelist. The two points of view in *This Side of Paradise* – Amory's within the novel and the author's own omniscient voice – are not always consistent. Fitzgerald was still under the influence of the Wellsian problem novel, which made it difficult for him to resist editorializing.* He remained an

---

* See James E. Miller's *F. Scott Fitzgerald: His Art and His Technique* (New York: New York University Press, 1954) for a thorough examination of the influence of Wells's saturation techniques on *This Side of Paradise*.

author who interpolated his own comments into his narratives, but he would learn to avoid or control blatant intrusions.

This Side of Paradise is now read as a romantic novel. *Romanticism* is an open-ended term: according to the authorities, it embraces such elements as primitivism, love of nature, imagination, individualism, mysticism, intuition, humanitarianism, political revolution, idealism, love of the past, escapism. The most obvious romantic quality in Fitzgerald is imaginative aspiration or illusion, the theme of all his best work. Fitzgerald and his heroes aspire to an emotional perfection, to a level of experience that transcends the 'unreality of reality.'[8] The closest he came to explicating this yearning was in his analysis of Jay Gatsby: '. . . there was something gorgeous about him, some heightened sensitivity to the promises of life, as if he were related to one of those intricate machines that register earthquakes ten thousand miles away. This responsiveness has nothing to do with that flabby impressionability which is dignified under the name of the 'creative temperament' – it was an extraordinary gift for hope, a romantic readiness. . . . '[9] Fitzgerald believed in the individual's capacity to seek a unique destiny, although the quest is doomed in his best work. Disenchantment or disillusionment are the concomitants of aspiration. The quest often appears as the ideal of heroism; but Fitzgerald noted, 'Show me a hero and I will write you a tragedy.'[10] Lionel Trilling, one of Fitzgerald's justest critics, observed that he 'was perhaps the last notable writer to affirm the Romantic fantasy, descended from the Renaissance, of personal ambition or heroism, of life committed to, or thrown away for, some ideal of self.'[11]

Romanticism is frequently defined in terms of oppositions: intuition vs. reason, imagination vs. realism. These neat contrasts do not work for Fitzgerald. His life and writings reveal a constant process of judgment and a search for values. Character is a moral problem for Fitzgerald. Far from being unrealistic or anti-realistic, his fiction is distinguished by accuracy of observation. His contemporary readers frequently acknowledged the effectiveness of Fitzgerald's social presentation by saying, 'That's the way it was.' When his daughter was trying to make a start as a writer of fiction, he provided her with a theory of realism that characteristically involved the author's emotional commitment to his material: 'But when in a freak moment you will want to give the low-down, not the scandal, not the merely *reported* but the *profound* essence of what happened at a prom or after it, perhaps that honesty will come to you – and then you will understand how it is possible to make even a forlorn Laplander *feel* the importance of a trip to Cartier's!'[12] Fitzgerald's concern for the 'forlorn Laplander' contributed to his achievement as a social historian, but his historical method did not utilize extensive documentation. As a chronicler he relied on evocative details to convey the moods of time and place, and these effects were intensified through style.

In his 1926 review of Hemingway's *In Our Time*, Fitzgerald stated that 'material, however closely observed, is as elusive as the moment in which it has its existence unless it is purified by an incorruptible style and by the catharsis of a passionate emotion.'[13] It is too much to claim that *This Side of Paradise* has an incorruptible style; there are manifold styles – one of which is Fitzgerald's. What is recognizable in his first novel as the authentic Fitzgerald is the warm voice of his prose: the tone or inflection that expresses a generous and acute sensitivity. Though he was still a self-conscious or self-indulgent writer with a weakness for the ostentatious passage, he was a natural writer. Fitzgerald's own feelings – as distinguished from Amory's poses – permeate his novel. In 1925 he wrote in his copy: 'I like this book for the enormous emotion, mostly immature and bogus, that gives every incident a sort of silly "life". . . . But the faked references and intellectual reactions + cribs from MacKenzie, Johnston, Wells, Wilde, Tarkington give me the pip.'[14] Yet despite its debts *This Side of Paradise* is Fitzgerald's novel.

Every great writer writes like no one else. Whatever differentiates one great writer from another is most truly expressed not by his material or themes, but by his style – those inevitable combinations of words and tones that produce lines only Hemingway or Faulkner or Fitzgerald could have written. Near the end of his life Fitzgerald offered his daughter another hard-learned lesson:

> If you have anything to say, anything you feel nobody has ever said before, you have got to feel it so desparately that you will find some way to say it that nobody has ever found before, so that the thing you have to say and the way of saying it blend as one matter – as indissolubly as if they were conceived together.
>
> Let me preach again for a moment: I mean that what you have felt and thought will by itself invent a new style, so that when people talk about style they are always a little astonished at the newness of it, because they think that it is only *style* that they are talking about, when what they are talking about is the attempt to express a new idea with such force that it will have the originality of the thought.[15]

For Fitzgerald, style was inseparable from the emotion it expressed. His rationale of style was to multiply meaning through lyrical language, and the liquefaction of his prose becomes an incantation. The obvious marks of his style are its flowing rhythms, sense of color, striking imagery, wit, delicate modulations of mood, and clarity. Gertrude Stein observed that Fitzgerald was 'the only one of the younger writers who wrote naturally in sentences.'[16] His remarkably flexible style permitted him to be playful, profound, or poetic. At its best it was always the vehicle for the emotions inherent in his material.

15

This Side of Paradise

[April 1920]

This Side of Paradise is the 300-page history of Amory Blaine from his indulged childhood with his eccentric mother through prep school and Princeton, culminating in an unhappy love affair and a renewed quest for values upon which to erect a fulfilling life. The novel is divided into two sections which trace the formulation of the two concepts that shape the hero.

'Book One: The Romantic Egotist' takes Amory through Princeton and the inception of his quest for a great destiny. Aristocratic individualism is as accurate a term for his attitudes as romantic egotism, for Fitzgerald nurtured a code of aristocracy founded on duty, courage, and honor. Amory is motivated by a sense of noblesse oblige. He does not doubt that a great destiny is reserved for him, but the exact nature of his destiny remains unclear. The greatest influence on the evolving Amory is Monsignor Darcy, the Fay figure, who responds to his ambitions and encourages his compulsive self-analysis. While unsuccessfully trying to point him toward Rome, Darcy intensifies Amory's sense of evil, which is dramatized by supernatural occurrences in the novel. The most puzzling and unconvincing episode occurs when it becomes clear to Amory that he and a Princeton classmate are expected to spend the night at the apartment of a couple of

New York showgirls: Amory, who is sober, hallucinates. He sees a devil figure that pursues him in the streets until he recognizes the apparition as Humbird, a Princetonian who was killed in a car wreck. The meaning of this Bensonian episode remains obscure, but the idea seems to be that Humbird has come not to warn Amory but to possess him. It is not clear why the inoffensive Humbird has become the embodiment of 'infinite evil,' but the explanation may be that he did not aspire to high goals. The episode is unconvincing and faintly absurd; nonetheless, it dramatizes the connection in Amory's mind between sex and evil.

Each of the books of *This Side of Paradise* has a love story. Book One describes Amory's unsuccessful courtship of Isabelle Borgé, who is based on Ginevra King. Separating the two books is a six-page 'interlude' which reports that Amory has been overseas in the Great War but provides no details. Having no firsthand knowledge of the war, Fitzgerald did not attempt to invent Amory's battle experiences.

'Book Two: The Education of a Personage,' which covers most of 1919, is built on Monsignor Darcy's distinction between a personality and a personage, and traces Amory's revived quest for personage-hood after he loses Rosalind Connage because of his poverty. Reared in the expectation of wealth, Amory finds himself penniless after the family fortune has been dissipated. Amory's feelings about Rosalind are obviously drawn from Fitzgerald's for Zelda, but the girls' backgrounds differ markedly; Rosalind is a New York debutante.* Book Two includes the chapter 'Young Irony,' in which Amory encounters self-destructive Eleanor Savage after losing Rosalind: 'Eleanor was, say, the last time that evil crept close to Amory under the mask of beauty, the last weird mystery that held him with wild fascination and pounded his

* Rosalind's break with Amory echoes the language of Beatrice Normandy's break with George Ponderevo in Wells's *Tono-Bungay*. Rosalind: 'I can't be shut away from the trees and flowers, cooped up in a little flat, waiting for you. You'd hate me in a narrow atmosphere. I'd make you hate me.' Beatrice: 'It's because I love you that I won't go down to become a dirty familiar thing with you amidst the grime.'[17]

soul to flakes.'[18] She is the kind of reckless romantic that Amory cannot be. Fitzgerald later commented on the Eleanor material in his marked copy of *This Side of Paradise*: 'This is so funny I can't even bear to read it.'[19]

Another supernatural manifestation occurs in Book Two when Amory makes a 'supercilious sacrifice,' taking the blame for Rosalind's brother who is caught with a whore in a hotel room. Here Amory perceives that 'over and around the figure crouched on the bed there hung an aura, gossamer as a moonbeam, tainted as stale, weak wine, yet a horror, diffusively brooding over the three of them . . . and over by the window among the stirring curtains stood something else, featureless and indistinguishable, yet strangely familiar. . . . '[20] Five days later Amory learns that Monsignor Darcy had died that night: 'He knew then what it was that he had perceived among the curtains of the room in Atlantic City.'[21] These apparitions in *This Side of Paradise* were intended to dramatize Amory's sense of spiritual corruptibility, for, despite the novel's iconoclastic reputation, he is committed to moral and social order. Amory is fundamentally conservative. His individualism is not of the Nietzschean Übermensch variety. He yearns to lead, but he expects to serve the race by leading. In fulfilling his destiny, he will fulfill his talents. For Amory Blaine failure is a form of death-in-life, a mark of spiritual bankruptcy.

This Side of Paradise ends with a burst of rhetoric as Amory walks to Princeton at the beginning of a pilgrimage:

> Long after midnight the towers and spires of Princeton were visible, with here and there a late-burning light – and suddenly out of the clear darkness the sound of bells. As an endless dream it went on; the spirit of the past brooding over a new generation, the chosen youth from the muddled, unchastened world, still fed romantically on the mistakes and half-forgotten dreams of dead statesmen and poets. Here was a new generation, shouting the old cries, learning the old creeds, through a revery of long days and nights; destined finally to go out into that dirty gray turmoil to follow love and pride; a new generation dedicated more than the last to the fear of poverty

and the worship of success; grown up to find all God's dead, all
wars fought, all faiths in man shaken. . . .

Amory, sorry for them, was still not sorry for himself – art,
politics, religion, whatever his medium should be, he knew he
was safe now, free from all hysteria – he could accept what was
acceptable, roam, grow, rebel, sleep deep through many
nights. . . .

There was no God in his heart, he knew; his ideas were still
in riot; there was ever the pain of memory; the regret for his
lost youth – yet the waters of disillusion had left a deposit on
his soul, responsibility and a love of life, the faint stirring of
old ambitions and unrealized dreams. But – oh, Rosalind!
Rosalind! . . .

'It's all a poor substitute at best,' he said sadly.

And he could not tell why the struggle was worth while, why
he had determined to use to the utmost himself and his
heritage from the personalities he had passed. . . .

He stretched out his arms to the crystalline, radiant sky.

'I know myself,' he cried, 'but that is all.'[22]

Fitzgerald had not really met Perkins's objection that the hero
of 'The Romantic Egotist' did not get anywhere. It is arguable
whether Amory does know himself, but it is appropriate for a
quest novel to end with the hero embarking on a new quest.

Although *This Side of Paradise* is autobiographical,
Fitzgerald assembled a cast that included copied and invented
characters. Amory Blaine is a rather idealized Fitzgerald;
Monsignor Darcy is Fay; Thomas Parke D'Invilliers is John
Peale Bishop; and Burne Holiday is loosely based on Henry
Strater.[23] Other Princetonians are composites, as Fitzgerald
combined several of his friends to form one character. Of the
principal women, Isabelle is recognizably Ginevra King, but
Rosalind is a combination of Zelda and Beatrice Normandy
from *Tono-Bungay*. Eleanor Savage was invented from Fay's
experiences, and Beatrice Blaine was drawn from the mother
of one of Fitzgerald's friends. In writing his first novel
Fitzgerald worked towards the method of 'transmuted
autobiography,' which subsequently allowed him to combine
his own emotions with the qualities of an actual figure in his

most enduring characters. Fitzgerald worked close to life, but after *This Side of Paradise* he rarely transcribed real people.

The Princeton material generated some of the popularity of *This Side of Paradise*, which was regarded as the first realistic American college novel. Moreover, it was about Princeton at a time when Princeton was a glamorous and exclusive place. (*Stover at Yale* [1911], which preceded it as an Ivy League document, was populated by unconvincing characters.) As a Princeton novel, *This Side of Paradise* appealed to young readers who wanted inside information about the American Oxbridges, and it was read as a handbook for collegiate conduct. Fifteen-year-old John O'Hara, dreaming of Ivy League triumphs in Pottsville, Pennsylvania, never forgot his first reading of *This Side of Paradise*. Twenty-five years later he wrote in his introduction to the *Portable F. Scott Fitzgerald* that half a million men and women between fifteen and thirty fell in love with the book.[24] The timing was perfect. In 1920 America was entering the collegiate decade memorialized in the drawings of John Held, Jr. Nonetheless, Fitzgerald's aristocrats would have been appalled by Held's creatures. *This Side of Paradise* is set at a pre-World War I Princeton committed to restrained behavior. ('Running it out' was the Princeton term of censure for overdoing things.)

Fitzgerald later described his novel as 'A Romance and a Reading List,'[25] for it is virtually a bibliography of the books that shape Amory Blaine. Sixty-four titles and ninety-eight writers are mentioned.[26] Amory and his friends are bookish if not necessarily scholarly; they seek codes and personal models in literature. This approach to literature became one of the characteristics of the American college novel.

Much of the impact of *This Side of Paradise* derived from its depiction of the new American girl in rebellion against the strictures of her mother. The novel was even credited, incorrectly, with having invented the American flapper. Newspapers and magazines of 1920 announced that girls read it as an instruction book. Yet Fitzgerald's sexual revolution amounted to a few pre-engagement kisses.

('Petting' in *This Side of Paradise* refers to what later generations would call 'necking.') Amory is as chaste as the girls he loves. *This Side of Paradise* seemed fresh – and even sensational – because it was the first American novel of the post-war period to treat college life and the liberated woman with a mixture of realism and romanticism. It was a serious book, and Fitzgerald's audience took it seriously.

On 27 May 1920 John Grier Hibben, the president of Princeton, wrote Fitzgerald a pained letter. After praising 'The Four Fists,' he expressed his distress over *This Side of Paradise*.

> It is because I appreciate so much all that is in you of artistic skill and certain elemental power that I am taking the liberty of telling you very frankly that your characterization of Princeton has grieved me. I cannot bear to think that our young men are merely living for four years in a country club and spending their lives wholly in a spirit of calculation and snobbishness.
>
> Your descriptions of the beauty and charm of Princeton are the most admirable that I have ever read and yet, I miss something in the book which I am sure you, yourself, could not wholly have missed in your college course.
>
> You must not think that my point of view is merely that of an older man and that that accounts for my differing with you in reference to the Princeton life. From my undergraduate days I have always had a belief in Princeton and in what the place could do in the making of a strong vigorous manhood. It would be an overwhelming grief to me, in the midst of my work here and my love for Princeton's young men, should I feel that we have nothing to offer but the outgrown symbols and shells of a past whose reality has long since disappeared.[27]

Fitzgerald replied on 3 June:

> I want to thank you very much for your letter and to confess that the honor of a letter from you outweighed my real regret that my book gave you concern. It was a book written with the bitterness of my discovery that I had spent several years trying to fit in with a curriculum that is after all made for the average student. After the curriculum had tied me up, taken away the honors I'd wanted, bent my nose over a chemistry book and

said, 'No fun, no activities, no offices, no Triangle trips – no, not even a diploma if you can't do chemistry' – after that I retired. It is easy for the successful man in college, the man who has gotten what he wanted to say

'It's all fine. It makes men. It made me, see'–

– but it seems to me it's like the Captain of a Company when he has his men lined up at attention for inspection. He sees only the tightly buttoned coat and the shaved faces. He doesn't know that perhaps a private in the rear rank is half crazy because a pin is sticking in his back and he can't move, or another private is thinking that his wife is dying and he can't get leave because too many men in the company are gone already.

I don't mean at all that Princeton is not the happiest time in most boys lives. It is of course – I simply say it wasn't the happiest time in mine. I love it now better than any place on earth. The men – the undergraduates of Yale + Princeton are cleaner, healthier, better-looking, better dressed, wealthier and more attractive than any undergraduate body in the country. I have no fault to find with Princeton that I can't find with Oxford and Cambridge. I simply wrote out of my own impressions, wrote as honestly as I could a picture of its beauty. That the picture is cynical is the fault of my temperament.

My view of life, President Hibben, is the view of the Theodore Driesers and Joseph Conrads – that life is too strong and remorseless for the sons of men. My idealism flickered out with Henry Strater's anti-club movement at Princeton. 'The Four Fists,' latest of my stories to be published, was the first to be written. I wrote it in desperation one evening because I had a three inch pile of rejection slips and it was financially necessary for me to give the magazine what they wanted. The appreciation it has received has amazed me.

I must admit however that This Side of Paradise does over accentuate the gayiety + country club atmostphere of Princeton. For the sake of the readers interest that part was much overstressed, and of course the hero, not being average, reacted rather unhealthily I suppose to many perfectly normal phenomena. To that extent the book is inaccurate. It is the Princeton of Saturday night in May. Too many intelligent classmates of mine have failed to agree with it for me to consider it really photographic any more, as of course I did when I wrote it.[28]

One of the problems with *This Side of Paradise* was that it was full of errors – misspellings and misusages. Even the dedication to 'Sigorney Fay' misspelled the Monsignor's first name. Franklin P. Adams devoted two of his 'Conning Tower' columns in the *New York Tribune* to listing 'instances of Mr. Fitzgerald's disregard for accuracy.'[29] Eventually, forty-two corrections were made in the first edition. The sloppy text of *This Side of Paradise* established the image of Fitzgerald as a careless or illiterate writer.* He was a bad speller (he never learned the i-before-e rule and all his life he wrote 'ect.,' 'apon,' 'critisism,' and 'yatch'); but the printed texts of Fitzgerald's books had errors because they were not properly copy-edited. At a trade house a book normally goes through a separate copy-editing process apart from literary editing; Perkins was reluctant to let anyone else work on Fitzgerald, and the great editor was a poor proofreader. Fitzgerald's manuscripts provide abundant evidence that he spelled and punctuated by ear. They also provide abundant evidence that he was a painstaking reviser. Fitzgerald was concerned with sentence structure and word choice when he polished his prose; he left spelling to editorial hands. His punctuation also required editorial intervention, but study of Fitzgerald's manuscripts reveals that the Scribners' house-styling imposed on him was more formal than his habitual light punctuation – especially with commas.[30]

Charles Scribner, Jr., who succeeded to the presidency of the firm in 1952, states: 'Perkins was totally useless when it came to copyediting or correcting a text. Such details meant very little to him. Consequently, the early editions of such books as Scott Fitzgerald's *The Great Gatsby* were textually corrupt to a nauseating degree.'[31] Fitzgerald was not indifferent to factual accuracy; he was particularly sensitive to the associations of time and place. Since his reliance upon Perkins and the editorial staff extended to details, errors of geography and chronology mar his novels and distract readers.[32]

* Fitzgerald was not unique among major authors in being an orthographic phenomenon. John Steinbeck is reported to have been a poor speller, and Hemingway's manuscripts look like the work of a child.

16

A Jazz-Age Marriage

[Spring 1920]

On 30 March 1920 – four days after publication of *This Side of Paradise* – Fitzgerald wired Zelda:

> TALKED WITH JOHN PALMER AND ROSALIND AND WE THINK BEST TO GET MARRIED SATURDAY NOON WE WILL BE AWFULLY NERVOUS UNTIL IT IS OVER AND WOULD GET NO REST BY WAITING UNTIL MONDAY FIRST EDITION OF THE BOOK IS SOLD OUT ADDRESS COTTAGE UNTIL THURSDAY AND SCRIBNERS AFTER THAT LOVE SCOTT[33]

Zelda came to New York with her sister Marjorie Brinson. (Rosalind Smith and Clothilde Palmer were living in New York.) The marriage service took place in the vestry of St. Patrick's Cathedral on Saturday, 3 April, at noon. Zelda's three sisters were present, but neither the bride's nor the groom's parents attended the wedding. Fitzgerald was nervous and insisted that the ceremony begin before the Palmers arrived. Ludlow Fowler was the best man, and Rosalind Smith was the matron of honor.* There was no

---

* The service was performed by Father William B. Martin – not by Father Thomas Delihant, as has been claimed.

151

party or wedding lunch – an uncharacteristic discourtesy for which Rosalind never forgave Fitzgerald. Mr. and Mrs. F. Scott Fitzgerald simply left the church together. They honeymooned at the Biltmore Hotel at 43rd Street and Vanderbilt Avenue. Zelda later wrote: 'Alabama lay thinking in room twenty-one-o-nine of the Biltmore Hotel that her life would be different with her parents so far away. David David Knight Knight Knight, for instance, couldn't possibly make her put out her light till she got good and ready. No power on earth could make her do anything, she thought frightened, any more, except herself.'[34]

Their marathon talks provided one of the pleasures of marriage. Fitzgerald later recalled in a memo: 'I have often thought that those long conversations we used to have late at night, that began at midnight + lasted till we could see the first light dawn that scared us into sleep, were something essential in our relations, a sort of closeness that we never achieved in the workaday world of marriage. We talked usually about abstractions but at a pitch where no personalities scarcely intruded and revelations were as free as alcoholic revelations but were revealing, illuminating and essentially healing rather than merely defiant. They stopped somewhere in Europe about five years ago.'[35]

Another pleasure for Zelda was spending her husband's money, at which she became adept with his encouragement. Since she had arrived in New York with frilly Southern dresses, one of their first priorities was to purchase a chic New York wardrobe – including a Patou suit.

Their marriage coincided with the beginning of the Boom, the Era of Wonderful Nonsense, the Roaring Twenties, what Fitzgerald named the Jazz Age and described as 'the greatest, gaudiest spree in history.'[36] In point of fact, Fitzgerald knew almost nothing about jazz and did not write about it. His explication of the term in 'Echoes of the Jazz Age' (1931) reveals that he used it to connote a mood or psychological

Opposite: Zelda at the time of her marriage to Fitzgerald

condition: 'The word jazz in its progress toward respectability has first meant sex, then dancing, then music. It is associated with a state of nervous stimulation, not unlike that of big cities behind the lines of a war.'[37] Fitzgerald began as a spokesman for the Jazz Age and became its symbol. With his capacity for becoming identified with his times, he came to represent the excesses of the Twenties – its Prince Charming and its fool.

The Twenties have been called a decade of confidence, of cynicism, of disillusionment, of ebullience, of moral upheaval. 'It was an age of miracles, it was an age of art, it was an age of excess and it was an age of satire,' Fitzgerald wistfully recollected in 1931.[38] America emerged from the Great War as the most powerful nation, but the war left a sour aftertaste as the ideals for which Americans fought – or had been told they were fighting for – were sacrificed to expediency and European corruption. The war generation was supposed to feel embittered, betrayed, lost – and some did. But Fitzgerald insisted that 'we were the great believers.'[39] One of the things they believed in was literature, and the Twenties produced an American Renaissance. Some of the younger writers who achieved recognition in the Twenties were Hemingway, Faulkner, Dos Passos, Lewis, Wolfe, Cozzens, Barry, O'Neill, Cummings, Stevens, Williams.

Fitzgerald's generation also believed in heroes. An era that requires heroes will create them. The Twenties produced a configuration of quasi-mythic figures: Babe Ruth, Jack Dempsey, George Gershwin, Greta Garbo, Bessie Smith, Bix Beiderbeck, Rudolph Valentino, Charlie Chaplin. Al Capone was the gangster. Man O'War was the horse. Another young Minnesotan flew the Atlantic and became the most admired American of his time.

The Roaring Twenties were typified by the bull market and Prohibition. Because of the small margin requirements, stock speculation could be strikingly successful. Some bootblacks, bartenders, and barbers did make paper fortunes. Not everyone was in the market – Fitzgerald wasn't. Nonetheless, the stories about quick fortunes made on a tip gave the big cities a boom-town mentality. Even if it didn't happen to you, it happened to somebody you knew or knew about. Anything was possible.

Although revisionist historians now argue that Prohibition was a success because it reduced alcohol consumption in rural areas and among the working class, it was a distinct failure among the urban upper classes. Drinking increased among people for whom defying the bluenose Prohibitionists was a gesture of intellectual respectability. Many of the new crop of expatriates would claim that life seemed intolerable in a country where alcohol was banned, because the enactment of the Prohibition law indicated that America was controlled by ignorant reformers who would stifle culture. A then-current definition was that a reformer was someone who was afraid that somebody somewhere was having a good time.

The Twenties brought about the first American children's crusade as the youth cult altered manners and morals; and the elders sometimes tried to imitate liberated youth. 'Flaming youth,' given currency by novelist Samuel Hopkins Adams, started as a term of disapproval but soon evolved into an unpejorative slogan.

The Fitzgeralds' first months in New York were heady. Any couple might have been spoiled by the same exciting circumstances. The twenty-three-year-old author and the nineteen-year-old Alabama girl were celebrities – young, handsome, rich (so it seemed), with no one to exercise authority over them. They were interviewed; they rode on the roofs of taxis; they jumped into fountains; there was always a party to go to. Regarding the days of his conquest of New York from the perspective of 1932, Fitzgerald wrote: ' . . . I remember riding in a taxi one afternoon between very tall buildings under a mauve and rosy sky; I began to bawl because I had everything I wanted and knew I would never be so happy again.'[40] The Fitzgeralds found themselves cast as the models for the new worship of youth. At first it may have rather bewildered them, but they soon accepted their roles as pioneers. Yet all the while a judging process was operating in Fitzgerald's mind. Like Nick Carraway in *The Great Gatsby*, Fitzgerald was simultaneously within and without, participating and observing. He later admitted to his daughter: 'Sometimes I wish I had gone along with that gang [musical comedy writers], but I guess I am too much a moralist at heart, and really want to preach at people in some acceptable form, rather than to entertain them.'[41]

Zelda drank along with her husband, and their social activities were fueled by alcohol. But there was a difference in the way they handled drink. Zelda got tight because she enjoyed it. Fitzgerald was an incipient alcoholic whose drinking behavior became increasingly unpredictable. In the early days of their marriage they simply fell asleep when they were tight. They would arrive at parties a little drunk and take a nap before joining the other guests. Zelda would sometimes come to a party and take a bath. Fitzgerald's growing dependence on alcohol is reflected by the admission of a character in 'A New Leaf' (1931): ' "About the time I came into some money I found that with a few drinks I got expansive and somehow had the ability to please people, and the idea turned my head. Then I began to take a whole lot of drinks to keep going and have everybody think I was wonderful." '[42] His need to impress people sometimes seemed desperate. If he couldn't please them, then he would try to get attention through conspicuous behavior. Fitzgerald had the ability to perform spontaneous acts of high-spirited charm. When he was in the Scribner Building and learned that Edith Wharton was in Charles Scribner's office, he burst into the room and knelt at her feet in homage.

As at Princeton, in New York Fitzgerald's friends were convinced that he pretended to be drunker than he was in order to excuse his outrageous conduct. The celebrating Fitzgeralds were not just nuisances; and people did not put up with them only because they were celebrities. Edmund Wilson has described their authentic appeal: 'The remarkable thing about the Fitzgeralds was their capacity for carrying things off and carrying people away by their spontaneity, charm, and good looks. They had a genius for imaginative improvisations. . . .'[43] Wilson has also testified to the attraction of Zelda's conversation as 'so full of felicitous phrases and unexpected fancies that, in spite of the fact that it was difficult to talk to her consecutively about anything, you were not led, especially if you yourself had absorbed a few Fitzgerald highballs, to suspect any mental unsoundness from her free "flight of ideas." '[44] Others were put off by her habit of making personal comments about the people she was talking to.

At parties Fitzgerald enjoyed performing 'Dog! Dog! Dog!,' a song he had written with Wilson's assistance:

> In Sunny Africa they have the elephant
> And in India they have the zebera –
> Up in Canada the Rocky Mountain goat
> And in Idaho the shoat
>   (You've heard about it!)
> But of all these animals
> You will find the best of pals –
>   Is!
>
> Dog, dog – I like a good dog –
> Towser or Bowser or Star –
> Clean sort of pleasure –
> A four-footed treasure –
> And faithful as few humans are!
> Here, Pup: put your paw up –
> Roll over dead like a log!
> Larger than a rat!
>   More faithful than a cat!
>   Dog! Dog! Dog![45]

The Fitzgeralds' marriage brought an ascendancy change in their relationship. Before the wedding Zelda was a Montgomery celebrity and Fitzgerald was one of a crowd of suitors. In New York, Fitzgerald was the famous one. At first Zelda did not appear to mind the role reversal because her stronger personality dominated their marriage; but it became increasingly difficult for her to accept the subordinate role of wife to F. Scott Fitzgerald.

Early Success

This Side of Paradise went through printing after printing: April, 3,025 and 5,000; May, 5,000; June, 5,050; July 5,000; August, 5,000; September, 5,000; October, 5,000. The novel achieved additional exposure when abridged versions were serialized in the *Chicago Herald and Examiner*, the *Atlanta Georgian*, and the *New York Daily News*. By the end of 1921 it had required twelve printings totaling 49,075 copies. Even so, it was not one of the ten best-selling novels for 1920 – although it would prove to be Fitzgerald's most popular book. *This Side of Paradise* made the *Publishers Weekly* best-seller list only twice: it was fourth in August and eighth in September.* Sinclair Lewis's *Main Street*, published in 1920, became the best-selling novel of 1921 with 295,000 copies.

The sales of *This Side of Paradise* did not make Fitzgerald rich. Scribners paid a royalty of 10 percent on the first 5,000 copies and 15 percent thereafter. For a $1.75 novel, this meant royalties of 17½¢ and 26¼¢ per copy. In 1920 the income from the novel was $6,200. Most of Fitzgerald's 1920 money came from other sources. Eleven stories brought $4,650 as Fitzgerald's price rose from $400 to $900; the movies paid $7,425 for three stories ('Head and Shoulders,' 'Myra Meets His Family,' and 'The Offshore Pirate') and an option on future stories. Fitzgerald earned $18,850 after commissions during his first full year as a professional writer – on which he paid $1,444.25 federal income tax. His income did not cover expenditures, and he began the custom of borrowing from Harold Ober and from Scribners.†

In March 1920 Fitzgerald had made an attempt to provide for the future, probably in anticipation of his responsibilities as a husband. He invested in two $500 bonds of Fair & Co., which paid 7½ percent interest. These bonds became a

---

* The best-selling novels of 1920 included *The Man of the Forest* by Zane Grey, *Kindred of the Dust* by Peter B. Kyne, *The Re-Creation of Brian Kent* by Harold Bell Wright, and books by James Oliver Curwood, Irving Bacheller, Eleanor H. Porter, Joseph C. Lincoln, E. Phillips Oppenheim, Ethel M. Dell, and Kathleen Norris.
† Ober received a 10 percent commission on Fitzgerald's magazine and movie sales, but for his books Fitzgerald always dealt directly with Scribners.

travesty of prudence when Fitzgerald was unable to sell them. He claimed that they were returned to him when he left them in the subway. In 1924 he managed to dispose of them for a $600 loss.

When the Biltmore asked the Fitzgeralds to leave because they were disturbing other guests, they transferred two blocks to the Commodore Hotel on 42nd Street, where they celebrated their move by spinning in the revolving door. New York seemed full of Princetonians who joined the group the Fitzgeralds partied with. Wilson and Bishop were on the staff of *Vanity Fair* (Fitzgerald sent Donald Ogden Stewart to them when he was trying to get started as a writer); Townsend Martin, Alexander McKaig, Lawton Campbell, and Ludlow Fowler were also in the city. A new friend was George Jean Nathan, co-editor of *The Smart Set*. Nathan instituted an elaborate wooing of Zelda, which sometimes annoyed Fitzgerald. Zelda noted that '[I] *cut* my *tail* on a broken bottle' during one of Nathan's parties.[46]

They met Nathan's partner, H. L. Mencken, on his trips from Baltimore. Then at the peak of his influence as a literary critic, Mencken had fought for the recognition of Theodore Dreiser and was one of Joseph Conrad's staunchest partisans. Although the stolid Mencken and the flamboyant Fitzgerald were too different to become close friends, they developed mutual respect. Fitzgerald said that Mencken was the only man in America for whom he had complete admiration. Mencken recognized Fitzgerald's potential but suspected that he would be deflected from great work by his style of living.

Another 1920 influence on Fitzgerald was the work of Mark Twain, resulting from Perkins's present of *The Ordeal of Mark Twain*. Since Van Wyck Brooks's study argued that Mark Twain had been damaged by the forces of respectability, the volume may have been Perkins's way of warning Fitzgerald against selling out to popularity. Fitzgerald was impressed by it and subsequently read Albert Bigelow Paine's biography of Twain. He admired *Tom Sawyer* and *Huckleberry Finn* (the Duke and the Dauphin were his favorite characters in the novel) and once ranked 'The Mysterious Stranger' among the '10 Best Books I Have Read'; but Mark Twain's direct influence on Fitzgerald's writing was minimal. (None of Mark Twain's books appears on the reading lists Fitzgerald later prepared for Sheilah Graham.) He cited Mark Twain as the source for 'The Curious Case of Benjamin Button' (1922), and the idea for 'The Diamond as Big as the Ritz' (1922) may have been suggested by the mountain of coal in *The Gilded Age*. When Fitzgerald was asked to provide a statement for the banquet marking the centenary of Samuel Langhorne Clemens's birth in November 1935, he wrote: 'Huckleberry

H. L. Mencken and George Jean Nathan

A Jazz-Age Marriage [Spring 1920]

Finn took the first journey *back*. He was the first to look *back* at the republic from the perspective of the west. His eyes were the first eyes that ever looked at us objectively that were not eyes from overseas. There were mountains at the frontier but he wanted more than mountains to look at with his restless eyes – he wanted to find out about men and how they lived together. And because he turned back we have him forever.'[47]

Scribners arranged for Fitzgerald to speak at Wanamaker's department store and at the National Arts Club. Surprisingly, he found that he was ill at ease addressing an audience and thereafter avoided public speaking engagements. In April, Fitzgerald prepared a self-interview for Scribners. Despite his brilliant-young-author pose, this document reveals Fitzgerald's sense of career and his ambition to place himself in the line of great writers:

' . . . The scope and depth and breadth of my writings lie in the laps of the Gods. If knowledge comes naturally, through interest, as Shaw learned his political economy or as Wells devoured modern science – why, that'll be slick. On study itself – that is, in 'reading up' a subject – I haven't ant-hill moving faith. Knowledge must cry out to be known – cry out that only I can know it, and then I'll swim in it to satiety, as I've swum in – in many things.'

'Please be frank.'

'Well, you know if you've read my book, I've swum in various seas of adolescent egotism. But what I meant was that if big things never grip me – well, it simply means I'm not cut out to be big. This conscious struggle to find bigness outside, to substitute bigness of theme for bigness of perception, to create an objective *Magnum Opus* such as "The Ring and the Book" – well, all that's the antithesis of my literary aims.

'Another thing,' he continued. 'My idea is always to reach my generation. The wise writer, I think, writes for the youth of his own generation, the critics of the next, and the schoolmasters of ever afterward. Granted the ability to improve what he imitates in the way of style, to choose from his interpretation of

161

the experiences around him what constitutes material, and we get the first-water genius.'

. . . .

'By style, I mean color,' he said. 'I want to be able to do anything with words: handle slashing, flaming descriptions like Wells, and use the paradox with the clarity of Samuel Butler, the breadth of Bernard Shaw and the wit of Oscar Wilde. I want to do the wide sultry heavens of Conrad, the rolled-gold sundowns and crazy-quilt skies of Hichens and Kipling as well as the pastel dawns of Chesterton. All that is by way of example. As a matter of fact I am a professed literary thief, hot after the best methods of every writer in my generation.'[48]

When Heywood Broun included this interview in his *Tribune* column, he commented: 'Having heard Mr. Fitzgerald, we are not entirely minded to abandon our notion that he is a rather complacent, somewhat pretentious and altogether self-conscious young man.'[49] Fitzgerald liked this self-interview so much that he borrowed from it for 'The Author's Apology,' a signed leaf inserted in copies of *This Side of Paradise* distributed by Scribners at the May 1920 meeting of the American Booksellers Association, in which he announced: 'I don't want to talk about myself because I'll admit I did that somewhat in this book. In fact, to write it took three months; to conceive it – three minutes; to collect the data in it – all my life. The idea of writing it came on the first of last July: it was a substitute form of dissipation.'[50]

17

Westport

[Summer 1920]

During the spring of 1920, Fitzgerald tried to be a writer in the confusion of hotel rooms. Zelda was not interested in house-keeping. She was bored when he was writing and would go off by herself to seek amusement; then Fitzgerald couldn't write because he was worried about what she was doing. Nonetheless, he admired her escapades and reported them with pride. Zelda's attentions to Fitzgerald's friends sometimes upset him. She would neck with party acquaintances. Once she tried to sleep with Bishop, although her intentions were not sexual; another time she wanted Townsend Martin to bathe her. The pattern of quarrels and reconciliations established during their courtship continued.

Fitzgerald was unable to work on his second novel. The only substantial piece he produced in New York was the long story 'May Day,' which may have been salvaged from an abandoned novel. Probably written in March, before his marriage, 'May Day' is one of Fitzgerald's best stories; but he discovered that it was too pessimistic for the popular magazines, and it went to *The Smart Set* for $200. At this time Fitzgerald was under the influence of naturalism – the deterministic development of realism that he had found in Frank Norris and Theodore Dreiser – but 'May Day' is the only story in which he fully developed this method. An account of the events culminating in the suicide of Gordon Sterrett, a poverty-ridden failed artist, in New York on the morning after 1 May 1919, the story is built around the contrast between the anti-socialist riots and the Yale dance at Delmonico's on May Day. Sterrett feels his hopelessness when he meets old college friends and is humiliated when he tries to borrow money from a wealthy classmate. He shoots himself when he wakes up married to a domineering lower-class girl. Although the material is naturalistic, the style is far richer and more flexible than the ploddings of Dreiser. Fitzgerald rapidly mastered the art of conveying meanings through tone. Here is the author setting the mood in a quasi-Biblical preamble:

There had been a war fought and won and the great city of the conquering people was crossed with triumphal arches and vivid with thrown flowers of white, red, and rose. All through the long spring days the returning soldiers marched up the chief highway behind the strump of drums and the joyous, resonant wind of the brasses, while merchants and clerks left their bickerings and figurings and, crowding to the windows, turned their white-bunched faces gravely upon the passing battalions.

Never had there been such splendor in the great city, for the victorious war had brought plenty in its train, and the merchants had flocked thither from the South and West with their households to taste of all the luscious feasts and witness the lavish entertainments prepared – and to buy for their women furs against the next winter and bags of golden mesh and varicolored slippers of silk and silver and rose satin and cloth of gold.

So gaily and noisily were the peace and prosperity impending hymned by the scribes and poets of the conquering people that more and more spenders had gathered from the provinces to drink the wine of excitement, and faster and faster did the merchants dispose of their trinkets and slippers until they sent up a mighty cry for more trinkets and more slippers in order that they might give in barter what was demanded of them. Some even of them flung up their hands helplessly, shouting:

'Alas! I have no more slippers! and alas! I have no more trinkets! May Heaven help me, for I know not what I shall do!'

But no one listened to their great outcry, for the throngs were far too busy – day by day, the foot-soldiers trod jauntily the highway and all exulted because the young men returning were pure and brave, sound of tooth and pink of cheek, and the young women of the land were virgins and comely both of face and of figure.

So during all this time there were many adventures that happened in the great city, and, of these, several – or perhaps one – are here set down.[51]

Fusing several stories into a single narrative, 'May Day' displays the marked technical advances Fitzgerald made during his first months as a professional writer.

The speculation whether Fitzgerald would have persevered with naturalistic material if it had been remunerative raises the more important problem of whether he trivialized his stories for the slick market. Over the next twenty years Fitzgerald put the major part of his writing time into 160 short stories, which he resented and disparaged. Most of them were written just for money; but admitting that he wrote potboilers is not the same as demonstrating that Fitzgerald deliberately spoiled stories to make them marketable. In *A Moveable Feast* Ernest Hemingway reports he warned Fitzgerald in 1925 that the *Post* stories would ruin his ability to write seriously. Fitzgerald explained that he wrote the real story first, then cheapened it for the *Post* – thereby nullifying the damage to his artistic judgment.[52] Fitzgerald may have made this claim; he often said unlikely things when he was drinking. But there is no evidence in Fitzgerald's preserved manuscripts of a story in which this process occurred.

In May 1920 *Metropolitan* magazine, which was fighting a losing circulation war, took an option on Fitzgerald's stories at $900 each – when the *Post* was paying him $500. The proposition, intended to capture Fitzgerald from the *Post*, provides an indication of the rapid popularity of his stories. Five were submitted under this contract in 1920–21 – 'The Jelly Bean,' 'His Russet Witch', 'Two For a Cent,' 'The Curious Case of Benjamin Button' (declined), and 'Winter Dreams' – before the *Metropolitan* went into receivership.

Fitzgerald did not regard his novels as uncommercial endeavors written for literature's sake; he expected them to make a great deal of money while bringing him artistic satisfaction and acclaim. He denigrated his stories because they interfered with his recognition as a serious writer. Early in his professional career Fitzgerald developed the rationale that he would do magazine stories only to underwrite his novels – to get financially ahead so that he could devote six months or a year to uninterrupted work on a novel. Like most of his practical plans, this one did not work out. He was rarely ahead; when he was, he usually wasted his time and money. It may well be that the stories are what we have, not instead of more novels but instead of nothing.

Fitzgerald wanted to show off his success and his bride at Princeton. On 25 April they went down in the implausible capacity of chaperones for a house party weekend. Fitzgerald shocked undergraduates by introducing Zelda as his mistress and during the course of the visit received a black eye during a scuffle in Harvey Firestone's car. He returned to Princeton on 1 May with Wilson and Bishop to attend a *Nassau Lit* banquet. Having provided themselves with lyres and wreaths, they called on Professor Gauss. Then Fitzgerald went to the Cottage Club, where he was told that he had been suspended from membership because he and his wife had disgraced the club. The members expressed their moral outrage by shoving him out a window. Fitzgerald was bitterly hurt and left on the first train.* The suspension was later lifted, and Fitzgerald always

---

* Wilson wrote a verse report of their Princeton trip:
Poor Fitz went prancing into the Cottage Club
With his gilt wreath and lyre,
Looking like a tarnished Apollo with the two black eyes

thought of himself as a member of Cottage, visiting the house whenever he was in Princeton.

After a month of New York hotel life the Fitzgeralds were in need of a place where he could work without distractions and she could swim and amuse herself. They bought a secondhand Marmon touring car and headed up U.S. 1 in search of tranquillity. Fitzgerald soon discovered that his bride was a terrifying driver, only partly because she had defective vision in one eye and refused to wear glasses. At Westport, Connecticut, they rented the Wakeman house, a gray-shingled eighteenth-century farmhouse on Compo Road near the Long Island Sound. About fifty miles from the city, Westport was still country, not suburbia. A Japanese houseboy named Tana was hired, and the Fitzgeralds intended to settle down to an orderly life, allowing for only an occasional guest. Instead, there were alcoholic weekend parties that had a way of lasting through Monday. The Westport authorities were not understanding when a false fire alarm was turned in from the Fitzgerald residence during one of their parties. Legend has it that when the firemen asked where the fire was, Zelda pointed to her breast and said, 'Here!' It may not have happened that way, but it was the kind of anecdote people liked to tell about the Fitzgeralds. George Jean Nathan was a regular visitor. He and Fitzgerald cooked up the gag that Tana was really a German spy named Tannenbaum; they improved the joke by sending him messages from the German High Command. Inevitably the

---

That he had got, when far gone in liquor, in some unintelligible fight,
But looking like Apollo all the same, with the sun on his pale yellow hair;
And his classmates who had been roaring around the campus all day
And had had whiskey, but no Swinburne,
Arose as one man and denounced him
And told him that he and his wife had disgraced the club and that he was no
    longer worthy to belong to it
(Though really they were angry with him
Because he had achieved great success
Without starting in at the bottom in the nut and bolt business).[53]

Fitzgeralds made frequent excursions to New York, leaving a trail of impulsive checks.

Fitzgerald planned to complete a novel, a play, and a story by 16 October 1920. He was a methodical planner all his professional life, preparing schedules and charts for his work; that he rarely kept to these plans did not discourage him from making them. The summer work schedule was interrupted by a trip to Montgomery. Zelda was homesick for the South and complained that she missed peaches and biscuits for breakfast. Perhaps she too wanted to show off her marriage – to return to Montgomery as one who had conquered the North as well as the South.

They departed on 15 July in the Marmon, now called 'the Rolling Junk,' and managed to get to Montgomery after many mechanical problems and a few social ones as they scandalized the 'surrounding yokelry' with their matching knickers. After celebrating in Montgomery for two weeks, they abandoned the Marmon and returned to Westport by train. In 1922 Fitzgerald wrote 'The Cruise of the Rolling Junk,' a humorous three-part travel article about the trip, which also expresses his response to the underside of the Twenties, that he found in the Main Streets of the South.

Fitzgerald wrote three stories during the summer: 'The Jelly Bean' (*Metropolitan*), 'The Lees of Happiness' (*Chicago Tribune*), and 'The I.O.U.' (unsold). The two published stories show him working with different kinds of material. In 'The Jelly Bean' a Southern loafer is temporarily inspired to reform by his love for a reckless girl. Although Fitzgerald quickly came to be regarded as a writer of entertaining short stories about young love, many of his stories had what he called 'a touch of disaster.' An attempt at pathos that does not rise above sentimentality, 'The Lees of Happiness' treats a young wife's eleven-year devotion to her paralyzed husband.

The Sayres came to Westport in August, but the visit was uncomfortable because the Judge did not conceal his disapproval of the way the Fitzgeralds lived. That month Fitzgerald got down to work on his next novel, which had as working titles 'The Beautiful Lady Without Mercy' and 'The Flight of the Rocket.' On the twelfth he explained to Charles Scribner that it 'concerns the life of one Anthony Patch between his 25th and 33rd years (1913–21). He is one of those many with the tastes and weaknesses of an artist but with no actual creative inspiration. How he and his beautiful young wife are wrecked on the shoals of dissipation is told in the story. This sounds sordid but it's really a most sensational book + I hope won't disapoint the critics who liked my first one.'[54] He stuck to his plan and made steady progress through the fall.

Fitzgerald summarized his twenty-third year, which brought him both Zelda and literary recognition, as 'Revelry and Marriage. The rewards of the year before. The happiest year since I was 18.' In October 1920 they moved to an apartment at 38 West 59th Street between Fifth and Sixth avenues – conveniently near the Plaza Hotel, from which they could order meals.

18

New York
and First Trip Abroad

[Fall 1920–Summer 1921]

It was the custom for Scribners to follow a successful novel with a volume of short stories. On 10 September 1920 they published Fitzgerald's first collection, *Flappers and Philosophers*. (The rejected titles for the volume included 'We are Seven,' 'Table D'hote,' 'A La Carte,' 'Journeys and Journey's End,' 'Bittersweet,' and 'Shortcake.')[55] Dedicated to Zelda, *Flappers and Philosophers* included eight stories: 'The Offshore Pirate,' 'The Ice Palace,' 'Head and Shoulders,' 'The Cut-Glass Bowl,' 'Bernice Bobs Her Hair' (illustrated on the dust jacket), 'Benediction,' 'Dalyrimple Goes Wrong,' and 'The Four Fists.' Only three – 'Pirate,' 'Bernice,' and 'Ice Palace' – are really first-rate, but the volume sold surprisingly well for a collection of stories. By November 1922 there were six printings with a total of 15,325 copies. The income seemed like found money to Fitzgerald because all the stories had appeared in magazines. The reviews of *Flappers and Philosophers* were mixed, with some critics finding it a letdown after *This Side of Paradise*. Mencken in *The Smart Set* was among the first to call attention to the split in Fitzgerald between the entertainer and the serious novelist: 'Fitzgerald is curiously ambidextrous. Will he proceed via the first part of

This Side of Paradise to the cold groves of beautiful letters, or will he proceed via 'Head and Shoulders' into the sunshine that warms Robert W. Chambers and Harold McGrath?'[56] Fitzgerald sent Mencken a copy of the collection with an inscription rating the stories. *Worth reading*: 'The Ice Palace,' 'The Cut-Glass Bowl,' 'Benediction,' 'Dalyrimple Goes Wrong'; *Amusing*: 'The Offshore Pirate'; *Trash*: 'Head and Shoulders,' 'The Four Fists,' 'Bernice Bobs Her Hair.'[57] Fitzgerald's ranking of 'Benediction' and 'Dalyrimple' was influenced by the circumstance that they had been published in *The Smart Set*.

The fall and winter in New York were relatively dull for the Fitzgeralds as he worked on his novel, and they began to feel lonely after quarreling with some of their friends. While writing his novel in the fall Fitzgerald produced only one story, 'His Russet Witch' (*Metropolitan*, February 1921), claiming that he wrote this fantasy to relax from the discipline of his novel.* The story deals with the response of a dreary bookstore proprietor to a woman who represents youth and daring.

Fitzgerald became interested in other projects while he was working on his novel. He considered converting *This Side of Paradise* into a play and wrote an unidentified movie scenario for Dorothy Gish that was rejected. The scenario may have been submitted to D. W. Griffith, whom he tried to persuade that the public would be interested in a movie about the movies, but Fitzgerald reported that Griffith was 'contemptuous' of the idea. In October Fitzgerald tried to enlist Mencken's support for a collected edition of Frank Norris;[58] Mencken offered to help, but the project never developed. (In 1928 Doubleday published a ten-volume Norris edition, in which Fitzgerald was not involved.) Fitzgerald was convinced that Norris was forgotten. During a lunch with George Horace Lorimer he asserted that he was probably the only one in the room who had heard of Norris; Lorimer replied that he had serialized two of Norris's novels in *The Saturday Evening Post*.[59] Norris's *Vandover and the Brute* (1914),

---

* Fitzgerald changed the title to 'O Russet Witch!' when he collected the story.

a study of character deterioration in which a promising young Harvard man becomes a derelict, obviously influenced the conception of Anthony Patch in Fitzgerald's second novel.*

When Bob Clark, a St. Paul friend, sent him a letter urging him to write about 'real people,' Fitzgerald wrote a Menckenian reply in February: 'The Rousseaus, Marxes, Tolstois – men of thought, mind you, "impractical" men, "idealist" have done more to decide the food *you* eat and the things *you* think + do than all the millions of Roosevelts and

Zelda and Scott, winter 1921–1922

* During their courtship Fitzgerald had tried to interest Zelda in Frank Norris's *McTeague*, but she complained that 'All authors who want to make things true to life make them *smell bad* – '[60] Fitzgerald remained a Norris partisan. At the end of his life he sent Edmund Wilson a copy of *McTeague* marked to show how John Steinbeck had imitated it in *Of Mice and Men*.

Rockerfellars that strut for 20 yrs. or so mouthing such phrases as 100% American (which means 99% village idiot), and die with a little pleasing flattery to the silly and cruel old God they've set up in their hearts.' His letter included a purported historical document:

Stratford-on-Avon
June 8th 1595

Dear Will:

Your family here are much ashamed that you could write such a bawdy play as Troilus and Cressida. All the real people here (Mr. Beef, the butcher and Mr Skunk, the village undertaker) say they will not be satisfied with a brilliant mind and a pleasant manner. If you really want to ammount to something you've got to be respected for yourself as well as your work

Affectionately
Your Mother, Mrs. Shakespeare[61]

Zelda found she was pregnant in February 1921. After she visited Montgomery, where Fitzgerald joined her in March, they planned a trip to Europe before Zelda's pregnancy became too advanced. At this time they were considering an extended stay in Italy and the trip was in the nature of a scouting expedition. By the end of April, Fitzgerald was able to send Harold Ober a typed draft of the novel – now titled *The Beautiful and Damned* – for serialization. They sailed on the Cunard liner *Aquitania* on 3 May 1921, traveling first class. Before their departure Fitzgerald was beaten in the Jungle Club speak-easy when Zelda egged him into fighting the bouncer;[62] it is impossible to tell whether she wanted to see her husband get hurt, whether she believed he could handle the bouncer, or whether they were both too drunk to be responsible for their behavior. When Fitzgerald reached a certain stage of insobriety he was ready to fight anyone – all five foot seven of him. He thought he was – or should be – a proficient fighter. He wasn't, and his bar fights usually resulted in beatings for him.

The *Aquitania* docked at Southampton on 10 May, and the

Fitzgeralds checked into the Cecil Hotel in London. Perkins had provided an introduction to John Galsworthy; and Charles Kingsley, the Scribners London representative, arranged for the Fitzgeralds to meet other literary people. They were invited to tea by Galsworthy, who disappointed Fitzgerald: 'I can't stand pessimism with neither irony nor bitterness.'[63] There was a reunion with Shane Leslie, who conducted them on a nighttime walking tour of the London docks with Zelda dressed in men's clothing for safety in this criminal district; when she tired, the two men took turns carrying her. Lady Randolph Churchill had them to lunch, and Zelda talked at length with Winston Churchill. In London Fitzgerald invested in English tailoring, ordering suits from Davies & Sons and shirts from Hilditch and Key. Oxford – the setting of *Sinister Street* – impressed Fitzgerald as the most beautiful place he'd ever seen, and for a while he considered living there.

While the Fitzgeralds were abroad, Ober sold the serial rights for *The Beautiful and Damned* to *Metropolitan* for $7,000. The novel appeared in seven installments, from September 1921 to March 1922. On 17 May the Fitzgeralds were in Paris, where they unsuccessfully waited outside Anatole France's house for a glimpse of him. They were in Venice on 26 May, in Florence on 3 June, and in Rome on the twenty-second. In Italy, Fitzgerald wrote an unidentified scenario for Metro Pictures that was rejected.

The trip to the Continent was disappointing. For the Fitzgeralds places were associated with people they knew, and they were bored with unrelieved sightseeing. Apart from his emotional response to the house by the Spanish Steps in Rome where Keats had died, Fitzgerald was appalled by Italy. He was not prepared to make obeisance to European civilization, and he wrote Wilson in July:

> God damn the continent of Europe. It is of merely antiquarian interest. Rome is only a few years behind Tyre + Babylon. The negroid streak creeps northward to defile the

nordic race. Already the Italians have the souls of blackamoors. Raise the bars of immigration and permit only Scandinavians, Teutons, Anglo Saxons and Celts to enter. France made me sick. It's silly pose as the thing the world has to save. I think its a shame that England and America didn't let Germany conquor Europe. Its the only thing that would have saved the fleet of tottering old wrecks. My reactions were all philistine, anti-socialist, provincial + racially snobbish. I believe at last in the white man's burden. We are as far above the modern frenchman as he is above the negro. Even in art! Italy has no one. When Anatole France dies French literature will be a silly rehashing of technical quarrels. They're thru + done. You may have spoken in jest about N.Y. as the capitol of culture but in 25 years it will be just as London is now. Culture follows money + all the refinements of aestheticism can't stave off its change of seat (Christ! what a metaphor). We will be the Romans in the next generation as the English are now.[64]

On 30 June they were back in London, where they stayed at Claridge's and at the Cavendish. One of the reasons for the return to London was that *This Side of Paradise* had been published by Collins on 26 May and Fitzgerald wanted to witness the English reception of his novel. If he expected a repetition of the New York response, he was disappointed. A few reviews were uncomprehendingly favorable, but most of the English critics dismissed *This Side of Paradise* as trivial and unconvincing. *The Times Literary Supplement*, the most influential English review journal, commented: 'As a novel it is rather tiresome; its values are less human than literary, and its characters, men and women alike, with hardly an exception, a set of exasperating *poseurs*, whose conversation, devoted largely to minute self-analysis, is artificial beyond belief.'[65] The *Manchester Guardian* review concluded: 'But what people! What a set! They are well lost.'[66] None of Fitzgerald's books sold well in England during his lifetime. After a Fourth of July trip to Cambridge, which was combined with a pilgrimage to Grantchester to pay homage to Rupert Brooke, the Fitzgeralds cut short their tour and returned to America on the White Star liner *Celtic*.

19

St. Paul and Revising

The Beautiful and Damned

[Summer 1921]

They were in Montgomery on 27 July, intending to stay there for the birth of their child in October; but the combination of the Alabama heat and the Montgomery attitude toward pregnancy drove them north. In those days a lady in the family way was expected to stay home when her 'delicate condition' became obvious. Zelda shocked the locals by swimming in a public pool when she was large with child.

Fitzgerald's *Ledger* summary for his twenty-fourth year was: 'Work at the beginning but dangerous at the end. A slow year, dominated by Zelda + on the whole happy.' At the end of August 1921 the Fitzgeralds were at Dellwood on White Bear Lake outside St. Paul; they had rented the Mackey J. Thompson house for a year, but the owner asked them to leave in October because of damage involving a burst water pipe, for which he held Fitzgerald responsible. The Thompson house had been found for them by Xandra Kalman, who also helped with the preparations for the impending birth. Xandra and her husband, banker Oscar

Kalman, were a wealthy St. Paul couple with homes on
Summit Avenue and at Dellwood. Considerably younger than
Oscar, who was forty-eight, Xandra was the only close friend
Zelda made in St. Paul. Zelda's reaction to the Midwest was
similar to Sally Carrol Happer's in 'The Ice Palace': she found
the women dull and missed the attention that she had
received from men in the South and in New York.

Zelda had apparently not met her husband's family before
the summer of 1921. She and Fitzgerald had made three trips
to Montgomery before they went to St. Paul. The reason for
the delay is not known, for Fitzgerald was not estranged from
his parents. The circumstance that Zelda was not a Catholic
would hardly have kept Mollie away from her son for a year
and a half. The separation was almost certainly of Fitzgerald's
making. As a child he had discouraged his mother from
visiting him at camp and had entertained the fantasy that he
was a royal foundling; now as a young literary star he was
embarrassed by his mother because she did not fit the
glamorous image that was evolving about him. He loved his
father, but Fitzgerald was always sensitive to – and perhaps
resentful of – Edward's failure. There is a report that
Edward Fitzgerald enjoyed being driven in his son's Buick
touring car to the Grotto Pharmacy, where his favorite Tom
Moore cigars were available. Fitzgerald and Zelda saw little of
his parents and Annabel in St. Paul, but not because there
were family clashes. Zelda was bored by her husband's family,
and she and Fitzgerald were active in the so-called young
married set.

Fitzgerald relished his return to St. Paul as a famous
author. In August he was interviewed by Thomas A. Boyd,
literary editor of the *St. Paul Daily News*, under the headline
SCOTT FITZGERALD HERE ON VACATION; 'RESTS' BY OUTLINING
NEW NOVELS, and he was frequently mentioned in the St. Paul
papers. Despite his discomfort as a public speaker, he
addressed the St. Paul Women's City Club on 1 December
1921. His announced topic, 'South America,' was a joke; he
spoke about his work and literary enthusiasms. After denying

that he was especially interested in flappers, he praised Mencken as having done more for American letters than any other man. Fitzgerald became friends with Boyd and his wife Peggy, who wrote as Woodward Boyd. Boyd was also a partner in the Kilmarnock Bookstore at 84 East Fourth Street, which was a regular stop for Fitzgerald.

In St. Paul, Fitzgerald assumed the self-appointed role of talent scout or acquisitions editor for Scribners – partly out of his desire to help other writers and partly out of a sense of loyalty to his publisher. Fitzgerald came to regard Scribners as a literary club in which he wanted to assemble all the promising young American writers. His first find was Peggy Boyd's novel *The Love Legend*, which Scribners published in the fall of 1922. Fitzgerald knew the novel was not important but felt that the author was worth encouraging. He was far more impressed by *Through the Wheat*, twenty-three-year-old Thomas Boyd's novel about the Marines in World War I, which Scribners published in the spring of 1923.

Fitzgerald's identification with the house of Scribner – as well as his desire to be thought of as a man of affairs – is demonstrated by the plan for a cheap reprint series he sent Charles Scribner in April 1922. Impressed by The Modern Library and the Lambskin Library, he proposed a series restricted to the Scribners list and recommended eighteen titles: *The House of Mirth* or *Ethan Frome* by Edith Wharton, *Predestined* by Stephen French Whitman, *This Side of Paradise*, *The Little Shepherd of Kingdom Come* by John Fox, Jr., *In Ole Kentucky* [*In Ole Virginia*] by Thomas Nelson Page, *Sentimental Tommy* by J. M. Barrie, *Saint's Progress* by John Galsworthy, *The Ordeal of Richard Feverel* by George Meredith, *Treasure Island* by Robert Louis Stevenson, *The Turn of the Screw* by Henry James, *The Stolen Story* or *The Frederic Carrolls* by Jesse Lynch Williams, *The Damnation of Theron Ware* by Harold Frederic, *Soldiers of Fortune* by Richard Harding Davis, *Simple Souls* by John Hastings Turner, and novels by 'George Barr Cable' [George Washington Cable], Henry Van Dyke, Jackson Gregory, and Mary Raymond Shipman Andrews.[67] This list does not represent Fitzgerald's favorite novels; rather, it is a sampling of titles from the Scribners backlist that he thought would have a steady sale at less than a dollar. Arthur Scribner replied that it was too late to compete with the established reprint series.

When they were evicted from the lake house, the Fitzgeralds moved to the Commodore, an apartment hotel in the Summit Avenue area, and Fitzgerald rented a downtown office. His first project in St. Paul was to revise *The Beautiful and Damned* for book publication. (He was not responsible for the serial version, which had been cut by some 40,000 words and edited at *Metropolitan*.)

A novel of character deterioration, *The Beautiful and Damned* chronicles Anthony and Gloria Patch as they wait to inherit his grandfather's fortune. It opens in 1913 with Anthony, four years out of Harvard, idling gracefully on his income and fostering his self-image as an immaculate intellectual. He marries Gloria Gilbert, and they both undergo an inexorable decline fueled by alcohol and the spending of capital. Anthony's grandfather, a rabid reformer, invades one of their drunken parties and disinherits him. After the grandfather's death the Patches initiate a long process of breaking the will. Anthony is drafted during the war and has an affair with a lower-class Southern girl. While the inheritance case is being decided after the war, Anthony becomes a sloppy drunk and Gloria's beauty coarsens. They get the money in 1921, but Anthony's mind and health are broken.

Because Fitzgerald did not share the Patches' conviction that the only lesson to be learned from life is that there is no lesson to be learned from life, the novel does not maintain a consistent attitude toward its characters. At times the author seems to credit Anthony and Gloria with a certain integrity of irresponsibility, casting them as victims of philistia; but Fitzgerald's moralizing compulsion takes over as the novel becomes a warning prophecy for the Fitzgeralds' own marriage. When he began the novel after six months of marriage, Fitzgerald perceived that his wife was not prepared to build her life around his work and that she was the stronger – or less flexible – character. He wrote to Zelda in 1930: 'I wish the Beautiful and Damned had been a maturely written book because it was all true. We ruined ourselves – I have never honestly thought that we ruined each other.'[68] But in 1940 he told his daughter: 'Gloria was a much more trivial and vulgar person than your mother. I can't really say there was any resemblance except in the beauty and certain terms of expression she used, and also I naturally used many circumstantial events of our early married life. However the emphases were entirely different. We had a much better time than Anthony and Gloria had.'[69] Fitzgerald's self-disapproval in *The Beautiful and Damned* is divided between Anthony Patch and Dick Caramel, a writer who becomes a supplier of commercial entertainment.* Both Anthony and Caramel are projections of what Fitzgerald feared for himself. Another character, Maury Noble, drawn from George Jean Nathan, represents the successful cynic that Anthony cannot become.

Although Fitzgerald's second novel is not structurally distinguished, it marks an improvement over the looseness of *This Side of Paradise*. Nevertheless, he was still relying on subtitles to separate episodes within chapters; and *The Beautiful and Damned* is flawed by sideshows as well as by inconsistencies in tone and style. Fitzgerald was unable to resist interpolating passages of philosophizing – sometimes in playlet form. The 'Flash-Back in Paradise,' in which Beauty (Gloria) is sent to earth by The Voice, is a violation of the novel's naturalistic or deterministic approach.

The point-of-view problems in *The Beautiful and Damned* result from Fitzgerald's ambivalent narrative stance as he fluctuates between approval of Anthony's adherence to the doctrine of futility and contempt for Anthony's weakness. The novel is told by a third-person omniscient narrator, but

---

* Caramel's complaint about the success of *This Side of Paradise* represents a lapse in Fitzgerald's judgment.

Revising The Beautiful and Damned [Summer 1921]

Fitzgerald does not maintain his perspective. The authorial voice is intrusive and usurps the qualities of a first-person narrator; it analyzes, soliloquizes, and engages in discourses with the reader. This indulgent narrative manner was encouraged by Fitzgerald's magazine story market, which welcomed his personal or didactic manner. He would not become a complete novelist until he learned the techniques for controlling point of view and disciplining his habit of invading the narrative.

Fitzgerald had proofs of *The Beautiful and Damned* by mid-October. He regarded proofs as a kind of typescript and used them as an opportunity to make final alterations that went far beyond corrections. Like many writers, Fitzgerald felt he could not make final decisions about his prose until he saw it in print. He told both Ober and Wilson that he had 'almost completely rewritten parts' of his novel in St. Paul;[70] but it is impossible to be certain about the extent of his proof revisions because the setting typescript and the proofs do not survive. The only pre-publication form of *The Beautiful and Damned* is Fitzgerald's manuscript with typed inserts at the Princeton University Library.* If the typescript that Scribners used as setting copy for the galley proofs was an unrevised copy made from Fitzgerald's manuscript, collation of the book text against the manuscript reveals that he made no proof deletions or additions that change the meaning of the novel – except for the conclusion. There were more cuts than insertions in proof. Passages were shifted ('A Flash-Back in

* The manuscript has two title pages. The first has the title 'The Beautiful Lady Without Mercy' changed to *The Beautiful and Damned* with a canceled epigraph from Keats's 'La Belle Dame Sans Merci' and another epigraph credited to Samuel Butler ('Life is one long process of getting tired.'). This page lists seven other possible titles: 'The House of Pain,' 'Misfortune's Street,' 'O, Beautiful,' 'The Broken Lute,' 'The Corruption of Anthony,' 'A Love Affair,' and 'Corruption.' The second title page uses *The Beautiful and Damned* with the Butler epigraph, which was replaced in the book with 'The victor belongs to the spoils. – Anthony Patch.' In the manuscript table of contents the three books of the novel are titled 'The Pleasant Absurdity of Things,' 'The Romantic Bitterness of Things,' and 'The Ironic Tragedy of Things.' These headings were not retained in the published volume.

Paradise,' for example), and thousands of spot changes were made as Fitzgerald polished his wording. Maury Noble's account of his education in the 'Symposium' chapter was rewritten. Almost every page was revised, but the published novel did not alter the plot or structure of the manuscript. Anthony and Gloria Patch were not significantly changed, although in a few places Fitzgerald made Gloria less culpable for Anthony's deterioration. At the opening of the 'Symposium' chapter, after the statement 'Gloria had lulled Anthony's mind to sleep,' Fitzgerald deleted the manuscript comment: 'This, of course, was desperately bad; halting that play and interplay of ideas which is at all times the salvation of such men as he.'[71] In the manuscript Anthony urges Gloria to have an abortion during what proves to be a false pregnancy. Fitzgerald also cut the manuscript analysis of Anthony and Gloria's despair after his grandfather's intrusion on their drunken party:

> And then, two evil people finding themselves ringed round by high portentous walls, ran to and fro in a panic, each crying out that the other had built the walls or that this agency and that had built them – then, sitting down to weep, confessed piteously that they had built the walls themselves. Who can doubt that they were wicked people? For if they were not wicked, who is – And what is there we may call evil?[72]

The moralistic tone of this authorial invasion is confusing, and it is not clear whether Fitzgerald intended irony in his application of the word 'evil.'

One of the chief purposes of Fitzgerald's revisions was to clarify the novel's judgment of Anthony and Gloria. He did not succeed, and his work with the ending reveals his uncertainty about the final impression he wanted to leave with the reader. The manuscript closes with Beauty's return to Paradise:

> 'Back again,' the voice whispered.
> 'Yes.'
> 'After fifteen years.'

Revising The Beautiful and Damned [Summer 1921]

'Yes.'

The voice hesitated.

'How remote you are,' it said, 'Unstirred ... You seem to have no heart. How about the little girl? The glory of her eyes is gone – '

But Beauty had forgotten long ago.

Fitzgerald replaced this finale with the didactic conclusion of the serial, which unconvincingly pays tribute to Anthony's and Gloria's idealism:

> That exquisite heavenly irony which has tabulated the demise of many generations of sparrows seems to us to be content with the moral judgments of man upon fellow man. If there is a subtler and yet more nebulous ethic somewhere in the mind, one might believe that beneath the sordid dress and near the bruised heart of this transaction there was a motive which was not weak but only futile and sad. In the search for happiness, which search is the greatest and possibly the only crime of which we in our petty misery are capable, these two people were marked as guilty chiefly by the freshness and fullness of their desire. Their disillusion was always a comparative thing – they had sought glamor and color through their respective worlds with steadfast loyalty – sought it and it alone in kisses and in wine, sought it with the same ingenuousness in the wanton moonlight as under the cold sun of inviolate chastity. Their fault was not that they had doubted but that they had believed.
>
> The exquisite perfection of their boredom, the delicacy of their inattention, the inexhaustibility of their discontent – were disastrous extremes – that was all. And if, before Gloria yielded up her gift of beauty, she shed one bright feather of light so that someone, gazing up from the grey earth, might say, 'Look! There is an angel's wing!' perhaps she had given more than enough in exchange for her tinsel joys.
>
> ... The story ends here.[73]

On 23 December 1921 Fitzgerald wired Perkins: LILDA THINKS BOOK SHOULD END WITH ANTHONY'S LAST SPEECH ON SHIP SHE THINKS NEW ENDING IS A PIECE OF MORALITY LET ME

KNOW YOUR ADVICE. . . . [74] Perkins agreed with Zelda. The book text ends with the sardonic view of the broken Anthony whispering to himself: 'I showed them,' he was saying. 'It was a hard fight, but I didn't give up and I came through!'

Perkins's editorial manner with Fitzgerald is revealed in their disagreement about Maury Noble's account of the Bible as a work of skepticism and irony, which Perkins thought would offend readers unnecessarily. Fitzgerald reacted with an emotional letter invoking Mark Twain, Anatole France, and George Bernard Shaw, charging Perkins with cowardice. On 12 December, Perkins replied: 'Don't ever *defer* to my judgment. You won't on any vital point, I know, and I should be ashamed, if it were possible to have made you; for a writer of any account must speak for himself.'[75] Fitzgerald then apologized: 'The thing *was* flippant – I mean it was the sort of worst of Geo. Jean Nathan. I have changed it now – changed "godalmighty" to deity, cut out "bawdy" + changed several other words so I think it is all right.'[76] The revised version was included in the novel. Fitzgerald liked Noble's oration so much that he also published it in the February *Smart Set*.

In 1922 Perkins was troubled by including 'Tarquin of Cheapside' in *Tales of the Jazz Age* because it dealt with rape, but he yielded when Fitzgerald reminded him that the story had appeared in the *Nassau Lit* without trouble.[77] Perkins confined himself to offering structural suggestions or spot queries and did not attempt to rewrite Fitzgerald. As their editorial relationship developed, he became the strongest influence on Fitzgerald's professional life. It has been suggested that Perkins, who had five daughters and wanted a son, saw his authors as surrogate sons – of whom Fitzgerald was the firstborn. Despite their mutual affection, they did not reach the Max and Scott stage until 1923.*

---

* The process took longer with Harold Ober. In 1925 they dropped 'Mr.' in their letters and moved to 'Dear Ober'/'Dear Fitzgerald'; not until 1927 were they on a first-name basis.

20

Birth of Scottie

[Fall 1921]

The Fitzgeralds' daughter was born on 26 October 1921 at the Miller Hospital in St. Paul. Fitzgerald made a note in his *Ledger* on Zelda's post-delivery remarks while she was still partly anesthetized: 'Oh God, goofo I'm drunk.* Mark Twain. Isn't she smart – she has the hiccups. I hope its beautiful and a fool – a beautiful little fool.' The last sentence was subsequently given to Daisy in *The Great Gatsby*. Writers waste nothing. Fitzgerald wired the Sayres: LILLIAN GISH IS IN MOURNING CONSTANCE TALMADGE IS A BACK NUMBER AND A SECOND MARY PICKFORD HAS ARRIVED.[78] Mencken recommended that the child be named Charlotte in honor of Charles Evans Hughes. The parents had been hoping for a boy and had not settled on a girl's name. The baby was named Scotty on her birth certificate and christened Frances Scott Fitzgerald at the Convent of the Visitation; but for several years Zelda also referred to her daughter as Patricia.

During the fall Fitzgerald wrote three stories for ready cash: 'Two for a Cent,' 'The Popular Girl' (a long story set in St. Paul which the *Post* published in two parts), and 'The

---

* Zelda called Fitzgerald 'Goofo' or 'Goofy' in the early days of their marriage; in her letters she later addressed him as 'Deo' or 'D.O.' or 'Do-Do' – possibly from the Latin word for god.

Diamond as Big as the Ritz.' The masterpiece, 'Diamond,' was declined by the high-paying magazines to which Ober offered it, even after Fitzgerald cut it from 20,000 words to 15,000. The story seemed baffling to some editors and blasphemous to others. Those who understood 'Diamond' saw it as a satirical attack on the American success ethic or at least on the faith that equates wealth with virtue – a message that might offend the advertisers. Commercial magazines exist to sell advertising space, not to publish great fiction. Fitzgerald reported to Ober, 'I am rather discouraged that a cheap story like *The Popular Girl* written in one week while the baby was being born brings $1500.00 + a genuinely imaginative thing into which I put three weeks real enthusiasm like *The Diamond in the Sky* [the original title] brings not a thing. But, by God + Lorimer, I'm going to make a fortune yet.'[79] The story went to *The Smart Set* for $300.

'The Diamond as Big as the Ritz,' Fitzgerald's most brilliant fantasy, is much more than a supreme fairy tale. The diamond of the title is a diamond mountain in the West owned by the Washingtons, making them by far the richest family in the world. Nevertheless, the necessity of protecting the secret of the diamond interferes with the benefits of ownership. The Washington children invite schoolmates for vacations, knowing that the visitors will be murdered. When the diamond is discovered by the authorities, Braddock Washington offers God a bribe before blowing it up. The story is susceptible to allegorical interpretations, but it is unlikely that Fitzgerald intended it as allegory. The meanings of 'Diamond' are sufficiently clear. Absolute wealth corrupts absolutely and possesses its possessors.

In November 1921 the Fitzgeralds rented a Victorian frame house at 626 Goodrich Avenue in the Summit Avenue neighborhood. The winter was a difficult time for them. Zelda hated the Minnesota cold and wrote Ludlow Fowler that she was grateful to be spared the fate of the monkey – referring to the current expression that it was cold enough to freeze the balls off a brass monkey.[80] She was sensitive about the weight she had gained during her pregnancy. At a time when ladies did not smoke on the streets, Zelda enjoyed making a point of it. When Fitzgerald asked people to the house, Zelda told them not to come because company noise made the baby cry; Fitzgerald would then insist that the invited people come because Zelda needed diversion. There were parties and dances. A Bad Luck Ball was held at the University Club on Friday the 13th of January 1922, and Fitzgerald was responsible for a parody newspaper, *The St. Paul Daily Dirge*, distributed at the dance. The *Dirge* reported the dance under the headline COTILLION IS SAD FAILURE and included gag stories about St. Paul friends.[81] In April he wrote and directed a musical revue, *Midnight Flappers*, for the Junior League Frolic vaudeville – with Zelda cast as one of the flappers.

Between 1921 and 1923, Fitzgerald wrote eleven book reviews for the *St. Paul Daily News*, the New York papers, and literary magazines.* Some of these reviews were written as friendly gestures to the authors; but Fitzgerald's responses were not perfunctory, as his assessment of Booth Tarkington's *Gentle Julia* shows: 'It is a pity that the man who writes better prose than any other living American was brought up in a generation that considered it a crime to tell the truth.'[82] He called Sherwood Anderson's *Many Marriages* 'a rather stupendous achievement' for creating a hero who exists in a vacuum, but complained: 'I do not like the man in the book. The world in which I trust, in which I seem to set my feet, appears to me to exist through a series of illusions.'[83] His review of Dos Passos's *Three Soldiers* is significant in announcing his renunciation of the H. G. Wells influence; after rating Dos Passos 'the best of all the younger men on this side,' Fitzgerald warns, 'such a profound and gifted man as John Dos Passos should never

---

* H. L. Mencken's *Prejudices, Second Series*, John Dos Passos's *Three Soldiers*, Charles Norris's *Brass*, Aldous Huxley's *Crome Yellow*, Booth Tarkington's *Gentle Julia*, John V. A. Weaver's *Margey Wins the Game*, Shane Leslie's *The Oppidan*, Woodward Boyd's *The Love Legend*, Grace Flandrau's *Being Respectable*, Sherwood Anderson's *Many Marriages*, and Thomas Boyd's *Through the Wheat*.

enlist in Wells' faithful but aenemic platoon along with Walpole, Floyd Dell and Mencken's latest victim, Ernest Poole. The only successful Wellsian is Wells. Let us slay Wells, James Joyce and Anatole France that the creation of literature may continue.'[84]

While waiting for publication of *The Beautiful and Damned* by Scribners, Fitzgerald decided to write a play that 'is to make my fortune.'[85] In January 1922 he sought Ober's advice about the commercial value of another project: 'When I finish my play I plan to write a series of twelve articles which will ostensibly be the record of a trip to Europe but will really be a mass of impressions and heavily laden with autobiography. . . . The twelve will not be connected and could go to different magazines if advisable, though I intend to publish them afterwards in one book.'[86] Ober's reply is lost, and the travel series was never begun.

21

The Beautiful and Damned

[March 1922]

The Beautiful and Damned was published on 4 March
1922 in a first printing of 20,600 copies. The
Fitzgeralds went to New York for the publication of the novel
and for Zelda to have an abortion because she did not want a
second child so soon. Sara Mayfield, one of Zelda's childhood
friends, states that Zelda had three abortions during her
marriage.[87] When Zelda suffered a mental breakdown in
1930, her sister Rosalind asked Fitzgerald, 'Do you think
Zelda's abortions could have had anything to do with her
illness?'[88] There is no documentation for the chronology of
the abortions.

The reception of The Beautiful and Damned was disappointing. Some reviewers – and readers – had expected a sequel to
This Side of Paradise or a novel like it. They were put off by
Fitzgerald's naturalistic material in this novel, which showed
the influence of Dreiser and the Norris brothers. The deterioration of Anthony Patch from immaculate intellectual to ruined
drunk drew upon similar treatments in Sister Carrie, Vandover
and the Brute, and Salt. Some reviewers mistakenly thought the
novel was intended as satire, possibly because of the dust-jacket
copy: ' . . . it reveals with devastating satire a section of American society which has never before been recognized as an
entity.' The more perceptive critics – among them Henry Seidel

189

Canby – recognized that *The Beautiful and Damned* was a transitional novel and that it revealed Fitzgerald's attempt to improve on the loose structure of *This Side of Paradise*.

Mencken commented in *The Smart Set*:

> Opportunity beckoned him toward very facile jobs; he might have gone on rewriting the charming romance of 'This Side of Paradise' for ten or fifteen years, and made a lot of money out of it, and got a great deal of uncritical praise for it. Instead, he tried something much more difficult, and if the result is not a complete success, it is nevertheless near enough to success to be worthy of respect. There is fine observation in it, and much penetrating detail, and the writing is solid and sound. After 'This Side of Paradise' the future of Fitzgerald seemed extremely uncertain. There was an air about that book which suggested a fortunate accident. The shabby stuff collected in 'Flappers and Philosophers' converted uncertainty into something worse. But 'The Beautiful and the Damned' delivers the author from all those doubts. There are a hundred signs in it of serious purpose and unquestionable skill. Even in its defects there is proof of hard striving. Fitzgerald ceases to be a *Wunderkind*, and begins to come into his maturity.[89]

Although Mencken was not included in the triple dedication to SHANE LESLIE, GEORGE JEAN NATHAN AND MAXWELL PERKINS IN APPRECIATION OF MUCH LITERARY HELP AND ENCOURAGEMENT, he may have been the strongest influence on Fitzgerald's attempt to write a deterministic novel; and Mencken's admiration for Conrad strengthened Fitzgerald's concern with structure and form.

The longest review was by John Peale Bishop in the *New York Herald*, which called *The Beautiful and Damned* an advance over *This Side of Paradise* but made just charges against it:

> ... Fitzgerald is at the moment of announcing the meaninglessness of life magnificently alive. His ideas are too often treated like paper crackers, things to make a gay and pretty noise with and then be cast aside; he is frequently at the

mercy of words with which he has only a nodding acquaintance; his aesthetics are faulty; his literary taste is at times extremely bad. The chapter labeled 'Symposium,' pictorially good, does not seem clearly thought out or burdened with wisdom. The episode entitled 'Flash Back in Paradise' might, except for its wit, have been conceived in the mind of a scenario writer. But these are flaws of vulgarity in one who is awkward with his own vigor.[90]

Edmund Wilson wrote a long unsigned 'Literary Spotlight' analysis of Fitzgerald's career for the March *Bookman*, citing the Midwest and his Irishness as two key influences on Fitzgerald's work. Before publication he sent the article to Fitzgerald, who asked him to cut a third influence: alcohol. Fitzgerald felt that publicizing his drinking would hurt him both with 'respectable friends' and financially. About his Irishness, Fitzgerald noted: 'I'm not Irish on Father's side – that's where Francis Scott Key comes in.' His claim is curious as well as incorrect because his paternal grandfather, Michael Fitzgerald, was Irish. Fitzgerald's attempt to rewrite his pedigree supports Wilson's theory that his erratic behavior resulted from his insecurity as an Irish Catholic. Wilson complied with Fitzgerald's request to remove the drinking material and an unidentified anecdote about his army days; but he did not act on Fitzgerald's assertion that 'the most enormous influence on me in the four + ½ yrs since I met her has been the complete fine and full hearted selfishness and chill-mindedness of Zelda.'[91]

Wilson's assessment of Fitzgerald's literary intelligence was harsh. It opened by repeating the comment by 'a celebrated person' (Edna St. Vincent Millay) that he was like 'a stupid old woman with whom someone has left a diamond.' Wilson concurred that Fitzgerald did not know what to do with his gifts: 'For he has been given imagination without intellectual control of it; he has been given the desire for beauty without an aesthetic ideal; and he has been given a gift for expression without very many ideas to express.'[92] This condescending judgment expressed a standard approach to Fitzgerald for the next thirty years – that he was a natural, but not an artist. The blame cannot be attributed solely to Wilson, of course, for it was shared or repeated by other critics who refused to take Fitzgerald seriously. The effects not only damaged Fitzgerald's contemporary reputation, but perhaps also impeded the fulfillment of his genius by depriving him of the critical esteem he sought. The popular or mythic view of Fitzgerald still retains the idea that he threw away his genius in orgiastic revelry.

The review of *The Beautiful and Damned* that has attracted the most attention is Zelda Fitzgerald's 'Friend Husband's Latest' in the *New York Tribune* – her first professional publication. Although the review is partly a joke, it points out the inconsistencies in Gloria's birth date and makes one serious literary judgment: 'The other things I didn't like in the book – I mean the unimportant things – were the literary references and the attempt to convey a profound air of erudition. It reminds me in its more soggy moments of the essays I used to get up in school at the last minute by looking up strange names in the Encyclopaedia Brittanica.' Her criticism is just, for the novel is intellectually pretentious, particularly in the set-piece seminars conducted by Anthony, Maury Noble, and Dick Caramel. At this stage Fitzgerald was still self-conscious about his spotty education.

Zelda's review also includes her claim that some of her writing went into *The Beautiful and Damned* by the back door: 'It seems to me that on one page I recognized a portion of an old diary of mine which mysteriously disappeared shortly after my marriage, and also scraps of letters which, though considerably edited, sound to me vaguely familiar.* In fact, Mr. Fitzgerald – I believe that is how he spells his name – seems to believe that plagiarism begins at home.'[93] In view of the later competition between the Fitzgeralds, this charge requires examination. Indeed, there is a school of Zelda partisans which asserts that

---

* In February 1920 – before his marriage – Fitzgerald wrote Perkins: 'I'm just enclosing you the typing of Zelda's diary. . . . You'll recognize much of the dialogue. Please don't show it to anyone else.'[94] The diary does not survive.

The Beautiful and Damned [March 1922]

she was his collaborator on his best work. It should be noted that Zelda does not say she collaborated on *The Beautiful and Damned*: only that Fitzgerald incorporated a portion of her diary 'on one page' and that he revised 'scraps' of her letters. None of Fitzgerald's surviving manuscripts shows her hand, though Zelda's manuscripts bear his revision. She did play an important role in his work – apart from providing him with a model – because he trusted her literary judgment and acted on her criticisms. But Zelda was never his collaborator.

In addition to her $15 review of *The Beautiful and Damned*, Zelda sold three articles in 1922 – 'The Super-Flapper' (presumably unpublished), 'Eulogy on the Flapper' (*Metropolitan*), and 'Does a Moment of Revolt Come Sometime to Every Married Man?' (a companion piece to a Fitzgerald article in *McCall's*) – for which she received a total of $815. The articles appeared under Zelda's byline with the explanation that she was the wife of F. Scott Fitzgerald. She does not seem to have harbored any literary ambitions at this time, and her articles were just part of the fun of being married to a celebrity.

While in New York, Fitzgerald was interviewed by the *New York World* and delivered some surprisingly conventional remarks about Prohibition society. He said that the young married set could only be saved by work: 'I think that just being in love, really in love – doing it well, you know – is work enough for a woman. If she keeps her house the way it should be kept and makes herself look pretty when her husband comes home in the evening and loves him and helps him with his work and encourages him – oh, I think that's the sort of work that will save her.'[95] His comments about a wife's duties have a rueful sound.

The three Scribners printings of *The Beautiful and Damned* in 1922 totaled 50,000 copies, and the novel made the *Publishers Weekly* monthly best-seller lists for March (tenth), April (sixth), and May (tenth).* Nonetheless, Fitzgerald was

* The most successful novel of 1922, *If Winter Comes* by A. S. M. Hutchinson,

193

disappointed because the $15,000 (plus $7,000 for the serial rights) from royalties was not enough to free him from his bondage to the magazines. Scribners had increased his royalty rate to a straight 15 percent, but it was 15 percent of $2. In the Twenties, the main income from a book stopped with the cloth sale. There were no paperback or lucrative book club deals (the Book-of-the-Month Club began in 1926), and movie rights brought modest figures – only $2,500 in 1922 for *The Beautiful and Damned*.

---

sold more than 350,000 copies. Other best-sellers of the year were Edith M. Hull's *The Sheik*, Tarkington's *Gentle Julia*, Frances Hodgson Burnett's *The Head of the House of Coombe*, Robert Keable's *Simon Called Peter*, Mary Roberts Rinehart's *The Breaking Point*, Hutchinson's *This Freedom*, Louis Hémon's *Maria Chapdelaine*, Zane Grey's *To the Last Man*, Lewis's *Babbitt*, and Harold Bell Wright's *Helen of the Old House*. *Simon Called Peter*, a sensational religious novel which Fitzgerald detested, sold 152,000 copies.

22

Writing The Vegetable

[Spring–Summer 1922]

In March 1922 Thomas Boyd published a three-part interview with Fitzgerald in the *St. Paul Daily News* that provided a description of his working habits: 'His writing is never thought out. He creates his characters and they are likely to lead him into almost any situation. His phrasing is done in the same way. It is rare that he searches for a word. Most of the time words come to his mind and then spill themselves in a riotous frenzy of song and color all over the page. Some days he writes as many as 7,000 or 8,000 words; and then, with a small *Roget's Thesaurus*, he carefully goes over his work, substituting synonyms for any unusual words that appear more than once in seven or eight consecutive pages.'[96] This article is the only indication that Fitzgerald ever relied on the *Thesaurus*, a dependency he seems to have broken.

Fitzgerald worked steadily on his play in the early months of 1922. Originally titled 'Gabriel's Trombone,' *The Vegetable* is a flapper comedy combined with political satire and parody of the American success story. When it was published, the title page carried an epigraph attributed to 'a current magazine': 'Any man who doesn't want to get on in the world, to make a million dollars, and maybe even park his toothbrush in the White House hasn't got as much to him as a good dog has –

he's nothing more or less than a vegetable.'

Jerry Frost, a railway clerk who really wants to be a postman, is nagged by his wife because he lacks large ambitions. In an alcohol-induced delirium he becomes president and makes a terrible mess of it. At the end of the play he is a happy postman. *The Vegetable* was ready for circulation in March 1922, and Fitzgerald informed Ober that 'Acts I + III are probably the best pieces of dramatic comedy written in English the last 5 years.'[97] The second act, the White House fantasy, gave Fitzgerald trouble throughout the history of the play. Wilson was sent a copy and responded with warm praise: 'As I say, I think that the play as a whole is marvelous – no doubt, the best American comedy ever written. I think you have a much better grasp on your subject than you usually have – you know what end and point you are working for, as isn't always the case with you. . . . I think you have a great gift for comic dialogue – even if you never can resist a stupid gag – and should go on writing plays. . . . By the way, the great question is, have you read James Joyce's *Ulysses*? Because if you haven't, the resemblance between the drunken-visions scene in it and your scene in the White House must take its place as one of the great coincidences in literature.'[98] Fitzgerald had not read *Ulysses* and asked Wilson how he could obtain a copy of the book, which was then banned in America.

Since two leading Broadway producers, William Harris and Charles Frohman (for whom Alec McKaig worked), had expressed interest in his play, Fitzgerald anticipated little difficulty in getting it staged. Wilson submitted it to the Theatre Guild and to actor Frank Craven, and Wilson and Nathan sought Eugene O'Neill's advice. No one was willing to produce the play, and Fitzgerald revised it through the summer of 1922, reworking the presidential fantasy in Act II. In one of the omitted scenes America is at war with the Buzzard Islands, and Jerry distinguishes himself by capturing the buzzards with worms. Another canceled scene shows the effects of the announcement by Jerry's senile father, the Secretary of the Treasury, that the end of the world is imminent – for which he has prepared by buying up the world supply of coffins.[99] The play is just not very funny, scarcely rising above the level of an undergraduate production. Despite Fitzgerald's apprenticeship as a playwright, his talent was novelistic – not dramatic. His stage dialogue does not stand up alone, and many of his jokes depend on the stage directions.

Fitzgerald wrote only one story in the first half of 1922, 'The Curious Case of Benjamin Button,' which traces the life of a man who is born old and grows up into infancy. The story was hard to place, but *Collier's* took it for $1,000. While his play was making the rounds of the producers, Fitzgerald considered moneymaking projects – including another play, which never developed.

He still regarded the movies as a potential source of easy money. During the March 1922 trip to New York David O. Selznick asked Fitzgerald to write a movie synopsis for actress Elaine Hammerstein. In April he submitted a 1,500-word synopsis for 'Trans-Continental Kitty.' If Selznick accepted it, Fitzgerald was to be paid $2,500 for expanding the synopsis into an 8,000-word screen story; but the synopsis was declined. It is not hard to understand why Fitzgerald's movie ventures failed. Although he had no trouble inventing plots, his magazine stories depend upon verbal elements that were lost on the silent screen. Moreover, he did not take the movies seriously as a vehicle for his own work and supplied synopses or plots that were trivial or imitative. After the advent of the talkies Fitzgerald came to see the movies as having a greater potential than the novel, but even then he could not adapt his techniques to the screen.

In June 1922 Fitzgerald sent Ober 'The Cruise of the Rolling Junk,' a 25,000-word serial based on the 1920 car trip to Montgomery and intended for the *Post*. After the *Post* rejected it and Ober was unable to place it in any of the other high-paying magazines, Fitzgerald cut it down to 17,000 words and sold it to *Motor* for $300. Gag photos of the

Fitzgeralds illustrated the three-part article, which was published in 1924.

The Fitzgeralds spent the summer of 1922 at the White Bear Yacht Club in Dellwood. It was mostly a time of relaxation, although Fitzgerald began planning his third novel. In June he informed Perkins: ' . . . I may start my novel and I may not. Its locale will be the middle west and New York at 1885 I think. It will concern less superlative beauties than I run to usually + will be centered on a smaller period of time. It will have a catholic element. I'm not quite sure whether I'm ready to start it quite yet or not.'[100] And to Perkins in July: 'I want to write something *new* – something extraordinary and beautiful and simple + intricately patterned.'[101] But a year would go by before Fitzgerald started serious work on the novel that became *The Great Gatsby*.

During the summer of 1922 he prepared his second story collection for Scribners. *Tales of the Jazz Age* was published on 22 September 1922 with eleven stories divided into three groups: *My Last Flappers* ('The Jelly Bean,' 'The Camel's Back,' 'May Day,' 'Porcelain and Pink'); *Fantasies* ('The Diamond as Big as the Ritz,' 'The Curious Case of Benjamin Button,' 'Tarquin of Cheapside,' 'O Russet Witch!'); *Unclassified Masterpieces* ('The Lees of Happiness,' 'Mr. Icky,' 'Jemina'). Despite the inclusion of two major stories, 'May Day' and 'Diamond,' the collection was a grab bag; Fitzgerald did not have enough good material for a volume and padded it with pieces that had been left out of *Flappers and Philosophers*, including a parody that had appeared in the *Nassau Lit*. 'Myra Meets His Family,' 'The Smilers,' and 'The Popular Girl' were omitted from the new collection because Fitzgerald regarded them as 'cheap.' *Tales of the Jazz Age* was attractively – if inappropriately – packaged in a dust jacket by popular cartoonist John Held, Jr., and sold well.* The first printing was 8,000 copies, and there

---

* John O'Hara's 1961 comment in his story 'Mrs. Stratton of Oak Knoll' is instructive: ' "For years I've been hearing and reading people talking about John Held's girls and Fitzgerald's, as though they were one and the same thing. They just simply weren't. From the literary point of view, one of the

were two more 1922 printings. Royalties on this volume amounted to $3,056 in 1922.

The working titles for the collection had been 'Youth and Death,' 'In One Reel,' and 'Sideshow.' Against the advice of the Scribners salesmen, Fitzgerald decided on *Tales of the Jazz Age* after convincing himself that it would not damage his reputation as a serious novelist. Fitzgerald claimed the phrase 'jazz age' as his contribution to the language. The volume was dedicated QUITE INAPPROPRIATELY TO MY MOTHER. None of Fitzgerald's books was dedicated to his father.

A feature of *Tales of the Jazz Age* that attracted attention and probably helped sales was the annotated table of contents in which Fitzgerald commented on each piece – mostly with tongue in cheek. Thus:

> These next stories are written in what, were I of imposing stature, I should call my 'second manner.' 'The Diamond as Big as the Ritz,' which appeared last summer in the 'Smart Set' was designed utterly for my own amusement. I was in the familiar mood characterized by a perfect craving for luxury, and the story began as an attempt to feed that craving on imaginary foods.
>
> One well-known critic has been pleased to like this extravaganza better than anything I have written. Personally I prefer 'The Off-Shore Pirate.' But, to tamper slightly with Lincoln: If you like this sort of thing, this, possibly, is the sort of thing you'll like.[103]

---

worst things that ever happened to Fitzgerald was the simultaneous popularity of John Held's drawings. Those damn editorial writers were largely to blame. Who would ever want to take Fitzgerald seriously if all they ever knew about him was that he wrote about those John Held girls? Held was a very good satirist, and he didn't *want* his girls to be taken seriously. Of course Fitzgerald was partly to blame. He called one book *Flappers and Philosophers,* and in the public mind the flapper was the John Held girl. Actually, of course, Fitzgerald and Held and the editorial writers were all misusing the word flapper. A flapper was English slang, and it meant a society girl who had made her debut and hadn't found a husband. On the shelf, they used to say. It wasn't an eighteen-year-old girl with flapping galoshes." '[102]

Though widely reviewed, the collection was judged as popular entertainment. Neither 'May Day' nor 'Diamond' was recognized as a masterpiece. Edmund Wilson's *Vanity Fair* review pronounced *Tales of the Jazz Age* much better than *Flappers and Philosophers* because 'he lets his fancy, his humor and his taste for nonsense run wild.' Wilson described 'The Diamond as Big as the Ritz' as 'a sustained and full-rounded fantasy' but made no attempt to identify its meanings.[104] His record as a judge of Fitzgerald's early work is spotty, showing a preference for Fitzgerald's entertainments – revealed by his praise of *The Vegetable*. It is likely that their Princeton association interfered with Wilson's ability to gauge Fitzgerald's work. For Wilson, Fitzgerald remained the undergraduate who had submitted material to him for the *Nassau Lit.* Indeed, Wilson never broke the habit of patronizing Fitzgerald. Although his affection was genuine, he was finally unable to believe that Fitzgerald was a major writer – in fact, a greater figure than himself.

Taken together, Fitzgerald's two story collections, which drew upon three years of writing, exhibit an impressive range of material and technique. He was not writing sheik-meets-flapper stories to magazine specifications. He was mastering his trade and refining his style as he wrote entertainments ('The Camel's Back,' 'The Offshore Pirate'), didactic stories ('The Four Fists,' 'The Cut-Glass Bowl'), realistic or naturalistic stories ('The Lees of Happiness,' 'May Day'), and fantasies ('The Diamond as Big as the Ritz,' 'O Russet Witch!'). In addition to demonstrating the fecundity of his ideas and flexibility of style, this variety of material and techniques suggests that Fitzgerald was deliberately testing his talents.

During the summer of 1922 Fitzgerald became involved in another movie project. Outlook Photoplays, which had made a movie of Sinclair Lewis's *Free Air* in St. Paul, took a $3,000 option on *This Side of Paradise*; and there was some consideration of having the Fitzgeralds take the roles of Amory and Rosalind. The schemes fell through when

Outlook failed to pay the option money. The rights were sold to Famous Players – Lasky in 1923, but the movie was never made.

The Fitzgeralds were asked to leave the White Bear Yacht Club in August because their rowdy parties disturbed the other members. They were ready to leave St. Paul anyway; they missed New York, and Fitzgerald wanted to be there for the anticipated Broadway production of his play. Before moving east, Fitzgerald wrote his second 1922 story in September, 'Winter Dreams' (*Metropolitan*, December). The most important of the *Gatsby* cluster stories – that is, those 1922–24 stories related to the germinating novel – 'Winter Dreams' is virtually a preview of *The Great Gatsby*. Dexter Green, a caddy at Black Bear Lake, encounters the rich and imperious eleven-year-old Judy Jones, who intensifies his dreams of success. He meets her again when he is twenty-three and on his way to a fortune. After Judy jilts him twice, Dexter moves to New York and becomes richer. When he is thirty-two he hears a report that Judy's beauty has faded and that she is unhappily married:

> For the first time in years the tears were streaming down his face. But they were for himself now. He did not care about mouth and eyes and moving hands. He wanted to care, and he could not care. For he had gone away and he could never go back any more. The gates were closed, the sun was gone down, and there was no beauty but the gray beauty of steel that withstands all time. Even the grief he could have borne was left behind in the country of illusion, of youth, of the richness of life, where his winter dreams had flourished.[105]

One distinction of 'Winter Dreams' is Fitzgerald's control of the narrative voice. The story is told by the third-person omniscient author, who freely comments on the action but whose sensibility is scarcely distinguishable from the hero's; Fitzgerald thereby achieved the effect of immediacy while retaining the impression of perspective. As Dexter Green's meditation on mutability demonstrates, 'Winter Dreams' is one of the stories in which Fitzgerald strikingly achieved what is the mark of his best work: the multiplication of meaning through style and tone.

'Winter Dreams' clearly anticipates the major ideas and emotions in *The Great Gatsby*: the ambitious boy whose dreams of success become blended with the image of a rich girl; her inconstancy; his faithfulness; and the inevitable sense of change and loss. Although Dexter Green does not match Jay Gatsby's romantic commitment, he is a preliminary sketch for Gatsby. So close are the reactions of Green and Gatsby to the rich girl's ambiance that the description of Judy's home was lifted from the magazine text of the story and written into *The Great Gatsby* for Daisy Fay's house.*

* In April 1943 Zelda wrote Oscar Kalman that 'Scott's story "Winter Dreams" written about you and Sandra has just been published in an anthology.' Kalman replied: 'I could not see how it in any way described Xandra or me but that may be because I was too close to the situation or perhaps don't know what goes on.'[106] There is no other evidence to connect the Kalmans with 'Winter Dreams.'

23

Great Neck
and Ring Lardner

[Fall 1922–Fall 1923]

Fitzgerald felt that the year in St. Paul had been largely wasted; the only substantial work he had accomplished was an unproduced play. The *Ledger* summary for his twenty-fifth year was: 'A bad year. No work. Slow deteriorating repression with outbreak around the corner.'

In September 1922 the Fitzgeralds left the baby in St. Paul while they went house-hunting in New York. They met John Dos Passos and took him along to look at houses in Great Neck, Long Island, where they called on Ring Lardner, who was drunk. There is no record of a previous meeting between Fitzgerald and Lardner, but Dos Passos's report of the visit indicates that they were already acquainted at this time. Dos Passos's first impressions of Fitzgerald parallel those of other friends; annoyance at his personal quizzing yielded to a surprised recognition of his literary intelligence: 'When he talked about writing his mind, which seemed to me full of preposterous notions about most things, became clear and hard as diamond.' At Zelda's insistence they stopped at an amusement park on the way back to New York. Fitzgerald remained in the car with a bottle while Zelda rode the Ferris

203

wheel with Dos Passos, who sensed that there were unreachable territories of her mind: 'The gulf that opened between Zelda and me, sitting up on that rickety Ferris wheel, was something I couldn't explain. It was only looking back at it years later that it occurred to me that, even the first day we knew each other, I had come up against that basic fissure in her mental processes that was to have such tragic consequences. Though she was so very lovely I had come upon something that frightened and repelled me, even physically. . . . Through it all I felt a great respect for her, a puzzled but affectionate respect.'[107]

In New York, Fitzgerald learned that his play had been declined by all the producers who had read it. For $300 a month the Fitzgeralds rented a small house at 6 Gateway Drive in Great Neck which Zelda described as a 'nifty little Babbit-home.'[108] About fifteen miles from the city, on the Long Island Sound side or North Shore of Long Island, Great Neck was favored by show business types. Among the residents were Ed Wynn, Eddie Cantor, Herbert Bayard Swope, Tom Mieghan, Gene Buck, and Lew Fields. Zelda went to St. Paul for Scottie, and the family settled down with a live-in servant couple ($160 a month), a nurse for the baby ($90 a month), and a part-time laundress ($36 a month).

Fitzgerald's friendship with Lardner, who lived nearby, became very close. It was an unlikely friendship because the thirty-seven-year-old humorist was a reserved man who shared few of Fitzgerald's interests and none of his ebullience. Fitzgerald later admitted that he never penetrated his friend's 'noble dignity.'[109] After achieving prominence as a sports columnist and humorist on the *Chicago Tribune*, Lardner had moved east to write a syndicated humor column and a comic strip based on his *You Know Me Al* stories. Although his use of the American vernacular in his fiction was beginning to attract critical attention, Lardner did not regard himself seriously as a writer. Fitzgerald, who does not seem to have been a Lardner fan before they met, soon became one of his strongest admirers and tried to promote Lardner's reputation. He saw Lardner as a writer whose achievement fell short of his

Ring Lardner

RING LARDNER, JR.

potential because of a cynical attitude toward his work, and concluded that Lardner had been stunted by his early years as a baseball reporter. 'A writer can spin on about his adventures after thirty, after forty, after fifty, but the criteria by which these adventures are weighted and valued are irrevocably settled at the age of twenty-five.'[110] Lardner and his wife Ellis were intrigued by Zelda; and he began an elaborate mock courtship of 'The Queel of Alabam,' addressing humorous poems to her. Here is the first stanza of a Christmas poem he sent her, probably in 1923:

> Of all the girls for whom I care,
> And there are quite a number,
> None can compare with Zelda Sayre,
> Now wedded to a plumber.[111]

Fitzgerald and Lardner had liquor in common – Lardner was an alcoholic – and they spent nights talking and drinking. When Joseph Conrad was visiting the Doubleday estate at Oyster Bay, Long Island, they decided to pay homage to him by performing a dance on the lawn; the anticipated meeting did not occur because the two votaries of Bacchus and Terpsichore were thrown off the property for trespassing. In April 1923 Fitzgerald contributed to the newspaper feature '10 Best Books I Have Read,'[112] citing Conrad's *Nostromo* as 'The great novel of the past fifty years, as "Ulysses" is the great novel of the future.'*

A source of amusement for Fitzgerald and Lardner was the behavior of Gene Buck, a songwriter of almost impenetrable egocentricity who worked with Florenz Ziegfield. Lardner wrote Buck into his story 'The Love Nest' and worked the Fitzgeralds into his articles. His retelling of 'Cinderella' explains that 'Her name was Zelda, but they called her Cinderella on account of how the ashes and clinkers clung to her when she got up noons'; Prince Charming is named

---

* The other books on Fitzgerald's list were Samuel Butler's *Notebooks*, Mencken's *The Philosophy of Friedrich Nietzsche*, Joyce's *Portrait of the Artist as a Young Man*, Beerbohm's *Zuleika Dobson*, Mark Twain's *The Mysterious Stranger*, Thackeray's *Vanity Fair*, *The Oxford Book of English Verse*, France's *Thaïs*, and Tarkington's *Seventeen* ('The funniest book I've ever read').

Scott.[113] Lardner's article 'In Regards to Geniuses' includes this comment:

> Another prominent writer of the younger set is F. Scott Fitzgerald. Mr. Fitzgerald sprung into fame with his novel *This Side of Paradise* which he turned out when only three years old and wrote the entire book with one hand. Mr. Fitzgerald never shaves while at work on his novels and looks very funny along towards the last five or six chapters. His hobby is leashing high bred dogs and when not engaged on a book or a story, can be seen most any day on the streets of Great Neck leashing high bred dogs of which there is a great number. He cannot bear to see any of them untied.[114]

Fitzgerald's interest in advancing other writers' careers found ready material in Ring Lardner. Despite Lardner's large newspaper and magazine following, his books had never sold well – not even the classic *You Know Me Al* – and he had given up on reaching a book-reading audience. Fitzgerald was dismayed to learn that Lardner considered his stories dead once they had appeared in magazines and did not bother to keep copies of them. He brought Lardner and Perkins together and conceived the plan for a new collection of Lardner's stories. Evidence of Fitzgerald's efforts survives in the form of an 11 December 1923 Chatham Hotel lunch menu on which he and Perkins made notes for possible Lardner collections.[115] Fitzgerald provided the title for the first Lardner volume under the Scribners imprint, *How to Write Short Stories*, which initiated a reappraisal of Lardner's fiction when it was published in May 1924. Scribners published six more Lardner volumes and a collected edition during his lifetime.

Great Neck was not condusive to serious work, and twenty-two-year-old Zelda required amusement. Amy Besser Sinberg has described an afternoon with Zelda when Fitzgerald was in the city. During lunch at Gateway Drive, Zelda and Helen Buck finished a shaker of orange blossoms (gin and orange juice). A thermos of cocktails accompanied them to the Sound View Golf Club, where Zelda and Helen became drunk on the course, with Zelda singing 'You can throw a silver dollar down upon the ground, And it'll roll, because it's round . . .' When Zelda wandered away on the course, Besser phoned Ring Lardner; he came and helped round up Zelda and Helen and bring them to the Fitzgerald house. 'I asked Ring what Scott would say, coming home and finding Zelda in that condition. He replied, "What can a drinking husband say to a drinking wife?" ' Fitzgerald was unperturbed when he arrived home with Townsend Martin.[116]

Fitzgerald started reading Dostoevski, probably at Lardner's recommendation. He was impressed by *The Brothers Karamazov* and later said he reread it before starting work on a new novel. He acknowledged to Mencken the indirect effect of Dostoevski on *The Great Gatsby*: 'the influence on it has been the masculine one of *The Brothers Karamazof*, a thing of incomparable form, rather than the feminine one of *The Portrait of a Lady*.'[117] Lardner may also have encouraged Fitzgerald to read Dickens; and *Bleak House* became his favorite Dickens novel.

Fitzgerald revised *The Vegetable* for at least the third time in Great Neck (he later claimed the play was revised six times) and decided to publish it as a book before it was produced. He believed that his name on the book was sure to bring sales; moreover, the exposure of the book might result in a stage production. Writing to Perkins about publication plans for *The Vegetable*, Fitzgerald admitted what was wrong with the play: 'To be advertised, it seems to me rather as a book of humor, like the Parody outline of History or Seventeen than like a play – because of course it is written to be read.'[118]

While the latest version of *The Vegetable* was being considered by impresarios, Fitzgerald again tried to earn what he regarded as easy money from the movies. At that time movies were still being produced in New York, and Fitzgerald made contact with movie people living in the Great Neck area. Townsend Martin was a partner in the Film Guild, which paid Fitzgerald $2,000 for his original story for *Grit*.* Starring Glen

* The scenario was written by James Ashmore Creelman; Fitzgerald received credit for the 'source.' Fitzgerald's screen story does not survive.

Hunter and Clara Bow, the crook melodrama shows that Fitzgerald approached movie work with the conviction that the movies required cheap plots. A young man overcomes his fear of guns to expose a gang of criminals and win an underworld girl named Orchid McGonigle. In 1923 Fitzgerald also earned $500 by writing the titles – most of which were not used – for the silent version of Edith Wharton's *Glimpses of the Moon*. With the $10,000 sale of *This Side of Paradise*, the movies paid him a total of $13,500 in 1923. Part of the movie money was put into $4,000 worth of Liberty Bonds, which were soon cashed in to meet the expenses of Great Neck life.

The March 1923 contract with Famous Players-Lasky for *This Side of Paradise* required Fitzgerald to prepare a treatment for the silent movie. He was initially enthusiastic about the project: 'I'm doing the continuity and the titleing and the editing + the treatment so if it's a bad picture I'm entirely responsible. But it's going to be amazing.'[119] A typed synopsis survives among Fitzgerald's papers, but there is no way to be sure that it is his work. In this proposed movie version Rosalind betrays Amory by eloping with the wealthy Burne Holiday, who is killed immediately after the wedding. Rosalind renounces a fortune by concealing the marriage and thereby sets up a noble happy ending: 'Amory takes her in his arms and we realize that, at last, he is strong enough to work out the destinies of both of them.'[120] Fitzgerald was to be paid an additional $2,500 for collaborating on the scenario or continuity, but the movie project was dropped.

Scribners published *The Vegetable or from President to postman* on 27 April 1923 in a printing of 7,650 copies at $1.50. Again the dust jacket was by Held. The dedication read: TO KATHERINE TIGHE AND EDMUND WILSON, JR. WHO DELETED MANY ABSURDITIES FROM MY FIRST TWO NOVELS I RECOMMEND THE ABSURDITIES SET DOWN HERE. The book was widely reviewed, but most of the critics regarded it as minor Fitzgerald and found the political satire labored. There was only one printing.

Eager to increase his short-story price from the $900

Metropolitan figure, Fitzgerald sold the Hearst organization an option on his 1923 output for $1,500. Under the terms of the agreement Hearst was to accept at least six stories for $1,500 each. The deal proved to be complicated and unsatisfactory.* The first of the Hearst stories, 'Dice, Brass Knuckles & Guitar,' was written in January. While not a major story, it has connections with *The Great Gatsby*. A farce, 'Dice' does not make a serious statement; but the story deals with the cruelty of the rich toward the outsider. A Southerner comes north with the improbable scheme of teaching the arts of crap shooting, jazz, and self-defense to the children of the wealthy. His school is a success, but he is bitterly hurt to discover that he is regarded as a servant. He is befriended by a girl who belongs with the rich by virtue of family though not of money. She delivers the judgment 'You're better than all of them put together'[121] – anticipating Nick Carraway's tribute to Gatsby.† 'Hot and Cold Blood,' written in April 1923, shows Fitzgerald reverting to his early didacticism. A young businessman is rebuked by his wife for allowing people to take advantage of his generosity and he decides to harden himself. After inadvertently making her the victim of his new selfishness, he returns to his natural kindness.

The first half of 1923 was a time of parties and drinking while Fitzgerald waited for *The Vegetable* to be accepted by a producer; he was reluctant to start his third novel because it would be interrupted when the play went into rehearsal. During the early months of 1923 he conferred with Perkins about the publication of Thomas Boyd's *Through the Wheat*.

* In 1923 and 1924 Fitzgerald submitted 'Dice, Brass Knuckles & Guitar' (*Hearst's International*), 'Hot and Cold Blood' (*International*), 'Our Own Movie Queen' (mostly written by Zelda; declined but published under Fitzgerald's name by the *Chicago Sunday Tribune*), and 'One of My Oldest Friends' (declined; published by *Woman's Home Companion*). ' "The Sensible Thing" ' (*Liberty*) and 'Rags Martin-Jones and the Pr-nce of W-les' (*McCall's*) were paid for by *International* but later returned; 'Diamond Dick and the First Law of Woman' and 'The Baby Party' were accepted in their place.
† One of the wealthy families in the story is named *Katzby*, which may have provided the sound for the name *Gatsby* that James Gatz invents for himself – combined with 'gat,' the slang word for a pistol.

When the book appeared in May he wrote a strong review for the *New York Evening Post*, describing it as the only novel that gave him the feeling of Conrad's 'Youth' and praising its unintellectualized realism 'and unmistakable note of heroism.' Fitzgerald's review concluded: 'To my mind this is not only the best combatant story of the great war, but also the best war book since "The Red Badge of Courage." ' Fitzgerald had reviewed Dos Passos's *Three Soldiers* for Boyd's *St. Paul Daily News* book page in 1921, placing it above *Red Badge*. In the interval Fitzgerald decided that Dos Passos had falsified the reactions of American soldiers 'and in so doing attributed the emotions of exhausted nations to men who for the most part were neither exhausted nor emotional.'[122] Some of his praise for Boyd must be discounted as an act of friendship; nonetheless, Fitzgerald's patriotic stance seems sincere. Perhaps it was an expression of his regret at having missed battle or perhaps it represented his disappointment with Europe, but Fitzgerald concluded that the American soldiers of the Great War were different from the Europeans. Although *Through the Wheat* achieved a period of respect, its reputation did not last. Boyd became a productive novelist and biographer, but none of his later books matched the success of his first novel.

Despite his own fame, Fitzgerald was almost boyishly eager to meet great writers. In the spring of 1923 he pleaded with Mencken, Ernest Boyd, and Carl Van Vechten to take him along to a party Theodore Dreiser was giving at his Greenwich Village apartment. They declined; but Fitzgerald later arrived tight at the extremely dull stag gathering, bearing a bottle of champagne as a gift for Dreiser – who carefully put it away. Fitzgerald was unable to start a conversation with his taciturn host.[123]

During 1923 the Fitzgeralds developed a friendship with Carl Van Vechten, who would record his impressions of them as David and Rilda Westlake in his 1930 novel *Parties*: 'Rilda and David tortured each other because they loved one another devotedly.'[124]

24

Alcohol and the Failure of The Vegetable

[1923]

Long Island provided material for Fitzgerald's third novel as impressions from that 'riotous island' went into the writer's process of cerebration. Jay Gatsby was inspired in part by a local figure, Max Gerlach. Near the end of her life Zelda Fitzgerald said that Gatsby was based on 'a neighbor named Von Guerlach or something who was said to be General Pershing's nephew and was in trouble over bootlegging.'[125] This identification is supported by a newspaper photo of the Fitzgeralds in their scrapbook, with a note dated 7/20/23: 'En route from the coast – Here for a few days on business – How are you and the family old Sport? Gerlach.'[126] Here is Gatsby's characterizing expression, *old sport*, from the hand of Gerlach. Attempts to fill in the history of Max Gerlach during the twenties have failed; the only clue is a 1930 newspaper reference to him as a 'wealthy yachtsman.'* ('Yachtsman' was

---

* Edmund Wilson's 'gentleman bootlegger' named Max Fleischman in his 1924 play *The Crime in the Whistler Room* drew upon Fitzgerald's ideas. In his copy of the play Fitzgerald noted 'I had told Bunny my plan for Gatsby' in the margin of Wilson's description of Fleischman: 'He lives like a millionaire. Gosh, I haven't seen so much to drink since prohibition. . . . Well, Fleischman

sometimes a euphemism for rum-runner.) In 1939 Max Von Gerlach, a former automobile dealer in Flushing, attempted suicide by shooting himself. In his suicide note he described himself as having been an officer in World War I.[128]

Some fifteen years after writing *The Great Gatsby* Fitzgerald noted the sources for the chapters on the endpaper of his copy of André Malraux's *Man's Hope* (1938):

I.	Glamor of Rumsies + Hitchcoks
II.	Ash Heaps. Memory of 125th. Gt Neck
III.	Goddards. Dwanns Swopes*
IV.	A. Vegetable days in N. Y.
	B. Memory of Ginevras Wedding
V.	The meeting all an invention. Mary
VI.	Bob Kerr's story. The 2nd Party.
VII.	The Day in New York
VIII.	The Murder (inv.)
IX.	Funeral an invention[129]

The material for Jay Gatsby's association with Dan Cody was provided by a Great Neck friend, Robert Kerr, who as a fourteen-year-old had warned Major Edwin R. Gilman that his yacht would break up when the tide ran out in Brooklyn's Sheepshead Bay. Gilman hired him, and Kerr lived aboard the yacht for three years. In the summer of 1924 Fitzgerald wrote Kerr: 'The part of what you told me which I am including in my novel is the ship, yatch I mean, + the mysterious yatchsman whose mistress was Nellie Bly.'[130]

Meyer Wolfsheim, 'the man who fixed the World Series

---

was making a damn ass of himself bragging about how much his tapestries were worth and how much his bathroom was worth and how he never wore a shirt twice – '[127] See Zelda Fitzgerald's reference to a bootlegger named Fleischman in her summer 1923 letter to the Kalmans on p. 214.

* Sculptor and polo player Charles Cary Rumsey was married to heiress Mary Harriman; they had an estate at Westbury, Long Island. Polo player and war hero Tommy Hitchcock was one of Fitzgerald's permanent idols. Goddard may have been screenwriter and playwright Charles William Goddard. Allan Dwan was a movie director. Herbert Bayard Swope was executive editor of the *New York World* and a famous Great Neck host.

back in 1919,' was obviously based on gambler Arnold Rothstein, whom Fitzgerald had met. Ring Lardner, who had
inside information on the Black Sox scandal, could have provided additional material on Rothstein. Aspects of Gatsby's
criminal career were suggested by the Fuller-McGee case of
1922, in which a brokerage house's assets were misappro-
priated by its owners – one of whom, Edward M. Fuller, had an
estate at Great Neck and was involved with Rothstein.

In the summer of 1923 Zelda reported to the Kalmans, who
had visited the Fitzgeralds at Great Neck: 'I have unearthed
some of the choicest bootleggers (including Fleischman). . . .
But Scott has started a new novel and retired into strict
seclusion and celibacy. . . . Besides, any minute he may have
to start going over to Famous Players about "T.S.O.P." '131

"THE BEAUTIFUL AND DAMNED"
DOES NOT LOOK ALL OF THAT

F. Scott Fitzgerald, his wife and their 2-year-old
daughter, "Scotty," at their summer home on Long
Island. Mrs. Fitzgerald is the heroine of her husband's successful novel, "The Beautiful and
Damned." —Fotograms

PRINCETON UNIVERSITY LIBRARY

The earliest draft of Fitzgerald's third novel has not been
preserved, so it is impossible to determine whether he began
working on his plan for a novel set in the Midwest in the
nineteenth century. The only clue to the 1923 draft is
provided by a 1925 letter to Willa Cather in which Fitzgerald
accounts for 'an instance of apparent plagiarism' from *A Lost
Lady* (1923) in *The Great Gatsby* by explaining that a
description of Daisy Buchanan was written before he read
Cather's description of Mrs. Forrester.[132] Fitzgerald enclosed

two pages of his first draft – all that survive. The locale is not specified in these pages. The characters named are Jordan Vance, Ada, and Carraway – who is not the narrator. The story is told by an omniscient authorial voice. Fitzgerald was not able to concentrate on his novel because of the distractions at Great Neck. Here, for example, is his *Ledger* entry for July 1923: 'Tootsie [Rosalind] arrived Intermittent work on novel Constant drinking. Some golf. Baby begins to talk. Parties at Allen Dwans. Gloria Swanson and the movie crowd Our party for Tootsie The Perkins arrive. I drive into the lake.'

By 1923–24 Fitzgerald had progressed from a party drinker to a steady drinker with increasingly erratic behavior. In *Tender Is the Night*, commenting on the alcoholic Abe North, he described the pleasurable effects he felt at a certain stage of drunkenness: 'The drink made past happy things contemporary with the present, as if they were still going on, contemporary even with the future as if they were about to happen again.'[133] Although Fitzgerald has the reputation of being one of the heaviest drinkers among American writers, his tolerance for alcohol was low and he became drunk on relatively small amounts of alcohol. He was not an expert drinker, and his palate for wine was untrained. His preferred tipple was straight gin, which gave him the quickest lift and which he thought was difficult to detect on his breath.

One textbook definition is that alcoholism is 'a chronic behavioral disorder manifested by an undue preoccupation with alcohol and its use to the detriment of physical and mental health, by loss of control when drinking is begun, and by a self-destructive attitude in dealing with personal relationships and life situations. Alcoholism results from a disturbance and deprivation in early life of experiences and the associated related alterations in basic physiochemical responsiveness; from the identification by the alcoholic person with significant figures who deal with life problems through an unhealthy preoccupation with alcohol, and from a sociocultural milieu that causes ambivalence, conflict and

215

guilt in the use of alcohol.'[134]

Alcoholism runs in families, but it is not clear that it is hereditary. Although it was formerly thought that the incidence of alcoholism among children of alcoholics was mainly the result of role emulation, recent studies have indicated that there may be genetic factors. This line of investigation cannot be developed in Fitzgerald's case because nothing is known about his father's drinking habits except that he went on occasional mild benders. There are also unconfirmed reports that Mollie's brothers were heavy drinkers.

Of the several psychoanalytic theories, R. P. Knight's formulation of the psychodynamics of alcoholism seems applicable to Fitzgerald:

> His [the alcoholic's] childhood experiences have given him a personality characterized by excessive demands for indulgence. These demands are doomed to frustration with intolerable disappointment and rage. The reaction impels him to hostile acts and wishes against the thwarting individuals for which he then feels guilt and punishes himself masochistically. As reassurance against guilt feelings and fears of dangerously destructive masochism and reality consequences of his behavior, he feels excessive need for affection and indulgence as proof of affection. Again, the excessive claims, doomed to frustration, arise, and the circle is complete. The use of alcohol as a pacifier for disappointment and rage, as a potent means of carrying out hostile impulses to spite his parents and friends, as a method of securing masochistic debasement, and as a symbolic gratification of the need for affection is now interweaving itself in the neurotic vicious cycle.[135]

Dr. Richard Hoffman, a psychiatrist who saw Fitzgerald while he was recovering from a 1939 bender, diagnosed that Fitzgerald suffered from hypoglycemia or hyperinsulinism, a condition in which the body produces an excess of insulin that causes a craving for sugar.[136] Alcohol is one way to replenish body sugar. True hypoglycemia results from a tumor on the islets of Langerhans in the pancreas, but the diagnosis can only be confirmed by a post-mortem examination or blood glucose tests. After examining Fitzgerald's medical records, pathologist William Ober concludes: 'There is no evidence for hypoglycemia whatsoever. The discharge note from Johns Hopkins Hospital on 3 January 1937 states that a blood sugar determination was done and reported as 78 mg. per 100 cc. This is perfectly normal, and the specimen was drawn after he had been in the hospital and not drinking for a couple of days.' Dr. Ober points out that all alcoholism induces hypoglycemia. 'However, the alcohol-induced low blood sugar levels were responsible for Fitzgerald's idiosyncratic eating habits, e.g. ice cream for breakfast, etc. He did not drink because his blood sugar level was low; he drank because he was a drunkard. "Drunkard" is the old-fashioned term for alcoholic, and, as we know today, it is an addiction, a form of escape for people with inadequate personalities, people with deep-seated insecurities, people with unresolved intra-psychic conflicts (often sexual but by no means always so), as well as people . . . who use it to drown out the still small voice of self-reproach. The superego can be defined as that portion of the personality that is soluble in alcohol.'[137] Fitzgerald's guilt about drinking may have generated the self-perpetuating situation whereby he sometimes drank to alleviate the feelings of guilt provoked by his drinking.

In his twenties Fitzgerald was partly playing a role. Writers were supposed to drink. His difficulty in controlling it – which in his case meant staying on the wagon – was compounded by the circumstance that his society ran on alcohol. His friends were drinkers, and the social gatherings he attended were drinking occasions. Zelda, though never an alcoholic, enjoyed getting tight.

The studies of literary alcoholism are inconclusive. Many of the best American writers of the twentieth century had alcohol problems: Fitzgerald, Faulkner, O'Neill, O'Hara, Wolfe, Lardner, Hemingway, Lewis, Chandler, Hammett. There is evidently a connection between alcoholism and the creative personality; but it remains unclear whether writers

Zelda and Scottie, 1923

drink because they are writers. Fitzgerald became convinced that alcohol was necessary to his creative process. During the Twenties he wrote sober, but he believed that pre-composition drinking intensified his responses to experience. He wrote eloquently about the effects of intoxication: 'A man drinking lives in a world of his own after a point for drink pays in pleasant tokens that have no value only because they melt away – checks written in disappearing ink.'[138] Writing and drinking are both forms of exhibitionism and escapism.

In the summer of 1923 Sam H. Harris agreed to produce *The Vegetable*.* The director was Sam Forrest, and the leading role of Jerry Frost was acted by Ernest Truex. Fitzgerald was involved in rehearsals, and in November he and Zelda went with the Lardners to Atlantic City, New Jersey, for the tryout. The play opened for a one-week run at Nixon's Apollo Theatre on 19 November 1923. Opening night was a disaster; and people walked out during the second act fantasy, which didn't work on the stage. Zelda reported to Xandra Kalman:

> In brief, the show flopped as flat as one of Aunt Jemimas famous pancakes – Scott and Truex and Harris were terribly disappointed and so was I as I had already spent the first weeks N.Y. royalty for a dress to wear to the opening night that could not be exchanged. . . . The first act went fine but Ernest says he has *never* had an experience on the stage like the second. I *heard* one woman hit the roof when the bible was mentioned. They seemed to think it was sacreligious or something. People were so obviously bored! And it was all very well done, so there was no use trying to fix it up. The idea was what people didn't like – Just hopeless! Scott suggested fixing it up by having Ernests teeth fall out when he heard about the Buzzard Islands, but I don't think anybody liked the suggestion except us – It is too terrible to contemplate.[139]

Fitzgerald did what he could to improve the play during the week at Atlantic City, but it was dead when its out-of-town

---

* Fitzgerald's May 1923 *Ledger* entry 'Play accepted by Williams' has not been explained.

tryouts ended.* The failure of *The Vegetable* terminated Fitzgerald's serious interest in the stage and its financial rewards. Although he would occasionally talk about writing another play, he never went beyond outlines. Superficially considered, it seems surprising that Fitzgerald did not persevere with the theater. His theatrical apprenticeship in St. Paul and Princeton had won him his first recognition; and his ability to write dialogue promised eventual success as a playwright. Nevertheless, much of the effectiveness of Fitzgerald's stories depends on elements of style and narrative technique that cannot be transferred to the stage. He was a storyteller, relying heavily on tone, style, and authorial voice. A Fitzgerald story or novel in dramatic form loses many of the qualities that make it a Fitzgerald work – as the disappointing movie versions of his novels have demonstrated.

---

* When the enormously successful Gershwin musical *Of Thee I Sing* was produced in 1931, Fitzgerald became convinced that the political satire by George S. Kaufman and Morrie Ryskind had been lifted from *The Vegetable*, and considered a plagiarism suit.

25

'How to Live
on $36,000 a Year'

[Winter 1923–Spring 1924]

The Vegetable left Fitzgerald in debt; he had written only two stories for *Hearst's International* in 1923 before the Atlantic City debacle. He went on the wagon at the end of 1923 and wrote ten stories by March 1924: 'Gretchen's Forty Winks,' 'Diamond Dick and the First Law of Woman,' 'The Third Casket,' ' "The Sensible Thing," ' 'Rags Martin-Jones and the Pr-nce of W-les,' 'The Unspeakable Egg,' 'John Jackson's Arcady,' 'The Baby Party,' 'The Pusher-in-the-Face,' and 'One of My Oldest Friends.' They brought $16,450, which paid off Fitzgerald's borrowings from Harold Ober and financed a summer of uninterrupted work on *The Great Gatsby.*

The 1924 stories were written on pots of coffee that made him irritable and sleepless, initiating the insomnia that troubled him for the rest of his life. Most of these stories were submitted to *Hearst's International Magazine* under the option agreement, but the magazine delayed payments. Fitzgerald resumed his association with *The Saturday Evening Post*, which for the next dozen years became his primary story market.

After 1924 Ober gave the *Post* first refusal on the stories. Of Fitzgerald's 113 published stories during the period he was a *Post* contributor, from 1920 to 1937, 65 (plus four articles) were in the *Post* – an average of 3.8 appearances a year. But he was not the *Post*'s most productive writer. That distinction belonged to Ben Ames Williams, with 160 fiction appearances during the Twenties; Joseph Hergesheimer, Octavus Roy Cohen, Hugh McNair Kahler, Clarence Buddington Kelland, and John P. Marquand all appeared more often than Fitzgerald. Despite his boast that he was the highest-paid short-story writer in America, it is unlikely that he was ever the *Post*'s highest-paid fiction contributor. In 1924 the *Post* paid Fitzgerald $1,750 for a story. His top price of $4,000 was not reached until 1929.

Most of Fitzgerald's 1924 stories are routine commercial efforts. He admitted to Mencken: 'my whole heart was in my first trash. . . . I never really "wrote down" until after the failure of the *Vegetable*.'[140] 'Gretchen's Forty Winks,' written in January, describes how a man with an important project drugs his spoiled wife until his work is done. At this time Fitzgerald could still turn his domestic problems into moneymaking humor. 'Rags Martin-Jones and the Pr-nce of W-les' was an obvious reprise of 'The Offshore Pirate': a wealthy young man wins a bored heiress by staging an elaborate spectacle for her. 'The Baby Party,' a story about parental anger resulting from a children's party, was written overnight.

' "The Sensible Thing" ' is the only one of the ten stories with particular merit, and it is one of the strongest *Gatsby* cluster stories. Drawing on his courtship of Zelda, Fitzgerald wrote about a young man who loses a Southern girl because he is too poor to marry her. After one of the sudden reversals of fortune that characterize Fitzgerald's stories, George O'Kelley comes back for Jonquil Cary a year later with money and a promising future. Now she is ready to marry him; but O'Kelley realizes that during the year something has been irretrievably lost:

All the time in the world – his life and hers. But for an instant as he kissed her he knew that though he search through eternity he could never recapture those lost April hours. He might press her close now till the muscles knotted on his arms – she was something desirable and rare that he had fought for and made his own – but never again an intangible whisper in the dark, or on the breeze of night. . . .

Well, let it pass he thought; April is over, April is over. There are all kinds of love in the world, but never the same love twice.[141]

O'Kelley can accept the mutability of love, but Gatsby will insist on nothing less than total restoration: he wants the same love twice.*

The 1923 start on the novel had included an account of the hero's boyhood in the Midwest. In April 1924 Fitzgerald told Perkins that he had converted part of the discarded opening into the story 'Absolution' for the *American Mercury*, Mencken's and Nathan's new magazine.[143] The connection between 'Absolution' and *The Great Gatsby* has engendered considerable speculation, with the common assumption that the boy is young Gatsby. This view is supported by Fitzgerald's 1934 statement to a critic: 'It might interest you to know that a story of mine, called "Absolution" . . . was intended to be a picture of his [Gatsby's] early life, but that I cut it because I preferred to preserve the sense of mystery.'[144] Nonetheless, it is not certain that Rudolph Miller, the boy whose dreams of metropolitan glamour are reinforced by his encounter with the deranged priest, is Jimmy Gatz. As Fitzgerald told Perkins, 'Absolution' was salvaged from a discarded version before he approached the novel from 'a new angle' – by which he meant a new plot. While Miller and Gatz share a romantic disposition, there is no clear evidence that they are the same characterization from the same novel. Fitzgerald's 1922 plan was that his third novel would have a

* Fitzgerald stated that ' "The Sensible Thing" ' and 'Rags Martin-Jones' were 'awfully good' stories 'before two editors cut them to pieces.'[142]

'catholic element' – which is entirely absent in *The Great Gatsby*, though central to 'Absolution.' Indeed, there is no clue to Gatsby's religious background beyond the fact that his funeral is conducted by a Lutheran minister. The safest way to regard Rudolph Miller is as a preliminary treatment of the figure who developed into Jay Gatsby; they share the conviction that 'There was something ineffably gorgeous somewhere that had nothing to do with God.'[145]

Because Fitzgerald was regarded as a spokesman for his generation, he was asked to write articles about love, marriage, and sex – four of which appeared in 1924: 'Why Blame It on the Poor Kiss if the Girl Veteran of Many Petting Parties Is Prone to Affairs After Marriage?' 'What Kind of Husbands Do "Jimmies" Make?' 'Does a Moment of Revolt Come Sometime to Every Married Man?' (with a companion article by Zelda) and 'Wait Till You Have Children of Your Own!' 'What Kind of Husbands Do "Jimmies" Make?' is an attack on the American 'wasting class,' in which Fitzgerald cites the lack of an American aristocracy. 'Here we come to something that sets the American "leisure class" off from the leisure class of all other nations – and makes it probably the most shallow, most hollow, most pernicious leisure class in the world. It has frequently no consciousness that leisure is a privilege, not a right, and that a privilege always implies a responsibility.'[146]

Great Neck proved to be expensive. Any place was expensive for the Fitzgeralds, but the proximity to New York City encouraged improvident evenings on the town. Although Fitzgerald earned $28,754.78 in 1923, it was not enough to pay his bills. With his penchant for making schedules, Fitzgerald worked out a budget proving that $2,000 was ample to cover their monthly expenses. But they were spending $3,000 – with $12,000 a year unaccounted for.* The only thing to do was to write about it; and the *Post*

* Fitzgerald's monthly budget for 1923 includes the following categories: 'House Liquor' ($80), 'Wild Parties' ($100), 'Subway (ect.)' ($29), 'Miscelaeneous Cash' ($276).[147]

bought 'How to Live on $36,000 a Year' for $1,000. Since $36,000 was an impressive figure in those days, the article attracted attention when it appeared in April 1924. Although 'How to Live on $36,000 a Year' was intended as humor, it provided an accurate view of Fitzgerald's circumstances and work habits at that time:

> Over our garage is a large bare room whither I now retired with pencil, paper and oil stove, emerging the next afternoon at five o'clock with a 7,000-word story. That was something; it would pay the rent and last month's overdue bills. It took twelve hours a day for five weeks to rise from abject poverty back into the middle class, but within that time we had paid our debts, and the cause for immediate worry was over.
>
> . . . .
>
> I wanted to find out where the $36,000 had gone. Thirty-six thousand is not very wealthy – not yacht-and-Palm-Beach wealthy – but it sounds to me as though it should buy a roomy house full of furniture, a trip to Europe once a year, and a bond or two besides. But our $36,000 had bought nothing at all.[148]

That was the mystery of the Fitzgeralds' finances: they never knew where their money had gone because they had nothing to show for it. The cycle of debt kept Fitzgerald in bondage to the magazines. It seemed he could always write another story, and his story price kept going up. Writing stories provided Fitzgerald with no satisfaction and generated guilt because he knew that his chance for greatness depended on novels. Even if Zelda understood her husband's potential, she did not share his contempt for his short stories and was pleased that they brought in what she regarded as easy money. After Fitzgerald's death Zelda said, 'I always felt a story in the Post was tops; a goal worth seeking. It really meant something, you know – they only took stories of real craftsmanship. But Scott couldn't stand to write them.'[149] Increasingly, Fitzgerald resented her inability to share his high literary ambitions. He later ruefully remarked: 'A strange thing was that I could never convince Zelda that I was

225

a first rate writer. She knew I could write well, but she didn't recognize how well. When I was making myself from a popular story writer into a serious writer, "a big shot," she did not understand or try to help me.'[150]

Every serious writer should ideally have a wife who puts his work ahead of everything, who runs an organized household and protects him from distractions; but Fitzgerald could not have fallen in love with a woman who would have provided the order and discipline he needed. He knew that Zelda was not domestically inclined when he married her. Despite his distress over the financial insecurity and the interruptions of his novels that were concomitants of life with Zelda, he shared the responsibility for the way they lived because it was what part of him wanted. They were collaborators in extravagance.

26

Second Trip Abroad:
Valescure and Betrayal

[Summer 1924]

In April 1924 Fitzgerald noted in his *Ledger*: 'Out of the woods at last + starting novel.' He sent Perkins a stock-taking letter declaring his resolves for *The Great Gatsby*:

A few words more relative to our conversation this afternoon. While I have every hope + plan of finishing my novel in June you know how those things often come out. And even if it takes me 10 times that long I cannot let it go out unless it has the very best I'm capable of in it or even as I feel sometimes, something better than I'm capable of. Much of what I wrote last summer was good but it was so interrupted that it was ragged + in approaching it from a new angle I've had to discard a lot of it – in one case 18,000 (part of which will appear in the Mercury as a short story.) It is only in the last four months that I've realized how much I've – well, almost *deteriorated* in the three years since I finished the Beautiful and Damned. The last four months of course I've worked but in the two years – over two years – before that, I produced exactly *one* play, *half a dozen* short stories and three or four articles – an average of about *one hundred* words a day. If I'd spent this time reading or travelling or doing anything – even staying healthy – it'd be different but I spent it uselessly, neither in study nor in contemplation but only in drinking and raising hell generally. If I'd written the B. + D. at the rate of 100 words a day it would have taken me *4 years* so you can imagine the moral effect the whole chasm had on me.

What I'm trying to say is just that I'll have to ask you to have patience about the book and trust me that at last, or at least for the 1st time in years, I'm doing the best I can. I've gotten in dozens of bad habits that I'm trying to get rid of

1. Laziness
2. Referring everything to Zelda – a terrible habit, nothing ought to be referred to anybody until its finished
3. Word consciousness + self doubt ect. ect. ect. ect.

I feel I have an enormous power in me now, more than I've ever had in a way but it works so fitfully and with so many bogeys because I've *talked so much* and not lived enough within myself to develop the necessary self reliance. Also I don't know anyone who has used up so. [much personal] experience as I have at 27. Copperfield + Pendennis were written at past forty while This Side of Paradise was three books + the B. + D. was two. So in my new novel I'm thrown directly on purely creative work – not trashy imaginings as in my stories but the sustained imagination of a sincere and yet radiant world. So I tread slowly and carefully – at times in considerable distress. This book will be a consciously artistic achievement + must depend on that as the 1st books did not.

If I ever win the right to any liesure again I will assuredly not waste it as I wasted this past time. Please believe me when I say that now I'm doing the best I can.[151]

Fitzgerald's working title was 'Among Ash Heaps and Millionaires' – which establishes that he had found one of the central symbols for the novel – but Perkins thought it was weak. In April, Perkins told Fitzgerald that he 'always thought that "The Great Gatsby" was a suggestive and effective title,' indicating that it was also an early possibility.[152]

The *Ledger* records 'Decision on 15th [April] to go to Europe.' The move was not based on a fondness for Europe or on cultural needs; it was mainly a financial imperative.

Since he could not settle down to steady work on his novel at Great Neck, the Fitzgeralds would go to the Riviera where life was simple and inexpensive. (The rate of exchange was nineteen francs to the dollar, and a meal with wine could be had for three francs.) His five months of story work had gotten him $7,000 ahead, and he hoped to be able to write *The Great Gatsby* on the Riviera without story interruptions.

Ring Lardner wrote Zelda an eight-stanza farewell poem:

> Zelda, fair queel of Alabam',
> Across the waves I kiss you!
> You think I am a stone, a clam;
> You think that I don't give a damn,
> But God! how I will miss you!
>
> . . . .
>
> My heart goes with you as you sail.
> God grant you won't be seasick!
> The thought of you abaft the rail,
> Diffusing meat and ginger ale,
> Makes both my wife and me sick.[153]

The Fitzgeralds sailed early in May on the *Minnewaska* with seventeen pieces of luggage, a hundred feet of copper screen, and the *Encyclopaedia Britannica*. The selection of a dry ship indicates Fitzgerald's resolve to remain sober. After nine days in Paris – where they had a reunion with Bishop and interviewed nannies for Scottie – they were at the Grimm's Park Hotel in Hyères on the Riviera. Fitzgerald sent Thomas Boyd a glowing report soon after his arrival at Hyères:

> Your letter was the first to reach me after I arrived here. This is the lovliest piece of earth I've ever seen without excepting Oxford or Venice or Princeton or anywhere. Zelda and I are sitting in the café l'Universe writing letters (it is 10:30 P.M.) and the moon is absolutely *au fait* Mediteraenean moon with a blurred silver linnen cap + we're both a a little tight and

very happily drunk if you can use that term for the less
nervous, less violent reactions of this side.

. . . .

I'm going to read nothing but Homer + Homeric literature
– and history 540–1200 A.D. until I finish my novel + I hope to
God I don't see a soul for six months. My novel grows more +
more extraordinary; I feel absolutely self-sufficient + I have a
perfect hollow craving for lonliness, that has increased for
three years in some arithmetical progression + I'm going to
satisfy it at last.

. . . .

Well, I shall write a novel better than any novel ever written
in America and become par excellence the best second-rater in
the world.[154]

The 'summer Riviera,' as it was called, was unfashionable
because the Riviera was then a winter resort; the hotel was
populated by elderly English invalids. The Fitzgeralds rented
the elegant Villa Marie in Valescure, 2.5 kilometers above St.
Raphaël, for $79 a month and bought a Renault for $750.
The English nanny, Lillian Maddock, was paid $26 a month;
and the cook and maid received $16 and $13 a month. Still,
the Riviera was not as cheap as the Fitzgeralds expected
because the servants and the local merchants took advantage
of them. As always, a good deal of money was spent in
restaurants and cafés.

Fitzgerald worked steadily on his novel, interrupting it to
write an account of life on the Riviera, 'How to Live on
Practically Nothing a Year,' for the *Post* in July. Although his
sanguine progress reports were exaggerated – for example,
the mid-July claim to Ober that 'the novel is almost done'[155] –
he made rapid progress on the manuscript draft. At first
Zelda seemed satisfied with their quiet life; but in July she
became involved with a French naval aviator, Edouard Jozan,
one of a group of young men the Fitzgeralds socialized with
on the beach and in the evenings. The Frenchmen competed

for Zelda's attention, and it must have seemed to her like a replay of Montgomery in 1918. Like the American pilots who had stunted above the Sayre house, Jozan buzzed the Villa Marie in his plane. The extent of this romantic attachment will probably never be known. Jozan has insisted that it was

'Villa Marie,' Valescure, France

only a flirtation.[156] Both Fitzgeralds wrote fictionalized versions of the events. In Zelda's novel, *Save Me the Waltz*, the affair is not consummated; the aviator wants a mistress but does not encourage her to leave her husband. Fitzgerald's *Ledger* notes 'The Big crisis – 13th of July.' He later reported that when Zelda asked him for a divorce he demanded a

Admiral Edouard Jozan in 1957
INTERNATIONAL HERALD TRIBUNE

confrontation with Jozan, which the aviator avoided.* Fitzgerald persuaded Zelda to drop her divorce plans, and in August he was able to write in his *Ledger*: 'Zelda and I close together.' He later wrote in his *Notebooks*: 'That September 1924, I knew something had happened that could never be repaired.'[157] Whether or not Zelda had slept with Jozan, Fitzgerald felt she had destroyed the basic trust that was essential to their marriage.

With their need for drama, the Fitzgeralds developed the Jozan affair into what was virtually a routine they performed, separately and jointly, for their friends. Ernest Hemingway reports his initial response to Fitzgerald's account: 'This first version that he told me of Zelda and a French naval aviator falling in love was truly a sad story and I believed it was a true story. Later he told me other versions of it as though trying them for use in a novel, but none was as sad as this first one and I always believed the first one, although any of them might have been true. They were better told each time; but they never hurt you the way the first one did.'[158] Hemingway is not always trustworthy on the Fitzgeralds, but his recollection is confirmed by his first wife, Hadley: 'It was one of their acts together. I remember Zelda's beautiful face becoming very, very solemn, and she would say how he had loved her and how hopeless it had been and then how he had committed suicide. Scott would stand next to her looking very pale and distressed and sharing every minute of it.'[159] Jozan did not commit suicide; he remained at St. Raphaël until he was transferred to Indo-China in October and he went on to a distinguished military career, becoming vice-admiral of the French navy in 1952.

Writing to Ludlow Fowler in August, Fitzgerald admitted: 'I feel old too, this summer – I have ever since the failure of my

---

* Both Fitzgeralds embroidered the details of the Jozan crisis in subsequent years. Zelda said Fitzgerald had locked her in the villa for a month. Near the end of his life Fitzgerald told Sheilah Graham the fabrication that he had fought a duel with Jozan and that this duel had been written into *Tender Is the Night*.

In my younger and more vulnerable years my father told me something that I've been turning over in my mind ever since.

"When you feel like criticizing anyone," he said, "just remember that everyone in this world hasn't had the advantages that you've had.

He didn't say any more but we've always been unusually communicative in a reserved way, and I understood that he meant a great deal more than that. In consequence I'm inclined to reserve all judgements, a habit that has opened up many curious natures to me and also made me the victim of not a few collossal bores. The abnormal mind is quick to detect and attach itself to this quality when it appears in a normal person, and so it came about that in college I was unjustly accused of being a politician, because I was privy to the secret griefs of wild, unknown men. Most of the confidences were unsought — frequently I have feigned sleep, preoccupation or a hostile levity when I realized by some unmistakeable sign that an intimate revelation was quivering on the horizon — for the intimate revelations of young men or at any rate the terms in which they express them vary no more than the heavenly messages which reach us over the psychic radio. Reserving judgements is a matter of infinite hope. I am still a little afraid of missing something if I forget that, as my father snobbishly suggested and I snobbishly repeat, a sense of the fundamental decencies is parcelled out unequally at birth.

And after boasting this way of my tolerance, I come to the admission that it has a limit. Conduct may be founded on the hard rock or the wet marshes but after a certain point I don't care what it's founded on. When I came back from the east last autumn I felt that I wanted the world to be in uniform and at a sort of moral attention forever; I wanted no more riotous excursions with privileged glimpses into the human heart. It was only Gatsby himself that was exempted from my

Opening page of the manuscript of **The Great Gatsby**

PRINCETON UNIVERSITY LIBRARY

And as I sat there brooding on the old unknown world I thought of Gatsby's ~~wonder~~ when he picked out the green light at the end of Daisy's dock. He had come a long way to this blue lawn but now his dream must have seemed so close that he could hardly fail to grasp it. He did not know that ~~he had left it behind~~ ~~long before~~, it lay ~~somew~~ it was all behind him, ~~somewhere~~ back in that vast obscurity on the other side of the city, where the dark fields of the republic rolled on under the night.

He believed in the green glimmer, in the orgastic future that year by year recedes before us. It eluded us then but never mind — tomorrow we will run faster, stretch out our arms farther. And one fine morning —

So we beat on, a boat against the current, borne back ceaselessly into the past

play a year ago. That's the whole burden of this novel – the loss of those illusions that give such color to the world that you don't care whether things are true or false as long as they partake of the magical glory.'[160] One of the lost illusions that informed *The Great Gatsby* was Fitzgerald's certainty in Zelda's love and fidelity.

The novel allowed Fitzgerald to dramatize the most powerful experiences in his love for Zelda: his courtship in 1918, the break in 1919, his triumphant restoration in 1920 (with its attendant financial rewards), and her betrayal in 1924. It is not known how much of *The Great Gatsby* had been written before the July 1924 Jozan crisis. The typescript was not sent to Scribners until the end of October, so Fitzgerald had at least three and a half months in which to write his disillusionment with Zelda into the novel. Like Fitzgerald, during the war Jay Gatsby falls in love with a girl who is incapable of matching his commitment. Daisy marries the wealthy Tom Buchanan, and Gatsby convinces himself that he lost her only because he was poor. He makes a fortune through mysterious and extralegal means, and sets himself up as a giver of lavish parties on Long Island, near Daisy's house. His parties are intended to attract Daisy, for he anticipates that some night she will appear at a party and his conspicuous show of affluence will win her back. The plan fails, and Gatsby arranges to meet Daisy through Nick Carraway, the narrator. Moved by Gatsby's fidelity, Daisy agrees to leave her adulterous husband. In a confrontation at the Plaza Hotel, Buchanan breaks Daisy's resolve by revealing that Gatsby is engaged in criminal activities. On the drive back to Long Island, Daisy kills her husband's mistress, Myrtle, in a hit-and-run accident. Gatsby takes the blame, and Buchanan sends Myrtle's husband to murder him. Jay Gatsby, the great believer, dies bereft of his illusions.

Despite the marital upset, Fitzgerald pushed ahead with his novel. But he did not work all the time, for – notwithstanding his claim to Boyd that he wanted a summer of isolation – he shared with Zelda a need for amusement and company.

There were trips to Monte Carlo, Antibes, and Cannes.

During the summer of 1924 the Fitzgeralds met Gerald and Sara Murphy, who would become their closest friends in France. They were probably introduced by Gerald's sister Esther, whom the Fitzgeralds had known in America. The Fitzgeralds could have met the Murphys in Paris in May, but it is more likely that the meeting came later on the Riviera, where the Murphys were staying at Cap d'Antibes, thirty miles east of St. Raphaël. Donald Ogden Stewart, who had met the Murphys in Paris in 1923, could have provided a connection. Since the Murphys do not appear in Fitzgerald's *Ledger* until August 1924, they may not have met until critic Gilbert Seldes and his bride came to visit the Fitzgeralds and the Murphys on their wedding trip in August.

Gerald and Sara Murphy were an American couple of

Sara and Gerald Murphy with their children

independent means who had determined to make an art of life, taking for their motto the Spanish saying 'Living well is the best revenge.' Gerald was the son of the owner of the Mark Cross leather goods store; Sara was one of the admired Wiborg sisters from Cincinnati, daughters of a wealthy ink manufacturer. Gerald had graduated from Yale in 1912 – where he had been tapped for Skull & Bones – and had worked in the family business, which he hated. Sara had spent much of her childhood touring Europe with her mother and had been presented at the Court of St. James in 1914. They were married in 1915. After Gerald was discharged from the army (he was trained as a pilot but never got overseas), the Murphys decided to make a break with American commercial life and family pressures. Gerald studied landscape architecture at Harvard, and in 1921 they settled in France with their three children to live well.

Eight years older than Fitzgerald, Gerald was handsome, witty, and charming. Sara matched his intelligence and had a strong streak of directness in her speech. Although the Murphys lived in luxury, with great originality and impeccable taste, they were not big rich. Gerald invaded his capital to maintain their good life, and Sara's income was only $7,000 a year. Their houses in Paris and at Cap d'Antibes were beautifully furnished and run by competent servants. Both were seriously interested in the arts. They studied painting with Natalie Goncharova and were active supporters of the Russian and Swedish ballets in Paris. Their close friends included Pablo Picasso, Philip Barry, Cole Porter, John Dos Passos, Archibald MacLeish, and Fernand Léger. Between 1922 and 1930 Murphy completed ten paintings that combined minute detail with abstract techniques. His first work was a large-scale arrangement of a safety razor, a fountain pen, and a matchbox; and art historians have credited him with anticipating the pop art school. Fitzgerald admired Murphy's virtuosity with people and felt that their shared Irish backgrounds provided a link between them. In *Tender Is the Night* he transferred Murphy's 'power of

arousing a fascinated and uncritical love' to Dick Diver:
'... people believed he made special reservations about
them, recognizing the proud uniqueness of their destinies,
buried under the compromises of how many years.'[161]
Murphy was what one part of Fitzgerald wistfully longed to
be, and Fitzgerald came to regard him as his social
conscience: '... a fourth man had come to dictate my
relations with other people when these relations were
successful: how to do, what to say. How to make people at
least momentarily happy.... This always confused me and
made me want to go out and get drunk, but this man had seen
the game, analyzed it and beaten it, and his word was good
enough for me.'[162]

Initially the Murphys were attracted more to Zelda.
Fitzgerald's drinking behavior put them off, and the
Murphys found it difficult to believe in him as a serious
writer. The Fitzgeralds visited the Murphys, who were staying
at the Hotel du Cap while renovating their Villa America at
Cap d'Antibes, and considered moving to Antibes to be near
the Murphys. One night Fitzgerald woke the Murphys with
the report that Zelda had taken an overdose of sleeping pills,
and they helped him keep her awake. It is not clear whether
her suicide gesture was related to the Jozan crisis.

During the summer of 1924 Fitzgerald found a new
intellectual enthusiasm in Oswald Spengler's *The Decline of the
West*. In 1940 he wrote Perkins, 'I read him the same summer
I was writing "The Great Gatsby"* and I don't think I ever
quite recovered from him.... [Spengler] prophesied gang
rule, "young peoples hungry for spoil," and more particularly
"The world as spoil" as an idea, a dominant supersessive

---

* Fitzgerald could not have read *The Decline of the West* at this time because it
was not translated into English until 1926 and he did not read German.
Nevertheless, there were prominent magazine articles about Spengler in
1924 that Fitzgerald probably read, e.g. W. K. Stewart's 'The Decline of
Western Culture: Oswald Spengler's "Downfall of Western Civilization"
Explained' in the July 1924 *Century*. Three installments of *The Decline of the
West* appeared in *The Dial* from November 1924 to June 1925, after
Fitzgerald had completed *The Great Gatsby*.

idea.'[163] It is unlikely that Spengler's synthesis of history, politics, and culture had a direct influence on *The Great Gatsby*. Because Fitzgerald was excited by large ideas about the movement of civilizations and felt insecure about his own education, he regarded *The Decline of the West* as a summation of intellectual history. (In *The Last Tycoon* Kathleen would explain that her lover had been educating her to read Spengler.) *The Decline of the West* presented an organic overview of Western history, contending that there has been a pattern of cultural movements that repeat the same cycle of development and collapse – with the twentieth-century Western world in the phase of decay.

By late August 1924 Fitzgerald was able to tell Perkins: 'The novel will be done next week. That doesn't mean however that it'll reach America before October 1st. as Zelda + I are contemplating careful revision after a weeks complete rest.' The reference to Zelda's editorial participation meant that Fitzgerald utilized her criticisms in revising the novel – not that she collaborated in rewriting it. In this letter Fitzgerald made another remark that has received attention: 'For Christs sake don't give anyone that jacket you're saving for me. I've written it into the book.'[164] Taking their lead from this statement, critics have assumed – on no firm evidence – that Fitzgerald borrowed the symbol of Dr. Eckleburg's billboard from the dust jacket that appeared on the published novel. However, it is unclear whether Fitzgerald was referring to preliminary dust-jacket art or the final one. If it was the jacket that appeared on the book, then there is no reason why Fitzgerald did not want anyone to see it. Since Fitzgerald refers to a dust jacket Perkins is 'saving' for him, it may well have been a lost trial sketch. Perkins replied on 10 September: 'There is certainly not the slightest risk of our giving that jacket to anyone in the world but you.'[165] Moreover, the book jacket does not present a billboard or any other scene from the novel. The striking painting by Francis Cugat shows a woman's face over an amusement park night scene; naked figures form the irises of the eyes, which do not at all resemble the bespectacled eyes of Dr. Eckleburg's billboard at the Valley of Ashes. Perkins's response when he read the manuscript does not clarify the problem: 'good as the wrap always seemed, it now seems a masterpiece for this book.'[166] After Fitzgerald saw the published book in 1925 he wrote Perkins: 'Thought the new

Francis Cugat's dust jacket for the first edition of The Great Gatsby

jacket was *great*.[167] The word 'new' almost certainly indicates that the final Cugat dust jacket replaced the preliminary jacket that Fitzgerald wrote into *The Great Gatsby*. A more probable source for the Eckleburg figure (who 'sank down himself into eternal blindness') and for the valley of ashes was T. S. Eliot's *The Waste Land* (1922), which Fitzgerald greatly admired. Eckleburg can be read as a Long Island version of the blind seer Tiresias, and the ash heaps are actually and symbolically a waste land.*

On 10 September, Fitzgerald informed Perkins: 'Now for a promise – the novel will absolutely + definately be mailed to you before the 1st of October. I've had to rewrite practically half of it – at present its stored away for a week so I can take a last look at it + see what I've left out – there's some intangible sequence lacking somewhere in the middle + a break in interest there inevitably means the failure of a book. It is like nothing I've ever read before.'[168] While the novel was put aside, the Lardners came to the Riviera for a visit. In a series of articles about his European trip Lardner remarked, 'Mr. Fitzgerald is a novelist and Mrs. Fitzgerald a novelty.'[169] If Lardner read the manuscript of *The Great Gatsby* during his visit, nothing is known about his response.†

During the summer Fitzgerald read his novel or parts of it to Seldes, Stewart, Dos Passos, Maxwell Struthers Burt '+ other literary gents who have done time with us.'[171] In September a Princeton friend, Frederick Yeiser, stopped off at St. Raphaël for a week. He detected no fissure in the Fitzgeralds' marriage, but he witnessed their heated

---

* In 1990 eight pieces of Cugat art related to the *Gatsby* dust jacket were acquired for the Bruccoli Collection. Five pastel sketches depict a cityscape with a woman's face; one of the sketches has pilings or mooring posts in the foreground. An oil painting shows a carnival night scene. Two ink-and-watercolor paintings illustrate railroad coal cars (with 'Long Island Railroad' on their sides) in a setting of slag heaps and shacks. It is not known whether Cugat read a prepublication form of the novel or whether he was provided with instructions.

† In March 1925 Lardner sent Fitzgerald corrections after reading the page proof; Lardner's letter does not indicate that he had any prior familiarity with the novel.[170]

arguments about religion and literature – after which they would not speak to each other. Fitzgerald and Yeiser had long talks about the Princeton social system. Although there was little literary conversation, Fitzgerald urged him to read *Ulysses, The Diary of Otto Braun,* and *The Journal of a Disappointed Man* by W. N. P. Barbillion.[172] Braun was a young German intellectual killed in the war; Fitzgerald viewed him as a cultural hero and was moved by his early death.

In his capacity as volunteer acquisitions editor for Scribners, Fitzgerald alerted Perkins to a promising writer in October 1924: 'This is to tell you about a young man named Ernest Hemmingway, who lives in Paris, (an American) writes for the transatlantic Review + has a brilliant future. Ezra Pount published a collection of his short pieces in Paris, at some place like the Egotist Press, I havn't it hear now but its remarkable + I'd look him up right away. He's the real thing.'[173] The work that prompted Fitzgerald's enthusiasm was *in our time* (Paris: Three Mountains Press, 1924), which Edmund Wilson, who reviewed it, may have called to Fitzgerald's attention. It is possible that Bishop, who had met Hemingway in 1922, told Fitzgerald about him during their May reunion in Paris. Donald Ogden Stewart also knew Hemingway. A thirty-two-page volume published in an edition of 170 copies, *in our time* consisted of eighteen vignettes or short impressionistic prose sketches. Hemingway's published work, which included another limited edition, *3 Stories & 10 Poems* (Paris: Contact, 1923), hardly justifies Fitzgerald's prediction of a 'brilliant future'; but Hemingway was already demonstrating his ability to attract attention, and he was regarded as one of the most promising American writers in Paris. Fitzgerald had not yet met Hemingway at the time he began promoting his career. He reminded Perkins about Hemingway through the fall and winter, but Perkins delayed making contact because he was unable to find a copy of *in our time* until February 1925, when he wrote to Hemingway at an old Paris address.

27

Rome and Capri

[Fall 1924–Spring 1925]

Zelda had been reading Henry James's novel *Roderick Hudson* and decided they would spend the winter of 1924–25 in Rome – despite their unfavorable impression of Italy in 1921. Since they had not economized on the Riviera, Italy also recommended itself because the rate of exchange was even more favorable there than in France. After the typescript of the novel was sent to Perkins on 27 October, the Fitzgeralds drove to Rome. Unable to find a suitable apartment, they settled at the Hotel des Princes in the Piazza di Spagna for $525 a month. The move proved a disaster. Fitzgerald disliked the Italians, whom he regarded as arrogant and dishonest. He drank heavily and was beaten by the police – an experience he regarded as the worst thing that had ever happened to him and which he later wrote into *Tender Is the Night*. In reply to Ober's suggestion that he write an article on Rome as a companion to 'How to Live on Practically Nothing a Year,' Fitzgerald announced: 'I hate Italy and the Italiens so violently that I can't bring myself to write about them for the *Post*. – unless they'd like an article called "Pope Siphilis the Sixth and his Morons" or something like that.'[174] Eventually he wrote 'The High Cost of Macaroni,' an article which Ober was unable to place.[175] The

Rome and Capri [Fall 1924–Spring 1925]

Fitzgeralds quarreled in Rome and were both sick. An operation to enable Zelda to become pregnant resulted in a lingering infection. The Jozan wound was temporarily healed; Fitzgerald was able to write Bishop in spring 1925 that 'Zelda and I sometimes indulge in terrible four-day rows that always start with a drinking party but we're still enormously in love and about the only truly happily married couple I know.'[176] An American movie crew was making *Ben Hur* in Rome and the Fitzgeralds joined their parties, forming a friendship with actress Carmel Myers.

Fitzgerald had been uncertain about the title while he was writing the novel. At various times he considered 'The Great Gatsby,' 'Among Ash-Heaps and Millionaires,' 'Trimalchio,' 'Trimalchio in West Egg,' 'On the Road to West Egg,' 'Gold-Hatted Gatsby,' 'The High-Bouncing Lover,' and 'Gatsby.' Two of these tentative titles were taken from his epigraph poem for the book.

> Then wear the gold hat, if that will move her;
>   If you can bounce high, bounce for her too,
> Till she cry 'Lover, gold-hatted, high-bouncing lover,
>   I must have you!'

(This poem is credited to Thomas Parke D'Invilliers, the character in *This Side of Paradise* based on Bishop.) Both Zelda and Perkins preferred 'The Great Gatsby,' and Fitzgerald reluctantly settled on it in December. His own choice was 'Trimalchio' or 'Trimalchio in West Egg' – after the ostentatious party-giver in Petronius's *Satyricon* – but he was persuaded by Lardner and others that the reference to Trimalchio would puzzle readers, who in any case would not know how to pronounce it.

The $7,000 stake they had brought to France was gone before they moved to Rome, and it was necessary for Fitzgerald to write stories during the time he was polishing his novel. Although 'Love in the Night' (*Post*, March 1925) is not an important work, it marks his first use of the Riviera setting.

This love story about an American heiress and a half-American Russian aristocrat pauperized by the Revolution includes an evocation of the lost Russian winter colony on the Riviera that was later incorporated into *Tender Is the Night*.* It was followed by 'The Adjuster' (*Redbook*, September 1925), written in Rome – one of the stories in which Fitzgerald seems to be lecturing at his wife. When a bored and selfish young woman is compelled to accept responsibilities after her husband's nervous collapse, she is instructed by a mysterious Dr. Moon: ' "We make an agreement with children that they can sit in the audience without helping to make the play," he said, "but if they still sit in the audience after they're grown, somebody's got to work double time for them, so that they can enjoy the light and glitter of the world." '[177]

On 20 November, Perkins sent Fitzgerald a long letter congratulating him on the novel and making three suggestions about the treatment of Gatsby: that his past be made less vague, that the source of his money be indicated, and that a long section of his autobiographical narrative be broken up.

> I think you have every kind of right to be proud of this book. It is an extraordinary book, suggestive of all sorts of thoughts and moods. You adopted exactly the right method of telling it, that of employing a narrator who is more of a spectator than an actor: this puts the reader upon a point of observation on a higher level than that on which the characters stand and at a distance that gives perspective. In no other way could your irony have been so immensely effective, nor the reader have been enabled so strongly to feel at times the strangeness of human circumstance in a vast heedless universe. In the eyes of Dr. Eckleberg various readers will see different significances; but their presence gives a superb touch to the whole thing: great unblinking eyes, expressionless, looking down upon the human scene. It's magnificent!
>
> I could go on praising the book and speculating on its

---

* The young hero of the story was based partly on Prince Val Engalitcheff, a friend of Fitzgerald's who committed suicide in 1923.

various elements and meanings, but points of criticism are more important now. I think you are right in feeling a certain slight sagging in chapters six and seven, and I don't know how to suggest a remedy. I hardly doubt that you will find one and I am only writing to say that I think it does need something to hold up here to the pace set, and ensuing. I have only two actual criticisms:–

One is that among a set of characters marvelously palpable and vital – I would know Tom Buchanan if I met him on the street and would avoid him – Gatsby is somewhat vague. The reader's eyes can never quite focus upon him, his outlines are dim. Now everything about Gatsby is more or less a mystery i.e. more or less vague, and this may be somewhat of an artistic intention, but I think it is mistaken. Couldn't *he* be physically described as distinctly as the others, and couldn't you add one or two characteristics like the use of that phrase 'old sport', not verbal, but physical ones, perhaps. I think that for some reason or other a reader – this was true of Mr. Scribner and of Louise – gets an idea that Gatsby is a much older man than he is, although you have the writer say that he is little older than himself. But this would be avoided if on his first appearance he was seen as vividly as Daisy and Tom are, for instance;– and I do not think your scheme would be impaired if you made him so.

The other point is also about Gatsby: his career must remain mysterious, of course. But in the end you make it pretty clear that his wealth came through his connection with Wolfsheim. You also suggest this much earlier. Now almost all readers numerically are going to be puzzled by his having all this wealth and are going to feel entitled to an explanation. To give a distinct and definite one would be, of course, utterly absurd. It did occur to me though, that you might here and there interpolate some phrases, and possibly incidents, little touches of various kinds, that would suggest that he was in some active way mysteriously engaged. You do have him called on the telephone, but couldn't he be seen once or twice consulting at his parties with people of some sort of mysterious significance, from the political, the gambling, the sporting world, or whatever it may be. I know I am floundering, but that fact may help you to see what I mean. The *total* lack of an explanation

through so large a part of the story does seem to me a defect;–
or not of an explanation, but of the suggestion of an explanation. I wish you were here so I could talk about it to you for
then I know I could at least make you understand what I mean.
What Gatsby did ought never to be definitely imparted, even if
it could be. Whether he was an innocent tool in the hands of
somebody else, or to what degree he was this, ought not to be
explained. But if some sort of business activity of his were
simply adumbrated, if would lend further probability to that
part of the story.

There is one other point: in giving deliberately Gatsby's
biography when he gives it to the narrator you do depart from
the method of the narrative in some degree, for otherwise
almost everything is told, and beautifully told, in the regular
flow of it, – in the succession of events or in accompaniment with
them. But you can't avoid the biography altogether. I thought
you might find ways to let the truth of some of his claims like
'Oxford' and his army career come out bit by bit in the course of
actual narrative. I mention the point anyway for consideration
in this interval before I send the proofs.

The general brilliant quality of the book makes me ashamed
to make even these criticisms. The amount of meaning you get
into a sentence, the dimensions and intensity of the impressions
you make a paragraph carry, are most extraordinary. The
manuscript is full of phrases which make a scene blaze with life.
If one enjoyed a rapid railroad journey I would compare the
number and vividness of pictures your living words suggest, to
the living scenes disclosed in that way. It seems in reading a
much shorter book than it is, but it carries the mind through a
series of experiences that one would think would require a book
of three times its length.

The presentation of Tom, his place, Daisy and Jordan, and
the unfolding of their characters is unequalled so far as I know.
The description of the valley of ashes adjacent to the lovely
country, the conversation and the action in Myrtle's apartment,
the marvelous catalogue of those who came to Gatsby's house,-
these are such things as make a man famous. And all these
things, the whole pathetic episode, you have given a place in
time and space, for with the help of T. J. Eckleberg and by an
occasional glance at the sky, or the sea, or the city, you have

248

imparted a sort of sense of eternity. You once told me you were not a *natural* writer – my God! You have plainly mastered the craft, of course; but you needed far more than craftsmanship for this.[178]

Perkins's suggestion that Fitzgerald 'let the truth of some of his claims like "Oxford" and his army career come out bit by bit' called for an extension of the narrative plan already present. Fitzgerald gave Perkins too much credit for improving the novel when he wrote after publication: 'Max, it amuses me when praise comes in on the "structure" of the book – because it was you who fixed up the structure, not me.'[179] Perkins did not restructure the novel. Fitzgerald did his own work, acting on Perkins's advice.

Around 20 December while waiting for the galley proofs – which were sent from New York in two batches on 22 and 30 December – Fitzgerald wrote Perkins from Rome that he knew how to improve his novel and that he planned a virtual rewrite in proof.

With the aid you've given me I can make 'Gatsby' perfect. The chapter VII (the hotel scene) will never quite be up to mark I've worried about it too long + I can't quite place Daisy's reaction. But I can improve it a lot. It isn't imaginative energy that's lacking – it's because I'm automaticly prevented from thinking it out over again *because I must get all those characters to New York* in order to have the catastrophe on the road going back + I must have it pretty much that way. So there's no chance of bringing the freshness to it that a new free conception sometimes gives.

The rest is easy and I see my way so clear that I even see the mental quirks that queered it before. Strange to say my notion of Gatsby's vagueness was O.K. What you and Louise + Mr. Charles Scribner found wanting was that:

I myself didn't know what Gatsby looked like or was engaged in + you felt it. If I'd known + kept it from you you'd have been *too impressed with my knowledge to protest*. This is a complicated idea but I'm sure you'll understand. But I know now – and as a penalty for not having known first, in other words to make sure I'm going to tell more.*

.   .   .   .

Anyhow after careful searching of the files (of a man's mind here) for the Fuller Magee case + after having had Zelda draw pictures until her fingers ache I know Gatsby better than I know my own child. My first instinct after your letter was to let him go + have Tom Buchanan dominate the book (I suppose he's the best character I've ever done – I think he and the brother in 'Salt' + Hurstwood in 'Sister Carrie' are the three best characters in American fiction in the last twenty years, perhaps and perhaps not) but Gatsby sticks in my heart. I had him for awhile then lost him + now I know I have him again. I'm sorry Myrtle is better than Daisy. Jordan of course was a great idea (perhaps you know its Edith Cummings)† but she fades out. Its Chap VII thats the trouble with Daisy + it may hurt the book's popularity that its *a man's book.*

Anyhow I think (for the first time since The Vegetable failed) that I'm a wonderful writer + its your always wonderful letters that help me to go on believing in myself.

Now some practical, very important questions. Please answer every one.

1. Montenegro has an order called *The Order of Danilo.* Is there any possible way you could find out for me there what it would look like – whether a courtesy decoration given to an American would bear an English inscription – or anything to give versimilitude to the medal which sounds horribly amateurish.‡

2. Please have *no blurbs of any kind on the jacket*!!! No Mencken or Lewis or Sid Howard or any thing. I don't believe in them *one bit* any more.

---

* This idea anticipates Hemingway's iceberg theory of composition which asserts that an author can omit anything he knows from a story without damaging it. Using the iceberg analogy, Hemingway argued that the force of a story results from its hidden part.
† Golfer Edith Cummings was a friend of Ginevra King.
‡ The Order of Danilo medal is enameled on both sides and could not have been engraved for Gatsby.

3. Don't forget to change name of book in list of works

4. Please shift exclamation point from end of 3d line to end of 4th line in title page poem. *Please!* Important!

5. I thought that the whole episode (2 paragraphs) about their playing the Jazz History of the world at Gatsby's first party was rotten.* Did you? ... Tell me frank *reaction* – personal. don't think! We can all think![180]

This letter mentions: 'I've got a new novel to write – title and all, that'll take about a year.' Nothing further is known about the projected work.

The first batch of galley proofs was returned by Fitzgerald on 24 January 1925, and in February he reported to Perkins:

After six weeks of uninterrupted work the proof is finished and the last of it goes to you this afternoon. On the whole its been a very successful labor.

(1.) I've brought Gatsby to life
(2.) I've accounted for his money
(3.) I've fixed up the two weak chapters (VI and VII) [Gatsby's second party and the hotel confrontation]
(4.) I've improved the first party
(5.) I've broken up the long narrative in Chap. VIII [Gatsby's autobiography][181]

* Nick Carraway's account of the 'Jazz History of the World' was deleted in galley 16: 'I know so little about music that I can only make a story of it – which proves, I've been told, that it must have been low-brow stuff. I don't mean that it had lonely music for the prehistoric ages, with tiger-howls from the traps and a strain from "Onward Christian Soldiers" to mark the year 2 B.C. It wasn't like that. It started out with a weird spinning sound, mostly from the cornets. Then there would be a series of interruptive notes which colored everything that came after them, until before you knew it they became the theme and new discords were opposed outside. But just as you'd get used to the new discord one of the old themes would drop back in, this time as a discord, until you'd get a weird sense that it was a preposterous cycle, after all. Long after the piece was over it went on and on in my head – whenever I think of that summer I can hear it yet.' The typescript for *The Great Gatsby* does not survive. Fitzgerald's revised galleys are at Princeton; a set of the unrevised galleys is in the Bruccoli Collection. The manuscript is reproduced in *The Great Gatsby: A Facsimile of the Manuscript.*
Fitzgerald's revised and rewritten galleys are in the Garland Press facsimile series.

Before deciding on the Plaza Hotel for the setting of the confrontation between Gatsby and Tom Buchanan, Fitzgerald wrote scenes set at the Polo Grounds during a baseball game and in Central Park. After the chapter was finished, he continued to worry that Daisy's reactions were unclear. Every chapter was revised in proof, and Chapters VI-VIII were rewritten. The most important structural alteration was shifting parts of Gatsby's history from Chapters VII and VIII to Chapter VI, thereby eliminating his autobiographical summary in Chapter VII as Perkins had recommended. The revised galleys with typed inserts reveal that the novel achieved its structural distinction during the time Fitzgerald reworked the proof in Rome.

Fitzgerald's technique in polishing his prose is demonstrated by Nick's closing meditation, which was moved and expanded from the first chapter of the manuscript.

MS, CHAPTER I, pp. 37–38

The sense of being in an unfamiliar place deepened on me and as the moon rose higher the unessential houses seemed to melt away until I was aware of the old island here that flowered once for Dutch sailors eyes – a fresh green breast of the new world. Its vanished trees, the very trees that had made way for Gatsby's house, had once pandered in whispers to the last and greatest of all human dreams – for a transitory and enchanted moment man must have held his breath in this presense of this continent, compelled into anaesthetic contemplation he niether understood nor desired, face to face for the last time in history with something commensurate to his capacity for wonder.

Book, CHAPTER IX, pp. 217–218

Most of the big shore places were closed now and there were hardly any lights except the shadowy, moving glow of a ferryboat across the Sound. And as the moon rose higher the inessential houses began to melt away until gradually I became aware of the old island here that flowered once for Dutch sailors' eyes – a fresh, green breast of the new world. Its vanished trees, the trees that had made way for Gatsby's house, had once pandered in whispers to the last and greatest of all human dreams; for a transitory enchanted moment man must have held his breath in the presence of this continent, compelled into an aesthetic contemplation he neither understood

And as I sat there brooding on the old unknown world I too held my breath and waited, until I could feel the motion of America as it turned through the hours – my own blue lawn and the tall incandescent city on the water and beyond that the dark fields of the republic rolling on under the night.

nor desired, face to face for the last time in history with something commensurate to his capacity for wonder.

And as I sat there brooding on the old, unknown world, I thought of Gatsby's wonder when he first picked out the green light at the end of Daisy's dock. He had come a long way to this blue lawn, and his dream must have seemed so close that he could hardly fail to grasp it. He did not know that it was already behind him, somewhere back in that vast obscurity beyond the city, where the dark fields of the republic rolled on under the night.

Gatsby believed in the green light, the orgastic future that year by year recedes before us. It eluded us then, but that's no matter – tomorrow we will run faster, stretch out our arms farther. . . . And one fine morning—

So we beat on, boats against the current, borne back ceaselessly into the past.

When Perkins queried 'orgastic,' Fitzgerald replied: ' "Orgastic" is the adjective from "orgasm" and it expresses exactly the intended ecstacy.'[182] (Edmund Wilson incorrectly changed it to 'orgiastic' in 1941.)

The time required for boat mail prevented Fitzgerald from seeing the reset proofs and giving his novel a last polish. Production was rushed because editor and author wanted to publish in April. Consequently the first printing of *The Great Gatsby* included errors: for example, the reference to Dr. Eckleburg's retinas and the mislocation of the Queensboro Bridge in Astoria, as well as chronological inconsistencies.

While working on the proofs Fitzgerald explored magazine serialization with Ober. He hoped to get $15,000 or $20,000, and serialization was a way to generate interest in the book before publication. The Hearst magazines had first refusal on serial rights under the 1923 option contract, and editor Ray Long declined the novel in December. Inoffensive as the material now seems, it was regarded as too strong for magazines whose readership was largely female. Fitzgerald thought John Wheeler would take it for *Liberty*, a weekly that was spending money to build circulation; but Wheeler informed Ober: 'It is too ripe for us. Running only one serial as we do, we could not publish this story with as many mistresses and as much adultery as there is in it.'[183] In January *College Humor* offered $10,000, which Fitzgerald turned down because he didn't want to delay book publication for the five months it would take to serialize it. He was also concerned about cheapening his novel: 'Most people who saw it advertised in *College Humor* would be sure that Gatsby was a great halfback and that would kill it in book form.'[184]

After dispatching the revised proofs in February, the Fitzgeralds moved to the Hotel Tiberio on Capri to get away from the damp winter of Rome. On Capri, Zelda spent time in bed with what was variously diagnosed as colitis and an ovarian problem, which she would be troubled by for the next two years. Fitzgerald drank while Zelda took painting lessons – her first formal art instruction. He was disappointed by his meeting with a former literary idol, Compton Mackenzie,[185] whom he reproached for abandoning serious fiction. A minor story, 'Not in the Guidebook' (*Woman's Home Companion*) was sent from Capri, and the novelette 'The Rich Boy' was started there.

On 7 March, Fitzgerald cabled Perkins to ask if it was too late to change the novel's title because he wanted to revert to 'Gold-Hatted Gatsby' or 'Trimalchio.'[186] Perkins replied on 9 March: 'Title change would cause bad delay and confusion.'[187] And on the nineteenth Fitzgerald cabled again: CRAZY ABOUT TITLE UNDER THE RED WHITE AND BLUE STOP WHART WOULD DELAY BE.[188] By then it was too late.

28

The Great Gatsby

[April 1925]

After two months on Capri the Fitzgeralds left in April for Paris. As publication date approached, Fitzgerald became increasingly jittery. On 11 April, the day after publication, he cabled Perkins for ANY NEWS.[189] The best Perkins could do was to report on 20 April: 'Sales situation doubtful excellent reviews.'[190] Perkins suspected that the thin size of the 218-page novel hurt its sales. Fitzgerald had two explanations:

1st The title is only fair, rather bad than good.

2nd *And most important* – the book contains no important woman character and women controll the fiction market at present. I don't think the unhappy end matters particularly.

This April letter to Perkins concluded with a depressed self-assessment: 'In all events I have a book of good stories for the fall. Now I shall write some cheap ones until I've accumulated enough for my next novel. When that is finished and published I'll wait and see. If it will support me with no more intervals of trash I'll go on as a novelist. If not, I'm going to quit, come home, go to Hollywood and learn the movie business. I can't reduce our scale of living and I can't stand this financial insecurity. Anyhow there's no point in trying to be an artist if you can't do your best. I had my chance back in 1920 to start my life on a sensible scale and I lost it and so I'll have to pay the penalty. Then perhaps at 40 I can start writing again without this constant worry and interruption.'[191] *The Great Gatsby* was published at $2 in a first printing of 20,870 copies. It was dedicated ONCE AGAIN TO ZELDA. A second printing of 3,000 copies was ordered in August, and some of these copies were still in Scribners' warehouse when Fitzgerald died.* At a 15 percent royalty, the first printing earned $6,261, canceling Fitzgerald's $6,000 debt to Scribners.

The reviews of *The Great Gatsby* were the best for any of Fitzgerald's books, although a few critics thought it was just a sensational story. Gilbert Seldes's outstanding *Dial* review did not appear until August: 'Fitzgerald has more than matured; he has mastered his talents and gone soaring in a beautiful flight, leaving behind him everything dubious and tricky in his earlier work, and leaving even farther behind all the men of his own generation and most of his elders.'[192] Other receptive reviews were written by William Rose Benet in *The Saturday Review of Literature*, Laurence Stallings in the *New York World*, Herbert S. Gorman in the *New York Sun*, and Harry Hansen in the *Chicago Daily News*. Especially gratifying were the letters of congratulation that came from writers Fitzgerald respected: Willa Cather, Edith Wharton, and T. S. Eliot – who declared, 'In fact it seems to me to be the first step American fiction has taken since Henry James.'[193] (Fitzgerald had sent Eliot a copy of *The Great Gatsby* inscribed to the 'Greatest of Living Poets from his enthusiastic worshipper.')[194] H. L. Mencken's long review in the *Baltimore Sun* dismissed the story as 'a glorified anecdote' but praised 'the

---

* The ten best-selling novels of 1925 were *Soundings* by A. Hamilton Gibbs, *The Constant Nymph* by Margaret Kennedy, *The Keeper of the Bees* by Gene Stratton Porter, *Glorious Apollo* by E. Barrington, *The Green Hat* by Michael Arlen, *The Little French Girl* by Anne Douglas Sedgwick, *Arrowsmith* by Sinclair Lewis, *The Perennial Bachelor* by Anne Parish, *The Carolinian* by Rafael Sabatini, and *Our Increasing Purpose* by A. S. M. Hutchinson. Lewis's three novels published in the same years as *This Side of Paradise, The Beautiful and Damned*, and *The Great Gatsby* vastly outsold Fitzgerald's novels.

charm and beauty of the writing' as well as Fitzgerald's social accuracy.[195] Fitzgerald responded to Mencken: 'I think the smooth, almost unbroken pattern makes you feel that. . . . It is in protest against my own formless two novels, and Lewis' and Dos Passos' that this was written.'[196]

Fitzgerald believed that the flaw in *The Great Gatsby* was the missing sequence he had told Perkins about in September 1924. He admitted to Wilson: 'The worst fault in it, I think is a BIG FAULT: I gave no account (and had no feeling about or knowledge of) the emotional relations between Gatsby and Daisy from the time of their reunion to the catastrophe. However the lack is so astutely concealed by the retrospect of Gatsby's past and by blankets of excellent prose that no one has noticed it – tho everyone has felt the lack and called it by another name.'[197]

The Great Gatsby marked an advance in every way over Fitzgerald's previous work. If he could develop so rapidly in the five years since *This Side of Paradise*, if he could write so brilliantly before he was thirty, his promise seemed boundless. Instead of addressing the reader, as he had done in *The Beautiful and Damned*, Fitzgerald utilized the resources of style to convey the meanings of *The Great Gatsby*. The values of the story are enhanced through imagery as detail is used with poetic effect. Thus the description of the Buchanans' house reveals how Fitzgerald's images stimulate the senses: 'The lawn started at the beach and ran toward the front door for a quarter of a mile, jumping over sun-dials and brick walks and burning gardens – finally when it reached the house drifting up the side in bright vines as though from the momentum of its run.'[198] In his richest prose there is an impression of movement; here the lawn runs, jumps, and drifts. Again and again, sentences are made memorable by a single word – often a color word, as in 'now the orchestra is playing yellow cocktail music.'[199]

The technique in *Gatsby* is scenic and symbolic. There are scenes and descriptions that have become touchstones of American prose: the first description of Daisy and Jordan,

Gatsby's party, Myrtle's apartment, the shirt display, the guest list, Nick's recollection of the Midwest. Within these scenes Fitzgerald endows details with so much suggestiveness that they acquire the symbolic force to extend the meanings of the story. Gatsby's car 'was a rich cream color, bright with nickel, swollen here and there in its monstrous length with triumphant hatboxes and supper-boxes and tool-boxes, and terraced with a labyrinth of wind-shields that mirrored a dozen suns.'[200] Its ostentation expresses Gatsby's gorgeous vulgarity. There is something overstated about everything he owns, and Daisy recognizes the fraudulence of his attempt to imitate the style of wealth. His car, which Tom Buchanan calls a 'circus wagon,' becom the 'death-car.'

Jimmy Gatz/Jay Gatsby confuses the values of love with the buying power of money. He is sure that with money he can do anything – even repeat the past. Despite his prodigious faith in money, Gatsby does not know how it works in society and cannot comprehend the arrogance of the rich who have been rich for generations. As a novelist of manners Fitzgerald was fascinated by class stratification, which he perceived from a privileged outsider's angle. In *The Great Gatsby* social commentary is achieved by economy of means as detail is made to serve the double function of documentation and connotation. The 595-word guest list for Gatsby's parties provides an incremental litany of the second-rate people who used Gatsby's house for an amusement park:

> Clarence Endive was from East Egg, as I remember. He came only once, in white knickerbockers, and had a fight with a bum named Etty in the garden. From farther out on the Island came the Cheadles and the O. R. P. Schraeders, and the Stonewall Jackson Abrams of Georgia, and the Fishguards and the Ripley Snells. Snell was there three days before he went to the penitentiary, so drunk out on the gravel drive that Mrs. Ulysses Swett's automobile ran over his right hand. The Dancies came, too, and S. B. Whitebait, who was well over sixty, and Maurice A. Flink, and the Hammerheads, and Beluga the tobacco importer, and Beluga's girls.

The Great Gatsby [April 1925]

The inventory ends with Nick's understated summation: 'All these people came to Gatsby's house in the summer.'[201]

This famous catalog is the most brilliant expression of Fitzgerald's list-making habit. He compiled chronological lists of girls, football players, songs, and even of the snubs he had suffered. One of his major resources as a social historian was his ability to make details evoke the moods, the sensations, and the rhythms associated with a specific time and place. Fitzgerald referred to the 'hauntedness' in *The Great Gatsby*.[202] He was haunted by lost time and borrowed time.

Much of the endurance of *The Great Gatsby* results from its investigation of the American Dream as Fitzgerald enlarged an Horatio Alger story into a meditation on the New World myth. He was profoundly moved by the innocence and generosity he perceived in American history – what he would refer to as 'a willingness of the heart.'[203] Gatsby becomes an archetypal figure who betrays and is betrayed by the promises of America. The reverberations of the fable still echo.

The greatest advance of *The Great Gatsby* over his previous novels is structural. Fitzgerald's narrative control solved the problem of making the mysterious – almost preposterous – Jay Gatsby convincing by letting the truth about him emerge gradually during the course of the novel. Employing a method he learned from reading Joseph Conrad, Fitzgerald constructed Nick Carraway as the partially involved narrator who is reluctantly compelled to judgment. Everything that happens in the novel is filtered through Nick's perceptions, thereby combining the effect of first-person immediacy with authorial perspective. As Carraway remarks, 'I was within and without, simultaneously enchanted and repelled by the inexhaustible variety of life.'[204] This sense of perspective became one of the distinguishing qualities of Fitzgerald's finest fiction.

Fitzgerald accurately gauged his achievement in *The Great Gatsby* and resolved to build on it: '*Gatsby* was far from perfect in many ways but all in all it contains such prose as has never been written in America before. From that I take heart. From that I take heart and hope that some day I can combine the verve of *Paradise*, the unity of the *Beautiful and Damned* and the lyric quality of *Gatsby*, its aesthetic soundness, into something worthy of the admiration of those few—.'[205]

THE
DRUNKARD'S
HOLIDAY

[1925–1931]

29

Paris and Ernest Hemingway

[Spring 1925]

Despite the parties and the drinking and the marital upset Fitzgerald accomplished an impressive amount of work during his first six years as a professional writer – three novels, a play, forty-one stories, and twenty-seven articles or reviews, as well as movie scenarios. This was the most productive period of his life. After 1925 it became increasingly difficult for him to devote consecutive months to writing.

That spring in Paris the Fitzgeralds rented a furnished apartment at 14 rue de Tilsitt on the Right Bank at the corner of the avenue Wagram near the Arc de Triomphe. The fifth-floor walk-up was a gloomy place, full of imitation eighteenth-century furniture, and as usual there were servant problems. All their Paris apartments proved to be unsatisfactory. Fitzgerald wanted to leave one immediately after moving in when he detected nasal mucus on the wallpaper, but Zelda said that hygiene did not matter in Paris because no one stayed home there. Fitzgerald took a studio nearby to write in but does not appear to have used it.

One of Fitzgerald's first projects in Paris was to locate

Ernest Hemingway. The meeting took place at the Dingo bar on the rue Delambre in Montparnasse sometime before 1 May. The only record of their first encounter is in Hemingway's *A Moveable Feast* – written some thirty-two years after the event – which portrays Fitzgerald as a fool, a nuisance, and a hopeless drunk. As reported by Hemingway, Fitzgerald embarrassed him by praising his work, asking personal questions ('Did you sleep with your wife before you were married?'), and passing out.* From the start of their friendship the famous and successful Fitzgerald was intimidated by Hemingway, the twenty-six-year-old apprentice. He was impressed by Hemingway's talent and awed by his inflated reputation as a war hero and athlete. Fitzgerald's regret at having missed battle was exacerbated by what he believed was Hemingway's record as a combat veteran. His response to Hemingway was not unusual: early and late Hemingway had the ability to charm and dominate; and the Hemingway legend was already forming in 1925.

Fitzgerald was disappointed to learn that Hemingway had signed a three-book option with Boni & Liveright for publication of his short-story volume *In Our Time* (1925), which seemed to end the possibility of bringing him to Scribners. At that time Hemingway was living on the Left Bank with his first wife, Hadley, and their son, who was called Bumby. Their poverty has been exaggerated by Hemingway. Hadley had a modest income, and they were not dependent on his meager earnings from the little magazines after he gave up journalism.

After a subsequent meeting at the Closerie des Lilas café convinced him that Fitzgerald could behave properly, Hemingway accepted an invitation to go to Lyon for the

---

* *A Moveable Feast* stipulates that Fitzgerald came to the Dingo with Princetonian Duncan Chaplin, thereby providing another witness to Fitzgerald's conduct. But Chaplin was not in Europe in 1925.[1] Hemingway's statements about Fitzgerald are not always reliable; and it is well to keep in mind Hemingway's warning in *A Moveable Feast*: 'If the reader prefers, this book may be regarded as fiction. But there is always the chance that such a book of fiction may throw some light on what has been written as fact.'[2]

Fitzgeralds' Renault, which had been left there for repair. The Lyon excursion turned into a series of annoyances for Hemingway, who nursed Fitzgerald through hypochondria and alcoholic misconduct. Hemingway blended facts and malice; but his account of the trip is partly documented by his wire from Lyon: SCOTT MISSED TRAIN.[3] A few days later Fitzgerald gave Hemingway *The Great Gatsby*: 'When I had finished the book I knew that no matter what Scott did, nor how he behaved, I must know it was like a sickness and be of any help I could to him and try to be a good friend.'[4]

When Hemingway met Zelda there was instant mutual antipathy. He thought she was crazy and told Fitzgerald so. Hemingway believed that Zelda was jealous of Fitzgerald's work and that she fostered his drinking in order to interfere with his writing. Another of Hemingway's charges against Zelda was that she sought out lesbian company in Paris as a way to impede Fitzgerald's work: 'Scott was afraid for her to pass out in the company they kept that spring and the places they went to. . . . Zelda did not encourage the people who were chasing her and she had nothing to do with them, she said. But it amused her and it made Scott jealous and he had to go with her to the places. It destroyed his work, and she was more jealous of his work than anything.'[5] Zelda's reaction to Hemingway was that he was a phony – 'a materialistic mystic,' 'a professional he-man,' 'a pansy with hair on his chest.'[6] Fitzgerald summarized June and July in his *Ledger* as '1000 parties and no work.'

Hemingway's mixture of affection and condescension toward Fitzgerald is shown in a letter written on 1 July 1925 from Spain while he was en route to the Fiesta of San Fermín at Pamplona that would provide the material for *The Sun Also Rises*:

> I wonder what your idea of heaven would be – A beautiful vacuum filled with wealthy monogamists all powerful and members of the best families all drinking themselves to death. And hell would probably be an ugly vacuum full of poor polygamists unable to obtain booze or with chronic stomach disorders that they called secret sorrows.
>
> To me heaven would be a big bull ring with me holding two

> barrera seats and a trout stream outside that no one else was
> allowed to fish in and two lovely houses in the town; one where
> I have my wife and children and be monogamous and love
> them truly and well and the other where I would have my nine
> beautiful mistresses. . . . I would write out at the Hacienda and
> send my son in to lock the chastity belts onto my mistresses
> because someone had just galloped up with the news that a
> notorious monogamist named Fitzgerald had been seen riding
> toward the town at the head of a company of strolling
> drinkers.[7]

This first surviving letter between them is a checklist of the
Hemingway tests that Fitzgerald had failed – indicating that
Fitzgerald was a bad drinker, sexually inexperienced, and
dazzled by money.

In July, Edith Wharton invited the Fitzgeralds to tea at her
Pavillon Colombe, fourteen miles outside Paris. She had
acknowledged receipt of an inscribed copy of *The Great Gatsby*
in June, congratulating Fitzgerald on its great advance over
his previous work but regretting that he had not filled in
Gatsby's career: 'That would have situated him, + made his
final tragedy a tragedy instead of a "fait divers" for the
morning papers – '[8] Zelda declined the invitation, saying she
did not want to be patronized by a grande dame. Fitzgerald
went with Theodore Chanler, a young American composer.
Stephan Parrott, who had taken up residence in Paris, was
also invited but did not attend. A break in the Fitzgerald-
Parrott friendship had occurred, and it was never mended.
Although Fitzgerald inscribed a copy of a portrait of himself
to Parrott 'from his brother' after 1920,[9] the real basis of their
friendship had been Father Fay's affection for both his
protégés.

The widely disseminated story of Fitzgerald's visit to Mrs.
Wharton has it that he arrived drunk and tried to shock her
by announcing that he and his wife had lived for two weeks in
a Paris brothel; when Mrs. Wharton squelched him,
Fitzgerald is supposed to have fled back to Paris and
confessed to Zelda, 'They beat me! They beat me! They *beat*

Stephen Parrot
for his brother
F. Scott Fitzgerald

Gordon Bryant
Aug. 1924

Portrait by Gordon Bryant

me!' This account requires correction.* Chanler's eyewitness
report is that Fitzgerald was not drunk, although he had
stopped for wine on the way. Fitzgerald tried to make
conversation with Mrs. Wharton through his usual ploy of
complimenting her, but she would not play along with him.
Because the gathering was so dull, Fitzgerald asked
permission to tell an anecdote about an American couple who
had mistakenly spent their first Paris days in a brothel.
Apparently missing the point of the story, Mrs. Wharton
asked what they did there. Chanler's summary is that Edith
Wharton's 'unyielding formality and stiffness might have
driven him to this desperate conversational measure even
without the help of alcohol.' Fitzgerald had been trying to
make her dull party go better. 'I cannot of course say whether
or not he made the remark "She beat me" on his return. But it
seems most likely that this is someone's invention. On the way
back to Paris he showed no sign of feeling squelched, or that
the failure of the occasion was due to him rather than to Mrs.
Wharton.'[10]

By 1 May, while his disappointment with the sales of *Gatsby*
was still fresh, Fitzgerald sent Perkins an ambitious
announcement: 'The happiest thought I have is of my new
novel – it is something really NEW in form, idea, structure –
the model for the age that Joyce and Stien are searching for,
that Conrad didn't find.'[11] And on 4 May Fitzgerald wrote
Mencken that his new novel would be about himself:
'Moreover it will have the most amazing form ever
invented.'[12] These statements of purpose expressed his new
concern with form and structure that developed from his
work on *The Great Gatsby*. The title for the novel was 'Our
Type'; but he probably did not have a clear plan until August
1925, when the *Ledger* notes 'Concieve novel.' The only

* Esther Murphy appears to have circulated this distorted version, but she
was not present. The first publication of the story in *The Far Side of Paradise*
cites the source as Richard Knight – who also was not there. Knight was an
eccentric friend of Zelda's, a disbarred lawyer who died under mysterious
circumstances.

writing Fitzgerald did in spring–summer 1925 was on the novelette 'The Rich Boy,' which he had brought with him from Capri. One of Fitzgerald's major stories – probably his best story – 'The Rich Boy' is an extension of *The Great Gatsby*, enlarging the examination of the effects of wealth on character: 'Let me tell you about the very rich. They are different from you and me. They possess and enjoy early, and it does something to them, makes them soft where we are hard, and cynical where we are trustful, in a way that, unless you were born rich, it is very hard to understand. They think, deep in their hearts, that they are better than we are because we had to discover the compensations and refuges of life for ourselves. Even when they enter deep into our world or sink below us, they still think they are better than we are. They are different.'[13]

The model for Anson Hunter was Fitzgerald's Princeton classmate and best man, Ludlow Fowler. Fitzgerald alerted Fowler: 'I have written a fifteen thousand-word story about you called *The Rich Boy** – it is so disguised that no one except you and me and maybe two of the girls concerned would recognize, unless you give it away, but it is in large measure the story of your life, toned down here and there and symplified. Also many gaps had to come out of my imagination. It is frank, unsparing but sympathetic and I think you will like it – it is one of the best things I have ever done.'[15] Fitzgerald gave Fowler the opportunity to read the story before it was published, and Fowler asked for cuts that were not made until it was collected in *All the Sad Young Men*.†

'The Rich Boy' is a key document for understanding

---

* 'The Rich Boy' had started as a regulation-length magazine story, but on 13 April 1925 Fitzgerald wrote Ober that he was stretching it into a 'three parter.'[14]

† Fowler's list of alterations does not survive; but he probably asked Fitzgerald to delete two anecdotes about Anson Hunter's drinking and womanizing that appear on page 144 of the first *Redbook* installment. There are more than 500 substantive changes between publication of the story in *Redbook* and *All the Sad Young Men*. In general, the effect of Fitzgerald's revisions was to make Anson more self-centered and Paula more appealing.[16]

Fitzgerald's much-discussed and much-misunderstood attitudes toward the rich. He was not an envious admirer of the rich who believed they possessed a special glamour. In 1938 he observed: 'That was always my experience – a poor boy in a rich town; a poor boy in a rich boy's school; a poor boy in a rich man's club at Princeton. . . . I have never been able to forgive the rich for being rich, and it has colored my entire life and works.'[17] But his feelings were more complex than this statement indicates. He knew that the lives of the rich had greater possibilities, but he recognized that they failed to use these possibilities fully. He also perceived that money corrupts the will to excellence. Believing that work is the only dignity (even though he could not live up to that doctrine), he condemned the self-indulgent rich for wasting the freedom of wealth. Fitzgerald admired the rich only at their best – exemplified for him by the Murphys – when leisure was combined with charm and culture. The world of the well-to-do provided him with material he could respond to from the perspective of a privileged outsider – the man who didn't fully belong. The narrator of 'The Rich Boy' – another outsider – concludes: 'I don't think he was ever happy unless some one was in love with him, responding to him like filings to a magnet, helping him to explain himself, promising him something. What it was I do not know. Perhaps they promised him that there would always be women in the world who would spend their brightest, freshest, rarest hours to nurse and protect that superiority he cherished in his heart.'[18]

Fitzgerald's judgments on the rich were complicated by his attitudes toward his own money, which he could never manage. He knew what money could buy – even more than luxury, a fuller life with time to write. He would have subscribed to Somerset Maugham's pronouncement that money is the sixth sense without which the other five senses cannot be used properly. Yet it is not entirely paradoxical that he threw his money away. His carelessness with money expressed his superiority to it. If he could waste it, then it didn't own him. The inevitable result was that he was in bondage to it after all because he had to earn the money he was squandering. The illusions attendant upon love and money – which went together – were Fitzgerald's material. A writer does not really choose his themes. With luck and talent he treats his material more profoundly as he develops, but the themes do not change.

At the time 'The Rich Boy' appeared in the January and February 1926 issues of *Redbook* (which paid $3,500 after the *Post* declined it), Ring Lardner expressed regret that Fitzgerald had not expanded it into a novel. Fitzgerald insisted that 'The Rich Boy' had come to him in the form of a story and that it would have been impossible for him to extend it. This explanation is not entirely convincing. The long story is written novelistically, employing the partially involved narrator Fitzgerald had developed in *The Great Gatsby*; but the writing stretched out over four or five months, during which he was drinking heavily and working with many interruptions (one of which was for 'A Penny Spent,' a *Post* story written in July). If he had been writing under more orderly conditions, the 17,000-word novelette might have evolved into a *Gatsby*-length novel of 50,000 words and reinforced the critical respect *The Great Gatsby* had elicited. Instead, nine years elapsed before Fitzgerald had another novel in the bookstores.

The Collins contract for *This Side of Paradise* granted first-refusal rights for British publication of Fitzgerald's subsequent books; they had published *Flappers and Philosophers*, *The Beautiful and Damned*, and *Tales of the Jazz Age*. None of these books sold well, although the two novels did better than the story collections. Collins declined *The Great Gatsby*, which was published by Chatto & Windus in 1926.* The novel was not a success, although it elicited some of the best reviews Fitzgerald received in England. The *Times Literary Supplement* called it 'undoubtedly a work of art and of great promise,'

* T. S. Eliot, an editor at Faber, had hoped his firm could publish the novel in England.

271

commending the structure but complaining about the unpleasantness of the characters.[19] In the *New Criterion* American poet Conrad Aiken praised the characters and 'excellence of form' but expressed concern that Fitzgerald would be spoiled by commercial work: 'If only he can refrain altogether in future from the sham romanticism and sham sophistication which the magazines demand of him, and give another turn of the screw to the care with which he writes, he may well become a first-rate writer.'[20] English critics and readers did not respond to the American themes of the novel. Gatsby's American dreams were not yet exportable.

During June 1925 Fitzgerald began selecting stories for his third collection, which had to be held up until 'The Rich Boy' appeared in *Redbook*. *All the Sad Young Men*, published by Scribners on 26 February 1926, was Fitzgerald's strongest collection, with four major stories ('The Rich Boy,' 'Winter Dreams,' 'Absolution,' and ' "The Sensible Thing" ') as well as five commercial stories ('The Baby Party,' 'Rags Martin-Jones and the Pr-nce of W-les,' 'The Adjuster,' 'Hot and Cold Blood,' and 'Gretchen's Forty Winks'). The volume was dedicated TO RING AND ELLIS LARDNER. As was his custom, Fitzgerald polished the magazine texts of these stories. He was convinced that the book publication of stories affected his reputation, whereas the magazine appearances were ignored by critics. A particular concern was to remove from the stories any passages that had been incorporated into *The Great Gatsby*, for he believed that it was dishonest to use the same phrases in different books.

All the Sad Young Men was successful for a story volume – three printings and 16,170 copies in 1926, which brought $3,894. There was no British edition. The reviewers were for the most part friendly, with the warmest praise appearing in an unsigned *Bookman* review: 'As F. Scott Fitzgerald continues to publish books, it becomes apparent that he is head and shoulders better than any writer of his generation.'[21] Yet the critics did not realize just how good the best stories were, and 'The Rich Boy' was not singled out for admiration.

30

Paris and Antibes

[Spring–Summer 1925]

Hemingway was well connected in the Paris expatriate literary colony and introduced Fitzgerald to some of the American writers living on the Left Bank. Fitzgerald went with Hemingway to 27 rue de Fleurus to meet Gertrude Stein, whom he charmed. She regarded Fitzgerald as the most promising of the young American novelists and delivered her pronouncement on *The Great Gatsby*.

Here we are and have read your book and it is a good book. I like the melody of your dedication it shows that you have a background of beauty and tenderness and that is a comfort. The next good thing is that you write naturally in sentences and that too is a comfort. You write naturally in sentences and one can read all of them and that among other things is a comfort. You are creating the modern world much as Thackeray did his in Pendennis and Vanity Fair and this isn't a bad compliment. You make a modern world and a modern orgy strangely enough it was never done until you did it in This Side of Paradise. My belief in This Side of Paradise was alright. This is as good a book and different and older and that is what one does, one does not get better but different and older and that is always a pleasure.[22]

273

Alice B. Toklas, Stein's companion, has reported a 1926 meeting: 'He was distinguished, highly intelligent and completely attaching. He came to see G.S. on his thirtieth birthday and said it was unbearable for him to have to face the fact that his youth was over. But you've been writing like a man of 30, she said. Have I, he said questioningly. He never believed what she told him about his work. It was too comforting to be true.'[23] Although Fitzgerald was intrigued by Stein and flattered by her praise, he did not become a disciple of her theories or a member of her coterie. He felt that *Three Lives* was a solid achievement, but that her later books were 'coo-coo.'

Fitzgerald probably met Robert McAlmon through Hemingway or Stein. McAlmon was an American writer and proprietor of Contact Editions, a Paris imprint that published expatriate writers – including himself. He envied the success of Fitzgerald and Hemingway, and later spread gossip about them culminating in the fabrication that they were homosexuals. Fitzgerald tried to rehabilitate Harold Stearns, the editor of *Civilization in the United States*, who was permanently drunk in Paris, although Hemingway warned him that nothing could be done about Stearns. He became friendly with Sylvia Beach, whose Shakespeare & Co. bookshop on the rue de l'Odéon in Montparnasse was a gathering place for American writers. Except for virtually mandatory contacts such as with Stein and Beach, Fitzgerald did not participate in the expatriate literary life. He wrote nothing for the little magazines and remained indifferent to the Paris movements and schools. By the time he arrived in Paris his own techniques and subjects were fully developed; and he was beyond writing experimental pieces for the pleasure of seeing them printed.

Scottie, now four, was left largely to the care of nannies, but Fitzgerald was a concerned father. He made sure that her nannies were good to her, and he spent time with her. One of his amusements was to work up routines in which she played the straight man. Fitzgerald: 'Do you know the story of the dirty shirt?' Scottie: 'No, I don't. What is it?' Fitzgerald: 'That's one on you!' Later in Paris he spent hours staging battles with the soldiers he avidly collected at the Nain Bleu toyshop – with Scottie on the losing side. Agincourt was his favorite battle. Zelda was bored by the chores of motherhood, but when her imagination was captured she devoted a good deal of effort to projects for Scottie – toy castles, playhouses, and elaborate Christmas trees. Both parents were careful to prevent their domestic discord from reaching Scottie, and she was untouched by their marital conflicts. It was not until she was an adolescent that Scottie understood her father was an alcoholic.

Believing that his mother's indulgence had weakened his character, Fitzgerald was a strict parent. Speaking through Dick Diver in *Tender Is the Night*, he observed: ' "Either one learns politeness at home . . . or the world teaches it to you with a whip and you may get hurt in the process. What do I care whether Topsy 'adores' me or not? I'm not bringing her up to be my wife." '[24] But he was not a severe disciplinarian, and Scottie was rarely punished. A toy gendarme from Nain Bleu was employed to serve as the intermediary in discipline. Once when Scottie had been sent to her room without toys or books, Fitzgerald caught her reading a popular French children's work, *Jean Qui Grogne et Jean Qui Rit*. Instead of administering the threatened spanking, he became so interested in the book's illustrations that he made Scottie read it aloud to him in English.

One of the Paris anecdotes about Fitzgerald was that he had insisted on being served a club sandwich at Voisin, an elegant restaurant.[25] The point of this story – that he remained a tourist – was largely true. Fitzgerald never felt at home in France as the Murphys and Hemingways did in their different ways. He spoke restaurant French, and he was indifferent to the music and art of Paris. He knew French literature only in translation, and Proust became his most admired French writer. He retained a streak of xenophobia, suspecting that the French shopkeepers and servants he dealt with were trying to cheat him. His favorite resorts were the American bars of the Right Bank. The Fitzgeralds liked to go out at night and apparently ate at home only reluctantly. In addition to their almost obligatory appearances at the Left Bank cafés (the Dôme, the Coupole, the Sélect, Lipp's, the Deux Magots, and the Closerie des Lilas), the Fitzgeralds frequented the cabarets of Montmartre. They became favorite patrons at Bricktop's, a nightclub presided over by a Black American singer, who later claimed that she took protective custody over Fitzgerald's money when he flashed a large roll. The Fitzgeralds were also regulars at Zelli's and le Perroquet. Legend has it that one night they jumped into the pool at the Lido cabaret. Once Fitzgerald commandeered a three-wheeled delivery cart and rode it around the Place de la Concorde pursued by two gendarmes on bikes. It is impossible to document all the stunts they were credited with; escapades were assigned to them because they were the sort of thing the Fitzgeralds might have done. Fitzgerald drank at the Ritz and Crillon bars, which were patronized by wealthy Americans. He often lunched at Ciro's, la Reine Pédauque, and Foyot, and liked to dine at the Trianon on the Left Bank because it was James Joyce's favorite restaurant. No matter how favorable the rate of exchange was, a good deal of his money simply vanished during riotous nights. He was a generous tipper and the size of his tips increased with his alcoholic intake.

Fitzgerald did not reserve part of every day for writing, usually working in concentrated bursts when a story had to be finished. In Paris his routine was to rise at 11 in the morning and try to start writing at 5 P.M. He claimed that he worked intermittently until 3:30 A.M., but too often his nights were spent on the town. In 'Babylon Revisited' Fitzgerald has Charles Wales reassess his Paris nights:

> All the catering to vice and waste was on an utterly childish
> scale, and he suddenly realized the meaning of the word
> 'dissipate' – to dissipate into thin air; to make nothing out of

something. In the little hours of the night every move from place to place was an enormous human jump, an increase of paying for the privilege of slower and slower motion.

He remembered thousand-franc notes given to an orchestra for playing a single number, hundred-franc notes tossed to a doorman for calling a cab.

But it hadn't been given for nothing.

It had been given, even the most wildly squandered sum, as an offering to destiny that he might not remember the things most worth remembering. . . . [26]

When Fitzgerald went pub-crawling by himself, it was sometimes hard to terminate his revels. William L. Shirer has reported a night when Fitzgerald showed up drunk at the *Paris Tribune* around midnight, where he sat at the copy desk and ripped up copy. He sang and insisted that the reporters join in. Shirer, James Thurber, and Eugene Jolas tried to take him home, but Fitzgerald insisted on touring the bars. When he passed out, they delivered him to the rue de Tilsitt, where he refused to go in and fought with the three of them until they carried him into his apartment.[27] The wonder of this account and similar ones is that the people who had to handle a drunken Fitzgerald usually forgave his misconduct. His talent and charm often rescued him from the social morasses he created.

Even if Fitzgerald did not take to the French, he enjoyed the stimulation of Paris and the beauty of the Riviera. Moreover, France seemed populated by interesting Americans. In Fitzgerald's fiction France is a place where Americans deteriorate or sometimes demonstrate their superiority over the natives. The chief contribution to his writing from his residence abroad was a new perspective on American character. Unlike fashionable expatriates who sneered at American vulgarity, Fitzgerald found that France intensified his identification with his native land.

In August 1925 the Fitzgeralds joined the Murphys at Cap d'Antibes, where they probably stayed at the Hotel du Cap. Fitzgerald wrote to Bishop in September: 'I'm crazy to see your novel. I'm starting a new one myself. There was no one at Antibes this summer except me, Zelda, the Valentino, the Murphy's, Mistinguet, Rex Ingram, Dos Passos, Alice Terry, the Mclieshes, Charlie Bracket, Maude Kahn, Esther Murphy, Marguerite Namara, E. Phillips Openhiem, Mannes the violinist, Floyd Dell, Max and Chrystal Eastman, ex-Premier Orlando, Ettienne de Beaumont – just a real place to rough it, an escape from all the world.'[28] As he later wrote, 'One could get away with more on the summer Riviera, and whatever happened seemed to have something to do with art.'[29] To be included in the Murphys' Riviera life was to be admitted to a world of elaborately simple pleasures. When

Fitzgerald and Scottie on the Riviera

Scottie said she wanted to marry him, Gerald Murphy staged a grand mock wedding. In *Tender Is the Night* Fitzgerald evoked the Murphys' hospitality as an incantation: 'Just for a moment they seemed to speak to everyone at the table, singly and together, assuring them of their friendliness, their affection. And for a moment the faces turned up toward them were like the faces of poor children at a Christmas tree. Then abruptly the table broke up – the moment when the guests had been daringly lifted above conviviality into the rarer atmosphere of sentiment, was over before it could be irreverently breathed, before they had half realized it was there.'[30]

The strong affection between the Murphys and Fitzgeralds is documented by Gerald's September letter to the Fitzgeralds after they had left the Riviera:

> There *really* was a great sound of tearing heard in the land as your train pulled out that day. Sara and I rode back together saying things about you both to each other which only partly expressed what we felt separately. Ultimately, I suppose, one must judge the degree of one's love for a person by the hush and the emptiness that descends upon the day, – after the departure. We heard the tearing because it was there, – and because we were'nt able to talk much about how much we do love you two. We agreed that it made us very sad, and sort of hurt a little – for a 'summer holiday.'
>
> Most people are dull, without distinction and without value, even *humanly*, – I believe (even in the depths of my expansive Irish heart). For Sara most people are guilty of the above until they are proved innocent. All this one can believe without presumption or personal vanity, – and the proof that it's true is found for me in the fact that you two belong so irrevocably to that rare race of people who are *valuable*. As yet in this world we have found four. One only *really* loves what is rare and valuable to one, in spite of the fact that one loves first.
>
> We four communicate by our presence rather than any means: so that where we meet and when will never count. Currents race between us regardless: Scott will uncover for me values in Sara, just as Sara has known them in Zelda through her affection for Scott.[31]

At this time Zelda became interested in resuming her ballet training – after at least a seven-year interruption. The Murphys recommended their daughter Honoria's Paris teacher, Lubov Egorova, but it has not been determined when Zelda began working with her.

One of Fitzgerald's intellectual enthusiasms was behaviorism, a physiological approach to human adjustments. (He may have acquired this interest through Mencken, who admired behaviorism.) Fitzgerald sent Judge Sayre an inscribed copy of John B. Watson's *Behaviorism* (1925): 'Since Europe in its exhaustion and political disillusion has been looking toward us for ideas our paucity in that regard has become particularly apparent. In fact the only American idea treated there with any respect or attention is Behaviorism, of which this book is the statement and the bible. With all its rawness and arrogance it is quite able to speak for itself – and has I believe been hurt by being confused with the various bastard sciences that have sprung from Freud. I'll be so interested to hear your reactions to it.'[32] Behaviorism did not influence Fitzgerald's work; his inscription seems to have been mainly prompted by a desire to impress the Judge with his seriousness.

31

Paris and Planning a Fourth Novel

[Fall 1925–Spring 1926]

The novel Fitzgerald planned in the summer of 1925 was about a young American traveling in France with his mother, whom he would murder. On 28 August, Fitzgerald informed Perkins: '*Our Type* is about several things, one of which is an intellectual murder on the Leopold-Loeb idea. Incidently it is about Zelda + me + the hysteria of last May + June in Paris. (Confidential).'[33] Other sources for the novel were Dorothy Ellingson, a San Francisco girl who murdered her mother in 1925; Dreiser's *An American Tragedy* (1925); and the appearance of Walker Ellis – Fitzgerald's collaborator on *Fie! Fie! Fi-Fi!* – on the Riviera. After a brilliant Princeton career and a degree from Harvard Law School, Ellis had abandoned the law for acting, at which he did not succeed. Fitzgerald saw Ellis as a case history in deterioration. Theodore Chanler, Fitzgerald's companion on the visit to Edith Wharton, was another source for the novel. Having grown dissatisfied with the irregularity of his life in France, Chanler decided to break with his friends. When Fitzgerald heard about it, he spoke of Chanler as the basis for a novel about a talented young American who is taken up by a charming expatriate group and undergoes a breakdown.

Actual writing on the novel probably did not commence until 1926. The earliest surviving drafts are the manuscripts and typescripts for parts of three chapters.* The protagonist is Francis Melarky, a twenty-one-year-old Southerner traveling in Europe with his domineering mother. The novel opens with their arrival on the Riviera, by which time Francis has been beaten by the police because of a drunken brawl in Rome. Before that he had been dismissed from West Point and had worked as a technician in Hollywood, where he had gotten into unspecified trouble. Francis has a quick temper, which his mother triggers by her efforts to control his life.

On the Riviera, Francis is taken up by an American couple, Seth and Dinah Roreback (who are also named Rorebeck and Piper). The Rorebacks' closest friend is Abe Herkimer, an alcoholic composer. Francis and Abe serve as seconds in a duel between Gabriel Brugerol and writer Albert McKisco. The Rorebacks invite Francis to Paris to see Abe off for America. In Paris, Francis falls in love with Dinah, who does not encourage his passion. At this point, the early drafts break off, but Fitzgerald's plan was to have Francis suffer an alcoholic breakdown and murder his mother. The drafts offer no indication of insanity in Dinah; this element would not be introduced into the novel until after 1930. Although Fitzgerald had told Perkins and Mencken that his novel would be structurally innovative, the early drafts are written in straightforward third-person narrative. The connections between this material and *Tender Is the Night* are obvious: the Rorebacks (based on the Murphys) become the Divers; Abe Herkimer (mostly based on Ring Lardner) is Abe North; Brugerol (partly based on Edouard Jozan) becomes Tommy Barban; and Francis evolves into Rosemary Hoyt (based on Lois Moran).

---

* The twelve drafts of the novel are traced in Bruccoli, *The Composition of* Tender Is the Night: *A Study of the Manuscripts* (Pittsburgh: University of Pittsburgh Press, 1963). The Garland facsimile series includes seven volumes of *Tender Is the Night* drafts.

The name Francis Melarky, chosen for the principal character, is puzzling. While the shared given name identifies the character with the author, the surname indicates that Fitzgerald had reservations about the character. Since 'malarkey' is a common expression for something exaggerated or unbelievable, it may well be that Fitzgerald's willingness to ridicule his protagonist with a ludicrous name indicates his reservations about his ability to deal with the matricide subject. At the time he was working with the Melarky plot, he wrote a fifty-four line comic ballad which he recited for friends:

> Just a boy who killed his mother
>   I was always up to tricks
> When she taunted me I shot her
>   Through her chronic appendix
> I was always very nervous
>   And it really isn't fair
> I bumped off my mother but never no other
>   Will you let me die in the chair?[34]

The Fitzgeralds were back in Paris in September 1925. Fitzgerald summarized his twenty-eighth year in his *Ledger* as 'The year of Zelda's sickness and resulting depression. Drink, loafing + the Murphys.' Little work was accomplished that fall, except for two commercial love stories – 'Presumption' and 'The Adolescent Marriage' – which brought a raise in Fitzgerald's *Post* price to $2,500. Their Paris life became increasingly disturbed as Zelda experienced at least one episode of 'nervous hysteria' that required a morphine injection.

In November there was a trip to London during which the Fitzgeralds partied with the Marchioness of Milford Haven, whom they met through Zelda's girlhood friend Tallulah Bankhead. While in London, Fitzgerald called at Chatto & Windus, the British publishers of *The Great Gatsby*. He had not made an appointment and none of the partners was there. Novelist Frank Swinnerton, an editor at the firm, received him without introducing himself. Fitzgerald was 'brusque to the point of truculence' until Swinnerton praised *Gatsby*; then Fitzgerald asked his name. When Swinnerton told him, Fitzgerald was dismayed. 'Snatching up his hat in consternation, he cried: "Oh, my God! *Nocturne's* one of my favorite books!' and dashed out of the premises.'[35]

France stimulated Fitzgerald's interest in the Great War. He collected war books and recommended some of them to Perkins for publication. At Brentano's Paris bookshop he was fascinated by books with photos of mutilated soldiers. He also acquired a set of glass slides of battle scenes. A fall trip to the Western Front battlefields inspired one of the most admired passages in *Tender Is the Night*, in which Fitzgerald expressed his sense that trench warfare had marked the termination of the old faiths:

'This western-front business couldn't be done again, not for a long time. The young men think they could do it but they couldn't. They could fight the first Marne again but not this. This took religion and years of plenty and tremendous sureties and the exact relation that existed between the classes. The Russians and Italians weren't any good on this front. You had to have a whole-souled sentimental equipment going back further than you could remember. You had to remember Christmas, and postcards of the Crown Prince and his fiancée, and little cafés in Valence and beer gardens in Unter den Linden and weddings at the mairie, and going to the Derby, and your grandfather's whiskers.... This kind of battle was invented by Lewis Carroll and Jules Verne and whoever wrote Undine, and country deacons bowling and marraines in Marseilles and girls seduced in the back lanes of Wurtemburg and Westphalia. Why, this was a love battle – there was a century of middle-class love spent here. This was the last love battle.'[36]

During the fall and winter of 1925 Fitzgerald was occupied with his friendship for Hemingway and his efforts to advance Hemingway's career. They spent a lot of time in cafés arguing about writing, with Fitzgerald trying to act as Hemingway's mentor. Although Hemingway's Boni & Liveright contract seemed to preclude bringing his books to the house of Scribner, Fitzgerald urged him to send stories to Perkins for *Scribner's Magazine.* Fitzgerald persuaded him to cut an anecdote about boxer Benny Leonard from the opening of 'Fifty Grand,' but Hemingway subsequently decided that it had been bad advice. Fitzgerald's alcoholic nocturnal visits annoyed Hemingway because they disturbed Hadley and woke the baby. Since his head for alcohol was strong, Hemingway could work after an evening of drinking; but Fitzgerald often wanted to prolong the party until morning. Hemingway began to suspect that Fitzgerald resented his self-discipline and was deliberately trying to impede his writing.

In the summer of 1925 Hemingway had written the first draft of *The Sun Also Rises,* his first novel, in two months and then put it aside for a few weeks before rewriting it. Fitzgerald was eager to read the novel, but Hemingway stalled him by explaining that it was bad for him to talk about his work before it was finished. While he was cooling off from *The Sun Also Rises,* Hemingway wrote *The Torrents of Spring* – a book-length parody of Sherwood Anderson, whose 1925 novel *Dark Laughter* he regarded as fraudulent. Hemingway presented the carbon copy of his burlesque to the Fitzgeralds, inscribed: 'To Scott and Zelda with love from Ernest.'[37] He had written Fitzgerald into *Torrents*:

> It was at this point in the story, reader, that Mr. Scott Fitzgerald came to our home one afternoon, and after remaining for quite a while suddenly sat down in the fireplace and would not (or was it could not, reader?) get up and let the fire burn something else so as to keep the room warm.[38]

Fitzgerald could not have been pleased by this depiction of him as helplessly drunk, but does not seem to have made an attempt to have it deleted from the published book.

The Torrents of Spring was submitted in December 1925 under the Boni & Liveright three-book contract, which would become invalid if the publishers declined any of the books Hemingway offered. Because Sherwood Anderson was one of Boni & Liveright's most important authors, it has been generally assumed that Hemingway deliberately wrote *Torrents* as a contract-breaker – with Fitzgerald acting as co-conspirator. Hemingway was determined to leave Boni & Liveright and was negotiating with Harcourt, Brace at the same time that he was negotiating with Scribners. Whatever Hemingway's motives were, Fitzgerald played it straight by urging Horace Liveright and T. R. Smith, the head editor at Boni & Liveright, to publish *Torrents*, calling it 'the best comic book ever written by an American.' He continued, 'Frankly, I hope you won't like it – because I am something of a ballyhoo man for Scribners and I'd some day like to see all my generation that I admire (3) rounded up in the same coop – but knowing my entheusiasm and his own trepidation Ernest agreed with me that such a statement from the former might break the ice for what is an extraordinary and unusual production.'[39]

After Boni & Liveright declined the parody, Fitzgerald persuaded Perkins to make an offer sight unseen for both *The Torrents of Spring* and *The Sun Also Rises*; the deal was consummated when Hemingway went to New York to meet Perkins. While these negotiations were going on, Fitzgerald sent Perkins advice on dealing with Hemingway, indicating that his ethics were shaky: 'In any case he is temperamental in business, made so by these bogus publishers over here. If you take the other two things get a signed contract for the *Sun Also Rises* (novel).'[40]

That Christmas a photo was taken of the three Fitzgeralds doing a kick step in front of their tree. It has been frequently published because it seems to preserve the insouciant image of the Fitzgeralds at the peak of his fame as the author of *The Great Gatsby* – young, handsome and confident.

Zelda continued to have abdominal pains through the end of the year, and in January 1926 the Fitzgeralds tried a cure at Salies de Béarn, a spa in the French Pyrenees. It was a dull place, and they left after two months. At Salies de Béarn,

Fitzgerald wrote two minor stories: 'The Dance' (*Redbook*, June 1926) and 'Your Way and Mine' (*Woman's Home Companion*, May 1927). 'The Dance' was his only detective story after 1909. He also wrote an essay-review of Hemingway's *In Our Time* entitled 'How to Waste Material: A Note on My Generation.' After discussing the failure of American writers to use American material properly – developing his longstanding conviction that the back-to-the-soil novels were fakes – Fitzgerald assessed *In Our Time* and identified 'Big Two-Hearted River' as the best story in the volume. The article concludes: 'And many of us who have grown weary of admonitions to "watch this man or that" have felt a sort of renewal of excitement at these stories wherein Ernest Hemingway turns a corner into the street.'[41] Declined by Mencken's *American Mercury* because it discussed Mencken, 'How to Waste Material' appeared in the May 1926 *Bookman*.

Fitzgerald, Zelda, Scottie, Christmas 1925, Paris

32

Juan-les-Pins

[Spring–Fall 1926]

The year 1926 should have provided ideal working conditions for the new novel because of the subsidiary income from *The Great Gatsby*. A successful stage version by Owen Davis and a Famous Players silent movie brought a windfall of some $25,000 before commissions, and the post-publication serial rights were sold for $1,000 to *Famous Story* magazine. Fitzgerald did not work on the play or the movie. In March the Fitzgeralds went to the Riviera for what was intended to be a repetition of their productive 1924 stay; but there were too many people and too many distractions. They rented the Villa Paquita at Juan-les-Pins. The house didn't suit them; in May or June they turned it over to the Hemingways and moved to the Villa St. Louis, where they remained until the end of 1926. The center of the swimming activities at Cap d'Antibes was the Plage de la Garoupe. The Murphys and their friends went there every day and established territorial rights over the part of the beach that Gerald had raked. Robert Benchley and Dorothy Parker had come to France with Hemingway, and Fitzgerald saw a good deal of them.

In April 1926 Fitzgerald optimistically reported to Ober that his new novel was 'about one fourth done and will be delivered for possible serialization about January 1st. It will be about 75,000 words long, divided into 12 chapters, concerning tho this is absolutely confidential such a case as that girl who shot her mother on the Pacific coast last year.'[42] On the basis of this prediction Ober negotiated a first-refusal agreement with *Liberty* for the serial rights.

Fitzgerald's belief in Hemingway's future remained undiminished. Hemingway – who resented any proprietary claims – always acknowledged that Fitzgerald had more concern for Hemingway's career than for his own. After a Riviera conversation in which Fitzgerald urged novelist Glenway Wescott to help promote Hemingway's reputation, Wescott concluded that Fitzgerald's admiration for Hemingway damaged Fitzgerald by convincing him he could delegate his literary responsibilities to Hemingway.[43] This view is hyperbolic. Fitzgerald's and Hemingway's styles and materials were so different that Fitzgerald could not have felt then that Hemingway had made him redundant.* Although he would designate Hemingway his artistic conscience, Fitzgerald was not directly influenced by Hemingway's techniques. He acknowledged in 1936: 'That a third contemporary had been an artistic conscience to me – I had not imitated his infectious style, because my own style, such as it is, was formed before he published anything, but there was an awful pull toward him when I was on a spot.'[44]

In June, Fitzgerald finally had the opportunity to read *The Sun Also Rises* only after it had been sent to Scribners. In *A Moveable Feast* Hemingway denies that Fitzgerald's advice was useful to him; but the ten-page report that Fitzgerald wrote shows that Hemingway did act on Fitzgerald's editorial judgment in revising the proof of *The Sun Also Rises*:

> Dear Ernest: Nowdays when almost everyone is a genius, at least for awhile, the temptation for the bogus to profit is no

---

* There is a report in *The Far Side of Paradise* that Fitzgerald told Thornton Wilder: 'I don't write any more. Ernest has made all my writing unnecessary' (p. 279). The statement seems to have been made during Fitzgerald's last Hollywood years, when he sometimes played the has-been writer.

greater than the temptation for the good man to relax (in one mysterious way or another) – not realizing the transitory quality of his glory because he forgets that it rests on the frail shoulders of professional entheusiasts. This should frighten all of us into a lust for anything honest that people have to say about our work. I've taken what proved to be excellent advice (on the B. + Damned) from Bunny Wilson who never wrote a novel, (on Gatsby – change of many thousand wds) from Max Perkins who never considered writing one, and on T. S. of Paradise from Katherine Tighe (you don't know her) who had probably never read a novel before.

[This is beginning to sound like my own current work which resolves itself into laborious + sententious preliminaries].*

Anyhow I think parts of *Sun Also* are careless + ineffectual. As I said yestiday (and, as I recollect, in trying to get you to cut the 1st part of 50 Grand) I find in you the same tendency to envelope or (and as it usually turns out) to *embalm* in mere wordiness an anecdote or joke thats casually appealed to you, that I find in myself in trying to preserve a piece of 'fine writing.' Your first chapter contains about 10 such things and it gives a feeling of condescending *casuallness*

P. 1.   'highly moral story'
        'Brett said' (O. Henry stuff)
        'much too expensive
        'something or other'
(If you don't want to tell, why waste 3 wds. saying it. See P. 23–'*9 or 14*' and 'or how many years it was since 19XX' when it would take two words to say   That's what youd kid in anyone else as mere 'style' – mere horse-shit   I can't find this latter but anyhow you've not only got to write well yourself but you've also got to scorn NOT-DO what anyone can do and I think that there are about 24 sneers, superiorities, and nose-thumbings-at-nothing that mar the whole narrative up to p. 29 where (after a false start on the introduction of Cohn) it really gets going. And to preserve these perverse and willful non-essentials you've done a lot of writing that *honestly* reminded me of Michael Arlen.

[You know the very fact that people have committed

---

* The brackets in this letter are Fitzgerald's.

themselves to you will make them watch you like a cat. + if they don't like it creap away like one]

For example.

Pps. 1 + 2. Snobbish (not in itself but because the history of English Aristocrats in the war, set down so verbosely so uncritically, so exteriorly and yet so obviously inspired from within, is *shopworn*.) You had the same problem that I had with my Rich Boy, previously debauched by Chambers ect. Either bring more thot to it with the realization that that ground has already raised its wheat + weeds or cut it down to seven sentences. It hasn't even your rythm and the fact that may be 'true' is utterly immaterial.

That biography from you, who allways believed in the superiority (the preferability) of the *imagined* to the *seen   not to say to the merely recounted.*

P. 3.   'Beautifully engraved shares' (Beautifully engraved 1886 irony) All this is O.K. but so glib *when* its glib + *so* profuse.

P. 5.   Painters are no longer *real* in prose. They must be minimized. [This is not done by making them schlptors, backhouse wall-experts or miniature painters]

P. 8.   'highly moral urges' 'because I believe its a good story' If this paragraph isn't maladroit then I'm a rewrite man for Dr. Cadman.

P. 9.   Somehow its not good. I can't quite put my hand on it – it has a ring of 'This is a true story ect.'

P.10.   'Quarter being a state of mind ect.' This is in all guide books. I havn't read Basil Swoon's but I have fifty francs to lose.

[About this time I can hear you say 'Jesus this guy thinks I'm lousy, + he can stick it up his ass for all I give a Gd Dm for his "critisism." ' But remember this is a new departure for you, and that I think your stuff is great. You were the first American I wanted to meet in Europe – and the last. (This latter clause is simply to balance the sentence. It doesn't seem to make sense tho I have pawed at it for several minutes. Its like the age of the French women.

P.14   (+ thereabout) as I said yesterday I think this anecdote is flat as hell without naming Ford which would be cheap.

It's flat because you end with mention of Allister Crowly. If he's nobody its nothing. If he's somebody, its cheap. This is a novel. Also I'd cut out actual mention of H. Stearns earlier.

Why not cut the inessentials in Cohens biography? His first marriage is of no importance. When so many people can write well + the competition is so heavy I can't imagine how you could have done these first 20 pps. so casually. You can't *play* with peoples attention – a good man who has the power of arresting attention at will must be especially careful.

From here Or rather from p. 30 I began to like the novel but Ernest I can't tell you the sense of disappointment that beginning with its elephantine facetiousness gave me. Please do what you can about it in proof. Its 7500 words – you could reduce it to 5000. And my advice is not to do it by mere pareing but to take out the worst of the *scenes*.

I've decided not to pick at anything else, because I wasn't at all inspired to pick when reading it. I was much too excited. Besides this is probably a heavy dose. The novel's damn good. The central theme is marred somewhere but hell! unless you're writing your life history where you have an inevitable pendulum to swing you true (Harding metaphor), who can bring it entirely off? And what critic can trace whether the fault lies in a possible insufficient thinking out, in the biteing off of more than you eventually cared to chew in the impotent theme or in the elusiveness of the lady character herself. My theory always was that she dramatized herself in terms of Arlens dramatization of somebody's dramatizatatg of Stephen McKenna's dramatization of Diana Manner's dramatization of the last girl in Well's *Tono Bungay* – who's original probably liked more things about Beatrix Esmond than about Jane Austin's Elizibeth (to whom we owe the manners of so many of our wives.)

Appropos of your foreward about the Latin quarter – suppose you had begun your stories with phrases like: 'Spain is a peculiar place – ect' or 'Michigan is interesting to two classes – the fisherman + the drummer.'

Pps 64 + 25 with a bit of work should tell all that need be known about *Brett*'s past.

(Small point) 'Dysemtry' instead of 'killed' is a clichês to avoid a clichê. It stands out. I suppose it can't be helped. I suppose all the 75,000000 Europeans who died between 1914–1918 will always be among the 10,000,000 who were killed in the war.

God! The bottom of p. 77 Jusque the top p. 78 are wonderful, I go crazy when people aren't always at their best. This isn't picked out – I just happened on it.*

The heart of my criticism beats somewhere apon p. 87.† I think you can't change it, though. I felt the lack of some crazy torturing tentativeness or insecurity – horror, all at once, that she'd feel – and he'd feel – maybe I'm crazy. He isn't *like an impotent man. He's like a man in a sort of moral chastity belt.*

Oh, well. It's fine, from Chap V on, anyhow, in spite of that – which fact is merely a proof of its brilliance.

Station Z.W.X. square says good night. Good night all.[45]

Fitzgerald's response to the novel was complicated by his dislike for Duff Twysden, the model for Brett Ashley. In the typescript and galleys of *The Sun Also Rises*, Chapter I provides a history of Brett Ashley's marital background; Chapter II describes Jake's Paris life and friends. Hemingway took Fitzgerald's advice and killed all this expository material up to 'Robert Cohn was once middleweight boxing champion of Princeton' in Chapter II, which opens the published novel.

Fitzgerald's document was supplemented by long talks with Hemingway, for they saw each other daily at Juan-les-Pins. Beyond providing a memo on particular points in the typescript, Fitzgerald's report served to prepare Hemingway for discussion – and to protect himself. As his opening paragraph shows, Fitzgerald knew he was playing with fire in criticizing the novel. Hemingway not only took Fitzgerald's advice about cutting the novel, but decided it was his own idea. On 5 June, Hemingway wrote Perkins that Fitzgerald

---

* Chapter six: the scene in which Frances Clyne berates Cohn for leaving her.
† Chapter seven: the scene in which Brett comes to Jake's flat.

was reading the novel and agreed that the first two chapters should be cut.[46] Hoping to get more money for Hemingway's short stories, Fitzgerald tried to persuade him to let Harold Ober represent him, but Hemingway was unwilling to have an agent.

Zelda also read *The Sun Also Rises*. When asked what it was about, she said, 'Bullfighting, bullslinging, and bull. . . . '[47] Fitzgerald cut her off, telling her not to speak about Hemingway that way. The Zelda-Hemingway relationship did not improve. When Zelda asked him if he didn't think Al Jolson was greater than Christ, Hemingway became convinced that she was truly insane.[48]

Except for a trip to Paris in June for Zelda's appendectomy, the Fitzgeralds remained on the Riviera that summer and did not join the Hemingways and Murphys on their July trip to Pamplona for the San Fermín Fiesta. (Fitzgerald never attended a bullfight with Hemingway.) He did not make significant progress on his novel, which Zelda remarked 'goes so slow it ought to be serialized in the Encyclopedia Britannica.'[49] He considered changing the title from 'Our Type' to 'The World's Fair.' Though he continued to send Perkins and Ober sanguine forecasts, Fitzgerald's work in the summer and fall of 1926 was devoted mainly to rewriting the opening of the first draft, adding a narrator. He was aware that much of the effectiveness of *The Great Gatsby* resulted from the use of Nick Carraway as narrator. It was therefore natural that he would attempt to adapt this technique to his next novel; however, he did not do so until after he had tried a third-person narrative. The narrator Fitzgerald supplied in 1926 is a nameless American who is not integrated into the plot. He interjects comments but does not certify the story or control the narrative. The manuscript for the 1926 narrator version advances the plot by a chapter that covers Francis's trip to Paris with the Pipers and Abe. A fuller typescript for the narrator version probably represents a later stage of revision.

Fitzgerald's drinking behavior became increasingly erratic on the Riviera in 1926, placing a strain on his friendship with the Murphys. At this time Fitzgerald began introducing himself to new acquaintances by announcing, 'I'm an alcoholic.' When the Murphys gave a party for the Hemingways at the Juan-les-Pins casino, Fitzgerald threw ashtrays until Gerald left his own party. Fitzgerald could not bear to be ignored, and his attempts to get attention were too often atrocious. At one Villa America dinner party he threw a fig at the Princesse de Caraman-Chimay, punched Murphy, and smashed the Venetian stemware. This exhibition got him banished from the Murphys' villa for three weeks. Moreover, having chosen the Murphys as the models for Seth and Dinah Piper in his novel, Fitzgerald subjected them to steady interrogation and analysis. Sara protested in writing:

> – But you can't expect anyone to like or stand a *Continual* feeling of analysis + sub-analysis, + criticism – on the whole unfriendly – Such as we have felt for quite awhile. It is definitely in the air, – + quite unpleasant. – It certainly detracts from any gathering, – + Gerald, for one, simply curls up at the edges + becomes someone else in that sort of atmosphere. And last night you even said 'that you had never seen Gerald so silly + rude' – It's hardly likely that I should Explain Gerald, – or Gerald me – to you. If you don't know what people are like it's *your* loss – And if Gerald was 'rude' in getting up + leaving a party that had gotten *quite bad*, – then he was rude to the Hemingways + MacLeishes too – No, it is hardly likely that you would stick at a thing like *Manners* – it is more probably some theory you have, – (it *may* be something to do with the book). – But *you ought to know at your age* that you *Can't have Theories about friends* – If you Can't take friends largely, + without suspicion – then they are not friends at all –. We *Cannot* – Gerald + I – at our age – + stage in life – *be bothered* with Sophomoric situations – like last night – We are very simple people – (unless we feel ourselves in a collegiate quagmire) – and we are *literally* + *actually* fond of you both – (There is no reason for saying this that I know of – unless we meant it.)[50]

This letter was written less than a year after Gerald's tribute to the deep understanding between the two couples.

The Fitzgeralds' behavior as a couple became ominous and dangerous. One evening the Murphys were dining with them in the hills above the Mediterranean at St. Paul-de-Vence, where they encountered Isadora Duncan. When Fitzgerald responded to the dancer's attentions, Zelda wordlessly threw herself headfirst down a flight of stone steps. Their frequent quarrels were known to their friends because Zelda would pack a trunk and leave it outside their villa. Zelda dared Fitzgerald to match her risky antics, and their competition sometimes seemed to reveal a mutual destructive compulsion. One night he accepted her challenge to do a series of dangerous high dives from the cliffs into the sea. Their alcoholic car trips were a peril to themselves and anyone else on the road. Some nights they didn't make it home, falling asleep in their car. Gerald Murphy's assessment of the Fitzgeralds' nocturnal habits is that they wanted something to happen every night: 'I don't think it was parties that started Scott and Zelda on their adventures. . . . Their idea was that they never depended upon parties. I don't think they cared very much for parties, so called, and I don't think they stayed at them very long. They were all out, always searching for some kind of adventure *outside* of the party. . . it didn't need, take a party to start them or anything of that kind. And they didn't stay around very much. They usually had their own funny little plans – they'd be with you for awhile and then they'd disappear and go on to some other place – and then you'd see them again somehow – they'd seek you out again.'[51] When Sara Murphy warned Zelda about their behavior, she replied, 'But Sara, didn't you know? We don't believe in conservation.'[52] A decade later Sara recalled her impressions of Zelda in a letter to Fitzgerald

> – I think of her face so often + so wish it had been *drawn* (not painted, drawn.) It is rather like a young Indian's face, except for the smouldering eyes. At night, I remember, if she was excited, they turned black – + impenetrable – but always full of impatience – at *something* –, the world I think – she wasn't of it anyhow – not really.

I loved her. + felt a sympathetic vibration to her violence. But she *wasn't throttled*, – you mustnt ever think she was except by herself – She had an inward life + feelings that I don't suppose anyone ever touched – not even you – She probably thought terribly dangerous secret thoughts – + had pent-in rebellions. Some of it showed through her eyes, – but only to those who loved her.[53]

Under Hemingway's influence Fitzgerald – who was normally puritanical in his speech. – developed a streak of scatological humor. He sent Hemingway a parody of the *In Our Time* vignettes: 'We were in a back house in Juan-les-Pins. Bill had lost controll of his splincter muscles. There were wet *Matins* in the rack beside the door. There were wet *Éclairers de Nice* in the rack over his head. When the King of Bulgaria came in Bill was just firing a burst that struck the old limeshit twenty feet down with a *splat-tap*. All the rest came just like that. The King of Bulgaria began to whirl round and round.'[54] Hemingway announced that he was planning to insert a subtitle in his novel:

THE SUN ALSO RISES (LIKE YOUR COCK IF YOU HAVE ONE)
A Greater Gatsby
(Written with the friendship of F. Scott FitzGerald.
(Prophet of THE JAZZ AGE)[55]

Zelda – who was by no means prudish – was put off by Hemingway's bawdry.

Fitzgerald's boon companion on the Riviera that summer was playwright Charles MacArthur, with whom he collaborated in alcoholic pranks. They threatened to saw a waiter in half with a musical saw; they lured a band to the Villa St. Louis and locked them in a room to provide music for them; they took the waiters from a café to the edge of a cliff and threatened to murder them. Some of MacArthur's qualities were transferred to Abe North in *Tender Is the Night*. With Ben Finney they made a movie at Grace Moore's villa on the grounds of the Hôtel du Cap; called *Love's Betrayal, or a Simple Story of Incest*, it featured obscene titles written on the walls of the villa. Finney, an American bon vivant, was a popular figure at Antibes. Fitzgerald respected his judgment and discussed the novel-in-progress with him. Egon, Finney's police dog, liked to aquaplane but could not mount the board by himself, so he would pester Fitzgerald to help him.[56]

Another Riviera acquaintance was Mario Braggiotti,* a young musician staying with the Murphys, who has described Fitzgerald as a 'mood-picker' – referring to his habit of quizzing people and analyzing them. Braggiotti had the impression that Fitzgerald 'discovered Zelda every minute.' Other people sometimes found her conversation hard to follow, but Fitzgerald encouraged her to talk and always understood her. Braggiotti had a crush on Zelda, which did not seem to bother Fitzgerald. Although twelve years younger than Fitzgerald, Braggiotti regarded him as unsophisticated; Fitzgerald seemed almost boyishly eager for knowledge and was trying to read his way through the *Britannica*.[57] Braggiotti, an American born in Italy, went into the amalgam of models for Tommy Barban in *Tender Is the Night*.

When the Riviera season was over in September 1926, Fitzgerald tried to settle down to work on his novel; but it was a wasted year, as indicated by his *Ledger* summary: 'Futile, shameful useless but the $30,000 rewards of 1924 work. Self disgust. Health gone.' In December the Fitzgeralds sailed for America from Genoa after two and a half years abroad. With the exception of his work on *The Great Gatsby* in 1924, the European sojourn had been a failure. They had not saved money; their lives had become increasingly disorganized; he had become an acknowledged alcoholic; their marriage had developed permanent strains; and he had not done any steady work for more than a year. Having gone to France to escape the distractions of New York, they now returned to America to escape the dissipations of France.

---

* Braggiotti is not sure which summer he knew the Fitzgeralds, but his recollections tie in with the events of 1926.

33

Hollywood and 'Ellerslie'

[January 1927–Spring 1928]

Fitzgerald professed to be dismayed by the American scene. In his 1927 interviews he made the obligatory comparisons between France and America: 'The best of America drifts to Paris. The American in Paris is the best American. It is more fun for an intelligent person to live in an intelligent country. France has the only two things toward which we drift as we grow older – intelligence and good manners.'[58]

The Fitzgeralds spent Christmas in Montgomery and considered where to settle in America. In January producer John W. Considine of United Artists asked Fitzgerald to come to Hollywood and write an original flapper comedy for Constance Talmadge. The deal called for $3,500 down and $12,500 when the script was accepted. Fitzgerald was confident of his ability to meet the Hollywood standards within a month. Leaving Scottie with his parents, who had moved to Washington, he and Zelda went to California for what proved to be a two-month stint. They took an apartment on the grounds of the Ambassador Hotel, where they shared a unit with Carmel Myers, John Barrymore, and Carl Van Vechten.

Although Fitzgerald intended to finish the job as quickly as possible, they inevitably became involved in Hollywood social life, being invited to many parties and crashing others.

The most important event in Fitzgerald's first Hollywood trip was his meeting with actress Lois Moran, probably through Van Vechten. Not yet eighteen, she had made her first movie success in *Stella Dallas* in 1925. Fitzgerald, who was thirty, was attracted to her because she was young, beautiful, and intelligent – and because he could show off for her. She was impressed by him and flattered by his attention, but she did not fall in love with him. In fact, Fitzgerald was never alone with Lois Moran, who lived with her widowed mother. An indication of Fitzgerald's involvement is that he took a screen test with the idea of acting with her, but nothing resulted from it. She had been carefully raised by her mother, whom Fitzgerald admired. But even with the Morans his behavior was unpredictable. When they invited the Fitzgeralds to a large tea, he collected the watches, purses, and wallets of the guests and tried to make soup out of them.[59]

Zelda recognized Lois Moran's appeal to Fitzgerald, describing her as 'a young actress like a breakfast food that many men identified with whatever they missed from life.'[60] When the Fitzgeralds quarreled about his interest in Lois, he said that he admired her because she did something with her talents that required work and discipline. Zelda expressed her resentment by burning her clothes in the bathtub.

The script Fitzgerald delivered to United Artists was called 'Lipstick.' Set at Princeton, its heroine is a girl who has been unjustly imprisoned and now has a magic lipstick that makes every man want to kiss her.[61] It was a thin screenplay, for Fitzgerald had again written down to the movies. While working on it, he quarreled with Constance Talmadge, which probably hurt the project's chances. The script was rejected, and Fitzgerald did not receive the $12,500 balance. Instead of supplying easy money, the Hollywood excursion consumed more than the $3,500 advance. On the way east the Fitzgeralds again quarreled about Lois Moran, and Zelda threw her platinum wristwatch – the first expensive thing he had given her, in 1920 – from the train window. Although Fitzgerald would see Lois Moran only three or four times again, she became a presence in his work and provided the model for Rosemary Hoyt in *Tender Is the Night*.

Fitzgerald met another figure in Hollywood who would

Lois Moran

yield him material for a novel: Irving Thalberg, the 'boy wonder' head of production at M-G-M. Some twelve years later Fitzgerald made a memo for *The Last Tycoon* of his first impressions of Thalberg:

> We sat in the old commissary at Metro and he said, 'Scottie, supposing there's got to be a road through a mountain – a railroad and two or three surveyors and people come to you and you believe some of them and some of them you don't believe; but all in all, there seems to be half a dozen possible roads through those mountains each one of which, so far as you can determine, is as good as the other. Now suppose you happen to be the top man, there's a point where you don't exercise the faculty of judgment in the ordinary way, but simply the faculty of arbitrary decision. You say, "Well, I think we will put the road there," and you trace it with your finger and you know in your secret heart and no one else knows, that you have no reason for putting the road there rather than in several other different courses, but you're the only person that knows that you don't know why you're doing it and You've got to stick to that and you've got to pretend that you know and that you did it for specific reasons, even though you're utterly assailed by doubts at times as to the wisdom of your decision because all these other possible decisions keep echoing in your ear. But when you're planning a new enterprise on a grand scale, the people under you mustn't ever know or guess that you're in any doubt because they've all got to have something to look up to and they mustn't ever dream that you're in doubt about any decision. Those things keep occurring.'
>
> At that point, some other people came into the commissary and sat down and first thing I knew there was a group of four and the intimacy of the conversation was broken, but I was very much impressed by the shrewdness of what he said – something more than shrewdness – by the largeness of what he thought and how he reached it at the age of 26 which he was then.[62]

The Fitzgeralds began house-hunting in the Wilmington, Delaware, area – possibly at the suggestion of Maxwell Perkins, who thought it would be sufficiently remote from the temptations of New York. John Biggs, Fitzgerald's Princeton roommate whose first novel, *Demigods*, had been published by Scribners in 1926 at Fitzgerald's recommendation, was a Wilmington lawyer. He helped them to find 'Ellerslie,' a nineteenth-century Greek Revival mansion at Edgemoor on the Delaware River. The house was too large for them; but the rent was only $150 a month, and they took a two-year lease. Zelda later wrote: 'The squareness of the rooms and the sweep of the columns were to bring us a judicious tranquility.'[63] The anticipated reclusion was delayed by a series of house parties. One of the first was for Lois Moran and her mother on the weekend of 21 May 1927, when Lindbergh flew the Atlantic. The guests included Charles MacArthur, Carl Van Vechten, and critic Ernest Boyd. Zelda kept her resentment of Lois under control, and there was no unpleasantness. Another weekend, when Cousin Ceci's daughter Teah was invited to 'Ellerslie,' Fitzgerald organized a polo match with farm horses and croquet mallets, but the party was spoiled because he drank too much in an effort to make things go.

Fitzgerald tried to promote Hemingway's reputation in America, although *The Sun Also Rises* had already launched his fame. He was eager to obtain Mencken's endorsement for Hemingway, but the Baltimore Sage did not share his judgment that Hemingway was 'the best we have.'[64] When Fitzgerald read Hemingway's story 'In Another Country,' he wrote him that ' "In the fall the war was always there but we did not go to it any more" is one of the most beautiful prose sentences I've ever read.'[65] Fitzgerald enclosed a $100 check to help Hemingway until his books started earning money.

At 'Ellerslie,' Zelda initiated a period of creative activity – almost certainly in reaction to Fitzgerald's admiration for Lois Moran – and went with Scottie to Philadelphia three times a week for lessons with Catherine Littlefield, director of the Philadelphia Opera ballet. She also resumed writing and in 1927 sold three articles: 'The Changing Beauty of Park Avenue' to *Harper's Bazaar*, 'Looking Back Eight Years' to

303

College Humor, and 'Editorial on Youth' to *Photoplay* (published as 'Paint and Powder' by the *Smart Set* in 1929 under Fitzgerald's byline). Most of her work was published under the joint byline 'F. Scott and Zelda Fitzgerald' because the magazines insisted on using his name. At first Zelda seemed amused that her writing was salable only with her husband's name on it; but as their marriage became openly competitive, Zelda resented the arrangement.* Her creative

'Ellerslie'

* In his *Ledger* Fitzgerald punctiliously identified her five articles and five stories that were published as collaborations. One article and two stories by Zelda were published under Fitzgerald's byline.

energies also found expression in designing oversized furniture for the large rooms at 'Ellerslie' and in constructing an elaborate doll house for Scottie. She lavished time on several series of detailed paper dolls for historical figures and fairy tales with changes of costume painted in thick watercolor: the Knights of the Round Table, the Court of Louis XIV, Joan of Arc, Goldilocks, and Red Riding Hood. A set of dolls for the family featured Fitzgerald with angel's wings.

To avoid distractions the top-floor room in which Fitzgerald wrote was furnished with only a kitchen table and a chair. He had promised to complete his novel in 1927, but little progress was made. In June he considered changing the title to 'The Boy Who Killed his Mother.' It is difficult to gauge Fitzgerald's progress on his novel during 1927–28. The sporadic effort he put into it seems to have been revision of the narrator version of the Melarky plot. He received an advance from Scribners in 1927, which was to be repaid from the serial sale. With his sometimes arcane system of accounting he carefully listed this advance as $5,752.06. His account with the Reynolds agency shows that in the fall-winter of 1927 he received at least one advance against stories each week: 1 September, $500; 8 September, $500; 15 September, $500; 22 September $300. He borrowed $1,450 in October, $2,200 in November, and $2,650 in December.[66]

The subsidiary-rights money from *The Great Gatsby* had been spent, and Fitzgerald resumed writing magazine stories in June 1927 after a fifteen-month break. The first 1927 *Post* story, 'Jacob's Ladder,' is permeated by Lois Moran. A cultivated man of thirty-three helps a sixteen-year-old shopgirl to become a movie star. Pygmalion-like, he falls in love with his creation but loses her to her success. Passages from the story were later incorporated into *Tender Is the Night*; and the girl's name, Jenny Prince, was an early name for Rosemary Hoyt in the novel drafts. Full of regret, loss, and loneliness, 'Jacob's Ladder' is a projection of Fitzgerald's feelings at thirty.

Another June project was the article 'Princeton' for *College Humor*. Fitzgerald's proximity to Princeton revived his love for the university and recalled his years of aspiration:

> Looking back over a decade one sees the ideal of a university
> become a myth, a vision, a meadow lark among the smoke
> stacks. Yet perhaps it is there at Princeton, only more elusive
> than under the skies of the Prussian Rhineland or
> Oxfordshire; or perhaps some men come upon it suddenly
> and possess it, while others wander forever outside. Even these
> seek in vain through middle age for any corner of the republic
> that preserves so much of what is fair, gracious, charming and
> honorable in American life.[67]

Again, the concluding mood is one of loss.

Fitzgerald wrote four other *Post* stories in 1927: 'The Love
Boat' (written in August, it brought a raise to $3,500), 'A Short
Trip Home' (October), 'The Bowl' (November), and 'Magnetism' (December). In 'A Short Trip Home,' which he described
as 'the first real ghost story I ever wrote,'[68] an undergraduate
frees a college girl from a spectre. Once more, Fitzgerald
connected sexual corruption with death. Work on 'The Bowl,'
a football story, rekindled Fitzgerald's interest in Princeton
football as he made trips to watch practice or attend games. He
began offering football coach Fritz Crisler advice – sometimes
in the form of late-night phone calls.[69] On one of his Princeton
trips he rearranged the furniture in a room at the Cottage Club
so that it would be the same as when he was an undergraduate.

There were regular trips from Wilmington to New York,
where the Fitzgeralds stayed at the Plaza. Zelda remarked, 'We
come up for a weekend, then wake up and it's Thursday.'[70] On
one of these excursions they went to a party for heavyweight
champion Gene Tunney with the Morans and George Jean
Nathan. Fitzgerald stuck close to Tunney all evening and did
not want to leave. Going back to the Plaza in a cab, he saw a
forlorn newsboy in the rain and bought all his papers.

The year 1927 brought a series of nervous ailments, which
may be what Fitzgerald was referring to in three puzzling
Ledger notes for August–September: 'Terrible incessant
stoppies begin'; 'Stoppies worse'; 'Stoppies now reached its

height.' When Perkins visited 'Ellerslie' in September, he came away worried that Fitzgerald was in danger of a nervous breakdown related to his inability to settle down to steady work on the novel. Perkins reported to Hemingway that 'tobacco was hurting him more than drink,' and persuaded Fitzgerald to switch from Chesterfields to Sano denicotinized cigarettes.[71] Fitzgerald remained a heavy cigarette smoker all his life, but he stuck with Sanos. At Perkins's urging he went on the wagon in October – or claimed he did. Like most alcoholics, Fitzgerald had his own interpretations of what being on the wagon meant at various times; sometimes it meant restricting himself to beer and wine. Perkins also tried to have him take up deck tennis as a form of regular exercise.

Fitzgerald's *Ledger* summary of his thirtieth year was 'Total loss at beginning. A lot of fun. Work begins again.' Although Fitzgerald did not publish a book in 1927, his income for the year had reached a new high of $29,757.87 after commissions – including $15,300 from five stories. His total book royalties were $153.23. He paid federal tax of $1,330.29.

Stimulated by his revived love of Princeton, Fitzgerald accepted an invitation to speak at a Cottage Club dinner in late January 1928. In the afternoon he talked movingly about Princeton to an informal group of undergraduates at Cottage. Anxious to make a good impression, he was intimidated and probably drunk when he began his formal speech in the evening; after a few nervous sentences he sat down. During this visit Fitzgerald was distressed to discover that the honor system was being diluted. He arrived home crying drunk over his speaking fiasco and his concern about the honor system. While Zelda's sister Rosalind was visiting 'Ellerslie' with her husband, during Fitzgerald's absence, Zelda had broken into the liquor cabinet. Fitzgerald and Zelda quarreled violently when he ordered her to bed, and he gave her a bloody nose.

In February they accepted a trip to Montreal from the Canadian railways, but Fitzgerald found nothing to write about there. From Canada he sent Scottie a series of postcards signed 'The man with three noses,' a comic figure he had invented for her.[72] That month Thornton Wilder – whose first novel, *The Cabala*, had been published in 1926 – visited 'Ellerslie'; he and Fitzgerald exchanged admiring letters, but no close friendship developed.[73]

34

Third Trip Abroad: A Summer in Paris

[1928]

Zelda pursued her ballet ambitions with increasing intensity in 1928. She spent hours every day in almost furious practice to make her twenty-eight-year-old body capable of professional dancing. Fitzgerald began to resent her discipline, feeling that it reflected on his own work habits. In April 1928 the Fitzgeralds went to Paris for the summer – crossing on the *Paris* – partly because they were bored in Wilmington but mostly because Zelda wanted to work with the Russian ballet. They rented an apartment at 58 rue de Vaugirard on the Left Bank; and Zelda took lessons from Lubov Egorova, a former ballerina who was regarded as one of the leading teachers.

Fitzgerald perceived that Paris had changed appallingly – or rather that the Americans coming there were grotesque. Paris had been transmogrified from the intellectual capital of the world to a vast tourist attraction. 'With each new shipment of Americans spewed up by the boom the quality fell off, until toward the end there was something sinister about the crazy boatloads. . . . There were citizens travelling in luxury in 1928 and 1929 who, in the distortion of their new condition, had

the human value of Pekinese, bivalves, cretins, goats.'[74]

The Paris trip was financed by the Basil Duke Lee stories for the *Post*, nine of which were written between March 1928 and February 1929: 'The Scandal Detectives' (March), 'The Freshest Boy' (April), 'A Night at the Fair' (May), 'He Thinks He's Wonderful' (July), 'The Captured Shadow' (September), 'The Perfect Life' (October), 'Forging Ahead' (January 1929), 'Basil and Cleopatra' (February). Fitzgerald's first series,* these stories examine Basil from boyhood in the Midwest through prep school in the East and into Yale. The identification between Basil and Fitzgerald is close; the chief episodes were drawn from the author's experiences – the production of *The Captured Shadow*, his unpopularity at Newman, his love for Ginevra King. The timing was right for a retrospective self-assessment by Fitzgerald, whose professional life and personal life were breaking down at thirty-one. Like many writers, he could best understand things by writing about them. After tracing his adolescent struggles for popularity and recognition, the series ends with a matured Basil in control of his romantic destiny in 'Basil and Cleopatra' after he relinquishes the girl he has loved: 'There was a flurry of premature snow in the air and the stars looked cold. Staring up at them he saw that they were his stars as always – symbols of ambition, struggle and glory. The wind blew through them, trumpeting that high white note for which he always listened, and the thin-blown clouds, stripped for battle, passed in review. The scene was of an unparalleled brightness and magnificence, and only the practiced eye of the commander saw that one star was no longer there.'[75]

Fitzgerald may not have planned a series of Basil stories, but they were easy to write because he had ample material; and they brought $31,500. He was a little embarrassed by the

---

* Unlike a serial, which continues a novel through installments, a series repeats the same characters in unconnected or loosely connected stories. Series stories were a staple of *The Saturday Evening Post*. The readers liked them, and the writers usually found them easier than inventing new characters.

Basil series: not by the stories themselves, most of which were excellent, but by the circumstance that he was writing stories about adolescents for the *Post*. Concerned that he was going the way of Booth Tarkington, he refused to publish the Basil stories as a separate volume. He believed that Tarkington had wasted one of the best talents in American prose and wrote himself a warning note about Tarkington's career: 'I have a horror of going into a personal debauch and coming out of it devitalized with no interest except an acute observation of the behavior of colored people, children, and dogs.'[76]

Fitzgerald had gone to Paris with the intention of finishing his novel there and sent optimistic reports to Perkins and Ober. On 3 June 1928 he cabled Ober: TWO MORE CHAPTERS FINISHED ALL COMPLETED AUGUST CAN YOU DEPOSIT ONE-FIFTY AT ONCE AND ONETHOUSAND WHEN STORY IS PAID.[77] In July he wrote Perkins: 'The novel goes fine. I think its quite wonderful + I think those who've seen it (for I've read it around a little) have been quite excited. I was encouraged the other day, when James Joyce came to dinner, when he said, 'Yes, I expect to finish my novel [*Finnegans Wake*] in three or four years more at the *latest* + he works 11 hrs a day to my intermittent 8. Mine will be done <u>sure</u> in September.'[78] He had met Joyce on 27 June at a dinner given by Sylvia Beach. Also present were Adrienne Monnier (proprietor of the bookstore La Maison des Amis des Livres), Nora Joyce, Zelda, and André and Lucie Chamson. Beach's copy of *The Great Gatsby* preserves Fitzgerald's drawing – captioned the 'Festival of St. James' – of Fitzgerald kneeling before the haloed Joyce.[79] At one of their meetings Fitzgerald upset Joyce by offering to jump out the window as an expression of admiration.* When Joyce

* Sylvia Beach's dinner is described in her *Shakespeare & Co.*[80] Herbert Gorman reports a Beach dinner for the Joyces and Fitzgeralds at which the Gormans were present but the Chamsons were absent. Gorman records that Fitzgerald had previously called on the Joyces and threatened to jump from the sixth-floor window unless Nora declared her love for him. It is impossible to be sure whether there were two separate Beach dinners or whether Gorman's account is untrustworthy.[81]

inscribed *Ulysses* for Fitzgerald, he enclosed a note referring to Fitzgerald's gesture:

> Dear Mr. Fitzgerald: Here with is the book you gave me signed and I am adding a portrait of the artist as a once young man with the thanks of your much obliged but most pusillanamous guest.
>
> Sincerely yours
> James Joyce[82]
>
> 11.7.928

The Joyces came to dinner at the Fitzgeralds' apartment, and Fitzgerald was annoyed because Zelda did not share his adulation for Joyce. Zelda's ballet work was a continuing source of strife. Fitzgerald resented her dedication to the dance and was angry when she was too tired to go out with him at night. He went drinking by himself and landed in jail twice that summer.

Fitzgerald had never become involved in French literary life, but in June he had asked Sylvia Beach to introduce him to a young French writer whom she thought he would like. She had brought him together with André Chamson, a twenty-eight-year-old civil servant and novelist. That Chamson spoke little English and Fitzgerald poor French was not an impediment to their friendship – the only literary friendship Fitzgerald formed with a Frenchman. As always, Fitzgerald's instinct was to help a younger writer. He urged Perkins to consider Chamson's *Les Hommes de la Route*, which Scribners published as *The Road* in 1929. (Chamson's books were not popular in America, but he became a distinguished novelist and a member of the French Academy.) The Chamsons, who lived in modest circumstances, were sometimes embarrassed by Fitzgerald's lavish hospitality. He gave Chamson his ties and handkerchiefs that Zelda had bought. When she protested, Fitzgerald explained that he wouldn't have given them to Chamson if he hadn't liked them. Chamson had his share of the problems caused by Fitzgerald's alcoholic behavior. Fitzgerald perched on the window railing of the Chamsons' sixth-floor apartment and proclaimed to Paris, 'I am Voltaire! I am Rousseau!' When Fitzgerald tried to buy the bicycles from two gendarmes who concluded that they were being insulted, it required considerable eloquence by Chamson to persuade the *flics* that Fitzgerald was a great American writer and shouldn't be arrested. Fitzgerald's generosity impressed Chamson as an American characteristic. He felt that Fitzgerald was never happy at the time of their friendship, but that he pretended he was by trying to make his friends happy.

King Vidor, the American movie director, was in Paris that summer. Fitzgerald introduced him to Chamson, and the three planned a movie that Chamson was supposed to write for Vidor: 'a mountain community, cut off from the world, puts itself to a huge collective task in order to be able to live.'[83] The collaboration was abandoned when Chamson declined an invitation to Hollywood. (In 1934 Vidor made *Our Daily Bread*, which resembled the Chamson project.) Fitzgerald also introduced Vidor to Gerald Murphy. When Vidor made *Hallelujah!* (1929), the first major all-black movie, Murphy — who collected spirituals — went to Hollywood as an adviser.

Thornton Wilder was in Paris with Gene Tunney, who had intellectual ambitions, and arranged a gathering at the Ritz Bar that included Fitzgerald and Robert and Maude Hutchins. When Fitzgerald took his usual approach to a woman by flattering the young wife of the Yale Law School dean, she told him off for patronizing her and left with her husband. According to her report, Fitzgerald followed the Hutchinses' cab in another cab and tried to placate her whenever he caught up with them.[84]

John Peale Bishop had married a wealthy woman and was living in a château at Orgeval outside Paris. He and Fitzgerald met for literary talk, though their intimate friendship was over — partly because Margaret Bishop didn't like her husband's friends and they disliked her. Sara Murphy commented on Margaret Bishop's conversational style, 'There *can't* be that many words.' Despite the leisure provided

313

by his wife's money, Bishop had not published a book since *The Undertaker's Garland*, written with Edmund Wilson in 1922. Fitzgerald reported to Perkins that Bishop's novel was 'impossible' (it was never published); but that his Civil War novelette was excellent.[85] At Fitzgerald's urging the novelette was submitted to *Scribner's Magazine*, which turned it down because it was too long. The story was probably 'The Cellar,' later collected in *Many Thousands Gone* (Scribners, 1931).

The Fitzgeralds returned to America on 7 October 1928 in a 'blaze of work + liquor,' crossing on the *Carmania* in a bad storm. The novel was still unfinished. Fitzgerald's *Ledger* summary of his thirty-first year replaces harsh judgment with resignation: 'Perhaps its the Thirties but I can't even be very depressed about it.'

Fitzgerald brought a Paris taxi driver named Philippe back to 'Ellerslie' as butler-chauffeur-sparring partner. Zelda disliked him because he was insubordinate to her. Fitzgerald took Philippe drinking with him, and John Biggs had to respond to late-night phone calls to get them out of jail. With a nice concern for social distinction, the Wilmington police would put Philippe in a cell but hold Fitzgerald in custody until Biggs arrived.

In October, Fitzgerald promised to begin sending Perkins two chapters a month until the novel was finished in eight chapters.[86] Perkins acknowledged receipt of the first two chapters on 13 November 1928; there were no further chapters. Perkins reserved criticism, but his letter makes it clear that these chapters were the opening of the Melarky version on the Riviera.[87]

On 19 November 1928 Hemingway and his second wife, Pauline, attended the Princeton-Yale football game at Princeton with the Fitzgeralds and spent the night at 'Ellerslie.' Hemingway's account of their first meeting in two years survives in an incomplete chapter intended for *A Moveable Feast*, which describes Fitzgerald's drunken behavior on the train after the game and at 'Ellerslie,' where he passed out.[88] The next day there was an altercation with the police at the Wilmington train station.* On 6 December Hemingway was on the train from New York to Florida when he was informed that his father had died in Oak Park, Illinois. He wired Perkins, Mike Strater, and Fitzgerald to send money to the North Philadelphia station so he could go west. Fitzgerald delivered the money in person.

Fitzgerald made no progress on his novel in the fall and winter of 1928–29. In November he interrupted the Basil Duke Lee series to write 'The Last of the Belles,' one of the best of the retrospective stories he wrote in 1928 and 1929.

Fitzgerald allegedly judging a Woodbury soap beauty contest

* A. E. Hotchner's account of this visit in *Papa Hemingway* (New York: Random House, 1966) is untrustworthy.

Set in Tarleton, Georgia, Fitzgerald's version of Montgomery, the story deals with the Yankee narrator's response to the South as expressed through his feelings for Ailie Calhoun, whom he meets while stationed in Tarleton during World War I. Six years later he returns, 'looking for my youth in a clapboard or a strip of roofing or a rusty tomato can . . . All I could be sure of was that this place that had once been so full of life and effort was gone, as if it had never existed, and that in another month Ailie would be gone, and the South would be empty for me forever.'[89] In addition to expressing Fitzgerald's pervasive mood of loss, 'The Last of the Belles' is Fitzgerald's last fictional attempt to explain the South and its women.

Fitzgerald picked up a windfall of $1,500 in 1928 and 1929 by lending his name to the Woodbury soap beauty contest. The other judges were John Barrymore and Cornelius Vanderbilt, Jr. The judges' photos and names were used in a series of ads, but it is unlikely that they selected the beauties.[90]

Zelda continued her dancing with an obsessive concentration, working in front of a large mirror that Fitzgerald called her 'whorehouse mirror.' The Fitzgeralds were having sexual problems. They accused each other of indifference, and Zelda complained he was an unsatisfactory lover.

35

Fourth Trip Abroad

[Spring 1929]

When the lease on 'Ellerslie' expired in the spring of 1929, the Fitzgeralds decided to return to Europe – partly so that Zelda could resume work with Egorova and partly because there was nothing to keep them in America. Fitzgerald may have hoped that he would be able to make progress on his novel if he worked in its setting.

At John Biggs's urging Fitzgerald applied for a $60,000 insurance policy with the Sun Life Assurance Company of Canada before returning to Europe. Somewhat to his surprise, he passed the physical examination. The premium was $741.91 per quarter. (The policy, which Fitzgerald maintained with difficulty, would constitute the bulk of his estate.) Despite the reassuring verdict of the insurance company's doctor, Fitzgerald remained convinced that his tuberculosis was active. That September he was examined by a radiologist in Cannes. Although Fitzgerald interpreted it as a virtual death sentence, the report does not indicate an active case of tuberculosis. The x-rays showed that he had had tuberculosis, but in 1929 there was no evidence of an infiltrate or cavity. A smear test for acid-fast bacilli, which would have been conclusive, was not performed.[91]

In March the Fitzgeralds took the Mediterranean route on

the *Conte Biancamano*. Fitzgerald had promised Perkins that he would revise the third and fourth chapters on the boat and send them from Genoa, but failed to do so. An American woman who met them aboard ship kept a diary in which she noted that they were both 'lit.' When Fitzgerald asked, 'Do women like a man's private parts large or small?' Zelda said, 'Shut up Scott, you fool.'[92] They spent March at the Beau Rivage hotel in Nice, and again Fitzgerald was jailed for disorderly conduct. By early April they were in Paris, where they rented an apartment on the rue Mézières near St. Sulpice.

Early in 1929 Fitzgerald helped Zelda plan a series of stories about types of girls for *College Humor*. Although the stories appeared with the byline 'F. Scott and Zelda Fitzgerald,' they were written by Zelda and only polished by him. 'The Original Follies Girl,' 'The Southern Girl,' 'The Girl the Prince Liked,' 'The Girl with Talent,' and 'The Poor Working Girl' were published between July 1929 and January 1931 at prices from $400 to $800. Fitzgerald thought they were worth more money, explaining to Ober in late September that 'most of them have been pretty strong draughts on Zelda's and my common store of material. This ['The Girl with Talent'] is Mary Hay for instance + the 'Girl the Prince Liked' was Josephine Ordway both of whom I had in my notebook to use.'[93] A sixth story by Zelda, 'A Millionaire's Girl,' appeared in the *Post* in 1929 under Fitzgerald's name alone, and it brought $4,000. Ober explained: 'I really felt a little guilty about dropping Zelda's name from that story . . . but I think she understands that using the two names would have tied the story up with the College Humor series and might have got us into trouble.'[94]

One of the motivations for Zelda's short-story work was her desire to pay for her ballet lessons. Her morning and afternoon lessons at Egorova's studio over the Olympia Music Hall cost $300 a month. There is no indication that Fitzgerald balked at paying for them, although he regarded her ambitions as impossible. She wanted the ballet to be something of her own and resented accepting his money for her lessons. Writing rapidly at the same time that she was dancing for hours every day increased the strain on her. Friends noticed Zelda's distracted behavior: her silences interrupted by puzzling remarks and her inappropriate smiles. Fitzgerald later replied to Sara Murphy's charge that he did not understand people – not even Zelda: 'In an odd way, perhaps incredible to you, she was always my child. . . . Outside of the realm of what you called Zelda's "terribly dangerous secret thoughts" I was her great reality, often the only liaison agent who could make the world tangible to her—'[95]

The fiction Zelda began writing in 1929 is characterized by wit, striking metaphors, words applied in unusual ways, and a rich sense of atmosphere. The opening of 'A Millionaire's Girl,' written in February 1930, displays Zelda's lush style and her sensitivity to the moods of time and place:

> Twilights were wonderful just after the war. They hung above New York like indigo wash, forming themselves from asphalt dust and sooty shadows under the cornices and limp gusts of air exhaled from closing windows, to hang above the streets with all the mystery of white fog rising off a swamp. The far-away lights from buildings high in the sky burned hazily through the blue, like golden objects lost in deep grass, and the noise of hurrying streets took on that hushed quality of many footfalls in a huge stone square. Through the gloom people went to tea. On all the corners around the Plaza Hotel, girls in short squirrel coats and long flowing skirts and hats like babies' velvet bathtubs waited for the changing traffic to be suctioned up by the revolving doors of the fashionable grill. Under the scalloped portico of the Ritz, girls in short ermine coats and fluffy, swirling dresses and hats the size of manholes passed from the nickel glitter of traffic to the crystal glitter of the lobby.[96]

The principal defect of her fiction is that it lacks story form and is essayistic. Fitzgerald acknowledged that Zelda was 'a great original in her way, with perhaps a more intense flame at its highest than I ever had,' but insisted that she lacked education and discipline.[97] 'She isn't a "natural story-teller" in the sense that I am, and unless a story comes to her fully developed and crying to be told she's liable to flounder around rather unsuccessfully among problems of construction.'[98] With her writing, as with her dancing, she started late and missed the apprenticeship that most professionals require.

Hemingway was in Paris in 1929, and Fitzgerald anticipated a resumption of their 1925–26 intimacy. He was hurt to learn that Hemingway was concealing his address from him because the Hemingways did not want to deal with Fitzgerald's drunken visits. Moreover, Pauline Hemingway disapproved of the Fitzgeralds. The status of the two writers had altered in the four years since their first meeting. Hemingway had become the most promising figure in American fiction, whereas Fitzgerald was regarded by many of their friends as a ruined drunk.

Fitzgerald was again eager to preview Hemingway's new novel. Now convinced that Fitzgerald's editorial advice was worthless, Hemingway reluctantly gave him a typescript of *A Farewell to Arms*, probably in June after serialization of the novel had begun in the May issue of *Scribner's Magazine*. Fitzgerald prepared a nine-page holograph memo, on which Hemingway wrote 'Kiss my ass.'

114–121 is slow + needs cutting – it hasn't the incisiveness of other short portraits in this book or in yr. other books. The characters too numerous + too much nailed down by gags. *Please* cut! There's absolutely no psychical justification in introducing those singers – its not even bizarre – if he got stewed with them + in consequence thrown from hospital it would be O.K. At least reduce it to a sharp + self sufficient vignette. It's just rather gassy as it is, I think.

For example – your Englishman on the fishing trip in T.S.A.R. contributes to the tautness of waiting for Brett. You seem to have written this to try to 'round out the picture of Milan during the war' during a less inspired moment.

(Arn't the Croats Orthodox Greeks? or some Byzantine Christian Sect – Surely they're not predominantly Mohamedens + you can't say their not Christans.

122^{ect}

In 'Cat in the rain' + in the story about 'That's all we do isn't it, go + try new drinks ect,' you were really listening to women – here you re only listening to yourself, to your own mind beating out facily a sort of sense that isn't really interesting, Ernest, nor really much except a sort of literary exercise – it seems to me that this ought to be *thoroughly* cut, even re-written.

(Our poor old friendship probably won't survive this but there you are – better me than some nobody in the Literary Review that doesn't care about you + your future.)

P. 124 *et sequitur*

This is definately *dull* – it's all right to say it was meant all the time + that a novel can't have the finesse of a short story but this has got to. This scene as it is seems to me a shame.*

Later I was astonished to find it was only about 750 wds. which only goes to show the pace you set yourself up to that point. Its dull because the war goes further + further out of sight every minute. 'That's the way it was' is no answer – this triumphant proof that races were fixed!

– I should put it as *400* word beginning to Chap XXI

Still later Read by itself it has points, but coming on it in the novel I still believe its dull + slow

———————

———————

Seems to me a last echo of the war very faint when Catherine is dying and he's drinking beer in the Cafe.

———————

Look over Switzerland stuff for cutting
(ie. 2nd page numbered 129)

———

* Chapter 20: The account of Frederic and Catherine at the race track.

321

129 (NW)* Now here's a great scene – your comedy used as part of you + not as mere roll-up-my sleeves- + pull-off a tour-de-force as on pages 114–121

P. 130—

This is a comedy scene that really becomes offensive for you've trained everyone to read every word – now you make them read the word cooked (+ fucked would be as bad) *one dozen times*. It has ceased to become amusing by the 5th, for they're too packed, + yet the scene has possibilities. Reduced to five or six *cooked* it might have rythm like the word 'wops' in one of your early sketches. You're a little hypnotized by yourself here.†

133–138

This could stand a good cutting. Sometimes these conversations with her take on a naive quality that wouldn't please you in anyone else's work. Have you read Noel Coward? Some of its wonderful – about brave man 1000 deaths ect. Couldn't you cut a little‡

134

Remember the brave expectant illegitimmate mother is an old situation + has been exploited by all sorts of people you wo't lower yourself to read – so be sure every line rings *new* + has some claim to being incarnated + inspired truth or you'll have the boys apon you with scorn,

By the way – that buying the pistol is a *wonderful* scene.

Catherine is too glib, talks too much physically. In cutting their conversations cut some of her speeches rather than his. She is too glib—

I mean – you're seeing him in a sophisticated way as now you see yourself then – but you're still seeing her as you did in 1917 thru nineteen yr. old eyes. In consequence unless you make her a bit fatuous occasionally the contrast jars – either the writer is a simple fellow or she's Eleanora Duse disguised as a

---

* Chapter 22: Miss Van Campen's discovery of the bottles in Frederic's hospital room.
† Chapter 21: Frederic's report of the British officer's analysis of the war.
‡ Chapter 21: Catherine's announcement that she is pregnant.

Red Cross nurse. In one moment you expect her to prophecy
the 2nd battle of the Marne – as you probably did then.
Where's that desperate, half-childish dont-make-me-think
V.A.D. feeling you spoke to me about? It's there – here – but
cut *to* it! Don't try to make her make sense – she probably
didn't!

The book, by the way is between 80,000 + 100,000 wds – not
160,000 as you thought
   P. 241 is one of the best pages you've ever written, I think

   P. 209 – + 219 I think if you use the word cocksuckers here
the book will be suppressed + confiscated within two days of
publication.

———————

All this retreat is marvellous the confusion ect.
   The scene from 218 on is the best in recent fiction*
   I think 293–294 need cutting but perhaps not to be cut
altogether.†
   It is the most eloquent in the book + could end it rather
gently + well.
   A beautiful book it is!

Kiss my ass
EH   99

Fitzgerald's main criticism was that Catherine Barkley's
speech was sometimes stagy and that her role as 'brave
expectant illegitimmate mother' had to be made fresh; he was
also concerned about the typescript ending of the novel,
which included a forecast of the characters' lives after
Catherine dies: 'I could tell how Rinaldi was cured of the
syphilis and lived to find that the technic learned in wartime
surgery is not of much practical use in peace. . . .'[100] He
recommended that Hemingway replace this ending with
Frederic Henry's meditation after his reunion with Catherine
at Stresa: 'If people bring so much courage to this world the

———

* Chapter 30: Frederic's arrest by the *carabinieri* and his escape.
† Opening of Chapter 40.

world has to kill them to break them, so of course it kills them. The world breaks every one and afterward many are strong at the broken places. But those that will not break it kills. It kills the very good and the very gentle and the very brave impartially. If you are none of these you can be sure it will kill you too but there will be no special hurry.'[101] Fitzgerald wrote on page 241 of the typescript, 'This is one of the most beautiful pages in all English literature.'[102] Although Hemingway repeatedly ridiculed Fitzgerald's advice, he acted on some of it in revising *A Farewell to Arms* in proof. Henry's cosmic ruminations at the opening of Chapter 40 (typescript pp. 293–94) were deleted. Hemingway tried to replace the original ending with the passage on typescript page 241 that Fitzgerald admired, before he wrote the famous understated published ending: 'After a while I went out and left the hospital and walked back to the hotel in the rain.' Hemingway later insisted that Fitzgerald gave him the terrible advice to have Henry read about the American troops at Belleau Wood while Catherine was dying.[103] This suggestion is not in Fitzgerald's memo, but it could have been made in conversation. It was substantially the same advice that Perkins had offered Hemingway in May about recombining the love and war themes at the end of the novel.

As reported in *A Moveable Feast*, Fitzgerald sought Hemingway's counsel about Zelda's complaint that his penis was too small to satisfy her.* It is an indication of Fitzgerald's respect for Hemingway's expertise in masculine matters that he turned to him for help; but he should have known that his admission would provoke Hemingway's contempt. After checking him in the men's room, Hemingway assured him that he was normal and urged him to repair his confidence by sleeping with somebody else. 'Zelda just wants to destroy you.'[105]

---

* The publication of *A Moveable Feast* resulted in public calibration of Fitzgerald's penis. Two witnesses – Arnold Gingrich, who once saw Fitzgerald with his bathrobe open, and Sheilah Graham, who slept with him – attested that it was normal.[104]

Zelda extended her attack on Fitzgerald's masculinity by charging that he was involved in a homosexual liaison with Hemingway, which hurt him more than anything else she said: 'The nearest I ever came to leaving you was when you told me you thot I was a fairy in the Rue Palatine. . . . '[106] She cited as evidence his muttering 'No more baby' in his sleep after coming home drunk from a meeting with Hemingway.[107] Zelda's accusation was especially painful to Fizgerald because he had always been outspokenly contemptuous of 'fairies.' It is fashionable to claim that men who are strongly biased against homosexuals are masking their sexual insecurities or compensating for impulses of which they are ashamed. (This charge has been frequently brought against Hemingway.) Anyone can be called a latent homosexual, but there is no evidence that Fitzgerald was ever involved in a homosexual attachment. His close friendships with men were expressions of his hero worship and generosity. If Father Fay was a homosexual, as has been asserted without proof, Fitzgerald was unaware of it. Fitzgerald observed in his *Notebooks*: 'The great homosexual theses – that all great pansies were pansies.'[108]

It is not known whether he reported Zelda's accusation to Hemingway, but Fitzgerald began to worry that he was acquiring a reputation as a homosexual. He was not ready to dismiss Zelda's charge as an indication that she was becoming deranged. (Suspicion about other people's sexual behavior is one of the symptoms of schizophrenia; and impotence is sometimes a side-effect of alcoholism.) Intending to verify his masculinity, Fitzgerald decided to try sleeping with a whore and purchased condoms; Zelda found them, and a bitter argument ensued.[109] At the same time she was expressing these suspicions about her husband, Zelda became concerned that she was a latent lesbian. Fitzgerald was furious when Dolly Wilde, a notorious Paris 'amazon,' made a pass at Zelda in May 1929.[110] Although Zelda developed close attachments to several women, there is no evidence that she ever engaged in a lesbian affair.

Three of the seven *Post* stories Fitzgerald wrote in 1929 –
'The Rough Crossing' (March), 'The Swimmers' (July–
August), and 'Two Wrongs' (October–November) – belong
with his cycle of marriage-problem stories, which probe with
increasing openness the wounds in the Fitzgerald marriage.
In 'The Rough Crossing,' based on the storm during the
Fitzgeralds' return to America in 1928, a marital crisis
accompanies a storm at sea. A successful playwright and his
wife are en route to Europe to get away from the distractions
in America – a recurring situation in Fitzgerald's fiction.
When he becomes infatuated with a younger woman, his wife
retaliates by involving herself with another man. At the
height of the storm she throws her pearls overboard, recalling
Zelda's gesture with her watch in 1927. Since this was a *Post*
story, the troubles pass with the storm. But the crisis could not
be resolved so neatly in the Fitzgeralds' marriage. Their
resentments, betrayals, and retaliations festered. A more
serious examination of marital betrayal is 'Two Wrongs,' in
which a Broadway producer loses his success and health
through dissipation and egoism. At the same time, his wife
begins her ballet career. When he develops tuberculosis and is
sent west to die, she lets him go alone because she has earned
the right to the career she has worked for. The story includes
an analysis of the wife's feelings about the dance, which was
also Fitzgerald's attempt to understand Zelda's commitment:
'She wanted to use herself on something she could believe in,
and it seemed to her that the dance was woman's
interpretation of music; instead of strong fingers, one had
limbs with which to render Tschaikowsky and Stravinski; and
feet could be as eloquent in Chopiniana as voices in "The
Ring." '[111]

The most interesting of the 1929 stories is 'The Swimmers.'
Although it is flawed by a trick plot and – as Fitzgerald
admitted – has too much material for its form, this story
represents Fitzgerald's attempt to synthesize his feelings
about France and America after four trips abroad. Henry
Clay Marston, an American living in Paris with his French

-46-

passenger was through at the window. When she ~~twined~~ turned they both

started; ~~he~~ and saw it was the girl.

"Oh, hello," she cried " I'm glad you're ~~along~~ going. I was

just asking when the pool opened. The thing about this ship

is that you can always get a swim."

"Why do you like to swim?" he demanded.

"You always ask me that." ~~She smiled.~~

"Perhaps you'd tell me, if we ~~dine~~ together to-night."

But when he ~~lift~~ her he knew that she could never tell

him, she was ~~another.~~ France was a land, England a people, but

America, ~~was~~ the graves at Shiloh and the tired, drawn nervous

faces of its great men, and a

~~And~~ the country boys/in the Argonne for a phrase that

was empty before their ~~body~~ withered. ⫶ It was a willingness

of the heart.

having about it still that quality of the
idea, was harder to ~~utter~~ — it was

Revised typescript for 'The Swimmers'
BRUCCOLI COLLECTION

wife, suffers a nervous breakdown after finding her in a compromising situation. His recovery is assisted by an American girl who teaches him to swim. Marston and his wife move to America, but she is again unfaithful. As he embarks for Europe after their divorce, Marston's feelings about America are expressed in an eloquent peroration:

> Watching the fading city, the fading shore, from the deck of the Majestic, he had a sense of overwhelming gratitude and gladness that America was there, that under the ugly débris of industry the rich land still pushed up, incorrigibly lavish and fertile, and that in the heart of the leaderless people the old generosities and devotions fought on, breaking out sometimes in fanaticism and excess, but indomitable and undefeated. There was a lost generation in the saddle at the moment, but it seemed to him that the men coming on, the men of the war, were better; and all his old feeling that America was a bizarre accident, a sort of historical sport, had gone forever. The best of America was the best of the world.
>
> . . . .
>
> France was a land, England was a people, but America, having about it still the quality of the idea, was harder to utter – it was the graves at Shiloh and the tired, drawn, nervous faces of its great men, and the country boys dying in the Argonne for a phrase that was empty before their bodies withered. It was a willingness of the heart.[112]

Though too profound for 'The Swimmers,' this summary demonstrates that Fitzgerald's response to his expatriate experience was a reinforcement of his identification with America – not just patriotism, but a deep emotional sense of its history and hopes. By one of the ironies that abound in Fitzgerald's career, 'The Swimmers' appeared in the *Post* issue for 19 October 1929, just before the Wall Street crash that terminated the era of American life Fitzgerald responded to so richly. The concluding passage from 'The Swimmers' also served as Fitzgerald's rebuttal to Gertrude Stein's 'lost generation' catch phrase that had achieved currency through Hemingway's use of it as an epigraph for *The Sun Also Rises*.

Fourth Trip Abroad [Spring 1929]

Whereas Stein had identified the lost generation with the war veterans, Fitzgerald insisted that the lost generation was the prewar group and expressed confidence in 'the men of the war.'

In May, Fitzgerald wrote a skillful commercial story for the *Post* in which he again created one of his determined young women. In 'Majesty' a beautiful American heiress rebels against her family's conventional expectations and takes up with a seedy claimant to a Middle European kingdom; with her help the weakling becomes ruler over rich mineral deposits, and she becomes his queen. The plot is unlikely, but Fitzgerald managed to make the heroine convincing. 'At Your Age,' another commercial story written in June about the attempt of a fifty-year-old man to win a young woman, brought a raise to Fitzgerald's peak *Post* price of $4,000. In 1929 Fitzgerald earned $27,000 from eight stories and $31.71 from book royalties.

May and June 1929 in Paris were months of drinking and trouble for Fitzgerald. A May *Ledger* entry indicates the kind of mess he got into when drunk: 'Nigger affair – Buck, Michell in prison. Dane.' This reference to a squabble he became involved in with blacks in Montmartre found its way into *Tender Is the Night*, where the episode marks Abe North's deterioration.

36

Paris and Cannes

[Summer 1929]

The young Canadian novelist Morley Callaghan, who had just become a Scribners author, was in Paris during the spring and summer of 1929 and looked up Fitzgerald to thank him for recommending his work to Perkins. Callaghan had known Hemingway when they were on the *Toronto Star*, and they boxed regularly in Paris. Fitzgerald was anxious to attend one of these private bouts and in June was invited to come along as timekeeper. According to Callaghan's detailed account in *That Summer in Paris* (1963), Fitzgerald was surprised to see the smaller Callaghan handle Hemingway with ease. Fitzgerald believed in Hemingway's reputation as a fighter of professional caliber, but Callaghan and others who boxed with him have attested that Hemingway was clumsy and easy to hit. In the second round Fitzgerald became so interested in the action as Hemingway tried to nail Callaghan with a knockout punch that he let the three-minute round run a minute long. When Callaghan knocked Hemingway down, Fitzgerald exclaimed, 'Oh, my God! I let the round go four minutes.' Hemingway angrily replied, 'All right, Scott. If you want to see me getting the shit knocked out of me, just say so. Only don't say you made a mistake.'[113] According to Callaghan, Fitzgerald was

330

shocked by Hemingway's accusation; but the matter was patched up and the rest of the day went amicably.* That summer, while Fitzgerald was on the Riviera and Hemingway was following the bullfights in Spain, they exchanged friendly letters – in which the Callaghan bout was not mentioned. Hemingway's 1929 letters to Fitzgerald show him trying to bolster Fitzgerald's confidence at a time when Fitzgerald was painfully aware that *A Farewell to Arms* was a brilliant success while his own novel was still unfinished after four years. When Fitzgerald reported that he was really working hard on his novel and was ashamed of all the time he had wasted, Hemingway assured him that the parts of the novel he had seen were better than anything except the best parts of *Gatsby*, and repeated his pet theory that Fitzgerald's novel writing had been blocked by Gilbert Seldes's favorable review of *Gatsby*, which compelled him to try to write a masterpiece.[115]

By July 1929 the Fitzgeralds were renting the Villa Fleur des Bois on the Boulevard Eugène Gazagnaire in Cannes, where they remained through September. Fitzgerald's *Ledger* has this July entry: 'Zelda dancing in Nice + Cannes.' It is unknown whether she had professional engagements or was taking lessons on the Riviera. In September she was offered a solo role in *Aïda* with the San Carlo Opera ballet company in Naples. It was the best ballet offer she ever received, and there is no explanation for her decision to decline it.

Fitzgerald informed Perkins in July: 'I am working night + day on novel from new angle that I think will solve previous difficulties.'[116] He had almost certainly dropped the matricide story for a new plot about Lew and Nicole Kelly, a movie director and his wife who are going to Europe because he feels he has grown stale in Hollywood. Aboard the ship are a girl named Rosemary and her mother, who hope that Kelly

---

* Fitzgerald never wrote about his timekeeping error. The eyewitness reports are by Callaghan and Hemingway, and Hemingway's versions changed over the years. This account is based on Callaghan's *That Summer in Paris* (New York: Coward-McCann, 1963). In 1951 Hemingway made the absurd claim that Fitzgerald had let the round go 13 minutes.[114]

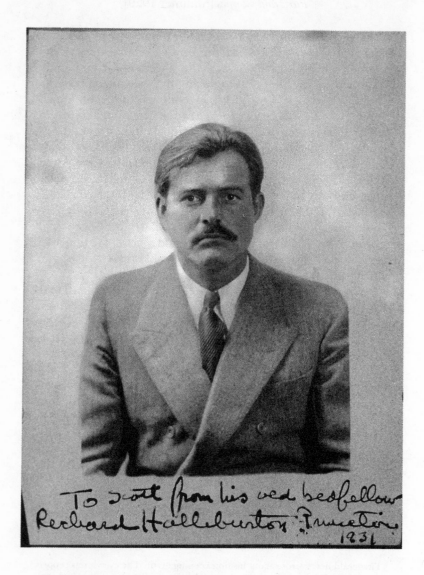

*Hemingway's inscription. Halliburton was a Princetonian who
wrote travel-adventure books*

will help Rosemary get a start in the movies. Lew Kelly was probably based on Rex Ingram, the director of *The Four Horsemen of the Apocalypse*, *The Prisoner of Zenda*, and *Scaramouche*, who had left Hollywood and set up a studio at Nice in 1927. Fitzgerald knew Ingram, who, like Kelly, was Irish and had attended Yale. The young actress introduces the Lois Moran-Rosemary Hoyt figure into the stream of composition. Only two shipboard chapters, comprising about fifty manuscript pages, survive from the Kelly version. The opening describes the Kellys walking the deck and chanting a nonsense song – 'Oh-oh-oh-oh/Other flamingoes than me' – which was salvaged for Book II of *Tender Is the Night*. When Fitzgerald read the Kelly opening to Zelda, she was distressed by the point that the director cannot devote all his attention to his wife and probably annoyed by the Lois/Rosemary character.

Fitzgerald dispatched optimistic progress reports during the summer and fall of 1929, but it is unlikely that he wrote more than the two extant chapters. On 29 August he cabled Ober: SENDING THREE FOURTH OF NOVEL SEPT 30 TH STARTING NEW STORY NEXT WEEK CAN YOU DEPOSIT THREE-FIFTY.[117] Writing in the tone of self-denigration that had come to characterize his letters to Hemingway, Fitzgerald admitted on 9 September:

> Just taken another chapter to typists + its left me in a terrible mood of depression as to whether its any good or not.* In 2½ mos. I've been here I've written 20,000 words on it + one short story, which is superb for me of late years. I've paid for it with the usual nervous depression and such drinking manners as the lowest bistrop (bistrot?) boy would scorn. My latest tendency is to collapse about 11:00 and, with tears flowing from my eyes or the gin rising to their level and leaking over, + tell interested friends or acquaintances that I havn't a friend in the world and likewise care for nobody, generally including Zelda, and often implying current company – after which current company tend to become less

* No typed chapters for the Kelly version survive.

current and I wake up in strange rooms in strange palaces. The rest of the time I stay alone working or trying to work or brooding or reading detective stories – and realizing that anyone in my state of mind who has in addition never been able to hold his tongue, is pretty poor company. But when drunk I make them all pay and pay and pay.

. . . .

Your analysis of my inability to get my serious work done is too kind in that it leaves out dissipation, but among acts of God it is possible that the 5 yrs between my leaving the army and finishing *Gatsby* 1919–1924 which included 3 novels, about 50 popular stories + a play + numerous articles + movies may I have taken all I had to say too early, adding that all the time we were living at top speed in the gayest worlds we could find.

. . . .

Here's a last flicker of the old cheap pride: – the *Post* now pays the old whore $4,000. a screw. But now it's because she's mastered the 40 positions – in her youth one was enough.[118]

The 20,000-word claim is high for fifty manuscript pages. Reconstructing the stages of *Tender Is the Night* is difficult because of Fitzgerald's exaggerated progress reports. He also claimed that he destroyed drafts; and Gerald Murphy witnessed one such incident. Fitzgerald's summer work on his novel was not steady, because he wrote 'The Swimmers' in July and August, which proved to be a difficult job. Hemingway replied:

> Oh Hell. You have more stuff than anyone and you care more about it and for Christ sake just keep on and go through with it now and dont please write anything else until it's finished. It will be damned good—
> (They never raise an old whore's price – she may know 850 positions – they cut her price all the same – So either you arent old or not a whore or both) The stories arent whoring They're just bad judgement – You could have and can make enough to live on writing novels.[119]

When Harold Ober gave up his partnership in the Reynolds agency in September 1929, Fitzgerald cabled him:

FOLLOWING YOU NATURALLY.[120] Ober prospered on his own, building a list of important clients that included William Faulkner. For the next decade he would serve as Fitzgerald's banker and eventually as his editor. In the early years of the Twenties, Fitzgerald requested payment for a story when he delivered it to Ober but before it was sold to a magazine. Their arrangement changed to a system whereby Fitzgerald would borrow against his next unwritten story, so that by 1928 he had spent the money before the story was written.

Fitzgerald's *Ledger* summary for the year was: 'Thirty two years old (And sore as hell about it) OMINOUS No Real Progress in ANY way + *wrecked myself with dozens of people.*'

In October the Fitzgeralds returned to Paris by car, through Aix, Arles, Pont du Gard, Vichy, and the château country. During this trip Zelda grabbed the steering wheel and tried to drive over a cliff, claiming that the car was responding to its own will. They rented an apartment at 10 rue Pergolèse near the Bois de Boulogne. During October and November Fitzgerald worked on 'Two Wrongs.' When the story was finished, he wrote Perkins: 'For the first time since August I see my way clear to a long stretch on the novel, so I'm writing you as I can't bear to do when its in one of its states of posteponement + seems so in the air.'[121] Nonetheless, Fitzgerald made no significant progress on the novel in Paris, and he felt increasingly resentful of Zelda's absorption in the dance. In *Save Me the Waltz* Zelda described the exhaustion of her work with Egorova:

> Alabama rubbed her legs with Elizabeth Arden muscle oil night after night. There were blue bruises inside above the knee where the muscles were torn. Her throat was so dry that at first she thought she had a fever and was disappointed to find that she had none. In her bathing suit she tried to stretch on the high back of a Louis Quartorze sofa. She was always stiff, and she clutched the gilt flowers in pain. She fastened her feet through the bars of the iron bed and slept with her toes glued outwards for weeks. Her lessons were agony.
> . . . . At night she sat in the window too tired to move, consumed

by a longing to succeed as a dancer. It seemed to Alabama that, reaching her goal, she would drive the devils that had driven her – that, in proving herself, she would achieve that peace which she imagined went only in surety of one's self – that she would be able, through the medium of the dance, to command her emotions, to summon love or pity or happiness at will, having provided a channel through which they might flow.[122]

Even though Fitzgerald angrily told Zelda that she would never become a first-rate dancer, he understood the desperation of her efforts and probably realized that she was close to the breaking point. He would compel her to turn in early when she showed signs of fatigue. Morley Callaghan, who was present at some of these occasions, was perplexed by Zelda's meekness in accepting her husband's authority and wondered about the reasons behind Fitzgerald's command over her. In retrospect, Callaghan concluded that Zelda had already begun to show symptoms of her impending breakdown.

Gertrude Stein caused an additional strain in the friendship between Fitzgerald and Hemingway that fall by telling them that Fitzgerald was the most talented writer of his generation, the one with the brightest flame. Her compliment upset Fitzgerald, who interpreted it as a slight to Hemingway or as an implied criticism of himself. Hemingway wrote Fitzgerald that Stein had been sincere, assuring him that he didn't feel any resentment or sense of competition with Fitzgerald because any comparison of flames was 'pure horseshit': 'There can be no such thing between serious writers – They are all in the same boat. Competition within that boat – which is headed toward death – is as silly as deck sports are – The only competition is the original one of making the boat and that all takes place inside yourself – You're on the boat but you're getting touchy because you haven't finished your novel – that's all – I understand it and you could be a lot more touchy and I wouldn't mind.'[123]

There was a delayed reaction to the Callaghan-Hemingway boxing episode after incorrect reports appeared in American newspapers. On 24 November 1929 the *New York Herald Tribune* printed an article stating that Callaghan had knocked out Hemingway for disparaging his boxing stories.* When Callaghan saw the article in Canada, he sent the *Trib* a correction that appeared on 8 December; but in the meantime Fitzgerald cabled Callaghan at Hemingway's insistence: HAVE SEEN STORY IN HERALD TRIBUNE ERNEST AND I WAIT YOUR CORRECTION SCOTT FITZGERALD.[124] Since Callaghan had not been responsible for the story, he was angry with Fitzgerald and sent him an abusive reply. The situation was further complicated by Hemingway's suspicion that Callaghan had repeated Robert McAlmon's gossip about his alleged homosexuality. McAlmon – who was a homosexual – also claimed that Fitzgerald was one. Fitzgerald believed that McAlmon's gossip about him and Hemingway helped to spoil the friendship. He observed in his *Notebooks*: 'I really loved him, but of course it wore out like a love affair. The fairies have spoiled all that.'[125] Hemingway is not named in this note, but the reference is clear.

With Perkins trying to act as peacemaker for three of his authors, the crisis ended after a four-sided exchange of letters; but Callaghan's friendship with Fitzgerald and Hemingway was finished. Although Callaghan became convinced that Fitzgerald's admiration for Hemingway was permanently ruined, Hemingway's letters to Fitzgerald about the Callaghan contretemps show him trying to patch their friendship. In December he wrote Fitzgerald that he did not suspect him of having deliberately let the round go long: 'I know you are the soul of honor. I mean that. If you remember I made no cracks about your time keeping until after you had told me over my objections for about the fourth time that you were going to deliberately quarrel with me. . . .

* The report first appeared in Caroline Bancroft's *Denver Post* article and was reprinted in Isabel M. Paterson's 'Turns with a Bookworm' column in the *Herald Tribune*. Bancroft later informed Callaghan that her source was Virginia Hersch, who heard it in Paris. Hemingway believed that Paris journalist Pierre Loving had been responsible for the false account.

I was so appalled at the idea of you saying that you were going
to deliberately quarrel with me that I didnt know (just having
heard those vile stuff from McA and C. which I thought I
should have heard a long time sooner, if I was to hear it, and
it was to go so long unresented) where the hell I stood on
anything.'[126]

37

Paris: Zelda's Collapse

[Fall 1929–Spring 1930]

The Wall Street crash on 29 October 1929 did not
directly affect Fitzgerald because he owned no
securities and had never played the market. The inventory of
the Fitzgeralds' possessions in 'Auction – Model 1934'
concludes: 'We shall keep it all – the tangible remnant of the
four hundred thousand we made from hard words and spent
with easy ones these fifteen years. And the collection, after all,
is just as valuable now as the Polish and Peruvian bonds of our
thriftier friends.'[127] Nonetheless, the Crash would reduce
Fitzgerald's earning power.* With his capacity for becoming
identified with the moods of his times, Fitzgerald would come
to symbolize the excesses of the Boom Decade. The Twenties
had spoiled and rewarded him. The Thirties would disparage
him.

Fitzgerald later made this assessment of the Twenties: 'It is
the custom now to look back ourselves of the boom days with
a disapproval that approaches horror. But it had its virtues,
that old boom: Life was a great deal larger and gayer for most
people, and the stampede to the spartan virtues in times of
war and famine shouldn't make us too dizzy to remember its

---

* Between 1920 and 1929 the Fitzgeralds' writings brought him $244,967
after commissions.

339

hilarious glory. There were so many good things. These eyes have been hallowed by watching a man order champagne for his two thousand guests, by listening while a woman ordered a whole staircase from the greatest sculptor in the world, by seeing a man tear up a good check for eight hundred thousand dollars.'[128] These moments represent more than extravagance. They share a generosity of gesture, a sense of infinite possibilities, that Fitzgerald responded to eloquently and complexly as 'the most expensive orgy in history.'[129] The identification of Fitzgerald with the Twenties – which represented half his professional life – has contributed to the distorted popular impression of him as the totemic figure who embodied or was even somehow responsible for the excesses of the boom and the punitive Depression. The ways in which his career duplicated the national moods are almost too neat – like something inept novelists invent. After achieving sudden success with *This Side of Paradise* in the spring of 1920, for the next decade he was rewarded for retelling people their favorite fables about youth and love and ambition and success and happiness. It wasn't that simple, of course, for amidst the echolalia of his parties there was a quest for values operating in his work. As the Twenties lurched or sprinted forward, Fitzgerald's warning notes became clearer. Yet the preacher was unable to heed his own sermons. He could only send out messages from within the hysteria. The moralist had to be a participant. By 1929 Fitzgerald knew he had lost something. Not his genius, not his capacity to feel intensely, not even his capacity for work. He had lost his belief that 'life was something you dominated if you were any good.'[130]

Continuing to serve as talent scout for Scribners, in January 1930 Fitzgerald called Perkins's attention to Robert Cantwell, Erskine Caldwell, Gerald Sykes, Cary Ross, Murry Godwin, and René Crevel. At the same time he sent Perkins 'some memoirs by an ex-marine doorman at my bank here' and proposed a plan for a series of translated French and German military volumes. Perkins interviewed Cantwell and Caldwell;

and Scribners published two of Caldwell's books, including *Tobacco Road*.

Throughout the fall and winter of 1929–30 Zelda's behavior showed the effects of the increasing strain of her intensive ballet work and her writing. At a flower market she told Fitzgerald that the flowers were talking to her. In February 1930 the Fitzgeralds took a trip to North Africa, mainly to provide Zelda with a rest. She later wrote: 'It was a trying winter and to forget bad times we went to Algiers. The Hôtel du l'Oasis was laced together by Moorish grills; and the bar was an outpost of civilization with people accentuating their eccentricities. Beggars in white sheets were propped against the walls, and the dash of colonial uniforms gave the cafés a desperate swashbuckling air. Berbers have plaintive trusting eyes but it is really Fate they trust.'[131] The trip was not a success because Zelda was anxious about the lessons she was missing. They quarreled bitterly in Biskra.

Zelda's devotion to Egorova grew steadily as she saw in her teacher a noble figure who endured poverty for the sake of art. Zelda desperately wanted Egorova's approval and competed with the other dancers for her attention. The ballet studio was a breeding place for the resentments and jealousies associated with the artistic temperament, and Zelda's fatigue was intensified by her nervous anxiety. Her concentration on dancing seemed to border on the pathological during the Kalmans' March 1930 visit to Paris. When Oscar Kalman was taking her to the studio, she became so upset about the possibility of being late that she changed into dancing clothes in the cab and ran to the studio when the cab was stuck in traffic.

There is a report that Zelda had a ballet recital in Paris early in 1930. Fitzgerald later recalled that Zelda was terribly disappointed when she thought a representative from Diaghilev's Ballet Russe had come to the studio to see her dance but discovered that he was actually someone from the Folies Bergère who was interested in making her a shimmy dancer.

With his novel stalled again, he resumed short-story work to maintain the expensive and unhappy life that the Fitzgeralds had evolved. He wrote eight stories in 1930, which brought $32,000 from the *Post*; but even so, he had to borrow $3,700 from Scribners against his novel. The first 1930 story, written in January, was 'First Blood,' the start of a five-story series ('First Blood,' 'A Nice Quiet Place,' 'A Woman with a Past,' 'A Snobbish Story,' and 'Emotional Bankruptcy') about Josephine Perry, a Chicago debutante at the time of World War I. The Josephine stories, based on Ginevra King, were not a companion series to the Basil stories because there was no overlap in material or characters; but they resulted from the same retrospective impulse, as Fitzgerald again reassessed his generation against his own decade of deterioration. Unlike Basil, who develops discipline, Josephine is self-destructive. She uses herself up on a series of trivial romances that provide no preparation for a responsible life, until in 'Emotional Bankruptcy' she has nothing left for the man she really wants to love. The concept of emotional bankruptcy became a key idea for Fitzgerald. He believed that people have a fixed amount of emotional capital; reckless expenditure results in early bankruptcy, which leaves the person unable to respond to the events that require true emotion. Appropriately, Fitzgerald developed a theory of character in terms of a financial metaphor.

Ten years and twenty days after her wedding Zelda Fitzgerald entered Malmaison clinic outside Paris. The Malmaison report reads:

Mrs. FITZ-GERALD entered on 23 April 1930 in a state of acute anxiety, restlessness, continually repeating: 'This is dreadful, this is horrible, what is going to become of me, I have to work, and I will no longer be able to, I must die, and yet I have to work. I will never be cured, let me leave. I have to go see 'Madame' (dance teacher), she has given me the greatest joy that can exist, it is comparable to the light of the sun that falls on a block of crystal, to a symphony of perfume, the most perfect chord from the greatest composer in music.

. . . .
    Finally, we are in the presence of a lady exhausted from
work in an environment of professional dancers. Some
obsessive ideas, the main one of which is her fear of becoming
a homosexual. She thinks she is in love with her dance teacher
(Madame X) as she had already thought in the past of being in
love with another woman.[132] [Translated from the French]

While Zelda was at Malmaison, Fitzgerald was involved in a
round of parties for the wedding of Ludlow Fowler's brother
Powell. He saw this wedding as the last manifestation of the
American Twenties in Paris. In May he wrote 'The Bridal
Party,' based on the Fowler wedding, which concluded that
American confidence had not been diminished by the Crash.
The story includes an inventory of the drinking habits among
the Americans in Paris that may indicate Fitzgerald's own
consumption: ' . . . for weeks they had drunk cocktails before
meals like Americans, wines and brandies like Frenchmen,
beer like Germans, whisky-and-soda like the English, and as
they were no longer in their twenties, this preposterous
mélange, that was like some gigantic cocktail in a nightmare,
served only to make them temporarily less conscious of the
mistakes of the night before.'[133]
In March 1930 Fitzgerald promised to start sending his
novel to Ober in sections, as he had tried to do with Perkins in
1928. Zelda's breakdown intervened, and in May Fitzgerald
explained to Ober:

> At one time I was about to send four chapters out of eight
> done to you. Then I cut one of those chapters absolutely to
> pieces. I know you're losing faith in me + Max too but God
> knows one has to rely in the end on one's own judgement. I
> could have published four lowsy, half baked books in the last
> five years + people would have thought I was at least a worthy
> young man not drinking myself to pieces in the south seas –
> but I'd be dead as Michael Arlen, Bromfield, Tom Boyd,
> Callaghan + the others who think they can trick the world with
> the hurried and the second rate. These *Post* stories *in* the *Post*
> are at least not any spot on me – they're honest and if their

form is stereotyped people know what to expect when they pick up the *Post*. The novel is another thing – if, after four years I published the Basil Lee stories as a book I might as well get tickets for Hollywood immediately.[134]

Even allowing for exaggeration, the 1930 material must have been a return to the Melarky-matricide story; the Kelly version never reached eight chapters. The four 1930 chapters cannot be identified because they were dismantled and incorporated into the final version of *Tender Is the Night*. Fitzgerald's report to Ober shows the nature of his problem with the novel: the longer the interval after *The Great Gatsby*, the better the new novel would have to be to justify the delay. As Hemingway had observed, Fitzgerald felt that he was in the position of having to write nothing less than an acknowledged masterpiece.

38

Prangins

[Summer–Fall 1930]

Zelda discharged herself from Malmaison on 11 May against her doctor's advice. She attempted to go back to ballet training but experienced hallucinations that resulted in a suicide attempt. On 22 May she entered Val-Mont clinic at Glion, Switzerland, which did not specialize in psychiatric problems. Dr. H. A. Trutmann of Val-Mont made this report on the case:

> At the beginning of the story Mrs. F. declared that she had never been ill and had been brought by force to the clinic. Every day she repeated that she wanted to return to Paris to resume her ballet work in which she thought she found the only satisfaction of her life. In addition, the patient related, in a rather obscure manner, the physical sensations which she felt, and which she connected with her homosexuality. This represented another reason for returning to Paris. The visits of her husband often offered the occasion for violent arguments, always provoked by the husband's attempts to reason with the patient and to refute the patient's insinuations because the patient suspected the husband of homosexuality. Mrs. F. put herself into a state of excitement at the thought that on one hand she was losing precious time, and on the other that the things most precious to her were being taken away: her work as a dancer and her Lesbian tendencies.[135]
> [Translated from the French]

Dr. Oscar Forel was brought in for a consultation on 3 June. He diagnosed Zelda as schizophrenic and agreed to treat her at his clinic, stipulating that she would have to agree to the transfer and that a temporary separation from her husband would be required.

On 5 June, Zelda entered Forel's Les Rives de Prangins clinic at Nyon on Lake Geneva between Geneva and Lausanne, accompanied by Fitzgerald and her brother-in-law Newman Smith. The Smiths, who were living in Brussels, represented the Sayre family during Zelda's treatment in Switzerland. Rosalind blamed Fitzgerald's drinking for Zelda's breakdown and wrote him, 'I would almost rather she die now than escape only to go back to the mad world you and she have created for yourselves.'[136] Fitzgerald argued in his defense that Zelda had always been eccentric and reckless, that their way of life was largely the result of her refusal to accept any domestic responsibility, and that there was a long history of nervous disorder in the Sayre family. According to Fitzgerald's inventory, Zelda's three sisters were neurotics; Judge Sayre had experienced a nervous breakdown; Mrs. Sayre's mother had committed suicide; there were some reputedly unbalanced uncles; and Zelda's brother was unstable.[137] (Anthony Sayre would commit suicide in 1933.)

Prangins had a resort-like atmosphere, and no expense was spared to provide Zelda with the most pleasant living conditions. Fitzgerald wanted to be near Zelda and spent the summer commuting between Paris and Switzerland – staying in hotels at Glion, Vevey, Caux, Lausanne, and Geneva. Scottie remained with her governess at 21 rue des Marionniers in Paris, where she attended the Cours Dieterlin. Concerned that the stock market crash would diminish his earning power, Fitzgerald made his last attempt to build an estate for his family when he invested $212 in a Northern Pacific Railway bond and an American Telephone & Telegraph debenture in June 1930.

Fitzgerald was anxious to resume sexual relations with Zelda at Prangins, but Dr. Forel did not allow him to visit her until a course of treatment had been established. During Zelda's fifteen months at Prangins she and Fitzgerald exchanged many letters – possibly more than a hundred – as they tried to explain their situation to each other and sometimes blamed each other for what had happened to them. In addition, Fitzgerald wrote long letters to Dr. Forel analyzing his relationship with Zelda and suggesting courses of treatment. Since neither of the Fitzgeralds dated letters to each other, it is impossible to establish a definite chronology; but a pattern can be seen. In the beginning their letters are often vituperative, expressing hurt and anger at the betrayals they assign to each other. Two of the 1930 letters reveal their wrenching need to justify themselves to each other. A seven-page memo, which may not have been sent, shows Fitzgerald attempting to account for the destruction of their happiness and the collapse of his career – which were intertwined.

" Les Rives de Prangins " Zelda's room + bath are around the corner facing the lake

The Drunkard's Holiday

Written with Zelda gone to the Clinique

I know this then – that those days when we came up from the south, from Capri, were among my happiest – but you were sick and the happiness was not in the home.

I had been unhappy for a long time then – When my play failed a year and a half before, when I worked so hard for a year, twelve stories and novel and four articles in that time with no one believing in me and no one to see except you + before the end your heart betraying me and then I was really alone with no one I liked. In Rome we were dismal and was still working proof and three more stories and in Capri you were sick and there seemed to be nothing left of happiness in the world anywhere I looked.

Then we came to Paris and suddenly I realized that it hadn't all been in vain. I was a success – the biggest man in my profession everybody admired me and I was proud I'd done such a good thing. I met Gerald and Sara who took us for friends now and Ernest who was an equeal and my kind of an idealist. I got drunk with him on the Left Bank in careless cafés and drank with Sara and Gerald in their garden in St Cloud but you were endlessly sick and at home everything was unhappy. We went to Antibes and I was happy but you were sick still and all that fall and that winter and spring at the cure and I was alone all the time and I had to get drunk before I could leave you so sick and not care and I was only happy a little while before I got too drunk. Afterwards there were all the usuall penalties for being drunk.

Finally you got well in Juan-les-Pins and a lot of money came in and I made of those mistakes literary men make – I thought I was 'a man of the world – that everybody liked me and admired me for myself but I only liked a few people like Ernest and Charlie McArthur and Gerald and Sara who were my peers. Time goes bye fast in those moods and nothing is ever done. I thought then that things came easily – I forgot how I'd dragged the great Gatsby out of the pit of my stomach in a time of misery. I woke up in Hollywood no longer my egotistic, certain self but a mixture of Ernest in fine clothes and Gerald with a career – and Charlie McArthur with a past. Anybody that could make me believe that, like Lois Moran did, was precious to me.

348

Prangins [Summer–Fall 1930]

Ellerslie, the polo people, Mrs. Chanler the party for Cecelia were all attempts to make up from without for being undernourished now from within. Anything to be liked, to be reassured not that I was a man of a little genius but that I was a great man of the world. At the same time I knew it was nonsense – the part of me that knew it was nonsense brought us to the Rue Vaugirard.

But now you had gone into yourself just as I had four years before in St. Raphael – And there were all the consequences of bad appartments through your lack of patience ('Well, if you were [   ] why don't you make some money') bad servants, through your indifference ('Well, if you don't like her why don't you send Scotty away to school') Your dislike for Vidor, your indifference to Joyce I understood – share your incessant entheusisam and absorbtion in the ballet I could not. Somewhere in there I had a sense of being exploited, not by you but by something I resented terribly no happiness. Certainly less than there had ever been at home – you were a phantom washing clothes, talking French bromides with Lucien or Del Plangue – I remember desolate trips to Versaille to Rhiems, to La Baule undertaken in sheer weariness of home. I remember wondering why I kept working to pay the bills of this desolate menage. I had evolved. In despair I went from the extreme of isolation, which is to say isolation with Mlle Delplangue, or the Ritz Bar where I got back my self esteem for half an hour, often with someone I had hardly ever seen before. In the evenings sometimes you and I rode to the Bois in a cab – after awhile I preferred to go to Cafe de Lilas and sit there alone remembering what a happy time I had had there with Ernest, Hadley, Dorothy Parker + Benchley two years before. During all this time, remember I didn't blame anyone but myself. I complained when the house got unbearable but after all I was not John Peale Bishop – I was paying for it with work, that I passionately hated and found more and more difficult to do. The novel was like a dream, daily farther and farther away.

Ellerslie was better and worse. Unhappiness is less accute when one lives with a certain sober dignity but the financial strain was too much. Between Sept when we left Paris and March when we reached Nice we were living at the rate of forty thousand a year.

349

But somehow I felt happier. Another spring – I would see Ernest whom I had launched, Gerald + Sarah who through my agency had been able to try the movies. At least life would less drab; there would be parties with people who offered something, conversations with people with something to say. Later swimming and getting tanned and young and being near the sea.

It worked out beautifully didn't it. Gerald and Sara didn't see us. Ernest and I met but it was a more irritable Ernest, apprehensively telling me his whereabouts lest I come in on them tight and endanger his lease. The discovery that half a dozen people were familiars there didn't help my self esteem. By the time we reached the beautiful Rivierra I had developed such an inferiority complex that I couldn't fase anyone unless I was tight. I worked there too, though, and the unusual combination exploded my lungs.

You were gone now – I scarcely remember you that summer. You were simply one of all the people who disliked me or were indifferent to me. I didn't like to think of you – You didn't need me and it was easier to talk to or rather at Madame Bellois and keep full of wine. I was grateful when you came with me to the Doctors one afternoon but after we'd been a week in Paris and I didn't try any more about living or dieing. Things were always the same. The apartments that were rotten, the maids that stank – the ballet before my eyes, spoiling a story to take the Troubetskoys to dinner, poisoning a trip to Africa. You were going crazy and calling it genius – I was going to ruin and calling it anything that came to hand. And I think everyone far enough away to see us outside of our glib presentation of ourselves guessed at your almost meglomaniacal selfishness and my insane indulgence in drink. Toward the end nothing much mattered. The nearest I ever came to leaving you was when you told me you thot I was a fairy in the Rue Palatine but now whatever you said aroused a sort of detached pity for you. For all your superior observation and your harder intelligence I have a faculty of guessing right, without evidence even with a certain wonder as to why and whence that mental short cut came. I wish the Beautiful and Damned had been a maturely written book because it was all true. We ruined ourselves – I have never honestly thought that we ruined each other.[138]

350

In July, Zelda developed severe eczema, which tortured her until the fall. In the depth of her misery she wrote Fitzgerald a forty-two page summary of their marriage:

I have just written to Newman to come here to me. You say that you have been thinking of the past. The weeks since I haven't slept more than three or four hours, swathed in bandages sick and unable to read so have I.

There was:

The strangeness and excitement of New York, of reporters and furry smothered hotel lobbies, the brightness of the sun on the window panes and the prickly dust of late spring: the impressiveness of the Fowlers and much tea-dancing and my eccentric behavior at Princeton. There were Townsend's blue eyes and Ludlow's rubbers and a trunk that exhuded sachet and the marshmallow odor of the Biltmore. There were always Ludow and Townsend and Alex and Bill Mackey and you and me. We did not like women and we were happy. There was Georges appartment and his absinth cock-tails and Ruth Findleys gold hair in his comb, and visits to the 'Smart Set' and 'Vanity Fair' – a collegiate literary world puffed into wide proportions by the New York papers. There were flowers and night clubs and Ludlow's advice that moved us to the country. At West Port, we quarrelled over morals once, walking beside a colonial wall under the freshness of lilacs. We sat up all night over 'Brass Knuckles and Guitar.' There was the road house where we bought gin, and Kate Hicks and the Maurices and the bright harness of the Rye Beach Club. We swam in the depth of the night with George before we quarrelled with him and went to John Williams parties where there were actresses who spoke French when they were drunk. George played 'Cuddle up a Little Closer' on the piano. There were my white knickers that startled the Connecticut hills, and the swim in the sandaled lady's bird-pool. The beach, and dozens of men, mad rides along the Post Road and trips to New York. We never could have a room at a hotel at night we looked so young, so once we filled an empty suit case with the telephone directory and spoons and a pin-cushion at The Manhattan – I was romantically attached to Townsend and he went away to Tahatii – and there were your episodes of Gene Bankhead and

351

Miriam. We bought the Marmon with Harvey Firestone and went south through the haunted swamps of Virginiia, the red clay hills of Georgia, the sweet rutted creek-bottoms of Alabama. We drank corn on the wings of an aeroplane in the moon-light and danced at the country-club and came back. I had a pink dress that floated and a very theatrical silver one that I bought with Don Stewart.

We moved to 59th Street. We quarrelled and you broke the bathroom door and hurt my eye. We went so much to the theatre that you took it off the income tax. We trailed through Central Park in the snow after a ball at the Plaza, I quarrelled with Zoë about Bottecelli at the Brevoort and went with her to buy a coat for David Belasco. We had Bourbon and Deviled Ham and Christmas at the Overmans and ate lots at the Lafayette. There was Tom Smith and his wall-paper and Mencken and our Valentine party and the time I danced all night with Alex and meals at Mollats with John and I skated, and was pregnant and you wrote the 'Beautiful and Damned.' We came to Europe and I was sick and complained always. There was London, and Wopping with Shane Leslie and strawberries as big as tomatoes at Lady Randolph Churchills. There was St. Johns Ervines wooden leg and Bob Handley in the gloom of the Cecil – There was Paris and the heat and the ice-cream that did not melt and buying clothes – and Rome and your friends from the British Embassy and your drinking, drinking. We came home. There was 'Dog' and lunch at the St. Regis with Townsend and Alex and John: Alabama and the unbearable heat and our almost buying a house. Then we went to St. Paul and hundreds of people came to call. There were the Indian forests and the moon on the sleeping porch and I was heavy and afraid of the storms. Then Scottie was born and we went to all the Christmas parties and a man asked Sandy 'who is your fat friend?' Snow covered everything. We had the Flu and went lots to the Kalmans and Scottie grew strong. Joseph Hergesheimer came and Saturdays we went to the university Club. We went to the Yacht Club and we both had minor flirtations. Joe began to dislike me, and I played so much golf that I had Tetena. Kollie almost died. We both adored him. We came to New York and rented a house when we were tight. There was Val Engelicheff and Ted Paramour and dinner with Bunny in Washington Square and pills and Doctor Lackin. And we had a violent quarrell on the train going back, I don't remember why. Then I brought Scottie to New York. She was round and funny in a pink coat and bonnet and you met us at the station. In Great Neck there was always disorder and quarrels: about the Golf Club, about the Foxes, about Peggy Weber, about Helen Buck, about everything. We went to the Rumseys, and that awful night at the Mackeys when Ring sat in the cloak-room. We saw Esther and Glen Hunter and Gilbert Seldes. We gave lots of parties: the biggest one for Rebecca West. We drank Bass Pale Ale and went always to the Bucks or the Lardners or the Swopes when they weren't at our house. We saw lots of Sydney Howard and fought the week-end that Bill Motter was with us. We drank always and finally came to France because there were always too many people in the house. On the boat there was almost a scandal about Bunny Burgess. We found Nancy and went to Hyeres – Scottie and I were both sick there in the dusty garden full of Spanish Bayonet and Bourgainvilla. We went to St. Raphael. You wrote, and we went sometimes to Nice or Monte Carlo. We were alone, and gave big parties for the French aviators. Then there was Josen and you were justifiably angry. We went to Rome. We ate at the Castelli di Cesari. The sheets were always damp. There was Christmas in the echoes, and eternal walks. We cried when we saw the Pope. There were the luminous shadows of the Pinco and the officer's shining boots. We went to Frascati and Tivoli. There was the jail, and Hal Rhodes at the Hotel de Russie and my not wanting to go to the moving-picture ball at the Excelsior and asking Hungary Cox to take me home. Then I was horribly sick, from trying to have a baby and you didn't care much and when I was well we came back to Paris. We sat to-gether in Marseilles and thought how good France was. We lived in the rue Tilsitt, in red plush and Teddy came for tea and we went to the markets with the Murphies. There were the Wimans and Mary Hay and Eva La Galliene and rides in the Bois at dawn and the night we all played puss-in-the-corner at the Ritz. There was Tunti and nights in Mont Matre. We went to Antibes and I was sick always and took too much Dial.* The Murphys were at the Hotel du Cap and we saw them constantly. Back in Paris I began dancing lessons because I had nothing to

* A sedative.

do. I was sick again at Christmas when the Mac Leishes came and Doctor Gros said there was no use trying to save my ovaries. I was always sick and having picqures* and things and you were naturally more and more away. You found Ernest and the Cafe des Lilas and you were unhappy when Dr. Gros sent me to Salies-de-Bearn. At the Villa Paquita I was always sick. Sara brought me things and we gave a lunch for Geralds father. We went to Cannes and listned to Raquel Miller and dined under the rain of fire-works. You couldn't work because your room was damp and you quarrelled with the Murphys. We moved to a bigger villa and I went to Paris and had my appendix out. You drank all the time and some man called up the hospital about a row you had had. We went home, and I wanted you to swim with me at Juan-les-Pins but you liked it better where it was gayer: at the Garoupe with Marice Hamilton and the Murphys and the Mac Leishes. Then you found Grace Moore and Ruth and Charlie and the summer passed, one party after another. We quarrelled about Dwight Wiman and you left me lots alone. There were too many people and too many things to do: every-day there was something and our house was always full. There was Gerald and Ernest and you often did not come home. There were the English sleepers that I found downstairs one morning and Bob and Muriel and Walker and Anita Loos, always somebody – Alice Delamar and Ted Rousseau and our trips to St. Paul† and the note from Isadora Duncan and the countryside slipping by through the haze of Chamberry-fraises and Graves – That was your summer. I swam with Scottie except when I followed you, mostly unwillingly. Then I had asthma and almost died in Genoa. And we were back in America – further apart than ever before. In California, though you would not allow me to go anywhere without you, you yourself engaged in flagrantly sentimental relations with a child. You said you wanted nothing more from me in all your life, though you made a scene when Carl suggested that I go to dinner with him and Betty Compson. We came east: I worked over Ellerslie incessantly and made it function. There was our first house-party and you and Lois – and when there was nothing more to

* Injections.
† St. Paul-de-Vence in the hills above the Mediterranean.

do on the house I began dancing lessons. You did not like it when you saw it made me happy. You were angry about rehearsals and insistent about trains. You went to New York to see Lois and I met Dick Knight the night of that party for Paul Morand. Again, though you were by then thoroughly entangled sentimentally, you forbade my seeing Dick and were furious about a letter he wrote me. On the boat coming over you paid absolutely no attention of any kind to me except to refuse me the permission to stay to a concert with whatever-his-name-was. I think the most humiliating and bestial thing that ever happened to me in my life is a scene that you probably don't remember even in Genoa. We lived in the rue Vaugirard. You were constantly drunk. You didn't work and were dragged home at night by taxi-drivers when you came home at all. You said it was my fault for dancing all day. What was I to do? You got up for lunch. You made no advances toward me and complained that I was un-responsive. You were literally eternally drunk the whole summer. I got so I couldn't sleep and I had asthma again. You were angry when I wouldn't go with you to Mont Matre. You brought drunken under-graduates in to meals when you came home for them, and it made you angry that I didn't care any more. I began to like Egorowa – On the boat going back I told you I was afraid that there was something abnormal in the relationship and you laughed. There was more or less of a scandal about Philipson,* but you did not even try to help me. You brought Philippe back and I couldnt manage the house any more; he was insubordinate and disrespectful to me and you wouldn't let him go. I began to work harder at dancing – I thought of nothing else but that. You were far away by then and I was alone. We came back to rue Palantine and you, in a drunken stupor told me a lot of things that I only half understood: but I understood the dinner we had at Ernests'. Only I didn't understand that it matterred. You left me more and more alone, and though you complained that it was the appartment or the servants or me, you know the real reason you couldn't work was because you were always out half the night and you were sick and you drank constantly. We went to Cannes. I kept up my lessons and we quarrelled. You wouldn't

* Unidentified.

let me fire the nurse that both Scottie and I hated. You
disgraced yourself at the Barry's party, on the yacht at Monte
Carlo, at the casino with Gerald and Dotty. Many nights you
didn't come home. You came into my room once the whole
summer, but I didn't care because I went to the beach in the
morning, I had my lesson in the afternoon and I walked at
night. I was nervous and half-sick but I didn't know what was
the matter. I only knew that I had difficulty standing lots of
people, like the party at Wm J. Locke's and that I wanted to get
back to Paris. We had lunch at the Murphy's and Gerald said to
me very pointedly several times that Nemchinova* was at
Antibes. Still I didn't understand. We came back to Paris. You
were miserable about your lung, and because you had wasted
the summer, but you didn't stop drinking. I worked all the time
and I became dependent on Egorowa. I couldn't walk in the
street unless I had been to my lesson. I couldn't manage the
appartment because I couldn't speak to the servants. I couldn't
go into stores to buy clothes and my emotions became blindly
involved. In February, when I was so sick with bronchitis that I
had ventouses† every day and fever for two weeks, I had to work
because I couldn't exist in the world without it, and still I didn't
understand what I was doing. I didn't even know what I wanted.
Then we went to Africa and when we came back I began to
realize because I could feel what was happening in others. You
did not want me. Twice you left my bed saying 'I can't. Don't you
understand' – I didn't. Then there was the Harvard man who
lost his direction, and when I wanted you to come home with me
you told me to sleep with the coal man. At Nancy Hoyt's dinner
she offerred her services but there was nothing the matter with
my head then, though I was half dead, so I turned back to the
studio. Lucienne was sent away but since I knew nothing about
the situation, I didn't know why there was something wrong. I
just kept on going. Lucienne came back and later went away
again and then the end happened. I went to Malmaison. You
wouldn't help me – I don't blame you by now, but if you had
explained I would have understood because all I wanted
was to go on working. You had other things: drink and tennis,

* Ballerina Nemtchinova.
† French medical term for cuppings.

and we did not care about each other. You hated me for asking you not to drink. A girl came to work with me but I didn't want her to. I still believed in love and I thought suddenly of Scottie and that you supported me. So at Valmont I was in tortue, and my head closed to-gether. You gave me a flower and said it was 'plus petite et moins etendue' – We were friends – Then you took it away and I grew sicker, and there was nobody to teach me, so here I am, after five months of misery and agony and desperation. I'm glad you have found that the material for a Josepine story and I'm glad that you take such an interest in sports. Now that I can't sleep any more I have lots to think about, and since I have gone so far alone I suppose I can go the rest of the way – but if it were Scottie I would not ask that she go through the same hell and if I were God I could not justify or find a reason for imposing it – except that it was wrong, of cource, to love my teacher when I should have loved you. But I didn't have you to love – not since long before I loved her.

I have just begun to realize that sex and sentiment have little to do with each other. When I came to you twice last winter and asked you to start over it was because I thought I was becoming seriously involved sentimentally and preparing situations for which I was morally and practicly unfitted. You had a song about Gigolos: if that had ever entered my head there was, besides the whole studio, 3 other solutions in Paris.

I came to you half-sick after a difficult lunch at Armonville and you kept me waiting until it was too late in front of the Guaranty Trust.

Sandy's tiny candle was not much of a strain, but it required something better than your week of drunkenness to put it out. You didn't care: so I went on and on – dancing alone, and, no matter what happens, I still know in my heart that it is a Godless, dirty game; that love is bitter and all there is, and that the rest is for the emotional beggars of the earth and is about the equivalent of people who stimulate themselves with dirty postcards—[139]

From the start Dr. Forel was convinced that Zelda's recovery depended on her relinquishing her hopes for a ballet career. Fitzgerald wrote to Egorova in June requesting an assessment of Zelda's capabilities.* Her 9 July verdict was less discouraging than Dr. Forel had anticipated:

1) According to my conviction, Zelda will not be able to become a first-class dancer; she started too late to succeed in it.
2) I cannot imagine Zelda being on the same level as Nikitina or Danilowa.†
4) I am quite certain that in the Massine ballets, without being the star, Zelda could perform with success some important roles. However, she can possibly become a good dancer.
5) Having started her dancing lessons quite late, it is certain that Zelda will not be able to reach some results that are only accessible to dancers who have been studying since childhood. Nevertheless, Zelda is very capable and does very well some steps that do not require years of work.
6) Zelda is as good a student as Galia, but I will not keep it from you that among my students, particularly among the professional ones, many of them are superior to her.
7) I can only repeat that Zelda is capable of becoming a very good dancer without however equalling stars like Nemtchinova or Nikitina.[141] [Translated from the French]

Zelda was badly disappointed by Egorova's report, for she had been sure that she could achieve distinction. She did not recommence her ballet training, although she continued to dance as a means of self-expression.

---

* Dr. Forel wrote to Fitzgerald on 23 June 1930: 'I've taken notice of the attached letter which shows how Mrs. Fitzgerald still clings to her career as a dancer. On the other hand, Dr. de Jonge and myself, we are certain that it is not in this direction that she will find her equilibrium and the possibility of resuming a normal life. Therefore, if you write to the teacher of your wife as she demands it, it would be preferable (although it will be a big disappointment to her) that, in the answer, one makes her understand that *there* is not her real calling. She wants to start work again, but at this point in time, it is not a question of dance, but medical treatment which she urgently needs.'[140] [Translated from the French]
† Fitzgerald's 22 June 1930 letter to Egorova listed seven questions about Zelda's dancing. His third question was how long would Zelda need to reach the level of Nikitina and Danilowa.

Prangins [Summer–Fall 1930]

Perhaps as a way to compensate Zelda for the loss of her ballet career, Fitzgerald tried to arrange for publication of the stories she wrote at Prangins. In July he offered Perkins 'three stories which Zelda wrote in the dark middle of her nervous breakdown.'[142] *Scribner's Magazine* declined 'A Workman,' 'The Drouth and the Flood,' and 'The House' as too specialized for a general audience, and Ober was unable to place them elsewhere.*

Dr. Forel was in fact treating both Fitzgeralds, for Zelda's recovery depended on her relationship with her husband. When Dr. Forel recommended that he stop drinking, Fitzgerald refused to accept Zelda's charge that his drinking had caused her collapse. He drafted a self-justifying letter to Dr. Forel minimizing his dependence on alcohol and insisting on his right to wine with meals:

> Now when that old question comes up again as to which of two people is worth preserving, I, thinking of my ambitions once so nearly achieved of being part of English literature, of my child, even of Zelda in the matter of providing for her – must perforce consider myself first. I say that without defiance but simply knowing the limits of what I can do. To stop drinking entirely for six months and see what happens, even to continue the experiment thereafter if successful – only a pig would refuse to do that. Give up strong drink permanently I will. Bind myself to foreswear wine forever I cannot. My vision of the world at its brightest is such that life without the use of its amenities is impossible. I have lived hard and ruined the essential innocense in myself that could make it that possible, *and the fact that I have abused liquor* is something *to be paid with suffering and death perhaps but not with renunciation.* For me *it would be as illogical as permanently giving up sex because I caught a disease* (which I hasten to assure you I never have) I cannot consider one pint of wine at the days end as anything but one of the rights of man.
>
> Does this sound like a long polemic composed of childish stubborness and ingratitude? If it were that it would be so

* These three stories are lost.

much easier to make promises. What I gave up for Zelda was women and it wasn't easy in the position my success gave me – what pleasure I got from comradeship she has pretty well ruined by dragging me of all people into her homosexual obsession. Is there not a certain disingenuousness in her wanting me to give up all alcohol? Would not that *justify her* conduct completely to herself and prove *to her relatives, and our friends that it was my drinking that had caused this calamity, and that I thereby admitted it? Wouldn't she finally get to believe herself that she had consented to 'take me back' only if I stopped drinking? I could only be silent.* And any human value I might have would disappear *if I condemned myself to a life long ascetisim to which I am not adapted either by habit, temperament* or the circumstances of my metier.[143]

The correspondence between Dr. Forel and Fitzgerald shows that the psychiatrist permitted Fitzgerald to feel that he was a consultant on the case.

Fitzgerald's *Ledger* summary of his thirty-third year – '*The Crash! Zelda + America*' – reveals how he identified the events of his life with the history of his time. He regarded Zelda and himself as eponymic figures – which they became.

39

Switzerland
and Recovery

[Fall 1930–Summer 1931]

After Zelda suffered relapses in the fall of 1930, Dr. Paul Eugen Bleuler was called in for a consultation on 22 November. He was the leading authority on schizophrenia, which he had named. The consultation cost $500, and Zelda thought it was a waste of money. Dr. Bleuler confirmed Dr. Forel's diagnosis and offered as hope that three out of four cases of schizophrenia were curable. Concerned that Zelda's parents held him responsible for her collapse, Fitzgerald relayed to the Sayres Dr. Bleuler's assurance: 'This is something that began about five years ago. Let us hope it is only a process of re-adjustment. Stop blaming yourself. You might have retarded it but you couldn't have prevented it.'[144]

Despite the worry and distractions of the Prangins period, Fitzgerald steadily wrote *Post* stories to pay for Zelda's treatment and his residence in Switzerland. He did not touch his novel for months. Zelda's bills at Prangins totaled 70,561 Swiss francs, or more than $13,000. In 1930–31 Fitzgerald sold seventeen stories and in 1931 achieved his peak pre-Hollywood earnings of $37,599. The stories provided him with opportunities to explain the collapse of his life; and two of the 1930 stories – 'One Trip Abroad' (August) and 'Babylon Revisited' (December) – are among his masterpieces. 'One Trip Abroad' re-examines the familiar situation of the hopeful young American couple who go to Europe seeking artistic or intellectual enrichment. Nicole and Nelson Kelly, having come into money, go to France to study painting and music. Instead they are caught up in dissipation and idleness, until at the end of the story they are patients in a Swiss clinic: 'Switzerland is a country where very few things begin, but many things end.'[145] Throughout the story the Kellys notice another young American couple who become increasingly unwholesome. At the end the Kellys realize that *they* are that other couple. Fitzgerald's use of the doppelgänger device is entirely successful in this story. He did not reprint 'One Trip Abroad,' perhaps because he felt that it was too close to *Tender Is the Night.*

'Babylon Revisited' is usually regarded as Fitzgerald's best story. Here he transferred his guilt to Charlie Wales, an American businessman who went to Paris with his wife and daughter during the boom and became involved in the alcoholic life of rich Americans. After a drunken quarrel with his wife he had locked her out in the snow, contributing to her death from heart disease. While suffering an alcoholic collapse he had given custody of his daughter, Honoria, to his sister-in-law, who detests him. (Wales's sister-in-law is obviously based on Rosalind Smith, who felt that Fitzgerald was not fit to raise Scottie, but the guardianship in the story is an invention; Fitzgerald never considered giving up Scottie, whom he visited regularly in Paris while living close to Zelda in Switzerland.) At the opening of 'Babylon Revisited' Wales returns to Paris in 1930 sober and solvent, intending to regain custody of Honoria; but his hopes are ruined by the appearance of drunken friends from his past. As the title indicates, 'Babylon Revisited' is about what it was like to be a rich American in Paris during the Twenties: ' – The men who locked their wives out in the snow, because the snow of twenty-nine wasn't real snow. If you didn't want it to be snow you just paid some money.'[146] Although considerable self-pity is expressed through Wales, Fitzgerald is clear in assigning blame to the abandonment of traditional values. This exchange between Wales and the Ritz barman reveals Wales's acceptance of his culpability:

> 'I heard you lost a lot in the crash.'
> 'I did,' and he added grimly, 'but I lost everything I wanted in the boom.'
> 'Selling short.'
> 'Something like that.'[147]

They are using the term 'selling short' in different ways. The barman is referring to selling stocks short in a bull market, which Wales did not do. Wales is referring to the love and loyalty he sold short to bring about another kind of bankruptcy.

During one of Fitzgerald's June 1930 trips to Paris he met Thomas Wolfe, who had been asked by Maxwell Perkins to look him up. Wolfe was Perkins's most recent discovery, and *Look Homeward, Angel* had been a brilliant success in 1929. With his feeling of loyalty to Scribners and Perkins, Fitzgerald was eager for Wolfe's friendship. He was greatly impressed by Wolfe's talent, but he had reservations about the validity of his almost mystical identification with America. Wolfe regarded Fitzgerald as a superannuated Princeton undergraduate and wrote a description of him at the Ritz Bar into a letter: 'I finally departed from his company at ten that night in the Ritz Bar where he was entirely surrounded by Princeton boys, all nineteen years old, all drunk, and all half-raw. He was carrying on a spirited conversation with them about why Joe Zinzendorff did not get taken into the Triple-Gazzaza Club. I heard one of the lads say "Joe's a good boy, Scotty, but you know he's a fellow that ain't got much background." – I thought it was time for Wolfe to depart, and I did.'[148] His almost pathological suspicion led Wolfe to

363

believe that Perkins had arranged the meeting to get Fitzgerald's judgment of him.*

After reading *Look Homeward, Angel* Fitzgerald reported to Perkins: 'You have a great find in him – what he'll do is incalculable. He has a deeper culture than Ernest and more vitality, if he is slightly less of a poet that goes with the immense surface he wants to cover. Also he lacks Ernests quality of a stick hardened in the fire. He is more susceptible to the world. John Bishop told me that he needed advice about cutting ect, but after reading his book I thought that was nonsense. He strikes me as a man who should be let alone as to length, if he had to be published in five volumes.'[150] Fitzgerald subsequently changed his mind and urged Wolfe to be selective: 'You never cut anything out of a book that you regret later.'[151]

During September, Fitzgerald encountered Wolfe in Montreux, Vevey, and Geneva. Fitzgerald relished telling the story of how the six-foot-six Wolfe caused a power failure in a Swiss town by breaking overhead electric wires while gesticulating. By this time Wolfe had decided that Fitzgerald was deliberately interfering with his work and avoided him. Given Wolfe's method of transposing people into his novels, it was inevitable that he would make use of Fitzgerald, who became Hunt Conroy in *You Can't Go Home Again*.

In the fall of 1930 Fitzgerald's base was Lausanne, where he lived at the Hotel de la Paix, but with excursions to Swiss resorts. During Zelda's hospitalization he began sleeping with other women, and he had an affair with an Englishwoman named Bijou O'Conor.[152] These brief affairs may have been partly a way of countering Zelda's charges that he was a homosexual.

---

* Wolfe made this entry in his notebook: 'There was once a young man who came to have a feeling of great trust and devotion for an older man. He thought that this older man had created liberty and hope for him. He thought that this older man was brave and loyal. Then he found that this older man had sent him to a drunken and malicious fellow, who tried to injure and hurt his work in every way possible. He found moreover that this older man had sent him to this drunk in order to get the drunk's "opinion" of him. That is the real end of this story.'[149]

Fitzgerald brought Scottie to visit Zelda for Christmas 1930, but the reunion was unhappy because Zelda behaved irrationally. Father and daughter went skiing at Gstaad for the rest of her Christmas vacation. In January 1931 Fitzgerald's father died in Washington, and he went home for the burial. Before sailing, he wrote Dr. Forel suggesting the theory that Zelda's eczema was caused by 'some lack of normal elimination of poison' which attacked the nerves:

> Now (I know you're regarding this as the wildest mysticism but please read on) – now just as the mind of the confirmed alcoholic accepts a certain poisoned condition of the nerves as the one to which he is most at home and in which, therefore, he is the most comfortable, Mrs. F. *encourages* her nervous system to absorb the continually distilled poison. Then the exterior world, represented by your personal influence, by the shock of Eglantine,* by the sight of her daughter causes *an effort of the will toward reality, she is able to force this poison out of her nerve cells* and the process of elimination is taken over again *by her skin.*
>
> In brief my idea is this. *That the eczema is not relative but is the clue to the whole business. I believe that the eczema is a definite concurrent product of every struggle back toward the normal.* . . . [153]

Westbound on the *New York* Fitzgerald met a lively blonde who convinced him that she was a professional card sharp. She called herself Bert Barr, but she was Bertha Weinberg Goldstein, the wife of a Brooklyn judge.[154] Fitzgerald was so charmed by her cleverness that he invited her to collaborate on stories with him, though nothing resulted from this plan. He saw Bert Barr in New York and again in Paris, and wrote her into his 1931 story 'On Your Own,' which expressed Fitzgerald's feelings about his father through an American actress returning from England for her father's funeral in

---

* The house at Prangins reserved for the most difficult patients, where Zelda was transferred in the summer of 1930.

Maryland. The story was declined by all the magazines Ober offered it to.*

Edward Fitzgerald was buried at St. Mary's Church in Rockville, Maryland. In a draft of an unfinished essay, 'The Death of My Father,' Fitzgerald assessed his father's influence on him:

> I loved my father – always deep in my subconscious I have referred judgements back to him, what he would have thought or done. He loved me – and felt a deep responsibility for me – I was born several months after the sudden death of my two elder sisters + he felt what the effect of this would be on my mother, that he would be my only moral guide. He became that to the best of his ability. He came from tired old stock with very little left of vitality and mental energy but he managed to raise a little for me.[155]

Fitzgerald felt that his father was his link with the American past. In *Tender Is the Night* he salvaged a passage from 'On Your Own' to express the filial feelings he shared with Dick Diver: 'These dead, he knew them all, their weather-beaten faces with blue flashing eyes, the spare violent bodies, the souls made of new earth in the forest-heavy darkness of the seventeenth century.

' "Good-by, my father – good-by, all my fathers." '[156]

While in America, Fitzgerald went to Montgomery to report on Zelda's condition to the Sayres. He knew that the Judge disapproved of him, and Fitzgerald wanted him to believe that he was competent to take care of Zelda and Scottie. In New York, he visited Charles MacArthur and his wife Helen Hayes. They saw each other infrequently after the Twenties, but MacArthur and Fitzgerald always appreciated each other. The two authors went to see the play *Grand Hotel* and were ejected for being drunk.[157]

When he returned to Europe at the end of February, Fitzgerald found that Zelda had made marked improvement

---

* 'On Your Own' was published in *The Price Was High* (1979).

during his absence; by April she was allowed to take trips with him to Montreux and Geneva. Her letters to Fitzgerald became affectionate and hopeful, expressing her dependence on him:

> Darling, Berne is such a funny town: we bumped into Hansel and Gretel and the Babes in the Wood were just under the big clock. It must be a haven for all lost things, painted on itself that way. Germanic legends slide over those red, peeling roofs like a fantastic shower and the ends of all stories probably lie in the crevasses. We climbed the cathedral tower in whispers, and there it was hidden in the valley, paved with sugar blocks, the home of good witches, and I asked of all they painted statues three wishes
>
> That you should love me
> That you love me
> You love me!
> O can you? I love you so.
>
> The train rode home through a beautiful word: 'alpin-glun.' The mountains had covered their necks in pink tulle like coquettish old ladies covering scars and wrinkles and gold ran down the hill-sides into the lake.
>
> When we got home they said you had 'phoned, so I phoned back as indiscreetly as possible since I couldn't bear not having heard your voice, that lovely warm feeling like an emotional massage.
>
> O my love – how can you love a silly girl who buys cheese and plaited bread from enchanted princes in the public market and eats them on the streets of a city that pops into life like a cucoo-clock when you press the right note of appreciation
>
> I *love* you, dear.[158]

At the end of 1930 Zelda resumed writing short stories at Prangins. Ober tried to place them, but only one was published, 'Miss Ella,' in the December 1931 *Scribner's*. Fitzgerald also tried to have them published under the blanket title 'Stories from a Swiss Clinique.'[159] With the ballet taken away from her, Zelda was again seeking some form of creative achievement. The clear difficulty was that in returning to fiction she was competing with her husband at an endeavor in which she couldn't win. 'Miss Ella' resembles the girl-series for *College Humor* in technique. An atmosphere story set in the Deep South, it narrates the empty life of an old maid whose wedding had been canceled by the suicide of a rejected suitor. As is characteristic of her fiction, there is little dialogue; the story is told by the author rather than dramatized. Perkins wrote Fitzgerald that Zelda's style distracted the reader: 'But when we send the proof I was going to ask Zelda if she would consider whether her figures of speech – I suppose they would be called similes – were not too numerous, and sometimes too remote. – That is, sometimes she likens something in the story to something too distant from it; and this has the effect sometimes of putting the emphasis on the figure of the simile instead of the thing to which it is likened.'[160]

When Fitzgerald claimed credit for naming the Jazz Age, Perkins responded in May 1931 with an invitation from Alfred Dashiell, managing editor of *Scribner's Magazine*, to write an article about it. 'Echoes of the Jazz Age' appeared in the November issue. This post-mortem on 'the most expensive orgy in history' shows the operation of that part of Fitzgerald that needed to analyze, judge, and assess his experiences and the collective experiences of his time that he had assimilated. His view of the Jazz Age fully recognizes the vulgarity and waste, but it also evokes the sense of boundless possibility that he felt: 'It bore him up, flattered him and gave him more money than he had dreamed of, simply for telling people that he felt as they did, that something had to be done with all the nervous energy stored up and unexpended in the war.' The essay concludes on a note of loss – regret for lost opportunity, regret for lost youth, and that characteristic Fitzgerald recognition of the loss of the ability to feel:

> Now once more the belt is tight and we summon the proper expression of horror as we look back at our wasted youth. Sometimes, though, there is a ghostly rumble among the

drums, an asthmatic whisper in the trombones that swings me back into the early twenties when we drank wood alcohol and every day and in every way grew better and better, and there was a first abortive shortening of the skirts, and girls all looked alike in sweater dresses, and people you didn't want to know said 'Yes, we have no bananas,' and it seemed only a question of a few years before the older people would step aside and let the world be run by those who saw things as they were – and it all seems rosy and romantic to us who were young then, because we will never feel quite so intensely about our surroundings any more.[161]

The evocation of unrecapturable emotions – one of the defining qualities of Fitzgerald's best work – would become increasingly difficult for him in the Thirties.

Fitzgerald sold nine stories in 1931: 'Indecision' (written in January and February), 'A New Leaf' (April), 'Flight and Pursuit' (April), 'Emotional Bankruptcy' (June; the last Josephine story), 'Between Three and Four' (June), 'A Change of Class' (July), 'Six of One – ' (July), 'A Freeze-Out' (September), and 'Diagnosis' (October). None of these is distinguished, and the *Post* complained to Ober that Fitzgerald's stories weren't up to his standard. 'Six of One – ' was rejected by the *Post* and published by *Redbook*. The story, which contrasts the sons of wealth with poor boys, arraigns the wastage of the privileged class. Nonetheless, Fitzgerald remained sensitive to the attractions of aristocracy: 'The young princes in velvet gathered in lovely domesticity around the queen amid the hush of rich draperies may presently grow up to be Pedro the Cruel or Charles the Mad, but the moment of beauty was there.'[162] In response to the *Post*'s recommendation that he write more fiction with American settings, Fitzgerald provided two plodding stories about the Depression, 'Between Three and Four' and 'A Change of Class.'

Mollie Fitzgerald came to Paris in May for a short visit. Although Fitzgerald had prepared for his mother's arrival by warning his Paris friends that she was eccentric, they found her behavior unexceptionable. In July 1931 Fitzgerald, Zelda, and Scottie spent two happy weeks together. Zelda later wrote of this time of hope:

> But we went to Annecy for two weeks in summer, and said at the end that we'd never go there again because those weeks had been perfect and no other time could match them. First we lived at the Beau-Rivage, a rambler rose-colored hotel, with a diving platform wedged beneath our window between the sky and the lake, but there were enormous flies on the raft so we moved across the lake to Menthon. The water was greener there and the shadows long and cool and the scraggly gardens staggered up the shelved precipice to the Hôtel Palace. We played tennis on the baked clay courts and fished tentatively from a low brick wall. The heat of summer seethed in the resin of the white pine bath-houses. We walked at night towards a café blooming with Japanese lanterns, white shoes gleaming like radium in the damp darkness. It was like the good gone times when we still believed in summer hotels and the philosophies of popular songs. Another night we danced a Wiener waltz, and just simply swep' around.[163]

In August the Fitzgeralds visited the Murphys in the Austrian Tyrol, where their son Patrick was being treated for tuberculosis. Zelda was relaxed and had a good time; but Fitzgerald was upset when Scottie mistakenly reported that she had been bathed in the same water the Murphy children had used. His concern about his own tuberculosis made him uneasy about exposing Scottie to Patrick. The small crisis was written into *Tender Is the Night*.

During the summer of 1931, when she was virtually an outpatient at Prangins, Zelda steadily gained confidence in her ability to face the world and was hopeful that they would be able to build a new life. She wrote Fitzgerald encouragingly:

> Please don't be depressed: nothing is sad about you except your sadness and the frayed places on your pink kimona and that you care so much about everything – You are the only

Recovered

Zelda at the time of her discharge from Prangins clinic

person who's ever done all they had to do, damn well, and had enough left over to be dissatisfied. You are the best – the best – the best and genius is so much a part of you that when you find a person you like you think they have it too because it's your only conception – O my love, I love you so – and I want you to be happy. Can't you possibly be just a little bit glad that we are alive and that all the year that's coming we can be to-gether and work and love and get some peace for all the things we've paid so much for learning? Stop looking for solace: there isn't any and if there were, life would be a baby affair.[164]

On 15 September 1931 Zelda was discharged from Prangins after sixteen months. The Fitzgeralds drove to Paris and sailed for America on 19 September aboard the *Aquitania*, the ship that first took them to Europe in 1921. They had lived abroad four and a half years – three in France, of which twenty-two months were spent in Paris. One of their albums has a photo of Zelda – perhaps a passport picture – taken at this time, which Fitzgerald captioned 'Recovered.' She looks older than thirty-one, and her features have lost their hawklike edge. The eczema had coarsened her skin, and she had developed a strained expression. It is the photograph of a woman who has been worn down by something. Fitzgerald's *Ledger* summary for his thirty-fourth year was: '*A Year in Lausanne. Waiting. From Darkness to Hope.*'

THE
LONG WAY
OUT

[1931–1934]

40

Montgomery and Hollywood: Relapse

[Fall–Winter 1931]

The Fitzgeralds *went* to Montgomery with the intention of settling there. Zelda needed a quiet environment and wanted to be with her parents because Judge Sayre's health was failing. They rented a house at 819 Felder Avenue in the Cloverdale section, and Fitzgerald began to replan his novel – perhaps considering a return to the Kelly material. After writing 'A Freeze-Out' and 'Diagnosis' for the *Post* in the fall, he had enough money to finance a period of uninterrupted work on his novel. Zelda, too, wrote stories that fall; two of her September–October stories are known only by their titles: 'All About the Downs Case' (also titled 'Crime Passionel') and 'There's a Myth in a Moral' (possibly retitled 'A Couple of Nuts').* Her best story, 'A Couple of Nuts,' had been written at Prangins. *Scribner's Magazine*

* Ober's memo on 'All About the Downs Case' reads: 'Difficult – cleverly written but doesn't get anywhere. Reminiscent of Nixon-Nordlinger case. Woman married to very rich man who gives her everything but treats her as a part of his possessions. She and a musician fall in love and he sees them kiss each other. He takes her to Europe and won't let her speak to anyone. She shoots him in the end. Strong language on p. 20.'[1] The story was declined by *College Humor*, *The Delineator*, and *Harper's Bazaar*. The Harold Ober Associates archives include memos on seven other stories by Zelda: 'Cotton Belt' (1932), 'Duck Supper,' 'Getting Away from It All,' 'Gods and Little Fishes,' 'One And, Two And' (1932), 'The Story Thus Far,' and 'Sweet

rejected the first version in October 1931 and published it in August 1932. The nuts are a young American couple who make a hit as entertainers in France during the Twenties but are corrupted by their rich patrons. The story ends on a characteristic Fitzgerald note of regret: 'Poor kids! Their Paris address turned up just the other day when I was looking for my trunk keys, along with some dirty postcards and a torn fifty-franc note and an expired passport. I remembered the night Larry gave it to me: I had promised to send them some songs from home – songs about love and success and beauty.'[2]

Fitzgerald blamed Zelda's literary disappointments on her inability to take a professional approach to writing. She wrote in bursts of energy without a sense of long-range achievement. He analyzed her misdirected activity in 'A Portrait':

> She will never be able to build a house. She hops herself up on crazy arrogance at intervals and wanders around in the woods chopping down everything that looks like a tree (vide: sixteen or twenty short stories in the last year *all of them* about as interesting as the average high-school product and yet all of them 'talented.') When she comes near to making a clearing it looks too much to her like all the other clearings she's ever seen so she fills it up with rubbish and debris and is ashamed even to speak of it afterwards. Driven, ordered, organized from without, she is a very useful individual – but her dominant idea and goal is freedom without responsibility which is like gold without metal, spring without winter, youth without age, one of those maddening, coo-coo mirages of wild riches which make her a typical product of our generation. She is by no means lazy yet when she chops down a tree she calls it work – whether it is in the clearing or not. She makes no distinction between *work* and mere sweat – less in the last few years since she has had arbitrarily to be led or driven.[3]

Early in November, Fitzgerald was contacted by Metro-

Chariot.' Most of these stories appear to have been written in 1932, but some may have been reworkings of Prangins stories.

Goldwyn-Mayer with an offer of six weeks at $750 to work on Katherine Brush's novel *Red-Headed Woman*, a Jean Harlow vehicle.* He didn't want to leave Zelda; he didn't want to delay his novel again; and he didn't want to go to Hollywood. When M-G-M raised the offer to $1,200 a week because Irving Thalberg wanted him for the job, he accepted. In Hollywood, Fitzgerald feuded with his collaborator, Marcel de Sano, whom he described as a studio hack. Fitzgerald wanted to appeal directly to Thalberg for permission to work alone but was advised that this would be considered improper conduct.

At a Sunday party the Thalbergs gave for English playwright Freddie Lonsdale, Fitzgerald, inspired by alcohol, performed his humorous song 'Dog' with a piano accompaniment by Ramon Navarro and was booed by John Gilbert and Lupe Velez. Thalberg told Charles MacArthur to take Fitzgerald home. The next day Fitzgerald received a telegram from Norma Shearer, Thalberg's wife: I THOUGHT YOU WERE ONE OF THE MOST AGREEABLE PERSONS AT OUR TEA.[4] He drank in Hollywood, but, except for the Thalberg exhibition, he behaved himself. Fitzgerald was not fired by Thalberg, as has been claimed.

While Fitzgerald was in Hollywood, Zelda wrote him daily loving, dependent letters assuring him that she was well. Some of these letters are so overstated that they were obviously intended as playful irony: 'Its wonderful that we have never had a cross word or done bad things to each other. Wouldn't it be awful if we had?'[5] Yet, according to her Montgomery friend Sara Mayfield, Zelda investigated the possibility of a divorce at this time.[6]

Fitzgerald was concerned about a relapse when Judge Sayre died on 17 November 1931, but Zelda took it well. In December she began to have asthma attacks and decided to drive to Florida to get away from dampness in Montgomery. Alarmed that asthma might signal the start of another breakdown, Fitzgerald persuaded her to travel with a nurse.

---

* Fitzgerald was needed to rewrite a screenplay by Bess Meredyth and C. Gardner Sullivan.

Fitzgerald finished his screenplay in five weeks and returned to Montgomery in time for Christmas. He had earned $6,000, but was convinced that M-G-M regarded his departure as running out on them because he had been asked to stay on for rewrites. His screenplay for *Red-Headed Woman* was not used because his treatment of the story of a woman who advances by means of sex was regarded as too serious. The movie was made from a new screenplay by Anita Loos. Zelda organized a gala Christmas for his return from Hollywood, constructing an historical panorama in papier-mâché around the tree – Hannibal crossing the Alps, a Roman village, a desert with Egyptian soldiers, and a train that stopped at several periods in history, ending with the War of the Roses.

Fitzgerald promised to write an article on 'Hollywood Revisited' for *Scribner's Magazine* but in January 1932 wrote instead the story 'Crazy Sunday.' Combining himself with screenwriter Dwight Taylor, he enlarged his humiliation at the Thalbergs' party into a story about the marital problems of a brilliant movie director.[7] The story was declined by the *Post* as too sexually frank, and it was not accepted by any of the other mass-circulation magazines. Fitzgerald later wrote Ober: 'Do you remember how the Hearst publicity men killed my story "Crazy Sunday" for *Cosmopolitan*. That was in case someone should get hurt, that it might offend Norma Shearer, Thalberg, John Gilbert or Marion Davies, etc. etc. As a matter of fact I had mixed up those characters so thoroughly that there was no character who could have been identified except possibly King Vidor and he would have been very amused by the story.'[8] 'Crazy Sunday' was published in Mencken's *American Mercury*.

In January, Fitzgerald took Zelda back to Florida for her asthma and informed Perkins of his writing plans from St. Petersburg: 'At last for the first time in two years + ½ I am going to spend five consecutive months on my novel. I am actually six thousand dollars ahead Am replanning it to include what's good in what I have, adding 41,000 new words + publishing. Don't tell Ernest or anyone – let them think what they want – you're the only one whose ever consistently felt faith in me anyhow.'[9]

In St. Petersburg what Fitzgerald described as a spot of eczema (more likely a hive) appeared on Zelda's neck, an ominous sign when accompanied by irrational outbursts. She was working hard on a novel, and the strain was showing. On the trip back to Montgomery she drank the contents of Fitzgerald's flask during the night and woke him to complain that terrible things were being done to her with his knowledge. Fitzgerald tried to talk her out of her fears, but Zelda insisted that she wanted to be hospitalized. He informed Dr. Forel, who advised him to bring Zelda back to Prangins; but that seemed out of the question.[10] On 12 February 1932 – five months after her release from Prangins – Fitzgerald took Zelda to the Henry Phipps Psychiatric Clinic of the Johns Hopkins University Hospital in Baltimore. He returned to Montgomery to wait for news of her progress and to try to resume work on his novel. That winter he spent considerable time with Scottie, reading *Great Expectations* to her and teaching her chess, which he loved to play. He was always teaching her something. In the spring there was a treasure hunt for which Fitzgerald wrote all the clues in verse, greatly impressing her classmates at Miss Margaret Booth's School.

Zelda did not respond well to Dr. Adolf Meyer, director of the Phipps clinic, whom she found dull and humorless; but she felt close to Dr. Mildred Squires. Fitzgerald was unable to achieve a collaborative relationship with Dr. Meyer, as he had with Dr. Forel. Wanting to participate in Zelda's treatment, he felt that Dr. Meyer did not regard him as a serious man. At Phipps, Zelda was permitted to work for two hours a day on her novel, and Dr. Squires informed Fitzgerald on 9 March that Zelda had finished it. Zelda sent it to Perkins, explaining: 'Scott being absorbed in his own has not seen it. . . . As soon as I hear that you have safely received the copy, I want to mail the ms. to Scott, so could you wire?'[11] She also wrote to Fitzgerald promising to send her novel to him. By 16 March, a week after Zelda's typescript had been sent to Perkins, Fitzgerald wrote an angry letter to Dr. Squires. He had read the novel and felt betrayed because she had preempted material from his work-in-progress.

As you may know I have been working intermittently for four years on a novel which covers the life we led in Europe. Since the spring of 1930 I have been unable to proceed *because* of the necessity of keeping Zelda in sanitariums. However about 50,000 words exist and this Zelda has heard and literally one whole section of her novel is an imitation of it, of its rhythm materials even statements and speeches. Now you say that the experiences which two people have undergone in common is common property – one transmutes the same scene through different temperaments and it 'comes out different'. As you will see from my letter to her there were only two episodes both of which *she* has reduced to anecdotes *but upon which whole sections of my book turn* that I have asked her to cut. Her own material – her youth her love for Jozan her dancing her observation of Americans in Paris the fine passages about the death of her father – any criticisms of that will be simply impersonal and professional. But do you realize that 'Amory Blaine' was the name of the character in my first novel to which I attached my adventures and opinions in effect my autobiography? Do you think that his turning up in a novel signed by my wife as a somewhat anemic portrait painter with a few ideas lifted from Clive Bell Leger ect could pass unnoticed? In short it puts me in an absurd and Zelda in a ridiculous position. If she could choose to examine our life together from an inimicable attitude + print her conclusions I could do nothing but answer in kind or be silent as I chose – but this mixture of fact and fiction is simply calculated to ruin us both or what is left of us and I can't let it stand. Using the name of a character I invented to put intimate facts in the hands of the friends and enemies we have accumulated *en route* – My God, my books made her a legend and her single intention in this somewhat thin portrait is to make me a non-entity. That's why she sent the book directly to New York.[12]

Fitzgerald did not feel threatened by Zelda's writing ability, though he was probably chagrined by her display of concentration in completing her novel so rapidly. His feeling of betrayal was aggravated by his conviction that it had been written on time paid for by him with money earned by time taken away from his own novel. On 16 March he wired Perkins: PLEASE DO NOT JUDGE OR IF NOT ALREADY DONE EVEN CONSIDER ZELDAS BOOK UNTIL YOU GET REVISED VERSION LETTER FOLLOWS.[13]

When Zelda learned of Fitzgerald's reaction, she attempted to pacify him:

> Dr. Squires tells me that you are hurt that I did not send my book to you before I mailed it to Max. Purposely I didn't – knowing that you were working on your own and honestly feeling that I had no right to interrupt you to ask for a serious opinion. Also, I know Max will not want it and I prefer to do the corrections after having his opinion. Naturally, I was in my usual rush to get it off my hands – You know how I hate brooding over things once they are finished: so I mailed it poste haste, hoping to have yours + Scribner's criticisms to use for revising.
>
> Scott, I love you more than anything on earth and if you were offended I am miserable. We have always shared everything but it seems to me I no longer have the right to inflict every desire and necessity of mine on you. I was also afraid we might have touched on the same material. Also, feeling it to be a dubious production due to my own instability I did not want a scathing criticism such as you have mercilessly – if for my own good given my last stories, poor things. I have had enough discouragement, generally, and could scream with that sense of inertia that hovers over my life and everything I do. So, Dear, my own, please realize that it was not from any sense of not turning first to you – but just time and other ill-regulated elements that made me so bombastic about Max.
>
> Goofo, please love me – life is very confusing – but I love you.
> . . . .
> Try, dear – and then I'll remember when you need me too sometime, and help.[14]

381

Fitzgerald wrote on Zelda's letter 'This is an evasion.' He was right, but he should have been prepared for her wish to keep her novel her own.

On 25 March – nine days after he read the novel – Fitzgerald wired Perkins: THINK NOVEL CAN SAFELY BE PLACED ON YOUR LIST FOR SPRING IT IS ONLY A QUESTION OF CERTAIN SMALL BUT NONE THE LESS NECESSARY REVISIONS MY DISCOURAGEMENT WAS CAUSED BY THE FACT THAT MYSELF AND DAUGHTER WERE SICK WHEN ZELDA SAW FIT TO SEND MANUSCRIPT TO YOU YOU CAN HELP ME BY RETURNING MANUSCRIPT TO HER UPON HER REQUEST GIVING SOME PRETEXT FOR NOT HAVING AS YET TIME READ IT AM NOW BETTER AND WILL WRITE LETTER TOMORROW IN MY OPINION IT IS A FINE NOVEL STOP WILL TAKE UP ARTICLE AS SOON AS I HAVE FINISHED CURRENT POST STORY WHICH WILL BE ON ARRIVAL BALTIMORE WEDNESDAY BEST REGARDS FAITHFULLY SCOTT FITZGERALD.[15] And on 28 March: READ MANUSCRIPT BUT IF YOU HAVE ALREADY RETURNED IT WIRE AND ILL SEND MY COPY STOP IF YOU LIKE IT AND WANT TO USE IMMEDIATELY REMEMBER ALL MIDDLE SECTION MUST BE RADICALLY REWRITTEN STOP TITLE AND NAME OF AMORY BLAINE CHANGED STOP ARRIVING BALTIMORE THURSDAY TO CONFER WITH ZELDA WILL IMMEDIATELY DECIDE ON NEW TITLE AND NAME CHANGES REVISING SHOULD TAKE FORTNIGHT SCOTT FITZGERALD.[16]

Although Zelda agreed to withdraw the novel and revise it, she tried to take a firm stand on the question of their joint material: the things that had happened to them were community literary property.

> Of cource, I glad submit to anything you want about the book or anything else. I felt myself that the thing was too crammed with material upon which I had not the time to dwell and consequently lost any story continuity. Shall I wire Max to send it back? The real story was the old prodigal son, of cource. I regret that it offended you. The Pershing incident which you accuse me of stealing occupies just one line and will not be missed. I willingly relinquish it. However, I would like

you to thoroughly understand that my revision will be made on an aesthetic basis: that the other material which I will elect is nevertheless legitimate stuff which has cost me a pretty emotional penny to amass and which I intend to use when I can get the tranquility of spirit necessary to write the story of myself versus myself. That is the book I really want to write.[17]

The original title of the novel is unknown. Zelda found 'Save Me the Waltz' in a record catalogue. The drafts of her novel are lost along with Fitzgerald's letters of editorial advice, so it is impossible to determine how much work he put into the revision – whether he confined himself to editorial advice or whether he revised it himself. The surviving setting copy and proofs show only a few galley revisions in Fitzgerald's hand. On 30 March he left Alabama and lived at the Hotel Rennert in Baltimore, where he was able to consult with Zelda during the revision process. She made a thorough revision in a month, and by the end of April Fitzgerald reported to Perkins: 'Zelda's novel is now good, improved in every way. It is new. She has largely eliminated the Speakeasy-nights-and-our-trip-to-Paris atmosphere. You'll like it. It should reach you in ten days. I am too close to it to judge it but it may be even better than I think.' He warned Perkins to keep his compliments conservative and avoid exciting Zelda's hopes. 'If she has a success coming she must associate it with work done in a workmanlike manner for its own sake, + part of it done fatigued and uninspired, and part of it done even when to remember the original inspiration and impetus is a psychological trick. She is not twenty-one and she is not strong, and she must not try to follow the pattern of my trail which is of course blazed distinctly on her mind.'[18]

In the middle of May, Fitzgerald sent Zelda's rewritten novel to Perkins:

Now, about its reception. If you refuse it, which I don't think you will, all communication should come through me. If you accept it write her directly and I withdraw all restraints on

383

whatever meed of praise you may see fit to give. The strain of
writing it was bad for her but it had to be written – she needed
relaxation afterwards and I was afraid that praise might
encourage the incipient egomania the doctors noticed, but she
has taken such a sane common sense view lately (at first she
refused to revise – then she revised completely, added on her
own suggestion + has changed what was a rather flashy and
self-justifying 'true confessions' that wasn't worthy of her into
an honest piece of work. She can do more with the galley but I
cant ask her to do more now.)[19]

This letter includes the warning not to discuss Zelda's novel
with Hemingway, who would expect Perkins's full allegiance
to his new book, *Death in the Afternoon*. Perkins accepted *Save
Me the Waltz* for fall 1932 publication.

41

'La Paix'
and Save Me the Waltz

[Spring–Fall 1932]

In May, Fitzgerald rented 'La Paix,' a fifteen-room Victorian frame house on the twenty-eight acre Turnbull estate at Towson, outside Baltimore. He also acquired an impressive used Stutz. Although the Fitzgeralds lived at 'La Paix' until the end of 1933, the house retained the bare look of a temporary residence. Zelda described it for Perkins: 'We have a soft shady place here that's like a paintless play-house abandoned when the family grew up. It's surrounded by apologetic trees and [morning] meadows and creaking insects and is gutted of its aura by many comfortable bed rooms which do not have to be floated up to on alcoholic inflation past the cupolas and cornices as did the ones at "Ellerslie".'[20] Fitzgerald had found 'La Paix' with the help of Edgar Allen Poe, Jr., a Baltimore lawyer who had been at Princeton with him. During the period Fitzgerald lived in Maryland, Poe handled his legal affairs. At first Zelda spent mornings at 'La Paix,' returning to Phipps after lunch. On 26 June she was discharged from Phipps; but she was not regarded as cured, and both Fitzgeralds went to Phipps for regular conferences with her doctors.

When Zelda became a full-time resident at 'La Paix,' Fitzgerald insisted that he have control over her and that she live according to a strict schedule of exercise and rest he had prepared. She resented his authority and chafed at the restraints put on her writing by him and Dr. Meyer; nonetheless, Fitzgerald blamed Dr. Meyer for encouraging her to write. Fitzgerald was concerned that Zelda would again poach on the material for his novel, particularly in the area of psychiatry, and he encouraged her to resume painting instead. Among the paintings she worked on after 1932 are ballet studies in which the dancers have swollen feet and legs, expressing the pain of her own ballet experiences.* Her paintings were, like her prose, often surprising and even startling. There was also a witty series of New York and Paris cityscapes.[21] Zelda painted for the rest of her life, but she preferred writing as a form of expression because she did not feel confident about her command of painting. She also believed that her poor eyesight hampered her work as a painter.

Although she had relinquished her ballet ambitions, Zelda continued to practice and often wore a tutu. She had developed the nervous habit of picking at her face, perhaps as the result of the eczema she had suffered at Prangins. At 'La Paix' there were frequent arguments during which the Fitzgeralds shouted at each other, but there were also interludes of tenderness. Visitors were impressed by the Fitzgeralds' enjoyment of each other's wit and the way they responded to recollections of past happiness.

During April and May 1932 Fitzgerald wrote three *Post* stories for ready money: 'Family in the Wind,' 'What a Handsome Pair!' and 'The Rubber Check.' 'What a Handsome Pair!' was an oblique response to the crisis over Zelda's novel. In this story the marriage between two keen sporting people turns into bitter rivalry. Another marriage in the story, that of a composer to an uncultured

* Since Zelda did not date her paintings, it is impossible to place them in a chronology.

woman who knows nothing about music, is contrastingly comfortable because the wife is just a wife. Too much mutuality of interests may ruin a marriage; one kind of good marriage – especially for a creative man – requires a wife without competing ambitions. 'Family in the Wind' expresses Fitzgerald's determination to fulfill his responsibilities to Scottie. Based on a recent cyclone in Alabama, the story treats a once-brilliant surgeon who has become the alcoholic proprietor of a small-town drugstore. He assumes responsibility for a little girl who has been orphaned by the cyclone and resumes his medical career. There were two more stories later in the year: 'One Interne' and 'On Schedule.' The *Post* cut his payments from $4,000 to $3,500, $3,000, and $2,500. In one year Fitzgerald's story price fell to its 1925 level. The *Post* was feeling the Depression with diminished advertising revenues, but the editors were also complaining to Ober that these stories were not up to the Fitzgerald standard. Fitzgerald admitted that one of his 1932 stories, 'Nightmare' (also titled 'Fantasy in Black'), set at an insane asylum, was

'La Paix,' Towson, Maryland

unsalable to any of the slick magazines. Ober ignored Fitzgerald's suggestion that it be offered to the pulps.[22] Fitzgerald's 1932 earnings were $15,832.40 – the lowest annual total since 1919.

Fitzgerald maintained his friendship with H. L. Mencken in Baltimore, but Mencken's domestic situation prevented resumption of the roistering times of 1920. Mencken had married an invalid, Sara Haardt – a girlhood friend of Zelda's from Montgomery – with whom he lived quietly. Although Mencken regarded him as the 'white hope of American letters,' he was convinced that Fitzgerald would not fulfill his promise as long as he remained with Zelda and continued to drink.

During August 1932 Fitzgerald made his first trip to Johns Hopkins Hospital with a tentative diagnosis of typhoid fever. His stay in the hospital provided him with 'One Interne,' a competently plotted doctor-nurse love story reinforced by

Zelda's watercolor of Notre Dame Cathedral

details of Hopkins customs. Fitzgerald was hospitalized at Hopkins eight more times between 1933 and 1937, both for alcoholism and for chronic inactive fibroid tuberculosis. One of his Baltimore physicians was Benjamin Baker, a thirty-one-year-old former Rhodes scholar. At Mencken's urging Dr. Baker took a personal interest in Fitzgerald and tried to keep him on the wagon. He managed it for several months by getting Fitzgerald to phone when he wanted to take a drink; Dr. Baker went to Washington and Richmond in response to these calls.[23]

Inevitably, Fitzgerald spent hours pumping Dr. Baker about his personal life. In search of story material he began visiting the Hopkins emergency room, where he made a friend of the eighty-year-old man – supposedly a disgraced English aristocrat – who registered the patients. Fitzgerald eventually wrote half a dozen Hopkins stories, some of which were unsalable.

Save Me the Waltz – dedicated to Dr. Squires – was published at $2 by Scribners on 7 October 1932 in a printing of 3,010 copies. The reception was disappointing. Sales were only about 1,400 copies, and the reviewers did not treat it respectfully. The novel was probably hurt by the circumstance that it apparently never received thorough copy editing and was peppered with errors. Fitzgerald had written into the contract the stipulation that half the royalties up to $10,000 were to be credited against his Scribners debt; but the 1932 earnings from *Save Me the Waltz* were only $120.73 – partly because of the cost of proof revisions.

Zelda's impressionistic technique and lush style puzzled readers. Passages like this are frequent: 'A shooting star, ectoplasmic arrow, sped through the nebulous hypothesis like a wanton hummingbird. From Venus to Mars to Neptune it trailed the ghost of comprehension, illuminating far horizons over the pale battlefields of reality.'[24] Flowers always enriched Zelda's life, and her letters often expressed her intense responses to them. *Save Me the Waltz* includes a lavish synesthesic description of the flowers of Paris.

Yellow roses she bought with her money like Empire satin brocade, and white lilacs and pink tulips like moulded confectioner's frosting, and deep-red roses like a Villon poem, black and velvety as an insect wing, cold blue hydrangeas clean as a newly calcimined wall, the crystalline drops of lily of the valley, a bowl of nasturtiums like beaten brass, anemones pieced out of wash material, and malignant parrot tulips scratching the air with their jagged barbs, and the voluptuous scrambled convolutions of Parma violets. She bought lemon-yellow carnations perfumed with the taste of hard candy, and garden roses purple as raspberry puddings, and every kind of white flower the florist knew how to grow. She gave Madame gardenias like white kid gloves and forget-me-nots from the Madeleine stalls, threatening sprays of gladioli, and the soft, even purr of black tulips. She bought flowers like salads and flowers like fruits, jonquils and narcissus, poppies and ragged robins, and flowers with the brilliant carnivorous qualities of Van Gogh. She chose from windows filled with metal balls and cactus gardens of the florists near the rue de la Paix, and from the florists uptown who sold mostly plants and purple iris, and from florists on the Left Bank whose shops were lumbered up with the wire frames of designs, and from outdoor markets where the peasants dyed their roses to a bright apricot, and stuck wires through the heads of the dyed peonies.[25]

Openly autobiographical, *Save Me the Waltz* is Zelda's attempt to comprehend her collapse. The novel makes it clear that her parents were a powerful presence in her life. Judge Sayre, despite his remoteness, provided Zelda with a standard of conduct against which she rebelled while accepting its justness. *Save Me the Waltz* is divided into four sections. In the opening section Alabama Beggs, the daughter of a Southern judge, meets a painter during World War I and marries him. David Knight, like Fitzgerald, has a quality of romantic promise. He achieves rapid success, and the Knights become New York celebrities: 'They were having the bread line at the Ritz that year. Everybody was there. People met people they knew in hotel lobbies smelling of orchids and plush and detective stories, and asked each other where they'd been since last time.'[26] When her parents make a disastrous visit to the Knights' Connecticut home, Alabama realizes she is permanently estranged from the Judge's certainties. The Knights have a daughter, Bonnie: and in the second section of *Save Me the Waltz* they go to the Riviera, where Alabama falls in love with a French naval aviator, Jacques Chevre-Feuille. She does not sleep with him, and the aviator discourages Alabama's offer to leave her husband. David tries to force a fight with Jacques, who refuses because he is much stronger than David.

The Knights move to Paris: 'Nobody knew whose party it was. It had been going on for weeks. When you felt you couldn't survive another night, you went home and slept and when you got back, a new set of people had consecrated themselves to keeping it alive.'[27] When David has an affair with an actress, Alabama determines to seek a ballet career. The third section of the novel details the strain of Alabama's ballet work and her concomitant estrangement from David as 'Madame,' the head of the studio, becomes the artistic and spiritual center of her life. In the final section Alabama accepts a position with a ballet company in Naples (the same offer Zelda had declined), and is separated from her husband and daughter. Alabama develops blood poisoning from an infected blister, and the operation makes it impossible for her to dance again. Reconciled, the Knights return to America. After Judge Beggs dies in November 1931, as did Judge Sayre, the Knights prepare to leave the South. They are together again with their shared sense of regret and loss. Even in its rewritten version, *Save Me the Waltz* is transparently about the Fitzgeralds and rehearses the crises of the first decade of their marriage – with the omission of the psychiatric episodes and accusations of homosexuality. But it is not simply Zelda's exercise in self-justification. The Knights' betrayals are mutual.

42

Work on
Tender Is the Night

[Summer 1932]

At *'La Paix'* Fitzgerald hired his first full-time secretary, Isabel Owens, for $12 a week and prepared for the final assault on his novel. Inevitably Mrs. Owens became companion for Zelda, surrogate mother for Scottie, and household manager. Abandoning the Melarky-matricide and Kelly-shipboard material, he conceived a new plot set in Europe about an American psychiatrist who is ruined by his marriage to a wealthy mental patient. If his inability to complete the early versions of the novel can be blamed on his lack of commitment to the matricide material, in 1932 Fitzgerald had material that he felt strongly about: Zelda's breakdown and his own deterioration. When he resumed work on the novel that would have to recoup his reputation, he had a store of painful emotions to draw on. *Tender Is the Night* became in the writing his attempt to understand the loss of everything he had won, the loss of everything he had ever wanted.

In August 1932 he noted in his *Ledger*, 'The novel now plotted + planned, never more to be permanently interrupted.' The plan consists of sixteen pages of story digest, character sketches, charts, and work schedules.

392

Work on Tender Is the Night [Summer 1932]

GENERAL PLAN
Sketch

The novel should do this. Show a man who is a natural idealist, a spoiled priest, giving in for various causes to the ideas of the haute Burgeoise, and in his rise to the top of the social world losing his idealism, his talent and turning to drink and dissipation. Background one in which the liesure class is at their truly most brilliant + glamorous such as Murphys.

———————

———————

The hero born in 1891 is a man like myself brought up in a family sunk from haute burgeoisie to petit burgeoisie, yet expensively educated. He has all the gifts, and goes through Yale almost succeeding but not quite but getting a Rhodes scholarship which he caps with a degree from Hopkins, + with a legacy goes abroad to study psychology in Zurich. At the age of 26 all seems bright. Then he falls in love with one of his patients who has a curious homicidal mania toward men caused by an event of her youth. Aside from this she is the legendary *promiscuous* woman. He 'transfers' to himself + she falls in love with him, a love he returns.

After a year of non-active service in the war he returns and marries her + is madly in love with her + entirely consecrated to completing the cure. She is an aristocrat of half American, half European parentage, young, mysterious + lovely, *a new character*. He has cured her by pretending to a stability + belief in the current order which he does not have, being in fact a communist-liberal-idealist, a moralist in revolt. But the years of living under patronage ect. + among the burgeoisie have seriously spoiled him and he takes up the marriage as a man divided in himself. During the war he has taken to drink a little + it continues as secret drinking after his marriage. The difficulty of taking care of her is more than he has imagined and he goes more and more to pieces, always keeping up a wonderful face.

At the point when he is socially the most charming and inwardly corrupt he meets a young actress on the Rivierra who falls in love with him. With considerable difficulty he contains himself out of fear of all it would entail since his formal

393

goodness is all that is holding his disintegration together. He knows too that he does not love her as he has loved his wife. Nevertheless the effect of the repression is to throw him toward all women during his secret drinking when he has another life of his own which his wife does not suspect, or at least he thinks she doesn't. In one of his absensces during which he is in Rome with the actress having a disappointing love affair too late he is beaten up by the police. He returns to find that instead of taking a rest cure she has committed a murder and in a revulsion of spirit he tries to conceal it and succeeds. It shows him however that the game is up and he will have to perform some violent + Byronic act to save her for he is losing his hold on her + himself.

He has known slightly for some time a very strong + magnetic man and now he deliberately brings them together. When he finds under circumstances of jealous agony that it has succeeded he departs knowing that he has cured her. He sends his neglected son into Soviet Russia to educate him and comes back to America to be a quack thus having accomplished both his burgeoise sentimental idea in the case of his wife and his ideals in the case of his son, + now being himself only a shell to which nothing matters but survival as long as possible with the old order.

(Further Sketch)   *Approach*

The Drunkard's Holiday will be a novel of our time showing the break up of a fine personality. Unlike *The Beautiful and Damned* the break-up will be caused not by flabbiness but really tragic forces such as the inner conflicts of the idealist and the compromises forced upon him by circumstances.

The novel will be a little over a hundred thousand words long, composed of fourteen chapters, each 7,500 words long, five chapters each in the first and second part, four in the third – one chapter or its equivalent to be composed of retrospect.

CHARACTERS + NAMES
Dick

The hero was born in 1891. He is a well-formed rather athletic and fine looking fellow. Also he is very intelligent, widely read – in fact he has all the talents, including especially great personal charm. This is all planted in the beginning. He is a superman in possibilities, that is, he appears to be at first sight from a burgeoise point of view. However he lacks that tensile strength – none of the ruggedness of Brancusi, Leger, Picasso. For his external qualities use anything of Gerald, Ernest, Ben Finny, Archie Mcliesh, Charley McArthur or myself. He looks, though, like me.

The faults – the weakness such as the social-climbing, the drinking, the desparate clinging to one woman, finally the neurosis, only come out gradually.

We follow him from age 34 to age 39.

Actual Age of

DICK

September	1891	Born
September	1908	Entered Yale
June	1912	Graduated Yale aged 20
June	1916	Graduated Hopkins. Left for Vienna (8 mo. there)
June	1917	Was in Zurich after 1 year and other work. Age 26
June	1918	Degree at Zurich. Aged 26
June	1919	Back in Zurich. Aged 27
September	1919	Married – aged 28 { after his refusing fellowship at University in neurology and pathologist to the clinic. Or does he accept?
July	1925	After 5 years and 10 months of marriage is aged almost 34 Story starts
July	1929	After 9 years and 10 months of marriage is aged almost 38.

Nicole's Age

Always one year younger than century.
Born July 1901
    courtship for two and one half years before that, since she was 13.

Catastrophe June 1917 Age almost 16
Clinic   Feb. 1918 Age 17
                                   To middle October bad period
                                   After Armistice good period
                                   He returns in April or May 1919
                                   She discharged June 1, 1919. Almost 18
                                   Married September 1919. Aged 18
Child born August 1920
Child born June 1922
    2nd Pousse almost immediately to October 1922 and
        thereafter Frenchman (or what have you in summer
        of 1923 after almost 4 years of marriage
In July 1925 when the story opens she is just 24
    (One child almost 5 (Scotty in Juan les Pins)
    One child 3 (Scotty in Pincio)
In July 1929 when the story ends she is just 28

The heroine was born in 1901. She is beautiful on the order of Marlene Dietrich or better still the Norah Gregor-Kiki Allen girl with those peculiar eyes. She is American with a streak of some foreign blood. At fifteen she was raped by her own father under peculiar circumstances – work out. She collapses, goes to the clinic and there at sixteen meets the young doctor hero who is ten years older. Only her transference to him saves her – when it is not working she reverts to homicidal mania and tries to kill men. She is an innocent, widely read but with no experience and no orientation except what he supplies her. Portrait of Zelda – that is, a part of Zelda.

We follow her from age 24 to age 29

Method of Dealing with Sickness Material
(1) Read books and decide the general type of case
(2) Prepare a clinical report covering the years 1916–1920
(3) Now examine the different classes of material selecting not
    too many things for copying.
    (1) From the sort of letter under E
    (2) From the sort of letter under F
        (In this case using no factual stuff)
    (3) From the other headings for atmosphere, accuracy

and material being careful not to reveal basic
ignorance of psychiatric and medical training yet
not being glib. Only suggest from the most remote
facts. *Not* like doctor's stories.
Must avoid Faulkner attitude and not end with a novelized
Kraft-Ebing – better Ophelia and her flowers.

Classification of the Material on Sickness
A. Accounts
B. Baltimore
C. Clinics and clipping
D. Dancing and 1st Diagnoses
E. Early Prangins – to February 1931
F. From Forel (include Bleuler Consultation)
H. Hollywood
L. Late Prangins
M. My own letters and comments
R. Rosalind and Sayre Family
S. Squires and Schedule
V. Varia

The plan includes a sheet on which Zelda's case history is
charted with that of the novel's heroine (see page 398).

The actress was born in 1908. Her career is like Lois or Mary
Hay – that is, she differs from most actresses by being a lady,
simply reeking of vitality, health, sensuality. Rather gross as
compared to the heroine, or rather *will be* gross for at present
her youth covers it. Mimi-Lupe Velez
We see her first at the very beginning of her carreer. She's
already made one big picture.

We follow her from age 17 to age 22.

The Friend was born in 1896. He is a wild man. He looks
like Tunte and like that dark communist at the meeting. He is
half Italian or French + half American. He is a type who hates
all sham + pretense. (See the Lung type who was like Foss
Wilson) He is one who would lead tribesmen or communists –
utterly aristocratic, unbourgeoise king or nothing. He fought

three years in the French foreign legion in the war and then painted a little and then fought the Riff. He's just back from there on his first appearance in the novel and seeking a new outlet. He has money + this French training – otherwise he *would* be a revolutionist. He is a fine type, useful or destructive but his mind is not quite as good as the hero's. Touch of Percy Pyne, Denny Holden also.

We see him from age 28 to age 33.[28]

In replanning his novel Fitzgerald was guided by Émile Zola's documentary method for assembling material, as described in Matthew Josephson's *Zola and His Time* (1928).*

* When *Tender Is the Night* was published, Fitzgerald sent Josephson an inscribed copy: 'Save for the swell organization of "Zola" + your reproduction of it, this would never have reached the stalls—'[29]

Fitzgerald departed from his preliminary plan in the course of writing the novel; for example, Nicole is not homicidal in the book. The plan reveals that from the inception of the final plot in 1932 the novel was not a direct transcription from life. The characters are composites. Nicole is a 'Portrait of Zelda – that is, a part of Zelda' compounded with an invented character and invented action. There is no evidence that Zelda had been the victim of incest.

The manuscripts for the novel, which now had the working title 'The Drunkard's Holiday' (the title of one of Fitzgerald's projected novels in 1919), show that while salvaging the best parts from the earlier versions, the book Fitzgerald planned in the summer of 1932 was a new work which synthesized many events and figures from the Fitzgeralds' expatriate years. Zelda's insanity – transferred to Nicole Diver – was the catalytic experience; but the subject of the novel is Fitzgerald's betrayal of his genius expressed through the career of Dr. Richard Diver, who represents Fitzgerald's self-judgment and self-condemnation. The characterization of Diver is complex because Fitzgerald brought to it both self-pity and self-contempt. The name 'Diver' reveals the ambivalence of Fitzgerald's feelings both about the hero and about himself. Dick Diver is of course the man who plunges from great promise to disgraced failure; but the name also has the slang meaning 'cocksucker.' Diver is the victim of corrupting influences, but he is corrupted because he is corruptible. On the simplest level he is ruined by the rich; but the true source of his collapse is his need to be loved and admired, which compels him to squander his emotional capital. Dr. Diver succeeds in curing his patient-wife at the cost of his own career. In achieving Zelda's impossible cure in fiction Fitzgerald may have been trying to absolve himself of whatever guilt he felt for his wife's madness – as well as to punish himself for his self-indulgence and self-betrayal.

The dedication of *Tender Is the Night* – 'TO/GERALD AND SARA/MANY FÊTES' – has led the incautious to assume that the Divers are the Murphys. This assumption does not hold up under scrutiny. The Pipers (Rorebacks) in the matricide version were modeled on the Murphys, but as Fitzgerald wrote and rewrote he worked away from the Murphys. Social qualities or background details from the Murphys were transferred to the Divers; but the Divers are invented – or synthesized – characters who finally are much closer to the Fitzgeralds than to the Murphys. As Fitzgerald's 'General Plan' shows, even at that preliminary stage the Divers were not straight transcriptions of the Murphys. Dick's external qualities were assembled from Murphy, Hemingway, Finney, MacLeish, MacArthur, and Fitzgerald. John O'Hara later told Gerald Murphy: 'Scott wrote the life, but not the lives. And that is true partly because Scott was always writing about the life. Sooner or later his characters always come back to being Fitzgerald characters in a Fitzgerald world. . . . And of course as he moved along, he got farther away from any resemblance to the real Murphys. Dick Diver ended up as a tall Fitzgerald. . . .'[30]

Except for *This Side of Paradise*, Fitzgerald never wrote a *roman à clef*, in which the characters and action are directly based on actual people and real events. He did, however, always draw some of his characters from life – sometimes closely. Abe North is obviously modeled on Ring Lardner with a suggestion of Charles MacArthur, but the events of North's life were invented. Tommy Barban is an amalgam of five people – Edouard Jozan, Mario Braggiotti, Tommy Hitchcock, and Princetonians Percy Pyne and Denny Holden. Although Fitzgerald did not stipulate Hemingway as one of the models for Barban, there are clear connections: just as Barban usurps Diver's Riviera kingdom, so Hemingway had eclipsed Fitzgerald's literary reputation. Baby Warren was drawn from Sara Murphy's sister, Hoyt; but her name was given to Rosemary Hoyt.

The most instructive example of Fitzgerald's method of character creation in *Tender Is the Night* is Rosemary, who evolved from the combination of the fictional Francis

Melarky with Lois Moran. Rosemary resembles the actress while performing some of the action salvaged from the Melarky drafts. In the process Fitzgerald converted the protagonist of the early version into the observer or reflector figure in the published novel. Because Rosemary's point of view is not maintained throughout the novel, Fitzgerald was unable to achieve the impression of distance from Diver that Carraway provides for Gatsby. In the Melarky version Fitzgerald had tried and rejected the partially involved narrator method – probably because the scope of the *Tender* story is too great to be observed by one character.

The material from the early drafts was not simply transferred to the Diver version. Fitzgerald revised or rewrote what he salvaged, and he wrote new material for the new characters. 'The Drunkard's Holiday' is based on the Melarky material up to Abe's departure from Paris in Chapter 19 of Book I. The rest of the novel is new – except for the account of Dick's beating in Rome, which was originally intended as the prologue for the matricide plot. The novel achieved its final form through layers of drafts. He paced when he worked, especially if he had been drinking. Owens recalled: 'If he was sober, he worked well and very smoothly. He was disciplined and would write for two hours and then stop and go back to it later. If he was drinking, he had a hard time sitting still. He'd be in and out of his office.'[31] As was his invariable practice, Fitzgerald wrote the novel in pencil on unlined legal-size sheets, with his secretary typing sections or chapters as they were written. Owens prepared a ribbon copy (triple-spaced to allow room for revision) and two carbons. Fitzgerald revised the ribbon and carbon copies. Then the best revision was retyped, and the revision process continued. At every stage Fitzgerald polished his prose by tightening sentences and finding richer language.

The complete typescript of 'The Drunkard's Holiday,' prepared for serialization in *Scribner's Magazine*, was some 700 double-spaced pages. Fitzgerald revised the ribbon copy (which he retitled 'Doctor Diver's Holiday: A Romance') and then the carbon copy (retitled *Tender Is the Night: A Romance*). The subtitle 'A Romance' indicates that Fitzgerald regarded his book as a departure from the realistic or novelistic modes of fiction.* Fitzgerald later described it to James Thurber as 'my testament of faith.'[32] *The Last Tycoon* would also be subtitled 'A Romance.'

Although the title 'Doctor Diver's Holiday' was an improvement over 'The Drunkard's Holiday,' Fitzgerald worried that it would give potential readers the impression that it was a medical story. The title *Tender Is the Night* – from Keats's 'Ode to a Nightingale' (a poem Fitzgerald claimed he could never read without tears) pleased him; but Perkins or some of the Scribners people required persuasion because it was not a selling title that gave the customers a clue to the nature of the work, and Fitzgerald briefly considered the neutral title 'Richard Diver.' *Tender Is the Night* with its epigraph ('Already with thee! tender is the night . . ./. . . But here there is no light,/Save what from heaven is with the breezes blown/Through verdurous glooms and winding mossy ways.') evokes the mood of disenchantment that pervades Fitzgerald's romance. Keats's poem expresses an attempt to flee painful reality and the consequent return to despair. The final lines of the ode express Dick Diver's mood of loss at the end of the novel: 'Was it a vision, or a waking dream?/Fled is that music: – Do I wake or sleep?'

* It is not known whether Fitzgerald was familiar with Hawthorne's explanation of his designating *The House of the Seven Gables* a romance, but Fitzgerald's application of the term accords with Hawthorne's usage to designate a form or technique that grants itself, 'a right to present that truth [of the human heart] under circumstances, to a great extent, of the writer's own choosing or creation. If he think fit, also, he may so manage his atmospherical medium as to bring out or mellow the lights and deepen and enrich the shadows of the picture.'

43

Competition
and Scandalabra

[1932–1933]

▚▚ *Fitzgerald was lonely* at 'La Paix' and spent time with
▚▚ Scottie and the three Turnbull children – Eleanor,
Frances, and Andrew – inventing games and writing skits for
them. He shared an interest in football with eleven-year-old
Andrew, who would become his biographer in 1962, and took
him to Princeton games.[33] Fitzgerald tried to compensate for
Zelda's absences and withdrawal from family life by devoting
attention to Scottie, who was approaching eleven. Concerned
that she might be influenced by exposure to her parents'
weakness, he endeavored to train her to be disciplined. He
expected her to excel at her studies and was harsh with her
when she disappointed him. Scottie was very much under her
father's influence, and Zelda resented it when the child
indicated that Daddy's decisions were the ones that counted.

Fitzgerald shared his pleasure in verbal play with Scottie,
teaching her riddles (the farmer, the goose, the fox, and the
bag of grain) and limericks, ('There was a Young Lady of
Niger . . . '). He played the word game Hangman with her
and encouraged her to read his favorite children's books,

Thackeray's *The Rose and the Ring* and Kipling's *Just-So Stories*. There were also croquet and tennis at 'La Paix,' and Fitzgerald gave his daughter boxing lessons. He played chess with both Scottie and Zelda.

In Baltimore, Fitzgerald looked up his college friend Eben Finney, Princeton '19. The Finneys had a daughter, Peaches, who was Scottie's age. The girls attended the Calvert and Bryn Mawr schools together, and Peaches Finney became Scottie's closest friend.

Mollie Fitzgerald's visits to 'La Paix' from Washington irritated her son because she could not conceal her anxiety about him. She would bring him candy, hoping that it would help him to cut down his drinking. Annabel Fitzgerald had married Clifton Sprague, a naval officer, and she rarely saw her brother. (Sprague, whom Fitzgerald admired but felt no rapport with, became an admiral and distinguished himself in the Battle of Leyte Gulf during World War II.)

Relations between the Fitzgerald and Turnbull households were cordial but not close. For one thing, the Turnbulls ran a dry house. Bayard Turnbull, an architect, was put off by Fitzgerald, who nevertheless developed a warm friendship with Margaret Turnbull. He talked books with her and sought her advice on Scottie. Fitzgerald respected women who represented for him the old standards of manners and impeccable conduct, and he was on his best behavior with Mrs. Turnbull. (He was amused by her reaction when the banks closed in March 1933 and he was the only one at 'La Paix' with money – $1,800 in gold.) When T. S. Eliot lectured on the metaphysical poets at Johns Hopkins University in February 1933, the Turnbulls invited Fitzgerald to a dinner they gave for Eliot. Fitzgerald regarded him as the greatest living poet and had been gratified by his praise of *The Great Gatsby*. On this occasion Fitzgerald was asked to read Eliot's poems aloud, which he did effectively.* Reporting on the

---

* On 2 February, Eliot inscribed Fitzgerald's copy of *Ash-Wednesday* 'with the author's homage.'[34]

meeting to Edmund Wilson, Fitzgerald described Eliot as 'Very broken and sad + shrunk inside.'[35]

While Zelda was at 'La Paix' during the summer of 1932, Fitzgerald kept in close touch with her doctors at Phipps. Zelda responded better to Dr. Thomas Rennie, a young psychiatrist, than she did to Dr. Meyer, and Fitzgerald wrote him analyses of her behavior. More and more Fitzgerald blamed Mrs. Sayre's indulgence of Zelda as a child for making her selfish and irresponsible. There were frequent arguments at 'La Paix,' for Zelda resented Fitzgerald's control over her daily activities.

Fitzgerald was unable to give up gin, which he was convinced made it possible for him to work. He reserved the times of the day when he was sober for his novel; but he took alcohol every day, and he went on binges. He later admitted to Perkins that drinking had interfered with his work on *Tender* and marred the pacing of the novel:

> It has become increasingly plain to me that the very excellent organization of a long book or the finest perceptions and judgment in time of revision do not go well with liquor. A short story can be written on a bottle, but for a novel you need the mental speed that enables you to keep the whole pattern in your head and ruthlessly sacrifice the sideshows as Ernest did in 'A Farewell to Arms.' If a mind is slowed up ever so little it lives in the individual part of a book rather than in a book as a whole; memory is dulled. I would give anything if I hadn't had to write Part III of 'Tender is the Night' entirely on stimulant. If I had one more crack at it cold sober I believe it might have made a great difference. Even Ernest commented on sections that were needlessly included and as an artist he is as near as I know for a final reference.[36]

Dr. Meyer regarded the Fitzgeralds as a joint case and insisted that Zelda would not be cured unless Fitzgerald gave up drinking, referring to him as 'a potential but unwilling patient.'[37] But Fitzgerald refused to undergo psychiatric treatment because he thought it would damage his writer's equipment. Again he had to defend or minimize his drinking;

drafting a letter to Dr. Meyer, he wrote:

> The witness is weary of strong drink and until very recently
> He had the matter well in hand for four years and has it in
> hand at the moment, and needs no help in the matter being
> normally frightened by the purely physical consequences of it.
> He does work and is not to be confused with the local
> Hunt-Club-Alcoholic and asks that his testimony be con-
> sidered as of prior value to any other.
> P.S. . . . . In answer to your points – I can concieve of giving up
> all liquor but only under conditions that seem improbable –
> Zelda suddenly a help-mate or even divorced and insane. Or,
> if one can think of some way of doing it, Zelda marrying some
> man of some caliber who would take care of her, *really* take
> care of her   This is a possibility   Her will to power must be
> broken without that – the only alternative would be to break
> me and I am forwarned + forearmed against that[38]

Fitzgerald's *Ledger* summary for his thirty-fifth year was:
'*Recession + Procession* Zelda Well, Worse, Better. Novel
intensive begins.'

Fitzgerald complained about Zelda's withdrawal from
family life at 'La Paix.' They did not entertain and rarely went
out together. An undated memo by Fitzgerald provides a
sense of the domestic conditions under which he wrote his
novel: 'As I got feeling worse Zelda got mentally better, but it
seemed to me as she did she was also coming to the conclusion
she had it on me, if I broke down it justified her whole life –
not a very healthy thought to live with about your own
wife. . . . Finally four days ago I told her frankly + furiously
that had got + was getting a rotten deal trading my health for
her insanity and from now on I was going to look out for
myself + Scotty exclusively + let her go to Bedlam for all I
cared.'[39]

The most serious crisis resulted from her plan to write a
novel about insanity – probably dealing with Nijinsky, the
Russian dancer who had gone mad. Since Fitzgerald was
treating psychiatric material in his novel, he charged that she
was again poaching and insisted that she could not write

about this subject until his novel was published. Zelda felt that she had earned the right to the material, that it was her material more than his, but she yielded and wrote a play instead. *Scandalabra*, 'a farce-fantasy,' was completed in the fall of 1932; in October, Zelda sent it to Harold Ober for circulation to Broadway producers, but there was no interest. The play can be described as a reversal of *The Beautiful and Damned*. A wealthy man leaves a fortune to his nephew on the condition that he live a dissipated life. After working at dissipation, the young man and his wife decide they'd rather be good – which is what the uncle had really intended. The dialogue is filled with Zelda's inversions and paradoxes, and much of it has a neo-Wildean quality: 'Influence, madam, is when there's somebody fond enough of us to justify our blaming them for our mistakes.'[40]

Fitzgerald worked steadily on his book during the fall and winter of 1932. The only distraction he allowed himself, apart from conferences with Zelda's doctors, was a growing concern with politics as he read Karl Marx. A November *Ledger* note reads: 'Political worries, almost neurosis.' Zelda wrote Perkins, 'The Community Communist comes and tells us about a kind of Luna-Park Eutopia.'[41] Although Fitzgerald had called himself a socialist in the Twenties and always regarded himself as a liberal, he remained essentially nonpolitical. Indeed, in 'Echoes of the Jazz Age' Fitzgerald stated, 'It was characteristic of the Jazz Age that it had no interest in politics at all.'[42] He approached politics as an aspect of history, and his interest was in main currents of thought. Nonetheless, in the Thirties he felt a pull toward political activity. The far left was beginning to dominate the literary scene. As politics and literature merged, Fitzgerald felt the need to identify with the ideas that were shaping literary standards. When he drew up the plan for his novel, he described Dick Diver as 'a communist-liberal-idealist, a moralist in revolt' and intended to end it with Diver's decision to send his son to be educated in Russia. This idea was not carried out.

Fitzgerald was incapable of submitting to political discipline, especially in his writing. He observed in his *Notebooks*: 'To bring on the revolution it may be necessary to work inside the communist party'[43] – which he could not do. His interest in communism was probably stimulated by Edmund Wilson's activities. He thought of Wilson as his intellectual conscience, and Wilson – though he did not join the party – was deeply involved with communism. However, Fitzgerald came to believe that Wilson's political commitment had narrowed him. After he went on a bender in New York in January 1933 and quarreled with both Hemingway and Wilson, Fitzgerald reported to Perkins: 'Am going on the water-wagon from the first of February to the first of April but don't tell Ernest because he has long convinced himself that I am an incurable alcoholic, due to the fact that we almost always meet on parties. I am *his* alcoholic just like Ring is mine and do not want to disillusion him, tho even *Post* stories must be done in a state of sobriety. I thought he seemed in good shape, Bunny less so, rather gloomy. A decision to adopt Communism definitely, no matter how good for the soul, must of necessity be a saddening process for anyone who has ever tasted the intellectual pleasures of the world we live in.'[44] At this time he wrote Wilson: 'I little thought that when I left politics to you + your gang in 1920 you would devote your time cutting up Wilson's shroud into blinders! Back to Mallarmé.'[45] And in 1934 Fitzgerald summarized his terminated political involvement for his cousin Ceci Taylor: ' . . . it will interest you to know that I've given up politics. For two years I've gone half haywire trying to reconcile my double alliegence to the class I am part of, and the Great Change I believe in. . . . I have become disgusted with the party leadership + have only health enough left for my literary work, so I'm on the sidelines. It had become a strain making speeches at 'Leagues against Imperialistic War,' + their treatment of the negro question finished me.'*[46] There is no

---

* The American communists were trying to win Negro adherents; the party line called for self-determination in the South.

record of any speeches he made in Baltimore except for a talk on 'How the war came to Princeton' for the Student Congress Against War.[47] A very different public appearance came in March 1933 when Fitzgerald served as one of the judges for a Baltimore children's talent contest sponsored by Metro-Goldwyn-Mayer.

On 28 May 1933 Fitzgerald, Zelda, and Dr. Rennie met at 'La Paix' with a stenographer, who prepared a 114-page typescript. The angry discussion ranged over many of the fissures in the Fitzgeralds' marriage, but the crux was Fitzgerald's insistence on the authority to veto Zelda's writing. In addition to the problem of who had first call on their shared experience, Fitzgerald was convinced that her name on novels would damage his reputation. He was also concerned that she might reveal too much about their lives in her fiction. The transcript shows how resentment and dependence were compounded in their relationship:

Extracts

Fitzgerald: I say I am a different sort of person than Zelda, that my equipment for being a writer, for being an artist, is a different equipment from hers. Her theory is that anything is possible and that a girl has just got to get along and so she has the right therefore to destroy me completely in order to satisfy herself. . . . She has certain experiences to report but she has nothing essentially to say. . . . The first time I met her I saw she was a drunkard. . . . Zelda was spoiled. She was made the baby and told that she had no obligations, that other people had obligations and so long as she was pretty she would never have to do anything except just be pretty. Then Zelda ceased being the prettiest person in the world as women inevitably will – and ceased to be so at twenty-five, though to me she is the most sexually attractive woman in the world. . . . I did not care whether you were a writer or not if you were any good. It is a struggle. It has been a struggle to me. It is self-evident to me that nobody cares about anything. It is a perfectly lonely struggle that I am making against other writers who are finely gifted and talented. You are a third-rate writer and a

409

third-rate ballet dancer. . . . If you want to write modest things you may be able to turn out one collection of short stories. For the rest, you are compared to me is just like comparing – well, there is just not any comparison. I am a professional writer with a huge following. I am the highest paid short story writer in the world. I have at various times dominated—

Zelda: It seems to me you are making a rather violent attack on a third-rate talent, then. . . . Why in the hell you are so jealous, I don't know. If I thought that about anybody I would not care what they wrote.

Fitzgerald: Because you are broaching at all times on my material just as if a good artist came into a room and found something drawn on the canvas by some mischievous little boy.

Zelda: Well, what do you want me to be?

Fitzgerald: I want you to do what I say. That is exactly what I want you to do and you know it. . . . Now, one of the agreements made between Dr. Adolph Meyer and Dr. Rennie and myself was that it was extremely inadvisable for you to write any novels which were a resumé of your insanity or discussed insanity. I gave you a clipping one day about Nijinsky which I had in my files, and immediately you founded upon that the idea that you would write a novel about insanity. You have been sneakingly writing that novel for a period of some months. What good that could have brought you or given you, I don't know, against any wish of mine that you should [not] publish a book before I publish another book and with the use of my name. . . . I don't want you for your own sake to write a novel about insanity because you know there is certain psychiatric stuff in my books; and if you publish a book before me or even at the same time in which the subject of psychiatry is taken up and people see 'Fitzgerald,' why that is Scott Fitzgerald's wife. They read that and that spells the whole central point of being a novelist, which is being yourself. You picked up the crumbs I drop at the dinner table and stick them into books. . . . She wants to write a novel against everybody's advice and it is discovered about three weeks ago

410

that she is doing it. . . . Everything that we have done is mine – if we make a trip – if I make a trip to Panama and you and I go around – I am the professional novelist and I am supporting you. That is all of my material. None of it is your material.

Dr. Rennie: We know that if you are writing a personal, individual study on a psychiatric topic, you are doing something that we would advise you right along not to do and that is not to write anything personal on psychiatric material.

Zelda: Well, Dr. Rennie, didn't we discuss some time ago and didn't I say to you that I was miserable because I could not write short things? . . . And didn't we decide that it would perhaps be better to go on and write long things?

Dr. Rennie: But didn't I also say very emphatically and haven't I said all along that for you to dabble with psychiatric material is playing with fire and you ought not to do it, and didn't you promise me really once that you would put the psychiatric novel away for five years and would not touch it in that period?

Fitzgerald: Well, we have had no relations for more than three or four months. The fact of the thing is we have various social connections with each other, one of which I blame you chiefly for, this course you are taking, because I think that course is egotistic, and I think that I am trying to be social and you are trying to be individual; and that we cannot in these times, that everything is so hard and tough, that we cannot come to any understanding on that basis, and I have got all the worries that everybody also has of making a living and I find an enemy in the family, treachery behind my back, or what I consider that. I may be hypersensitive to what I consider logical from the traditions of my profession.

Zelda: You think it is personally all right that you feel that way and you accuse me of everything in the world, with having ruined your life, not once, but over and over again.

Fitzgerald: When did that first happen?

The Long Way Out

Zelda: You did that last fall. You sat down and cried and cried. You were drunk, I will admit, and you said I had ruined your life and you did not love me and you were sick of me and wished you could get away, and I was strained and burdened. You said that when you came back from New York, also drunk, and that is the kind of life I am expected to live together with you, and make whatever adjustment I can.

Fitzgerald: What do you think caused these two things?

Zelda: It is impossible to live with you. I would rather be in an insane asylum where you would like to put me.

Fitzgerald: What do you think causes those things?

Zelda: I think the cause of it is your drinking. That is what I think is the cause of it. . . . Dr. Rennie, I am perfectly willing to put aside the novel, but I will not have any agreement or arrangements because I will not submit to Scott's neurasthenic condition and be subjected to these tortures all the time. I cannot live in this kind of a world, and I would rather live in any insane asylum. That is my ultimatum on the subject.

Fitzgerald: Our sexual relations were very pleasant and all that until I got the idea you were ditching me. They were all very nice to then, weren't they?

Zelda: Well, I am glad you considered them satisfactory.

Fitzgerald: I want you to stop writing fiction. . . . Whether you write or not does not seem to be of any great importance.

Zelda: I know. Nothing I do seems to be of any great importance.

Fitzgerald: Why don't you drop it then?

Zelda: Because I don't want to live with you, because I want to live someplace that I can be my own self.

Competition and Scandalabra [1932–1933]

Fitzgerald: Would you like to go to law about it?

Zelda: Yes, I would. . . . I think honestly the only thing is to get a divorce because there is nothing except ill will on your part and suspicion.

Fitzgerald: I am perfectly determined that I am going to take three or four drinks a day. . . . And then the fact that if I ever stop drinking her family and herself would always think that that was an acknowledgement that I was responsible for her insanity, which is not so.

Zelda: What is the matter with Scott is that he has not written that book and if he will ever get it written, why, he won't feel so miserable and suspicious and mean towards everybody else.

Fitzgerald: It has got to be an unconditional surrender on her part. That is the only promise I can have. Otherwise I would rather go to law because I don't trust her. . . . The unconditional surrender is that it is necessary for her to give up the idea of writing anything. . . . the important point is that she must only write when under competent medical assistance I say that she can write. Now that sounds awfully egotistical, but it is the only way that I can ever organize my life again.

Zelda: I want to write and I am going to write. I am going to be a writer, but I am not going to do it at Scott's expense if I can possibly avoid it. So I agree not to do anything that he does not want, a complete negation of self until that book is out of the way, because the thing is driving me crazy the way it is, and I cannot do that. And if he cannot adjust it and let me do what I want to do and live with me after that, I would rather do what I want to do.

Fitzgerald: The thing that used to crop up in the days before Zelda collapsed, she would continually make this statement, that she was working to get away from me. Now, you see, that sticks with me.

Zelda: Dr. Rennie, that is not true. . . . Here is the truth of the

413

matter: that I have always felt some necessity for us to be on a more equal footing than we are now because I cannot possibly – there is just something, one thing, that I simply cannot live in a world that is completely dependent on Scott when he does not care anything about me and reproaches me all the time. . . . I want to be able to say, when he says something that is not so, then I want to do something so good that I can say, 'That is a goddamned lie,' and have something to back it up – that I can say it.

Fitzgerald: Now we have found rock bottom.

Zelda: What is our marriage, anyway? It has been nothing but a long battle ever since I can remember.

Fitzgerald: I don't know about that. We were about the most envied couple in about 1921 in America.

Zelda: I guess so. We were awfully good showmen.

Fitzgerald: We were awfully happy. . . . You say that you will put off your writing another book, you will stop everything, and you have said that a number of times before in the presence of Dr. Rennie. And you did not mean it. You will start it up in twenty-four hours. You mean I will have to write this whole book in the next three months with the sense that you wait hating me, waiting for me to get away. That is not the social arrangement that I can live under. . . . I want my own way. I earned the right to my own way—. . .

Zelda: And I want the right of my own way.

Fitzgerald: And you cannot have it without breaking me so you have to give it up. It all comes to the same thing: I have to sacrifice myself for you, and you have got to sacrifice yourself for me, and no more writing of fiction.

Zelda: Of any kind?

Fitzgerald: If you write a play, it cannot be a play about

414

psychiatry and it cannot be a play laid on the Riviera, and it cannot be a play laid in Switzerland, and whatever the idea is it will have to be submitted to me.

Zelda: Scott, you can go on and have your way about this thing and do anything until you finish the book, and when you finish the book I think we'd better get a divorce, and any decision you choose to make with regard to me is all right because I cannot live on those terms, and I cannot accept them.[48]

Fitzgerald consulted Poe about a divorce for the first time after this conference.

The tensions in the household are documented by one of the case histories Fitzgerald prepared at this time:

PART III
'Self Expression'

Husband works with great success	
Woman flirts	Both drink

In Hollywood at 25 woman discovers there are still young girls.

One of them wants her husband to take screen test. Husband reluctantly consents for the money but director judges his face too old.

That night wife gets drunk, imagines her husband is with the screen stars when in reality he is at a banquet given to President Hillen. She burns her clothes in the bath tub and throws away a platinum and diamond wrist watch of large sentimental and material value.

They are reconciled but husband repelled by the outburst now becomes interested in screen star.

After an unhappy month husband and wife return East where screen star visits them. Finis actress.

Wife at first is nicer to husband, more womanly. Then, plunging into ballet, she grows odd, secretive. Conjugal difficulties on both sides with wife's announcement that she is working to set up for herself.

Schizophrenia.

Recovery, reunion and happiness for eight months.

Husband goes to Hollywood. Period of strain at home

415

agravated by asthma. Probably jealous suspicion of husband because of former event.

Jealousy again takes form as rivalry. When husband reads her beginning of his book in which movie director does not and cannot be with his wife every minute, she has sudden return of psychosis.

Not realizing the cause of the old jealousy 'I'm as good as you and a whole lot better' and loving husband and child she turns against

A. governess
B. butler

This of course is illogical and her personality again disintegrates.

In Phipps she charms woman psychiatrist who not understanding author's profession. Document blames author deeply, uses much of his material is calculated to harm him professionally. He is struggling with money worries and takes it hard.

Improved wife issues from clinic. No more documents dealing with husband or psychiatry order doctors. Patient agrees.

Lives in country and agrees.

Her book fails – just as husband had accumulated enough capital to take up his own novel interrupted by her sickness.

Immediately she changes. Again she wants to write novel, is apparently persuaded out of it.

All old jealousy of husband flares up, but still not projected upon him but upon

A. The psychiatrists. Rage at psychiatrists.
B. The child. Trouble with child.

Situation now becoming too difficult for husband; wants to hospitalize her temporarily but psychiatrists refuse. Husband begins drinking.

Unpleasant episodes begin again between husband and wife – quarrels, suspicions, scenes, disagreements, also between mother and daughter, throwing father toward daughter and thus further estranging wife and husband. Husband overworked and overworried goes away for a week. No improvement. Wife's painting fails to achieve much recognition. Miserable winter.

He has at least the solace of his novel and she thinks she needs the same and begins, *semi-secretly*, the very book she was asked not to write, a book based on her own going insane dancing.

But she is up against husband's observation of parallel with dancing crises. She suggests going to a clinic but it is apparent she wants to be sent away to write. She no longer wants integration but justification.

Manner to world now meek and mild. Young doctor (not psychiatrist) sees distraught author drunk and hysterical, announces falsely he could certify him and woman clings to this as a straw. She gets drunk – husband gets nurse.

From now on parallel with her dancing days just before the crash. Sinks into herself – world vague to her, foolish impulses and remarks, separation of spirit from her husband who as the wheel moves around has at last come to seem to her the enemy, emerging from behind figures of

1. Governess
2. Child
3. Dr. Squires
4. Dr. Rennie
5. Dr. Myers

Husband forcibly seizes book she had agreed not to write. It is stored away and in long scene she is made unwillingly to admit principal of communality of obligation in marriage. Will stop till husband finishes in September.[49]

44

A Novel
of Deterioration

[1933–1934]

◤◤ *Scandalabra was accepted* for production by the Junior
Vagabonds, a Baltimore little theater group, in the
spring of 1933. Zelda designed the sets, and the play opened
for a one-week run on 26 June. Fitzgerald did not attend the
rehearsals; but when the dress rehearsal ran five hours, Zelda
asked him to cut her script. In an all-night session he read the
play to the cast and excised lines that could not be defended.*
Fitzgerald tried to promote *Scandalabra*. He invited friends
down from New York for the opening, and praised it in front
of the theater to attract passers-by. The Baltimore reviewers
found the play confusing and lacking in action. Zelda did
nothing further with *Scandalabra* after the Baltimore
production.

Tender Is the Night was approaching completion in
September 1933, but Fitzgerald was out of money. In 1933 he

---

* This account of Fitzgerald's revision of *Scandalabra* is substantiated by
members of the Junior Vagabonds. Another report is that Fitzgerald began
cutting the play after opening night and worked on it through the week.[50]
The play survives in two texts: the longer version deposited for copyright in
1932 and the shorter version at Princeton, which was published in 1980.

sold three stories to the *Post* for $8,500. Another 1933 story, 'What to Do About It,' was unsalable. Even with a $4,200 advance from Scribners his income for the year came to only $16,328.03. The days when he could dependably grind out commercial fiction were over. Of the three *Post* stories – 'More than Just a House' (written in April), 'I Got Shoes' (July), and 'The Family Bus' (September) – only the first is noteworthy. 'More than Just a House' examines the decline of a Southern family through the three daughters' feelings about the family house. The story brought a fan letter from John O'Hara, who was not yet a novelist. 'You've written another swell piece, doing again several of the things you do so well, and doing them in a single piece. Miss Jean Gunther, of the More than Just a House Gunthers, was one of those girls for the writing about of whom you hold the exclusive franchise, if you can puzzle out that sentence. . . . And that easily we get to the second thing you've done so well: Lowrie, the climber; and I wonder why you do the climber so well. Is it the Irish in you? *Must* the Irish always have a lot of climber in them?'[51] Fitzgerald replied on 18 July (see p. 26 above) with an assessment of his social insecurities, blaming them on the conflict between his 'black Irish' and 'old American' backgrounds.

Fitzgerald probably began organizing his *Notebooks* after he moved to Maryland in 1932. The pages were typed by secretaries from Fitzgerald's manuscript notes and marked tear sheets of his stories. There are twenty-three sections: Anecdotes; Bright Clippings; Conversations and Things Overheard; Description of Things and Atmosphere; Epigrams, Wise Cracks and Jokes; Feelings & Emotions (without girls); Descriptions of Girls; Descriptions of Humanity (Physical); Ideas; Jingles and Songs; Karacters; Literary; Moments (what people do); Nonsense and Stray Phrases; Observations; Proper Names; Rough Stuff; Scenes and Situations; Titles; Unclassified; Vernacular; Work References; Youth and Army.* Fitzgerald's *Notebooks* assembled ideas

---

* Selections from the *Notebooks* were included in *The Crack-Up* (1945); *The Notebooks of F. Scott Fitzgerald* was published in 1978.

for stories and autobiographical material; they also provided a place to bank passages from his uncollected stories that he intended to salvage for use in novels. But, as he admitted in 'One Hundred False Starts,' a March 1933 *Post* article, the 'book of mistakes' did not help to break his short-story block.

> Mostly, we authors must repeat ourselves – that's the truth. We have two or three great and moving experiences in our lives – experiences so great and moving that it doesn't seem at the time that anyone else has been so caught up and pounded and dazzled and astonished and beaten and broken and rescued and illuminated and rewarded and humbled in just that way ever before.
>
> Then we learn our trade, well or less well, and we tell our two or three stories – each time in a new disguise – maybe ten times, maybe a hundred, as long as people will listen.

This article explains why Fitzgerald was unable to use other people's experiences for stories: 'Whether it's something that happened twenty years ago or only yesterday, I must start out with an emotion – one that's close to me and that I can understand.'[52] In 1933 he was concerned that he had used up his emotions – not just his material, but his capacity to invest his characters with authentic feeling. As he later observed in Hollywood, 'Taking things hard – from Genevra King to Joe Mank –: that's stamp that goes into my books so that people can read it blind like brail.'[53] 'One Hundred False Starts' includes Fitzgerald's citation of 'the idea that it is pleasantest to live with – the idea of heroism.' At this stage of his career he was doubting his 'immaculateness of purpose.' Heretofore, despite his self-indulgences, he had believed in his destiny and in his ability to preserve the best part of his genius. Now, struggling with his novel and grinding out unfelt stories, he came to feel that he was starting out all over again without the confident illusions that had sustained him in 1920.

In 1933 after ninety commercial stories Fitzgerald felt depleted. What had seemed spontaneous in his stories now showed signs of labor.* The retrospective or self-assessing mood of 'One Hundred False Starts' also informed another 1933 essay, 'My Lost City,' written for *Cosmopolitan* and unpublished until 1945. In 'My Lost City' Fitzgerald evoked the feelings of triumph and romance that New York gave him during his first success and mourned his lost exhilaration, lost confidence, lost illusions: 'For the moment I can only cry out that I have lost my splendid mirage. Come back, come back, O glittering and white!'[55]

The completion of *Tender Is the Night* was financed by Scribners and Ober. Fitzgerald's accounting system is puzzling, but between 1927 and 1933 he received some $16,000 in advances from Scribners and borrowed from Ober against the anticipated serial rights sale. *Liberty* had asked for first refusal on the serial in 1927, and Fitzgerald expected between $30,000 and $40,000 from them. When *Scribner's Magazine* offered $10,000, Fitzgerald accepted it because he thought serialization in a quality magazine would be better for the novel. Six thousand dollars of the serial fee was credited against the Scribners advances; $4,000 was paid to Ober, who turned it over to Fitzgerald as needed.[56] Scribners lent Fitzgerald an additional $2,000 at 5 percent interest, and there were other borrowings from Ober. The collateral for these loans was the anticipated sale of movie rights. During the summer of 1933 Fitzgerald began borrowing money from his mother, a difficult thing for the son who had boasted to her in 1930: 'All big men have spent money freely. I hate avarice or even caution'.[57]

Perkins worried about Fitzgerald but never gave up on him. Publishing *The Great Gatsby* had been one of the warmest satisfactions of Perkins's career. In August 1933 he wrote Fitzgerald: 'Whenever any of these new writers come up who

---

* James Gould Cozzens commented after Fitzgerald's death: 'On the other hand, there is no trade better calculated to drive you to drink, especially if you practice as he did the Saturday Evening Post end of it – it is a perfect example of the truth that writing short stories is living on your capital if you are naturally a novelist – you can get through in a few years all the subjects, even if you have a lot, that you could have written books on.'[54]

are brilliant, I always realize that you have more talent and more skill than any of them;- but circumstances have prevented you from realizing upon the fact for a long time.'[58]

There was a fire at 'La Paix' in August 1933 when Zelda burned some papers in a fireplace, causing damage to the second floor. The *Baltimore News* exaggerated the extent of the loss by reporting that 'valuable manuscripts, books and paintings which never can be replaced were destroyed.'[59] No important manuscripts were lost, but many of Fitzgerald's World War I books were ruined.

Ring Lardner died in September 1933 at forty-eight from a heart attack, after a long struggle with tuberculosis and alcoholism. Fitzgerald had seen him infrequently since the Great Neck days, but he regarded Lardner with enduring affection combined with regret for his unfulfilled genius – feelings that he expressed through Abe North in *Tender Is the Night*. Lardner's death moved him to write a tribute for *The New Republic* in which he stated that 'Ring got less percentage of himself on paper than any other American of the first flight.'

> At no time did I feel that I had known him enough, or that anyone knew him – it was not the feeling that there was more stuff in him and that it should come out, it was rather a qualitative difference, it was rather as though, due to some inadequacy in one's self, one had not penetrated to something unsolved, new and unsaid. That is why one wishes that Ring had written down a larger proportion of what was in his mind and heart. It would have saved him longer for us, and that in itself would be something. But I would like to know what it was, and now I'll go on wishing – what did Ring want, how did he want things to be, how did he think things were?[60]

'Ring' attracted wide attention and brought Fitzgerald letters of appreciation from other writers. Dorothy Parker wrote him that it was 'the finest + most moving thing I have ever read.'[61] John O'Hara told Fitzgerald that when he asked for the magazine at a newsstand the vendor said, 'You want it

422

for the article on Lardner I guess.'[62] Fitzgerald's grief for Lardner was genuine, but some of the power of 'Ring' derived from his identification with his friend's despair. A decade before, they had met when they were both at their peaks. Now at thirty-seven, after years of waste and tragedy, Fitzgerald was attempting to reestablish or justify himself so as not to die with too much of what was in his own mind and heart unwritten. When Perkins asked him to help with the selection of the material and write the introduction for a Ring Lardner collection, he declined because of the pressure of seeing *Tender Is the Night* through the press and recommended Gilbert Seldes for the assignment.[63] Seldes's Lardner volume, *First and Last* (1934), disappointed Fitzgerald, but it was well received.

In the fall of 1933 Fitzgerald began checking into Johns Hopkins Hospital to taper off from benders and for treatment of fevers which were related to his tuberculosis. He was given sedatives and an alcohol ration, and was permitted to discharge himself. Between September 1933 and January 1937 he was in Hopkins eight times: 1–5 September 1933; 29 October–1 November 1933; 30 April–7 May 1934; 21–27 July 1934; 14–17 January 1936; 13–15 February 1936; 26 December–3 January 1937; 11–14 January 1937.

On 25 September 1933 Fitzgerald was able to promise Perkins delivery of *Tender Is the Night* by the end of October: 'You can imagine the pride with which I will enter your office a month from now. *Please do not have a band as I do not care for music.*'[64] When the novel was completed, Fitzgerald gave up 'La Paix' and rented a town house at 1307 Park Avenue in Baltimore. His *Ledger* summary for the year in which he wrote the novel was '*A strange year of Work + Drink. Increasingly unhappy. – Zelda up + down. 1st draft of novel complete Ominous!*'

Fitzgerald brought the revised typescript of *Tender Is the Night* to Scribners for serialization on or about 27 October 1933. Because the serial appeared while the book was in production for April 1934 publication, he worked on the magazine and book texts at the same time – revising the serial proof for the magazine and then revising the serial again for the book. Between the serialization and the book publication he altered the chapter divisions. The serial proof revisions were so extensive that the second, third, and fourth installments had to be reset. In late November, Fitzgerald took a break from the proofs and went with Zelda to Bermuda for a week, but the trip was spoiled by his pleurisy.

45

Publication of
Tender Is the Night

[April 1934]

Tender Is the Night opens on the Riviera in the summer of 1925, when the young actress Rosemary Hoyt meets a dazzlingly attractive American couple, Dick and Nicole Diver. The Divers' circle includes alcoholic composer Abe North and Tommy Barban, a Franco-American soldier of fortune, who is in love with Nicole. Rosemary becomes infatuated with Dick. A flashback provides the information that Dick was a brilliant young psychiatrist when he married Nicole Warren, a rich mental patient who had been raped by her father. As husband and doctor to Nicole, Dick finds it increasingly difficult to maintain his professional viewpoint, and he neglects his research while living up to the style of Nicole's wealth. With the Warren money he becomes a partner in a Swiss clinic but is forced out because he has lost his commitment to his work – symptomized by his drinking. On a trip to Rome he sleeps with Rosemary and is beaten by the police as the result of a drunken brawl. In 1929 the Divers return to the Riviera, where Dick's drinking increases and Nicole leaves him for Tommy Barban. Dick tries to resume his career in America but disappears as an unsuccessful small-town doctor.

In chronicling Dick Diver's decline Fitzgerald was trying to account for his own loss of purpose after 1925, recognizing that in both cases the causes could be traced back to a romantic concept of character. Thus Dick 'used to think that he wanted to be good, he wanted to be kind, he wanted to be brave and wise, but it was all pretty difficult. He wanted to be loved, too, if he could fit it in.'[65] Dick's susceptibilities were established before he met Nicole – just as Fitzgerald's character was formed before he met Zelda. The decision to marry Nicole is not determined by the Warren money, although her money eventually erodes his commitment to his work. He marries her out of his need to be needed and to be used. But Dick's generosity is not disinterested, for he requires the 'carnivals of affection' that he inspires. His infatuation with Rosemary is a clear signal that his process of deterioration is well advanced by the opening of the novel. The price of the admiration he elicits is a steady drain on the energies a serious man reserves for work. When the rising line of Nicole's strength has crossed the slope of his decline, Dick makes the professional decision to discharge his patient-wife. Nicole is ready for the break, but Dick forces her to declare her independence: 'The case was finished. Doctor Diver was at liberty.'[66] The spectacle of Dick Diver's collapse is harrowing because he is destroyed by the same elements in his character that might have made him a great figure. His heroic aspirations dwindle into a 'fatal pleasingness.'[67]

The novel was serialized in four issues of *Scribner's Magazine*, beginning in the January 1934 issue with Fitzgerald's portrait on the cover. Edward Shenton's pen-and-ink illustrations for the magazine were so successful that they were retained in the book. The serial text has twelve long chapters, which had been Fitzgerald's plan in 1932. (The book text is divided into three sections compromising sixty-one chapters.) The first magazine installment included what became the first eighteen chapters of Book I of the

426

novel – through Abe North's departure from Paris. The February installment completed Book I and included the first nine chapters of the flashback section in Book II of the novel – up to Dick's decision to marry Nicole. The March installment completed the flashback and concluded Book II with Dick's beating in Rome. The April installment comprised all of Book III.

Fitzgerald and Scribners anticipated that serialization would generate effective visibility and promote book sales, but serialization may have damaged the initial reception of *Tender Is the Night.* The structure of the novel, with its break in chronology and point of view between Books I and II, was probably blurred by the thirty-day intervals. Fitzgerald suspected that some of the critics reviewed his novel from the serial and urged his friends to reread it in book form. He wrote to Edmund Wilson a month before publication date: 'Any attempt by an author to explain away a partial failure in a work is of course doomed to absurdity – yet I could wish that you, and others, had read the book version rather than the mag. version which in spots was hastily put together. The last half for example has a *much* more polished facade now.'[68] Fitzgerald inscribed the book for Dorothy Parker: 'This is better than the magazine.'[69] The serial version included six short scenes that were dropped from the book.* The only passages added to the book were the sexual material that was unpublishable in the magazine – notably an expansion of Warren's confession of his incestuous relationship with Nicole.

While the book text was being set, Fitzgerald made New York trips in January and February 1934 to work on the proofs. Twenty years later Scribners editor John Hall

* The scenes deleted from the book text were two sequences describing Abe North in the Ritz Bar (Book I); Dick's involvement with a woman at Innsbruck (Book II); and three sequences on the ship during Dick's return to Europe after his father's funeral (Book II). Fitzgerald cut from the typescript *before* serialization the account of Tommy and Nicole's visit to an American gangster on the Riviera in Book III.

Wheelock remarked that Fitzgerald was the only author he knew who could make delicate stylistic revisions while obviously drunk. During these trips Fitzgerald spent time with John O'Hara and Dorothy Parker. O'Hara, who was trying to finish his first novel, *Appointment in Samarra*, was grateful for Fitzgerald's encouragement.* Fitzgerald offered to lend him money, but O'Hara declined the loan because he knew that Fitzgerald had no money to spare.

Fitzgerald's layers of extensive proof revision complicated the job of the proofreaders. The published book has dozens of spelling errors as well as inconsistencies of chronology which obscure the rate of Dick Diver's decline. The fault was the author's, but meticulous editing would have called the problem to his attention.

On 12 February 1934, exactly two years after she had been moved from Montgomery to Baltimore, Zelda reentered the Phipps clinic. When she failed to show improvement, Fitzgerald had her transferred to Craig House, a resort-like sanitarium at Beacon, New York, where the minimum fee was $175 a week. With writing interdicted, Zelda worked at painting in 1933 and 1934. Fitzgerald arranged a New York show for her with Cary Ross, a friend from the Paris years. Although the show was planned to boost Zelda's morale, she felt that Fitzgerald was taking it over and withdrew from active participation. It was held at Ross's gallery from 29 March to 30 April, with a smaller exhibit at the Hotel Algonquin, and was a joint show of Zelda's paintings with the photographs of Dr. Marion Hines of the Johns Hopkins Medical School. Since Zelda's show overlapped publication of *Tender Is the Night*, Fitzgerald was probably trying to compensate Zelda for compelling her to abandon her novel. The catalogue – with the motto PARFOIS LA FOLIE EST LA SAGESSE ('Sometimes madness is wisdom') – listed thirteen paintings and fifteen drawings by Zelda. The biographical

---

* When *Appointment in Samarra* was published in August 1934, Fitzgerald provided a blurb that was used in ads: 'John O'Hara's novel indicates the tremendous strides that American writers have taken since the war.'[70]

note read in part: 'Her work crystallizes the qualities of
imagination and poetry which have made her an almost
legendary figure since the days just after the last war when
she and her husband became symbols of young America in
the Jazz Age.'[71] The paintings that attracted the most
attention were two · portraits of Fitzgerald: 'The Cornet
Player' (bought by Dorothy Parker) and 'Portrait in Thorns'
(not sold). Neither of these portraits has been located.*

'Circus' by Zelda Fitzgerald
MONTGOMERY MUSEUM OF FINE ARTS

* Many of Zelda's paintings were destroyed after her death when a shed in
which they were stored in Montgomery burned. 'The Cornet Player' is
believed to have been lost in another fire.

Zelda was permitted to leave Craig House for the opening of her exhibition. The reception was disappointing and the gross receipts were only $328.75. Commenting on Zelda's 'latest bid for fame,' *Time* noted: 'The work of a brilliant introvert, they were vividly painted, intensely rhythmic. A pinkish reminiscence of her ballet days showed figures with enlarged legs and feet – a trick she may have learned from Picasso. An impression of a Dartmouth football game made the stadium look like the portals of a theatre, the players like dancers. *Chinese Theatre* was a gnarled mass of acrobats with an indicated audience for background. There were two impressionistic portraits of her husband, a verdant *Spring in the Country* geometrically laced with telephone wires.'[72] Zelda told the *Time* reporter that her greatest wish was to earn her own living; but this bid for independence failed.

Because of the bitterness resulting from the Fitzgeralds' quarrels about their material, Zelda did not read *Tender Is the Night* until it was serialized. After congratulating him on the installments, she wrote him in April from Craig House:

> The book is grand. The emotional lift sustained by the force of a fine poetic prose and the characters *subserviated* to forces stronger than their interpretations of life is very moving. It is tear-evoking to witness individual belief in individual volition succumbing to the purpose of a changing world. That is the purpose of a good book and you have written it – Those people are helpless before themselves and the prose is beautiful and there is manifest an integrity in the belief of both those expressions. It is a reverential and very fine book and the first literary contribution to what writers will be concerning themselves with some years from now.[73]

Zelda did not improve at Craig House, and on 19 May 1934 she was admitted in a catatonic condition to the Sheppard and Enoch Pratt Hospital outside Baltimore. By this time Fitzgerald had come to accept that Zelda's full recovery was impossible and that they would never be able to resume life together. He wrote in his *Notebooks*: 'I left my capacity for hoping on the little roads that led to Zelda's sanitarium.'[74]

46

Reception of
Tender Is the Night

[1934]

Tender Is the Night was published on 12 April 1934 at $2.50. It had been nine years since *The Great Gatsby*. One of the Fitzgerald myths is that the novel was a failure when it was published. It was a failure in terms of Fitzgerald's expectations; otherwise, it had a respectable sale for a Depression-year novel. The first printing of 7,600 copies sold out promptly, and in the spring there were two more printings of 5,075 and 2,520 copies. *Tender Is the Night* was tenth on the *Publishers Weekly* best-seller lists for April and May.* Even so, the royalties did not pay off Fitzgerald's debts. At 37½ cents per copy royalty, the book sales earned him $5,104.65.

John O'Hara endorsed the generally held view that *Tender Is the Night* was a victim of the Depression: 'The book

---

* By 1934 the Book-of-the-Month Club and the Literary Guild were in operation, but *Tender Is the Night* was not a main selection of either. The Literary Guild used the novel as an alternate, which meant that it filled orders. On 15 April 1935 Fitzgerald wrote Perkins: 'Things happen all the time which make me think that it is not destined to die quite as easily as the boys-in-a-hurry prophesied. However, I made many mistakes about it from its delay onward, the biggest of which was to refuse the Literary Guild subsidy.'[75] The nature of this offer is unknown.

came out at precisely the wrong time in the national history. No matter how good it was, it was about the Bad People, the well fed, well housed, well educated, well born – the villains of the depression. It was a time for Odets and the imitators of Odets, and of Steinbeck and the imitators of Steinbeck. . . . I am proud to say I did not go along with the gutless thinking that all but destroyed TENDER IS THE NIGHT and without a doubt broke Fitzgerald's heart.'[76] Nonetheless, a list of the ten best-selling novels of 1934 does not suggest that the Depression readers rejected *Tender* in favor of sociopolitical tracts. The most successful book of the year was Hervey Allen's *Anthony Adverse*, followed by Caroline Miller's *Lamb in His Bosom*, Stark Young's *So Red the Rose*, James Hilton's *Goodbye, Mr. Chips*, Margaret Barnes's *Within This Present*, Sinclair Lewis's *Work of Art*, Phyllis Bottome's *Private Worlds*, Mary Ellen Chase's *Mary Peters*, Alice Tisdale Hobart's *Oil for the Lamps of China*, and Isak Dinesen's *Seven Gothic Tales*. There is no proletarian novel in this typical mixture. That the three top sellers of the year were historical novels and the number four book was *Goodbye, Mr. Chips* indicates that historical romance and sentimental books about schoolmasters sell well, boom or bust. *Private Worlds* was a novel about psychiatry; and Fitzgerald protested when the Houghton Mifflin publicity compared it with *Tender Is the Night*.[77]

The reviews were not hostile, nor did the reviewers uniformly attack Fitzgerald for reverting to the unfashionable subject of expatriate life in the Twenties. There were twice as many favorable as unfavorable reviews, but even the favorable reviews expressed disappointment that it was not a better novel. The years of waiting since *The Great Gatsby* had generated high expectations among critics; Fitzgerald was competing with his own reputation. *Tender* had become a legend before it was published. In an unfinished preface Fitzgerald attempted to account for the long period of gestation:

> This is the first novel the writer have published in nine years. Since then there has scarcely a week when some party didn't ask me the state of its progress and the probable time of its publication. For awhile I told what I believed to be the

truth, 'this fall,' 'next spring,' 'next year.' Then growing weary I
lied and lied, announced that I had given it up or that it was now
a million words long and would eventually be published in five
volumes. Since some of those inquiries were inspired by interest
instead of mere curiosity I append a word of explanation.

When I finished my last novel at the end of 1924 I felt pretty
empty, nothing much to say, nothing *long* to say, but after a little
more than a year I had formulated a new idea and during 1926
I began work on it very slowly indeed. I picked it up and
dropped it.[78]

The most frequent criticism was that *Tender Is the Night*
failed to achieve a strong single effect. Some influential
reviewers contended that the causes of Dick Diver's
destruction were not sufficiently clear. Henry Seidel Canby
(*Saturday Review of Literature*), Clifton Fadiman (*New Yorker*), J.
Donald Adams (*New York Times*), Edith Walton (*New York
Sun*), Horace Gregory (*New York Herald Tribune*), and William
Troy (*Nation*) claimed that because Dick was not convincing as
a character, his collapse failed to produce a clear response in

Dust jacket for the first edition of Tender Is the Night

the reader. Other critics cited faulty organization or lack of unity. In the 13 April *Times* John Chamberlain commented that when Rosemary leaves at the end of Book I 'one could almost guarantee that "Tender Is the Night" is going to be a failure. But, as a matter of fact, the novel does not really begin until Rosemary is more or less out of the way.' He concluded, 'By the time the end is reached, the false start is forgotten.'[79] After Adams complained in the *Times* on the fifteenth that 'the wrecking of his [Dick's] morale seems contrived rather than the product of his inability to withstand the pressure to which he is subjected,'[80] Chamberlain interrupted a review of Faulkner's *Dr. Martino* the next day with a rebuttal of Adams: 'The wonder to us is that Dick didn't collapse long before Mr. Fitzgerald causes him to break down. And when he does collapse, his youth is gone, it is too late to catch up with the Germans who have been studying new cases for years. This seems to us to be a sufficient exercise in cause-and-effect. Compared to the motivation in Faulkner, it is logic personified.'[81]

Malcolm Cowley's tardy mixed review in the 6 June *New Republic* introduced the double-vision approach to Fitzgerald's sensibility that Cowley developed in his later critical pieces. He explained that Fitzgerald had the ability to be simultaneously an observer and a participant in his work: 'Part of him has been a little boy peeping in through the window and being thrilled by the music and the beautifully dressed women – a romantic but hardheaded little boy who stops every once in a while to wonder how much it all cost and where the money comes from.'* Cowley also proposed an influential explanation for the 'technical faults' of *Tender*: that as it was written over a long period parts of it became fixed so that the early and late sections do not agree.[82] This view can be challenged. Fitzgerald intermittently worked on the three versions of his novel for eight years, but the final version was

---

* Compare William Butler Yeats's comment on Keats in 'Ego Dominus Tuus': 'I see a schoolboy when I think of him,/With face and nose pressed to a sweet-shop window.'

written in a little over a year. Nonetheless, Fitzgerald felt that the years of false starts had cost him some of the control over his material. As he remarked to Baltimore journalist Louis Azrael, 'The man who started the novel is not the man who finished it.'[83]

Fitzgerald was particularly pleased by the review in the *Journal of Nervous and Mental Disease,* which stated that the novel was 'an achievement which no student of the psychobiological sources of human behavior, and of its particular social correlates extant today, can afford not to read.'[84] The receptive reviewers included Burton Rascoe (*Esquire*), Harry Hansen (*New York World-Telegram*), Herschel Brickell (*North American Review*), C. Hartley Grattan (*Modern Monthly,* a Marxist journal), and Cameron Rogers (*San Francisco Chronicle*). Gilbert Seldes, who had recognized Fitzgerald as the best of his generation at the time of *The Great Gatsby,* announced in the *New York Evening Journal*: 'He has gone behind generations, old or new, and created his own image of human beings. And in doing so has stepped again to his natural place at the head of the American writers of our time.'[85]

Tender Is the Night was published in London by Chatto & Windus in September 1934 and was the last Fitzgerald book published in England during his lifetime. The English reviews were sparse. G. B. Stern praised both Fitzgerald and his work in the London *Daily Telegraph; The Times Literary Supplement* commented respectfully on the quality of the writing and the sensitivity of feeling but complained that 'It is almost all of it tragedy without nobility, and therefore the less tragedy.'[86] The most substantial English review was by D. W. Harding in the December issue of the prestigious critical journal *Scrutiny.* Harding found the spectacle of Dick's decline so harrowing that he tried to discover an 'emotional trick' behind it, questioning whether the reader has been 'trapped into incompatible attitudes' toward Dick. Failing to make a case against Fitzgerald, he concluded rather lamely: 'The difficulty of making a convincing analysis of the painful quality of this novel, and the conviction that it was worth while trying to, are evidence of Scott Fitzgerald's skill and effectiveness. . . . I am prepared to be told that this attempt at analysis is itself childish – an attempt to assure myself that the magician didn't really cut the lady's head off, did he? I still believe there was a trick in it.'[87] Harding's response was symptomatic of a critical resistance to Fitzgerald in England and America, a reluctance to credit him with the fulfillment of deliberate intentions.

As a consequence of Fitzgerald's commercial magazine work and his playboy image it had become increasingly difficult for critics to appraise the serious novelist. A writer's career is organic. Fitzgerald's magazine work and his novels have to be judged by the same standards; but the gauge of a writer's achievement must be his best work. Hemingway could get away with writing for *Esquire* – or with not writing at all – because he had compelled the critics to regard him as a dedicated artist. Fitzgerald's flamboyant reputation impeded the recognition of his best work.

Having learned the importance of structure with *The Great Gatsby*, Fitzgerald undertook to achieve a structure for *Tender* that again would involve the reader in reordering the story. The novel has a flashback plan, opening in 1925 and then going back to 1917 in Book II. The first twenty-five chapters – all of Book I – describe two weeks on the Riviera and Paris mostly from the point of view of Rosemary Hoyt, the eighteen-year-old actress who idealizes the Divers. At the opening of Book II Rosemary is dropped, and the novel reverts to the true beginning of the story when Dr. Diver meets Nicole, a patient at a Swiss psychiatric clinic during World War I. The first nine chapters of Book II relate Dick's participation in Nicole's recovery up to his decision to marry her in 1919. The tenth chapter is the time bridge in which the course of the Divers' marriage is summarized in Nicole's interior monologue up to the opening of the novel on the beach in 1925: 'Yes, I'll look. More new people – oh, that girl – yes. Who did you say she looked like. . . . No, I haven't, we don't get much chance to see the new American pictures over here. Rosemary who? Well, we're getting very fashionable for July – seems very peculiar to

me. Yes, she's lovely, but there can be too many people.'
Thereafter the novel is presented in straight chronology.
Dick's affair with Rosemary and his beating by the Rome police
in 1928 conclude Book II, which has twenty-three chapters.
The thirteen chapters of Book III cover Dick's resignation
from his clinic through his departure from the Riviera in 1929
and the epilogue report of his humiliated wanderings in
upstate New York.

The structure of the novel is not complicated and makes no
heavy demands on the reader. The important reviews did not
specifically question the flashback – apart from the
disappearance of Rosemary at the end of Book I – but
Fitzgerald came to believe that the flashback was responsible
for the critics' complaints that Dick Diver was not a
convincing character. On 23 April 1934 Fitzgerald defended
his plan in a letter to H. L. Mencken, who had not reviewed
Tender Is the Night:

> . . . I would like to say in regard to my book that there was a
> deliberate intention in every part of it except the first. The
> first part, the romantic introduction, was too long and too
> elaborated, largely because of the fact that it had been written
> over a series of years with varying plans, but everything else in
> the book conformed to a *definite intention* and if I had to start to
> write it again tomorrow I would adopt the same plan,
> irrespective of the fact of whether I had, in this case, brought it
> off or not brought it off. That is what most of the critics fail to
> understand (outside of the fact that they fail to recognize and
> identify anything in the book) that the motif of the 'dying fall'
> was absolutely deliberate and did not come from any
> diminuition of vitality but from a definite plan.
>
> That particular trick is one that Ernest Hemmingway and I
> worked out – probably from Conrad's preface to 'The
> Nigger'* – and it has been the greatest 'credo' in my life ever
> since I decided that I would rather be an artist than a careerist.

---

* Other examples of the understated ending or fade-off cited by Fitzgerald
were from David Garnett's *The Sailor's Return* and *Lady into Fox*, Dostoevski's
The Brothers Karamazov, and Proust's *Time Regained*. Fitzgerald sent Garnett
an inscribed copy of *Tender*: 'Notice how neatly I stole + adapted your

I would rather impress my image (even though an image the size of a nickel) upon the soul of a people than be known, except in so far as I have my natural obligation to my family – to provide for them. I would as soon be as anonymous as Rimbaud, if I could feel that I had accomplished that purpose – and that is no sentimental yapping about being disinterested. It is simply that having once found the intensity of art, nothing else that can happen in life can ever again seem as important as the creative process.[89]

Here Fitzgerald is dealing with the emotional plan – in particular with the understatement of Book III – rather than with the structure.

In 1936 Fitzgerald proposed a new edition of *Tender Is the Night* for The Modern Library, in which the time scheme would be clarified. He explained to publisher Bennett Cerf: 'That the parts instead of being one, two and three . . . would include in several cases sudden stops and part headings which would be to some extent explanatory; certain pages would have to be inserted bearing merely headings. Part two, for example, should say in a terse and graceful way that, The scene is now back on the Riviera in the fall after these events have taken place, or that, This brings us up to where Rosemary first encounters the Divers. . . . There is not more than one complete sentence that I want to eliminate, one that has offended many people and that I admit is out of Dick's character: "I never did go in for making love to dry loins.". . . I don't want to change anything in the book but sometimes by a single word change one can throw a new emphasis or give a new value to the exact same scene or setting.'[90] These projected alterations made the book impossible for The Modern Library, which kept costs down by reprinting from existing plates.

---

magnificent ending to *Lady into Fox* (which I know practically as I used to know the X's Prayer in my Catholic days) "By heart."[88] The last paragraph of *Lady into Fox* (1922) reads: 'For a long while his life was despaired of, but at last he rallied, and in the end he recovered his reason and lived to be a great age, for that matter he is still alive.'

For the rest of his life Fitzgerald brooded about what he regarded as the stillbirth of *Tender Is the Night*. In 1938 he wrote to Perkins: 'But I am especially concerned about *Tender* – that book is not dead. The *depth* of its appeal exists. . . . It's great fault is that the *true* beginning – the young psychiatrist in Switzerland – is tucked away in the middle of the book. If pages 151–212 were taken from their present place and put at the start the improvement in appeal would be enormous. In fact the mistake was noted and suggested by a dozen reviewers.'[91] At Fitzgerald's death his books included a revised disbound copy of *Tender* with the chapters in chronological order beginning with Dick Diver's 1917 arrival in Switzerland: 'This is the *final version* of the book as I would like it.'[92] (Fitzgerald's revisions in this copy end on page 212.) Malcolm Cowley's edition of the 'author's final version' was published by Scribners in 1951; but after a flurry of attention it was discontinued. Whatever its flaws, the 1934 version has been vindicated by reader preference.

The most likely cause for the critics' feeling that Dick's collapse is unconvincing is that the time-scheme of *Tender* is unclear or even contradictory, and this problem bears on the structure. Because it is impossible to be sure of the years in which certain crucial events take place after 1925, it is difficult for the reader to gauge the rate of Dick's deterioration. The causes of his decline are clear, but the timing is blurred. The novel opens with Dick at the peak of his charm in the summer of 1925, and by the Rome episodes in 1928 he has lost control. Fitzgerald does not specifically account for the intervening years, beyond noting that the Divers had been at the clinic for a year and a half in 1928 – which leaves 1926 unaccounted for. Moreover, it is not clear how much time elapses between Dick's withdrawal from his clinic in 1928 and his final departure from the Riviera at the end of the novel. Almost certainly the last Riviera scenes are supposed to take place in 1929 before the Wall Street crash. Tommy's remark at the end of the novel that his stocks are doing well indicates that the time is pre-October 1929; but

Malcolm Cowley has made a case for 1930. Fitzgerald's plans for *Tender* do not clarify the time scheme.*

Rosemary's return to the Riviera in Book III confuses the chronology. Three times the novel specifies that it has been five years since she first came to the Riviera in 1925; however, Fitzgerald seems to have confused five summers with five calendar years. In 1929 five summers – but only four years – have elapsed since 1925. The chronology is further obscured by the contradictory ages stipulated for characters at different points in the novel.

Whereas *The Great Gatsby* was a dramatic novel, Fitzgerald classified *Tender* as a philosophical or psychological novel. The writing is less concentrated than in *Gatsby*, but the expansiveness of *Tender* allowed Fitzgerald to achieve his effects by accumulation. In *Tender* Fitzgerald evoked what he called 'lingering after-effects,' leaving the reader with a sense of regret generated by the action and reinforced by the language. The mood of loss and waste pervades the novel. Again, as with *Gatsby*, there are scenes and passages that are classics of American prose: the Divers' party in Paris, Nicole's shopping excursion, Dick's meditation at the trenches, the funeral of Dick's father, the haunting understatement of the final paragraph:

> After that he didn't ask for the children to be sent to America and didn't answer when Nicole wrote asking him if he needed money. In the last letter she had from him he told her that he was practising in Geneva, New York, and she got the impression that he had settled down with some one to keep house for him. She looked up Geneva in an atlas and found it was in the heart of the Finger Lakes Section and considered a pleasant place. Perhaps, so she liked to think, his career was biding its time, again like Grant's in Galena; his latest note was post-marked from Hornell, New York, which is some distance from Geneva and a very small town; in any case he is almost certainly in that section of the country, in one town or another.

* In 1935 Fitzgerald inscribed a copy of the novel: 'F Scott Fitzgerald requests the pleasure of Laura Guthrie's Company in Europe 1917–1930.'[93]

47

Baltimore

[1934]

Fitzgerald was anxious to have Hemingway's response to *Tender Is the Night*. When Hemingway did not communicate with him, Fitzgerald wrote on 10 May, a month after publication: 'Did you like the book? For God's sake drop me a line and tell me one way or another. You can't hurt my feelings. I just want to get a few intelligent slants at it to get some of the reviewers jargon out of my head.'[94] Hemingway – who had replaced Fitzgerald as the Murphys' great friend – had already told Perkins that *Tender* was unsound because the Divers act in ways that the Murphys would never behave: 'Scott can't invent true characters because he doesn't know anything about people. . . he has so lousy much talent and he has suffered so without knowing why, has destroyed himself and destroyed Zelda, though never as much as she has tried to destroy him, that out of this little children's, immature, misunderstood, whining for lost youth death-dance that they have been dragging into and out of insanity to the tune of, the guy all but makes a fine book, all but makes a splendid book.'[95]

On 28 May, Hemingway sent Fitzgerald a three-page typed letter saying that even though the writing was brilliant, *Tender* was untrue because it distorted the Murphys.

Goddamn it you took liberties with peoples pasts and futures that produced not people but damned marvellously faked case histories. You, who can write better than anybody can, who are so lousy with talent that you have to – the hell with it. Scott for gods sake write and write truly no matter who or what it hurts but do not make these silly compromises. You could write a fine book about Gerald and Sara for instance if you knew enough about them and they would not have any feeling, except passing, if it were true.

There were wonderful places and nobody else nor none of the boys can write a good one half as good reading as one that doesn't come out by you, but you cheated too damn much in this one. And you don't need to.

In the first place I've always claimed that you can't think, all right we'll admit you can think. But say you couldn't think; then you ought to write, invent, out of what you know and keep the people's antecedent's straight. Second place a long time ago you stopped listening except to the answers to your own questions. That's what dries a writer up (we all dry up. That's no insult to you in person.) not listening. And we sprout again as grass does after rain when we listen. That is where it all comes from. Seeing, listening. You see well enough. But you stop listening.

. . . .

Forget your personal tragedy. We are all bitched from the start and you especially have to be hurt like hell before you can write seriously. But when you get the damned hurt use it – don't cheat with it....

. . . .

You see Bo, you're not a tragic character. Neither am I. All we are is writers and what we should do is write. Of all people on earth you needed discipline in your work and instead you marry someone who is jealous of your work, wants to compete with you and ruins you. It's not as simple as that and I thought Zelda was crazy the first time I met her and you complicated it even more by being in love with her and, of course you're a rummy. But you're no more of a rummy than Joyce is and most good writers are. But Scott good writers always come back. Always. You are twice as good now as you were at the time you think you were so marvellous. You know I never

442

thought so much of Gatsby at the time. You can write twice as
well now as you ever could. All you need to do is write truly
and not care about what the fate of it is.[96]

Hemingway added on the envelope that he had not
commented on the good parts of *Tender* but Fitzgerald knew
what they were. Fitzgerald wrote a restrained six-page typed
reply on 1 June.

Next to go to the mat with you on a couple of technical
points. The reason I had written you a letter was that Dos
dropped in in passing through and said you had brought up
about my book what we talked about once in a cafe on the
Avenue de Neuilly about composite characters. Now, I don't
entirely dissent from the theory but I don't believe you can try
to prove your point on such a case as Bunny using his own
father as the sire of John Dos Passos, or in the case of this book
that covers ground that you personally paced off about the
same time I was doing it. In either of those cases how could
you trust your own detachment? If you had never met any of
the originals then your opinion would be more convincing.

Following this out a little farther, when does the proper and
logical combination of events, cause and effect, etc. end and
the field of imagination begin? Again you may be entirely right
because I suppose you were applying the idea particularly to
the handling of the creative faculty in one's mind rather than
to the effect upon the stranger reading it. Nevertheless, I am
not sold on the subject, and especially to account for the big
flaws of *Tender* on that ground doesn't convince me. Think of
the case of the Renaissance artists, and of the Elizabethan
dramatists, the first having to superimpose a medieval
conception of science and archeology, etc. upon the bible
story; and in the second, of Shakespeare's trying to interpret
the results of his own observation of the life around him on the
basis of Plutarch's Lives and Hollinshed's Chronicles. There
you must admit that the feat of building a monument out of
three kinds of marble was brought off. You can accuse me
justly of not having the power to bring it off, but a theory that
it can't be done is highly questionable. I make this point with
such persistence because such a conception, if you stick to it,

might limit your own choice of materials. The idea can be reduced simply to: you can't say *accurately* that composite characterization hurt my book, but that it only hurt it for you.

To take a case specifically, that of Gerald and Sara. I don't know how much you think you know about my relations with them over a long time, but from certain remarks that you let drop, such as one 'Gerald threw you over,' I guess that you didn't even know the beginning of our relations. In that case you hit on the exact opposite of the truth.

I think it is obvious that my respect for your artistic life is absolutely unqualified, that save for a few of the dead or dying old men you are the only man writing fiction in America that I look up to very much. There are pieces and paragraphs of your work that I read over and over – in fact, I stopped myself doing it for a year and a half because I was afraid that your particular rhythms were going to creep in on mine by process of infiltration. Perhaps you will recognize some of your remarks in *Tender*, but I did every damn thing I could to avoid that. . . .

To go back to my theme song, the second technical point that might be of interest to you concerns direct steals from an idea of yours, an idea of Conrad's and a few lines out of David-into-Fox-Garnett. The theory back of it I got from Conrad's preface to *The Nigger*, that the purpose of a work of fiction is to appeal to the lingering after-effects in the reader's mind as differing from, say, the purpose of oratory or philosophy which leave respectively leave people in a fighting or thoughtful mood. The second contribution to the burglary was your trying to work out some such theory in your troubles with the very end of *A Farewell to Arms*. I remember that your first draft – or at least the first one I saw – gave a sort of old-fashioned Alger book summary of the future lives of the characters: 'The priest became a priest under Fascism,' etc., and you may remember my suggestion to take a burst of eloquence from anywhere in the book that you could find it and tag off with that; you were against this idea because you felt that the true line of a work of fiction was to take a reader up to a high emotional pitch but then let him down or ease him off. You gave no aesthetic reason for this – nevertheless, you convinced me. The third piece of burglary contributing to this

444

symposing was my admiration of the dying fall in the aforesaid Garnett's book and I imitated it as accurately as it is humanly decent in my own ending of *Tender*, telling the reader in the last pages that, after all, this is just a casual event, and trying to let *him* come to bat for *me* rather than going out to shake his nerves, whoop him up, then leaving him rather in a condition of a frustrated woman in bed. (Did that ever happen to you in your days with MacCallagan or McKisco, Sweetie?)[97]

Sara Murphy shared Hemingway's view that Fitzgerald did not understand people: 'I have always told you you haven't the faintest idea what anybody else but yourself is like. . . .'[98] Fitzgerald regarded her view as a dismissal of his career, and in August 1935 he tried to convince Sara that he had captured the essence of her personality in *Tender*:

> In my theory, utterly opposite to Ernest's, about fiction, i.e. that it takes half a dozen people to make a synthesis strong enough to create a fiction character – in that theory, or rather in despite of it, I used you again + again in *Tender*.
>   'Her face was hard + lovely + pitiful'
>   and again
>   'He had been heavy, belly-frightened with love of her for years' – in those + in a hundred other places I tried to evoke not *you* but the effect that you produce on men – the echoes + reverberations – a poor return for what you have given by your living presence, but nevertheless an artist's (what a word!) sincere attempt to preserve a true fragment rather than a 'portrait' by Mr. Sargent. And someday, in spite of all the affectionate scepticism you felt toward the brash young man you met on the Rivierra eleven years ago, you'll let me have my little corner of you where I know you better than anybody – yes, even better than Gerald.[99]

At the end of 1935, in a time of unhappiness, Gerald admitted to Fitzgerald: 'I know now that what you said in "Tender is the Night" is true. Only the invented part of our life, – the unreal part – has had any scheme any beauty.'[100]

Hemingway sent Perkins a message about the novel in 1935: 'How is Scott? I wish I could see him. A strange thing is that in retrospect his Tender Is the Night gets better and better.'[101] On 15 April 1935 Fitzgerald replied to Perkins, who had become a relay station for their communications: 'Thanks for the message from Ernest. I'd like to see him too and I always think of my friendship with him as being one of the high spots of my life. But I still believe that such things have a mortality, perhaps in reaction to their very excessive life, and that we will never again see very much of each other. I appreciate what he said about "Tender is the Night." '[102] Later Hemingway wrote Perkins: 'I found Scott's Tender Is the Night in Cuba and read it over. It's amazing how excellent much of it is. If he had integrated it better it would have been a fine novel (as it is) much of it is better than anything else he ever wrote. How I wish he would have kept on writing. Is it really all over or will he write again? If you write him give him my great affection. (I always had a very stupid little boy feeling of superiority about Scott – like a tough little boy sneering at a delicate but talented little boy.) But reading that novel much of it was so good it was frightening.'[103] Fitzgerald preserved Hemingway's messages in his scrapbook for *Tender*.

The disappointment of Hemingway's 1934 response to *Tender* was compensated for by the warm letters Fitzgerald received from James Branch Cabell, Bennett Cerf, Carl Van Vechten, John O'Hara, Richard Simon, Christian Gauss, G. B. Stern, Robert Benchley, John Dos Passos, Matthew Josephson, Louis Bromfield, and John Peale Bishop. Archibald MacLeish wrote: 'Great God Scott you can write. You can write better than ever. You are a fine writer. Believe it. Believe It – not me.'[104] Despite the resentment he had felt toward Fitzgerald in Europe, Thomas Wolfe wrote after reading the magazine installments: 'I thought you'd be interested to know that the people in the book are even more real and living now than they were at the time I read it. It seems to me you've gone deeper in this book than in anything you ever wrote. . . . I think it's the best work you've done so far, and I know you'll understand what I mean and won't mind it if I get a kind of selfish hope and joy out of your own success.'[105]

Through his interest in the Junior Vagabonds theater group Fitzgerald had met Charles Marquis Warren, a young Baltimorean who had written and directed the musical revue called *So What?* Fitzgerald was greatly impressed by Warren's talent and appointed himself his patron. Nearly all the information about their friendship derives from Warren, whose statements cannot be verified.* Warren reports that Zelda resented him and scratched his face so badly that he had to be treated at a hospital. He also reports that once, while he played tennis with Zelda, she stripped off all her clothes as Fitzgerald watched impassively. Warren's most important claim is that he collaborated on Book III of *Tender Is the Night.* The manuscripts provide no evidence of the collaboration; however, on page 320 of the book the name of Nicole's father is given as Charles Warren, although it is Devereux Warren earlier. This name change, according to Charles Marquis Warren, was Fitzgerald's way of acknowledging his help; in the third printing of 1934 the name was changed back to Devereux.

Warren did collaborate with Fitzgerald on the movie treatment and provided a musical score. Hoping that *Tender Is the Night* would solve his money problems, Fitzgerald was eager to exploit the movie and play rights. Since the Hollywood studios made no offers for the novel, Fitzgerald and Warren prepared a treatment for the movies in April and May 1934. This work clearly shows the differences between Fitzgerald's concepts of literary material and movie material, for it reads like a version of *Tender Is the Night* rewritten by Lloyd C. Douglas. A melodramatic happy ending is achieved when Dick operates on Nicole after their separation (see Appendix I).

---

* Warren has said that he was seventeen when he met Fitzgerald, but *Filmgoer's Companion* gives his birth year as 1912 – which would make him twenty-one or twenty-two in 1934; his entry in *Who's Who in America* omits the year of his birth. Warren's account of his relationship with Fitzgerald has been included in Aaron Latham's *Crazy Sundays* (1971).

In the quiet, mechanical smoothness of the operating room, in the midst of his delicate work – with the newness and mystery of this particular operation – and the burning sensation that he is trying to save Nicole for another man, Dick's nerve fails.

But Nicole, deep in the oblivion of the anesthetic murmurs once 'Dick' and his hand does not falter after that.[106]

The inscription in Warren's copy of *Tender Is the Night* reads: 'For Charles (Bill) Warren with the hope that our co-operation will show us to prosperity. April 1st (fool's day) 1934.'[107] This message does not stipulate cooperation or collaboration on the novel and almost certainly refers to the movie project. An undated receipt signed by Warren shows that Fitzgerald paid him $250 'for my work on treatment of *Tender is the Night* and permission to use what I contributed to it as his own creation and property as he may see fit, this not to include my music to which I reserve full copyright.'[108]

Ober was unable to interest Hollywood in the treatment. At the end of May, Fitzgerald staked Warren to a Hollywood trip for the double purpose of looking for a writing job and selling their treatment. Fitzgerald armed him with letters of introduction,* one of which, to M-G-M story editor Samuel Marx, offered this high appraisal of Warren's abilities: 'His talents are amazingly varied – he writes, composes, draws and has this aforesaid general gift for the theatre – and I have a feeling that he should fit in there somewhere within a short time and should go close to the top, in fact I haven't believed in anybody so strongly since Ernest Hemingway.'[109] Warren failed to find Hollywood employment in 1934. (He later became a movie and television producer-director and created the *Gunsmoke* and *Rawhide* series.)

Against Ober's advice Fitzgerald assigned the stage rights to another young Baltimore writer, Robert Spafford. Fitzgerald did not collaborate with Spafford, and the play does

---

* Fitzgerald wrote letters to John Monk Saunders, Myron Selznick, Bess Meredyth, George Cukor, Roland Young, Sonia Levien, Dwight Taylor, Zoë Akins, Al Lewin, and Richard Barthelmess.

not seem to have been completed. The dramatic version written by Cora Jarrett and Kate Oglebay in 1938 was not produced.

Probably through the Vagabonds, Fitzgerald met Rita Swann, a Baltimore newspaper writer whose children were active in the theater group. Mrs. Swann's home on Park Avenue was a gathering place for stage-struck young people and Baltimore bohemians, and Fitzgerald enjoyed showing off for them. He planned an unproduced musical revue with her son Francis and worked on another project with eighteen-year-old Garrison Morfit – who would become a prominent radio and television figure as Garry Moore. Fitzgerald had the idea of combining Ring Lardner's nonsense plays with horror plays and invited Morfit to work with him. Unlikely as this plan seems, Fitzgerald was serious about it and discussed it with Gilbert Seldes in May 1934: ' . . . it seems to me that an evening of five nonsense plays would be monotonous no matter how funny they were, but just suppose, taking over the technique of the Grand Guignol, two of these plays were alternated with something macabre.'[110]

Morfit's home was near 1307 Park Avenue, and he worked with Fitzgerald in the evenings over the course of four months. Fitzgerald dictated dialogue to him, with the requirement that he use a different color of pencil for each character's speech. Morfit thought this method was silly, and Fitzgerald was furious when he caught him ignoring his orders. Once when Morfit was driving Fitzgerald past the statue of Francis Scott Key at Eutaw Place, Fitzgerald jumped out of the car and hid in the bushes, calling: 'Don't let Frank see me drunk.' Morfit had to wave a handkerchief at the statue to distract Key while Fitzgerald sneaked away. One night Fitzgerald needed a secretary and Morfit got his sister to help. When Fitzgerald showed an amorous interest in her, Morfit left with her and the collaboration ended. Morfit never saw Fitzgerald sober or charming.[111]

Disappointed by the reception of *Tender* and faced with Zelda's incurable state, Fitzgerald was drunk during much of spring and summer of 1934. Louis Azrael recalls that Fitzgerald tried to ration himself to an ounce of gin every hour but that he would borrow ounces ahead.

While she was at Craig House and Sheppard-Pratt in 1934, Zelda and Fitzgerald exchanged letters that were permeated with memories of unrecoverable happiness and wasted possibilities. From Fitzgerald in April: 'The sadness of the past is with me always. The things that we have done together and the awful splits that have broken us into war survivals in the past stay like a sort of atmosphere around any house that I inhabit. The good things and the first years together, and the good months that we had two years ago in Montgomery will stay with me forever, and you should feel like I do that they can be renewed, if not in a new spring, then in a new summer. I love you my darling, darling.'[112] And from Zelda in June:

> I wish we could spend July by the sea, browning ourselves and feeling water-weighted hair flow behind us from a dive. I wish our gravest troubles were the summer gnats. I wish we were hungry for hot-dogs and dopes [Coca-Cola] and it would be nice to smell the starch of summer linens and the faint odor of talc in blistering bath-houses. Or we could go to the Japanese gardens with Kay Laurel and waste a hundred dollars staging conceptions of gaiety. We could lie in long citroneuse beams of the five-o'clock sun in the plage at Juan-les-Pins and hear the sound of the drum and piano being scooped out to sea by the waves. Dust and alfalfa in Alabama, pines and salt at Antibes, the lethal smells of city streets in summer, buttered pop-corn and axel grease at Coney Island and Virginia beaches – and the sick-sweet smells of old gardens at night, verbena or phlox or night-blooming stock – we could see if all those things are still there.[113]

After *Tender Is the Night* was published, Fitzgerald withdrew his interdiction of Zelda's writing. He provided editorial help and tried to arrange for publication of her short pieces. In June 1934 he reported to Zelda that he was trying to persuade Perkins to publish a collection of her stories and essays.[114] The Fitzgeralds both put time into polishing the material, but nothing came of this project.

Letter from Zelda to Scott, c. October 1934

IN THE
DARKEST
HOUR

[1934–1937]

48

False Starts

[1934]

When it became clear that *Tender Is the Night* would not solve Fitzgerald's financial problems, he once again undertook to write himself out of debt with magazine stories. In April 1934 he began working on a historical novel in the form of a series of stories that could be sold separately. Fitzgerald's only mature attempt at historical fiction (aside from two Civil War stories written later), 'The Count of Darkness,' or Philippe, stories, set in ninth-century France, were the chronicle of the recovery of his father's territory by Philippe, the young Count of Villefranche. The hero was based on Hemingway, but not recognizably so. (If Hemingway saw himself in Philippe, his reaction is unknown.) Fitzgerald wrote in his *Notebooks*: 'Just as Stendahl's portrait of a Byronic man made *Le Rouge et Noir* so couldn't *my* portrait of Ernest as Phillipe make the real modern man.'[1] The plan was 'tremendously ambitious – there was to have been Philippe as a young man founding his fortunes – Philippe as a middle-aged man participating in the Captian founding of France as a nation – Philippe as an old man and the consolidation of the feudal system. It was to have covered a span of about sixty years from 880 A.D. to 950.'[2] Fitzgerald planned to call the novel 'The Castle.' He invested a great deal of research time in the stories, compiling reading lists and preparing historical charts. When Louis Azrael dropped by the Park Avenue house one night, he found Fitzgerald constructing Philippe's fort with building blocks. A history buff all his life, Fitzgerald kept a Histomap on his study wall and invented a game for Scottie played with picture cards of French historical figures.

Ober had difficulty placing the Philippe stories, but Edwin Balmer of *Redbook* agreed to take a chance on them. Fitzgerald wrote the four Philippe stories on alcohol, receiving $1,250 for the first and $1,500 each for the others. *Redbook* published the first three with increasing reluctance compounded by Fitzgerald's inability to meet deadlines, but held 'The Gods of Darkness' until after his death.* In the first story, 'In the Darkest Hour' (published October 1934), twenty-year-old Philippe returns to his ravaged ancestral lands in the Loire Valley and organizes the peasants to defeat a Viking band. The second story, 'The Count of Darkness' (June 1935), covers the building of Philippe's fort. The third, 'The Kingdom in the Dark' (August 1935), describes how Philippe gives protection to Griselda, the mistress of King Louis the Stammerer. Although Philippe warns the king about a Viking ambush, Louis burns his fort. In the fourth story, 'The Gods of Darkness,' Philippe rebuilds his fort and defends it against the Duke de Maine. When Philippe is threatened with being deposed by a witch cult, Griselda saves him by revealing that she is a priestess of the cult. In 1935 Fitzgerald planned four more stories for a total of 60,000 words:

5 Decision to build castle leads to raid to kidnap artisans + fight to death
6 Called to serve King. His Castle Stormed (Usurper has made surfs mutiny) The Fief absolute
7 Hard boiled Counts with Eclessiastics inventing Bogus rights to give chivalry a sacrosanct aspect
8 Love Story[3]

* The cover of the September 1935 *Redbook* lists Fitzgerald as a contributor, but the issue prints nothing by him.

The Philippe stories were among the worst fiction Fitzgerald published. He was proud of his knowledge of French history, but the stories never come alive because he could not work well with researched material. The mixture of archaisms and modern slang was intended to make the material less remote for the reader, but Fitzgerald's attempt to render the speech of the Middle Ages is often inadvertently funny. The peasants sound like Southern sharecroppers, and Philippe talks like somebody in a hard-boiled novel: ' "Call me 'Sire!' . . . And re*mem*ber; There's no bedroom talk floating around this precinct!" '⁴ Moreover, all four stories are flawed by inconsistencies of characterization. It is remotely possible that the Philippe stories were intended as political allegory, that Fitzgerald was suggesting comparisons between the Middle Ages and the Depression; but the point is lost. He did not entirely abandon the project and several times revived the scheme of enlarging the stories into a book.

In May–August 1934 Fitzgerald wrote 'No Flowers,' 'New Types,' and 'Her Last Case,' which the *Post* bought for $3,000 each – warning Ober that these stories were not what was expected from F. Scott Fitzgerald. During 1934 he found a market at *Esquire*, a new fifty-cent men's magazine that enjoyed surprising success during the Depression by combining contributions of well-known writers, fashion material, and pinups. The editor, Arnold Gingrich, who was a staunch admirer of Fitzgerald's prose, accepted nearly everything he submitted. In addition to its reliability as a source of emergency money, *Esquire* appealed to Fitzgerald because Ernest Hemingway was its star contributor. The drawback was that *Esquire* paid Fitzgerald a top price of $250. Fitzgerald dealt directly with Gingrich; Ober was not involved in the *Esquire* transactions. The relationship with Gingrich became personal as Fitzgerald's dealings with *Esquire* were complicated by his pleas for advances. They did not become close friends, but the editor tried to help him for the rest of Fitzgerald's life.

Fitzgerald's first bylines in *Esquire* appeared on two articles written by Zelda and polished by him, which were credited to

'F. Scott and Zelda Fitzgerald' – 'Show Mr. and Mrs. F. to Number – ' (published May and June 1934) and 'Auction – Model 1934' (July). Both were probably written at Craig House and are attempts to account for the squandered years. They are the most effective articles Zelda wrote because her style was suited to the mixture of nostalgic detail and wry humor.

'Show Mr. and Mrs. F. to Number – ,' a catalogue of the hotels they had stayed at, provides a cumulative impression of the quest for pleasure that had once been simple. Fitzgerald's technique in polishing Zelda's prose is shown by his holograph revisions in the typescript.

Typescript

In Salies-de-Bearn, I took a cure and rested in a white pine room flushed with thin sun rolled down from the Pyranees. There was a bronze statue of Henry IV on the mantel in our room and many medicine bottles and a lone uncapturable fly. The casino was closed. The boarded windows were splotched with bird droppings and Salies awaited the return of its own special season. Idling along the smoky streets we bought canes with spears on the end and authentic beret Basques and whatever there was in the souvenir shops.

Revised Text

In Salies-de-Béarn in the Pyrenees, we took a cure for colitis, disease of that year, and rested in a white pine room in the Hôtel Bellevue, flush with thin sun rolled down from the Pyrenees. There was a bronze statue of Henry IV on the mantel in our room, for his mother was born there. The boarded windows of the Casino were splotched with bird droppings – along the misty streets we bought canes with spears on the end and were a little discouraged about everything. We had a play on Broadway and the movies offered $60,000, but we were china people by then and it didn't seem to matter particularly.[5]

Fitzgerald's revisions add details to Zelda's impressionistic flow and point up the lesson in his final sentence.

'Auction – Model 1934' is an inventory of the possessions accumulated by the Fitzgeralds during their peripatetic years:

'A white sweater next that really can't be disposed of, though the front is clotted with darns and the back all pulled apart to make the worn places elsewhere meet; it was used while writing three books when the house grew cold at night after the heat went off. Sixty-five stories were forced through its sagging meshes.'[6] This passage was almost certainly Fitzgerald's interpolation.

Fitzgerald's 1934 contributions to *Esquire* were an essay, 'Sleeping and Waking,' and a pair of atypical stories. 'The Fiend' analyzes the relationship between a man and the murderer of his wife and child as the desire for revenge turns into dependence. 'The Night Before Chancellorsville'* is a whore's uncomprehending report of a Civil War battle. These *Esquire* stories were an attempt to find new material, for he had pretty much exhausted the *Post* vein of gold. They had the attraction for Fitzgerald of being easy to write because *Esquire* did not use *Post*-length stories of 5,000 or 6,000 words. Fitzgerald's *Esquire* stories ranged from 1,100 words to 2,250 words.

'Sleeping and Waking,' written in the fall, was the first of what would be a series of confessional articles for *Esquire*. An account of his struggles with insomnia, it evokes his feelings of guilt and loss as he assessed his life in the sleepless nights: ' – Waste and horror – what I might have been and done that is lost, spent, gone, dissipated, unrecapturable.' Sleep comes with a happy dream:

> In the fall of '16 in the cool of the afternoon
> I met Caroline under a white moon
> There was an orchestra – Bingo-Bango
> Playing for us to dance the tango
> And the people all clapped as we arose
> For her sweet face and my new clothes—[7]

These six lines have become Fitzgerald's best-known verse. He incorporated them in a six-stanza poem, 'Thousand-and-First Ship,' which *The New Yorker* declined in 1935.

* Fitzgerald retitled this story 'The Night of Chancellorsville' when he collected it in 1935.

Fitzgerald sought other sources of income to supplement his falling magazine earnings. When Clark Gable came to Baltimore on a personal-appearance tour, Fitzgerald revised Gable's stage act and tried to interest him in a sound remake of *The Great Gatsby*. Fitzgerald met George Burns and Gracie Allen, also on tour in Baltimore, and wrote a movie treatment for them on speculation, 'Gracie at Sea,' which was not bought.[8] He collaborated on the Burns & Allen project with Robert Spafford, who was working on the stage version of *Tender Is the Night*.

In September 1934 Fitzgerald approached Dean Gauss about the possibility of delivering eight formal lectures 'on the actual business of creating fiction' under the sponsorship of the Princeton English Department, promising to stay sober while on campus. Gauss tactfully replied that the university was not prepared to sponsor these lectures and suggested that Fitzgerald speak to an undergraduate club instead. Fitzgerald wanted some recognition from the English Department and decided to wait for a proper invitation, which never came.[9]

September 1933–September 1934 was the last year for which Fitzgerald wrote a summary in his *Ledger*, although he continued to make entries through 1936. For his thirty-seventh year he commented: '*Zelda breaks, the novel finished. Hard times begin for me, slow but sure. Ill health throughout.*' His income in 1934 was $20,032.33, of which all his books (including *Tender Is the Night*) contributed $58.35; $6,481.98 was listed as an advance against his next collection of stories. Part of this advance was in fact a loan from Scribners, and there were additional loans from Ober.

Perkins wanted to publish Fitzgerald's next story volume as soon as possible to take advantage of the attention *Tender* had received. In May 1934 Fitzgerald proposed four possible plans: (1) an omnibus volume of collected and uncollected stories; 2) a volume of the Basil and Josephine stories with new stories that would bring the characters together; 3) a volume of stories written since *All the Sad Young Men*; 4) a collection of articles and personal writings. Perkins favored the Basil and Josephine plan, but Fitzgerald then decided against the volume because he was concerned that a collection of stories about teenagers would diminish his reputation and because he did not feel up to writing the new stories.[10] He decided on a collection of previously uncollected stories, but told Perkins that it would not be ready for 1934 publication. There were some fifty stories to choose from, and it would take time to edit out the phrases and passages that had been incorporated into *Tender*. When Perkins advised him not to worry about the repeated material, citing Hemingway as a precedent, Fitzgerald took a firm stand: 'The fact that Ernest has let himself repeat here and there a phrase would be no possible justification for me doing the same. Each of us has his virtues and one of mine happens to be a great sense of exactitude about my work. He might be able to afford a lapse in that line where I wouldn't be and after all I have got to be the final judge of what is appropriate in these cases.'[11]

Fitzgerald was pleased when Bennett Cerf asked him to write the introduction for a ninety-five-cent Modern Library reprint of *The Great Gatsby* in 1934 and used the opportunity to offer a defense of his career: 'Reading it over one can see how it could have been improved – yet without feeling guilty of any discrepancy from the truth, as far as I saw it; truth or rather the *equivalent* of truth, the attempt at honesty and imagination. I had just re-read Conrad's preface to *The Nigger*, and I had recently been kidded half haywire by critics who felt that my material was such as to preclude all dealing with mature persons in a mature world. But, my God! it was my material, and it was all I had to deal with.'[12] Fitzgerald was not satisfied with his introduction and asked Cerf to let him rewrite it for a second printing, but The Modern Library discontinued *The Great Gatsby* because of insufficient sales.

Perkins visited Fitzgerald in July 1934 and took him to meet Elizabeth Lemmon in Middleburg, Virginia. Miss Lemmon was Perkins's cousin, to whom he had a longstanding attachment. Fitzgerald was impressed by her intelligence and charm, and saw her in Virginia and

Baltimore; but he was too burdened by worry and illness to maintain a close relationship. After a visit to 'Welbourne,' the Lemmon family home, he rose to the occasion by writing 'The True Story of Appomattox,' which he had printed to look like a newspaper clipping:

> We have learned that when Grant had decided to surrender his milk-fed millions to Lee's starving remnants and the rendezvous was arranged at Appomattox Court House, Lee demanded that Grant put his submission into writing. Unfortunately Grant's pencil broke, and, removing his cigar from his mouth, he turned to General Lee and said with true military courtesy: 'General, I have broken my pencil; will you lend me your sword to sharpen it with?' General Lee, always ready and willing to oblige, whipped forth his sword and tendered it to General Grant.[13]

'Her Last Case,' a *Post* story about alcoholism written in August, is set at 'Welbourne.'

In October, Perkins warned Fitzgerald that Scribners would not be able to make further advances against future books, but Fitzgerald continued to get small personal loans from Perkins. Concerned that Perkins was giving up on him, Fitzgerald defended himself against unspoken charges on 8 November 1934:

> I know you have the sense that I have loafed lately but that is absolutely not so. I have drunk too much and that is certainly slowing me up. On the other hand, without drink I do not know whether I could have survived this time. In actual work since I finished the last proof of the novel in the middle of March, eight months ago, I have written and sold three stories for the *Post*, written another which was refused, written two and a half stories for the *Redbook*, rewritten three articles of Zelda's for *Esquire* and one original for them to get emergency money, collaborated on a 10,000-word treatment of 'Tender Is the Night', which was no go, written an 8,000-word story for Gracie Allen, which was also no go, and made about five false starts on stories which went from 1000 to 5000 words, and a preface to the Modern Library edition of 'The Great Gatsby',

which equalizes very well what I have done in other years. I am
good for just about one good story a month or two articles.[14]

Much of this work was wasted – two unsold movie treatments,
five aborted stories, and one rejected story. Fitzgerald was
working, but to little purpose and for little income. He again
borrowed from his mother as his debts mounted. Gertrude
Stein, who was making an American lecture tour, came to
Park Avenue with Alice B. Toklas during the 1934 Christmas
holidays, and Zelda was upset when Fitzgerald insisted on
giving them one of her paintings.

In December 1934 Ober felt compelled to tell Fitzgerald that
his unreliability was destroying his magazine markets. Ober
also complained about Fitzgerald's attempts to interpose himself in negotiations with editors when he was drinking.

> Up to a couple of years ago if you had sent me word that a story
> would arrive on a certain date, I would have been as certain that
> the story would arrive as that the sun would rise the next day.
> Lately when you have wired me that a story would be sent on a
> certain date I have no faith at all that it will come. . . . I do think
> it would be better if you would make it a rule not to call up or
> write editors, and while I am on the subject I think it would be
> better if you did not call up or write to moving picture exe-
> cutives. . . . You are apt to use the telephone when you are not
> in your most rational state of mind and when you do call anyone
> up in that way it only adds to the legend that has always been
> ready to crop out – that you are never sober.[15]

From November 1934 to January 1935 Fitzgerald worked
on assembling his fourth story collection. With some
misgivings he titled it *Taps at Reveille*, expressing concern that
women would not know how to pronounce 'reveille.' The
alternate titles included 'Basil, Josephine and Others,' 'When
Grandma Was a Boy,' 'Last Year's Steps,' 'The Salad Days,'
'Many Blues,' 'Just Play One More,' 'Dance Card,' 'Last
Night's Moon,' 'In the Last Quarter of the Moon,' 'Golden
Spoons,' and 'Moonlight in My Eyes.' Fitzgerald wrote a short
foreword that he decided to omit:

Before the last of these stories were written the world that they represented passed. In consequence the reviewer may be tempted to apply the title harshly to the fate of the collection. Yet almost all these stories, the winnowing of fifty odd, meant a great deal to the author at the time of the writing: all of them tried for an arduous precision in trying to catch one character or one emotion or one adventure – which is all that one can do in the length of a short story.[16]

After considerable juggling of the contents, Fitzgerald settled on eighteen stories: five Basil stories ('The Scandal Detectives,' 'The Freshest Boy,' 'He Thinks He's Wonderful,' 'The Captured Shadow,' 'The Perfect Life'), three Josephine stories ('First Blood,' 'A Nice Quiet Place,' 'A Woman with a Past'), 'Crazy Sunday,' 'Two Wrongs,' 'The Night of Chancellorsville,' 'The Last of the Belles,' 'Majesty,' 'Family in the Wind,' 'A Short Trip Home,' 'One Interne,' 'The Fiend,' and 'Babylon Revisited.' *Taps at Reveille* was Fitzgerald's largest collection. Despite the two uncharacteristic *Esquire* stories, 'The Fiend' and 'The Night of Chancellorsville,' it was a balanced volume, beginning with Basil and Josephine and including strong stories from the Thirties. Nonetheless, good stories were omitted – 'One Trip Abroad,' 'The Swimmers,' 'Jacob's Ladder' – because Fitzgerald had borrowed from them in *Tender*.

Published on 10 March 1935 in a printing of 5,100 copies, *Taps* was dedicated to Harold Ober. As was always the case with Fitzgerald's story volumes, the reviews were mainly favorable; but a $2.50 book of stories was a luxury item in 1935, and the collection was not reprinted. The reviews by John Chamberlain in *The Times* and William Troy in *The Nation* were respectful appraisals of Fitzgerald's career and material, expressing the hope that he would write more ambitious stories worthy of his social and moral insights. Chamberlain made a point of defending Fitzgerald against the charge that his material was trivial, asserting that his characters were no more futile than those of Faulkner, Proust, Flaubert, or Lewis.[17]

Zelda repeatedly attempted suicide at Sheppard-Pratt. During one of his visits Fitzgerald prevented her from throwing herself under a train while they were taking a walk. John O'Hara stopped off in Baltimore to see Fitzgerald early in 1935 and later described a Sunday afternoon when 'I had Scott and Zelda in my car and I wanted to kill him. Kill. We were taking her back to her Institution, and he kept making passes at her that could not possibly be consummated. We stopped at a drug store to get him some gin. The druggist would not give it to him. I had to persuade the druggist to relent, and he got the gin. But I wanted to kill him for what he was doing to that crazy woman, who kept telling me that she had to be locked up before the moon came up.'[18] Although Fitzgerald's behavior with Zelda was sometimes cruel or irrational, he retained a fidelity to their past, a sense of regret that was not always distinguishable from self-pity. He wrote in his *Notebooks*: 'The voices fainter and fainter – How is Zelda, how is Zelda – tell us – how is Zelda.'[19] In grieving over her insanity he was also mourning the loss of his happiness. 'Lamp in a Window,' a poem addressed to Zelda which *The New Yorker* published in March 1935, shows this mixture of regret, nostalgia, and self-pity:

> Do you remember, before keys turned in the locks
> When life was a closeup, and not an occasional letter,
> That I hated to swim naked from the rocks
> While you liked absolutely nothing better?
>
> Do you remember many hotel bureaus that had
> Only three drawers? But the only bother
> Was that each of us argued stubbornly, got mad
> Trying to give the third one to the other.
>
> East, west, the little car turned, often wrong
> Up an erroneous Alp, an unmapped Savoy river.
> We blamed each other, wild were our words and strong,
> And, in an hour, laughed and called it liver.
>
> And, though the end was desolate and unkind:
> To turn the calendar at June and find December
> On the next leaf; still, stupid-got with grief, I find
> These are the only quarrels that I can remember.[20]

49

North Carolina

[1935]

On 3 February 1935, feeling desperate and concerned about his lungs, Fitzgerald took Scottie out of school and went to the mountains of North Carolina, which was an area for the treatment of tuberculosis. He picked the resort town of Tryon because he knew Nora and Lefty Flynn there. Nora was one of the celebrated Langhorne girls from Virginia, a sister of Lady Astor. Fitzgerald believed that Nora was in love with him. A former Yale football star and movie actor, Lefty Flynn had an alcohol problem and was on the wagon. Scottie stayed with the Flynns while Fitzgerald was at the Oak Hall hotel. The Flynns were talented musicians, and the entertainment at their house featured their performances. Lefty and Fitzgerald acted in a comic playlet, 'Love's Melody,' which Fitzgerald wrote for the occasion. Nora tried unsuccessfully to persuade Fitzgerald to accept Christian Science treatment for his alcoholism. He carefully noted in his *Ledger* for February: 'Went on wagon for all liquor + alcohol on *Thursday 7th* (or Wednesday 6th at 8:30 P.M.).' Fitzgerald's 1935 story, 'The Intimate Strangers,' was a thinly disguised account of the Flynns' marital histories.[21] They recognized themselves in the story, but were not upset. *McCall's* bought it for $3,000.

466

In February, Fitzgerald wrote a story about his domestic and financial predicament. In 'Lo, the Poor Peacock!' a returned expatriate whose business has been ruined by the Depression tries to raise his daughter while his wife is hospitalized (though she is not a psychiatric case). The story was declined by the *Post* and *Ladies' Home Journal* and was not published until 1971.* It is loosely organized and obviously padded as Fitzgerald tried to stretch it to commercial length. Structure and plotting became a problem in Fitzgerald's stories after 1934. They no longer came to him as 5,000-word units, and he had to fill them in with nonfunctional incidents or scenes. He observed in his *Notebooks*: 'It grows harder to write because there is much less weather than when I was a boy and practically no men and women at all.'[22]

After a couple of weeks in Tryon, Fitzgerald and Scottie returned to Baltimore. Fitzgerald's tuberculosis had been considered inactive because sputum tests failed to show acid-fast bacilli, but x-rays revealed progressive lung damage. By April 1935 it was active.† He returned to North Carolina for the summer, staying at the Grove Park Inn in Asheville while Scottie was at camp. Although he was trying to economize, Fitzgerald selected an expensive hotel by Depression standards and spent money on hotel meals which he rarely finished. He was supposed to be resting and writing stories in Asheville, but he needed company – someone to listen to him, to be impressed by him. At the Grove Park Inn he met Laura Guthrie, who was working there as a palmist; the encounter intrigued Fitzgerald because he was writing 'Fate in Her Hands,' a gimmick story about a fortune teller,

---

* The 1971 *Esquire* text was revised by an editorial hand. Fitzgerald's text was first published in *The Price Was High* (1979).
† Dr. J. W. Pierson's 23 April 1935 report on Fitzgerald's x-rays in Baltimore reads: 'Examination of the chest shows that a much more extensive involvement of the lungs has taken place since the previous examination of June 26, 1933. An area of infiltration is seen in the upper left lobe and the center of infiltration is not as dense as the peripheral portion, which would indicate the presence of a cavity. Large areas of infiltration are seen in the right, middle and upper lobes.'[23]

which was sold to *The American Magazine*. Mrs. Guthrie had literary ambitions and was separated from her husband; she soon became Fitzgerald's typist, companion, and confidante. There was no romance, but she spent long evenings with him while he drank beer – up to twenty bottles a day – and talked about himself. When they went to the movies, he restlessly changed seats and went out for quick beers.

Mrs. Guthrie kept a journal of her days and nights with Fitzgerald which includes an account of his affair with a married woman that summer.[24] Beatrice Dance was a wealthy Texan staying at the Grove Park Inn with her sister, who was suffering from nervous problems. Fitzgerald flirted with Beatrice – as he did with most attractive women – and she fell in love with him. According to Fitzgerald's reports to Mrs. Guthrie, Beatrice pushed their affair further than he wanted. It was not a casual infidelity for her; but he made it clear that he would never abandon Zelda, whom he referred to as 'my invalid.' When Beatrice's husband came to Asheville, her indiscreet conduct revealed that she was involved with Fitzgerald, and there was a confrontation. The affair turned messy, but Fitzgerald seems to have enjoyed himself. In addition to the reassurance provided by Beatrice's love, he liked being the center of attention and advising people. Beatrice left Asheville in August, and Fitzgerald closed their affair with a firm letter:

> This is going to be as tough a letter to read as it is to write. When I was young I found a line in Samuel Butler's *Notebooks* – the worst thing that can happen to a man is the loss of his health, the second worst the loss of his money. All other things are of minor importance.
>
> This is only a half truth but there are many times in life when most of us, and especially women, must live on half truths. The utter synthesis between what we want and what we can have is so rare that I look back with a sort of wonder on those days of my youth when I had it, or thought I did.
>
> The point of the Butler quotation is that in times of unhappiness and emotional stress that seemed beyond

endurance, I used it as a structure, upon which to build up a hierarchy of comparative values:

– This comes first.

– This comes second.

This is what you [Beatrice], *are not doing!*

Your charm and the heightened womanliness that makes you attractive to men depends on what Ernest Hemingway once called (in an entirely different connection) 'grace under pressure.' The luxuriance of your emotions under the strict discipline which you habitually impose on them makes that tensity in you that is the secret of all charm – when you let that balance become disturbed, don't you become just another victim of self-indulgence? – breaking down the solid things around you and, moreover, making *yourself* terribly vulnerable? – imagine having to have had to call in Doctor Cole in this matter! The *indignity*! I have plenty cause to be cynical about women's nervous resistance, but frankly I am concerned with my misjudgment in thinking you were one of the strong – and I can't believe I was mistaken.

The tough part of the letter is to send you this enclosure – which you should now read—

– now you've read it?

There are emotions just as important as ours running concurrently with them – and there is literally no standard in life other than a sense of duty. When people get mixed up they try to throw out a sort of obscuring mist, and then the sharp shock of a *fact* – a collision seems to be the only thing to make them sober-minded again. You once said, 'Zelda is your *love!*' (only you said 'lu-uv'). And I gave her all the youth and freshness that was in me. And it's a sort of investment that is as tangible as my talent, my child, my money: That you had the same sort of appeal to me, deep down in the gut, doesn't change the other.

The harshness of this letter will have served its purpose if on reading it over you see that I have an existence outside you – and in doing so remind you that you have an existence outside of me. I don't belittle your fine intelligence by supposing that anything written here *need* be said, but I thought maybe the manner of saying it might emphasize those old dull truths by

which we live. We can't just let our worlds crash around us like
a lot of dropped trays.

— *You have got to be good.*

— Your sense of superiority depends upon the picture of
yourself as being *good*, of being large and generous and
all-comprehending, and just and brave and all-forgiving. But
if you are not *good*, if you don't preserve a sense of
comparative values, those qualities turn against you — and your
love is a mess and your courage is a slaughter.[25]

Fitzgerald included a dependent letter from Zelda, probably
this one written from Sheppard-Pratt:

Dearest and always
Dearest Scott:

I am sorry too that there should be nothing to greet you but
an empty shell. The thought of the effort you have made over
me, the suffering this *nothing* has cost would be unendurable to
any save a completely vacuous mechanism. Had I any feelings
they would all be bent in gratitude to you and in sorrow that of
all my life there should not even be the smallest relic of the
love and beauty that we started with to offer you at the end.

You have been so good to me — and all I can say is that there
was always that deeper current running through my heart: my
life — you.

You remember the roses in Kinneys yard — you were so
gracious and I thought 'he is the sweetest person in the world'
and you said 'darling.' You still are. The wall was damp and
mossy when we crossed the street and said we loved the south.
I thought of the south and a happy past I'd never had and I
thought I was part of the south. You said you loved this lovely
land. The wistaria along the fence was green and the shade
was cool and life was old.

— I wish I had thought something else — but it was a
confederate, a romantic and nostalgic thought. My hair was
damp when I took off my hat and I was safe and home and you
were glad that I felt that way and you were reverent. We were
gold and happy all the way home.

Now that there isn't any more happiness and home is gone
and there isn't even any past and no emotions but those that

were yours where there could be any comfort – it is a shame that we should have met in harshness and coldness where there was once so much tenderness and so many dreams. Your song.

I wish you had a little house with hollyhocks and a sycamore tree and the afternoon sun imbedding itself in a silver tea-pot. Scottie would be running about somewhere in white, in Renoir, and you will be writing books in dozens of volumes. And there will be honey still for tea, though the house should not be in Granchester—

I want you to be happy – if there were justice you would be happy – maybe you will be anyway—

Oh, Do-Do

Do-Do—

Zelda.[26]

Fitzgerald continued to correspond with Beatrice, and she sent him gifts.

Fitzgerald became friendly with Tony Buttitta, the young proprietor of the bookshop in the George Vanderbilt Hotel in Asheville. Buttitta was an aspiring writer and took notes on their conversations, which he published forty years later in *After the Good Gay Times*. Fitzgerald made Buttitta privy to his affair with Beatrice and lectured him about literature. At Fitzgerald's request Buttitta introduced him to a call girl. He told her about his sexual difficulties with Zelda, and she assured him that he was normal – repeating Hemingway's diagnosis that Zelda had been trying to destroy his confidence.

During 1935 Fitzgerald sold seven stories: two to the *Post*, two to *McCall's*, and others to the *American, Liberty*, and *Esquire*. The magazine work he had once done dependably – if grudgingly – had become so hellishly difficult for him that his stories were labored and unconvincing. Two of the 1935 pieces are baffling. 'Shaggy's Morning' in *Esquire* is a narration by a dog that may or may not have been intended as a parody of Hemingway. 'The Passionate Eskimo,' for which *Liberty* paid $1,500, is a weak story about an Eskimo at the

471

World's Fair. Some magazines were still willing to pay for Fitzgerald's name, but not for long.

Since he was now writing to raise fast money for pressing debts, Fitzgerald was submitting what were really working drafts. The inevitable result was that his stories became harder to sell, forcing him to write more stories hastily. Dorothy Parker once remarked that although Fitzgerald could write a bad story, he couldn't write badly; but in 1935 his style was losing its distinction because he didn't have time to polish his prose. His plots had become loosely constructed and his characters were unconvincing. He was a sick, tired, depressed man of thirty-eight who thought he had lost the capacity to feel people intensely. For the first time in his career he was producing what was really hack work – as distinguished from commercial work. He explained to Ober in the summer of 1935 why he couldn't grind out successful commercial stories: ' . . . all my stories are conceived like novels, require a special emotion, a special experience – so that my readers, if such there be, know that each time it'll be something new, not in form, but in substance (it'd be better for me if I could write pattern stories but the pencil just goes dead on me. I wish I could think of a line of stories like the Josephine or Basil ones which could go faster + pay $3000. But no luck yet. If I ever get out of debt I want to try a second play. It's just possible I could knock them cold if I let go the vulgar side of my talent.)'[27] His search for story material reopened the Zelda-Jozan wound in 'Image on the Heart,' wasting his intense emotion on a minor story for *McCall's*.

In September 1935 Ober found Fitzgerald the assignment to write a short antiwar radio drama, 'Let's Go Out and Play,' for the *World Peaceways* program.[28] Fitzgerald was paid $700 and began considering other radio projects. He outlined a thirteen-week series about a father and his daughter, called 'With All My Heart,' but Ober was unable to sell the plan. Fitzgerald's thinking about the radio series yielded the idea for a *Post* series about a widower raising his teenage daughter. The girl, Gwen, was based on Scottie, and Fitzgerald hoped

Fitzgerald and Scottie in Baltimore

his feelings as a sole parent would make the Gwen stories as successful as the Basil and Josephine stories. In 1935 and 1936 he wrote four stories about Gwen. The *Post* took 'Too Cute for Words' and 'Inside the House' at $3,000 each, but declined the other two and recommended that Fitzgerald discontinue the series. The material was thin because Fitzgerald did not respond intensely to Scottie's interests, but the main difficulty with the Gwen stories was that they were hastily written. They were freighted with too many incidents and the plots were labored. By this point Ober was functioning as editor and even collaborator because the versions Fitzgerald sent him weren't in salable form. For one of the Gwen stories, 'The Pearl and the Fur,' Ober sent Fitzgerald a list of twenty-nine recommendations for revisions.[29] The two Gwen stories rejected by the *Post* – 'The Pearl and the Fur' and 'Make Yourself at Home' – were sold for $2,500 and $1,000 to the *Pictorial Review* with the names of the characters changed, but they were not published there. 'Make Yourself at Home' seems to have been resold to *Liberty*, where it appeared as 'Strange Sanctuary' in 1939. Some of the stories written in 1935–37 were not marketable at any price. A 1935 story called 'I'd Die for You' was rejected by the *Post, American, McCall's, Cosmopolitan, Redbook, Collier's,* and *Woman's Home Companion.**

Fitzgerald was treated in Asheville by lung specialist Dr. Paul Ringer. During August 1935 he drank steadily, and Dr. Ringer put him in the hospital in September to dry out. Upon his discharge Fitzgerald returned to Baltimore. For a while during the fall he had two apartments – one at the Cambridge Arms on Charles Street across from the Johns Hopkins University campus and another two blocks away at 3300 St. Paul Avenue. The Cambridge Arms became Fitzgerald's

---

* The unsold stories written during 1935–37 included 'Travel Together' (1935), 'Lo, The Poor Peacock!' (1935), 'I'd Die for You,' 'The Legend of Lake Lure' (1935), 'Cyclone in Silent Land' (1936), 'Thank You for the Light' (1936), 'They Never Grow Older' (1937), 'The Vanished Girl' (1937), and 'Offside Play' (also titled 'Athletic Interview' and 'Athletic Interval,' 1937).

Baltimore residence after December 1935.

When the Princeton Triangle Club came to Baltimore during its Christmas tour, Fitzgerald organized a theater party for Scottie and some of her friends, including Peaches Finney. He had a pre-theater chicken dinner sent to the Cambridge Arms and proceeded to give the boys a carving lesson using two carrots. His guests could not decide whether the demonstration was inspired by drunkenness or whether it was intended as an entertaining performance.

Fitzgerald felt the strain of being the sole parent of a teenager. He claimed that Scottie had played the record of 'Cheek to Cheek' (which he called 'Cheek by Jowl') so many times that every note was engraved on his innards. But he was interested in her friends and entertained them with stories when they came to the house. Always concerned about providing her with a career, he considered enrolling Scottie in a New York drama school, but she refused to leave the Bryn Mawr School.

50

The Crack-Up

[1935–1936]

In November 1935 Fitzgerald fled the Baltimore winter and went to Hendersonville, North Carolina. During his absences from Baltimore Scottie stayed with the Finneys or with Mrs. Owens. Taking a cheap room in the Skyland Hotel, Fitzgerald washed his own linen and lived on canned food. 'But it was funny coming into the hotel and the very deferential clerk not knowing that I was not only thousands, nay tens of thousands in debt, but had less than 40 cents cash in the world and probably a $13. deficit at my bank.'[30] Here he wrote 'The Crack-Up.' He had been asking for advances from *Esquire*, but Gingrich explained that he could not send money without something to show the accountants. 'I suggested that he put down anything that came into his head, as automatic writing in the Gertrude Stein manner, or that, if even that were beyond his powers of concentration, he simply copy out the same couple of sentences over and over, often enough to fill eight or ten pages, if only to say I can't write stories about young love for *The Saturday Evening Post*.'[31] The first of these articles was 'The Crack-Up,' followed by 'Pasting It Together' and 'Handle with Care,' which appeared in the February, March, and April 1936 issues of *Esquire*.* These

---

* When Edmund Wilson edited *The Crack-Up* in 1945, the titles for 'Pasting It Together' and 'Handle with Care' were transposed.

476

confessional pieces became Fitzgerald's best-known essays and provided the name for his 1935–37 period.

In the 'Crack-Up' series Fitzgerald analyzed his emotional bankruptcy and produced the irony of a writer writing brilliantly about his inability to write because of the loss of his capacity to care about the things and people he had once responded to so completely. Beginning with the proposition that 'the test of a first-rate intelligence is the ability to hold two opposed ideas in the mind at the same time, and still retain the ability to function,' Fitzgerald diagnosed that he had become depleted by 'mortgaging myself physically and spiritually up to the hilt.'[32] After describing the blows and failures that had produced his emotional bankruptcy in 'Pasting It Together,' he announced in 'Handle with Care' that he intended to survive by becoming just a writer – not a person giving himself to people. Nonetheless, the contempt with which he described this new man revealed that it was impossible for him to altogether relinquish 'the old dream of being an entire man in the Goethe-Byron-Shaw tradition, with an opulent American touch, a sort of combination of J. P. Morgan, Topham Beauclerk and St. Francis of Assisi.'[33]

The reactions to the 'Crack-Up' series further undermined Fitzgerald's position as a commercial writer. Public confession is contemptible to many people, and Fitzgerald had admitted that he was a broken man. Ober found that the magazine editors became even more suspicious of Fitzgerald's ability to deliver good stories, and the movie people who had expressed interest in hiring him now thought he was washed up.

The 'Crack-Up' articles dramatized Fitzgerald's condition, but they did not exaggerate it. He had suffered a lesion of confidence. With his facility for expressing the mood of an era in his life and work, he seemed to personify both the excesses of the Boom and the anguish of the Depression. Not only did he appear to be finished as a writer, but his name seemed to evoke shameful aspects of American experience. His friends were appalled by the articles, finding in them a

477

mixture of self-pity, egotism, and exhibitionism. It seemed to some of them that Fitzgerald was enjoying his humiliation. John Dos Passos rebuked him: 'I've been wanting to see you, naturally, to argue about your Esquire articles – Christ, man, how do you find time in the middle of the general conflagration to worry about all that stuff? If you dont want to do stuff on your own, why not get a reporting job somewhere. . . . We're living in one of the damndest tragic moments in history – if you want to go to pieces I think its absolutely o.k. but I think you ought to write a first rate novel about it (and you probably will) instead of spilling it in little pieces for Arnold Gingrich – '[34] Perkins found the 'Crack-Up' articles embarrassing and wished Fitzgerald had never written them. Hemingway regarded them as cowardly and shameful.

Fitzgerald knew that he and Hemingway would never again be close, but he continued to think of their 1925–26 friendship as one of the high spots of his life and kept in touch with him. Approaching the peak of his reputation as the most famous living writer, Hemingway was unable to generate much sympathy for Fitzgerald. His tactic was to kid Fitzgerald's troubles with bullying humor. When Fitzgerald sent him a depressed letter, Hemingway replied in December 1935 by offering to arrange for him to be killed in Cuba so that Zelda and Scottie could collect the insurance.

> . . . and I'll write you a fine obituary that Malcolm Cowley will cut the best part out of for the new republic and we can take your liver out and give it to the Princeton Museum, your heart to the Plaza Hotel, one lung to Max Perkins and the other to George Horace Lorimer. If we can still find your balls I will take them via the Ile de France to Paris and down to Antibes and have them cast into the sea off Eden Roc and we will get MacLeish to write a Mystic Poem to be read at that Catholic School (Newman?) you went to. Would you like me to write the mystic poem now. Let's see.
>
> Lines To Be Read At the Casting of Scott FitzGerald's balls into the sea from Eden Roc (Antibes Alpes Maritimes)

478

Whence from these gray
Heights unjockstrapped wholly stewed he
Flung
Himself?
No.
Some Waiter?
Yes.

Push tenderly oh green shoots of grass
Tickle not our Fitz's nostrils
Pass
The gray moving unbenfinneyed sea depths deeper than
our debt to Eliot
Fling flang them flung his own his two finally his one
Spherical, colloid, interstitial,
uprising lost to sight
in fright
natural
not artificial
no ripple make as sinking sanking sonking sunk[35]

Despite his falling magazine prices, Fitzgerald earned $16,845.16 in 1935, a good income in a Depression year; but his debts mounted as he continued to borrow from Ober and obtained small loans from Perkins and John Biggs. On 28 December he wired Ober: HAVE TRIED LIFE ON SUBSISTANCE LEVEL AND IT DOESN'T WORK STOP I THOUGHT IF I COULD HAVE THIS MONEY I COULD HOLD MY HEAD UP AND GO ON STOP WHAT YOU SUGGEST POSTPONES BY HALF A YEAR THE LIQUIDATION WE BOTH WANT STOP PLEASE CARRY ME OVER THE SECOND GWEN STORY AND GIVE ME TWENTY SEVEN HUNDRED[36]

During their 1930 trip to North Africa the Fitzgeralds had met L. G. Braun, manager of ballerina Olga Spessivtzewa. In 1936 Braun was in America trying to arrange a movie contract for Spessivtzewa with Samuel Goldwyn. Fitzgerald became interested in writing a screenplay for her, believing that Zelda's ballet experiences had provided him with material. He had probably already written a ballet synopsis called 'Lives of the Dancers.'* Fitzgerald asked Ober to arrange a meeting with Goldwyn, which did not occur; and in March 1936 he wrote a treatment for the movie called 'Ballet Shoes,' which combined a benevolent rumrunner, a 'little waif,' a long-lost father, and a great deal of coincidence.[37] Fitzgerald expected to 'deliver something entirely authentic in the matter full of invention and feeling,'[38] but his treatment offered the far-fetched situations that he believed the movies required. Nothing came of the project. Another movie possibility was a treatment for boy soprano Bobby Breen, suggested by Ober; Fitzgerald came up with an idea but was not encouraged to work on it.[39]

In March 1936 Simon & Schuster, in response to the attention the 'Crack-Up' articles were receiving, approached Fitzgerald about the possibility of publishing a volume of his autobiographical articles. Fitzgerald cleared the offer with Perkins, who suggested that Fitzgerald instead write 'a reminiscent book, – not autobiographical, but reminiscent' for Scribners. Believing that it would be as much work to write this book as a new novel, Fitzgerald tried to persuade Scribners to take over the autobiographical collection. Perkins felt the articles volume would spoil the chance for a book of reminiscences, but indicated that he would publish the collection if Fitzgerald insisted.[40] The project was dropped in June after Gilbert Seldes wrote Fitzgerald arguing against it – almost certainly at Perkins's request.[41]

Still hoping to develop a series for the *Post*, Fitzgerald in May 1936 wrote 'Cyclone in Silent Land,' the first of a projected series of stories about a nurse nicknamed Trouble. The *Post* declined it, and Fitzgerald wrote a second nurse story, ' "Trouble," ' in June. ' "Trouble" ' was reluctantly accepted, but the *Post* discouraged continuation of the series and advised Fitzgerald to invent a new character. The story was held until the March 1937 issue and was the last of

---

* 'The Lives of the Dancers' is in the 'Unclassified' section of the *Notebooks* (#1599). Its story line follows the Russian ballet to Paris and America after the 1917 revolution.

The Crack-Up [1935–1936]

Fitzgerald's sixty-five *Saturday Evening Post* stories.*
Although it was not intended as such, Fitzgerald's 5 June 1936 letter to fiction editor Adelaide W. Neall constituted his valedictory to the *Post* and to commercial stories:

> I appreciated your interest yesterday. I think that if one cares about a *metiér* it is almost necessary to learn it over again every few years. Somewhere about the middle of 'Tender is the Night' I seemed to have lost my touch on the short story – by touch I mean the exact balance, how much plot, how much character, how much background you can crowd into a limited number of words. It is a nice adjustment and essentially depends upon the enthusiasm with which you approach a given subject. In the last two years I've only too often realized that many of my stories were built rather than written.
>
> Still and however, one is limited by one's experience and I've decided to go on with the series of medical stories hoping to unearth something new – and as a beginning have decided to rewrite this story with the original as a skeleton.
>
> With best wishes to all of you and many thanks for your personal interest in the prospected series
>
> F Scott Fitzgerald
>
> (On re-reading this, it sounds somewhat stilted but I trust you'll understand that I dont need critisism a bit – the critics are always wrong (including you!) but they are always right in the sense that they make one re-examine one's artistic conscience.
>
> F.S.F.[42]

Zelda did not improve at Sheppard-Pratt and was experiencing a religious mania. On 8 April 1936 Fitzgerald transferred her to Highland Hospital at Asheville, where the minimum monthly fee was $240. Dr. Robert S. Carroll, the director of the sanitarium, had developed a treatment for mental problems on the theory that they resulted from toxic substances. (Fitzgerald had proposed a similar theory to Dr. Forel at Prangins.) The regimen at Highland was based on

---

* George Horace Lorimer retired from the *Post* at the end of 1936. He was succeeded by Wesley Winans Stout, with whom Fitzgerald had no connection.

controlled diet and exercise. Fitzgerald gave Dr. Carroll copies of *Tender Is the Night* and *Save Me the Waltz* with a letter about Zelda's novel in which he claimed that he could have beat Jozan in a fight: 'Parts of it made me angry – at the time of my quarrel . . . with her French friend I could have annialated him in two minutes. I boxed for some months with Tommy and Mike Gibbons* as a young man + this kid didn't know his left hand from his right. This is vain statement but the truth.'[43] Again hoping to provide Zelda with an outside interest to alleviate the dull routine of her sanitarium life, Fitzgerald asked Ober to investigate the possibility of publishing a book of Zelda's letters, but Ober was not encouraging.[44]

Zelda responded to the course of treatment at Highland. There were no further suicide attempts; her religious mania became less intense, although she still prayed a great deal. Her abandoned ballet career remained a permanent regret, and she would dance to the point of exhaustion unless stopped by a nurse. She often spoke wistfully about the lost days of her youth and celebrity.

After settling Zelda at Highland Hospital, Fitzgerald returned to Baltimore – partly to be near his mother, who was terminally ill in Rockville, Maryland. In the summer of 1936 he was back at the Grove Park Inn, but he saw Zelda only a few times because he broke his right shoulder in July. The accident occurred while he was diving, and Fitzgerald insisted that the shoulder actually broke before he hit the water. Placed in a body cast with his right arm elevated, he tried to work by dictation and then wrote on an overhead board. One of the stories Fitzgerald produced in his cast was originally titled 'Thumbs Up,' based on his father's Civil War recollections. It was declined by thirteen magazines before Kenneth Littauer of *Collier's* paid $1,500 down in 1937 against an acceptable rewrite. Another setback came when Fitzgerald

---

* The Gibbons brothers were St. Paul professionals. Mike claimed the middleweight title, and Tommy fought Jack Dempsey for the heavyweight championship. Fitzgerald's boast that he sparred with them is unsubstantiated.

fell in the bathroom while in the cast; he developed arthritis in the broken shoulder as a result of lying on the tile floor.

When his mother died at seventy-six in August 1936, Fitzgerald was unable to attend her funeral. He was not deeply affected by his mother's death, but he recognized that he had not been a good son. In a letter to Beatrice Dance he explained: 'She was a defiant old woman, defiant in her love for me in spite of my neglect of her, and it would have been quite within her character to have died that I might live.'[45] Before she died, Fitzgerald wrote an obituary for his mother in the September 1936 issue of *Esquire*. 'An Author's Mother' describes the death of an old woman who is confused by the modern world.* Though proud of her son, a successful writer, she does not understand his books. Her favorite authors are the nineteenth-century sentimental poets Alice and Phoebe Cary, who at the end 'had come to call upon her, and taken her hands, and led her back gently into the country she understood.'[46]

His mother's death brought Fitzgerald the expectation of temporary relief from his financial problems because his half share of her estate was $22,975.38 (less the $5,000 he had borrowed from her). Under Maryland law he had to wait six months for his inheritance, and by that time he had encumbered most of it – borrowing $7,500 from his St. Paul friend Oscar Kalman and $2,000 from Scribners. When his personal debts were paid, Fitzgerald was left with about $5,000. He spent $75 of his inheritance on a 1927 Packard roadster, which he kept in Asheville.

By the summer of 1936 Fitzgerald owed Scribners $9,000, and his debt to Ober had reached $11,000. Ober's business, like most others, was suffering from the Depression. He had two sons to educate and was concerned about the mounting total. It did no good to explain that he could not keep advancing money; Fitzgerald continued to wire desperate pleas for $50 or $100 when his bank account was overdrawn. In August, Fitzgerald secured $8,000 of his debt to Ober with

---

* Fitzgerald was undecided as to whether 'An Author's Mother' was an article or a story.

an insurance assignment, at the same time that he assigned $1,500 to Scribners in return for payment of two premiums. Since he carried only $60,000 in life insurance, he was jeopardizing Zelda's and Scottie's security by depleting the amount of money that would be available to them.

Scottie, who would be fifteen in October, was accepted by The Ethel Walker School in Simsbury, Connecticut, in 1936. The tuition was $2,200 a year, but Fitzgerald arranged for a reduction. From this time on the Obers became her foster parents. They visited her at school, and she stayed with them in Scarsdale during holidays. Fitzgerald maintained a steady flow of letters to Scottie in which he lectured her about self-indulgence and frequently warned her against following in the footsteps of her parents. He selected her courses and tried to prepare her for scientific studies – for which Scottie had no aptitude.

> Now, insofar as your course is concerned, there is no question of your dropping mathematics and taking the easiest way to go into Vassar, and being one of the girls fitted for nothing except to reflect other people without having any particular character of your own. I want you to take mathematics up to the limit of what the school offers. I want you to take physics and I want you to take chemistry. I don't care about your English courses or your French courses at present. If you don't know two languages and the ways that men chose to express their thoughts in those languages by this time, then you don't sound like my daughter. You are an only child, but that doesn't give you any right to impose on that fact. *I want you to know certain basic scientific principles*, and I feel that it is impossible to learn them unless you have gone as far into mathematics as coordinate geometry. *I don't want you to give up mathematics next year.* I learned about writing from doing something that I didn't have any taste for. If you don't carry your mathematics such as coordinate geometry (conic sections), you will have strayed far afield from what I had planned for you. I don't insist on the calculus, but it is certainly nothing to be decided by what is easiest. You are going into Vassar with mathematical credits and a certain side of your life there is going to be scientific.[47]

51

Debts

[1936–1937]

Apart from the Gwen series, the only high-priced story Fitzgerald sold in 1936 was ' "Trouble," ' for which the *Post* paid $2,000. There were nine stories and articles for *Esquire* in 1936 (which brought only $2,250), including two masterfully written essays that continued the 'Crack-Up' articles – 'An Author's House' and 'Afternoon of an Author.' 'An Author's House' allegorizes the rooms in terms of the influences that made him a writer and the conditions of a writer's life. There is a fresh grave in the cellar: ' "That is where I buried my first childish love of myself, my belief that I would never die like other people, and that I wasn't the son of my parents but a son of a king, a king who ruled the whole world." '⁴⁸ The August 1936 *Esquire* carried 'Afternoon of an Author,' an account of a tired and lonely writer trying to get an idea for a story: 'The problem was a magazine story that had become so thin in the middle that it was about to blow away. The plot was like climbing endless stairs, he had no element of surprise in reserve, and the characters who started so bravely day-before-yesterday couldn't have qualified for a newspaper serial.'⁴⁹ The irony that the critics have referred to him as 'indefatigable' brings tears to his eyes.* The lead story

---

* The writer recalls Stonewall Jackson's last words, 'Let us cross over the river

in the same issue of *Esquire* was Hemingway's 'The Snows of Kilimanjaro,' about a dying writer's loss of integrity, which included a contemptuous reference to Fitzgerald: 'The rich were dull and they drank too much or they played too much backgammon. They were dull and they were repetitious. He remembered poor Scott Fitzgerald and his romantic awe of them and how he had started a story once that began, "The very rich are different from you and me."* And how someone had said to Scott, Yes they have more money. But that was not humorous to Scott. He thought they were a special glamorous race and when he found they weren't it wrecked him just as much as any other thing that wrecked him.'[50] Though cruelly hurt by Hemingway's public betrayal of their friendship, Fitzgerald sent him a restrained letter on 16 July:

> Dear Ernest:
> Please lay off me in print. If I choose to write *de profundis* sometimes it doesn't mean I want friends praying aloud over my corpse. No doubt you meant it kindly but it cost me a night's sleep. And when you incorporate it (the story) in a book would you mind cutting my name?
> It's a fine story – one of your best – even though the 'Poor Scott Fitzgerald ect' rather spoiled it for me.
>
> Ever Your Friend
Scott
>
> Riches have *never* facinated me, unless combined with the greatest charm or distinction.[51]

Hemingway felt that by whining in *Esquire* Fitzgerald had relinquished his right to consideration. His lost reply to Fitzgerald has been described by Gingrich as 'brutal.'[52]

The anecdote about the crushing rejoinder to Fitzgerald – 'Yes, they have more money' – has become a standard element in Fitzgerald lore, with Hemingway identified as

---

and rest under the shade of the trees' – which were also the source for the title of Hemingway's novel *Across the River and Into the Trees* (1950).
* 'The Rich Boy' did not begin with this sentence.

having delivered the *coup de grâce*. Perkins explained to Elizabeth Lemmon (but not to Fitzgerald) in August – commenting on what he called the 'contemptible' reference to Fitzgerald in 'Snows' – that it was Hemingway who had been the recipient of the squelch.[53] Perkins, Hemingway, and critic Mary Colum were lunching together when Hemingway remarked, 'I am getting to know the rich.' Mrs. Colum replied, 'The only difference between the rich and other people is that the rich have more money.' If Hemingway felt so crushed by this exchange that he had to assign it to someone else, then 'poor Scott' was a target of opportunity because of 'The Crack-Up.' Beyond publicly shaming Fitzgerald, 'Snows' did so in *Esquire* – his last dependable market. Hemingway told Perkins that the reference to Fitzgerald was intended to help him by shocking him out of his self-pity.

On 15 September, Fitzgerald wrote Beatrice Dance that he had resisted continuing the quarrel with Hemingway: '. . . I wrote him a hell of a letter that would have been sudden death for somebody the next time we met, and decided, hell let it go. . . . He is quite as nervously broken down as I am but it manifests itself in different ways. His inclination is towards megalomania and mine toward melancholy.'[54] Four days later Fitzgerald wrote to Perkins:

> I feel that I must tell you something which at first seemed better to leave alone: I wrote Ernest about that story of his, asking him in the most measured terms not to use my name in future pieces of fiction. He wrote me back a crazy letter, telling me about what a great Writer he was and how much he loved his children, but yielding the point – 'If I should out live him –' which he doubted. To have answered it would have been like fooling with a lit firecracker.
>
> Somehow I love that man, no matter what he says or does, but just one more crack and I think I would have to throw my weight with the gang and lay him. No one could ever hurt him in his first books, but he has completely lost his head and the duller he gets about it, the more he is like a punch-drunk pug fighting himself in the movies.[55]

When 'The Snows of Kilimanjaro' was collected in *The Fifth Column and the First Forty-Nine Stories* (1938), Hemingway wanted to retain 'Scott' while dropping 'Fitzgerald.' It required Perkins's intervention to have the name changed to 'Julian.'

'Snows' was followed by another public humiliation in September 1936. Michel Mok of the *New York Post* interviewed Fitzgerald on his fortieth birthday when he was drinking and sick at the Grove Park Inn. Mok's front-page article appeared on 25 September, headlined: 'The Other Side of Paradise/Scott Fitzgerald, 40/Engulfed in Despair/Broken in Health He Spends Birthday Re-/gretting That He Has Lost Faith in His Star.' Fitzgerald was described as a drunk with the 'pitiful expression of a cruelly beaten child.' When asked how his generation had turned out, Fitzgerald replied:

> 'Some became brokers and threw themselves out of windows. Others became bankers and shot themselves. Still others became newspaper reporters. And a few became successful authors.'
> His face twitched.
> 'Successful authors!' he cried. 'Oh, my God, successful authors!'
> He stumbled over to the highboy and poured himself another drink.[56]

When Fitzgerald saw the article, he was so miserable that, as he reported to Ober, he swallowed an overdose of morphine, which he vomited up.[57] The newspaper article was picked up by *Time*, and Fitzgerald was concerned about preventing Scottie from seeing it at school. Surprisingly, he turned to Hemingway for support, asking him to respond to Mok.[58] Hemingway replied from Montana that he had not seen the article but was ready to help. Fitzgerald acknowledged his offer: WIRED UNDER IMPRESSION THAT YOU WERE IN NEW YORK NOTHING CAN BE DONE AT LONG RANGE AND ON COOLER

Debts [1936–1937]

CONSIDERATION SEEMS NOTHING TO BE DONE ANYHOW
THANKS BEST ALWAYS SCOTT.[59]
     Always needing the attention and admiration of women,
Fitzgerald developed friendships in Asheville with his nurse,
Dorothy Richardson, and with Martha Marie Shank, the
proprietor of a secretarial service whom he enlisted as his
business manager.* The Grove Park Inn regarded Fitzgerald
as a troublesome guest and refused to allow him to stay
without a nurse after he fired a revolver in a suicide threat.
Since he was not confined to bed, Miss Richardson's duties
mainly involved trying to limit his drinking and providing
company. Inevitably he prepared reading lists for her.[60] At
about this time Fitzgerald drafted a memo for Scottie on
'How Would I grade my Knowledge at 40' – in which he gave
himself a B+ in literature and attendant arts, B+ in history
and biography, B− in philosophy, and C in psychiatry, D+ in
military tactics and strategy, D in languages, D in architecture,
D in art, and D in Marxian economics. 'Everything else way
below educated average including *all* science, natural history,
music, politics, business, handicrafts ect. ect. – save for some
specialized sport knowledge – boxing, football, women ect.'[61]
     When Perkins urged him to use the inheritance from his
mother to write an autobiographical book, Fitzgerald
explained on 16 October that he needed at least $18,000 a
year for living expenses. 'I have a novel planned, or rather I
should say conceived, which fits much better into the
circumstances, but neither by this inheritance nor in view of
the general financial situation do I see clear to undertake it. It
is a novel certainly as long as Tender Is the Night, and
knowing my habit of endless corrections and revisions, you
will understand that I figure it at two years.' Nothing is known
about the subject of this projected novel; the circumstance
that Fitzgerald mentioned it a month after the death of Irving
Thalberg is intriguing. But Fitzgerald felt condemned to 'this

* Miss Shank preserved his working drafts and later donated them to
Princeton.

489

endless Post writing' for ready money. His carelessness with money was compounded by the conviction that penny-pinching would smother his response to experience. 'Such stray ideas as sending my daughter to a public school, putting my wife in a public insane asylum, have been proposed to me by intimate friends, but it would break something in me that would shatter the very delicate pencil end of a point of view.'[62]

In the fall of 1936 Perkins asked Marjorie Kinnan Rawlings to look up Fitzgerald while she was in North Carolina. At that time the Florida writer had published two books with Scribners but had not yet written her great success, *The Yearling* (1938). Since Rawlings had overcome bouts of depression, Perkins hoped she would be able to encourage Fitzgerald. Rawlings sent Perkins a reassuring report on the 'perfectly delightful time'; but her unpublished account reveals that in an effort to rise to the occasion Fitzgerald ordered a bottle of sherry, white wine, and 'a bottle of port, and as the afternoon wore on, another and another.'[63] The two writers liked each other and exchanged admiring letters after their meeting in Asheville, but geography prevented the development of a closer friendship.

Fitzgerald's total earnings fell to $10,180.97 in 1936. He continued to borrow from the reluctant but loyal Ober. In December he returned to Baltimore to give a tea dance for Scottie, at which he got drunk and ordered the guests to leave. Scottie was visiting her Baltimore friend Peaches Finney, and the two girls were taken home by Peaches's father. After the dance was over, Fitzgerald paid the band to keep playing while he sat alone in the middle of the Belvedere Hotel room with a bottle of gin. He spent the Christmas holidays in Johns Hopkins Hospital recovering from flu and drying out. In January 1937 he returned to the Oak Hall hotel in Tryon, where he struggled with stories that were unsalable to the high-paying magazines. When *Contemporary American Authors* sent him a biographical form in February, he listed his hobbies as 'Swimming, mild fishing, history, especially military, bucolic but civilized travel, food and wine, imaginary problems of organization, if this makes sense.'[64]

Works of F. Scott Fitzgerald

Novels

This Side of Paradise
The Beautiful + Damned
The Great Gatsby
Tender is the Night
In the Darkest Hour (2 Vols.)
Through the Night (Contemp.)
Last Word

	Pub. at
40	1st of Darkest
41	2nd of Darkest
42	Stories V
46	The Night
47	Stories VI
50	Last Word
51	Stories VI
53	Plays + Poetry
55	tins + last Words

Stories

Flappers
Jazz
Sad
Taps
More
More
Savings

Revised Edition
55 - 60
will contain
12 Volumes

Plays + Poetry
1 Vol. Vegetable, New One: 39   , New One: 42

Essays

(Total 17 Vols)

Fitzgerald's plan for his collected works, c. 1936

He sold five stories to *Esquire* and an excellent article, 'Early Success,' to *American Cavalcade*. Reassessing his career from the lowest point of his fortunes, Fitzgerald evoked the period 'when the fulfilled future and the wistful past mingled in a single gorgeous moment – when life was literally a dream.'

> – America was going on the greatest, gaudiest spree in history and there was going to be plenty to tell about it. The whole golden boom was in the air – its splendid generosities, its outrageous corruptions and the torturous death struggle of the old America in prohibition. All the stories that came into my head had a touch of disaster in them – the lovely young creatures in my novels went to ruin, the diamond mountains of my short stories blew up, my millionaires were as beautiful and damned as Thomas Hardy's peasants. In life these things hadn't happened yet, but I was pretty sure living wasn't the reckless, careless business these people thought – this generation just younger than me.[65]

Three of the 1937 *Esquire* stories – 'The Honor of the Goon,' 'In the Holidays,' and 'The Guest in Room 19' – were distinctly poor; but 'Financing Finnegan' was one of his best in *Esquire*. Partly a private joke about Fitzgerald's financial dependence on Perkins and Ober, the story describes the efforts of an editor and agent to maintain disaster-prone author Finnegan. 'His was indeed a name with ingots in it. His career had started brilliantly and if it had not kept up to its first exalted level, at least it started brilliantly all over again every few years. He was the perennial man of promise in American letters – what he could do with words was astounding, they glowed and corruscated – he wrote sentences, paragraphs, chapters that were masterpieces of fine weaving and spinning.'[66] After the *Post* declined the story because the editors thought it would not interest enough readers, it went to *Esquire* for the standard $250.

Fitzgerald calculated his minimum expenses in Tryon at $101 a week: $35 for himself, $41 for Zelda's reduced fees at Highland, and $25 for Scottie's reduced tuition at Ethel Walker. He was spending more than that, of course, and his earnings from *Esquire* did not support him. Through the spring of 1937 he sent Ober wires pleading for money to cover checks. On 11 May: TO REMAIN HERE AND EAT MUST HAVE ONE HUNDRED AND THIRTY TODAY PLEASE ASK PERKINS.[67]

'Financing Finnegan' ends with the statement that 'the movies are interested in him – if they can get a good look at him first and I have every reason to think that he will come through. He'd better.' Ober had been trying to get Fitzgerald on salary with a studio since 1935, but Fitzgerald had resisted the plan because he hated the collaborative writing system. As his earnings for the first half of 1937 fell to under $3,500, he admitted that he needed Hollywood. Ober's Hollywood associate H. N. Swanson – who had published the Fitzgeralds when he was editing *College Humor* – set about finding a movie job for him. In 1937 the movie people were reluctant to take a chance on hiring him because of his reputation as a hopeless alcoholic – a reputation which the 'Crack-Up' articles and the *New York Post* interview seemed to confirm.

By June of 1937 Fitzgerald had not sold a story, except to *Esquire*, for almost a year. Despite Ober's repeated reminders that he had lent him much more than he could afford, Fitzgerald continued to call on him as his debt climbed past $12,000. One of the unsalable 1937 stories was 'They Never Grow Older.' The magazine readers' reports were blunt in their judgment that Fitzgerald had lost the ability to construct a story:

> One of the most cockeyed nightmarish stories I have ever read.

> It is a confusing muddled story about a famous cartoonist, the girl he has loved since college days, and a rival who has also loved her all his life. For some reason which the author may know but I couldn't discover the cartoonist never proposes and the girl waits around until she is forty before they finally decide to get married. Just by way of pretending that it is a story, a madman breaks into the cartoonist's studio and shoots him in the middle of the story. This particular scene reminds

us that Fitzgerald can write but it has very little connection with what should be the thread of the story.[68]

In May, Fitzgerald sent Ober 'That Kind of Party,' an unpublished Basil story with the characters' names changed. He was trying to launch another series, but the story was declined by the *Ladies' Home Journal* and *Pictorial Review* because the magazine editors felt it gave too much attention to kissing games. In any case, it was not up to the standard of the Basil stories. That month Fitzgerald managed to raise enough money to take Zelda on a trip to Myrtle Beach, South Carolina. So desperate was his situation by June that he and Ober considered a feeler from the *Pontiac Varsity* show for him to serve as master of ceremonies on the radio program, which toured college campuses.[69]

On 4 June 1937 Hemingway delivered a denunciation of fascism at the meeting of the American Writers' Congress in Carnegie Hall. Fitzgerald was in New York that day, apparently having made a special trip from North Carolina to see him. They discussed Hemingway's next book, and Fitzgerald – reverting to his role as literary godfather – urged him to beef up *To Have and Have Not* with short stories. That day Carl Van Vechten photographed Fitzgerald in front of the Hotel Algonquin. He is wearing a checked jacket and a knit club tie with a white button-down shirt. His hair had darkened and thinned; the eyes appear older than forty years and eight months; his half-smile seems timid. The dapper outfit and the haunted expression suggest the specter of the author of *The Great Gatsby*.

Later in June, Fitzgerald returned to New York to be interviewed by M-G-M story editor Edwin Knopf, who had written *The Wedding Night* (1935), a thinly disguised movie portrait of Fitzgerald. Knopf reported to M-G-M that Fitzgerald was in good shape, and he was hired in July for six months at $1,000 per week with an option for another year at $1,250. Fitzgerald made his will on 17 June 1937 in North Carolina, appointing Biggs and Ober as executors.

Fitzgerald, 4 June 1937

PHOTOGRAPH BY CARL VAN VECHTEN, YALE UNIVERSITY LIBRARY

THE
LAST
OF THE
NOVELISTS

[1937–1940]

52

Hollywood

[Summer 1937]

'*Hollywood is a* Jewish holiday, a gentiles tragedy,' Fitzgerald observed.[1] But in 1937 it was his last hope. When he went to work for M-G-M, he was more than $22,000 in debt: $12,511.69 to Ober; $1,150 to Perkins; and at least another $9,000 to Scribners in loans and advances. The value of his life insurance policy had been reduced to $30,000. He was behind in the payments to Highland Hospital, where the annual charges for Zelda were $6,780 in 1938. His claim that he owed $40,000 when he went to California may have been close to the truth. He instructed Ober to divide his $1,000 weekly paychecks as follows:

100   to you – commission
150   to you on debt
 50   to Scribners on debt, as follows
     1st to be paid against Perkins loan
     2nd to be paid against insurance assignment held by
        Charles Scribner
     3d to be paid against their movie loan on *Tender*
     4th to be paid against my retail bill there
200   to be banked by you against taxes somewhere where I
     can get compound interest. Perhaps you can make a
     suggestion where

100   to be banked at 1st National Baltimore for 'vacation money' for I will be taking six to 8 weeks off a year.

400   to be put to my account out here for which I will pay expenses + $100 insurance. For the present we will call this one the expense check + when I find a bank in California will deposit it there.

———

$1000[2]

Out of his $400 a week allowance Fitzgerald paid for Zelda's treatment and Scottie's tuition, as well as his living expenses. He optimistically calculated that he would be able to discharge his debts in a year. Although he paid off Ober and Perkins at the end of 1938, he still owed Scribners more than $5,000 at his death.

Fitzgerald went west with high resolves and renewed ambition. Despite his two previous failures in Hollywood, he believed that this time he could launch a new career at forty. On the train he wrote to Scottie, reviewing his movie record and sharing his plan for coping with collaborators:

I feel a certain excitement. The third Hollywood venture. Two failures behind me though one no fault of mine. The first one was just ten years ago. At that time I had been generally acknowledged for several years as the top American writer both seriously and, as far as prices went, popularly. I had been loafing for six months for the first time in my life and was confident to the point of conciet. Hollywood made a big fuss over us and the ladies all looked very beautiful to a man of thirty. I honestly believed that with *no effort on my part* I was a sort of magician with words – an odd delusion on my part when I had worked so desperately hard to develop a hard, colorful prose style.

Total result – a great time + no work. I was to be paid only a small amount unless they made my picture – they didn't.

The second time I went was five years ago. Life had gotten in some hard socks and while all was serene on top, with your mother apparently recovered in Montgomery, I was jittery underneath and beginning to drink more than I ought to. Far from approaching it too confidently I was far too humble. I

500

ran afoul of a bastard named de Sano, since a suicide, and let myself by gyped out of command. I wrote the picture + he changed as I wrote. I tried to get at Thalberg but was erroneously warned against it as 'bad taste.' Result – a bad script. I left with the money, for this was a contract for weekly payments, but disillusioned and disgusted, vowing never to go back, tho they said it wasn't my fault + asked me to stay. I wanted to get East when the contract expired to see how your mother was. This was later interpreted as 'running out on them' + held against me.

(The train has left El Paso since I began this letter – hence the writing – Rocky Mountain writing.)

I want to profit by these two experiences – I must be very tactful but keep my hand on the wheel from the start – find out the key man among the bosses + the most malleable among the collaborators – then fight the rest tooth + nail until, in fact or in effect, I'm alone on the picture. That's the only way I can do my best work. Given a break I can make them double this contract in less than two years.[3]

He probably reported at M-G-M on Saturday, 10 July 1937; his first full working week started on Monday the twelfth. Ober had arranged for him to take a small apartment at the Garden of Allah, a raffish hotel at 8152 Sunset Boulevard favored by writers, where he shared a unit with screenwriter Edwin Justus Mayer. The rent was $400 a month. He acquired a 1934 Ford coupe to commute to the M-G-M lot in Culver City.

Fitzgerald had old friends among the Hollywood writers' colony, and he was pleased when the movie people made a fuss over him. Robert Benchley and Dorothy Parker were hospitable, but these two drinkers were surprised to find that he was on the wagon and diffident to the point of humility. His embarrassment about his position in Hollywood was intensified by Hemingway's arrival as a conquering hero to raise money for the Spanish loyalists. Fitzgerald was among the guests when Hemingway showed *The Spanish Earth* at the home of Fredric March on 12 July.* This was the last time

---

* Lillian Hellman's published account of the evening has been classified as an

Fitzgerald saw Hemingway, and there is no record that they talked. The next day he sent Hemingway a wire: THE PICTURE WAS BEYOND PRAISE AND SO WAS YOUR ATTITUDE = SCOTT.[5] Fitzgerald understood that their close friendship was over, admitting: 'I talk with the authority of failure – Ernest with the authority of success. We could never sit across the table again.'[6]

Fitzgerald was able to send Anne Ober an exuberant report on his first week in Hollywood:

> This letter is long overdue. Suffice to summarize: I have seen Hollywood – talked with Taylor, dined with March, danced with Ginger Rogers (this will burn Scottie up but its true) been in Rosalind Russel's dressing room, wise-cracked with Montgomery, drunk (gingerale) with Zukor and Lasky, lunched alone with Maureen OSullivan, watched Crawford act and lost my heart to a beautiful half caste Chinese girl whos name I've forgotten. So far Ive bought my own breakfasts.
>
> And this is to say Im through. From now on I go nowhere and see no one because the work is hard as hell, at least for me and I've lost ten pounds. So farewell Miriam Hopkins who leans *so* close when she talks, so long Claudette Clobert as yet unencountered, mysterious Garbo, glamorous Dietrich, exotic Shirley Temple – you will never know me. Except Miriam who promised to call up but hasn't. There is nothing left girls but to believe in reincarnation and carry on.[7]

Though Fitzgerald was returning to work he had no heart for, he was at the best studio in Hollywood.* Irving Thalberg

---

'apocryphism' by Martha Gellhorn, who establishes that Hellman could not have been present.[4]

* Fitzgerald did not become a mere Hollywood hack writer and never worked on a B picture. With one exception, his salary was at least $1,000 a week, which placed him among the highest-paid movie writers. (In the Forties, William Faulkner worked at Warner Bros. for $300 a week.) Fitzgerald's notes for *The Last Tycoon* include a Hollywood pay scale: 'Junior writers $300; Minor poets – $500 a week; Broken novelists – $850–1000; One play dramatists – $1500; Sucks – $2000. – Wits – $2500.'[8]

had died in 1936; but M-G-M retained the Thalberg style in its expensive, well-produced movies. M-G-M had the largest stable of cars and paid top salaries to writers. On 21 August, Fitzgerald signed the twenty-page M-G-M contract which stipulated: 'During the time the author is laid off pursuant to the provisions of this paragraph, the author shall have the right to write and/or work upon three (3) stories for the Saturday Evening Post, one (1) story for Collier's Magazine, three (3) short articles for Esquire Magazine and/or may complete the writing of that certain play tentatively entitled 'Institutional Humanitarianism,' heretofore commenced by the author, and the producer shall have no right or interest in such material.'[9] This play, which was to have a prison setting, did not advance beyond the planning stage.

Fitzgerald was assigned an office on the third floor of the writers' building on the M-G-M lot. He was expected to report between 9 and 10 A.M., and the studio day ended at 6 P.M.; Saturday was a half day. He got through the studio day with Cokes – as many as a dozen a day – and arranged the empties around the walls of his office until they formed a complete perimeter. If he had to be on the sound stages when shooting was in progress, he carried Cokes in his briefcase. Coca-Cola provided a stimulant and satisfied his craving for sweets when he was on the wagon; it probably also served to meet his need to have a glass in his hand. The studio work schedule was hard on him because he slept badly and was often tired during the day. Before going to bed, he took chloral and Nembutal to help him sleep. In the morning he took Benzedrine to get him started. After his heart trouble began, forty-eight drops of Digitalin were added to his nightly medication.

Determined to build a new career in Hollywood, Fitzgerald took notes on old movies and tried to learn the language of camera technique, even though he was told that it was unnecessary for a screen-writer to know these things – the director and the cameraman would take care of them. At the studio he was almost painfully humble with people who had known him in the old days. He would drop in at Anita Loos's office and apologize for bothering her. A character in Christopher Isherwood's *Prater Violet* describes Hollywood writers as feeling like married men meeting in a whorehouse, and Fitzgerald, too, seemed embarrassed by his situation. He did not mind the writing part of the job, but the waiting and the long story conferences wore him down.

At M-G-M, Fitzgerald became friendly with Albert Hackett and Frances Goodrich Hackett, who wrote the *Thin Man* movies. He seemed shy and miserable in the commissary and rarely joined the writers' table, which included Dorothy Parker, Ogden Nash, George Oppenheimer, S. J. Perelman, and the Hacketts. Occasionally he lunched at another table with Anita Loos, gagman Robert Hopkins, writers John Lee Mahin and Howard Emmett Rogers, Spencer Tracy and Clark Gable, and sometimes Aldous Huxley. Wit was the chief qualification for a seat at these tables, but Fitzgerald was conspicuously quiet. On the wagon, he experienced that sense of alienation heavy drinkers have after they stop. He was a displaced person in Hollywood. As late as 1940 he wrote to a friend in the East, 'Isn't Hollywood a dump – in the human sense of the word. A hideous town, pointed up by the insulting gardens of its rich, full of the human spirit at a new low of debasement.'[10] He felt forgotten and out of touch with the world, as documented in a postcard he wrote to himself: '*Dear Scott* – How are you? Have been meaning to come in and see you. I have living at The Garden of Allah Yours Scott Fitzgerald.'[11]

Among Fitzgerald's earliest correspondence from Hollywood is a letter urging Thomas Wolfe to curb his compulsion to put all of his material into his books: 'The novel of selected incidents has this to be said: that the great writer like Flaubert has consciously left out the stuff that Bill or Joe (in this case, Zola) will come along and say presently. He will say only the things that he alone sees. So *Madame Bovary* becomes eternal while Zola already rocks with age. . . .'[12] This letter may have been prompted by Fitzgerald's desire to believe that although he had sold himself to the movies, he was still part of Perkins's literary family. Wolfe replied on 26 July, remarking, 'I'll be damned if I'll believe anyone lives in a place called "The Garden of Allah." ' Since he had not invited Fitzgerald's advice, Wolfe's long response expressed impatience with what had become a familiar complaint against his work: 'Well, don't forget, Scott, that a great writer is not only a leaver-outer but also a putter-inner, and that Shakespeare and Cervantes and Dostoievsky were great putter-inners – greater putter-inners, in fact, than taker-outers – and will be remembered for what they put in – remembered, I venture to say, as long as Monsieur Flaubert will be remembered for what he left out.'[13]

Because he was regarded as an expert on collegiate matters, Fitzgerald's first M-G-M assignment was to polish the screenplay for *A Yank at Oxford*. The project involved one of the intricate script collaborations that Fitzgerald hated. The original story had been supplied by John Monk Saunders, and the first screenplay by Frank Wead was turned over to Fitzgerald for dialogue polishing. It was then rewritten by Malcolm Stewart Boyland and Walter Ferris, whose work was then doctored by George Oppenheimer.

English novelist Anthony Powell had come to Hollywood hoping to obtain work on *A Yank at Oxford*. When he learned that Fitzgerald was assigned to this movie, he arranged to meet him for lunch at the M-G-M commissary on 20 July. Powell was impressed by Fitzgerald's 'odd sort of unassuming dignity.' Their conversation about English university slang for the movie turned into a discussion of the cultural flow into America, which Fitzgerald diagrammmed. Powell was struck by Fitzgerald's pedagogical manner: 'He loved instructing. There was a schoolmasterish streak, if at the same time an attractive one; an enthusiasm, simplicity of exposition, that might have offered a career as a teacher or university don.'[14]

Fitzgerald's participation was not substantial enough to earn him a screen credit – the gauge by which a writer's success was measured. When the movie was released,

Fitzgerald wrote Mrs. Sayre: 'Very few lines of mine are left in "A Yank at Oxford." I only worked on it for eight days, but the sequence in which Taylor and Maureen O'Sullivan go out in the punt in the morning, while the choir boys are singing on Magdalene Tower, is mine, and one line very typically so – where Taylor says, "Don't rub the sleep out of your eyes. It's beautiful sleep." I thought that line had my trade mark on it.'[15]

53

Sheilah Graham
and M-G-M

[Summer–Winter 1937]

On 14 July, Robert Benchley – one of the most popular figures in Hollywood – gave a party at the Garden of Allah to celebrate the engagement of Sheilah Graham and the Marquess of Donegall, who had come from England to propose. She was a twenty-eight-year-old English Hollywood columnist. Fitzgerald dropped in at the party and left early without speaking to her, but he had noticed her extraordinary resemblance to the young Zelda. He later wrote his first impression of Sheilah into *The Last Tycoon:* 'Smiling faintly at him from not four feet away was the face of his dead wife, identical even to the expression. Across the four feet of moonlight, the eyes he knew looked back at him, a curl blew a little on a familiar forehead; the smile lingered, changed a little according to pattern; the lips parted – the same. An awful fear went over him, and he wanted to cry aloud.'[16] Benchley phoned Fitzgerald to rejoin the party after Sheilah and her fiancé had left, and Fitzgerald asked who was still there. When Benchley told him that a blond actress named Tala Birell was there, Fitzgerald returned, thinking she was Sheilah. (He had incorrectly remembered that the girl who interested him had been wearing a silver belt – a detail that went into *The Last Tycoon* for Monroe Stahr's meeting with Kathleen Moore.)

After Donegall returned to England, Fitzgerald saw Sheilah Graham again at the Screen Writers Guild dinner dance on 22 July in the Fiesta Room of the Ambassador Hotel, where he was Dorothy Parker's guest. His first words to her were 'I like you.' 'I like you, too,' she replied, and asked him to dance with

Fitzgerald and Sheilah Graham in 1939

her; but the party ended before they danced or spoke again. The following Saturday, 24 July, Eddie Mayer invited Sheilah to have dinner with him and Fitzgerald. She already had an engagement with her legman, Jonah Ruddy, who was therefore included in the invitation. The group went to the Clover Club, a nightclub and gambling house, where Fitzgerald and Sheilah spent most of the evening dancing.

F. Scott Fitzgerald was only a name to Sheilah. She knew that he was an author but did not know what he had written, and she had no knowledge of his past. He impressed her as charming and witty, and she was flattered by the close attention he paid her. Sheilah noticed that his friends treated him respectfully, yet she was puzzled by incongruities in his behavior – for example, that he dressed warmly in the Los Angeles summer and was nervous in auto traffic.

Fitzgerald phoned to cancel their next dinner date because Helen Hayes was bringing Scottie to California for a visit, but Sheilah said she'd like to meet his daughter. They went to the Trocadero with Scottie and some young people; Sheilah was dismayed to see the ebullient Fitzgerald of the Clover Club turn into a strict father as he corrected Scottie all evening. After Scottie was dropped off, Sheilah felt so sorry for Fitzgerald in his parental anxiety that she invited him into her house on King's Road in the Hollywood Hills.* Presumably their intimacy began that night.

Scottie enjoyed her first visit to California, despite her father's tendency to lecture her. He arranged for her to meet her idol, Fred Astaire, and other stars. (Her meeting with Astaire was reported in Sheilah's column.) Since Scottie stayed with Helen Hayes and Charles MacArthur, Fitzgerald was spared the strain of having a teenager on the premises.

---

* This account is based on Sheilah Graham's recollections in *Beloved Infidel, College of One,* and *The Real F. Scott Fitzgerald,* which telescope time. Her reports place the Screen Writers Guild dinner (which she also refers to as an Anti-Nazi League dinner) at the Cocoanut Grove a few days after 14 July, whereas it was held at the Ambassador on the twenty-second. Scottie and Helen Hayes departed by train from New York on 3 August, so the dinner at the Trocadero could not have been before 6 August.

During her visit he insisted that she take tap-dancing lessons.

If Sheilah knew little about Fitzgerald, all he knew about her was the autobiography she had invented: that she belonged to an upper-class English family and had become a chorus girl as a lark before turning to journalism. The truth, which she concealed, was that she had been born Lily Sheil in an East End London slum and was raised in an orphanage. She had married an older, Micawber-like gentleman named Graham who improved her manners and speech. Always short of money, he urged her to go on the stage and even encouraged her to date other men. As she began to move in London society without her husband, she worried that her lack of proper background would be exposed and tried to educate herself. After her marriage broke up, she decided to try her hand at journalism in America and by 1937 was writing a syndicated Hollywood column for the North American Newspaper Alliance. Hollywood was full of gossip columnists, and Sheilah Graham never achieved the power of Louella Parsons or Hedda Hopper; nor was she influential enough to advance Fitzgerald's movie career. In 1937 she earned $160 a week for five daily 'Hollywood Today' columns and a Saturday feature article.

Subjected to Fitzgerald's endless curiosity about her background, Sheilah tearfully told him the truth. Instead of being appalled as she had feared, he was fascinated by her efforts to rise and immediately volunteered to guide her education. He was, however, shocked when she admitted to having slept with eight men. In the early months of their relationship he was still on the wagon, and she had no idea that he was an alcoholic – or what his drinking behavior was like.

After his stint on *A Yank at Oxford* Fitzgerald received the important assignment to write the screenplay for Erich Maria Remarque's novel *Three Comrades* for Joseph Mankiewicz, one of the studio's top producers. It was a major movie, with four stars, to be directed by Frank Borzage. Mankiewicz was one of Hollywood's most literate producers and had been a successful screenwriter. His career later reached a peak when he wrote and directed *A Letter to Three Wives* (1949) and *All About Eve*

(1950). Fitzgerald was mistakenly assigned the office already occupied by Waldo Salt, who was also writing for Mankiewicz, and was profusely apologetic because he thought the younger writer's feelings were hurt by being moved out. After the mix-up was settled, Fitzgerald complimented Salt on *Shopworn Angel* and talked with him about the movies. Salt was impressed by Fitzgerald's seriousness about screenwriting.

At first Fitzgerald worked alone, and he wanted to keep it that way. By 4 September, before flying east to see Zelda, he had submitted about two-thirds of the screenplay to Mankiewicz, along with a letter requesting that he be allowed to finish without a collaborator. Mankiewicz wired that the screenplay was 'simply swell' and assured Fitzgerald that he could continue alone.[17] Fitzgerald spent a week with Zelda and Scottie in Charleston, South Carolina. The visit was tranquil, but he made no plans for bringing his wife to California. It was understood that they would live apart at least as long as she required treatment. He sent her weekly affectionate letters and saw to it that she was not denied any reasonable pleasures at Highland. His letters closed 'With dearest love'; hers were signed 'Devotedly.'

When he returned to Hollywood to resume work on *Three Comrades*, Fitzgerald was assigned E. E. Paramore as a collaborator. Best known for 'The Ballad of Yukon Jake,' a popular parody of the Robert W. Service poems, Ted Paramore was an experienced – if undistinguished – screenwriter. Fitzgerald had known Paramore, a friend of Edmund Wilson's in 1920, and had caricatured him in *The Beautiful and Damned* as Fred E. Paramore. Predictably, he began feuding with Paramore over who was in charge of the screenplay. He regarded Paramore as a hack who had been teamed with him to help with construction problems; but Paramore considered himself an equal partner.

At this stage of his screenwriting Fitzgerald still wrote novelistically and needed the help of an experienced Hollywood hand. His first screenplay for *Three Comrades* began with historical background on postwar Germany, including a graph showing German inflation. One sequence became something of a Hollywood legend. For the scene in which Erich (Robert Taylor) telephones Pat (Margaret Sullavan) for a date, Fitzgerald conceived a switchboard operated by St. Peter, an angel, and a satyr.

In October he fell off the wagon. A good deal is known about his drinking in California from Sheilah Graham's accounts in her books of reminiscence. She first saw what alcohol did to him when she was late phoning him after dining with writer Arthur Kober; Fitzgerald retaliated by getting drunk. Her discovery of his alcoholism was particularly upsetting because of her childhood memories of drunken men in London's East End. Having climbed a long way on ambition and determination, she was concerned about damaging her career by becoming involved with a drunk. At this point she had committed herself to Fitzgerald by breaking her engagement to the Marquess of Donegall.

When Ginevra King, now divorced, wired Fitzgerald that she was visiting Santa Barbara, Fitzgerald saw her for the first time in nineteen years and drank too much in an attempt to rise to the occasion. He found her still charming and phoned her for the next few days, but they did not see each other again. Sheilah became the woman in his life, and they settled down to a domestic routine while maintaining separate residences. His football interests revived in California, and he regularly took her to the college games in Los Angeles. He was a fan of UCLA's great black halfback, Kenny Washington, and gave his maid tickets to see Washington play.

Despite their antipathy, Fitzgerald and Paramore submitted six drafts of their screenplay. The final version, dated 1 February 1938, was then thoroughly revised by Mankiewicz. Fitzgerald felt betrayed, writing in his copy of the shooting script: '37 pages mine about ⅓, but all shadows + rythm removed.'[18] He protested to Mankiewicz on 20 January 1938 in an emotional letter that may not have been sent:

> To say I'm disillusioned is putting it mildly. I had an entirely

different conception of you. For nineteen years, with two years out for sickness, I've written best selling entertainment, and my dialogue is supposedly right up at the top. But I learn from the script that you've suddenly decided that it isn't good dialogue and you can take a few hours off and do much better.

. . . .

You are simply tired of the best scenes because you've read them too much and, having dropped the pilot, you're having the aforesaid pleasure of a child with a box of chalk. I know you are *or have been* a good writer, but this is a job you will be ashamed of before it's over. The little fluttering life of what's left of my lines and situations won't save the picture.

. . . .

My only hope is that you will have a moment of clear thinking. That you'll ask some intelligent and *disinterested* person to look at the two scripts. Some honest thinking would be much more valuable to the enterprise right now than an effort to convince people you've improved it. I am utterly miserable at seeing months of work and thought negated in one hasty week. I hope you're big enough to take this letter as it's meant – a desperate plea to restore the dialogue to its former quality – to put back the flower cart, the piano-moving, the balcony, the manicure girl – all those touches that were both natural and new. Oh, Joe, can't producers ever be wrong? I'm a good writer – honest. I thought you were going to play fair. Joan Crawford might as well play the part now, for the thing is as groggy with sentimentality as 'The Bride Wore Red,' but the true emotion is gone.[19]

Mankiewicz has defended himself against the charge of having tampered with a great writer's prose by insisting that Fitzgerald 'really wrote very bad spoken dialogue'[20] and that the cast – particularly Margaret Sullavan – had complained about their lines.*

Three Comrades ran into further trouble after it was made.

* Fitzgerald's original screenplay – without the revisions of Paramore and Mankiewicz – has been published as *F. Scott Fitzgerald's Screenplay for Erich Maria Remarque's Three Comrades* (Carbondale & Edwardsville: Southern Illinois University Press, 1978).

The German consul protested against its obvious anti-Nazi stance; and Joseph Breen, the movie industry censor, recommended that the Germans be appeased by making the villains communists. Mankiewicz refused to consider this change, for which Fitzgerald congratulated him by hugging him in the M-G-M commissary. Then when the movie was previewed for the exhibitors, they objected to the unhappy ending with the death of Pat. Her death was retained in the released movie, but Fitzgerald wanted a stronger ending with the two surviving comrades returning to fight against the Nazis, instead of leaving for South America. He wrote another angry letter (on which he noted 'Unsent – needless to say') to M-G-M executives Eddie Mannix and Sam Katz: 'In writing over a hundred and fifty stories for George Lorimer, the great editor of the Saturday Evening Post I found he made a sharp distinction between a sordid tragedy and a heroic tragedy – hating the former but accepting the latter as an essential and interesting part of life.'[21] Fitzgerald was slow to accept the condition that his Hollywood bosses did not care about his literary reputation. He was being well paid to give them what they wanted.

The reception of *Three Comrades*, featuring Robert Taylor, Margaret Sullavan, Franchot Tone, and Robert Young, countered Fitzgerald's dire predictions. It was a box-office hit and ranked as one of the ten best movies of 1938. Margaret Sullavan received an Academy Award nomination and won both the New York Critics Award and the British National Award for best actress of the year. *Three Comrades* brought Fitzgerald his only screen credit, which he shared with Paramore. Despite his difficulties with Paramore and Mankiewicz, his work won him a renewal of his contract at the end of 1937. For the next year his salary was raised to $1,250 per week.

54

Screenwriting

[1937–1938]

Sheilah had agreed to do a weekly radio talk on the movies – which Fitzgerald helped her write – but the first broadcast was a failure because she had trouble controlling her voice. The sponsor decided to have someone read the scripts for her, but Sheilah thought her problem was caused by the wait in the California studio while the network stations were connected across the country. She was sure she would be able to control her voice if the delay were removed and asked for the chance to do a broadcast from Chicago. Fitzgerald, who had been drinking, went with her – fortifying himself with gin at the airport. When Sheilah saw how drunk he was on the plane, she told him to get off at Albuquerque and return to California. He disembarked but reboarded the plane with a new supply of gin. Although Sheilah did not know it, he was AWOL from M-G-M. In Chicago he created a nuisance by directing Sheilah in the radio studio and punching the sponsor after which he was ejected. When Sheilah returned to their hotel she found Arnold Gingrich – whom Fitzgerald had summoned from the *Esquire* Chicago office – trying to sober him up by spoon-feeding him. Fitzgerald had turned it into a game by spitting out the food and trying to bite Gingrich's hand. At the airport the airline refused to board Fitzgerald because he was obviously drunk. Sheilah rode in a taxi with him for five or six hours until he looked sober. In California, Fitzgerald arranged for a drying-out process which required day and night nurses and intravenous treatment. The next week Sheilah went alone to Chicago, planning to go on to New York. Fitzgerald warned her that he would not be in California when she came back from the East, so she gave up the idea and returned from Chicago.

In January 1938 Fitzgerald went to visit Zelda and took her to Florida and Montgomery. The trip went without problems. He stayed sober, but the strain of taking care of Zelda tired him. After *Three Comrades* he was transferred to Hunt Stromberg's production unit and given what was supposed to be the choice assignment of working alone on a movie for Joan Crawford. M-G-M had acquired 'Infidelity,' a short story by Ursula Parrott, which was scrapped. Fitzgerald's job was to write what was virtually an original screenplay dealing with marital infidelity. When he told Joan Crawford that he was working on her next movie, she supposedly replied, 'Write hard, Mr. Fitzgerald. Write hard.' He studied her movies and made notes on her acting, because the role had to be tailored to her abilities. He found this requirement difficult explaining to Gerald Murphy in March 1938: 'She can't change her emotions in the middle of a scene without going through a sort of Jeckyll and Hyde contortion of the face, so that when one wants to indicate that she is going from joy to sorrow, one must cut away and then cut back. Also, you can never give her such a stage direction as 'telling a lie,' because if you did she would practically give a representation of Benedict Arnold selling West Point to the British.'[22] The problem that seems to have been ignored at the inception of the project was that in 1938 a movie about marital infidelity could not be made in Hollywood. The subject was taboo. No matter how the adultery was treated, there would have to be some kind of obligatory happy reconciliation reaffirming the sanctity of matrimony.

Fitzgerald approached the assignment with enthusiasm, hoping to bring off a sophisticated drama that would solve the problems of the material and satisfy both Joseph Breen and Louis B. Mayer. He was happy to be unencumbered with collaborators and enjoyed working with Stromberg, whom he described as 'a sort of one-finger Thalberg, without Thalberg's scope, but with his intense power of work and his absorption in his job.'²³ Known on the M-G-M lot as a writer's producer, Stromberg had a strong story sense but did not rewrite dialogue. He respected Fitzgerald and tried to make things agreeable for him.

Fitzgerald worked on 'Infidelity' from February to May 1938, writing a 104-page screenplay that lacks an ending.* The story Fitzgerald invented treats Nicolas and Althea Gilbert, a wealthy couple who are deeply in love. When Althea goes to Europe to look after her sick mother, Nicolas inexplicably has a one-night affair with a former sweetheart. Althea returns unexpectedly and finds them breakfasting in the Gilbert home under circumstances that make it obvious Nicolas has been unfaithful. The Gilberts continue to live together with no hope of reconciliation until Althea enters into a platonic attachment with a former suitor. Fitzgerald's screenplay breaks off when Althea has rejected her suitor's proposal and is being comforted by an attractive doctor. There was no way to resolve this situation in an M-G-M movie. At one point someone suggested outsmarting the censors by changing the title to 'Fidelity.' Fitzgerald was deeply disappointed when Stromberg gave up on the project; he had hoped his screenplay would establish him as a top movie writer.

During Scottie's 1938 spring vacation Fitzgerald flew east and took his wife and daughter on a disastrous trip to Virginia Beach and Norfolk, Virginia. After two days of arguing with Zelda, he got drunk and she persuaded people in their hotel that he was a dangerous madman. Fitzgerald and Zelda disagreed about the conditions of her release from

* The unfinished screenplay was published in the December 1973 issue of *Esquire*.

517

Highland. He insisted that any such trial be carefully controlled and under hospital supervision; but she wanted to travel, with a companion of her own choosing. When he returned to California, Fitzgerald wrote her a strong letter about her delusions and his finances, ending with a tender postscript: 'Oh, Zelda, this was to have been such a cold letter, but I dont feel that way about you. Once we were one person and always it will be a little that way.'[24]

In April 1938 Sheilah found a house for him at 114 Malibu Beach for $300 a month because she wanted to get him away from the Garden of Allah, a noisy gathering place for the gregarious, to a restful location. Convinced that it would aggravate his tuberculosis, Fitzgerald never swam at Malibu. Sheilah spent weekends at Malibu, where their pleasures included ping-pong and reading. Fitzgerald also liked to make fudge to satisfy his craving for sweets – a common condition in dried-out alcoholics. Their quiet ocean-front life was a far cry from the Riviera years when the Fitzgeralds partied every night. After 'Infidelity' was canceled, Sheilah suggested that they give a party at Malibu to exorcise the disappointment. Fitzgerald was the life of the party – on gin. He took writer Nunnally Johnson aside for a drunken fatherly talk to persuade him to leave Hollywood immediately before it ruined him. Johnson had been a *Post* writer and was doing well in Hollywood. He liked movie work and went on to become one of Hollywood's most successful writer-producers. He failed to react properly to his host's advice, and Fitzgerald wanted to fight him. As Johnson and his wife were leaving, Fitzgerald shouted at them that he knew they'd never visit him again because he was living with his 'paramour.'*

---

*.Charles Marquis Warren, Fitzgerald's Baltimore protégé, attended this party and lived at the beach house for a short time in 1938. Warren's account of his Malibu stay, included in Aaron Latham's *Crazy Sundays*, claims that Ernest Hemingway was a fellow house guest and was receiving an allowance from Fitzgerald while writing *For Whom the Bell Tolls*. This account is a fabrication. Hemingway did not visit Fitzgerald in Malibu. The only time they saw each other in California was in June 1937 when Hemingway came to raise money for the Spanish Loyalists.

518

Fitzgerald's feelings about his liaison with Sheilah were ambivalent. After his death she discovered that he had written 'Portrait of a Prostitute' on the back of his framed photo of her. (The note was almost certainly made after one of his drunken quarrels with Sheilah.) When Helen Hayes was appearing in a play in Los Angeles, Fitzgerald took Sheilah backstage, but the next day he sent the actress flowers with a note apologizing for introducing Sheilah to her. He needed Sheilah and loved her; yet his puritan streak disapproved of their arrangement, which was circumspect by Hollywood standards. Indeed, Sheilah has insisted that she was not really Fitzgerald's mistress because he never supported her. Though they maintained separate residences, Fitzgerald did not try to keep their relationship a secret. Certainly Scottie knew about it, and her father warned her not to mention Sheilah to Zelda or the Sayres. Scottie liked Sheilah, who went to considerable trouble making her

Fitzgerald's chart for 1931–1938

Seven years

	Fall		Winter	Spring	Summer
1931	Hollywood	1932	Montgomery Fla.	Pitts	Children La Paix
1932	Book	1933	Zelda's Play	Book	Book
1933	Book	1934	Bermuda	Drunk	Drunk
1934	Elizabeth	1935	Nora	T.B.	Beatrice
1935	Hendersonvle	1936	Scottie	Drunk	Back
1936	Nurses	1937	Tryon	Tryon	Hollywood
1937	Sheilah	1938	Maconw Fla	Easter	Malibu

California visits pleasant. Fitzgerald introduced Sheilah to the Murphys, Ober, Perkins, and Wilson when they went east.

In 'For Sheilah, a Beloved Infidel' Fitzgerald expressed gratitude to her earlier lovers for having made her more desirable. Still, the fifty-six-line poem reveals his uneasiness about her amatory history:

> That sudden smile across a room
> Was certainly not learned from me
> That first faint quiver of a bloom
> The eyes initial extacy
> Whoever taught you how to page
> Your lover so sweetly – now as then
> I thank him for my heritage
> The eyes made bright by other men.
>
> But when I join the other ghosts
> Who lay beside your flashing fire
> I must believe I'll drink their toasts
> To one who was a sweet desire
> And sweet fulfillment – all they found
> Was worth remembering. And then
> *He'll* hear us as the wine goes round
> – A greeting from us other men[25]

Fitzgerald worried about his responsibilities to Scottie as he tried to supervise her social life and education at a distance of 3,000 miles. His greatest anxiety was that, like the heroine of his Josephine stories, she would become emotionally bankrupt before she was twenty. Feeling that he had to compensate for the lack of close parental guidance by being strict, he bombarded her with admonishing letters. He was particularly troubled by her casual attitude toward school work and demanded that she be a good student – perhaps by way of penance for his own academic sins. Scottie was very bright; but she, like him, was too preoccupied with her surroundings to be a scholar. It troubled Fitzgerald that his daughter showed talent for writing and was repeating his involvement in school theatricals. He wanted her to study science and mathematics, warning her that parties and boys were threats to her development as a serious woman. When she was away from school on vacations, he pestered the Obers with telegrams and phone calls about her activities until Harold Ober told him – as forcefully as his gentlemanly nature would allow – to stop annoying them at home.

In 1938 Scottie graduated from Walker's and applied to Vassar, a decision Fitzgerald approved of because of Vassar's academic reputation. He did not attend her graduation but arranged for Zelda to go with her sister Rosalind. While remaining at school after graduation to study for college entrance exams, Scottie and a classmate broke bounds and thumbed their way to Yale for dinner with the girl's fiancé. They were found out and sent home. Fitzgerald was furious, feeling that she had lost her chance for Vassar. He was greatly relieved when she was accepted after he wrote a pleading letter to the dean of admissions. In June he got drunk when Scottie went to Baltimore – where she had friends and which she regarded as her hometown – without his permission. That summer he gave her a trip to France chaperoned by his old friend Alice Lee Myers, because he wanted her to see Europe again before the war he anticipated changed it. She came to California twice in the summer of 1938, before and after the trip to Europe. In July he wrote her a long letter sent to Paris in which he drew warnings from his and Zelda's mistakes:

> When I was your age I lived with a great dream. The dream grew and I learned how to speak of it and make people listen. Then the dream divided one day when I decided to marry your mother after all, even though I knew she was spoiled and meant no good to me. I was sorry immediately I had married her but, being patient in those days, made the best of it and got to love her in another way. You came along and for a long time we made quite a lot of happiness out of our lives. But I was a man divided – she wanted me to work too much for *her* and not enough for my dream. She realized too late that work was dignity and the only dignity and tried to atone for it by

521

working herself but it was too late and she broke and is broken forever.

It was too late also for me to recoup the damage – I had spent most of my resources, spiritual and material, on her, but I struggled on for five years till my health collapsed, and all I cared about was drink and forgetting.

The mistake I made was in marrying her. We belonged to different worlds – she might have been happy with a kind simple man in a southern garden. She didn't have the strength for the big stage – sometimes she pretended, and pretended beautifully, but she didn't have it. She was soft when she should have been hard, and hard when she should have been yielding. She never knew how to use her energy – she's passed that failing on to you.

For a long time I hated *her* mother for giving her nothing in the line of good habit – nothing but 'getting by' and conceit. I never wanted to see again in this world women who were brought up as idlers. And one of my chief desires in life was to keep you from being that kind of person, one who brings ruin to themselves and others. When you began to show disturbing signs at about fourteen, I comforted myself with the idea that you were too precocious socially and a strict school would fix things. But sometimes I think that idlers seem to be a special class for whom nothing can be planned, plead as one will with them – their only contribution to the human family is to warm a seat at the common table.

My reforming days are over, and if you are that way I don't want to change you. But I don't want to be upset by idlers inside my family or out. I want my energies and my earnings for people who talk my language.

I have begun to fear that you don't. You don't realize that what I am doing here is the last tired effort of a man who once did something finer and better. There is not enough energy, or call it money, to carry anyone who is dead weight and I am angry and resentful in my soul when I feel that I am doing this.[26]

After 'Infidelity' Fitzgerald worked briefly on a resuscitated Thalberg project, 'Marie Antoinette,' with producer Sidney Franklin. When the project was tabled, he was given another excellent assignment under Stromberg to write the screen-play for Claire Booth Luce's hit play *The Women*. Sober again, he worked on *The Women* from May to October 1938. The play was a melodrama with comedy, and Fitzgerald's dialogue was not regarded as bitchy enough. Since the cast included Norma Shearer, Joan Crawford, Paulette Goddard, and Rosalind Russell, he had the difficulty of providing them with equally good lines. Fitzgerald's job was complicated by Stromberg's health problems, for the producer was suffering from a back injury that required pain-killing drugs and was unable to give adequate attention to *The Women*. Toward the end of the assignment, Fitzgerald was teamed with Donald Ogden Stewart, who had become one of the highest-paid screenwriters; though he privately ridiculed Stewart's conversion to the left with its attendant guilt feelings, Fitzgerald offered suggestions for a speech Stewart was writing in reply to an attack on the Anti-Nazi League by Congressman Martin Dies. When it was decided that the screenplay required a woman's hand, Fitzgerald and Stewart were replaced by Jane Murfin and Anita Loos. Fitzgerald felt under pressure because his option was coming up for renewal. By the terms of his contract M-G-M would have to either raise him to $1,500 a week for another year or dismiss him. He received one screen credit in eighteen months and was taken off two important screenplays – not an impressive record.

55

College of One

[1938–1939]

▨ *Although work by* Fitzgerald appeared in *Esquire* and other magazines through 1937, it had all been written before he went to Hollywood. During his first eighteen months as a screenwriter he wrote nothing for publication. But he never stopped thinking of himself as a fiction writer, even when movie work left him without energy for his own writing. He made notes on Hollywood and probably began planning a Hollywood novel in 1938. Concerned that he was forgotten as a novelist, Fitzgerald showed his excitement in March 1938 when Perkins mentioned the 'secret hope' of publishing *This Side of Paradise, The Great Gatsby*, and *Tender Is the Night* as an omnibus volume – 'after a big success with a new novel.'[27] (It appears that Perkins hoped that The Modern Library, not Scribners, would publish the omnibus.) When Scribners reported in April that *This Side of Paradise* was out of print, Fitzgerald tried to persuade Perkins to undertake the omnibus as soon as possible.[28] Perkins informed him that the project was 'hopeless' at present and suggested he complete the Count of Darkness series instead.[29] Fitzgerald replied that he would rather write a new short novel. He asked Perkins to investigate the possibility of a 25 cent reprint of *This Side of Paradise* by Mercury Books, but Mercury declined it.[30] Fitzgerald believed that an edition of the novel with a glossary or with the names changed 'For those under Thirty Six' might find a new readership.[31]

On her return from France in August 1938, Scottie went to California with her Baltimore friend Peaches Finney. The short visit was difficult because her father berated her for past lapses and planned her Vassar life. Fitzgerald was opposed to Scottie's decision to room with Dorothy Burns, a beautiful girl from the Walker School to whom he had taken an odd dislike; but Scottie refused to change her roommate. Suspicious that parties would distract her from scholarship, Fitzgerald even forbade her to read the Baltimore newspapers while she was at Vassar. When his criticisms of Scottie became opprobrious, Peaches told him off. A letter of advice followed Scottie to Poughkeepsie on 19 September:

A chalk line is absolutely specified for you at present. . . . beside the 'cleverness' which you are vaguely supposed to have 'inherited', people will be quick to deck you out with my sins. If I hear of you taking a drink before you're twenty, I shall feel entitled to begin my last and greatest non-stop binge, and the world also will have an interest in the matter of your behavior. It would like to be able to say, and would say on the slightest provocation: 'There she goes – just like her papa and mama.' Need I say that you can take this fact as a curse – or you can make of it a great advantage?

Remember that you're there for four years. It is a residential college and the butterfly will be resented. You should never boast to a soul that you're going to the Bachelors' Cotillion. I can't tell you how important this is. For one hour of vainglory you will create a different attitude about yourself. Nothing is as obnoxious as other people's luck. And while I'm on this: You will notice that there is a strongly organized left-wing movement there. I do not particularly want you to think about politics, but I do *not* want you to set yourself against this movement. I am known as a left-wing sympathizer and would be proud if you were. In any case, I should feel outraged if you identified yourself with Nazism or Red-baiting in any form. Some of those radical girls may not look like much now but in

525

your lifetime they are liable to be high in the councils of the nation.

. . . .

Here is something you can watch happen during your college course. Always at the beginning of the first term, about half a dozen leaders arise. Of these at least two get so intoxicated with themselves that they don't last the first year, two survive as leaders and two are phonies who are found out within a year – and therefore discredited and rated even lower than before, with the resentment people feel for anyone who has fooled them.

Everything you are and do from fifteen to eighteen is what you are and will do through life. Two years are *gone* and half the indicators *already point down* – two years are left and you've got to pursue desperately the ones that point up![32]

When Scottie entered Vassar, Fitzgerald sent her a framed statement by Edison – 'There is no expedient to which a man will not go to avoid the real labor of thinking.' He continued his epistolary lectures, which she preserved even though she took most of the advice lightly.

Malibu was damp in the winter, and Fitzgerald left in November 1938 to take a house on the 'Belly Acres' estate of actor Edward Everett Horton in Encino. The rent was $200 a month, and the house-keeper received $60 a month. For $130 a month Fitzgerald hired a secretary, Frances Kroll, who started work in April 1939 and became devoted to him. Her 1985 memoir, *Against the Current*, provides a corrective to the sentimental and possibly apocryphal accounts of Fitzgerald's Hollywood life. Kroll's descriptions of his writing habits are particularly useful: 'Now and again he would ask me to read a page he had written out loud so he could listen to it for cadence. How it sounded was as important as the sight of the words on paper, as if a blind person had to hear it and a deaf one to read it.'[33]

Fitzgerald probably had begun preparing the curriculum for Sheilah's 'College of One' at Malibu, and it was in full operation at Encino. He outlined a two-year course of study restricted to the arts and humanities, since he was not prepared to tutor Sheilah in the sciences. His first plan was built around H. G. Wells's *Outline of History* and integrated sections of Wells with works of literature.[34] Fitzgerald's participation required more than providing reading lists; he reread the assignments and supplied Sheilah with background information and mnemonic aids, including a rhymed chronicle of French history with this quatrain:

> Catherine de Medici
> In fifteen hundred seventy-three
> With her sons (two lousy snots)
> Massacred the Hugenots[35]

Each required reading was discussed in a tutorial session, according to the Princeton preceptorial method. Although the program was heavy on literature and history, there were units for religion, politics, music, and art. Upon completing the two-year schedule, Sheilah would be ready to read Spengler's *Decline of the West* with Fitzgerald.

Most private educational projects fail for lack of supervision, but Sheilah received the equivalent of a college education in the areas Fitzgerald chose to survey. His inattentive years at Princeton had left gaps in his own education, and in the fields of music and art he was as much co-pupil as teacher. Nevertheless, the program worked because he was an enthusiastic tutor with a student who was eager to learn. The 'College of One' consumed a good deal of his time, but he enjoyed it. He had always tried to improve protégés, and Sheilah provided the perfect outlet for his Pygmalion compulsion.

Scottie did not entirely escape her father's pedagogy, and he sent her reading lists and quizzes at Vassar. With his curious bookkeeping system he made her an allowance of $13.85 a week; she extracted the checks and put the rest in a drawer marked 'Daddy's letters,' determined to go through college without her father looking over her shoulder. She respected his intelligence and admired his writing style, but in

Reading List

Well's Outline		159-184	Vanity Fair,	Thackeray
"	"	185-205	Man and Superman,	Shaw
"	"	205-226	The Red and the Black,	Stendhal
"	"	226-252	Bleak House (1st half),	Dickens
"	"	252-285	Seven Men,	Beerbohm
"	"	285-303	Bleak House (2nd half),	Dickens
"	"	303-322	Androcles & The Lion,	Shaw
"	"	322-344	Henry Esmond,	Thackeray
"	"	344-375	The Dolls House,	Ibsen
"	"	376-387	Sister Carrie,	Drieser
"	"	388-412	The Red Lily,	France
"	"	412-435	Youths Encounter,	McKenzie
"	"	435-454	Sinister Street,	McKenzie
"	"	455-480	(The Kreutzer Sonata and)	Tolstoi
"	"	480-501	Death In Venice,	Mann
"	"	501-523	Madam Bovary,	Flaubert
"	"	524-546	Custom of the Country,	Wharton
"	"	546-565	Brothers Karamazov,	Dostoevski
"	"	565-597	Tono Bungay,	Wells
"	"	599-617	Roderick Hudson,	James
"	"	617-634	The Pretty Lady,	Bennet
"	"	635-667	Tess of the Duburvilles,	Hardy
"	"	667-698	How to Write Short Stories,	Lardner
"	"	699-732	Cheri,	"Colette"
"	"	733-751	My Antonia,	Cather
"	"	751-778	The Sailors Return,	Garnett
"	"	778-803	The Financier,	Drieser
"	"	803-835	The Titan,	Drieser
"	"	835-866	The Lost Lady,	Cather
"	"	867-893	The Revolt of The Angels,	France
"	"	893-928	"Ariel" or The Life of Shelley,	Maurois
"	"	929-955	The Song of Songs,	Suderman
"	"	956-991	The Sun Also Rises,	Hemingway
"	"	991-1025	Growth of the Soil	Hamsun
"	"	1025-1050	Byron: The Last Journey,	Nicholson
"	"	1051-1076	Southwind,	Douglas
"	"	1076-1101	Man's Fate,	Malraux
"	"	1102-1128	The Woman Who Rode Away,	Laurence
"	"	1128-1152	The Cabala,	Wilder
"	"	1152-1170 &Chronology	Tender Is The Night	Shakespeare

Renar/s **Life of Christ**

Loyce's **Portrait of an Artist**

Stien's **Three Lives**

Pere Goriot

Esther Waters

Anna Karenina

Swanny

(4 muscar)

Cousin Betty

(Life of Christ)

Portrait of an Artist

Victory

Communist Manifesto

Open all Night

Loud all Night

Great Expectation

Reading list from the 'College of One'

the abstract only. 'In the particular, he gave me claustro-phobia,' she said in retrospect. 'Always picking, analyzing, probing. . . . children need to make their own mistakes, not the ones selected for them.' Scottie admitted that 'I knew even then that his letters were masterpieces. I wish I had shown him more appreciation, but of course I had no idea that he was going to die so soon.'[36]

Since his own college years had been among the most stimulating times of his life, Fitzgerald wanted to participate in his daughter's. Surprisingly, though, he seems to have visited her at Vassar only once. He tried to supervise her courses and friendships, convinced that she was not taking advantage of her exposure to education. When Scottie used up her allot-ment of four overnight leaves during her first term, he wrote an angry letter to her adviser, who replied: 'I can't see how any eighteen-year-old-girl could have behaved badly enough to merit so much parental misgiving and dispair – such dark bodings for the future.'[37]

But his letters to Scottie were not unrelieved expressions of a strict father's disappointment in a frivolous daughter. Often he was sharing his hard-bought wisdom and reflecting upon his own experiences.

I am not a great man, but sometimes I think the impersonal and objective quality of my talent and the sacrifices of it, in pieces, to preserve its essential value has some sort of epic grandeur.[38]

Once one is caught up into the material world not one person in ten thousand finds the time to form literary taste, to examine the validity of philosophic concepts for himself or to form what, for lack of a better phrase, I might call the wise and tragic sense of life.

By this I mean the thing that lies behind all great careers, from Shakespeare's to Abraham Lincoln's, and as far back as there are books to read – the sense that life is essentially a cheat and its conditions are those of defeat, and that the redeeming things are not 'happiness and pleasure' but the deeper satisfactions that come out of struggle. Having learned this in theory from the lives and conclusions of great men, you can get a hell of a lot more enjoyment out of whatever bright things come your way.[39]

Frances Goodrich Hackett had gone to Vassar, so Fitzgerald occasionally tried out on her his letters to Scottie.[40] Since the thing Fitzgerald knew best was writing, his comments on literature run through the letters, offering the lessons of one who had mastered his craft.

A good style simply doesn't form unless you absorb half a dozen top flight authors every year. Or rather it *forms* but instead of being a subconscious amalgam of all that you have admired, it is simply a reflection of the last writer you have read, a watered-down journalese.[41]

Anybody that can't read modern English prose by themselves is subnormal – and you know it. The chief fault in your style is its lack of distinction – something which is inclined to grow with the years. You had distinction once – there's some in your diary – and the only way to increase it is to cultivate *your own garden*. And the only thing that will help you is poetry which is the most concentrated form of style.

Example: You read *Melantha* which is practically poetry and sold a New Yorker story – you read ordinary novels and sink back to a Kitty-Foyle-Diary level of average performance. The only sensible course for you at this moment is the one on *English Poetry – Blake to Keats*. (English 241). I don't care how clever the other professor is, one can't raise a discussion of modern prose to anything above tea-table level. I'll tell you everything she knows about it in three hours and guarantee that what *each* of us tells you will be largely wrong, for it will be almost entirely conditioned by our responses to the subject matter. It is a course for Clubwomen who want to continue on from Rebecca and Scarlett O'Hara.[42]

All good writing is *swimming under water* and holding your breath.[43]

When he was in a cheerful mood, his wit enlivened his letters to Scottie. In his note about her charge account at Peck &

530

Peck, he wrote: 'Have paid Peck + Peck + Peck + Peck + Peck.'[44]

Fitzgerald encouraged Sheilah's ambitions to write fiction and began a collaboration with her on 'Dame Rumor,' a play about a Hollywood gossip columnist. In February 1938 he had Ober draw up a contract for the division of the anticipated income from the play, but the project did not develop beyond the first act.[45] He did not assist Sheilah with her column.*

Fitzgerald's last job at M-G-M was the important assignment to write *Madame Curie*, a movie that was planned for Greta Garbo. A treatment had been prepared by Aldous Huxley, but Fitzgerald and Huxley did not collaborate. Working on *Madame Curie* from November 1938 to January 1939, Fitzgerald submitted a seventy-four-page screenplay on 3 January that took the Curies up to their decision to marry – with her work on radium still to come – when work on the movie was suspended. Fitzgerald felt the movie was shelved because he and producer Sidney Franklin were 'bucking Bernie Hyman's preconception of the thing as a love story.'[47] Fitzgerald commented on Hyman, an executive producer: 'Bernie Hyman like Zero – looks like nothing, acts like nothing – add him to anything and he decreases it.'[48] (In 1943 *Madame Curie* was made with Greer Garson from a screenplay by Paul Osborn and Paul H. Rameau.) During his work on *Madame Curie* Fitzgerald was informed that the second option on his M-G-M contract would not be picked up. He admitted to Perkins, 'I just couldn't make the grade as a hack – that, like everything else requires a certain practised excellence—'[49]

During the last three weeks of his M-G-M contract, which expired on 27 January 1939, Fitzgerald was loaned to David O. Selznick on 6 January to revise the screenplay for *Gone with the Wind*. The author of *The Great Gatsby* and *Tender Is the Night* was required to use only dialogue that came from Margaret Mitchell's novel. His assignment was to polish

---

* The only item he is known to have supplied was a sneer at Constance Bennett in retaliation for insulting Sheilah: 'Poor Connie – faded flapper of 1919, and now symbolically cast as a ghost in her last production!'[46]

Oliver H. P. Garrett's revision of Sidney Howard's screenplay. He worked on the sequences from the bazaar through the burning of Atlanta, rewriting the scenes for Rhett's gift of the bonnet to Scarlett and for Ashley's leave. Fitzgerald's copy of the screenplay is annotated with his comments justifying his cuts and dialogue changes. His most frequent notes are 'Cut' and 'Book restored.' During the bazaar sequence Fitzgerald observed: 'We're running "the Cause" into the ground. Mitchell satirizes but does not burlesque.' He deleted Scarlett's statement to Ashley that the sash she made for him looks like gold, and noted 'This is technicolor.'* Fitzgerald liked working for Selznick, but he was not kept on *Gone with the Wind* because relays of writers, totaling sixteen, were being brought in. According to Sheilah's lecture on Hollywood, which Fitzgerald helped her write, he was dismissed after he was unable to find a way to make Aunt Pitty quaint enough for the cameras.

Fitzgerald continued to submit ideas for original screenplays to M-G-M producers, hoping to be hired to develop them. Almost inevitably he proposed a musical based on the Basil stories for Mickey Rooney, Judy Garland, and Freddie Bartholomew. Another proposed musical resulted from Fitzgerald's longstanding conviction that Hollywood had ignored the movies as movie material: 'Babes in Wonderland' was to deal with a group of hopeful actors and actresses hiding out in a studio. Probably in 1939 Fitzgerald wrote a treatment for a third movie story, 'The Feather Fan,' which is reminiscent of his early fiction. Set in 1919, the story deals with a Vassar girl named Genevra who discovers a feather fan that will grant her wishes. As she uses up her wishes, the fan diminishes in size and her health deteriorates:

> Then comes her fruitless and dramatic fight against death almost like that of the girl in 'Dark Victory' though of course

---

* The Fitzgerald Papers at Princeton have pp. 50–111 of his copy of the screenplay. Because the marginal annotations are typed, it is impossible to be certain that the notes are all Fitzgerald's; there are no alterations in his hand.

different and her death which symbolizes something that seems to me to have happened to women of that very generation of the twenties who thought that the world owed them happiness and pleasure if only they had the courage enough. The sanitariums are full of them and many are dead. I could name many names and after those wild five years from 1919–24 women changed a little in America and settled back to something more stable. The real lost generation of girls were those who were young right after the war because they were the ones with infinite belief.[50]

During his eighteen months on the M-G-M payroll Fitzgerald was paid some $85,000. (His 1938 salary was $58,783.10, on which he paid federal and state taxes of $2,942.36). This was more money than he had ever earned before; but when his paychecks stopped he had saved only a couple of thousand dollars, most of which was earmarked for taxes. Fitzgerald did not live extravagantly in California. He did not give Sheilah expensive presents, except for a fox jacket, but they ate at good restaurants and took trips to Santa Barbara and La Jolla. There wasn't much left from his salary after paying debt installments and maintaining Zelda and Scottie; and his own medical expenses were high. He had no other income from writing while he was at M-G-M.

The popular image of Fitzgerald as a broken-down, forgotten failure in Hollywood is a distortion as well as a simplification. His life there had a quiet order when he was not drinking. He knew that the movie work was unworthy of his genius and resented the power exercised over him by lesser men; but he earned an excellent salary at M-G-M and was proud that he was discharging his obligations. Though he and Sheilah avoided large cocktail parties, they had many friends and went to dinners at the Hacketts' and to Sunday afternoon teas at screenwriter Charles Brackett's. Fitzgerald was in top form at one party for Thomas Mann, speaking brilliantly about Mann's work. They enjoyed small parties with S. J. Perelman and his brother-in-law Nathanael West, where verbal play and charades were the entertainment.

Fitzgerald and Sheilah in Tijuana, Mexico

Fitzgerald was impressed by West, who uncomplainingly wrote junk movies to finance his unpopular novels.* As Sheilah became more deeply involved in the 'College of One,' she sent her legman to cover publicity events while she stayed home with Fitzgerald. When their studies reached music and art, they attended concerts at the Hollywood Bowl and visited museums.

Most of Fitzgerald's writer friends were active liberals, and his own political enthusiasms revived as he developed an interest in the Screen Writers Guild. An ardent anti-Nazi, he was excited by the outbreak of World War II – which he had been predicting – and followed the war news closely.

Fitzgerald regretted that his books were not being read, but he was planning a comeback. Despite the money worries after he left M-G-M, and the constant health problems, his three and a half years with Sheilah were mainly happy and often hopeful. He was sober most of the time in Hollywood. (Sheilah Graham estimated that he was drinking during nine of the forty-two months they were together; but Frances Kroll Ring has written that he continued to 'tipple' during 1939–40.) The excitements, aspirations, and expectations of the Twenties could not be revived; life would never again seem infinitely promising. Yet Fitzgerald's Hollywood exile was not a tragic period.

Zelda presumably never learned about Fitzgerald's relationship with Sheilah, although she almost certainly suspected that he had someone in California. Fitzgerald was concerned that any definite knowledge about Sheilah might cause Zelda's complete collapse. Sheilah did not try to push him into divorcing Zelda, but she felt that Fitzgerald would marry her if she insisted. She accepted the situation but shocked him by suggesting they have a child. A possible clue to Zelda's jealous recognition that her husband had found

* When West's novel *The Day of the Locust* (1939) was published, Fitzgerald provided an endorsement calling attention to 'the uncanny almost medieval feeling of some of his Hollywood background'; but this statement was not used on the dust jacket until 1950.

another heroine is provided by her response to Kathleen in *The Last Tycoon* when the unfinished novel was published posthumously in 1941: 'I confess that I didnt like the heroine, she seeming the sort of person who knows too well how to capitalize the unwelcome advances of the ice-man and who smells a little of the rubber-shields in her dress. However, I see how Stahr might have found her redolent of the intimacies of forgotten homely glamours, and his imagination have endowed her with the magical properties of his early authorities.'[51]

56

Free-lancing in Hollywood

[1939]

◥◤ *Since no other* studio offered him a contract, Fitzgerald ◣◢ became a free-lancer. Early in 1939 his Hollywood agent Swanson found him an assignment on *Winter Carnival*, which Walter Wanger was producing for United Artists. The salary was $1,250 a week. Again, to his dismay, he was being employed as a collegiate expert. His collaborator was Budd Schulberg, a recent Dartmouth graduate who had written a treatment that Fitzgerald was expected to improve. Schulberg's story was built around a young woman who is fleeing with her child to Canada and is stuck at the Dartmouth winter carnival; if her husband catches up with her before she crosses the border, she will lose her child.

Schulberg was a great admirer of Fitzgerald's fiction, though he had been under the impression that Fitzgerald was dead. In his awe he was happy to defer to Fitzgerald, and their collaboration was comfortable – so comfortable that instead of working they talked about books and the new college generation. The son of B. P. Schulberg, former head of production at Paramount, Budd Schulberg was a mine of inside information for the Hollywood novel Fitzgerald was planning. By the time the camera crew was ready to go to Dartmouth for location shooting, the writers had only a ten-page treatment and Wanger decided they should go to Dartmouth to get fresh ideas. Fitzgerald tried to get out of it, suspecting that Wanger wanted to return to his alma mater and show off the famous writer he had working for him, but Wanger insisted. B. P. Schulberg provided his son with two bottles of champagne for the flight; unaware that Fitzgerald was an alcoholic, Budd persuaded him to share them. Schulberg noticed that Sheilah Graham was on the plane, but he did not yet know about her relationship with Fitzgerald. She would stay in New York while Fitzgerald was at Dartmouth and return to California with him.

The champagne triggered a Fitzgerald bender. The writers were supposed to work on the plane and in New York before taking the train to Dartmouth; but they talked about everything except the screenplay, and Fitzgerald headed for a bar after they arrived in New York. Schulberg sobered him up and got him on the date train full of girls going to Dartmouth. Fitzgerald probably obtained alcohol on the train, for he began boasting to the girls about how famous he was. When the train stopped at a New England station, the writers got off for coffee and were left behind. They hired a car to take them to the next station, and the driver provided them with applejack against the cold. They managed to get back on their train, but Fitzgerald was never sober during his three days at Dartmouth, 10–12 February, and had caught a bad cold. He wandered around Hanover like a sorry wraith. When *The Dartmouth* interviewed Fitzgerald and Wanger, Fitzgerald could only mumble a few words.[52] Wanger fired both writers and ordered them out of town. Back in New York, Schulberg and Sheilah got Fitzgerald into Doctors Hospital. His admission record shows that he had a fever of 103.8 and a mild to moderate upper respiratory infection; he was described as confused, excitable, and restless, with difficulty in coordinating his speech. At Doctors Hospital, Dr. Richard Hoffman, a psychiatrist who had met Fitzgerald in

Paris, tried to assuage his anxiety that he had used up his talent. 'This is not your death,' Hoffman told him, 'it is the death of your youth. This is a transitional period, not an end. You will lie fallow for a while, then you will go on.'[53] After three days in the hospital and a week in a hotel, Fitzgerald returned to California with Sheilah.

Budd Schulberg was rehired by Wanger in California, and *Winter Carnival* was made into an undistinguished movie starring Ann Sheridan. In 1950 Schulberg published *The Disenchanted*, a novel largely based on his Dartmouth experiences with Fitzgerald. *The Disenchanted* has been read as a biographical treatment of Fitzgerald, despite Schulberg's insistence that Manley Halliday is a combination of several Hollywood writers – one of whom was Fitzgerald.

Without the discipline of reporting every day to the studio, Fitzgerald drank steadily at Encino, and his secretary Frances Kroll had as one of her assignments the removal of empty gin bottles from the premises. In March 1939 he worked for a month with Donald Ogden Stewart on 'Air Raid' for Madeleine Carroll at Paramount, but the movie was not made. Fitzgerald informed Scottie that although he planned to continue writing movies, he would avoid steady employment at a studio: 'But I'm convinced that maybe they're not going to make me Czar of the Industry right away, as I thought 10 months ago. It's all right, baby – life has humbled me – Czar or not, we'll survive. I am even willing to compromise for Assistant Czar! . . . It is the greatest of all human mediums of communication and it is a pity that the censorship had to come along + do this, but there we are. *Only* I will never again sign a contract which binds me to tell none other than children's stories for a year and a half!'[54]

During 1939 Sheilah Graham had to cope with Fitzgerald's violent behavior when he was drunk. In April they fought while she tried to take a revolver away from him, and Sheilah told him, 'Shoot yourself, you son-of-a-bitch! . . . I didn't pull myself out of the gutter to waste my life on a drunk like you!'[55] At this time Fitzgerald gave her a check for $2,000, as though to pay her off. The next day he went to Asheville and took Zelda to Cuba, where he continued drinking. In Havana, Zelda remained in the hotel praying while Fitzgerald wandered around the city; trying to stop a cockfight, he was beaten by the spectators. Zelda managed to get him back to New York, where he registered at the Algonquin. When she went to see her sister Tilde Palmer in Larchmont, he continued his bender until he was hospitalized. Although he later told Sheilah that he walked out of Bellevue Hospital's alcoholic ward and signed himself into Doctors Hospital, Fitzgerald was assisted by John Palmer and Frank Case, owner of the Algonquin. He was in the hospital 24–27 April and left against the advice of the doctors. A sputum test there revealed that his tuberculosis was active. Zelda returned to Highland by herself and covered for him with her doctors. It was the last time Scott and Zelda Fitzgerald were together. He wrote Zelda in May: 'You are the finest, loveliest, tenderest, most beautiful person I have ever known, but even that is an understatement because the length that you went to there at the end would have tried anybody beyond endurance.'[56]

Perkins and Ober had seen Fitzgerald during both New York benders, and Ober doubted that he would ever again be able to control his drinking. A fight with a cabdriver who took him to the Ober house in Scarsdale resulted in a black eye for Fitzgerald. After the Cuba trip he told Scribners that he was planning a Hollywood novel. When Charles Scribner, Jr., sent him an encouraging letter, Fitzgerald wrote Perkins denying that he was considering such a work and asking that the news not be circulated.[57] He was planning a novel about the movie industry, but he was concerned that the studios would not hire him if they knew he was writing it.

Fitzgerald and Sheilah were again reconciled, and he returned to short stories after Swanson placed him on the list of unavailable script writers. During his period of recuperation he was considered for Alfred Hitchcock's *Rebecca*. In May 1939 he informed Ober that he had 'blocked out' a 50,000-word novel to be written in three or four months, which probably meant only that he had a plot in mind. He asked Ober to report on the current short-story market, particularly at *The Saturday Evening Post*.[58] His first work of fiction in 1939 was the rewrite of 'Thumbs Up,' the Civil War story that he had owed *Collier's* since 1937. After rejecting at least two revisions, editor Kenneth Littauer accepted the version called 'The End of Hate' in June 1939 and paid the $1,000 balance due. During the spring and summer of 1939 Fitzgerald wrote 'Design in Plaster,' 'Mike Van Dyke's Christmas Wish' (which became 'Pat Hobby's Christmas Wish'), 'Three Hours Between Planes,' and possibly 'Last Kiss' and 'Director's Special' – all of which were declined by *Collier's*, where Fitzgerald was hoping to develop a connection through Littauer.

The story that took the most work was 'The Women in the House' (retitled 'Temperature'), written in June and intended for *The Saturday Evening Post*. Ober did not offer it to the *Post* because its 14,000-word length made it impossible for that magazine, but he met Fitzgerald's request for a $500 advance. Correctly anticipating that Fitzgerald was about to resume borrowing against unsold or unwritten stories, Ober wrote him a firm letter explaining that his family obligations prevented him from making further advances or loans; but Ober did not mail the letter, probably because he realized it would do no good.[59] After Fitzgerald cut 'Temperature' to 8,000 words, Ober reluctantly submitted the story to the *Post*, which rejected it on 18 July as too long and too slight. 'Temperature' is a gimmick story about a medical mix-up which occurs when a healthy young man gets the wrong electrocardiogram and is led to believe he has a serious heart condition. The women are his fiancée, his secretary, and a comic nurse. The characters are familiar magazine types, and the plot is predictable.

Fitzgerald's ability to write fresh, well-constructed commercial stories was irrecoverable. He tried to explain this loss to himself in his *Notebooks*: 'I have asked a lot of my emotions – one hundred and twenty stories. The price was high, right up with Kipling, because there was one little drop of something not blood, not a tear, not my seed, but me more intimately than these, in every story, it was the extra I had. Now it has gone and I am just like you now.'[60] On or about 3 July, Ober refused Fitzgerald's request for another advance, and Fitzgerald appealed to Perkins: HAVE BEEN WRITING IN BED WITH TUBERCULOSIS UNDER DOCTORS NURSES CARE SIS ARRIVING WEST. OBER HAS DECIDED NOT TO BACK ME THOUGH I PAID BACK EVERY PENNY AND EIGHT THOUSAND COMMISSION. AM GOING TO WORK THURSDAY IN STUDIO AT FIFTEEN HUNDRED CAN YOU LEND ME SIX HUNDRED FOR ONE WEEK BY WIRE TO BANK AMERICAN CULVERCITY. SCOTTIE HOSPITAL WITH APPENDIX AND AM ABSOLUTELY WITHOUT FUNDS. PLEASE DO NOT ASK OBERS COOPERATION.[61] Perkins came through. The job was for one week at Universal, where Fitzgerald prepared a treatment called 'Open That Door' for Charles Bonner's novel *Bull by the Horns*; the movie was not made.

On 13 July Fitzgerald wired Ober: STILL FLABBERGASTED AT YOUR ABRUPT CHANGE IN POLICY AFTER TWENTY YEARS ESPECIALLY WITH STORY IN YOUR HANDS STOP MY COMMERCIAL VALUE CANT HAVE SUNK FROM 60 THOUSAND TO NOTHING BECAUSE OF A SLOW HEALING LUNG CAVITY STOP AFTER 30 PICTURE OFFERS DURING THE MONTHS I WAS IN BED SWANSON NOW PROMISES NOTHING FOR ANOTHER WEEK STOP CANT YOU ARRANGE A FEW HUNDRED ADVANCE FROM A MAGAZINE SO I CAN EAT TODAY AND TOMORROW STOP WONT YOU WIRE SCOTT.[62] Ober refused.* The well was dry. Apart from the effect of having his dependable source of emergency money cut off after twenty years, Fitzgerald was hurt by the clear signal that Ober had given up on him. He subsequently explained to Perkins, 'When Harold withdrew from the questionable honor of being my banker I felt completely numb financially and I suddenly wondered what money was and where it came from. There had always

---

* Fitzgerald's wire was received in New York at 3:56 A.M. on 14 July. The preceding request for a loan and Ober's reply are lost.

seemed a little more somewhere and now there wasn't.'[63]
Fitzgerald sent Ober two long letters breaking off their
business arrangement but inviting him to make some gesture
of reconciliation or at least an expression of confidence. On
19 July:

> This is not a request for any more backing – there will be no
> more requests. I am quite sure that you would be as stubborn
> in any decision that I am through as you were up to 1934 about
> the value of my stories. Also I am writing this letter with, I
> hope, no touch of unpleasantness – simply from a feeling that
> perhaps you share, that I have depended too long on backing
> and had better find out at the source whether my products are
> considered deficient and why.
>
> . . . .
>
> I feel less hesitation in saying this because it is probably what
> you wanted for some time. You now have plenty of authors
> who produce correctly and conduct their affairs in a
> business-like manner. On the contrary, I have a neurosis about
> anyone's uncertainty about my ability that has been a principal
> handicap in the picture business. And secondly, the
> semi-crippled state into which I seem to get myself sometimes
> (almost like the hero of my story 'Financing Finnegan') fill me,
> in the long nights, with a resentment toward the absurd
> present which is not fair to you or to the past. Everything I
> have ever done or written is *me*, and who doesn't choose to
> accept the whole cannot but see the wisdom of a parting. One
> doesn't change at 42 though one can grow more tired and even
> more acquiescent – and I am very close to knowing how you
> feel about it all: I realize there is little place in this tortured
> world for any exhibition of shattered nerves or anything that
> illness makes people do.[64]

And on 2 August:

> I don't have to explain that even though a man has once
> saved another from drowning, when he refuses to stretch out
> his arm a second time the victim has to act quickly and
> desperately to save himself. For change you did, Harold, and
> without warning – the custom of lending up to the probable

543

yield of a next short story obtained between us for a dozen years. Certainly you haven't just discovered that I'm not any of the things a proper business man should be? And it wasn't even a run around – it was a walk-around that almost made me think the New York telegraph was closed. Finally I had to sell a pair of stories [probably 'Design in Plaster' and 'The Lost Decade'] to *Esquire* the longest one of which (2800 words) might have brought twice as much from *Liberty*.

Whatever I am supposed to guess, your way of doing it and the time you chose, was as dispiriting as could be. I have been all too hauntingly aware during these months of what you did from 1934 to 1937 to keep my head above water after the failure of *Tender*, Zelda's third collapse and the long illness. But you have made me sting none the less.[65]

Ober agonized over the decision but maintained his embargo on advances, and Fitzgerald began acting as his own agent. The Obers continued to provide a home for Scottie, with whom they had a loving relationship; and Ober handled the small amount of business for Fitzgerald's published work. *Collier's* declined the stories Fitzgerald submitted during the summer of 1939 although Fitzgerald tried to persuade Littauer that he was opening up a new vein of fiction: 'You see I not only announced the birth of my young illusions in "This Side of Paradise" but pretty much the death of them in some of my last *Post* stories like "Babylon Revisited.' . . . Nevertheless, an overwhelming number of editors continue to associate me with an absorbing interest in young girls – an interest that at my age would probably land me behind the bars.'[66]

The July 1939 issue of *Mademoiselle* carried Scottie's article 'A Short Retort' under the byline Frances Scott Fitzgerald. Her father was angered by Scottie's evaluation of her self-reliant generation because he saw it as an implied attack on his irresponsibility: ' . . . in the speakeasy era that followed, we were left pretty much to ourselves and allowed to do as we pleased. And so, we "know the score".' He asked her to publish her future work under 'any name that doesn't sound like mine.'[67] Probably at this time he wrote 'My Generation,' a reply to Scottie's article that was not published until 1968.

Fitzgerald's July letters to Scottie were harsh: 'You left a most unpleasant impression behind last autumn with many people, and I would much rather not see you at all than see you without loving you. Your home is Vassar.'[68] When Zelda rebuked him for writing this letter, Fitzgerald defended himself by explaining that he was an invalid and dreaded having his tranquillity disturbed.[69]

Scottie's August 1939 visit to 'Belly Acres' went well enough although Fitzgerald was drinking all that summer. She was planning a novel and he reworked the outline for her. Fitzgerald insisted that she take driving lessons – 'in case a man you are out with has too much to drink' – and read Keats and Shelley aloud to her. Always a great believer in the benefits of memorizing verse, he assigned her Keats's 'Ode on a Grecian Urn' and Thomas Gray's 'Ode on the Death of a Favorite Cat Drowned in a Tub of Goldfishes,' of which he relished the final lines:

> Not all that tempts your wandering eyes
> And heedless hearts is lawful prize;
> Nor all that glisters gold.

57

Planning
The Last Tycoon

[Fall 1939]

Fitzgerald wanted to begin a novel after his M-G-M contract expired but was undecided whether to salvage the Philippe medieval project, which Perkins encouraged, or to start a short novel about Hollywood. By May 1939 he had settled on the plan of writing the Hollywood novel for serialization in *Collier's* – since Kenneth Littauer was the only magazine editor who showed interest in his longer fiction – counting on the payments for each installment to finance his work. On 29 September he sent a synopsis to Littauer and Perkins, hoping for an advance from *Collier's*:

> This will be difficult for two reasons. First that there is one fact about my novel, which, if it were known, would be immediately and unscrupulously plagiarized by the George Kaufmans, etc., of this world. Second, that I live always in deadly fear that I will take the edge off an idea for myself by summarizing or talking about it in advance. But, with these limitations, here goes:
> The novel will be fifty thousand words long. As I will have to write sixty thousand words to make room for cutting I have figured it as a four months job – three months for the writing – one month for revision. The thinking, according to my

conscience and the evidence of sixty pages of outline and notes, *has already been done*. I would infinitely rather do it, now that I am well again, than take hack jobs out here.

The Story occurs during four or five months in the year 1935. It is told by Cecelia, the daughter of a producer named Bradogue in Hollywood. Cecelia is a pretty, modern girl neither good nor bad, tremendously human. Her father is also an important character. A shrewd man, a gentile, and a scoundrel of the lowest variety. A self-made man, he has brought up Cecelia to be a princess, sent her East to college, made of her rather a snob, though, in the course of the story, her character evolves *away from this*, That is, she was twenty when the events that she tells occurred, but she is twenty-five when she tells about the events, and of course many of them appear to her in a different light.

Cecelia is the narrator because I think I know exactly how such a person would react to my story. She is *of* the movies but not *in* them. She probably was born the day 'The Birth of a Nation' was previewed and Rudolf Valentino came to her fifth birthday party. So she is, all at once, intelligent, cynical but understanding and kindly toward the people, great or small, who are of Hollywood.

She focuses our attention upon two principal characters – Milton Stahr (who is Irving Thalberg – and *this is my great secret*) and Thalia, the girl he loves. Thalberg has always fascinated me. His peculiar charm, his extraordinary good looks, his bountiful success, the tragic end of his great adventure. The events I have built around him are fiction, but all of them are things which might very well have happened, and I am pretty sure that I saw deep enough into the character of the man so that his reactions are authentically what they would have been in life. So much so that he may be recognized – but it will also be recognized that *no single fact is actually true*. For example, in my story he is unmarried or a widower, leaving out completely any complication with Norma.

In the beginning of the book I want to pour out my whole impression of this man Stahr as he is seen during an airplane trip from New York to the coast – of course, through Cecelia's eyes. She has been hopelessly in love with him for a long time. She is never going to win anything more from him than an affectionate regard, even that tainted by his dislike of her father (parallel the deadly dislike of each other between Thalberg and Louis B. Mayer). Stahr is over-worked and deathly tired, ruling with a radiance that is almost moribund in its phosphorescence. He has been warned that his health is undermined, but being afraid of nothing the warning is unheeded. He has had everything in life except the privilege of giving himself unselfishly to another human being. This he finds on the night of a semi-serious earthquake (like in 1935) a few days after the opening of the story.

It has been a very full day even for Stahr – the bursted water mains, which cover the whole ground space of the lot to the depth of several feet, seems to release something in him. Called over to the outer lot to supervise the salvation of the electrical plant (for like Thalberg, he has a finger in every pie of the vast bakery) he finds two women stranded on the roof of a property farmhouse and goes to their rescue.

Thalia Taylor is a twenty-six year old widow, and my present conception of her should make her the most glamorous and sympathetic of my heroines. Glamorous in a new way because I am in secret agreement with the public in detesting the type of feminine arrogance that has been pushed into prominence in the case of Brenda Frazier, etc. People simply do not sympathize deeply with those who have had *all* the breaks, and I am going to dower this girl, like Rosalba in Thackeray's 'Rose in the Ring' with 'a little misfortune.' She and the woman with her (to whom she is serving as companion) have come secretly on the lot through the other woman's curiosity. They have been caught there when the catastrophe occurred.

Now we have a love affair between Stahr and Thalia, an immediate, dynamic, unusual, physical love affair – and I will write it so that you can publish it. At the same time I will send you a copy of how it will appear in book form somewhat stronger in tone.

This love affair is the meat of the book – though I am going to treat it, remember, as it comes through to Cecelia. That is to say by making Cecelia at the moment of her telling the story, an intelligent and observant woman, I shall grant myself the privilege, as Conrad did, of letting her imagine the actions of the characters. Thus, I hope to get the verisimilitude of a first person narrative, combined with a Godlike knowledge of all events that happen to my characters.

Two events beside the love affair bulk large in the intermediary chapters. There is a definite plot on the part of Bradogue, Cecelia's father, to get Stahr out of the company. He has even actually and factually considered having him murdered. Bradogue is the monopolist at its worst – Stahr, in spite of the inevitable conservatism of the self-made man, is a paternalistic employer. Success came to him young, at twenty-three, and left certain idealisms of his youth unscarred. Moreover, he is a worker. Figuratively he takes off his coat and pitches in, while Bradogue is not interested in the making of pictures save as it will benefit his bank account.

The second incident is how young Cecelia herself, in her desperate love for Stahr, throws herself at his head. In her reaction at his indifference she gives herself to a man whom she does not love. This episode is *not* absolutely necessary to the serial. It could be tempered but it might be best to eliminate it altogether.

Back to the main theme, Stahr cannot bring himself to marry Thalia. It simply doesn't seem part of his life. He doesn't realize that she has become necessary to him. Previously his name has been associated with this or that well-known actress or society personality and Thalia is poor, unfortunate, and tagged with a middle class exterior which doesn't fit in with the grandeur Stahr demands of life. When she realizes this she leaves him temporarily, leaves him not because he has no legal intentions toward her but because of the hurt of it, the remainder of a vanity from which she had considered herself free.

Stahr is now plunged directly into the fight to keep control of the company. His health breaks down very suddenly while he is on a trip to New York to see the stockholders. He almost dies in New York and comes back to find that Bradogue has seized upon his absence to take steps which Stahr considers unthinkable. He plunges back into work again to straighten things out.

Now, realizing how much he needs Thalia, things are patched up between them. For a day or two they are ideally happy. They are going to marry, but he must make one more trip East to clinch the victory which he has conciliated in the affairs of the company.

Now occurs the final episode which should give the novel its quality – and its unusualness. Do you remember about 1933 when a transport plane was wrecked on a mountain-side in the Southwest, and a Senator was killed? The thing that struck me about it was that the country people rifled the bodies of the dead.* That is just what happens to this plane which is bearing Stahr from Hollywood. The angle is that of three children who, on a Sunday picnic, are the first to discover the wreckage. Among those killed in the accident besides Stahr are two other characters we have met. (I have not been able to go into the minor characters in this short summary.) Of the three children, two boys and a girl, who find the bodies, one boy rifled Stahr's possessions; another, the body of a ruined ex-producer; and the girl those of a moving picture actress. The possessions which the children find, symbolically determine their attitude toward their act of theft. The possessions of the moving picture actress tend the young girl to a selfish possessiveness; those of the unsuccessful producer sway one of the boys toward an irresolute attitude; while the boy who finds Stahr's briefcase is the one who, after a week, saves and redeems all three by going to a local judge and making full confession.

The story swings once more back to Hollywood for its finale. During the story *Thalia has never once been inside a studio.* After Stahr's death as she stands in front of the great plant which he created, she realizes now that she never will. She knows only that he loved her and that he was a great man and that he died for what he believed in.

This is a novel – not even faintly of the propoganda type. Indeed, Thalberg's opinions were entirely different from mine in many respects that I will not go into. I've long chosen him for a hero (this has been in my mind for three years) because he is one of the half-dozen men I have known who were built on the grand scale. That it happens to coincide with a period in which the American Jews are somewhat uncertain in their morale, is for me merely a fortuitous coincidence. The racial angle shall scarcely be touched on at all. Certainly if

* On 6 May 1935 a TWA plane crashed at Atlanta, Missouri, killing Senator Bronson M. Cutting. Also aboard the plane were members of a Paramount crew bound for Annapolis. The crash was observed, and the local people aided in rescuing the injured. The wreckage was not plundered.

Ziegfield could be made into an epic figure than what about Thalberg who was literally everything that Ziegfield wasn't?

There's nothing that worries me in the novel, nothing that seems uncertain. Unlike *Tender is the Night* it is not the story of deterioration – it is not depressing and not morbid in spite of the tragic ending. If one book could ever be 'like' another I should say it is more 'like' *The Great Gatsby* than any other of my books. But I hope it will be entirely different – I hope it will be something new, arouse new emotions perhaps even a new way of looking at certain phenomena. I have set it safely in a period of five years ago to obtain detachment, but now that Europe is tumbling about our ears this also seems to be for the best. It is an escape into a lavish, romantic past that perhaps will not come again into our time. It is certainly a novel I would like to read. Shall I write it?

A carbon copy of the last page has Fitzgerald's note 'Orig Sent thru here' after 'Shall I write it?' The rest of the page reads:

As I said, I would rather do this for a minimum price than continue this in-and-out business with the moving pictures where the rewards are great, but the satisfaction unsatisfactory and the income tax always mopping one up after the battle.

The minimum I would need to do this with peace of mind would be $15,000., payable $3000. in advance and $3000. on the first of November, the first of December, the first of January and the first of February, on delivery of the last installment. For this I would guarantee to do no other work, specifically pictures, to make any changes in the manuscript (but not to having them made for me) and to begin to deliver the copy the first of November, that is to give you fifteen thousand words by that date.

Unless these advances are compatible with your economy, Kenneth, the deal would be financially impossible for me under the present line up. Four months of sickness completely stripped me and until your telegram came I had counted on a buildup of many months work here before I could *consider* beginning the novel. Once again a telegram would help tremendously, as I am naturally on my toes and[70]

As Fitzgerald acknowledged, his character Monroe Stahr was inspired by Irving Thalberg, the boy genius of Hollywood who was head of production at Universal when he was twenty and died in 1936 at thirty-seven. In the draft of the inscription for the copy he planned to give Norma Shearer, Thalberg's widow, Fitzgerald wrote:

> Dear Norma:
> You told me you read little because of your eyes but I think this book will interest you – and though the story is purely imaginary perhaps you could see it as an attempt to preserve something of Irving. My own impression shortly recorded but very dazzling in its effect on me, inspired the best part of the character of Stahr – though I have put in some things drawn from of other men and, inevitably, much of myself.
> I invented a tragic story and Irvings life was, of course, not tragic except his struggle against ill health, because no one has ever written a tragedy about Hollywood (a *Star is Born* was a pathetic story and often beautiful story but not a tragedy and doomed and heroic things do happen here.
> With Old Affection and Gratitude[71]

After Norma Shearer Thalberg read *The Last Tycoon* she was reported to have said that Monroe Stahr was not at all like her husband. Her comment is not really a criticism of Fitzgerald's achievement because he had not attempted to write a biographical novel about Irving Thalberg. Stahr is Fitzgerald's response to the heroic aspects of the Thalberg legend into which he projected himself. Although Fitzgerald was inspired by – and even identified with – the myth-making elements of Thalberg's career, he did not know him well. They probably had fewer than half a dozen meetings, the most important of which was the 1927 conversation in the M-G-M commissary during which the young producer gave Fitzgerald the short seminar on decision-making that Fitzgerald wrote into the first chapter of *The Last Tycoon*, when Stahr talks to the uncomprehending pilot (see pp. 259–60 above). Fitzgerald had worked for Thalberg at M-G-M – but not with him – in 1931, and 'Crazy Sunday' was an attempt to build a character only partly on Thalberg. When Thalberg died in 1936 Fitzgerald wrote to Oscar Kalman: 'Talbert's* final collapse is the death of an enemy for me, though I liked the guy enormously. He had an idea that his wife and I were playing around, which was absolute nonsense, but I think even so that he killed the idea of either Hopkins or Frederick Marsh doing "Tender is the Night".'[72] Fitzgerald had made a late-night alcoholic phone call to Thalberg in 1934 offering him the movie rights to *Tender*.†

Fitzgerald believed that Thalberg, the executive with taste and courage, represented the best of Hollywood. He responded to Thalberg's early success – always a stimulating concept for Fitzgerald – and to his efforts to raise the level of the movies. Having gone to Hollywood in 1937 with ambitions of winning elevation to producer or even director status, Fitzgerald saw Thalberg as a model for what could be done in the movies. (Ironically, though, Thalberg had been largely responsible for the team system of script writing, which Fitzgerald hated.) Thalberg's precarious health also helped Fitzgerald to identify with him. In his last months Fitzgerald was a cardiac case writing about a man dying of heart disease.

The elements of Stahr's emotional situation were drawn from Fitzgerald's life. Stahr's dead wife, Minna, was Zelda, and Kathleen Moore, Stahr's last love, was obviously based on Sheilah Graham. Kathleen looks like Sheilah. Both are British; and they share a history as girls who were educated by older men, although Kathleen's past is glamorized by making her the former mistress of a deposed king.

The Thalberg/Stahr figure permitted Fitzgerald to use the ideas about the movie industry that he had developed during his Hollywood years and to combine them with the themes that run through all his fiction. The most obvious is the

---

* Fitzgerald's typist made this error.
† Neither Miriam Hopkins nor Fredric March was under contract to M-G-M at this time, and Fitzgerald's suspicion that Thalberg blocked the movie sale of his novel is unsupported.

essential Fitzgerald concern with aspiration and the rewards of success. Stahr is the last in Fitzgerald's long line of inspired poor boys, and the novel is his most mature meditation on the American Dream.

Fitzgerald's unfinished novel was posthumously published in 1941 as *The Last Tycoon*, but it is not certain that this was his final title. The only surviving title page among the manuscripts reads 'Stahr: A Romance'; there is also Fitzgerald's note for another working title, 'The Love of the Last Tycoon: A Western.'[73] Another possible title was 'The Last of the Tycoons.' Whether or not Fitzgerald would have called his novel *The Last Tycoon*, the title bestowed on it by Edmund Wilson evokes the sense of 'lastness' that permeates it and informs much of Fitzgerald's fiction. He saw both his hero and himself as coming at the end of an American historical process and believed there would be no more Stahrs. A self-reliant leader, Stahr is under attack from the forces of both business and labor.

In his notes for the novel Fitzgerald wrote; 'I am the last of the novelists for a long time now.'[74] Fitzgerald and Stahr share an allegiance to traditional American values and ideals. Sensing that the politics of the Thirties and the impending world war would terminate the romantic reactions to life that had inspired his fiction, Fitzgerald saw himself as the last of a certain kind of novelist writing about the last of the old American heroes. Nurturing a heroic sense of American character, he found his essential American figure in his last novel.

Stahr is a lonely man working himself to death, but he is not an emotional bankrupt. Fitzgerald buttresses him with the language of heroism. The grandness of Stahr's vision is emphasized by the imagery of flight, making him a Daedalian figure and reinforcing his mythic qualities: 'He had flown up very high to see, on strong wings, when he was young. And while he was up there he looked on all the kingdoms, with the kind of eyes that can stare straight into the sun. Beating his wings tenaciously – finally frantically – and keeping on beating them, he had stayed up there longer than most of us, and then, remembering all he had seen from his great height of how things were, he had settled gradually to earth.'[75]

Fitzgerald's achievement in understanding and even identifying with Stahr is remarkable given their utterly different backgrounds: the New York Jew and the Midwestern Irish Catholic; the disciplined executive who consolidated his early achievement and the alcoholic writer who dissipated his success. Yet so thorough was Fitzgerald's identification with his hero that Stahr stands among the most compelling Jewish characters in American fiction. In its fragmentary form *The Last Tycoon* remains the best Hollywood novel. Even though he had the advantage of dealing with a myth-making industry, it is nonetheless strikingly ironic that Fitzgerald created one of the few heroic business figures in our literature – perhaps the most admirable one. Better than Howells, Norris, Dreiser, or O'Hara, Fitzgerald enforces the relationship between character and work. In a note for a projected scene in which Stahr is ordered to quit work by his doctor, Fitzgerald reminded himself: 'The idea fills Stahr with a horror that I must write a big scene to bring off. Such a scene as has never been written. . . . the words of the doctor fill Stahr with a horror that I must be able to convey to the laziest reader – the blow to Stahr and the utter unwillingness to admit that at this point, 35 years old, his body should refuse to serve him and carry on these plans which he has built up like a pyramid of fairy skyscrapers in his imagination.'[76]

58

Debts and
Esquire *Stories*

[1940]

Littauer refused to make an advance without seeing a substantial sample of the novel and asked for the first 15,000 words. If the opening of the novel was sufficiently impressive, *Collier's* would advance Fitzgerald $5,000 with an additional $5,000 for the next 20,000 words against a total price to be negotiated; $20,000 was a talking figure.[77] Fitzgerald was under the impression that *Collier's* was prepared to offer $15,000 (the figure he had suggested in the unsent part of his proposal), which he regarded as 'much too marginal.'[78] He explained to Perkins: 'But (without taking such steps as reneging on my income tax, letting go my life insurance for its surrender value, taking Scottie from college and putting Zelda in a public asylum) I couldn't last four months on that. Certain debts have been run up so that the larger part of the $15,000 has been, so to speak, spent already. A contraction of my own living expenses to the barest minimum, that is to say a room in a boarding house, abandonment of all medical attention (I still see a doctor once a week) would still leave me at the end not merely penniless but even more in debt than I am now.'[79] Perkins thought *Collier's* might go as high as $30,000. Fitzgerald was spoiling

556

the deal over a matter that could not be settled until after he had submitted a section of his novel.

In September, Fitzgerald picked up a week's work on *Raffles* for Samuel Goldwyn. The *Raffles* assignment was supposed to last longer, but Fitzgerald got caught in a disagreement between Goldwyn and director Sam Wood. He expressed in Goldwynese his reaction to working for Goldwyn: 'He liked Sam Goldwyn – you always knew where you stood with Goldwyn – nowhere.'[80]

Fitzgerald earned $21,466.67 (including $4,600 from stories) in 1939, yet in September he had difficulty paying Scottie's $615 tuition for her sophomore year at Vassar. He managed to meet the expense with the help of a $360 loan from Gerald Murphy and $250 from the radio rights to *Gatsby*: YOU CAN REGISTER AT VASSAR STOP IT COST A HEMORRHAGE BUT I RAISED SOME MONEY FROM ESQUIRE AND ARRANGED WITH COMPTROLLER TO PAY OTHER HALF OCTO-BER 15TH IF YOU DON'T PLAY STRAIGHT THIS WILL BE ALL STOP FORGIVE ME IF UNJUSTLY CYNICAL REMEMBER HARMONY MORE PRACTICAL THAN MUSIC HISTORY ALSO OTHER CHANGE STOP RETURN ME FORMER CHECK AIR MAIL LOVE DADDY.[81] Scottie was accustomed to the telegraphic fluctuations between affluence and dire poverty, and was not distressed.

He tried unsuccessfully to get an advance for the novel from Scribners in October. On 2 November Littauer agreed to decide on the basis of a 6,000-word sample. Late in the month Fitzgerald sent both *Collier's* and Perkins the first chapter of the novel – the airplane trip to California which introduces Monroe Stahr. On 28 November Littauer wired: FIRST SIX THOUSAND PRETTY CRYPTIC THEREFORE DISAPPOINTING. BUT YOU WARNED US THIS MIGHT BE SO. CAN WE DEFER VERDICT UNTIL FURTHER DEVELOPMENT OF STORY? IF IT HAS TO BE NOW IT HAS TO BE NO. REGARDS.[82] An hour later Fitzgerald replied to Littauer: NO HARD FEELINGS THERE HAS NEVER BEEN AN EDITOR WITH PANTS ON SINCE GEORGE LORIMER.[83]

That afternoon he wired Perkins to offer the serial rights to the *Post*; but the magazine was not interested because the material seemed too strong for its readership. Realizing how disappointed Fitzgerald would be by Littauer's rejection, Perkins wired Fitzgerald on the twenty-ninth: 'A beautiful start. Stirring and new. Can wire you two hundred fifty and a thousand by January.'[84] Perkins was not acting for Scribners; he was making a personal loan. Fitzgerald also wired Perkins on the twenty-ninth to explore with agent Leland Hayward the scheme of getting a studio to finance the novel in return for the movie rights – a reversal of his earlier position that the novel be kept a secret from Hollywood. Hayward told Perkins that he could do nothing until the novel was written. In December, Fitzgerald sent Perkins some of the second chapter, but there were no further progress reports until the end of 1940. Despite his refusal to make a commitment, Littauer did not abandon interest in the novel. *Collier's* editor Max Wilkinson came to see Fitzgerald in December 1939, when Fitzgerald was drunk and abusive. Late in 1940 Littauer discussed the novel with Fitzgerald in California.

Littauer's refusal to commit *Collier's* to the novel triggered an extended Fitzgerald bender in November 1939. His drinking aggravated his tuberculosis, and Fitzgerald reported lung hemorrhages to Zelda. Sheilah was never sure how sober he was during the fall and winter of 1939. One day she arrived at 'Belly Acres' to find Fitzgerald giving his clothes away to a couple of bums he had picked up. When she told them to leave, Fitzgerald hit her and threatened to kill her. Sheilah managed to get away by phoning the police. This time she had had enough and was determined to break off with him permanently. Fitzgerald made things worse by sending her threatening notes and stealing the fox jacket he had given her. After Fitzgerald dried out he began a campaign to win her back, which succeeded in January 1940. Thereafter she never saw him take another drink.

Dissatisfied with his Hollywood agent's handling of his screenwriting career, Fitzgerald switched from Swanson to Leland Hayward and then in February 1940 to the Phil Berg-Bert Allenberg agency; but there were no good job offers. With free time and sobriety he settled down to work on his novel, supporting himself with $250 checks from *Esquire*. Arnold Gingrich was still prepared to take almost anything Fitzgerald offered, but there were a few rejections because Fitzgerald submitted so much material. 'Design in Plaster' appeared in the November 1939 issue, followed by 'The Lost Decade' in December. 'Design in Plaster,' an unexceptional story about marital infidelity for which Fitzgerald drew upon his 1936 experience in a cast, was selected by Edward J. O'Brien for *The Best Short Stories* 1940. It did not deserve this recognition, but the inclusion indicated that Fitzgerald was not forgotten as a short-story writer. In January *Esquire* published 'Pat Hobby's Christmas Wish,' the first of seventeen Hobby stories. From November 1939 to July 1941 (seven months after his death) there was a Fitzgerald story in each issue of *Esquire*. As his stories accumulated at the magazine, Fitzgerald proposed to Gingrich the idea of publishing some of them under a pseudonym. 'I'm awfully tired of being Scott Fitzgerald anyhow, as there doesn't seem to be so much money in it, and I'd like to find out if people read me just because I am Scott Fitzgerald or, what is more likely, don't read me for the same reason.'[85] One *Esquire* story, 'On an Ocean Wave,' appeared after Fitzgerald's death under the byline Paul Elgin in February 1941.

When Zelda suggested that he resume writing for the *Post* in 1940, Fitzgerald admitted that it was now impossible for him:

> As you should know from your own attempts, high priced commercial writing for the magazines is a very definite trick. The rather special things that I brought to it, the intelligence and the good writing and even the radicalism all appealed to old Lorimer who had been a writer himself and liked style. The man who runs the magazine now [Wesley W. Stout] is an up and coming young Republican who gives not a damn about literature and who publishes almost nothing except escape stories about the brave frontiersmen, etc., or fishing, or football captains, nothing that would even faintly shock or

disturb the reactionary bourgeois. Well, I simply can't do it and as I say, I've tried not once but twenty times.

As soon as I feel I am writing to a cheap specification my pen freezes and my talent vanishes over the hill and I honestly don't blame them for not taking the things that I've offered to them from time to time in the past three or four years. An explanation of their new attitude is that you no longer have a chance of selling a story with an unhappy ending (in the old days many of mine *did* have unhappy endings – if you remember).[86]

This explanation is partly a rationalization. While it is true that Stout's taste differed from Lorimer's, the basic problem for Fitzgerald was not material but form or construction. As he observed in his *Notebooks*, 'In a short story, you have only so much money to buy just one costume. Not the parts of many. One mistake in the shoes or tie, and you're gone.'[87] All his published fiction after 1939 was in the short-short-story form, in which he could still develop a mood or portray a character effectively. 'The Lost Decade' is brilliantly written, but it is only 1,100 words. A once-famous architect, who had been drunk for ten years, spends an afternoon in New York; now sober, he tries to reassimilate the texture of reality: 'I simply want to see how people walk and what their clothes and shoes and hats are made of. And their eyes and hands.'[88] Nothing happens in terms of plot, but the image of a man trying to recover the impressions and rhythms of a decade has haunted readers.

Since his story work during the last year of his life included the Pat Hobby series, Fitzgerald has sometimes been incorrectly identified with this character. Pat Hobby is not a self-portrait of Fitzgerald in Hollywood. An illiterate ex-gag writer, Pat Hobby survives through petty dishonesty. When Frances Kroll's brother Nathan attempted to dramatize the Hobby stories, Fitzgerald explained that 'the series is characterized by a really bitter humor and only the explosive situations and the fact that Pat is a figure almost incapable of real tragedy or damage saves it from downright unpleasantness.'[89] Most of the Hobby stories are manipulations of a series character who lurches from disgrace to humiliation; only two, 'A Patriotic Short' and 'Two Old-Timers,' generate sympathy for Pat. Nevertheless, Fitzgerald put considerable effort into these stories, revising them and juggling the order of publication.[90] Since he wrote them while he was working on *The Last Tycoon*, he was careful not to use anything that might be novel material. A possible personal link between Fitzgerald and Pat Hobby is that the character's grotesque adventures in Hollywood provided a kind of therapy for the author and purged the bitterness that might otherwise have found its way into the novel. The most important contribution of the Hobby stories to the novel is that they earned $4,500 worth of writing time. (In 1940 Fitzgerald persuaded Gingrich to raise the price of the Hobby stories to $300.)

Fitzgerald wrote a strong Hollywood story outside of the Hobby series, 'Last Kiss,' which was declined by *Collier's* and *Cosmopolitan* and remained unpublished until 1949.* 'Last Kiss' shares the novel's mood of loss, and the heroine – like Kathleen – was drawn from Sheilah Graham. An English actress is befriended by a young producer, but her uncooperative conduct destroys her chances. After her death from pneumonia she comes to him for a goodnight kiss: 'Then sleep, he thought, as he turned away – sleep. I couldn't fix it. I tried to fix it. When you brought your beauty here I didn't want to throw it away, but I did somehow. There is nothing left for you now but sleep.'[91] Fitzgerald regarded 'Last Kiss' as 'unpleasant as hell'[92] and stripped it for his *Notebooks*. Another Hollywood story, 'Director's Special,' was salvaged by *Harper's Bazaar* as 'Discard' in 1948. 'Dearly Beloved,' a brilliantly written sketch, was rejected by *Esquire* and rescued in 1969. This 850-word piece is the only story in which Fitzgerald seriously treated a black character. The hero, a Pullman porter, has obvious connections with the philosophical black fisherman in *The Last Tycoon*.

---

* When *Collier's* published 'Last Kiss' in 1949, it paid $1,800 plus a $1,000 bonus for the best story in the issue.

59

Writing The Last Tycoon

[1940]

Since *Fitzgerald expected* to interrupt the novel for movie work, he needed a detailed plan that would permit him to break off work without losing control of his material. Five outline plans survive, all of which project a *Gatsby*-length novel of some 50,000 words. In the latest plan the story is divided into nine chapters (*Gatsby* also had nine chapters) of thirty episodes, with a five-act structure.

It is impossible to gauge the extent to which screenwriting influenced or even damaged Fitzgerald's structural powers in his fiction. The manuscripts show that he wrote the novel in sequences, like a screenplay; after the first chapter there are no complete chapters – only scenes or episodes that were to be fused into chapters during the rewrites. His material expanded as he wrote. Though he invented no new episodes, the projected episodes required more words than he had allotted. Fitzgerald had too much story for 50,000 words.

The Last Tycoon is thought of as two-thirds finished, but Fitzgerald progressed only a little more than halfway through his outline plan and a great deal of the plot was left undeveloped. At his death he had reached the beginning of Chapter 6 (episode 17) and had written 44,000 words for his latest – but not final – draft. Because little of this material

Episodes		
A 1. The plane June 28 2. Nashville 3. Up Forward. Different 6000	Chapter (A) Introduce Cecelia, Stahr, White, Schwartze.	Act I June (THE PLANE) 6000 STAHR
B 4. Johnny Swanson--Marcus leaving --Brady July 28th. 5. The Earthquake 6. The Back lot 3000	Chapter (B) Introduces Brady, Kathleen, Robinson and secretaries. Atmos- phere of night-sustain	Act II (THE CIRCUS July--early August 21,000
C 7. The Camera man. July 29 Stahr's work and health. From something she wrote 8. First Conference 9. Second conference and afterwards. 10. Commissary and Idealism about non- profit pictures. Rushes Phone call, etc. 5000	Chapters (C) & (D) are equal to guest list and Gatsby's party. Throw everything into this, with selection. They must have a plot, though, leading to 13	
D 11. Visit to rushes. 12. Second Meeting that night. Wrong girl--glimpse 2500		STAHR AND KATHLEEN
E 13. Cecelia and Stahr and Ball - Aug. 6th Football game. Cecelia and Wylie and Maude. 14. Malibu seduction. Try to get on lot. DEAD MIDDLE 15. Cecelia and father 16. Phone call & Wedding. 6000	Chapter (E) Three episodes Atmosphere in 15 most important. Hint of Waste Land of the house too late.	
F 17. The Dawn breaks with Brimmer 18. The Cummerbund - market-- (The theatre with Benchley) August 10th 19. The four meet. like Hop and Lefty. Renewal. Palomar 20. Wylie White in Office August 28th-Sept. 14th.	Chapter (F) This belongs to the women. It introduces Smith (for the 1st time?)	Act III Aug-early Sept. (The Underworld) 11,500 THE STRUGGLE
G 21. Sick in Washington. To quit? 22. Brady and Stahr--double blackmail. Quarrel with Wylie. 23. Throws over Cecelia who tells her father. Stops making pictures. A story conference--rushes and sets. Lies low after Cut. 24. Last fling with Kathleen. Old stars in heat wave at Encino. 6500	Chapter (G) The blows fall on Stahr. Sense of heat all through, culmina- ting in 25.	
H 25. Brady gets to Smith. Fleishacker and Cecelia. (S.G.&K) Sept. 15-30th. 26. Stahr hears plan. Camera man O.K. Stops it--very sick. 27. Resolve problem. Thalia at airport. Cecelia to college; Thalia at airport. S.G. 7000	Chapter (H). The suit and the price.	Act IV September (The Murderers) 7000 DEFEAT
I 28. The Plane falls. Fortaste of the future in Fleishacker Sept 30th-Oct. 29. Outside the studio. S.G. 30. Johnny Swanson at funeral 4500	Chapter (I) Stahr's death.	Act V October (The End) 4500 EPILOGUE
WRITTEN FOR TWO PEOPLE - FOR SF AT 17 AND FOR EW AT 45 - IT MUST PLEASE THEM BOTH		51,000

Latest outline from *The Last Tycoon*

seems expendable, *The Last Tycoon* might well have been almost twice as long as projected, while still conforming to the nine-chapter plan.

The outlines and notes show that Fitzgerald was planning to develop a blackmail-murder plot in the second half of the novel. Stahr's partner Brady (Bradogue) would blackmail him by threatening to inform Kathleen's husband after Kathleen and Stahr resume their affair; and Stahr would retaliate with information he has about Brady. After discovering that Brady intends to have him killed, Stahr would arrange for his murder while Stahr is away from Hollywood. On the plane Stahr would reject the plan because it debases him and decide to call off the murder from the next airport. But the plane would crash, killing Stahr.* These events are not mentioned in the plot summary Fitzgerald sent Littauer – nor is the complication of Kathleen's marriage.

Fitzgerald's early idea for the conclusion was to have the plane wreckage plundered by children whose characters would be shaped by the possessions they take. This ending appears to have been rejected or modified in favor of an account of Stahr's funeral, employing the final irony that a has-been actor, who is mistakenly asked to be a pallbearer, enjoys a restoration on the basis of his supposed friendship with Stahr.

Fitzgerald did not try to push through to a complete working draft. Instead, he rewrote each episode through several layers. Frances Kroll recalls the writing as a process of accretion:

> Fitzgerald's work patterns on TYCOON started with notes; then the sorting of notes into chapters; then brief biographies of the characters; then chapter outlines and finally roughly written chapters.
> He wrote everything out in longhand. He used the morning and some early noon hours for work. He was not much of a

---

* See Bruccoli, *'The Last of the Novelists': F. Scott Fitzgerald and the Last Tycoon*, for a study of the manuscripts.

sleeper, so during these fitful times, he made notes which would be on my table when I came to work.

He never dictated the novel, but did considerable revision from typescripts. He also switched chapter notes if they didn't work out in the designated chapters and assigned them to other chapters in the book.

That was basically the pattern without going into too much detail. Of course, all of this was not a continuous process. Work on the chapter notes and outlines were interrupted many times before they were completed and before the actual writing began.[93]

Fitzgerald polished the dialogue endlessly, reading it aloud to improve the speeches. When he felt stuck, he had his secretary read the Bible to him – not for divine inspiration, but because he admired the rhythms of the King James version.

Revising the typescripts through as many as four or five stages of typing, he accumulated some 1,100 pages of drafts for the seventeen episodes and more than 200 pages of notes and background material. None of the episodes was regarded as final. Even the completed opening chapter was marked 'Rewrite from mood. Has become stilted with rewriting. Don't look rewrite from mood.'[94] Fitzgerald was probably never entirely satisfied with his treatment of Kathleen and reminded himself in a note: 'Where will the warmth come from in this. Why does he think she's warm. Warmer than the voice in Farewell. My girls were all so warm and full of promise. The sea at night. What can I do to make it honest and different?'[95]

Some critics have concluded from the evidence of the manuscripts that Fitzgerald had lost his ability to hold a novel in his head while working on parts of it, and even that he had lost confidence in his capacity to write an extended work of fiction. Nevertheless, the drafts indicate that Fitzgerald was proceeding carefully without concern for a deadline. After the *Collier's* serial deal fell through, he wrote to satisfy his own standards. The pressure he felt was to produce a novel that would redeem him from neglect and reestablish him at the top of his profession. Despite all the revisions, he made steady progress in 1940, with time off for *Esquire* pieces and two movie jobs.

As Fitzgerald noted in his proposal for *Collier's*, *The Last Tycoon* was intended to be 'more "like" *The Great Gatsby* than any of my other books.' The resemblance was in form, not in content. The Hollywood novel was planned as a short, dramatic work like *Gatsby*. As with Jay Gatsby, Fitzgerald had to make the romantic figure Monroe Stahr a convincing character. Again he solved the problem by using another character in the novel to certify the action. In *The Last Tycoon* the narrator is Cecelia Brady,* the daughter of Stahr's treacherous partner. (Fitzgerald told Budd Schulberg that Cecelia was a combination of Scottie and Schulberg.†) Fitzgerald had explained the narrative rationale to Littauer: 'I hope to get the verisimilitude of a first person narrative, combined with a Godlike knowledge of all events that happen to my characters.' Cecelia's background qualifies her for this role. As a Hollywood insider she approaches the industry with clear eyes, and she is in love with Stahr. But Cecelia is not as effective a narrator as Nick Carraway in *Gatsby* because she is required to imagine too much. The scope of Stahr's activities is too great to be observed by Cecelia, and she does not document all of the narrative. The love scenes between Stahr and Kathleen – which Cecelia cannot witness or really imagine – are narrated by the author. Twice Fitzgerald was compelled to insert clumsy transitions (which may have been intended as notes to himself): 'This is Cecelia taking up the narrative in person'; 'This is Cecelia taking up the story.'[96] It is possible, of course, that Fitzgerald would have modified the narrative framework. There is a

* This character was named for Fitzgerald's cousin Cecilia Delihant Taylor, but he consistently spelled her name 'Cecelia' in the manuscripts.
† While Fitzgerald was writing *The Last Tycoon* Schulberg completed his own Hollywood novel, *What Makes Sammy Run?* Fitzgerald wrote publisher Bennett Cerf an admiring letter about it on 13 December 1940, which was used on the dust jacket.

discarded opening in which Cecelia tells the story to a narrator who reports it to the reader – a double-narrator effect.

John O'Hara's friendship with Fitzgerald was renewed in Hollywood, although they did not spend much time together. O'Hara had never altered his high opinion of Fitzgerald's work, which was later summed up in a statement to John Steinbeck: 'Fitzgerald was a better just plain writer than all of us put together. Just words writing.'[97] O'Hara provides a curious view of the Hollywood sexual stratification: 'But Scott had a personal cockiness that in the present fashion would be said to mask his basic insecurity. I don't believe that theory, at least as it applied to him. He told me about two movie stars that he wanted me to invite to a party Belle and I gave for him, implying that he had laid both of them. Well, he had laid one of them, but not the other, and the one he had laid he had laid in her dressing-room but not at home. He did not have a real affair with her.'[98] This report raises the question whether Fitzgerald was faithful to Sheilah; but there is no other evidence to support O'Hara's testimony.

When the O'Haras came to lunch at 'Belly Acres,' probably late in 1939, Fitzgerald allowed him to read the work-in-progress on his novel.

He was terribly nervous, disappearing for five and ten minutes at a time, once to get a plaid tie to give my wife because she was wearing a Glen plaid suit. Once to get a volume of Thackeray because I'd never read Thackeray, another time to get some tome about Julius Caesar which he assured me was scholarly but readable – but which he knew I would never read. Then we went out and took some pictures,* and when we finished that he suddenly said, 'Would you like to read what I've written, but first promise you won't tell anyone about it. Don't tell them anything. Don't tell them what it's about, or anything about the people. I'd like it better if you didn't even tell anyone

---

* These snapshots taken by Belle O'Hara may have been the last photos taken of Fitzgerald. He looks obviously unwell.

Fitzgerald and John O'Hara at 'Belly Acres'

PHOTOGRAPH BY BELLE O'HARA

I'm writing another novel.' So we went back to the house and I read what he had written. He saw that I was comfortable, with pillows, cigarettes, ashtrays, a coke. And sat there tortured, trying to be casual, but unhappy because he did not know that my dead pan was partly due to my being an extremely slow reader of good writing, and partly because this *was* such good writing that I was reading. When I had read it I said, 'Scott, don't take any more movie jobs until you've finished this. You work so slowly and this is so good, you've got to finish it. It's real Fitzgerald.' Then, of course, he became blasphemous and abusive, and asked me if I wanted to fight. I saw him a few times after that day, and once when I asked him how the book was coming he only said, 'You've kept your promise? You haven't spoken to anyone about it?'[99]

Sheilah's syndicate sent her on a speaking tour in November 1939. Fitzgerald reworked her anecdotal talk, making the serious point that the directors were the most important figures in the moviemaking system. After her Kansas City appearance a front-page editorial by publisher W. R. Wilkerson in the *Hollywood Reporter*, a movie trade paper, denounced Sheilah for disloyalty to the industry – objecting to her choice of anecdotes about movie stars.[100] Fitzgerald decided to force a retraction and asked O'Hara to accompany him when he went to the paper to beat up Wilkerson. O'Hara tried to talk him out of it, explaining that it was always a bad idea to hit a newspaperman: 'If you insist on going, I'll go with you, but I don't want you to go and I don't want to go with you.' 'That's all I wanted to know,' Fitzgerald said. 'I thought you were my one real friend in this town. I'll get Eddie [Mayer]. He's diabetic and doesn't get into fights, but he's a gentleman.'[101] Fitzgerald did not try to enlist Mayer's support, but went alone to the paper's office on Sunset Boulevard and demanded to see Wilkerson. A secretary stalled him, and he left after an hour of waiting. O'Hara never heard from Fitzgerald again.

60

Endings

[1940]

During 1939 and 1940 Fitzgerald engaged in a bitter and reproachful correspondence with the Sayres and Zelda over the question of her release from Highland. Mrs. Sayre and Zelda's sisters wanted her to live in Montgomery. Fitzgerald tried to arrange with Dr. Carroll for Zelda to have three or four months of furlough a year in the company of a nurse; but the Sayres objected to the nurse provision, and in any case he could not afford a full-time nurse after 1938. He insisted that Dr. Carroll was opposed to Zelda's release and would not take her back at Highland if she left against his advice. Zelda added to the epistolary pressure on Fitzgerald. After he asked her to 'leave me in peace with my hemorrhages and my hopes,'[102] Zelda wrote him in the fall of 1939: '. . . short of your paranoiacal self-defensive reflex I cant see any legitimization of keeping me under hospitalization much longer. . . . There is every reason to believe that I am more able to observe the social dictats than yourself – on the evidence of our "vacations" from the hospital – which have been to date a dread affair of doctors and drink and confirmation of the impossibility of any equitable reunion. Although you know this – and that the probabilities are much against our ever having any life to-gether again – you are persistent in not letting me have a chance to exist alone – at least in comfort – in Alabama and make my own orientation.

Or even in Ashville. I *might* be able to get a job. . . . '[103]

Fitzgerald was outraged that she was inclining toward Rosalind Smith's conviction that he was keeping Zelda confined to absolve himself of the blame for her collapse. He told Zelda that he would accede to her release only if they were divorced, so that he would not be responsible for her. Probably late in 1939, during the period of heavy drinking that followed the collapse of the *Collier's* serial deal, he drafted a nine-page vituperative letter which was not mailed:

> That a fifty dollar ticket to Montgomery would in some way purchase your eternal mental health is a proposition I will not debate. I wont even debate it with Dr Carrol – if he says it will, then Godspeed you. I should think that before Christmas – if I can get some peace – you could go south (to Montgomery) for a long trip *with* supervision. But the other story is too dreary – what would you do – because if you did go on your own I would fold up completely – for paints or amusements or clothes? Scottie would have to work + not be able to send you much for some time. Id lie very quietly in my grave out here but I think the spectre of you walking the streets of Montgomery in rags as the last of the Sayres, followed by curious urchins, would haunt me.
>
> . . . .
>
> Do you think she [Mrs. Sayre] cares or ever has cared about you or your impersonal interest? Do you think she would ever quarrel with you for your impersonal good? She constructed herself on a heroic romantic model as a girl and you were to be the stuffed dummy – true or false, screwed or chaste, honest or bogus – on which she was to satisfy her egotism. She chose me – and she did – and you submitted at the moment of our marriage when your passion for me was at as low ebb as mine for you – because she thought romanticly that her projection of herself in you could best be shown thru me. I never wanted the Zelda I married. I didn't love you again till after you became pregnant. You – thinking I slept with that Bankhead – making all your drunks innocent + mine calculated till even *Town Topics* protested. I'd been drunk, sure – but find any record of me as a drunk at Princeton – or in the army, except

one night when I retired to the locker room. You were the drunk – at *seventeen*, before I knew you – already notorious.

This is the very questionable element I bought and your mother asks to be given back – for some vague reason known fully in the depths of your family psycholoay. The assumption is that you were a great prize package – by your own admission many years after (and for which I have [never] reproached you) you had been seduced and provincially outcast. I sensed this the night we slept together first for you're a poor bluffer and I loved you – romantically – like your mother, for your beauty + defiant intelligence; but unlike her I wanted to make it useful. I failed, as she did, but my intentions were a hell of a lot purer and since you could have left me at any time I'd like to discover the faintest basis for your family's accusation that I drove you crazy. In so far as it was the conscious work of man, that old witch drove you crazy. You were 'crazy' in the ordinary sense before I met you. I rationalized your eccentricities and made a sort of creation of you. But dont fret – if it hadn't been you perhaps I would have worked with more stable material. My talent and my decline is the norm. Your degeneracy is the deviation[104]

In March 1940 Dr. Carroll informed Fitzgerald that Zelda was to be released from Highland. It is unclear whether Dr. Carroll was reversing himself or whether Fitzgerald had exaggerated the hospital's position in 1939. Fitzgerald was pleased by this development – happy for Zelda's sake and relieved to be freed from the burden of the Highland bills, on which he had fallen behind. The only stipulation he made was that there be provision for readmitting Zelda to Highland. Zelda was discharged in April 1940 and went to live with her mother in Montgomery. At Fitzgerald's insistence Dr. Carroll provided a letter absolving him of responsibility in the event of Zelda's relapse.

This is to certify that Mrs. Zelda Fitzgerald entered Highland Hospital April 8th, 1936, bringing a history of many months of acute disturbance. At the time of her admission she was entirely irresponsible, highly excitable, and had just emerged from a three months period of intense suicidal mania, at which time she was successfully protected at Sheppard Pratt Hospital, Baltimore, Md.

Mr. Fitzgerald made provision for every helpful treatment and through the months Mrs. Fitzgerald has gradually improved to the point that we are now cooperating with the husband in paroling her in the care of her family in Montgomery where she will live in her mother's home and carry out, we trust, a simple regime of normal living.

Mrs. Fitzgerald's history shows a definite cyclic tendency and we must look forward with apprehension to her inability to meet emotional situations, to face infections, or to indulge in alcohol, tobacco or drugs without a rapid return to her maniacal irresponsibility. Let it be known that Mrs. Fitzgerald is capable of being absolutely irresponsible and intensely suicidal. Her present condition, however, is one of gentleness, reasonable capacity for cooperation and yet with definitely reduced judgment maturity.[105]

Fitzgerald sent Zelda an allowance of $30 a week but made it clear that he was not prepared to bring her to California.

Brooding about his obscurity and the desertion of his literary friends, Fitzgerald wrote Perkins on 20 May 1940: 'Once I believed in friendship, believed that I *could* (if I didn't always) make people happy and it was more fun than anything. Now even that seems like a vaudevillian's cheap dream of heaven, a vast minstrel show in which one is the perpetual Bones.'[106] This rumination was prompted by John Peale Bishop's 1937 article 'The Missing All,'[107] which Fitzgerald read as a charge that he had been a 'suck around the rich.' Fitzgerald commented to Wilson, 'Maybe it's conscience – nobody ever sold himself for as little gold as he did.' In a postscript Fitzgerald added, 'This sounds like such a bitter letter – I'd rewrite it except for a horrible paucity of time. Not even time to be bitter.'[108]

Again in May 1940 Fitzgerald asked Perkins about the possibility of making his work available for a new reading generation: 'Professionally, I know the next move must come from me. Would the 25 cent press keep *Gatsby* in the public eye – or *is the book unpopular*. Has it *had* its chance? Would a popular

573

reissue in that series with a preface *not* by me but by one of its admirers – I can maybe pick one – make it a favorite with class rooms, profs, lovers of English prose – anybody. But to die, so completely and unjustly after having given so much. Even now there is little published in American fiction that doesn't slightly have my stamp – in a *small* way I was an original.'[109]

Fitzgerald was hoping to complete his novel by the end of 1940 – with time off for movie jobs. In February he had tried to interest Edwin Knopf at M-G-M in a Civil War movie idea based on his stories 'The Night of Chancellorsville' and 'The End of Hate.'[110] Probably around this time, he wrote an original movie scenario called 'Love Is a Pain,' about an American girl who returns from Europe with a secret weapon hidden in her trunk by foreign agents.[111]

Independent producer Lester Cowan bought the movie rights to 'Babylon Revisited' for $1,000 in March and hired Fitzgerald to write the screenplay for $500 a week, which brought him another $5,000. Cowan, who had made *My Little Chickadee* with W.C. Fields and Mae West, intended to produce 'Babylon Revisited' with the Columbia studios. The price for the story was low, and the weekly salary was less than half Fitzgerald's studio rate; but he was to receive a bonus if the movie was made. Fitzgerald needed the money and enjoyed working on one of his best stories at home without interference. At first he was suspicious of Cowan, but they settled down to a comfortable working relationship because Fitzgerald felt that Cowan respected him. Despite the bargain-rate salary, Fitzgerald put his best efforts into the assignment. When he completed his second draft for 'Cosmopolitan,' as the screenplay was titled, in August 1940, he included this 'Author's Note':

> This is an attempt to tell a story from a child's point of view *without* sentimentality. Any attempt to heighten the sentiment of the early scenes by putting mawkish speeches into the mouth of characters – in short by doing what is locally known as 'milking it,' will damage the *force* of the piece. Had the

present author intended, he could have broken down the sentimental section of the audience at many points, but the price would have been *the release of the audience too quickly from tension* – and one would wonder at the end where the idea had vanished – or indeed what idea had been purchased. So whoever deals with this script is implored to remember that it is *a dramatic piece* – not a homey family story. Above all things, Victoria is a *child* – not Daddy's little helper who knows all the answers.

Another point: in the ordinary sense, this picture has no more moral than 'Rebecca' or 'The Shop Around the Corner' – though one can draw from it any moral one wishes about the life of the Wall Street rich of a decade ago. It had better follow the example of 'Hamlet,' which has had a hundred morals read into it, all of them different – let it stand on its own bottom.

Finally – the author wishes to acknowledge the valuable help of Lester Cowan in keeping the line straight and giving many valuable suggestions.[112]

The movie was never made from Fitzgerald's screenplay. Cowan later sold the rights to 'Babylon Revisited' to M-G-M for a reported $40,000, and it was made as *The Last Time I Saw Paris* (1954) from a new screenplay by Philip G. Epstein, Julius J. Epstein, and Richard Brooks.

'Cosmopolitan' has the reputation of being Fitzgerald's best screenplay. It is not a close adaptation of 'Babylon Revisited,' for Fitzgerald invented a new plot which greatly enlarged the role of the child, Honoria. (In the screenplay the name of the child was changed to Victoria, in honor of Budd Schulberg's baby daughter. When Victoria Schulberg was born, Fitzgerald gave her father a telephone lecture on the responsibilities of raising a daughter.) The expansion of the child's part in the movie may have been required by the decision to seek Shirley Temple for the role; however, it is not clear whether the movie was regarded as a Temple vehicle from its inception. In July, Fitzgerald discussed the screenplay with Shirley Temple and her mother. Cowan and Mrs. Temple were unable to agree on terms, and the project was shelved.

In 'Cosmopolitan,' Charles Wales, a brilliant Wall Street speculator, decides to get out of the market in October 1929 because his wife's nerves have broken under the strain of his work. He is taking his wife and daughter to Europe for a long vacation. The market crashes while they are aboard ship, and Wales spends a day trying to save a friend's investments by cable. Feeling that the ticker tape will always dominate their lives, his wife jumps overboard. Wales has a nervous breakdown in Paris and turns Victoria over to his sister-in-law, who hates him. Wales's crooked partner bribes a French doctor to keep him drugged so that the firm can use Wales's money. With the help of an American nurse Wales escapes from Paris and goes to Switzerland to seek financial backing. Victoria follows him. Also in Switzerland is a killer hired by Wales's partner to murder him for the million-dollar insurance policy the firm had taken out on Wales. At the moment when the killer is about to shoot him, the phone rings. The murderer is distracted and Wales knocks him out. The call, of course, is from Victoria. In the last line of the screenplay Wales says, 'Ah, there's a lot to live for.'[113]

The technical device for the movie was the use of Victoria as a camera eye, shooting as many takes as possible from her point of view and even from her level up at the adults. 'Cosmopolitan' has been admired as a job of screenwriting, but it loses most of the values of Fitzgerald's short story. The scenes of Wales's rueful return to Paris are gone. Indeed, the idea of Babylon revisited is absent from the screenplay, because the events that cause the death of Wales's wife and the loss of his child occur before he arrives in Paris. Fitzgerald felt compelled to invent a new plot in order to provide action for the camera. 'Cosmopolitan' again demonstrates that he approached movies as a genre that required standards different from those of literature. When he wrote a movie, he tried to think in terms of Hollywood taste – with which he was never comfortable.

At the end of May 1940 Fitzgerald gave up the Encino house to get away from the summer heat of the San Fernando Valley and moved to an apartment at 1403 North Laurel Avenue in Hollywood, a block from Sheilah's apartment at 1443 North Hayworth Avenue. He described it as the least expensive apartment he could live in without looking poor; the rent was $110 per month.

Scottie attended the Harvard Summer School in 1940. She did not come to California because of the August wedding of her college roommate in Lake Forest, Illinois, which elicited her father's recollection: 'Once I thought that Lake Forest was the most glamorous place in the world. Maybe it was.'[114] The relationship between father and daughter became slightly more relaxed after her sophomore year. Fitzgerald acknowledged that she had earned more freedom and gradually stopped trying to interpose himself in her Vassar life. Except when she overspent her allowance, his scolding missives were replaced by letters according her partnership in family concerns. When she failed to write, he no longer threatened to dock her allowance; instead, he employed humor: 'I remember once a long time ago I had a daughter who used to write me letters but now I don't know where she is or what she is doing, so I sit here listening to Puccini "Someday she'll write (*Pigliano edda ciano*)".'[115] He continued to offer her advice, drawing lessons from his own self-indulgence as in this June 1940 admission: 'What little I've accomplished has been by the most laborious and uphill work, and I wish now I'd *never* relaxed or looked back – but said at the end of *The Great Gatsby*: I've found my line – from now on this comes first. This is my immediate duty – without this I am nothing.'[116]

Fitzgerald's last screenwriting assignment came when Twentieth Century-Fox hired him to prepare a screenplay from *The Light of Heart*, Emlyn Williams's play about an alcoholic actor. This job paid $1,000 per week from 26 August to 15 October. He submitted three drafts, but his version was rejected as too gloomy. The assignment was turned over to Nunnally Johnson – whom Fitzgerald had tried to save from Hollywood corruption in 1938. At Fox he was also involved in a story conference for *Everything Happens at Night*, a Sonja Henie vehicle, and may have worked briefly on 'Brooklyn Bridge,' a proposed movie about the building of the bridge.

Trying to finance working time on his novel, he prepared 'A Sept 1st Schedule at the end of My 44th Year 1940':

Sept 1st–22nd Sure job
   ''   22nd–Oct 20th Possible job (to save $2000)
Three days planning novel
Write on it to Dec 1st possible *finishing* 1st draft
Alternate   Feather Fan if job is not extended.

Or play or Phillipe. *Not* another story – no more stories.
Radio one-act plays.[117]

This memo includes the note that his nightly sleeping medication was one and a half grains of Seconal and one and a half to two and a half grains of Nembutal or one and a half grains of Seconal and five grains of Barbitol. Dr. William Ober has noted that 'the combination of alcohol and barbituates is dangerous. Both act as cortical depressants, and the effect is additive.'[118]

Through the fall of 1940 Fitzgerald reported on the progress of his novel in his weekly letters to Zelda: 'I expect to be back on my novel any day and this time to finish a two months' job' (11 October); 'I'm trying desperately to finish my novel by the middle of December and it's a little like working on "Tender is the Night" at the end – I think of nothing else. . . . My room is covered with charts like it used to be for "Tender is the Night" telling the different movements of the characters and their histories' (19 October); 'I am deep in the novel, living in it, and it makes me happy. It is a *constructed* novel like *Gatsby*, with passages of poetic prose when it fits the action, but no ruminations or sideshows like *Tender*. Everything must contribute to the dramatic movement. . . . Two thousand words today and all good' (23 October); 'The novel is hard as pulling teeth but that is because it is in its early character-planting phase. I feel people so less intently than I did once that this is harder. It means welding together hundreds of stray impressions and incidents to form the fabric of entire personalities' (2 November); 'It will, at any rate, be nothing like anything else as

Endings [1940]

I'm digging it out of myself like uranium – one ounce to the cubic ton of rejected ideas. It is a novel *a la Flaubert* without "ideas" but only people moved singly and in mass through what I hope are authentic moods' (23 November).[119]

While he was writing *The Last Tycoon*, Fitzgerald assessed the struggle to recoup his standing in American literature: 'I want to write scenes that are frightening and inimitable. I don't want to be as intelligible to my contemporaries as Ernest who as Gertrude Stein said, is bound for the Museums. I am sure that I am far enough ahead to have some small immortality if I can keep well.'[120] At the end of 1940 Fitzgerald was ruefully aware of Hemingway's great success with *For Whom the Bell Tolls*, which sold more than 270,000 copies in its first year. The young writer Fitzgerald had encouraged in 1925 was now America's foremost living literary figure. Hemingway sent him a copy of the novel inscribed 'To Scott with affection and esteem Ernest.'[121] Although Fitzgerald regarded *For Whom the Bell Tolls* as 'a thoroughly superficial book which has all the profundity of Rebecca,'[122] he responded with a warmly complimentary letter on 8 November: 'Congratulations too on your new book's great success. I envy you like hell and there is no irony in this. I always liked Dostoiefski with his wide appeal more than any other European – and I envy you the time to do what you want.'[123] Fitzgerald's remaining time was forty-three days.

At the end of November 1940 Fitzgerald had a coronary episode at Schwab's drugstore on Sunset Boulevard. (Alcoholic cardiomyopathy, or enlargement of the heart chambers, occurs in chronic alcoholics.) His symptoms of chest pains, pain running down the arms, and shortness of breath are typical of angina pectoris, the result of stenosing arteriosclerosis (hardening of the coronary arteries).[124] He was ordered to rest in bed, where he wrote for a couple of hours a day on a board. Fitzgerald's North Laurel Avenue apartment was on the top floor – and one of his neighbors disturbed him by exercising her dog on the roof – so he moved to Sheilah's ground-floor apartment on North Hayworth Avenue to avoid climbing stairs. He felt he was

26

"Oh no," he said "I was drunk." He
looked around ... this room —
somebody from ... dio."
"Somebody from New York."
"Well, I'll have to get you out of
here," he said in his old pleasant
way. "How would you like to go out to Doug Fairbanks's
ranch and spend the night?" He asked me—I
know we love to wander ...
That's how the two weeks started
that he and I went around together. It
only took one of them for ~~Hilda~~ Luella to leave
married

The last page of the working draft for The Last Tycoon

making a good recovery, reporting to Zelda on 13 December: 'The novel is about three-quarters through and I think I can go on till January 12 without doing any stories or going back to the studio. I couldn't go back to the studio anyhow in my present condition as I have to spend most of the time in bed where I write on a wooden desk. . . . The cardiogram shows that my heart is repairing itself but it will be a gradual process that will take some months. It is odd that the heart is one of the organs that does repair itself.'[125] On 14 December, Fitzgerald made a schedule for completing the working draft by 15 January. By writing 1,750 words per day, he expected to finish the last four chapters in 28,000 words.

Friday, 20 December 1940, Fitzgerald worked on episode 17 of his novel, the meeting between Stahr and the communist labor organizer Brimmer. It gave him trouble, but he told Sheilah he was satisfied when he finished. That night they had dinner at Lyman's on Hollywood Boulevard and attended the premiere of *This Thing Called Love*, a comedy with Melvyn Douglas and Rosalind Russell at the Pantages Theatre. While they were leaving the theater, he experienced a dizzy spell and had trouble walking to the car. He declined to see a doctor that night because Dr. Clarence Nelson was coming to examine him the next day.

F. Scott Fitzgerald died of occlusive coronary arteriosclerosis on 21 December 1940 with 44,000 words of his novel written. His books were not out of print, as has been claimed. Six of his books were in stock at Scribners.[126] His last royalty statement on 1 August 1940 reported sales of forty copies (including seven copies of *The Great Gatsby* and nine of *Tender Is the Night*) for a royalty of $13.13.

It may be ironically appropriate that Fitzgerald died in obscurity trying to complete a masterpiece, but the manner of his death does not accord with his legend. Thus John O'Hara: 'Scott should have been killed in a Bugatti in the south of France, and not to have died of neglect in Hollywood, a prematurely old little man haunting bookstores unrecognized (as he was the last-but-one time I saw him.)'[127]

61

Consequences

Harold Ober made notes during the call from Sheilah Graham informing him of Fitzgerald's death: 'S. doesn't think he would like to be buried in California because he really hated California. She thinks he would like to be buried where his father is buried because he admired him.'[128] The decision to send the body east was made by Zelda in telephone discussions with John Biggs, who had become a federal judge in Wilmington. There was a viewing of the body for Fitzgerald's California friends in the Wordsworth Room of the Pierce Brothers Mortuary at 720 West Washington Boulevard.

Permission to bury Fitzgerald at St. Mary's Church in Rockville, Maryland, was denied by an official at the Baltimore Diocese because he had not been a practicing Catholic at his death – not, as has been incorrectly stated, because his books were proscribed by the Church.* Burial was at Rockville Union Cemetery on 27 December, following a service conducted by an Episcopalian minister, Reverend

---

* None of his books was on the Index Librorum Prohibitorum. Judge Biggs went to Baltimore to appeal to the bishop, who declined to reverse the decision denying Fitzgerald a Catholic burial.

Raymond Black, at the Pumphrey Funeral Home in Bethesda. The funeral was attended by Scottie, the Murphys, Perkinses, Obers, Biggses, and Turnbulls, Cecilia Taylor and her daughters, Ludlow Fowler, Newman Smith, and those of Scottie's Baltimore friends who had known him – altogether about thirty people. Hemingway was in Cuba, and Perkins wrote him after the funeral, 'I thought of telegraphing you, but it didn't seem as if there were any use in it, and I shrank from doing it.'[129] Sheilah Graham did not attend the funeral in deference to propriety. Zelda did not feel well enough to come north from Montgomery, though she was involved in the arrangements.

Fitzgerald was strapped but not destitute during the last year of his life. His 1940 earnings were $14,570. Apart from personal possessions, $738.16 in the bank, and $486.34 in cash, the bulk of his estate was the reduced $44,225.15 value of his life insurance policy. His 1937 Ford convertible, which he had bought secondhand from S.J. Perelman, was sold for $265. He died owing $4,067.14 to Highland Hospital, $5,456.92 to Scribners, $802.13 to Ober (who waived $2,926 in accumulated interest on loans), and at least $1,500 to Perkins. His copyrights were regarded as virtually worthless, and the royalties from his writings were a trickle. The State of California appraised work-in progress for *The Last Tycoon* at $5,000 and all the other manuscripts at $1,000.

In his 1937 will Fitzgerald had appointed John Biggs and Harold Ober his executors, but on 10 November 1940 he crossed out Ober's name and substituted Maxwell Perkins. He also changed the provision for 'a suitable funeral and burial in keeping with my station in life' to 'the cheapest funeral and burial.'[130] Since Fitzgerald's alteration of his will raised legal problems, Ober and Perkins withdrew as executors in favor of Biggs; but both worked closely with Biggs in administering Fitzgerald's literary affairs. The will set up trusts for Zelda and Scottie from the insurance policy and stipulated that income from his writings also be held in trust for them. For the next seven years Biggs provided for Zelda and Scottie from an inheritance of less than \$35,000 – supplemented by royalties from posthumously published volumes. An annuity purchased for Zelda paid her \$49.16 a month; as a veteran's widow she qualified for a \$35 monthly pension. Scottie was able to finish Vassar with the help of loans from Ober, Perkins, and Murphy, which she repaid.

Maxwell Perkins was determined to salvage *The Last Tycoon* as a memorial and to earn a little money for the estate. At first he thought about having another writer complete the novel and approached John O'Hara and Budd Schulberg, who declined because they felt no other writer could finish Fitzgerald's work.[131] He even considered seeking Hemingway's help, an idea which Zelda opposed: 'May I suggest that rather than bringing into play another forceful talent of other inspiration it would be felicitous to enlist a pen such as Gilbert Seldes, whose talent depends on concision of idea and aptitude of word rather than the spiritual or emotional transports of the author.'[132] By the end of January 1941 Perkins informed Zelda: 'I don't think anybody ought to attempt to write an ending, or even could do it.'[133] After conferring with Gilbert Seldes, he decided to publish the novel in its unfinished form. Edmund Wilson, who agreed to donate his editorial services, recommended that *The Last Tycoon* be published with the 'Crack-Up' essays and Pat Hobby stories; but Perkins vetoed the proposal because he felt that 'The Crack-Up' had damaged Fitzgerald's reputation and regarded the Hobby pieces as minor efforts. The volume published on 27 October 1941 presented the edited fragments of *The Last Tycoon* with *The Great Gatsby* and five stories 'that seem most likely to have permanent interest'[134] ('May Day,' 'The Diamond as Big as the Ritz,' 'The Rich Boy,' 'Absolution,' and 'Crazy Sunday'). Wilson prepared a text of *The Last Tycoon* for the general reader, assembling the episodes into chapters. The effect of Wilson's redaction was to present the episodes in much more finished form than in Fitzgerald's draft. He also provided a summary of the unwritten chapters and a selection of the plans and notes. Wilson's edition remains the only published text of *The Last Tycoon*; for forty years it has been read in a form that obscures the work-in-progress quality of what Fitzgerald left.

The first printing was probably less than 5,000 copies; the book sold slowly but steadily – requiring reprintings in 1941, 1945, 1947, 1948 – and has never gone out of print. The 1941 reviews were respectful and regretful. Most of the critics agreed with Wilson's statement that *The Last Tycoon* is 'even in its imperfect state, Fitzgerald's most mature piece of work';[135] and the omnibus volume provided reviewers the opportunity to reassess Fitzgerald's career. J. Donald Adams, who had never been a partisan of his work, wrote the front-page *New York Times Book Review* article in which he called Fitzgerald's early death 'a heavy loss to American literature' and cautiously ventured that 'I think he will be remembered in his generation.'[136] Three months after the volume was published, James Thurber's review appeared in *The New Republic*. While approving publication of *The Last Tycoon*, Thurber warned that it was not to be judged as finished work: 'Fitzgerald's perfection of style and form, as in "The Great Gatsby," has a way of making something that lies between your stomach and your heart quiver a little.' Thurber believed that if Fitzgerald had lived to complete his work, he would have fulfilled his ambitions for the novel: 'I know of no one else who could.'[137] In 1945 Dos Passos wrote of *The Last Tycoon*: 'Even in this unfinished state these fragments, I believe, are of sufficient dimensions to raise the level of American fiction to follow in some such way as Marlowe's blank verse line raised the whole level of Elizabethan verse.'[138]

One of the dissenting opinions from the majority judgment on *The Last Tycoon* was Hemingway's. He informed Perkins that the writing is like moldy bacon and that the plan of the novel involves 'impossible dramatic tricks.' He compared Fitzgerald to a pitcher with a dead arm, reiterating his claim that Fitzgerald never knew enough about people to write a novel that did not depend on magic.[139]

The Last Tycoon epitomizes Fitzgerald's career in ways that are almost too neat. His quintessential theme of aspiration and his concomitant quest for heroism found their fullest expression in Monroe Stahr. Whereas *The Great Gatsby* treats the American Dream almost allegorically, *The Last Tycoon* shows the fable made actuality. Fitzgerald's long meditation on the promises of America culminated on the last American frontier, in a boom town built on a lode of illusions and hopes. But in 1935 Stahr is already an anachronism. The old faiths are wavering; the dream is fading. The romantic individualism that Fitzgerald had believed in so devoutly and the sense of life's infinite possibilities that he had evoked so eloquently were crumbling. In his notes for the novel he wrote: 'I look out at it – and I think it is the most beautiful history in the world. It is the history of me and of my people. And if I came here yesterday like Sheilah I should still think so. It is the history of all aspiration – not just the American dream but the human dream and if I came at the end of it that too is a place in the line of the pioneers.'[140] In *The Last Tycoon* – which Fitzgerald thought of as 'A Western' – 'the last of the novelists' was writing about the last of the pioneers in the last frontier town. The quondam playboy of American literature died like one of the overworked American leaders he admired, engaged in his final quest for heroism.

Zelda continued to live with her mother at 322 Sayre Street in Montgomery, voluntarily returning to Highland during periods of depression. She painted, worked on an unfinished novel, and took the long walks that were part of her therapy. Her last years were peaceful but also bitterly ironic: the most famous Montgomery belle returned home to live as an impoverished invalid. Old friends were kind to her – with the kindness reserved, especially in the South, for the broken and helpless. She returned to Highland in November 1947. On the night of 10 March 1948 a fire broke out in the building where she was sleeping, and she was one of the nine patients who died. The body that was positively identified as Zelda Sayre Fitzgerald was buried with her husband at Rockville

Union Cemetery. In 1975 they were interred in the Fitzgerald family plot at St. Mary's Church, Rockville.

During Zelda's last years there were indications that F. Scott Fitzgerald was not entirely forgotten.* Stephen Vincent Benet's review of *The Last Tycoon* ended with an accurate forecast: 'You can take off your hats now, gentlemen, and I think perhaps you had better. This is not a legend, this is a reputation – and seen in perspective, it may well be one of the most secure reputations of our time.'[141] In 1945 Edmund Wilson edited *The Crack-Up*, a selection from Fitzgerald's autobiographical essays, notebooks, and letters, with tributes from other writers. Published by New Directions, it was warmly received and has become a standard volume in the Fitzgerald canon. In his influential review of *The Crack-Up* Lionel Trilling identified Fitzgerald's 'heroic awareness': 'The root of Fitzgerald's heroism is to be found, as it sometimes is in tragic heroes, in his power of love.'[142] That year Dorothy Parker edited *The Portable F. Scott Fitzgerald* in which John O'Hara stated: 'All he was was our best novelist, one of our best novella-ists, and one of our finest writers of short stories.'[143] By 1951 what was then called 'the Fitzgerald revival' was in full progress, and by 1960 the revival had become a resurrection.

Despite his many moves, Fitzgerald preserved a large archive of his papers. In addition to his scrapbooks, photo albums, and notebooks, he kept the manuscripts, drafts, and proofs of his writings, as well as his correspondence. After her father's death Scottie declined to sell the legacy, refusing a token offer from the Princeton University Library and feelers from dealers who would have scattered the collection. In 1950 she donated the archive to Princeton. The manuscripts require fifty-seven boxes, forming one of the richest research collections for a major American author. Scottie's gift has been supplemented by Sheilah Graham's

---

* In February and March 1941 *The New Republic* published two groups of tributes under the title 'In Memory of F. Scott Fitzgerald,' with contributions by John Peale Bishop, John Dos Passos, John O'Hara, Budd Schulberg, and Glenway Wescott.

material and contributions by friends and admirers, and the Charles Scribner's Sons Archives have since been donated to Princeton. Although the Princeton University Library also houses the papers of Woodrow Wilson, John Foster Dulles, and James Forrestal, the F. Scott Fitzgerald Papers are the most frequently consulted collection at the library. Fitzgerald would have relished the circumstance that the Princeton undergraduate whose poor scholarship deprived him of a diploma now attracts scholars from all over the world to the library of his alma mater.

In the fifty years since Fitzgerald's death Scribners has sold at least twelve million copies of his books. Forty-three new collections of his writings have been published, along with some sixty biographical and critical books and pamphlets. His work has been translated into thirty-five languages. *The Great Gatsby* has become a classroom staple and sells some 300,000 copies a year in America.

F. Scott Fitzgerald is now permanently placed with the greatest writers who ever lived, where he wanted to be all along. Where he belongs.

After her husband's death Zelda Fitzgerald wrote an eight-page tribute, probably intended for *The Crack-Up*. It closes with this assessment:

> Fitzgeralds books were the first of their kind and the most indicative. If his people didn't have a good time, or things come out well at the end, the scene of their activity was always the arena of some new philosophic offensive, and what they did was allied with many salient projects of the era. The plush hush of the hotel lobby and the gala grandeur of the theatre port-cochiere; fumes of orchidaceous elevators whirring to plaintive deaths the gilded aspirations of a valiant and protesting age, taxis slumberously afloat on deep summer nights—
>
> Such Fitzgerald made into many tragic tales; sagas of people compelling life into some more commensurate and compassionate measure. His meter was bitter, and ironic and spectacular

Consequences

and enviting: so was life. There wasnt much other life during those times than to what his pen paid the tribute of poetic tragic glamour and offered the reconciliation of the familiarities of tragedy.

Rest in Peace.[144]

Scottie with Princeton University Librarian
Julian P. Boyd at the presentation of
F. Scott Fitzgerald's Papers, 18 November 1950.

PRINCETON ALUMNI WEEKLY

The Colonial Ancestors
of Francis Scott Key Fitzgerald

by Scottie Fitzgerald Smith

All his life – which may seem odd in one who is sometimes called 'the historian of the Jazz Age' – my father was fascinated by the poetic aspects of early times. His first success, at age sixteen, came with the production in St. Paul of a Civil War play, *Coward* . . . and his most abysmal failure, some twenty years later, with a series of stories about a medieval knight which were so inferior to his other work that *Redbook* asked him to discontinue them. He loved to study the 'Histomap' that hung on the wall of his workroom in Baltimore, to collect miniature soldiers which he deployed in marches around our Christmas trees, and to recite the kings and queens of England. I can still remember his annoyance when I kept falling asleep during his background briefings on *Ivanhoe*.

It seems, therefore, ironic and a little sad that he was almost totally unaware of what romantic cloth his own colonial ancestors were made. He knew, of course, that he was related to Francis Scott Key, but he dubbed him a great-great-uncle

Note: Genealogy is time-consuming work; even with the aid of modern copying machines and reprint houses, I could never have tracked down these people without the help over several years of Messrs. Theodore Brownyard, a professional genealogist in Washington; Harry Wright Newman, the Annapolis-based expert on ancient Maryland families; and Waverly Barbe, professor of genealogy at the University of Alabama.

whereas Key was, in fact, only a distant cousin. The snob in him dropped the names of some Dorsey and Ridgely forebears into his preface to Don Swann's *Colonial and Historic Homes of Maryland*, but they were hopelessly confused. I do wish he had been familiar with Adam Thoroughgood, Kenelm Cheseldyne, Marmaduke Tylden, and the other intrepid souls who set sail from England in the seventeenth century to settle along the rivers of Tidewater Maryland and Virginia, for surely he would have contributed their improbable-sounding names to literature.

The one with whom I fancy my father might have felt the closest bond is Thomas Gerard, Lord of the Manor of St. Clement's in St. Mary's County, Maryland, who arrived in 1638, four years after his cousin had made the celebrated voyage with the *Ark* and *Dove*. To get to be a Lord of the Manor, of which some eighty were created before the title was abolished toward the end of the century, you simply had to buy 1,000 acres and import enough indentured servants to populate them; but Gerard went on to become one of the province's largest landowners, with holdings of over 12,000 acres including what is now Capitol Hill in Washington. A poor relative of a titled family, he was a doctor by profession, referred to by Lord Baltimore as his 'beloved surgeon.' This staunch Catholic brought suit against a Jesuit priest who tried to coerce his Protestant wife and children into attending Catholic services. A tobacco planter like nearly all the Maryland landowners, he also manufactured bricks and a celebrated peach brandy ... of which he evidently partook with relish, being publicly accused of drunkenness and intemperate language at a meeting of the Provincial Council.

In 1659, after a characteristic scrap with his patron Lord Baltimore, Gerard joined a briefly successful rebellion against his government; when a furious Baltimore returned to power, he fined him 5,000 pounds of tobacco and exiled him to Virginia where he continued to practice medicine and bought several thousand more acres. Eventually he was pardoned and given back his confiscated lands, but though he returned temporarily he spent the end of his life in Virginia where he started what has been called the first country club on these shores. It consisted of a 'Banquetting House' at the point where his property joined with three others, and its bylaws called for a party once a year 'fit to entertain the undertakers thereof,' to be followed by a 'procession to every man's land for re-marking and bounding . . . this for the better preservation of that friendship which ought to be between neighbors.' He was, perhaps, among the earliest *bon vivants* in the New World.

Though Gerard kept a low political profile after his exile, his rebellious spirit seems to have transmitted itself to his family, for three of his numerous daughters married men who became, sixteen years after his death, important figures in the Maryland Revolution of 1689. This nonviolent event, which removed the Baltimores from office for a quarter of a century, had many causes – among them Protestant resentment of the favoritism shown by the Baltimores to their relatives and Catholic intimates. When England's Glorious Revolution of 1688 placed the Protestant William and Mary on the throne, the time seemed right for such ambitious malcontents as Kenelm Cheseldyne to make their move. The second son of the Vicar of Blaxham in Lincolnshire, a London-educated lawyer and husband of the well-to-do Mary Gerard, Cheseldyne joined with his two brothers-in-law and Henry Jowles, the father of his son-in-law, to play a prominent part in the overthrow of the Baltimores, the forming of the Associators' Convention (as the revolutionary government was called), and to a lesser extent in the royal government which was established in 1691. It was he who sailed for London with his brother-in-law, John Coode, to plead the cause of the Associators before the Crown.

I cannot resist inserting here that John Coode, the military commander of the revolution and by all accounts a fiery rascal, is a direct progenitor by way of his second marriage of my mother Zelda. There is no way my mother's sister Rosalind, who spent many years documenting their origins in southern Maryland, could not have known this, yet she so detested my father that she studiously omitted from her papers any reference to it or to the many other connections by marriage between their Maryland ancestors ... and carried her awful secrets to her grave.

At about the time that Thomas Gerard was establishing himself in southern Maryland – during the 1640's – a group of dissenters from England's established church, called Non-Conformists or Puritans, were running into trouble with the authorities at their settlement along the Elizabeth River in Virginia. For refusing to 'hear the Book of Common Prayer' and other offenses against the Crown, they were being threatened with arrest and imprisonment. Governor William Stone, Maryland's first Protestant governor, anxious for more colonists, took it upon himself during Lord Baltimore's absence in England to invite them to settle on the virgin territory along the Severn River near what is now Annapolis. Thus in about 1650 Edward Dorsey and Matthew Howard, whose descendants stayed in the foreground of Maryland affairs for many generations, were among those who made the move from Virginia northwards. They were granted between 200 and 500 acres each, according to how many children and indentured servants they transported with them, and the complete (for that time) religious freedom which allowed some, like Edward Dorsey's wife, even to become Quakers. Puritanism did not last much beyond the first generation, however; prosperity and the advent of slavery soon demanded a less exacting religion.

The first Anne Arundel County settlers were joined by Richard Warfield, an indentured servant who rose to become a commissioned officer in the Provincial Militia (how my father would have relished, during the scandal over King Edward VIII's abdication, knowing he was an eighth cousin to Wallis Warfield, Duchess of Windsor!) and by Richard Hill, 'a Scotchman, bold in speech, who spoke what others only dared to think,' and was often sent as ambassador to the neighboring colonies to try to work out a joint policy toward the marauding northern tribes of Indians. He wrote to the Governor on one of his trips that in 'lyeing out of doors both upon land and water I have taken a grievous cold, but as I am at your Lordship's Commands, I shall nevertheless readily obey them.' These were some of the immigrants whose names appear on the family tree for several generations; wives' maiden names are seldom recorded.

Things were turbulent in the earliest days of this puritan enclave within a predominantly Catholic-run province, culminating in the bloody 1655 Battle of the Severn between the established planters of St. Mary's and the new arrivals. No F.S.F. ancestor lost his life, but the brother of one did: Thomas Hatton, former Secretary of the Province, the man famous for bringing over on the boat from England the draft of Maryland's 'Act Concerning Religion,' the first formal declaration of religious tolerance in the New World. He had also brought along the widow of his brother Richard and her four children, and thereby hangs a tale.

Soon after their arrival in Maryland in 1648, one of the Widow Hatton's daughters married Captain Luke Gardiner, Lord of the Manor of St. Richard's, Justice of the County Court, High Sheriff of St. Mary's (the Sheriff was the Governor's Representative in each county), and member of the Assembly. He was so ardent a Catholic that after marrying Elizabeth Hatton, a Protestant, he kidnapped her twelve-year-old sister, Elinor, in an attempt to bring her up in the Roman faith. The Widow Hatton, by now remarried, elicited the help of her brother-in-law, then Secretary of State, in having Elinor forcibly returned to her. Hatton termed the abduction 'an insufferable dealing' and one of 'very dangerous and Destructive consequence in relacion to the peace and welfare of this Province,' terming Gardiner insolent and refractory. Elinor apparently suffered no lasting damage, later marrying twice most advantageously (both times to Catholics), but Luke's wife Elizabeth left his bed and board, declaring in court that she was 'delighted' to be released from him. After Luke's death she remarried – to a

Protestant. Luke left his large estate to his four young sons on condition that if any 'be no Catholic' his share be divided among his brothers.

A third region of Maryland was becoming populated in the mid-seventeenth century – as late as 1700, there were not many more than 25,000 people in the entire colony – across the Chesapeake Bay from the mainland, on what is now known as the Eastern Shore. Our ancestors were among the pioneers along its river banks: Dr. Richard Tilghman, 'Doctor in Physic,' who plied his trade from a boat and built a famed plantation house, 'The Hermitage'; Thomas Hynson, High Sheriff and later Justice of Kent County, who held the sessions of the court at 'Hinchingham,' his 2,200-acre property (when he died, his sons paid Dr. Tilghman 4,621 pounds of tobacco 'for care and physic'); Simon Wilmer, delegate from the new county to the Assembly at Annapolis, owner of 'White House Farm' on which part of Chestertown now stands; Marmaduke Tylden (changed to 'Tilden' in later generations), who inherited 'Great Oak Manor' from his father-in-law William Harris and was said to be the largest landowner in the county, with 13,000 acres. William Harris was one of the few Eastern shore planters to join the rebel side in 1689.

Dr. John Scott, another surgeon, was also one of the pioneer settlers, though not such a formidable landowner. From him seven generations of Scotts descend, all of whom lived in Chestertown, Kent County, until after the American Revolution when the fifth of the line, also a John Scott, moved to Baltimore. These were not the same Scotts for whom Francis Scott Key was named – no connection can be found – though F.S.F.'s mother, when naming him after his illustrious relative, must surely have taken into consideration the fact that the Chestertown Scotts were the longest continuous line in his American ancestry. Only the name 'Francis' was what one might call capricious, and even 'Francis' had been in the family before the birth of Francis Scott Key. Whatever her motives, Mollie Fitzgerald had legitimate cause for bestowing upon her son such a star-spangled name.

Before leaving the seventeenth century for the more worldly eighteenth, when all the known forebears on this side of the Atlantic were firmly planted on Maryland soil, we need to return to Virginia, setting the calendar back briefly to the year 1608. The first of our adventurers to arrive in America, Thomas Graves, landed that year at Jamestown as part of the 'Second Supply.' Shortly after, while on an exploring expedition, he was taken captive by hostile Indians and rescued just in time to avoid a premature death.

In 1619 Captain Graves was one of two representatives from 'Smythe's Hundred' (Southampton) to the first session of the House of Burgesses of Virginia – the first legislative assembly in the New World – held in an old wooden church at Jamestown. Later that year, referring to a feud at Smythe's Hundred, Governor Yeardley wrote, 'I have entreated Capt. Graves antient officer of this Company to take charge of the people and the workes.' He could not have been quite so 'antient' as implied, for several years later, as part of the census taken after the Indian Massacre of 1622, he is listed as Commander of the 'Plantation of Accomack' on Virginia's eastern shore.

In 1629 Graves represented the new county of Accomack-Northampton at the Assembly, later becoming a member of the first vestry of the Church of England parish. One of his daughters, Ann, set what must be some sort of record by marrying successively three rectors of this parish. Her third husband then accepted a rectorship in Charles County, Maryland, where her sister Verlinda was living with her husband, former governor William Stone, who had earlier in his career been Commissioner of Accomack, Virginia. When Stone died, Ann stayed on with Verlinda, sending her own husband back to Virginia alone. Her daughter by her first husband, the Reverend William Cotton, married a Charles County, Maryland, planter, thus ending the Virginia connection.

Another early bird, especially interesting to his descendants because his plantation house east of Norfolk – said to be the oldest brick dwelling still standing in America – is now a charming small museum, was Adam Thoroughgood. The seventh son of the Vicar of St. Botolph's, Norfolk, England, he is credited with giving America's Norfolk its name. He arrived in Virginia in 1621 as a seventeen-year-old indentured servant, earned his freedom in the customary five years, bought 150 acres, and returned to England where he married Sarah Offley, daughter of a well-to-do London merchant who was, lo and behold, a member of the Virginia Company. Soon Adam was back in Virginia with 105 new settlers, which entitled him to large amounts of land; within seven years, he was one of the wealthiest planters in the colony and a member of the prestigious King's Council. He died at thirty-five and the widow Sarah, though remarried as most affluent widows promptly were, appears to have remained devoted. When a woman importunely suggested that 'noone could get a bill' out of Sarah's late husband, she insisted that the offender publicly apologize in the middle of the following Sunday's church service. The Thoroughgoods had, of course, founded the church.

One more Virginia immigrant – doubtless the most blue-blooded of the lot, since he is listed by the Order of the Crown of Charlemagne in the United States as a descendant of that monarch – needs mention. Gerard Fowke of Gunston, Staffordshire, had been a Gentleman of the Bedchamber to Charles I and a colonel in the royal army before coming to Westmoreland County, Virginia, sometime before 1657 with his cousin George Mason. He became a colonel of troops but ran into serious trouble in 1661 when, along with Mason and two others, he was charged with having 'injured and affronted' Wahonganocke, King of the Potomac Indians. For the high misdemeanor of illegally imprisoning the King, they were ordered to pay him '100 arms length of Roanoke apiece or match coats instead at 20 arms length every coat,' to pay the Assembly 15,000 pounds of tobacco, and to relinquish all offices, civil or military. Fowke moved to Charles County, Maryland, where he married Anne, the daughter of Adam Thoroughgood, then a widow living at Port Tobacco. He was soon elected Burgess, then appointed Justice, despite his reputation for a 'hasty temper.' One of his granddaughters, Frances Fowke, married Dr. Gustavus Brown, which brings us back to the eighteenth century when two of the last colonial immigrants on the tree – and among the most appealing – are about to establish residence in southern Maryland.

Gustavus Brown, grandson of a minister of the Scottish Episcopal Church who was deposed for 'speaking out against the Covenant,' came in 1708 as a nineteen-year-old surgeon's mate on a royal ship bound for the Chesapeake Bay. While the ship lay at anchor, a storm arose and it put out to sea, leaving him ashore with nothing but the clothes on his back. According to an early report, 'he quickly made himself known, and informed the planters of his willingness to serve them if he could be provided with instruments and medicines, leaving them to judge if he was worthy of their confidence. He began his practice at Nansemond, Maryland, soon gained respect and succeeded beyond his expectations.' He married the heiress Frances Fowke, granddaughter of the Gerard Fowke above, and they had twelve children, the eleventh of whom, Cecilia, married a son of Philip Key. The young John Key was living with Dr. Brown while studying medicine, as was the custom of the day, when the romance was discovered by Cecilia's father. He wrote to his friend Philip to come and fetch his son at once, but despite their youth, the couple's wishes prevailed.

In 1723 Dr. Brown was one of seven trustees appointed by the county to find schoolteachers who were to be 'members of the Church of England, pious and exemplary in their lives, capable of teaching well the grammar, good writing and the mathematics, if such could conveniently be got.' The following story was told of him by a descendant:

> On one occasion Dr. Brown was sent for in haste to pay a professional visit in the family of a Mr. H., a wealthy citizen of King George Co., Va., who was usually very slow in paying his

598

physician for his valuable services, and who was also very ostentatious in displaying his wealth. In leaving the chamber of his patient it was necessary for Dr. B. to pass through the dining room, where Mr. H. was entertaining some guests at dinner. As Dr. B. entered the room a servant bearing a silver salver, on which stood two silver goblets filled with gold pieces, stepped up to him and said, 'Dr. B., master wishes you to take out your fee.' It was winter, and Dr. B. wore his overcoat. Taking one of the goblets he quietly emptied it into one pocket, and the second goblet into another, and saying to the servant, 'Tell your master I highly appreciate his liberality,' he mounted his horse and returned home.

Dr. Brown's son, also Dr. Gustavus Brown, was one of the two physicians with George Washington at the time of his death – not a glorious page, it is said, in medical history.

Philip Key, first of the Maryland line, was born in London and received his legal education at The Temple before settling in St. Mary's County in 1720 at 'Bushwood Lodge,' adjoining the St. Clement's Manor which had belonged to Thomas Gerard. He built a highly successful practice, held the offices of High Sheriff and Presiding Justice, served on a commission with Dr. Gustavus Brown to 'regulate the parishes of St. Mary's and Charles Counties,' and finally in 1763 received the highest honor, appointment to the Council of Maryland. When he died the following year, the *Maryland Gazette* extolled him as 'a pious and devout Christian, an affectionate and tender Husband, an indulgent and fond parent, a humane Master, a warm Friend, a friendly Neighbor, and a most agreeable and cheerful companion.'

His first wife was Susanna, daughter of John Gardiner, the grandson of the Luke Gardiner who had kidnapped his twelve-year-old sister-in-law some three-quarters of a century earlier. She was probably raised a Catholic, as the Gardiners were among the last of the old manorial Catholic families. Philip and Susanna had seven children, all but one of whom held high provincial offices: one was Francis, father of Philip Barton Key who sided with the British during the Revolution, but was later forgiven and elected to Congress. It was from him that my father was convinced he was descended, probably because of a chart made by a Baltimore genealogist erroneously stating that Eliza Key, wife of his great-grandfather John Scott, was Philip Barton Key's daughter. From Francis also came the father of the author of our national anthem. Dr. John Key was the only one of Philip and Susanna's children to choose a profession other than the law. He is supposed to have studied medicine at Edinburgh, but whether this was before or after his apprenticeship with Dr. Brown is unclear.

Philip Key was married again after the death of Susanna, to Theodosia Barton, who was so kind to her stepchildren (so goes the legend) that Philip Barton Key was named for her. She established the first free school for the poor in the vestry house of the church her husband had built at Chaptico with bricks 'brought from England.' A descendant wrote that 'so highly was Mr. Key honored while High Sheriff that the . . . congregation would not enter the Church until the Lord High Sheriff arrived.'

Dr. John Key and Cecilia Brown were married just long enough to have two children, Philip and Susanna, before he died. It is a commentary on the times – for today it would probably raise a hue and cry – that after her husband's death Cecilia married Major Thomas Bond, whose younger brother Richard married her daughter Susanna, making mother and daughter sisters-in-law. Philip, her son by Dr. John Key, went to London in 1767 to study law, was presented at the Court of St. James and, according to one source, 'was counted one of the handsomest men of his day.' At a Key family reunion held in June of 1877, the story was told that just before he left for London, he had become engaged to his cousin, Mary Key, but when he stayed abroad longer than expected, local gossips attributed this to an English love affair. Disconsolate, the fair Mary married another suitor in August of 1768. When Philip learned of this at the Annapolis inn where he spent the night on his return home, he became so distraught that he remained single for ten more years.

He then, however, wed Rebecca Jowles Sothoron, great-great-granddaughter of that Henry Jowles who had been prominent in the Revolution of 1689. Her father was Henry Greenfield Sothoron of 'The Plains,' Justice, delegate to the Assembly for five terms, delegate from St. Mary's to the Provincial Conventions held between 1774 and 1776 when independence was declared, and member for St. Mary's of the General Committee for the Revolution, which was charged with carrying out the policies of the Continental Congress. Philip Key was also a delegate to the Assembly (Speaker of the House for two terms), and active in the Revolution as a member of the Committee of Correspondence. He was elected to the second United States Congress in 1791, and 'declined the offer to become Governor of Maryland when that official was appointed by the Electoral College.'

After the Revolution, Philip and Rebecca bought Tudor Hall, a plantation house famous for its inset portico; it is now preserved as the public library at Leonardtown, county seat of St. Mary's. They had nine children, the youngest of whom, Eliza, born in 1792 at Tudor Hall, would have had to be my father's favorite ancestress. She is credited with saving the Leonardtown courthouse from the depredations of the British Navy in 1814 by rowing out in a boat, alone, to persuade the British Admiral against all evidence that the courthouse was sometimes used as 'a place of divine worship.' He is alleged to have been so charmed that he also gave protection to Tudor Hall, with the words, 'That is a deucedly fine woman; her house shall not be burned.' Eliza married John Scott, a Baltimore lawyer, thus becoming the great-grandmother of F.S.F. and bringing the large southern Maryland branch into the family tree.

Meanwhile, the descendants of the Puritan settlers of Anne Arundel County were prospering mightily. Captain John Dorsey, third son of Edward Dorsey the boatwright, served in both houses of the Assembly, on commissions to lay out the town and port of Annapolis, and on the Governor's Council.

He accumulated land, much of it in newly created Howard County near Baltimore, where the soil was not depleted by the continuous planting of tobacco. Having amply taken care of his sons in his will, he left the sons of his daughter Deborah, Charles and William Ridgely, a 2,000-acre Howard County estate which he called 'White Wine and Claret' because the surveyors he engaged, and supplied with potables, gave it such irregular boundaries. At this funeral in 1715 ten gallons of rum and thirty gallons of cider were consumed. His daughter Deborah's husband, Charles Ridgely, was a son of Robert Ridgely, a leading lawyer of the province who was at one time Deputy Secretary of Maryland. From him, Charles inherited a large estate in what is now Prince George's County. He left Deborah a widow only five years after they were married; as usual, the records frustratingly fail to suggest a cause. According to one account, she was nearly blind from a childhood case of smallpox, but 'so acute were her senses of hearing and feeling that she suffered no inconvenience from her misfortune.' She went on to marry Richard Clagett, another of Maryland's princely landowners, and by him to become the grandmother of the first Episcopal Bishop consecrated in America.

Deborah's son Charles, one of her three Ridgely children, became a Justice of Baltimore County. Public offices in those days were regarded more as a way of paying one's dues to society than making a living; his principal business was dealing in mortgages and liens on property, a lucrative endeavor at a time when Maryland's population was growing rapidly and banking was a private enterprise. Included in his vast estate at his death in 1773 were 125 gallons of spirits (whiskey), 25 gallons of rum, 111 bottles of canary wine, 115 bottles of red port wine, seven gallons of Lisbon wine, and 11 hogsheads of cider. His son Charles Ridgely III, brother of our ancestress Pleasance, built 'Hampton,' a magnificent mansion in the Dulaney Valley near Baltimore, now open to the public. Ridgely descendants still occupied the house when my father lived in Baltimore in the Thirties, and invited him to visit on several occasions; as I recall he was enthralled, asking many questions and taking copious notes. He had no idea, I am certain, that while Charles Ridgely's wife officially opened 'Hampton' with a prayer meeting, Charles held a card party in the attic with his fellow officers from the militia.

Charles Ridgely died childless in 1790, before 'Hampton' was completed, and left it (with the wherewithal to finish the job) to a nephew, on condition that he change his name to Ridgely. He was also generous to his sister Pleasance and her children by Lyde Goodwin, leaving them roughly a fourth of his fortune. One of her daughters, Elizabeth Goodwin, married her second cousin, Henry Hill Dorsey, in 1765, which returns us again to the Dorseys. We left the Dorseys, the reader will recall, when Deborah Dorsey married Charles Ridgely in about 1700. Four years later her brother Caleb married Elinor Warfield, daughter of the upwardly mobile Richard of early Annapolis, and he, too, parlayed his land holdings into a vast domain, smartly investing around Elk Ridge Landing, the new port about to burst into prosperity because of the iron ore which had been discovered nearby. They lived at 'Hockley-in-the-Hole' near Annapolis, the plantation left to Caleb by his father, and very well: his will, made in 1742, bequeathed thirty-four slaves to his wife Elinor and their eleven children. They actually had twelve children, but one had fallen into disfavor: 'Item, to daughter Elinor Lynch, who for her disobedience, I exclude from any part of my estate, five shilling sterling.'

It was Caleb's son Caleb who became the real tycoon, opening mines, building forges, and erecting furnaces on the Elk Ridge lands as Maryland inched from its tobacco economy into the industrial age. Known as 'the Iron Merchant of Elk Ridge,' it was said that he could ride ten miles in any direction on his properties. He ran his own fleet of ships directly to England. In 1735 he married Priscilla Hill, granddaughter of the immigrant Richard, after a romantic encounter described by a descendant:

On one of his long hunts after the elusive fox, young Caleb Dorsey, who was living at the time at his father's plantation, 'Hockley-in-the-Hole,' got lost in the vicinity of the West River, and made up his mind to spend the night in the woods, when to his surprise there came riding down a little lane a young damsel as beautiful as the goddess Diana.

'How may I get to Hockley, near Annapolis?' he inquired.

'I don't know,' replied the maiden, 'but if you keep down this lane for half a mile and turn to the left you will come to a mansion where they may direct you.' With that, she rode quickly away. The house she spoke of was her father's.

Caleb followed the lady's directions, and made the acquaintance of old Mr. Hill, a fox-hunter like himself. He not only spent the night under the hospitable roof of the Hill family, but remained their guest for several days. After that Caleb frequently renewed the chase in the same direction of the West River, and finally brought home Miss Priscilla Hill as his wife. Obtaining from his father the tract known as Moore's Morning Choice, he built the lordly *Belmont* for his bride.

'Belmont,' finished in 1738, is one of the great country houses of Maryland. It is terraced after the English fashion, with formal gardens bordered with box and lilac bushes, and has a graveyard behind the house where Caleb and Priscilla are buried. Two of its unusual features are the 'witches' crosses' Caleb put on the doors to ward off evil spirits and the plate with the initials 'C' and 'P' intertwined which is in the front wall. The property was inherited through marriage by Alexander Contee Hanson, another relative of Zelda's.

When Caleb and Priscilla's oldest son, Henry Dorsey, married his cousin Elizabeth Goodwin in 1765, he was doing the traditional thing: intermarriages between Dorseys, Ridgelys, Howards, Warfields, and a few other families of the squirearchy were everyday affairs. One of Henry's sisters married Charles Ridgely III, the builder of 'Hampton,' becoming his aunt as well when he married Elizabeth. Another sister married Charles Ridgely Carnan, who changed his name to Charles Carnan Ridgely to inherit 'Hampton'; he was Elizabeth's first cousin. Yet another sister

604

married Elizabeth's brother, and a brother married a Dorsey. Henry and Elizabeth's daughter, Elizabeth Goodwin Dorsey, broke the pattern when she married John Scott from Kent County, a Baltimore lawyer and state senator and later judge, in 1788.

Henry Dorsey died in 1772, in the same year as his father, and his brothers Samuel and Edward ran the ironworks throughout the Revolution, supplying guns, cannons, and ammunition to George Washington's troops. John Scott's father, Dr. John Scott, vaccinated 500 revolutionary soldiers against smallpox in the public square in Chestertown, refusing to take a fee.

John Scott himself was only eight years old at the time of the Declaration of Independence; he and Elizabeth Goodwin Dorsey were the last of the ancestors to have been born in America under the British flag. They carried a mighty lot of colonial history in their veins, and it seems appropriate that some of the furniture at Mount Vernon was given by Elizabeth Dorsey Scott at the time of its restoration. It is equally appropriate, and pleasing, that my father is buried in an ancient churchyard in Rockville, Maryland, just north of Washington . . . which is just about equidistant from where all these adventurous folks put down their strong, tenacious, and, I like to think romantic, roots.

Principal Sources

Anne Arundel Gentry, by Harry Wright Newman, Vols. I and II (privately printed), and all other writings of Mr. Newman's; *Maryland's Revolution of Government*, by Lois Green Carr and David William Jordan (Cornell University Press, 1974); *Founders of Anne Arundel & Howard Counties*, by J. D. Warfield (1905, reprinted by Regional Publishing Co., Baltimore, 1973); *Sidelights on Maryland History*, by Hester Dorsey Richardson (1903, reprinted by Tidewater Publishers, Cambridge, Md., 1967); *His Lordship's Patronage*, by Donnell M. Owings (Maryland Historical Society, 1953); *Virginia Genealogies*, by

Horace Edwin Hayden (1891, reprinted by Genealogical Publishing Co., Baltimore, 1973); *History of Old Kent County*, by George A. Hanson (1876, reprinted by Regional Publishing Co., Baltimore, 1967); *Adventurers of Purse & Person*, ed. Annie Josh Jester (reprinted by the Order of First Families of Virginia, 1964); *History of St. Mary's County, Maryland*, by Regina Combs Hammett (privately printed 1977, with an introduction by Edwin W. Beitzell); *Yesterday in Old St. Mary's*, by Robert E. T. Pogue (privately printed, 1968).

How Francis Scott Key Fitzgerald Got His Name

Philip Key (1697–1764)
m. Susanna Gardiner

Francis Key (1731–1770)
m. Anne Arnold Ross

Philip Barton Key (1757–1815)
m. Anne Plater

Philip Barton Key (1809–1854)
m. (1) Mary Brent Sewall
    (2) Maria Laura Sewall

Dr. John Key (1730–1755)
m. Cecilia Brown (b. 1731)

John Ross Key (1754–1821)
m. Phoebe Penn Dagworthy Charlton

Philip Key (1750–1820)
m. Rebecca Jowles Sothoron

Francis Scott Key (1779–1843)
m. Mary Tayloe Lloyd

Eliza Maynadier Key (1792–1866)
m. John Scott (1789–1840)

Cecilia Ashton Scott (1832–1924)
m. Michael Fitzgerald (d. 1855)

Edward Fitzgerald (1853–1931)
m. Mollie McQuillan (1860–1936)

Francis Scott Key Fitzgerald (1896–1940)
m. Zelda Sayre (1900–1948)

Therefore: Francis Scott Key Fitzgerald and Francis Scott Key were second cousins, three times removed.

APPENDIX 1

Summary Movie Treatment for
Tender Is the Night
by F. Scott Fitzgerald and Charles Warren*

There were no immediate movie offers for *Tender Is the Night* when the novel was published. Hoping to make the property more attractive to the studios, Fitzgerald prepared a movie treatment in 1934 with Charles Marquis Warren, a young Baltimore writer. It is impossible to differentiate the collaborators' contributions; but this treatment had Fitzgerald's approval. As such, it shows how Fitzgerald tried to satisfy Hollywood's requirements by providing melodramatic action and the obligatory happy ending. Even so, no studio was willing to buy *Tender Is the Night* at that time.

CAST OF CHARACTERS in the Treatment

Richard Diver	Paklin Troubetskoi
Nicole Diver	Prince from the Balkans
Baby Warren	Rosemary Hoyt

POSSIBLE CASTING OF THE ROLES

Dick Diver—Frederick March	Baby Warren—Kay Francis
Herbert Marshall	Ina Claire
Robert Montgomery	
Richard Barthelmess	Paklin Troubetskoi—
Paul Lukas	George Raft

*F. Scott Fitzgerald Papers, Princeton University Library.

Tender Is the Night *Movie Treatment*

Douglas Fairbanks, Jr.	Ronald Colman
Ronald Colman	Charles Bickford
Leslie Howard	Douglas Fairbanks, Jr.

Nicole Diver—Katherine Hepburn
            Miriam Hopkins
            Helen Hayes
            Ann Harding
            Myrna Loy
            Delores Del Rio
            Nora Gregor
            Marlene Dietrich
            Constance Bennett

Prince Paklin Troubetskoi, exiled Russian nobleman and ex-Cossack, has established a fashionable girls' riding school on the shores of Lake Geneva in Switzerland. It is his habit every afternoon to take his pupils, girls from a nearby school, for a short, hilarious gallop through the surrounding country side. It is on one of these escapades that Nicole Warren, seventeen year old American heiress and Troubetskoi's pet (though Troubetskoi is not cast as the type that would quite appeal to the average man as a son-in-law), loses control of her mount, and despite the valiant efforts of the Russian riding master to save her, is thrown in a nasty fall and dashed against the base of a tree. After having worked frantically to revive the unconscious girl, Troubetskoi dispatches one of his pupils to bring a doctor immediately.

A charity hospital is near the scene of the accident. Richard Diver, Assistant Resident therein, promising young brain surgeon and psychiatrist, is just completing a delicate operation. When word is brought to him of the accident he feels he is too busy to go, but when he is informed that the girl is an American and badly hurt he throws off his preoccupation and taking another horse rides to the scene. While hurriedly examining the injured girl, Dr. Dick Diver finds out what he can from the anxious Russian, Troubetskoi, and the distraught girl pupils. He learns that Nicole evidently suffered a severe blow on the head, and while she is still unconscious he has her removed to the hospital.

Word is sent to Nicole's elder sister, "Baby" Warren, living in Vienna. Two days later Baby arrives. Tall, handsome and distinctly

609

conscious of the prominence of the Warren name in America; she is slightly more irritated than sympathetic over her sister's accident. Although X-rays prove that the skull is not fractured or any obvious damage done Nicole remains in a coma for two days. At Dick's suggestion Baby puts up at a hotel not far from the hospital. Returning to consciousness Nicole shows some disturbing outward signs of mental disorder – nothing violent, but a tendency toward exaggerated elation and exaggerated melancholy, a sort of confusion. At the end of a week Dr. Dick Diver permits Baby to take Nicole to a cottage that she has found not far from the hospital and on the shore, where Nicole will get rest and quiet. At first only the anxious Troubetskoi and Dr. Diver are permitted to visit Nicole – Troubetskoi in the role of a man fast falling in love and Dick Diver purely as a physician. Even then, Dr. Diver calls rarely and only because he has a suspicion that there is some definite physical lesion in Nicole's brain, whether or not caused by the accident – a suspicion, however, that he does not reveal to anyone.

But it is a different case with Nicole. She finds this young doctor fascinating. And in the course of three months she falls in love with him. This has been a monotonous three months for Baby Warren and when she learns of Nicole's attraction to Dick she formulates a plan to "buy" Dick as Nicole's husband, thus insuring her sister's health and taking Nicole off her own hands.

In appreciation for his fine work at the hospital and out of respect for his tired condition, Dick Diver is granted a vacation. He plans to bicycle through Switzerland – and it is evening when he calls on the Warrens to say good-bye. Baby Warren, realizing that her plans to capture Dr. Dick Diver might run aground if she lets him get away, decides to put her proposition before him immediately. She takes Dick aside and in no uncertain terms tells him of the wealth of the Warren family, the sickness of her sister, the need of a medical man to take care of her, and the decision that, in return for Dick's marriage to Nicole, he will be supplied with the money he needs to continue his work. Dick flatly refuses. The cold indifference of this older sister has stunned him. What about Nicole? Hasn't Baby Warren considered her sister's feelings in this matter? Nicole, though a patient, is still a human being. Baby explains casually that Nicole thinks she is in love with him.

To Dick the entire proposition is preposterous. Nicole is only a child – but quite a lovely child. He leaves Baby Warren but on his way out of the cottage runs into Nicole. The various influences of the evening on the lakeside, of Nicole's beauty, and of her new-found love for him are not to be denied, and though he leaves somewhat abruptly with a few formal instructions for her as a patient, she has registered big on Dick Diver's heart.

Bicycling is not the best thing in the world to take a man's mind off a woman, and Dick finds himself constantly haunted by the girl, who has blossomed forth in his mind as a young woman. So, when by coincidence he meets Baby and Nicole in a funicular making the trip up a mountain for pleasure, his gaiety is somewhat forced. A casual conversation between two of the passengers about the possibilities of the cables that pull the car breaking seems to upset Nicole, and Dick again finds himself concerned about this delicate girl. Something goes wrong with the cable. The car begins to tremble and amid the terror of the passengers, Dick's one thought is for Nicole's safety. The cable splits and the funicular is precipitated down the incline for a horrible moment, then derailed. It crashes over on its side and amid the confusion that follows, Dick clutches Nicole tightly to his heart. Thankful that she is safe, and realizing that this girl and her future mean everything to him, he looks across her still body at Baby Warren, who is slightly shaken up and holding in his arms the girl that he now realizes is his love, indicates to Baby Warren his acquiescence in her proposition that he is to be her husband and private doctor for life.

This treatment must be broken off for a moment to explain the intention of what comes next. In the book, *Tender Is the Night*, there is much emphasis on the personal charm of the two Divers and of the charming manner in which they're able to live. In the book this was conveyed largely in description, "fine writing", poetic passages, etc. It has occurred to us that a similar effect can be transferred to the spectator by means of music, and to accomplish this we have interpolated in the way shown below a melody written and copyrighted by Charles M. Warren.

Now go on with the treatment.

There is a view of the frayed end of the split cable, which gradually changes into a thick dangling rope. This rope is suspended over a cliff ledge and falls down to the shore below. At the top of the cliff is 'Villa Diana', the luxurious house of the Divers. With the

Appendix 1

Warren money, Dick and Nicole have *literally* bought an old mountain village and converted it into the most charming place in Southern France. At the bottom of the cliff two French workmen contemplate the possibilities of using this suspended rope to hoist a giant grand piano to the house above.

'Who lives up there?'

'The Divers, and believe me they tip well.'

'They better.' (Adjusting rope to piano) 'Look at the size of the thing. It ought to be worth plenty to have this baby hauled up to that house.' (They look up at the cliff, that mounts like a wide staircase to the 'Villa Diana'.)

'If the road hadn't been washed away we could a used a truck. What do they want it for now? You said they already had one piano.'

'These crazy rich Americans! They're giving a party tonight.'

'Well, it's a good piano, anyway.'

Perching himself precariously on top of the piano he leans down and fingers the keys.

[music]

'Watch yourself!' comes a sharp caution from his co-worker.

But it is too late. On the top level of the cliff, eight farm horses, harnessed together and driven by a farmer, have begun to pull, and the piano is rising. Against his will the man is carried up with it. His fellow workman runs up a zig-zag staircase, cut on the side of the stone hill, crying in alarm to the driver on top to 'Stop the horses!' The driver does so and the piano swings into one of the indentations higher up on the cliff where it is allowed to come gently to rest. The danger over, the frightened workman hops off the piano and with forced bravado says:

'It wasn't anything. See – I'll play the rest of the tune.

He plays with one hand:

[music]

'It doesn't go like that,' says the first workman.

'*Sure* it does.'

They are interrupted by a woman's voice:

'No, it goes like *this*:'

Tender Is the Night *Movie Treatment*

[music]

It is Nicole, happy and the picture of health. She has played the tune
more fully than the workmen, who stand respectfully, listening. Dick
joins her and with one arm around Nicole improves on her version of
the music. As Nicole diminishes the melody to pianissimo Dick speaks
to the workmen:

'Careful with this piano! Don't let it bang now as it goes up!'

'We'll follow it, Monsieur Diver, and see that it won't scrape against
the stone, so it'll be in good condition for your party tonight.'

Dick turns to Nicole. 'Come along, young lady. You have to get
some good rest before the party – remember! Papa doesn't consider
you entirely strong yet.'

As they start trailing upward along the zig-zag walk we hear:

'. . . so damn glad to get a few minutes alone with you. We won't
have much time when that crowd comes.' Upon Nicole's encouragement they sit down and kiss then and there . . .

. . . Throughout this the tinkle of the piano is heard continuing as if
by itself. But now there is just the suggestion of an ominous note in its
melody as it reaches a still higher level, and swings from side to side
and then comes to rest like a pendulum might.

OVER THE HEADS OF:

Baby Warren and her latest 'royalty'. He is a small pudgy individual,
a Prince Somebody from the Balkans – a type with whom Baby is
invariably involved, and just as invariably discards.

Due to some difficulty overhead, the piano is temporarily lowered,
and, giggling, Baby's boy friend plays a repetition of the previous
melody but now comically in the highest octave of the piano. Again
there is an ominous note in the score as Baby Warren walks over to his
side and finishes the tune in the bass cleff.

[music]

The workmen, impatient to get their job done, signal the man above,
who lifts, and so almost snatches the piano from under Baby's hands.

'Crude fellow. Might hurt someone doing that sort of thing.'

'That reminds me. As I was telling you – you might say we – well,
why not come out with it – you'll understand – we *bought* this doctor,
and now it seems—' Their voices fade as they begin climbing—

—And up above, the driver looks over the edge and blusters down
to his companions:

'What is this – anyhow? You're hired to help them get the piano to the house "Villa Diana"? – or do you want 'em to play it on the side of this cliff? Tell those people to lay off this God—' The crack of his whip starting the team of horses behind him and the sound of the horses moving, drown out his description of the piano job.

And our piano, at first lazily spiraling as it moves upwards, begins to twist around and around so quickly that it, and the eccentric music accompanying it in its rise, blend into a whirling blur.

Finally it slows, and as it gently rights itself the keys are seemingly played by an unseen hand. Slowly a figure at the piano emerges and is playing. Blending into the picture is an orchestra surrounding the musician at the piano. *The orchestra is now rendering a full score of the melody that accompanied the piano up the cliff!*

The Divers are giving a dinner. Here all the charm of the menage which the Divers have created is apparent. The atmosphere of luxury and good taste of intimate friends has *not yet* been broken by the underlying sinister threat of cold hard calculating selfishness as personified by Baby Warren.

There is Dick, the compelling and magnetic host; there is Nicole, incomparable hostess and wife supreme; there is Rosemary Hoyt, motion picture star – young and beautiful and obviously infatuated with the enchanting Dick Diver; there is Prince Troubetskoi, with such attractions as women associate with romance, vainly endeavoring to conceal his passion for Nicole; there is Baby Warren, half-comic in her pretended aloofness; there is her little pudgy beau, pal of Troubetskoi and heir to the throne of some other vague Balkan principality, and there is an elderly English doctor from Cannes.

During the past three years of happy married life, the luxury and ample supply of the Warrens' money have caused Dick Diver's charm and ability to stage-manage his parties to overshadow his interest in the medical profession, even to the extent of dropping 'Doctor' as a prefix to his name. But inwardly there have been longings and old regrets, even though Dick is too proud to show them, and dreads the effect upon Nicole.

After dinner the men and women separate – the men following Prince Paklin to a series of small tables placed beside the cliff, the women going to the flat Moorish roof of the villa.

Dick and the old English doctor from Cannes remain at table – finishing a glass of champagne – they are naturally less interested in the visits from the cliff. The doctor has begun to take a paternal interest in Dick but his persistent remarks about getting back to work are irritating to Dick.

On the roof directly overhead the women closest to the edge are able to overhear the conversation that ensues. First Baby hears it, then Nicole, then Rosemary and a couple of curious guests.

Down below Dick has exploded.

'Stop it! Do you think I don't know? Do you think *you* are the *only* one who knows? Cooped up for three years! Private *doctor?* Private *nurse!*'

And he leaves the table and walks out on the terrace. Nicole is shocked and hurt. It is the first suspicion she has had that Dick was not entirely satisfied with their easy existence. Young Rosemary Hoyt's exaggerated sympathy for Dick tends to deepen Nicole's hurt. Baby Warren immediately takes possession of the situation. Her suspicions have been further aroused by Dick's outburst of discontent – and by Rosemary's tearing down the stairs to console Dick. Finding that Dick prefers to be alone, Rosemary kisses him lightly. Nicole arrives upon the scene at this moment and falsely interprets it as a love passage between Dick and Rosemary. The panic in Nicole's expression is the fade out on this sequence.

We open up on the Divers and their house guests on the beach next morning taking their customary dip in the blue Mediterranean and the inevitable sun bath on the beach. Dick suggests that they take the Divers' speed boat and do some aquaplaning. Nicole, with the jealousy of the previous evening still close to her, interprets Dick's desire to aquaplane as a method of showing off physically before Rosemary's exciting youth.

With Paklin Troubetskoi guiding the smooth little craft, each member of the party takes his turn on the board. When it comes to Dick's turn Nicole finds herself wondering with growing coldness if he will make a spectacle of himself, fumbling through stunts he had once done with ease. She compared him with the romantic figure of the Russian riding master beside her. For the first time Dick suffers from a comparison made by his wife.

Dick is preparing to do his old lifting trick – the object being to straighten all the way up, from a kneeling position, and carry a man on his shoulders. It is noticeable to the people in the boat, watching closely, that he is having difficulties. As the boat gathers momentum and the men on the board get their balance, Dick, with a last wrenching effort, stands upright, but the board slips side-wise simultaneously and they both topple off into the sea. Rosemary is enthused. 'Wonderful! They almost had it!' Baby Warren and Nicole are a little disgusted.

Dick – annoyed and perhaps a little embarrassed – tries again. He is more careful in this second attempt, and almost succeeds; but at the crucial moment his legs suddenly buckle, and both men are throne into the water again.

Dick is angry and asks for another chance, which, though he looks tired, is readily granted. As the speed of the boat increases, Dick rests for a moment, belly-down on the board. Then he crouches beneath the man and his muscles flex as he tries to rise. The passengers in the boat scarcely raise him-and-his-burden two inches from the board and exhausted, he collapses into the water. The boat races back to pick him up and Nicole's anxiety changes to contempt as she finds him floating exhaustedly but safely in the water. On the way in to the shore Baby Warren smiles as she remarks that the huge, well-built riding master beside him could have turned the trick easily 'with *three* men on his back!'

It is the last day of the week-end party and every one decides to go to a fair that is being held close to the Divers' home. On the way Dick senses Nicole's attitude towards the episode on the aquaplane that morning and this causes him to show more than ordinary interest in Rosemary. Arriving at the fair, Nicole suddenly opens the door of the car and leaps out. Dick and Baby follow her on the run while the riding master is left with Rosemary.

After bursting through countless tents and zig-zagging through the grounds of the entire fair, Dick finally sees Nicole riding on a ferris-wheel. As the car in which she is riding nears the top Nicole stands up and looks bewilderedly at the ground far below. Dick shouts to the operator of the wheel to stop it immediately. The man at first refuses, but Dick frantically presses money into his hand and the wheel is brought to a stop. Childishly, Nicole is reluctant to leave scolding Dick and Baby for following her. Dick and Baby realize that the mental disorder, which has been dormant for three years, has cropped up again. Baby accuses Dick.

'It's your fault that this happened. Your attitude towards that little kid, Rosemary—'

Dick and Baby lead Nicole against her will back to the car.

Tender Is the Night *Movie Treatment*

Nicole's mind wanders.

'I won't ride. I never want to see another horse. I had an accident riding a horse. They always frighten me now. Please don't make me ride – I'm afraid of horses.' (She sees Paklin Troubetskoi) 'But I'm not afraid if he's here. He was my riding master.'

Bewildered and uncertain, Nicole sits next to Dick who is driving. It is when Dick has stepped on the accelerator for a short straightaway run that Nicole, laughing hysterically, clutches the steering wheel and swerves the car off the road, down a little incline at the bottom of which it rolls over on its side. Dick's leg, unknown to the others, is pinned agonizingly under the side of the car. Rosemary is thrown against him in such a way that it looks as though he might have crawled over to her. Baby, unhurt, is draped awkwardly over the upright side of the car. Paklin Troubetskoi's first thought has been of Nicole and he scrambles out of the car with Nicole in his arms, holding her until she assures him, still hysterically, that she has not been hurt. Paklin has already hailed a passing car to take them home when the three women discover that Dick is hurt. But his injury doesn't succeed in quieting Nicole or curing the suspicion in Baby's mind that Dick's usefulness as Nicole's husband is over.

At the Divers' home Dick and Nicole are immediately put to bed in separate rooms. Baby Warren, who has been waiting for a chance to get another doctor's opinion on Nicole's case, calls in a physician from Cannes. He turns out to be the same old senile Englishman who aroused Dick Diver's ire during the dinner party. Being a simple country practitioner, it is comparatively easy for Baby to convince him, during the examination, that the sick girl's husband is responsible for her condition.

'He causes her worry over every new face he sees. He's lost all interest in my sister and thinks only of himself. How can we blame Nicole for getting sick when her husband, the man who should take care of her, does nothing but cause her mental anguish?'

Convinced, the small-time doctor prescribes a change of environment and urges that Nicole should be spared even seeing Dick.

This is all that Baby Warren needs and she goes into Dick's room and tells him as a matter of fact that Nicole would be better off without him. It is not in Baby's character to mince matters or situations; and without regard for Dick's injured condition she ends by telling Dick:

617

Appendix 1

'We hired you to take care of my sister – not to make her worse. The doctor and I have decided that it would be better for Nicole to forget you entirely. Nicole herself will realize that it is the best thing that could possibly happen to her.'

Dick, lying in bed with his leg badly crushed – physically and mentally hurt, and weary of Nicole's sickness, gives up. That Baby should come to him at a time like this and tell him flatly that they no longer require his service is more than he can stand. He murmurs:

'Do you think that I could have stood a moment with Nicole if I hadn't loved her? Would I have locked myself away from everything for three years if I hadn't cared? All right – I'm through. If you think Nicole can get along better without me – I'll leave. Perhaps I won't make such a mess of things alone.'

Impulsively, he topples out of bed and hobbles painfully to the door. The car is called and he leaves them. There is no restraining hand – they are glad to see him go. Baby and the doctor and Prince Paklin Troubetskoi watch the receding lights of his car as it threads its way down the steep descent to the road which leads away from the "Villa Diana". The case is finished. Doctor Diver is at liberty.

Now the flowers and foliage of the gardens and terraces which surround the 'Villa Diana' with their loveliness of spring have bared themselves in the lonely bleakness of winter. An atmosphere of restlessness prevails in the Divers' household. In particular, Baby Warren, a guest, cannot suppress her restless desire to leave the 'Villa Diana'. She intimates as much to the senile old English doctor from Cannes, who has been a regular visitor attending Nicole.

'I feel as though I'm shut off from the rest of the world – as though I'm a prisoner up here on this cliff.'

'That is what her husband said as he left,' says the doctor.

'This is different. I'm thinking of Nicole. She needs a change. The place gets on her nerves.'

'The young Russian who visits your sister so often – doesn't he relieve the monotony?'

'He can't change this place. This house is still the same, whether he's here or not. Besides, he thinks she should go away, too.'

Nicole is living in confusion. Something is missing. She cannot decide whether it is her condition or the loss of her husband that bewilders her. She had thought of Dick really as an inexhaustible energy, incapable of fatigue and she had forgotten the trouble she had caused him. Sometimes she has felt the old hypnotism of his intelligence, his kindness and patience with her. Yet, this Russian has been kind and undoubtedly patient. And most of all he has loved her for herself – not through the eyes of a professional man seeing only the work he revers so much.

Paklin enters even as Baby and the doctor are talking and goes into the next room to see Nicole. He comes right to the point.

'You've been keeping me waiting here for six months. Can't we go away? Your sister says you need the change.'

Comparative pictures of Dick and Paklin flash before Nicole's eyes. Doctor Diver – working, playing, knowing all. Paklin Troubetskoi – handsome, romantic, loving her because she is the rich Nicole Warren.

Baby Warren and the doctor enter. Baby explains that Nicole must leave 'Villa Diana' for her own good.

'The doctor and I have decided that a change—'

There follows a week of quiet, but thorough levity. The music, the dancing, and the gay nights are a tonic to Baby Warren's pent up nerves and incidentally serve as a change of environment for her sister. Back in circulation again, Baby nails one of her many admirers (the one who happened to attend the Divers' week-end party) and he invites them to his principality. Nicole and Paklin enjoy this rough little Balkan sea-side town (planted to be like Corfu or Ragusa) but Baby tires quickly and leaving the two alone, takes her Prince and goes to Vienna.

Meanwhile Doctor Diver has resumed his studies in Vienna, and has been practising brain surgery. He is badly in need of money. On his way home from one of the hospitals he sees Baby Warren sweeping grandly into the finest hotel, where she is staying. He enters and follows her into her suite in order to inquire after Nicole. Baby politely but coldly tells him that her sister is doing very well. A telephone call comes through at the moment from Nicole who is in trouble.

Upon Baby Warren's departure from the little Balkan resort Nicole and Paklin were elated to find themselves just as completely alone as though they had been stranded in mid-ocean. Nicole wanted an 'affair' – she did not want any vague spiritual romance; she wanted a change. And this Russian was making her thrill with delight in thinking of herself in a new way.

Driving through the pleasant countryside Nicole does not object when Paklin turns the car into a drive that leads to a small mountain hotel. She hovers, outwardly tranquil, as Paklin fills out the police blanks and registers the names – his real, hers false. Their room is simple, almost ascetic. Paklin orders brandy and when the waiter has brought it and left – they suddenly move together and meet standing up. Then he is kissing her as they sit on the bed.

Suddenly Nicole is conscious of that nameless fear which precedes all emotions, joyous or sorrowful, inevitably as a hum of thunder precedes a storm. Moment by moment all that Dick has taught her, all that he has grown to mean to her comes back. Realizing that she cannot go through with her 'affair', she tells Paklin so, as gently as she can. Paklin is astounded and at first does not believe her. When he is convinced that she means what she says, his hurt and disappointment turn to anger. He accuses her of being afraid of Dick, of being mentally still attuned to her doctor husband – unable to break away from his professional grip on her. But Nicole's mind is made up. She knows now that Dick matters more to her than anything else.

Paklin, who has drunk the remainder of the brandy, becomes defiant and drives Nicole back to town, telling her furiously that he will break this hold that Dick has on her.

'You don't know what a really good time is. You've never had one. You couldn't be gay – really gay, with a psychiatrist nagging you all the time. Now you're throwing over what could be the happiest part of your life—'

'Because I love Dick.'

'You don't love him. You didn't love him an hour ago. It's because you're always afraid of him. Well, tonight I'm going to get rid of that fear. You'll be gay tonight if it's the last thing you do.'

Frightened, Nicole is taken by Paklin to various bars and cafes. The Russian's method of showing her a gay time merely serves to disgust and frighten Nicole, and to make an objectionable drunk out of himself.

At last they reach a cabaret where a listless band is playing and a dozen couples cover the wide floor. Paklin has become somewhat noisy. With apparently no reason he picks a fight with one of the waiters. When they see that the big man is easily beating their co-worker, the other waiters join in the fight and before Nicole's

horrified eyes Paklin is beaten brutally to the floor. The police come
in and take Paklin to the police station. Nicole is left in the cabaret
with Paklin's drunken shouts for her to 'do something' still ringing in
her ears. 'Go to the American Ministry! Go to the Consulate! Go
somewhere and get me out of this filthy mess!'

In a daze Nicole goes to the Ministry to get help. It is late at night
and everyone there is asleep. She goes almost automatically through
the torture of shouting to half asleep men in their night shirts,
explaining to them why she is there, what has happened and what is
needed. But she runs up against a stone wall. They refuse to help
her saying it is impossible to assist a man who has started a street
brawl and resisted the police.

Nicole is frantic. The day and night has progressed at a staccato
rate and she is not habituated to such strains. She feels the old
mental reaction coming on and the need of her husband's steadying
hand. Hurrying to the last resource, the Consulate, she finally
succeeds in awakening the Consul and almost hysterically with her
impotence to get results, repeats her story. The Consul is galvanized
into activity and sends the vice-Consul with Nicole to rescue Paklin.

They find Paklin, under guard, slumped in a solitary chair in a
cell. His face is bruised and cut, his hair matted with blood. The
vice-Consul asks Nicole to call for a doctor. She does so, and then,
thoroughly exhausted, phones to her sister in the hotel in Vienna—

—where Baby Warren and Dick are talking. Nicole is at the
breaking point. At intervals a stupid central cuts in on the frantic
conversation – this serving further to upset Nicole.

'Baby – Baby! Come quickly. 'We're here – police station. It's
Paklin. He's – He'ss—' Hilarious hysterical laughter as Nicole sinks
to the floor still grasping the phone and her voice continuing:
'Where's Dick? Find him, bring him with you – I want him. Please
find Dick—' Nicole drops the phone as she slips into unconscious-
ness. At the other end of the line Baby is confused and worried. Dick
senses that it is Nicole who has phoned.

'What's the matter?'

'She's in trouble. Something wrong with Paklin, too. I'm going to
her.'

'I'm coming with you.'

'No. They don't need you.'

'Coming anyway.'

By the time Baby and Dick arrive, Nicole has been taken to a hospital. Doctors there consider her condition very serious and are at a loss as to the origin of it. When they hear that Dr. Diver has arrived they consult him on what to do. The implication is that it is a mysterious organic disease of the brain, something new to medical science. To operate calls for the skill of the best of brain surgeons and Dick is called upon to operate on his wife.

Whether he is operating on Nicole to save her for Paklin, Dick doesn't know, but he is making the attempt regardless.

In the quiet, mechanical smoothness of the operating room, in the midst of his delicate work – with the newness and mystery of this particular operation – and the burning sensation that he is trying to save Nicole for another man, Dick's nerve fails.

But Nicole, deep in the oblivion of the anesthetic murmurs once 'Dick' and his hand does not falter after that.

It takes weeks for Nicole to be able to sit up, but with her peace of mind and Dick's nearness it is made possible.

Finally when Baby Warren brings in Prince Paklin (whose face still shows the disfiguration of his battle with the police) to say goodbye before she (Baby) and Prince Paklin start on their newly planned love trip, both Nicole and Dick are happily content to look towards a future that promises brighter than it ever has before.

APPENDIX 2

From Fitzgerald's Ledger

Fitzgerald's *Ledger* includes a year-by-year accounting of his earnings from 1919 – his first year as a professional writer – through 1936. He stopped maintaining this record when he went to work for the movies in 1937.

This accounting is indispensable for understanding the shape of Fitzgerald's career as a professional writer – that is, the relationship between his magazine work and his novels. The record shows that his magazine stories brought most of his income. Moreover, by today's standards for a successful writer, he did not earn a great deal of money. Fitzgerald's earnings for 1919–36 were $386,382.96 after commissions – a total that includes movie work and all ancillary rights – for an average of $21,466 per year. During this period sales and serializations of his nine books brought $74,515. *This Side of Paradise* earned $14,375 plus $10,000 for movie rights; *The Beautiful and Damned*, $22,297 plus $2,250 for movie rights; *The Great Gatsby*, $8,397 plus $6,864 from the play and $18,910 for movie rights; *Tender Is the Night*, $16,307.* His first three volumes of stories brought a total of $11,270.

Fitzgerald's books did not enjoy steady backlist sales. In 1929, the year *The Saturday Evening Post* raised his story price to $4,000, his total royalties on seven books were $31.77.

---

*The figure for *Tender Is the Night* is uncertain because it is impossible to untangle the loans and advances against this novel.

Appendix 2

Money Earned by Writing since Leaving Army

	Record for 1919		
Stories	Babes in the Woods		
	[*Smart Set*]	$	30.00
	The Debutante (Play)		
	[*Smart Set*]		35.00
	The Four Fists		
	[*Scribner's*]		150.00
	The Cut Glass Bowl		
	[*Scribner's*]		150.00
	Porcelain + Pink (Play)		
	[*Smart Set*]		35.00
	Dalyrimple goes Wrong		
	[*Smart Set*]		40.00
	Benediction		
	[*Smart Set*]		40.00
	Head and Shoulders		
	[*Saturday Evening Post*]		360.00
	A Dirge (Poem)		
	[*Judge*]		4.00
	Mr. Icky (Play)		
	[*Smart Set*]		35.00
	Total Earnings		879.00*

	Record for 1920	
*Stories**	The Ice Palace	
	[*Saturday Evening Post*]	360.00
	Myra Meets His Family	
	[*Saturday Evening Post*]	360.00
	The Camels Back	
	[*Saturday Evening Post*]	450.00
	Bernice Bobs her Hair	
	[*Saturday Evening Post*]	450.00

*Editorial note: These figures are after agent's commissions were deducted. Bracketed material has been supplied. Fitzgerald's arithmetic has not been corrected.

From Fitzgerald's Ledger

	The Off-Shore Pirate	
	[*Saturday Evening Post*]	450.00
	The Smilers	
	[*Smart Set*]	35.00
	May Day	
	[*Smart Set*]	200.00
	Tarquin of Cheapside	
	[*Smart Set*]	50.00
	The Jellybean	
	[*Metropolitan*]	810.00
	The Russet Witch	
	[*Metropolitan*]	810.00
	Total	3,975.00
Movies	Head and Shoulders	
	[Metro]	2,250.00
	Myra Meets His Family	
	[Fox]	900.00
	The Off Shore Pirate	
	[Metro]	2,025.00
	Option on my output	
	[Metro]	2,700.00
	Total	7,425.00
Other Writings	This is a Magazine	
	[*Vanity Fair*]	75.00
	Total	75.00
From Books	This Side of Paradise	6,200.00
	Flappers and Philosophers	500.00
	Total	6,700.00
	Total	$18,175.00
	*Ommission – The Lees of Happiness	
	[*Chicago Tribune*]	675.00
	Total	$18,850.00

Appendix 2

	Record for 1921	
Stories	The Popular Girl	
	[*Saturday Evening Post*]	$ 1,350.00
	Total	1,350.00
Serial	The Beautiful + Damned	
	[*Metropolitan*]	6,300.00
	Total	6,300.00
Other Writings	Jemina	
	[*Vanity Fair*]	100.00
	The Baltimore Anti-Christ	
	[*Bookman*]	13.50
	The Far-seeing Skeptics	
	[*Smart Set*]	5.00
	Brass	
	[*Bookman*]	7.00
	Total	135.50
From Books	This Side of Paradise	5,636.68
	Flappers and Philosophers	2,730.00
	The Beautiful and Damned	
	(advance)	2,813.19
	Total	11,179.68
English Advance	(Add *Syndication*	
	Jelly Bean $5.00)	100.00
	Total	$19,065.18

	Record for 1922	
Stories	The Diamond as big as the Ritz	
	[*Smart Set*]	270.00
	Benjamin Button	
	[*Collier's*]	900.00
	Two for a Cent	
	[*Metropolitan*]	810.00
	Winter Dreams	
	[*Metropolitan*]	810.00
	Total	2,790.00

From *Fitzgerald's* Ledger

Movie	The Beautiful and Damned [Warner Bros.]	2,250.00
Other Writings	On Being Twenty five [*American*]	800.00
	Little Brother of the Flapper [unlocated]	900.00
	The Moment of Revolt [*McCall's*]	250.00
	Canadian Winter Dreams	90.00
	'Love Legend' (review) [*New York Evening Post*]	5.00
	'The Oppidan' (review) [*New York Tribune*]	3.00
	'Margie Wins the Game' (review) [*New York Tribune*]	5.00
	Movies and the Publisher [unlocated]	5.00
	Total	7,098.00
English Rights	Forty seven pounds	212.00
From Books	This Side of Paradise	1,200.00
	Flappers and Philosophers	350.00
	The Beautiful and Damned	12,133.00
	Tales of the Jazz Age	3.056.00
	The Vegetable (advance)	1,236.00
	Total (all these book figures estimated)	17,775.00
	Total	$25,135.00

Zelda's Earnings
The Super-Flapper
[unlocated] $ 500.00

The Moment of Revolt		
[*McCall's*]		250.00
Review of Beautiful + Damned		
[*New York Tribune*]		15.00
Eulogy on the Flapper		
[*Metropolitan*]		50.00
Total	$	815.00

Record for 1923

Stories	Option from Hearsts		
	[1923 stories]	$	1,350.00
	'Dice, Brassknuckles and Guitar'		
	[*Hearst's International*]		1,350.00
	Hot and Cold Blood		
	[*Hearst's International*]		1,350.00
	'Diamond Dick'		
	[*Hearst's International*]		1,350.00
	'Our Own Movie Queen' (half Zelda)		
	[*Chicago Tribune*]		900.00
	Gretchen's Forty Winks		
	[*Saturday Evening Post*]		1,080.00
	Winter Dreams (English Rights)		112.50
	Total		7,492.50

Movies	This Side of Paradise	
	[Famous Players]	10,000.00
	The Camel's Back	
	[Warner Bros.]	1,000.00
	Grit	
	[Film Guild]	2,000.00
	Titles for Glimpses of the Moon	
	[Famous Players]	500.00
	Total	13,500.00

From *Fitzgerald's* Ledger

Play Advance		450.00
Other Writings	Imagination and a few Mothers	
	[*Ladies Home Journal*]	900.00
	The Cruise of the Rolling Junk	
	[*Motor*]	270.00
	Making Monogamy Work	
	[Metropolitan Newspaper Service]	270.00
	Our Irresponsible Rich	
	[Metropolitan Newspaper Service]	315.00
	The Most Disgraceful Thing I Ever Did	
	[*Vanity Fair*]	20.00
	Review of Being Respectable	
	[*Literary Digest International Book Review*]	15.00
	Review of Many Marriages	
	[*New York Herald*]	5.00
	Review of Through the Wheat	
	[*New York Evening Post*]	5.00
	Total	1,800.00
	Syndicate Returns	67.28
Books	This Side of Paradise	880.00
	Flappers and Philosophers	98.00
	The Beautiful and Damned	292.00
	Tales of the Jazz Age	270.43
	Total (figures estimated)	1,510.00
	Advance on New Novel	
	(The Great Gatsby)	3,939.00
	Total	5,450.00
	Total	$28,759.78

Appendix 2

Stories*	**Record for 1924**	
	The Baby Party	
	[*Hearst's International*]	1,350.00
	The Sensible Thing	
	[*Liberty*]	1,575.00
	Rags Martin-Jones and the Pr-nce of W-les	
	[*McCall's*]	1,575.00
	The Third Casket	
	[*Saturday Evening Post*]	1,575.00
	One of My Oldest Friends	
	[*Woman's Home Companion*]	1,575.00
	The Pusher-in-the Face	
	[*Woman's Home Companion*]	1,575.00
	The Unspeakable Egg	
	[*Saturday Evening Post*]	1,575.00
	John Jackson's Arcady	
	[*Saturday Evening Post*]	1,575.00
	Love in the Night	
	[*Saturday Evening Post*]	1,575.00
	The Adjuster	
	[*Red Book*]	1,800.00
	Total	15,750.00
English Rights	The Third Casket	
	The Sensible Thing	
	Rags Martin-Jones and the Pr-nce of W-les	
	Total	241.20
Articles	Wait till You Have Children of Your Own	
	[*Woman's Home Companion*]	900.00
	How to Live on $36,000 a Year	
	[*Saturday Evening Post*]	900.00
	How to Live on Practically Nothing a Year	
	[*Saturday Evening Post*]	1,080.00
	Total	2,880.00

From Fitzgerald's Ledger

Syndicate		103.52
Other Rights	The Third Casket (German Rights)	17.50
From Books	This Side of Paradise	325.00
(inc. English	Flappers and Philosophers	16.00
and Syndicate)	The Beautiful and Damned	527.00
	Tales of the Jazz Age	7.00
	The Great Gatsby (further advance)	325.00
		1,200.00
	Total	$20,192.22
	*Ommission Absolution [*American Mercury*]	118.00
	Total	$20,310.22

Record for 1925

Stories	Not in the Guide Book [*Woman's Home Companion*]	1,575.00
	A Penny Spent [*Saturday Evening Post*]	1,800.00
	The Rich Boy [*Red Book*]	3,150.00
	Presumption [*Saturday Evening Post*]	2,250.00
	The Adolescent Marriage [*Saturday Evening Post*]	2,250.00
	Total	$11,025.00
Books	This Side of Paradise	26.24
	Flappers and Philosophers	21.65
	The Beautiful and Damned	144.30
	Tales of the Jazz Age	20.54
	The Great Gatsby	1,981.85
	All the Sad Young Men (advance)	2,717.33
	Total	4,906.61

Appendix 2

Misselaneous	Advance on Gatsby play	900.00
	Gatsby second serial	
	[*Famous Story*]	900.00
	Old New England Farmhouse	
	[*College Humor*]	180.00
	Syndicate	282.00
	Gretchen's Forty Winks	60.00
	(English)	
	Love in the Night (English)	80.00
	Total	2,402.00
	Total	$18,333.61

	Record for 1926	
Stories	Your Way and Mine	
	[*Woman's Home Companion*]	1,575.00
	The Dance	
	[*Red Book*]	1,800.00
	Total	3,375.00
English Rights	Love in the Night	
	(see previous page)	78.00
	One of Our Oldest Friends	83.45
	A Penny Spent	61.92
	The Adolescent Marriage	64.80
	Total	288.17
Syndicate ect	Adjuster, Pusher in the	
	Face, Oldest Friends	222.68
Article	How to Waste Material	
	[*Bookman*]	90.00
Books	This Side of Paradise	44.00
(inc. English)	Flappers and Philosophers	35.80
	The Beautiful and Damned	33.10
	Tales of the Jazz Age	21.20

	The Great Gatsby	508.25
	All the Sad Young Men	1,181.05
	Total	2,033.20
Foreign	Danish and Swedish Rights to Gatsby	213.00
Moving Picture	The Great Gatsby [Famous Players]	13,500.00
Play (The Great Gatsby)	New York Run	2,616.98
	Chicago Run	2,673.97
	Road Run	673.26
	(Detroit, Brklyn, Balt., St. Louis, Chi, Denver, Phila)	5,964.21
	Total	$25,686.05
	Love in the Night (English)	97.75
Stories	**Record for 1927** Jacob's Ladder [*Saturday Evening Post*]	$ 2,700.00
	The Love Boat [*Saturday Evening Post*]	3,150.00
	A Short Trip Home [*Saturday Evening Post*]	3,150.00
	The Bowl [*Saturday Evening Post*]	3,150.00
	Magnetism [*Saturday Evening Post*]	3,150.00
	Total	15,300.00
Movies	California work on 'Lipstick' [M-G-M]	3,500.00
	Additional Payment 'Gatsby'	2,910.00
	Total	6,410.00

Appendix 2

<table>
<tr><td rowspan="1">Other Writings
and Rights</td><td>Princeton
[College Humor]</td><td align="right">450.00</td></tr>
<tr><td></td><td>Editorial Photoplay (Zelda)
['Paint and Powder', Smart Set]</td><td align="right">450.00</td></tr>
<tr><td></td><td>Park Avenue ("   )
[Harper's Bazaar]</td><td align="right">300.00</td></tr>
<tr><td></td><td>Looking Back 8 Years ("   )
[College Humor]</td><td align="right">300.00</td></tr>
<tr><td></td><td>English 'Presumption'</td><td align="right">68.98</td></tr>
<tr><td></td><td>German 'Rags Martin Jones'</td><td align="right">25.00</td></tr>
<tr><td></td><td>Golden BK 'Pusher in Face'</td><td align="right">99.00</td></tr>
<tr><td></td><td>Anthology 'Pusher in Face'</td><td align="right">22.50</td></tr>
<tr><td></td><td>Anthology 'Jellybean'</td><td align="right">26.67</td></tr>
<tr><td></td><td>Syndicate 'Your Way + Mine'
ect</td><td align="right">137.44</td></tr>
<tr><td></td><td>German Rights to Gatsby</td><td align="right">141.00</td></tr>
<tr><td></td><td>All English Book Royalties</td><td align="right">95.32</td></tr>
<tr><td></td><td>Total</td><td align="right">2,096.11</td></tr>
<tr><td>Books</td><td>This Side of Paradise</td><td align="right">13.03</td></tr>
<tr><td></td><td>The Beautiful and Damned</td><td align="right">14.80</td></tr>
<tr><td></td><td>The Great Gatsby</td><td align="right">55.65</td></tr>
<tr><td></td><td>Flappers and Philosophers</td><td align="right">26.70</td></tr>
<tr><td></td><td>Tales of the Jazz Age</td><td align="right">16.35</td></tr>
<tr><td></td><td>All the Sad Young Men</td><td align="right">43.05</td></tr>
<tr><td></td><td>Advance on New Novel Serial
[Tender Is the Night]</td><td align="right">5,752.06</td></tr>
<tr><td></td><td>Total</td><td align="right">5,911.64</td></tr>
<tr><td></td><td>Total</td><td align="right">29,737.87</td></tr>
</table>

Tax Unpaid 1926

Adolescent Marriage	$ 64.80
Gatsby Road	320.15
	384.95

From *Fitzgerald's* Ledger

	Record for 1928	
Stories	The Scandal Detectives	
	[*Saturday Evening Post*]	3,150.00
	The Freshest Boy	
	[*Saturday Evening Post*]	3,150.00
	A Night at the Fair	
	[*Saturday Evening Post*]	3,150.00
	He Thinks he's Wonderful	
	[*Saturday Evening Post*]	3,150.00
	The Captured Shadow	
	[*Saturday Evening Post*]	3,150.00
	The Perfect Life	
	[*Saturday Evening Post*]	3,150.00
	The Georgia Belle	
	['The Last of the Belles,'	
	Saturday Evening Post]	3,150.00
	Total	22,050.00
Other Writings	Outside the Cabinet Makers	
	[*Century*]	135.00
	Who Can Fall in Love	
	after Thirty (Zelda)	
	[*College Humor*]	180.00
	Syndicate (Wheeler)	12.15
	Magnetism (English)	78.25
	Bell Syndicate	2.23
	Total	406.67
Advertisement	[Woodbury Soap]	1,000.00
Books	This Side of Paradise	22.05
	The Beautiful and Damned	22.40
	Flappers + Philosophers	12.30
	Tales of the Jazz Age	12.90
	The Vegetable	8.60
	The Great Gatsby	44.15
	All the Sad Young Men	25.05

	Further Advance on New Novel Serial	2,129.03
	Total	2,272.96
	Total	25,732.96

Record for 1929

Stories	Forging Ahead [*Saturday Evening Post*]	$ 3,150.00
	Basil + Cleopatra [*Saturday Evening Post*]	3,150.00
	Rough Crossing [*Saturday Evening Post*]	3,150.00
	Majesty [*Saturday Evening Post*]	3,150.00
	At Your Age [*Saturday Evening Post*]	3,600.00
	The Swimmers [*Saturday Evening Post*]	3,600.00
	Two Wrongs [*Saturday Evening Post*]	3,600.00
	First Blood [*Saturday Evening Post*]	3,600.00
	Total	27,000.00

Zelda's Sketches	Original Follies Girl [*College Humor*]	360.00
	Poor Working Girl [*College Humor*]	450.00
	Southern Girl [*College Humor*]	450.00
	Girl the Prince Liked [*College Humor*]	450.00
	Girl with Talent [*College Humor*]	720.00
	Total	2,430.00

From Fitzgerald's Ledger

Misselaneous	Talkie Rights B+D	900.00
	Girls Believe in Girls	
	[*Liberty*]	1,350.00
	Advertisement	
	[Woodbury Soap]	500.00
	Short Autobiography	
	[*New Yorker*]	90.00
	Golden Bk 'One of My Oldest'	90.00
	English 'Outside Cabinet'	34.56
	Reprints	21.85
	Total	2,986.41
Books	This Side of Paradise	4.80
	Flappers + Philosophers	11.70
	The Beautiful + Damned	3.60
	Tales of the Jazz Age	3.00
	Great Gatsby	5.10
	All Sad Young Men	2.10
	Vegetable	1.13
	English Gatsby	.34
	Total	31.77
	Grand Total	$32,448.18

Record for 1930

Stories	A Nice Quiet Place	
	[*Saturday Evening Post*]	$ 3,600.00
	The Bridal Party	
	[*Saturday Evening Post*]	3,600.00
	A Woman with a Past	
	[*Saturday Evening Post*]	3,600.00
	One Trip Abroad	
	[*Saturday Evening Post*]	3,600.00
	A Snobbish Story	
	[*Saturday Evening Post*]	3,600.00
	The Hotel Child	
	[*Saturday Evening Post*]	3,600.00

	Babylon Revisited	
	[*Saturday Evening Post*]	3,600.00
	Total	25,200.00
Other Items	Salesmanship in the Champs Elysee [*New Yorker*]	
	At Your Age – Modern Library	
	Two for a Cent – Golden Book	
	Jacob's Ladder English Reprints	
	Total	341.10
Zelda's Writings	The Millionaire's Girl	
	[*Saturday Evening Post*]	3,600.00
	Miss Bessie	
	['Miss Ella,' *Scribner's*]	150.00
	Total	3,750.00
Books	This Side of Paradise	10.20
	Flappers + Philosophers	10.05
	The Beautiful + Damned	4.80
	Tales of the Jazz Age	8.40
	The Vegetable	1.12
	The Great Gatsby	15.60
	All the Sad Young Men (+ Presentday Stories)	51.80
	Further Advances (Serial new novel + 1,583.06 against bk.	3,701.97
	Total	3,820.00
	Grand Total	$33,090.10

	Record for 1931	
Stories	Indecision	
	[*Saturday Evening Post*]	3,600.00

From Fitzgerald's Ledger

A New Leaf		
	[*Saturday Evening Post*]	3,600.00
Flight and Pursuit		
	[*Saturday Evening Post*]	3,600.00
Emotional Bankruptcy		
	[*Saturday Evening Post*]	3,600.00
Between Three and Four		
	[*Saturday Evening Post*]	3,600.00
A Change of Class		
	[*Saturday Evening Post*]	3,600.00
Half a Dozen of the Other		
	['Six of One,' *Redbook*]	2,700.00
A Freeze Out		
	[*Saturday Evening Post*]	3,600.00
Diagnosis		
	[*Saturday Evening Post*]	3,600.00
	Total	31,500.00

Other Items	Treatment Metro Goldwyn Mayer	
	[*Red Headed Woman*]	5,400.00
	Echoes of the Jazz Age	
	[*Scribner's*]	500.00
	Vegetable Performance	22.50
	New Leaf (English)	59.00
	Flight + Pursuit (English)	126.00
	John Jackson's Arcady	2.00
	Total	6,109.50

Books	This Side of Paradise	12.90
	Flappers + Philosophers	4.30
	The Beautiful + Damned	4.40
	Tales of the Jazz Age	3.90
	The Vegetable	1.13
	The Great Gatsby	17.90
	All the Sad Young Men	7.90
	Advance against Bk.	44.15
	Total	100.00

Appendix 2

	Less: Not paid in 1931 by Metro	−155.35
	Grand Total	37,554.00
	New Yorker sketch	45.00
		37,599.00

Record for 1932

Stories	Crazy Sunday		
	·[*American Mercury*]	$	200.00
	Family in the Wind		
	[*Saturday Evening Post*]		3,150.00
	What a Hansome Pair		
	[*Saturday Evening Post*]		2,250.00
	The Rubber Check		
	[*Saturday Evening Post*]		2,700.00
	Interne		
	[*Saturday Evening Post*]		3,150.00
	On Schedule		
	[*Saturday Evening Post*]		2,700.00
	Total		14,805.00

Other Items	Reprint of The New Leaf	
	Walter Baker Royalty	
	Flight + Pursuit (English)	
	Couple of Nuts (Zelda)	
	[*Scribner's*]	
	The Gourmets (Zelda)	
	[unlocated; possibly 'The Continental Angle,' *New Yorker*]	
	Total of all these	313.40

Books	All Royalties	20.00
	Advance on Novel	480.00
	Total	500.00
	Grand Total	15,823.40

From Fitzgerald's Ledger

Record for 1933

Stories	More than just a House	
	[*Saturday Evening Post*]	2,700.00
	I Got Shoes	
	[*Saturday Evening Post*]	2,250.00
	The Family Bus	
	[*Saturday Evening Post*]	2,700.00
Articles	My Lost City	
	[unpublished]	900.00
	One Hundred False Starts	
	[*Saturday Evening Post*]	1,080.00
Books	*Tender* and *Taps* Advance	4,200.00
	and new advance	
	of 1,690.21	
	Other Books	30.00
	Save me the Waltz	120.00
Sound Rights	The Great Gatsby	2,250.00
Other Items	Two for a Cent (English)	34.81
	New Leaf (Home Mag.	
	English)	63.03
	John Jackson (Royalties)	19.00
		16,328.03

Record for 1934

Stories	No Flowers	
	[*Saturday Evening Post*]	2,700.00
	New Types	
	[*Saturday Evening Post*]	2,700.00
	Her Last Case	
	[*Saturday Evening Post*]	2,700.00
	In the Darkest Hour	
	[*Redbook*]	1,125.00

641

	The Count of Darkness	
	[*Redbook*]	1,350.00
	A Kingdom in the Dark	
	[*Redbook*]	1,350.00
	The Fiend	
	[*Esquire*]	250.00
	The Night before	
	Chancellorsville	
	[*Esquire*]	250.00
		12,475.00
All Books		58.35
Misselaneous	Ring Lardner	
	[*New Republic*]	50.00
	Preface to Gatsby	
	[Modern Library]	50.00
	Broadcast of Diamond	45.00
	Family in the Wind (Swedish)	12.27
	Your Age (Modern)	3.16
	Show Mr + Mrs F.	
	[*Esquire*]	200.00
	Auction – Model 1934	
	[*Esquire*]	200.00
	Modern American Prose	37.50
	Smart Set Anthology	12.50
	Chatto + Windus	156.31
	American Short Story	1.02
	Gatsby Modern Library	250.00
		1,017.76
	On New Work	6,481.98
Scribner *Advance*		20,032.33

From *Fitzgerald's* Ledger

Record for 1935

Stories

The Intimate Strangers	
[*McCall's*]	2,700.00
Zone of Accident	
[*Saturday Evening Post*]	2,700.00
What You Don't Know	
['Fate in Her Hands,'	
American]	2,700.00
Too Cute for Words	
[*Saturday Evening Post*]	2,700.00
Gods of the Darkness	
[*Redbook*]	1,350.00
The Esquimo Boy	
['The Passionate Eskimo,'	
Liberty]	1,350 00
The Image on the Heart	
[*McCall's*]	1,125.00
	14,725.00

Misselaneous

Lamp in a Window	
[*New Yorker*]	22.50
Modern Library Royalty	17.89
English Sale – The Fiend	41.93
Columbia Broadcast 'Lets go	
Out'	630.00
Shaggy's Morning	
[*Esquire*]	250.00
Same – London	31.00
Sleeping + Waking	
[*Esquire*]	250.00
Your Age	10.88
Crack Up	
[*Esquire*]	250.00
Paste Together	
[*Esquire*]	250.00
Brittish Fiend	41.93
	1,796.13

Appendix 2

All Books	and Advance	$	342.03
			16,845.16

Record for 1936

Stories	Outside the House ['Inside the House,' *Saturday Evening Post*]		$ 3,000.00
	Make Yourself At Home [*Pictorial Review*; possibly published as 'Strange Sanctuary,' *Liberty*]		2,500.00
	The Pearl + the Fur [unpublished, *Pictorial Review*		1,000.00
	Trouble [*Saturday Evening Post*]		2,000.00
	−10%		7,650.00

Esquire Pieces	Handle with Care	250.00
	Three Acts of Music	''
	The Ants at Princeton	''
	Author's House	''
	Afternoon of an Author	''
	An Author's Mother	''
	I Didn't Get Over	''
	Please Send me in, Coach	''
	An Alcoholic Case	''
		2,250.00

Misscelaneous	Modern Library, British + Danish, John Jackson ect	199.79
All Books		81.18
	Total	10,180.97

From Fitzgerald's Ledger

	Record for 1937
Stories	The Goon
	[*Esquire*]
	The Long Way Out
	[*Esquire*]
	In the Holidays
	[*Esquire*]
	Room 13
	[*Esquire*]
	Financing Finnegan
	[*Esquire*]
Misselaneous	Obit on Parnassus
	[*New Yorker*]
	Book of Ones Own
	[*New Yorker*]
	Early Success
	[*American Cavalcade*]
	Foreign Sales (Gatsby)
	Random House
	Scribners (All Books)

[Fitzgerald stopped maintaining his *Ledger* when he went to California in June 1937.]

Zelda's Earnings

1922   Four articles ['The Super-Flapper,'
unpublished; 'Friend Husband's Latest,' *New
York Tribune*; 'Eulogy on the Flapper,'
Metropolitan; 'Does a Moment of Revolt
Come Sometime to Every Married Man?' $ 815.00*
McCall's]

1923   Our Own Movie Queen (Story – half mine)
       [*Chicago Sunday Tribune*]   450.00

*Editorial note: These figures are after agent's commissions were deducted.
Bracketed material has been supplied.

Appendix 2

1927	Editorial Photoplay (*unpublished*)	
	['Paint and Powder,' *Smart Set*]	450.00
	Park Avenue	
	[*Harper's Bazaar*]	300.00
	Looking Back Eight Years	
	[*College Humor*]	300.00
1928	Who Can Fall in Love After Thirty	
	[*College Humor*]	180.00
1929	The Original Follies Girl	
	[*College Humor*]	360.00
	The Poor Working Girl (*unpublished*)	
	[*College Humor*]	450.00
	The Southern Girl	
	[*College Humor*]	450.00
	The Girl the Prince Liked	
	[*College Humor*]	450.00
	The Girl with Talent	
	[*College Humor*]	720.00
	Total	5,075.00
1930	The Millionaire's Girl	
	[*Saturday Evening Post*]	3,600.00
	Miss Bessie	
	['Miss Ella," *Scribner's*]	135.00
1931	The Continental Angle	
	[*New Yorker*]	
1932	A Couple of Nuts	
	[*Scribner's*]	
1932	Save Me the Waltze	
	[novel]	
1934	Show Mr + Mrs F. to Number —	
	[*Esquire*]	
1934	Auction Model 1934	
	[*Esquire*]	

APPENDIX 3

F. Scott Fitzgerald's Publications, Zelda Fitzgerald's Publications, Principal Works about Fitzgerald

Books by Fitzgerald
(This chronological list omits privately printed pamphlets and keepsakes which were not for sale.)

Fie! Fie! Fi-Fi! Cincinnati, New York & London: The John Church Co., 1914. 17 song lyrics.

The Evil Eye. Cincinnati, New York & London: The John Church Co., 1915. 17 song lyrics.

Safety First. Cincinnati, New York & London: The John Church Co., 1916. 21 song lyrics.

This Side of Paradise. New York: Scribners, 1920; London: Collins, 1921. Novel.

Flappers and Philosophers. New York: Scribners, 1920; London: Collins, 1922. Stories: 'The Offshore Pirate,' 'The Ice Palace,' 'Head and Shoulders,' 'The Cut-Glass Bowl,' 'Bernice Bobs Her Hair,' 'Benediction,' 'Dalyrimple Goes Wrong,' 'The Four Fists.'

The Beautiful and Damned. New York: Scribners, 1922; London: Collins, 1922. Novel.

Tales of the Jazz Age. New York: Scribners, 1922; London: Collins, 1923. Stories: My Last Flappers: 'The Jelly-Bean,' 'The Camel's Back,' 'May Day,' 'Porcelain and Pink'; Fantasies: 'The Diamond as Big as the Ritz,' 'The Curious Case of Benjamin Button,'

647

'Tarquin of Cheapside,' 'O Russet Witch!'; Unclassified Master-
pieces: 'The Lees of Happiness,' 'Mr. Icky,' 'Jemina.'
The Vegetable. New York: Scribners, 1923. Play.
The Great Gatsby. New York: Scribners, 1925; London: Chatto &
Windus, 1926. Novel. *The Great Gatsby: A Facsimile of the
Manuscript,* ed. Matthew J. Bruccoli. Washington: Bruccoli
Clark/NCR Microcard Books, 1973.
All the Sad Young Men. New York: Scribners, 1926. Stories: 'The Rich
Boy,' 'Winter Dreams,' 'The Baby Party,' 'Absolution,' 'Rags
Martin-Jones and the Pr-nce of W-les,' 'The Adjuster,' 'Hot and
Cold Blood,' ' "The Sensible Thing," ' 'Gretchen's Forty Winks.'
John Jackson's Arcady, arranged for reading by Lilian Holmes Strack.
Boston: Baker, 1928. Story.
Tender Is the Night. New York: Scribners, 1934; London: Chatto &
Windus, 1934. Novel. *Tender Is the Night,* 'With the Author's Final
Revisions,' ed. Malcolm Cowley. New York: Scribners, 1951;
London: Grey Walls, 1953.
Taps at Reveille. New York: Scribners, 1935. Stories: Basil: 'The
Scandal Detectives,' 'The Freshest Boy,' 'He Thinks He's
Wonderful,' 'The Captured Shadow,' 'The Perfect Life';
Josephine: 'First Blood,' 'A Nice Quiet Place,' 'A Woman with a
Past'; 'Crazy Sunday,' 'Two Wrongs,' 'The Night of Chancel-
lorsville,' 'The Last of the Belles,' 'Majesty,' 'Family in the Wind,'
'A Short Trip Home,' 'One Interne,' 'The Fiend,' 'Babylon
Revisited.'
The Last Tycoon. New York: Scribners, 1941; London: Grey Walls,
1949. Unfinished novel. With *The Great Gatsby* and 5 stories.
The Crack-Up, ed. Edmund Wilson. New York: New Directions,
1945. Includes 'Echoes of the Jazz Age,' 'My Lost City,' 'Ring,'
' "Show Mr. and Mrs. F to Number —," ' 'Auction – Model 1934,'
'Sleeping and Waking,' 'The Crack-Up,' 'Handle with Care,'
'Pasting It Together,' 'Early Success,' selections from the
Notebooks, and letters.
The Stories of F. Scott Fitzgerald, ed. Malcolm Cowley. New York:
Scribners, 1951. 'The Diamond as Big as the Ritz,' 'Bernice Bobs
Her Hair,' 'The Ice Palace,' 'May Day,' 'Winter Dreams,' ' "The
Sensible Thing," ' 'Absolution,' 'The Rich Boy,' 'The Baby Party,'
'Magnetism,' 'The Last of the Belles,' 'The Rough Crossing,' 'The
Bridal Party,' 'Two Wrongs,' 'The Scandal Detectives,' 'The
Freshest Boy,' 'The Captured Shadow,' 'A Woman with a Past,'

'Babylon Revisited,' 'Crazy Sunday,' 'Family in the Wind,' 'An Alcoholic Case,' 'The Long Way Out,' 'Financing Finnegan,' 'A Patriotic Short,' 'Two Old-Timers,' 'Three Hours Between Planes,' 'The Lost Decade.'

Afternoon of an Author, ed. Arthur Mizener. Princeton, N.J.: Princeton University Library, 1957; New York: Scribners, 1958; London: Bodley Head, 1958. Stories and essays: 'A Night at the Fair,' 'Forging Ahead,' 'Basil and Cleopatra,' 'Princeton,' 'Who's Who – and Why,' 'How to Live on $36,000 a Year,' 'How to Live on Practically Nothing a Year,' 'How to Waste Material,' 'Ten Years in the Advertising Business,' 'One Hundred False Starts,' 'Outside the Cabinet-Maker's,' 'One Trip Abroad,' ' "I Didn't Get Over," ' 'Afternoon of an Author,' 'Author's House,' 'Design in Plaster,' ' "Boil Some Water – Lots of It," ' 'Teamed with Genius," 'No Harm Trying,' 'News of Paris – Fifteen Years Ago.'

The Pat Hobby Stories, ed. Arnold Gingrich. New York: Scribners, 1962; Harmondsworth: Penguin, 1967. 'Pat Hobby's Christmas Wish,' 'A Man in the Way,' ' "Boil Some Water – Lots of It," ' 'Teamed with Genius,' 'Pat Hobby and Orson Welles,' 'Pat Hobby's Secret,' 'Pat Hobby, Putative Father,' 'The Homes of the Stars,' 'Pat Hobby Does His Bit,' 'Pat Hobby's Preview,' 'No Harm Trying,' 'A Patriotic Short,' 'On the Trail of Pat Hobby,' 'Fun in an Artist's Studio,' 'Two Old-Timers,' 'Mightier than the Sword,' 'Pat Hobby's College Days.'

The Letters of F. Scott Fitzgerald, ed. Andrew Turnbull. New York: Scribners, 1963; London: Bodley Head, 1964.

The Apprentice Fiction of F. Scott Fitzgerald, ed. John Kuehl. New Brunswick, N.J.: Rutgers University Press, 1965. 'The Mystery of the Raymond Mortgage,' 'Reade, Substitute Right Half,' 'A Debt of Honor,' 'The Room with the Green Blinds,' 'A Luckless Santa Claus,' 'The Trail of the Duke,' 'Pain and the Scientist,' 'Shadow Laurels,' 'The Ordeal,' 'The Debutante,' 'The Spire and the Gargoyle,' 'Tarquin of Cheapside,' 'Babes in the Woods,' 'Sentiment – and the Use of Rouge,' 'The Pierian Springs and the Last Straw,' Appendix: 'The Death of My Father.'

Thoughtbook of Francis Scott Key Fitzgerald, ed. John Kuehl. Princeton, N.J.: Princeton University Library, 1965.

Dearly Beloved. Iowa City, Iowa: Windhover Press, 1970. Story.

F. Scott Fitzgerald in His Own Time: A Miscellany, ed. Matthew J. Bruccoli and Jackson R. Bryer. Kent, Ohio: Kent State University

Press, 1971. Poems and lyrics, contributions to the *Princeton Tiger* and the *Nassau Literary Magazine*, reviews, letters, articles, and interviews. Also material about Fitzgerald.

Dear Scott/Dear Max, ed. John Kuehl and Jackson R. Bryer. New York: Scribners, 1971; London: Cassell, 1973. The Fitzgerald/Maxwell Perkins correspondence.

As Ever, Scott Fitz—, ed. Matthew J. Bruccoli and Jennifer M. Atkinson. Philadelphia and New York: J.B. Lippincott, 1972; London: Woburn, 1973. The Fitzgerald/Harold Ober correspondence.

The Basil and Josephine Stories, ed. Jackson R. Bryer and John Kuehl. New York: Scribners, 1973. 'That Kind of Party,' 'The Scandal Detectives,' 'A Night at the Fair,' 'The Freshest Boy,' 'He Thinks He's Wonderful,' 'The Captured Shadow,' 'The Perfect Life,' 'Forging Ahead,' 'Basil and Cleopatra,' 'First Blood,' 'A Nice Quiet Place,' 'A Woman with a Past,' 'A Snobbish Story,' 'Emotional Bankruptcy.'

F. Scott Fitzgerald's Ledger (A Facsimile), ed. Matthew J. Bruccoli, Washington: Bruccoli Clark/NCR Microcard Books, 1973.

Bits of Paradise, ed. Matthew J. Bruccoli and Scottie Fitzgerald Smith. London: Bodley Head, 1973; New York: Scribners, 1974. Stories: 'The Popular Girl,' 'Love in the Night,' 'A Penny Spent,' 'The Dance,' 'Jacob's Ladder,' 'The Swimmers,' 'The Hotel Child,' 'A New Leaf,' 'What a Handsome Pair!' 'Last Kiss,' 'Dearly Beloved.' Also 10 stories by Zelda Fitzgerald.

Preface to This Side of Paradise. Iowa City, Iowa; Windhover Press, 1975.

The Cruise of the Rolling Junk. Bloomfield Hills, Mich. & Columbia, S.C.: Bruccoli Clark, 1976. 3 travel articles.

F. Scott Fitzgerald's Screenplay for Eric Maria Remarque's Three Comrades, ed. Matthew J. Bruccoli. Carbondale & Edwardsville: Southern Illinois University Press, 1978.

The Notebooks of F. Scott Fitzgerald, ed. Matthew J. Bruccoli. New York & London: Harcourt Brace Jovanovich/Bruccoli Clark, 1978.

F. Scott Fitzgerald's St. Paul Plays, ed. Alan Margolies. Princeton, N.J.: Princeton University Library, 1978. *The Girl from Lazy J, The Captured Shadow, 'Coward', Assorted Spirits*.

The Price Was High, ed. Matthew J. Bruccoli. New York & London: Harcourt Brace Jovanovich/Bruccoli Clark, 1979; London: Quartet, 1979. Stories: 'The Smilers,' 'Myra Meets His Family,'

'Two for a Cent,' 'Dice, Brassknuckles & Guitar,' 'Diamond Dick and the First Law of Woman,' 'The Third Casket,' 'The Pusher-in-the-Face,' 'One of My Oldest Friends,' 'The Unspeakable Egg,' 'John Jackson's Arcady,' 'Not in the Guidebook,' 'Presumption,' 'The Adolescent Marriage,' 'Your Way and Mine,' 'The Love Boat,' 'The Bowl,' 'At Your Age,' 'Indecision,' 'Flight and Pursuit,' 'On Your Own,' 'Between Three and Four,' 'A Change of Class,' 'Six of One—,' 'A Freeze-Out,' 'Diagnosis,' 'The Rubber Check,' 'On Schedule,' 'More than Just a House,' 'I Got Shoes,' 'The Family Bus,' 'In the Darkest Hour,' 'No Flowers,' 'New Types,' 'Her Last Case,' 'Lo, the Poor Peacock!' 'The Intimate Strangers,' 'Zone of Accident,' 'Fate in Her Hands,' 'Image on the Heart,' 'Too Cute for Words,' 'Inside the House,' 'Three Acts of Music,' ' "Trouble," ' 'An Author's Mother,' 'The End of Hate,' 'In the Holidays,' 'The Guest in Room Nineteen,' 'Discard' ['Director's Special'], 'On an Ocean Wave,' 'The Woman from Twenty-One.'

Correspondence of F. Scott Fitzgerald, ed. Matthew J. Bruccoli and Margaret M. Duggan, with Susan Walker. New York: Random House, 1980.

Poems 1911–1940, ed. Matthew J. Bruccoli. Bloomfield Hills, Mich. & Columbia, S.C.: Bruccoli Clark, 1981.

F. Scott Fitzgerald: Inscriptions. Columbia, S.C.: Matthew J. Bruccoli, 1988

The Short Stories of F. Scott Fitzgerald, ed. Matthew J. Bruccoli. New York: Scribners, 1989; London: Scribners, 1991, 'Head and Shoulders,' 'Bernice Bobs Her Hair,' 'The Ice Palace,' 'The Offshore Pirate,' 'May Day,' 'The Jelly-Bean,' 'The Curious Case of Benjamin Button,' 'The Diamond as Big as the Ritz,' 'Winter Dreams,' 'Dice, Brassknuckles & Guitar,' 'Absolution,' 'Rags Martin-Jones and the Pr-nce of W-les,' ' "The Sensible Thing," ' 'Love in the Night,' 'The Rich Boy,' 'Jacob's Ladder,' 'A Short Trip Home,' 'The Bowl,' 'The Captured Shadow,' 'Basil and Cleopatra,' 'The Last of the Belles,' 'Majesty,' 'At Your Age,' 'The Swimmers,' 'Two Wrongs,' 'First Blood,' 'Emotional Bankruptcy,' 'The Bridal Party,' 'One Trip Abroad,' 'The Hotel Child,' 'Babylon Revisited,' 'A New Leaf,' 'A Freeze-Out,' 'Six of One –,' 'What a Handsome Pair!,' 'Crazy Sunday,' 'More Than Just a House,' 'Afternoon of an Author,' 'Financing Finnegan,' 'The Lost Decade,' ' "Boil Some Water – Lots of It," ' 'Last Kiss,' 'Dearly Beloved.'

Appendix 3

Facsimile Collection

F. Scott Fitzgerald Manuscripts, ed. Matthew J. Bruccoli. New York & London: Garland, 1990-1991. 18 vols.: *This Side of Paradise, The Beautiful and Damned, The Great Gatsby* galleys, *Tender Is the Night, The Vegetable*, Stories, and Articles.

Critical Edition

The Cambridge Edition of the Works of F. Scott Fitzgerald, ed. Matthew J. Bruccoli. Cambridge, New York, Port Chester, Melbourne, Sydney: Cambridge University Press, 1991‒ ‒. 15 vols. projected. *The Great Gatsby* (1991); *The Love of the Last Tycoon: A Western*(1992).

Stories and Plays

(Entries provide first periodical appearance and first publication in a Fitzgerald collection.)

'The Mystery of the Raymond Mortgage,' *St. Paul Academy Now and Then*, II (October 1909), 4–8, *Apprentice Fiction*.
'Reade, Substitute Right Half,' *St. Paul Academy Now and Then*, II (February 1910), 10–11. *Apprentice Fiction*.
'A Debt of Honor,' *St. Paul's Academy Now and Then*, II (March 1910), 9–11. *Apprentice Fiction*.
'The Room with the Green Blinds,' *St. Paul Academy Now and Then*, III (June 1911), 6–9. *Apprentice Fiction*.
'A Luckless Santa Claus,' *Newman News*, IX (Christmas 1912), 1–7. *Apprentice Fiction*.
'Pain and the Scientist,' *Newman News* (1913), 5–10. *Apprentice Fiction*.
'The Trail of the Duke,' *Newman News*, IX (June 1913), 5–9. *Apprentice Fiction*.
'Shadow Laurels,' *Nassau Literary Magazine*, LXXI (April 1915), 1–10. *Apprentice Fiction*.
'The Ordeal,' *Nassau Literary Magazine*, LXXI (June 1915), 153–159; 'Benediction,' *Smart Set*, LXI (February 1920), 35–44. *Apprentice Fiction* and *F & P*.
'The Debutante,' *Nassau Literary Magazine*, LXXII (January 1917),

241–252; *Smart Set*, LX (November 1919), 85–96. *Apprentice Fiction.*

'The Spire and the Gargoyle,' *Nassau Literary Magazine*, LXXII (February 1917), 297–307. *Apprentice Fiction.*

'Tarquin of Cheapside,' *Nassau Literary Magazine*, LXXIII (April 1917), 13–18. *Apprentice Fiction.*

'Babes in the Woods,' *Nassau Literary Magazine*, LXXIII (May 1917), 55–64; *Smart Set*, LX (September 1919), 67–71. *Apprentice Fiction.*

'Sentiment – And the Use of Rouge,' *Nassau Literary Magazine*, LXXIII (June 1917), 107–123. *Apprentice Fiction.*

'The Pierian Springs and the Last Straw,' *Nassau Literary Magazine*, LXXIII (October 1917), 173–185. *Apprentice Fiction.*

'Porcelain and Pink (A One-Act Play),' *The Smart Set*, LXI (January 1920), 77–85. *TJA.*

'Dalyrimple Goes Wrong,' *The Smart Set*, LXI (February 1920), 107–116. *F & P.*

'Head and Shoulders,' *The Saturday Evening Post*, CXCII (21 February 1920), 16–17, 81–82, 85–86. *F & P.*

'Mister Icky: The Quintessence of Quaintness in One Act,' *The Smart Set*, LXI (March 1920), 93–98. *TJA.*

'Myra Meets His Family,' *The Saturday Evening Post*, CXCII (20 March 1920), 40, 42, 44, 46, 49–50, 53. *Price.*

'The Camel's Back,' *The Saturday Evening Post*, CXCII (24 April 1920), 16–17, 157, 161, 165. *TJA.*

'The Cut-Glass Bowl,' *Scribner's Magazine*, LXVII (May 1920), 582–592. *F & P.*

'Bernice Bobs Her Hair,' *The Saturday Evening Post*, CXCII (1 May 1920), 14–15, 159, 163, 167. *F & P.*

'The Ice Palace,' *The Saturday Evening Post*, CXCII (22 May 1920), 18–19, 163, 167, 170. *F & P.*

'The Offshore Pirate,' *The Saturday Evening Post*, CXCII (29 May 1920), 10–11, 99, 101–102, 106, 109. *F & P.*

'The Four Fists,' *Scribner's Magazine*, LXVII (June 1920), 669–680. *F & P.*

'The Smilers,' *The Smart Set*, LXII (June 1920), 107–111. *Price.*

'May Day,' *The Smart Set*, LXII (July 1920), 3–32. *TJA.*

'The Jelly-Bean,' *Metropolitan Magazine*, LII (October 1920), 15–16, 63–67. *TJA.*

'The Lees of Happiness,' *Chicago Sunday Tribune* (12 December 1920), Blue Ribbon Fiction Section, 1, 3, 7. *TJA.*

'His Russet Witch,' *Metropolitan Magazine*, LIII (February 1921), 11–13, 46–51. *TJA*.

'Tarquin of Cheapside,' *The Smart Set*, LXIV (February 1921), 43–46. *TJA*.

'The Far-seeing Skeptics,' *The Smart Set*, LXVII (February 1922), 48. Excerpt from B & D.

'The Popular Girl,' *The Saturday Evening Post*, CXCIV (11 February and 18 February 1922), 3–5, 82, 84, 86, 89; 18–19, 105–106, 109–110. *Bits*.

'Two for a Cent,' *Metropolitan Magazine*, LV (April 1922), 23–26, 93–95. *Price*.

'The Curious Case of Benjamin Button,' *Collier's*, LXIX (27 May 1922), 5–6, 22–28. *TJA*.

'The Diamond as Big as the Ritz,' *The Smart Set*, LXVIII (June 1922), 5–29. *TJA*.

'Winter Dreams,' *Metropolitan Magazine*, LVI (December 1922), 11–15, 98, 100–102, 104–107. *ASYM*.

'Dice, Brass Knuckles & Guitar,' *Hearst's International*, XLIII (May 1923), 8–13, 145–149. *Price*.

'Hot & Cold Blood,' *Hearst's International*, LXIV (August 1923), 80–84, 150–151. *ASYM*.

'Gretchen's Forty Winks,' *The Saturday Evening Post*, CXCVI (15 March 1924), 14–15, 128, 130, 132. *ASYM*.

'Diamond Dick and the First Law of Woman,' *Hearst's International*, XLV (April 1924), 58–63, 134, 136. *Price*.

'The Third Casket,' *The Saturday Evening Post*, CXCVI (31 May 1924), 8–9, 78. *Price*.

'Absolution,' *The American Mercury*, II (June 1924), 141–149. *ASYM*.

'Rags Martin-Jones and the Pr-nce of W-les,' *McCall's*, LI (July 1924), 6–7, 32, 48, 50. *ASYM*.

' "The Sensible Thing," ' *Liberty*, I (5 July 1924), 10–14. *ASYM*.

'The Unspeakable Egg,' *The Saturday Evening Post*, CXCVII (12 July 1924), 12–13, 125–126, 129. *Price*.

'John Jackson's Arcady,' *The Saturday Evening Post*, CXCVII (26 July 1924), 8–9, 100, 102, 105. *Price*.

'The Baby Party,' *Hearst's International*, XLVII (February 1925), 32–37. *ASYM*.

'The Pusher-in-the-Face,' *Woman's Home Companion*, LII (February 1925), 27–28, 143–144. *Price*.

'Love in the Night,' *The Saturday Evening Post*, CXCVII (14 March

1925), 18–19, 68, 70. *Bits.*

'One of My Oldest Friends,' *Woman's Home Companion*, LII (September 1925), 7–8, 120, 122. *Price.*

'The Adjuster,' *The Redbook Magazine*, XLV (September 1925), 47–51, 144–148. *ASYM.*

'A Penny Spent,' *The Saturday Evening Post*, CXCVIII (10 October 1925), 8–9, 160, 164, 166. *Bits.*

'Not in the Guidebook,' *Woman's Home Companion*, LII (November 1925), 9–11, 135–136. *Price.*

'The Rich Boy,' *The Redbook Magazine*, XLVI (January and February 1926), 27–32, 144, 146; 75–79, 122, 124–126. *ASYM.*

'Presumption,' *The Saturday Evening Post*, CXCVIII (9 January 1926), 3–5, 226, 228–229, 233–234. *Price.*

'The Adolescent Marriage,' *The Saturday Evening Post*, CXCVIII (6 March 1926), 6–7, 229–230, 233–234. *Price.*

'The Dance,' *The Redbook Magazine*, XLVII (June 1926), 39–43, 134, 136, 138. *Bits.*

'Your Way and Mine,' *Woman's Home Companion*, LIV (May 1927), 7–8, 61, 64, 67, 68. *Price.*

'Jacob's Ladder,' *The Saturday Evening Post*, CC (20 August 1927), 3–5, 57–58, 63–64. *Bits.*

'The Love Boat,' *The Saturday Evening Post*, CC (8 October 1927), 8–9, 134, 139, 141. *Price.*

'A Short Trip Home,' *The Saturday Evening Post*, CC (17 December 1927), 6–7, 55, 57–58. *TAR.*

'The Bowl, *The Saturday Evening Post*, CC (21 January 1928), 6–7, 93–94, 97, 100. *Price.*

'Magnetism,' *The Saturday Evening Post*, CC (3 March 1928), 5–7, 74, 76, 78. *Stories.*

'The Scandal Detectives,' *The Saturday Evening Post*, CC (28 April 1928), 3–4, 178, 181–182, 185. *TAR; Basil and Josephine.*

'A Night at the Fair,' *The Saturday Evening Post*, CCI (21 July 1928), 8–9, 129–130, 133. *Basil and Josephine.*

'The Freshest Boy,' *The Saturday Evening Post*, CCI (28 July 1928), 6–7, 68, 70, 73. *TAR; Basil and Josephine.*

'He Thinks He's Wonderful,' *The Saturday Evening Post*, CCI (29 September 1928), 6–7, 117–118, 121. *TAR; Basil and Josephine.*

'Outside the Cabinet-Maker's,' *The Century Magazine*, CXVII (December 1928), 241–244. *Afternoon.*

'The Captured Shadow,' *The Saturday Evening Post*, CCI (29

December 1928), 12–13, 48, 51. *TAR; Basil and Josephine.*

'The Perfect Life,' *The Saturday Evening Post,* CCI (5 January 1929), 8–9, 113, 115, 118. *TAR; Basil and Josephine.*

'The Last of the Belles,' *The Saturday Evening Post,* CCI (2 March 1929), 18–19, 75, 78. *TAR.*

'Forging Ahead,' *The Saturday Evening Post,* CCI (30 March 1929), 12–13, 101, 105. *Basil and Josephine.*

'Basil and Cleopatra,' *The Saturday Evening Post,* CCI (27 April 1929), 14–15, 166, 170, 173. *Afternoon; Basil and Josephine.*

'The Rough Crossing,' *The Saturday Evening Post,* CCI (8 June 1929), 12-13, 66, 70, 75. *Stories.*

'Majesty,' *The Saturday Evening Post,* CCII (13 July 1929), 6–7, 57–58, 61–62. *TAR.*

'At Your Age,' *The Saturday Evening Post,* CCII (17 August 1929), 6–7, 79–80. *Price.*

'The Swimmers,' *The Saturday Evening Post,* CCII (19 October 1929), 12–13, 150, 152, 154. *Bits.*

'Two Wrongs,' *The Saturday Evening Post,* CCII (18 January 1930), 8–9, 107, 109, 113. *TAR.*

'First Blood,' *The Saturday Evening Post,* CCII (5 April 1930), 8–9, 81, 84. *TAR; Basil and Josephine.*

'A Nice Quiet Place,' *The Saturday Evening Post,* CCII (31 May 1930), 8–9, 96, 101, 103. *TAR; Basil and Josephine.*

'The Bridal Party,' *The Saturday Evening Post,* CCIII (9 August 1930), 10–11, 109–110, 112, 114. *Stories.*

'A Woman with a Past,' *The Saturday Evening Post,* CCIII (6 September 1930), 8–9, 133–134, 137. *TAR; Basil and Josephine.*

'One Trip Abroad,' *The Saturday Evening Post,* CCIII (11 October 1930), 6–7, 48, 51, 53–54, 56. *Afternoon.*

'A Snobbish Story,' *The Saturday Evening Post,* CCIII (29 November 1930), 6–7, 36, 38, 40, 42. *Basil and Josephine.*

'The Hotel Child,' *The Saturday Evening Post,* CCIII (31 January 1931), 8–9, 69, 72, 75. *Bits.*

'Babylon Revisited,' *The Saturday Evening Post,* CCIII (21 February 1931), 3–5, 82–84. *TAR.*

'Indecision,' *The Saturday Evening Post,* CCIII (16 May 1931), 12–13, 56, 59, 62. *Price.*

'A New Leaf,' *The Saturday Evening Post,* CCIV (4 July 1931), 12–13, 90–91. *Bits.*

'Emotional Bankruptcy,' *The Saturday Evening Post,* CCIV (15 August

1931), 8–9, 60, 65. *Basil and Josephine.*
'Between Three and Four,' *The Saturday Evening Post,* CCIV (5 September 1931), 8–9, 69, 72. *Price.*
'A Change of Class,' *The Saturday Evening Post,* CCIV (26 September 1931), 6–7, 37–38, 41. *Price.*
'A Freeze-Out,' *The Saturday Evening Post,* CCIV (19 December 1931), 6–7, 84–85, 88–89. *Price.*
'Six of One—,' *Redbook Magazine,* LVIII (February 1932), 22–25, 84, 86, 88. *Price.*
'Diagnosis,' *The Saturday Evening Post,* CCIV (20 February 1932), 18–19, 90, 92. *Price.*
'Flight and Pursuit,' *The Saturday Evening Post,* CCIV (14 May 1932), 16–17, 53, 57. *Price.*
'Family in the Wind,' *The Saturday Evening Post,* CCIV (4 June 1932), 3–5, 71–73. *TAR.*
'The Rubber Check,' *The Saturday Evening Post,* CCV (6 August 1932), 6–7, 41–42, 44–45. *Price.*
'What a Handsome Pair!' *The Saturday Evening Post,* CCV (27 August 1932), 16–17, 61, 63–64. *Bits.*
'Crazy Sunday,' *The American Mercury,* XXVII (October 1932), 209–220. *TAR.*
'One Interne,' *The Saturday Evening Post,* CCV (5 November 1932), 6–7, 86, 88–90. *TAR.*
'On Schedule,' *The Saturday Evening Post,* CCV (18 March 1933), 16–17, 71, 74, 77, 79. *Price.*
'More Than Just a House,' *The Saturday Evening Post,* CCV (24 June 1933), 8–9, 27, 30, 34. *Price.*
'I Got Shoes,' *The Saturday Evening Post,* CCVI (23 September 1933), 14–15, 56, 58. *Price.*
'The Family Bus,' *The Saturday Evening Post,* CCVI (4 November 1933), 8–9, 57, 61–62, 65–66. *Price.*
'No Flowers,' *The Saturday Evening Post,* CCVII (21 July 1934), 10–11, 57–58, 60. *Price.*
'New Types,' *The Saturday Evening Post,* CCVII (22 September 1934), 16–17, 74, 76, 78–79, 81. *Price.*
'In the Darkest Hour,' *Redbook Magazine,* LXIII (October 1934), 15–19, 94–98. *Price.*
'Her Last Case,' *The Saturday Evening Post,* CCVII (3 November 1934), 10–11, 59, 61–62, 64. *Price.*
'The Fiend,' *Esquire,* III (January 1935), 23, 173–174. *TAR.*

Appendix 3

'The Night Before Chancellorsville,' *Esquire*, III (February 1935), 24, 165. *TAR*.

'Shaggy's Morning,' *Esquire*, III (May 1935), 26, 160.

'The Count of Darkness,' *Redbook Magazine*, LXV (June 1935), 20–23, 68, 70, 72.

'The Intimate Strangers,' *McCall's*, LXII (June 1935), 12–14, 36, 38, 40, 42, 44. *Price*.

'The Passionate Eskimo,' *Liberty*, XII (8 June 1935), 10–14, 17–18.

'Zone of Accident,' *The Saturday Evening Post*, CCVIII (13 July 1935), 8–9, 47, 49, 51–52. *Price*.

'The Kingdom in the Dark,' *Redbook Magazine*, LXV (August 1935), 58–62, 64, 66–68.

'Fate in Her Hands,' *The American Magazine*, CXXI (April 1936), 56–59, 168–172. *Price*.

'Image on the Heart,' *McCall's*, LXIII (April 1936), 7–9, 52, 54, 57–58, 62. *Price*.

'Too Cute for Words,' *The Saturday Evening Post*, CCVIII (18 April 1936), 16–18, 87, 90, 93. *Price*.

'Three Acts of Music,' *Esquire*, V (May 1936), 39, 210. *Price*.

'The Ants at Princeton,' *Esquire*, V (June 1936), 35, 201.

'Inside the House,' *The Saturday Evening Post*, CCVIII (13 June 1936), 18–19, 32, 34, 36. *Price*.

'An Author's Mother,' *Esquire*, VI (September 1936), 36. *Price*.

' "I Didn't Get Over," ' *Esquire*, VI (October 1936), 45, 194–195. *Afternoon*.

' "Send Me In, Coach," ' *Esquire*, VI (November 1936), 55, 218–221.

'An Alcoholic Case,' *Esquire*, VII (February 1937), 32, 109. *Stories*.

' "Trouble," ' *The Saturday Evening Post*, CCIX (6 March 1937), 14–15, 81, 84, 86, 88–89. *Price*.

'The Honor of the Goon,' *Esquire*, VII (June 1937), 53, 216.

'The Long Way Out,' *Esquire*, VIII (September 1937), 45, 193. *Stories*.

'The Guest in Room Nineteen,' *Esquire*, VIII (October 1937), 56, 209. *Price*.

'In the Holidays,' *Esquire*, VIII (December 1937), 82, 184, 186. *Price*.

'Financing Finnegan,' *Esquire*, IX (January 1938), 41, 180, 182, 184. *Stories*.

'Design in Plaster,' *Esquire*, XII (November 1939), 51, 169. *Afternoon*.

'The Lost Decade,' *Esquire*, XII (December 1939), 113, 228. *Stories*.

'Strange Sanctuary,' *Liberty*, XVI (9 December 1939), 15–20.

'Pat Hobby's Christmas Wish,' *Esquire*, XIII (January 1940), 45, 170–172. *Hobby*.

'A Man in the Way,' *Esquire*, XIII (February 1940), 40, 109. *Hobby*.

' "Boil Some Water – Lots of It," ' *Esquire*, XIII (March 1940), 30, 145, 147. *Hobby*.

'Teamed with Genius,' *Esquire*, XIII (April 1940), 44, 195–197. *Hobby*.

'Pat Hobby and Orson Welles,' *Esquire*, XIII (May 1940), 38, 198–199. *Hobby*.

'Pat Hobby's Secret,' *Esquire*, XIII (June 1940), 30, 107. *Hobby*.

'The End of Hate,' *Collier's*, CV (22 June 1940), 9–10, 63–64. *Price*.

'Pat Hobby, Putative Father,' *Esquire*, XIV (July 1940), 36, 172–174. *Hobby*.

'The Homes of the Stars,' *Esquire*, XIV (August 1940), 28, 120–121. *Hobby*.

'Pat Hobby Does His Bit,' *Esquire*, XIV (September 1940), 41, 104. *Hobby*.

'Pat Hobby's Preview,' *Esquire*, XIV (October 1940), 30, 118, 120. *Hobby*.

'No Harm Trying,' *Esquire*, XIV (November 1940), 30, 151–153. *Hobby*.

'A Patriotic Short,' *Esquire*, XIV (December 1940), 62, 269. *Hobby*.

'On the Trail of Pat Hobby,' *Esquire*, XV (January 1941), 36, 126. *Hobby*.

'Fun in an Artist's Studio,' *Esquire*, XV (February 1941), 64, 112. *Hobby*. Elgin, Paul [pseud.]. 'On an Ocean Wave,' *Esquire*, XV (February 1941), 59, 141. *Price*.

'Two Old-Timers,' *Esquire*, XV (March 1941), 53, 143. *Hobby*.

'Mightier than the Sword,' *Esquire*, XV (April 1941), 36, 183. *Hobby*.

'Pat Hobby's College Days,' *Esquire*, XV (May 1941), 55, 168–169. *Hobby*.

'The Woman from Twenty-One,' *Esquire*, XV (June 1941), 29, 164. *Price*.

'Three Hours Between Planes,' *Esquire*, XVI (July 1941), 41, 138–139. *Stories*.

'Gods of Darkness,' *Redbook Magazine*, LXXVIII (November 1941), 30–33, 88–91.

'The Broadcast We Almost Heard Last September,' *Furioso*, III (Fall 1947), 8–10.

'News of Paris – Fifteen Years Ago,' *Furioso*, III (Winter 1947), 5–10.

Appendix 3

Afternoon.

'Discard,' Harper's Bazaar, LXXXII (January 1948), 103, 143–144, 146, 148–149. *Price.*

'The World's Fair,' *The Kenyon Review*, X (Autumn 1948), 567–568.

'Last Kiss,' *Collier's*, CXXIII (16 April 1949), 16–17, 34, 38, 41, 43–44. *Bits.*

'That Kind of Party,' *The Princeton University Library Chronicle*, XII (Summer 1951), 167–180. *Basil and Josephine.*

'Dearly Beloved,' Fitzgerald/Hemingway Annual 1969, pp. 1–3. *Bits.*

'Lo, the Poor Peacock,' *Esquire*, LXXVI (September 1971), 154–158. *Price.*

'On Your Own,' *Esquire*, XCI (30 January 1979), 55–67. *Price.*

'A Full Life,' *Princeton University Library Chronicle*, XLIX (Winter 1988), 167-172.

Articles and Essays

(Entries provide first periodical appearance and first publication in a Fitzgerald collection.)

'S.P.A. Men in College Athletics,' *St. Paul Academy Now and Then*, III (December 1910), 7.

Untitled news feature about school election, *Newman News* (1912), 18.

Untitled news feature about school dance, *Newman News* (1913), 18.

'Who's Who – and Why,' *The Saturday Evening Post*, CXCIII (18 September 1920), 42, 61. *Afternoon.*

'Three Cities,' *Brentano's Book Chat*, I (September–October 1921), 15, 28. *In His Own Time.*

'What I Think and Feel at Twenty-Five,' *American Magazine*, XCIV (September 1922), 16, 17, 136–140. *In His Own Time.*

'How I Would Sell My Book if I Were a Bookseller,' *Bookseller and Stationer*, XVIII (15 January 1923), 8. *In His Own Time.*

'10 Best Books I Have Read,' *Jersey City Evening Journal* (24 April 1923), 9.

'Imagination – and a Few Mothers,' *The Ladies' Home Journal*, XL (June 1923), 21, 80–81.

'The Cruise of the Rolling Junk,' *Motor* XLI (February, March, April

1924), 24–25, 58, 62, 64, 66; 42–43, 58, 72, 74, 76; 40–41, 58, 66, 68, 70.

' "Why Blame It on the Poor Kiss If the Girl Veteran of Many Petting Parties Is Prone to Affairs After Marriage?" ' *New York American* (24 February 1924), LII-3. *In His Own Time.*

'Does a Moment of Revolt Come Sometime to Every Married Man?' *McCall's*, LI (March 1924), 21, 36. *In His Own Time.*

'What Kind of Husbands Do "Jimmies" Make?' *Baltimore American* (30 March 1924), ME-7. *In His Own Time.*

'How to Live on $36,000 a Year,' *The Saturday Evening Post*, CXCVI (5 April 1924), 22, 94, 97. *Afternoon.*

' "Wait Till You Have Children of Your Own!" ' Woman's Home Companion, LI (July 1924), 13, 105. *In His Own Time.*

'How to Live on Practically Nothing a Year,' *The Saturday Evening Post*, CXCVII (20 September 1924), 17, 165–166, 169–170. *Afternoon.*

'Our Young Rich Boys,' *McCall's*, LIII (October 1925), 12, 42, 69. *In His Own Time.*

'How to Waste Material: A Note on My Generation,' *The Bookman*, LXIII (May 1926), 262–265. *Afternoon.*

'Princeton,' *College Humor*, XIII (December 1927), 28–29, 130–131. *Afternoon*

'Ten Years in the Advertising Business,' *The Princeton Alumni Weekly*, XXIX (22 February 1929), 585. *Afternoon.*

'A Short Autobiography (With Acknowledgments to Nathan),' *The New Yorker*, V (25 May 1929), 22–23. *In His Own Time.*

'Girls Believe in Girls,' *Liberty*, VII (8 February 1930), 22–24. *In His Own Time.*

'Echoes of the Jazz Age,' *Scribner's Magazine*, XC (November 1931), 459–465. *Crack-Up.*

'One Hundred False Starts,' *The Saturday Evening Post*, CCV (4 March 1933), 13, 65–66. *Afternoon.*

'Ring,' *The New Republic*, LXXVI (11 October 1933), 254–255. *Crack-Up.*

'Introduction,' *The Great Gatsby*. New York: Modern Library, 1934.

'Sleeping and Waking,' *Esquire*, II (December 1934), 34, 159–160. *Crack-Up.*

'The Crack-Up,' *Esquire*, V (February 1936), 41, 164. *Crack-Up.*

'Pasting It Together,' *Esquire*, V (March 1936), 35, 182–183. *Crack-Up.*

'Handle with Care,' *Esquire*, V (April 1936), 39, 202. *Crack-Up.*

'Author's House,' *Esquire*, VI (July 1936), 40, 108. *Afternoon.*

'Afternoon of an Author,' *Esquire*, VI (August 1936), 35, 170. *Afternoon.*

'Early Success,' *American Cavalcade*, I (October 1937), 74–79. *Crack-Up.*

'Foreword,' *Colonial and Historic Homes of Maryland*, by Don Swann. Baltimore: Etchcrafters Art Guild, 1939.

'The Death of My Father,' *The Princeton University Library Chronicle*, XII (Summer 1951), 187–189. *Apprentice Fiction.*

'The High Cost of Macaroni,' *Interim*, IV, nos. 1 and 2 (1954), 6–15.

'My Generation,' *Esquire*, LXX (October 1968), 119, 121. *Profile.*

Prose Parody and Humor

(Entries provide first periodical appearance and first publication in a Fitzgerald collection.)

The *Princeton Tiger* contributions are reprinted in *F. Scott Fitzgerald In His Own Time.*

Untitled humor article, beginning 'There was once a second group student . . .,' *The Princeton Tiger*, XXV (December 1914), 5. *In His Own Time.*

'How They Head the Chapters,' *The Princeton Tiger*, XXVI (September 1915), 10. *In His Own Time.*

'The Conquest of America (as some writers would have it),' *The Princeton Tiger*, XXVI (Thanksgiving 1915), 6. *In His Own Time.*

'Three Days at Yale,' *The Princeton Tiger*, XXVI (December 1915), 8–10.

'Our Next Issue,' *Nassau Literary Magazine*, LXXII (December 1916), unpaged. *In His Own Time.*

'Jemina: A Story of the Blue Ridge Mountains by John Phlox, Jr.,' *Nassau Literary Magazine*, LXXII (December 1916), 210–215; *Vanity Fair*, XV (January 1921), 44. *TJA. In His Own Time.*

'The Usual Thing by Robert W. Shameless,' *Nassau Literary Magazine*, LXXII (December 1916), 223–228. *In His Own Time.*

'Little Minnie McCloskey: A Story for Girls,' *The Princeton Tiger*, XXVII (1 December 1916), 6–7. *In His Own Time.*

'A Litany of Slang,' *The Princeton Tiger*, XXVII (18 December 1916),

7. *In His Own Time.*

' "Triangle Scenery by Bakst," ' *The Princeton Tiger*, XXVII (18 December 1916), 7. *In His Own Time.*

'Futuristic Impressions of the Editorial Boards,' *The Princeton Tiger*, XXVII (18 December 1916), 7. *In His Own Time.*

' "A glass of beer kills him," ' *The Princeton Tiger*, XXVII (18 December 1916), 7. *In His Own Time.*

Untitled joke, beginning ' "When you find a man doing a little more . . .," ' *The Princeton Tiger*, XXVII (18 December 1916), 7. *In His Own Time.*

'Things That Never Change! Number 3333,' *The Princeton Tiger*, *XXVII (18 December 1916), 7. In His Own Time.*

'The Old Frontiersman: A Story of the Frontier,' *The Princeton Tiger*, XXVII (18 December 1916), 11. *In His Own Time.*

Untitled joke, beginning 'Boy Kills Self Rather than Pet . . .,' *The Princeton Tiger*, XXVII (3 February 1917), 12. *In His Own Time.*

'Things That Never Change. No. 3982,' *The Princeton Tiger*, XXVII (3 February 1917), 12. *In His Own Time.*

'Precaution Primarily,' *The Princeton Tiger*, XXVII (3 February 1917), 13–14.

Untitled joke, beginning 'McCaulay Mission – Water Street . . .,' *The Princeton Tiger*, XXVII (17 March 1917), 10. *In His Own Time.*

'The Diary of a Sophomore,' *The Princeton Tiger*, XXVII (17 March 1917), 11. *In His Own Time.*

'The Prince of Pests: A Story of the War,' *The Princeton Tiger*, XXVII (28 April 1917), 7. *In His Own Time.*

Untitled joke, beginning ' "These rifles *** will probably not be used . . .," ' *The Princeton Tiger*, XXVII (28 April 1917), 8. *In His Own Time.*

Untitled joke, beginning ' "It is assumed that the absence of submarines . . .," ' *The Princeton Tiger*, XXVII (28 April 1917), 8. *In His Own Time.*

Untitled joke, beginning 'Yale's swimming team will take its maiden plunge to-night,' *The Princeton Tiger*, XXVII (28 April 1917), 8. *In His Own Time.*

'The Staying Up All Night,' *The Princeton Tiger*, XXVIII (10 November 1917), 6. *In His Own Time.*

'Intercollegiate Petting-Cues,' *The Princeton Tiger*, XXVIII (10 November 1917), 8. *In His Own Time.*

'Cedric the Stoker (The True Story of the Battle of the Baltic),' *The*

663

Princeton Tiger, XXVIII (10 November 1917), 12. *In His Own Time.*

'This Is a Magazine,' *Vanity Fair*, XV (December 1920), 71. *In His Own Time.*

'Reminiscences of Donald Stewart by F. Scott Fitzgerald (in the Manner of ....),' *St. Paul Daily News* (11 December 1921), City Life Section, 6. *In His Own Time.*

'Some Stories They Like to Tell Again,' *New York Herald* (8 April 1923), magazine section, 11.

'The Most Disgraceful Thing I Ever Did: 2. The Invasion of the Sanctuary,' *Vanity Fair*, XXI (October 1923), 53. *In His Own Time.*

'My Old New England Homestead on the Erie,' *College Humor*, VI (August 1925), 18–19.

'Salesmanship in the Champs-Élysées,' *The New Yorker*, V (15 February 1930), 20. *In His Own Time.*

'The True Story of Appomattox,' privately printed (1934). *In His Own Time.*

'A Book of One's Own,' *The New Yorker*, XIII (21 August 1937), 19. *In His Own Time.*

Verse
(All of Fitzgerald's verse is collected in *Poems 1911–1940*)

' "Football," ' *Newman News*, IX (Christmas [1911]), 19.

'May Small Talk,' *The Princeton Tiger*, XXVI (June 1915), 10

'A Cheer for Princeton,' *The Daily Princetonian* (28 October 1915), I.

'Yais,' *The Princeton Tiger*, XXVII (June 1916), 13.

'To My Unused Greek Book (*Acknowledgments to Keats*),' *Nassau Literary Magazine*, LXXII (June 1916), 137.

'One from Penn's Neck,' *The Princeton Tiger*, XXVII (18 December 1916), 7.

Untitled verse beginning 'Oui, le backfield est from Paris . . .,' *The Princeton Tiger*, XXVII (18 December 1916), 7.

'Rain Before Dawn,' *Nassau Literary Magazine*, LXII (February 1917), 321.

'Popular Parodies – No. 1,' *The Princeton Tiger*, XXVII (17 March 1917), 10.

'Undulations of an Undergraduate,' *The Princeton Tiger*, XXVII (17 March 1917), 20.

Untitled verse beginning 'Ethel had her shot of brandy . . .,' *The*

Princeton Tiger, XXVII (28 April 1917), 8.

'Princeton – The Last Day,' *Nassau Literary Magazine*, LXXIII (May 1917), 95.

'On a Play Twice Seen,' *Nassau Literary Magazine*, LXXIII (June 1917), 149.

'The Cameo Frame,' *Nassau Literary Magazine*, LXXIII (October 1917), 169–172.

'Our American Poets,' *The Princeton Tiger*, XXVIII (10 November 1917), 11.

'City Dusk,' *Nassau Literary Magazine*, LXXIII (April 1918), 315.

'My First Love,' *Nassau Literary Magazine*, LXXIV (February 1919), 102.

'Marching Streets,' *Nassau Literary Magazine*, LXXIV (February 1919), 103–104.

'The Pope at Confession,' *Nassau Literary Magazine*, LXXIV (February 1919), 105.

'A Dirge (Apologies to Wordsworth),' *Judge*, LXXVII (20 December 1919), 30.

'Sleep of a University,' *Nassau Literary Magazine*, LXXVI (November 1920), 161.

'To Anne,' *Atlanta Journal* (30 September 1923), 5.

Untitled verse beginning 'For the lands of the village triumph . . .,' *Atlanta Journal* (30 September 1923), 5.

'Lamp in a Window,' *The New Yorker*, XI (23 March 1935), 18.

'Obit on Parnassus,' *The New Yorker*, XIII (5 June 1937), 27.

Book Reviews
(These reviews, except for 'The Defeat of Art,' are collected in *F. Scott Fitzgerald in His Own Time*.)

Untitled book review of *Penrod and Sam* by Booth Tarkington, *Nassau Literary Magazine*, LXXII (January 1917), 291–292.

Untitled book review of *David Blaize* by E.F. Benson, *Nassau Literary Magazine*, LXXII (February 1917), 343–344.

Untitled book review of *The Celt and the World* by Shane Leslie, *Nassau Literary Magazine*, LXXIII (May 1917), 104–105.

Untitled book review of *Verses in Peace and War* by Shane Leslie, *Nassau Literary Magazine*, LXXIII (June 1917), 152–153.

Untitled book review of *God, the Invisible King* by H.G. Wells, *Nassau*

Literary Magazine, LXXIII (June 1917), 153.

'The Baltimore Anti-Christ,' *The Bookman*, LIII (March 1921), 79–81. H.L. Mencken's *Prejudices. Second Series.*

'Three Soldiers,' *St. Paul Daily News* (25 September 1921), feature section, 6. John Dos Passos's *Three Soldiers.*

'Poor Old Marriage,' *The Bookman*, LIV (November 1921), 253–254. Review of Charles Norris's *Brass.*

'The Defeat of Art,' unlocated 1922 review of Heywood Broun's *The Boy Grew Older, Fitzgerald/Hemingway Annual 1977.*

'Aldous Huxley's "Crome Yellow," ' *St. Paul Daily News* (26 February 1922), feature section, 6.

' "Margey Wins the Game," ' *New York Tribune* (7 May 1922), section IV, 7. John V.A. Weaver's *Margey Wins the Game.*

'Tarkington's "Gentle Julia," ' *St. Paul Daily News* (7 May 1922), feature section, 6.

'Homage to the Victorians,' *New York Tribune* (14 May 1922), section IV, 6. Shane Leslie's *The Oppidan.*

'A Rugged Novel,' *New York Evening Post* (28 October 1922), 143–144. Woodward Boyd's *The Love Legend.*

'Minnesota's Capital in the Role of Main Street,' *Literary Digest International Book Review*, I (March 1923), 35–36. Grace Flandrau's *Being Respectable.*

'Sherwood Anderson on the Marriage Question,' *New York Herald* (4 March 1923), section 9, 5. Sherwood Anderson's *Many Marriages.*

'Under Fire,' *New York Evening Post* (26 May 1923), 715. Thomas Boyd's *Through the Wheat.*

'F. Scott Fitzgerald Is Bored by Efforts At Realism In "Lit," ' *The Daily Princetonian* (16 March 1928), 1, 3. March issue of *The Nassau Literary Magazine.*

Public Letters and Statements

(Entries provide first periodical appearance and first publication in a Fitzgerald collection.)

'The Claims of the *Lit.*,' *Princeton Alumni Weekly*, XX (10 March 1920), 514.

Self-Interview, 1920, *Saturday Review*, XLIII (5 November 1960), 26, 56. *In His Own Time.*

'Contemporary Writers and Their Work: A Series of Autobiographical Letters – F. Scott Fitzgerald,' *Editor*, LIII (Second July Number, 1920), 121–122.

Public letter to Thomas Boyd, *St. Paul Daily News* (20 February 1921), feature section, 8. *In His Own Time.*

'The Author's Apology,' tipped into copies of the third printing of *This Side of Paradise* (April 1920). *In His Own Time.*

'What I Was Advised to Do – and Didn't,' *Philadelphia Public Ledger* (22 April 1922), 11. *In His Own Time.*

'Confessions,' *Chicago Daily Tribune* (19 May 1923), 9. Public letter to Fanny Butcher. *In His Own Time.*

'Censorship or Not,' *The Literary Digest*, LXXVII (23 June 1923), 31, 61. *In His Own Time.*

'In Literary New York,' unlocated (fall-winter 1923). *In His Own Time.*

'Who's Who in this Issue,' *Woman's Home Companion*, LI (July 1924), 110.

'Fitzgerald Sets Things Right About His College,' *Washington Herald* (28 June 1929), II, 1. Public letter to Stanley Olmstead. *In His Own Time.*

'False and Extremely Unwise Tradition,' *The Daily Princetonian* (27 February 1930), 2. *In His Own Time.*

'Confused Romanticism,' *Princeton Alumni Weekly*, XXXII (22 April 1932), 647–648. *In His Own Time.*

'An Open Letter to Fritz Crisler,' *Princeton Athletic News*, II (16 June 1934), 3. *In His Own Time.*

'Anonymous '17,' *Nassau Literary Magazine*, XCV (June 1934), 9. *In His Own Time.*

'My Ten Favorite Plays,' *New York Sun* (10 September 1934), 19.

These Stories Went to Market, ed. Vernon McKenzie. New York: McBride, 1935, p. xviii. Comments on stories. *In His Own Time.*

Interviews

(Entries provide first periodical appearance and first publication in a Fitzgerald collection.)

Broun, Heywood. 'Books,' *New York Tribune* (7 May 1920), 14.

'More Than Hundred Notes of Rejection Failed to Halt Scott

Fitzgerald's Pen,' *St. Paul Pioneer Press* (12 September 1920), 2nd section, 8.

H.H. [Harry Hansen]. 'Have Faith in Fitzgerald,' *Chicago Daily News* (27 October 1920), 12.

Smith, Frederick James. 'Fitzgerald, Flappers and Fame,' *Shadowland*, III (January 1921), 39, 75. *In His Own Time*.

Boyd, Thomas Alexander. 'Scott Fitzgerald Here on Vacation; "Rests" by Outlining New Novels," *St. Paul Daily News* (28 August 1921), City Life Section, 6.

Boyd, Thomas Alexander. 'Scott Fitzgerald Speaks at Home,' *St. Paul Daily News* (4 December 1921), City Life Section, 6.

Boyd, Thomas Alexander. 'Literary Libels – Francis Scott Key Fitzgerald,' *St. Paul Daily News* (5, 12, 19 March 1922), City Life Section, 6. *In His Own Time*.

J.V.A.W. [John V.A. Weaver]. 'The Lion's Cage,' *Brooklyn Daily Eagle* (25 March 1922), 5.

Marshall, Marguerite Mooers. 'F. Scott Fitzgerald, Novelist, Shocked by "Younger Marrieds" and Prohibition,' *New York Evening World* (1 April 1922), 3. *In His Own Time*.

O'Donnell, John. 'Fitzgerald Condemns St. Paul Flappers,' *St. Paul Daily News* (16 April 1922), I, 1, 5.

'The Gossip Shop,' *The Bookman*, LV (May 1922), 333–334.

McCardell, Roy L. 'F. Scott Fitzgerald – Juvenile Juvenal of the Jeunesse Jazz,' *New York Morning Telegraph* (12 November 1922), magazine section, 3.

'Novelist Flays Drys, Exalting Our Flappers,' *New York Daily News* (24 January 1923), 18.

'Prediction Is Made About James Novel: F.S. Fitzgerald Believes "Ulysses" Is Great Book of Future,' *Richmond Times-Despatch* (24 June 1923), II, 5.

'What a "Flapper Novelist" Thinks of His Wife,' *Detroit News* (30 September 1923), Metropolitan Section, 3. *In His Own Time*.

Wilson, B.F. 'F. Scott Fitzgerald on "Minnie McGluke," ' *Picture-Play*, XIX (October 1923), 83–84, 102.

Wilson, B.F. 'F. Scott Fitzgerald Says: "All Women Over Thirty-five Should be Murdered," ' *Metropolitan Magazine*, LVIII (November 1923), 34, 75–76. *In His Own Time*.

Wilson, B.F. 'Notes on Personalities, IV – F. Scott Fitzgerald,' *Smart Set*, LXXIII (April 1924), 29–33.

Baldwin, Charles C. 'F. Scott Fitzgerald,' *The Men Who Make Our*

Fitzgerald's Publications

Novels. New York: Dodd, Mead, 1924. *In His Own Time*.
Wales, Henry. 'N.Y. "400" Apes Chicago Manner; Fails; So Dull,' *Chicago Daily Tribune* (7 December 1925), 12.
'Novelist Admires French,' *Baltimore Evening Sun* (21 December 1926), 11.
Salpeter, Harry. 'Fitzgerald, Spenglerian,' *New York World* (3 April 1927), 12M. *In His Own Time*.
Reid, Margaret. 'Has the Flapper Changed?' *Motion Picture Magazine*, XXXIII (July 1927), 28–29, 104. *In His Own Time*.
Shaw, Charles G. 'F. Scott Fitzgerald,' *The Low-Down*. New York: Henry Holt, 1928. *In His Own Time*.
'Fitzgerald Back from Riviera; Is Working on Novel,' *Paris Tribune* (9 April 1929), 8.
Whitman, William. 'They Write Books – The Gin and Jazz Age,' *Boston Globe* (13 April 1929), 14.
Bald, Wambly. 'La Vie de Boheme (As Lived on the Left Bank),' *Paris Tribune* (16 December 1929), 5.
Walling, Keith. 'Scott Fitzgeralds to Spend Winter Here Writing Books,' *Montgomery Advertiser* (8 October 1931), 1, 7. *In His Own Time*.
'Scott Fitzgerald Seeking Home Here,' *Baltimore Sun* (8 May 1932), 18, 12. *In His Own Time*.
'F. Scott Fitzgerald Is Hunting Trouble,' *Baltimore Evening Sun* (29 June 1932), 36.
'Fitzgeralds Felt Insecure in France; Now Live Here,' *Baltimore Evening Sun* (25 October 1932), 3.
' "No, Not Cellar-Door!" Baltimore Writers Cry,' *Baltimore Post*, (13 December 1932), 2.
'F. Scott Fitzgerald Is Visitor in City; New Book Appears Soon,' *Charlottesville Daily Progress* (25 May 1933), 1.
'Holds "Flappers" Fail As Parents,' *New York Times* (18 September 1933), 17.
Malcolm Cowley, 'Ivory Towers to Let,' *The New Republic*, LXXVIII (18 April 1934), 260–263.
'F. Scott Fitzgerald Staying at Hotel Here,' *Asheville Citizen-Times* (21 July 1935), 1–2. *In His Own Time*
Buttitta, Anthony. 'Fitzgerald's Six Generations,' *Raleigh News and Observer* (1 September 1935), 3. *In His Own Time*.
Mok, Michel. 'The Other Side of Paradise, Scott Fitzgerald, 40, Engulfed in Despair,' *New York Post* (25 September 1936), 1, 15. *In*

His Own Time.

Hess, John D. 'Wanger Blends Abruptness with Charm in Personality,' *The Dartmouth* (11 February 1939), 2, 13.

'An Interview with F. Scott Fitzgerald,' *Saturday Review*, LXIII (5 November 1960), 26, 56.

Buttitta, Anthony. 'An Encounter with Fitzgerald In a North Carolina Bookshop,' *San Francisco Chronicle*, 'This World' (26 August 1962), supplement, 38.

Unlocated Interviews

Untitled clipping: 'And whom did we see in New York? Well, there was F. Scott Fitzgerald, for one. . . . '

'Fitzgerald and Flappers.'

Fulton, Bart. 'Fitzgerald, Flapperdom's Fiction Ace, Qualifies as Most Brilliant Author, but Needs Press Agent, Says Scribe.'

'Middle West Girl More at Home in Kitchen Than in Ballroom, Says F. Scott Fitzgerald,' 1922/1923.

'American Writer Finds a Home in Rome.' Datelined Rome. Winter 1924–25.

' "Gatsby's' Author Boasts His Child, Not His Novel.' Possibly *New York Herald*, 1925.

Babcock, Muriel. 'F. Scott Fitzgerald Upholds His Own Generation,' Los Angeles, 1927. *In His Own Time.*

Millen, Gilmore. 'Scott Fitzgerald Lays Success to Reading,' Los Angeles, c. 1927.

'Fitzgerald Finds He Has Outgrown Jazz Age Novel.' c. 1929.

'Painted St. Paul's Name on Literary Signboard.'

'The Virtue of Persistence.'

Untitled clipping. Interview with Fitzgerald about movie version of *TSOP*, 'Grit,' and *VEG*.

Untitled clipping. Interview with Fitzgerald and Cornelius Vanderbilt, Jr., about beauty contest, 1929.

Movie-Writing Assignments

(This list does not include scenarios and synopses Fitzgerald wrote on speculation.)

Grit. Film Guild, 1924. Original story by Fitzgerald.

'Lipstick.' United Artists, 1927. Unproduced. (*Fitzgerald/Hemingway Annual 1978, pp. 5–33.*)

Red-Headed Woman. M-G-M, 1931. Fitzgerald's screenplay was rejected.

A Yank at Oxford. M-G-M, 1937. Fitzgerald polished the screenplay.

Three Comrades. M-G-M, 1937–1938. Fitzgerald received screen credit with E. E. Paramore. (Carbondale & Edwardsville: Southern Illinois University Press, 1978)

'Infidelity.' M-G-M, 1938. Unproduced. (*Esquire*, LXXX [December 1973], 193–200, 290–304.)

Marie Antoinette. M-G-M, 1938. Fitzgerald's screenplay was rejected.

The Women. M-G-M, 1938. The screenplay by Fitzgerald and Donald Ogden Stewart was rejected.

Madame Curie. M-G-M, 1938–1939. Fitzgerald's screenplay was rejected.

Gone With the Wind. Selznick International, 1939. Fitzgerald polished the screenplay.

Winter Carnival. United Artists (Walter Wanger), 1939. Fitzgerald was fired.

'Air Raid,' Paramount, 1939. With Donald Ogden Stewart. Unproduced.

'Open That Door.' Universal, 1939. Fitzgerald worked on the screenplay for one week.

Raffles. Goldwyn, 1939. Fitzgerald worked on the screenplay for one week. 'Cosmopolitan' ('Babylon Revisited'). Columbia (Lester Cowan), 1940. Unproduced.

Life Begins at Eight-Thirty. Twentieth Century-Fox, 1940. Fitzgerald's screenplay was rejected.

Works by Zelda Fitzgerald

Books

Save Me the Waltz. New York: Scribners, 1932; London: Grey Walls, 1953. Novel.

Bits of Paradise. London: Bodley Head, 1973; New York: Scribners, 1974. Includes 10 stories by Zelda: 'Our Own Movie Queen,' 'The Original Follies Girl,' 'The Southern Girl,' 'The Girl the Prince

Liked,' 'The Girl with Talent,' 'A Millionaire's Girl,' 'Poor Working Girl,' 'Miss Ella,' 'The Continental Angle,' 'A Couple of Nuts.'

Scandalabra. Bloomfield Hills, Mich. & Columbia, S.C.: Bruccoli Clark, 1980. Play.

Zelda Fitzgerald: The Collected Writings, ed. Matthew J. Bruccoli; Intro. by Mary Gordon. New York: Scribners, 1991. *Save Me the Waltz*, *Scandalabra*, 'Our Own Movie Queen,' 'The Original Follies Girl,' 'Southern Girl,' 'The Girl the Prince Liked,' 'The Girl With Talent,' 'A Millionaire's Girl,' 'Poor Working Girl,' 'Miss Ella,' 'The Continental Angle,' 'A Couple of Nuts,' 'Other Names for Roses,' 'Friend Husband's Latest,' 'Eulogy on the Flapper,' 'Does a Moment of Revolt Come Sometime to Every Married Man?,' 'What Became of the Flappers?,' 'Breakfast,' 'The Changing Beauty of Park Avenue,' 'Looking Back Eight Years,' 'Who Can Fall in Love After Thirty?,' 'Paint and Powder,' 'Show Mr. and Mrs. F. to Number — —,' 'Auction–Model 1934,' 'On F. Scott Fitzgerald,' Letters to F. Scott Fitzgerald.

Stories

'Our Own Movie Queen,' *Chicago Sunday Tribune* (7 June 1925), magazine section, 1–4. Partly by Fitzgerald; but published under his name only. *Bits.*

'The Original Follies Girl,' *College Humor*, XVII (July 1929), 40–41, 110. By-lined 'Zelda and F. Scott Fitzgerald,' but credited to Zelda in Ledger. *Bits.*

'Southern Girl,' *College Humor*, XVIII (October 1929), 27–28, 94, 96. By-lined 'F. Scott and Zelda Fitzgerald,' but credited to Zelda in Ledger. *Bits.*

'The Girl the Prince Liked,' *College Humor*, no. 74 (February 1930), 46–48, 121–122. By-lined 'F. Scott and Zelda Fitzgerald,' but credited to Zelda in Ledger. *Bits.*

'The Girl with Talent,' *College Humor*, no. 76 (April 1930), 50–52, 125–127. By-lined 'F. Scott and Zelda Fitzgerald,' but credited to Zelda in Ledger. *Bits.*

'A Millionaire's Girl,' *The Saturday Evening Post*, CCII (17 May 1930), 8–9, 118, 121. By-lined 'F. Scott Fitzgerald' but credited to Zelda in Ledger. *Bits.*

'Poor Working Girl,' *College Humor*, no. 85 (January 1931), 72–73,

122. By-lined 'F. Scott and Zelda Fitzgerald,' but credited to Zelda in Ledger. *Bits.*

'Miss Ella,' *Scribner's Magazine*, XC (December 1931), 661–665. *Bits.*

'The Continental Angle,' *The New Yorker*, VIII (4 June 1932), 25. *Bits.*

'A Couple of Nuts,' *Scribner's Magazine*, XCII (August 1932), 80–84. *Bits.*

'Other Names for Roses,' *Collected Writings.*

Articles

'Friend Husband's Latest,' *New York Tribune* (2 April 1922), magazine section, 11. Review of *B & D.*

'Eulogy on the Flapper,' *Metropolitan Magazine*, LV (June 1922), 38–39.

'Does a Moment of Revolt Come Sometime to Every Married Man?' *McCall's*, LI (March 1924), 82. Published with companion article by Fitzgerald.

'Breakfast,' *Favorite Recipes of Famous Women*, ed. Florence Stratton. New York & London: Harper & Brothers, 1925.

'What Became of the Flappers?' *McCall's*, LIII (October 1925), 12, 30, 66. Published with companion article by Fitzgerald.

'The Changing Beauty of Park Avenue,' *Harper's Bazaar*, LXII (January 1928), 61–63. By-lined 'Zelda and F. Scott Fitzgerald,' but credited to Zelda in Ledger.

'Looking Back Eight Years,' *College Humor*, XIV (June 1928), 36–37. By-lined 'F. Scott and Zelda Fitzgerald,' but credited to Zelda in Ledger.

'Who Can Fall in Love After Thirty?' *College Humor*, XV (October 1928), 9, 92. By-lined 'F. Scott and Zelda Fitzgerald,' but credited to Zelda in Ledger.

'Editorial on Youth,' written for *Photoplay* in 1927. Published as 'Paint and Powder,' *Smart Set*, LXXXIV (May 1929), 68. By-lined 'F. Scott Fitzgerald' but credited to Zelda in Ledger.

' "Show Mr. and Mrs. F. to Number —," ' *Esquire*, I–II (May and June 1934), 19, 154B; 23, 120. By-lined 'F. Scott and Zelda Fitzgerald,' but credited to Zelda in Ledger. *Crack-Up.*

'Auction – Model 1934,' *Esquire*, II (July 1934), 20, 153, 155. By-lined 'F. Scott and Zelda Fitzgerald,' but credited to Zelda in Ledger. *Crack-Up.*

Appendix 3

Principal Works about Fitzgerald

Bibliographies

Bruccoli, Matthew J. *F. Scott Fitzgerald: A Descriptive Bibliography*. Pittsburgh: University of Pittsburgh Press, 1972.

———. *Supplement to F. Scott Fitzgerald: A Descriptive Bibliography*. Pittsburgh: University of Pittsburgh Press, 1980.

———. *F. Scott Fitzgerald: A Descriptive Bibliography, Revised Edition*. Pittsburgh: University of Pittsburgh Press, 1987.

Bryer, Jackson R. *The Critical Reputation of F. Scott Fitzgerald*. Hamden, Conn.: Archon, 1967.

———. *Supplement One Through 1981*. Hamden, Conn.: Archon, 1984.

Biographies and Memoirs

Berg, Scott. *Maxwell Perkins: Editor of Genius*. New York: Congdon/ Dutton, 1978.

Bruccoli, Matthew J. *Scott and Ernest: The Authority of Failure and the Authority of Success*. New York: Random House, 1978.

Buttitta, Tony. *After the Good Gay Times*. New York: Viking, 1974; *The Lost Summer*. London: Robson, 1987.

Callaghan, Morley. *That Summer in Paris*. New York: Coward-McCann, 1963.

Donaldson, Scott. *Fool for Love*. New York: Congdon & Weed, 1983.

Graham, Sheilah. *College of One*. New York: Viking, 1967.

———. *The Real F. Scott Fitzgerald Thirty-five Years Later*. New York: Grosset & Dunlap, 1976; London: W.H. Allen, 1976.

Graham, Sheilah, and Gerold Frank. *Beloved Infidel*. New York: Holt, Rinehart & Winston, 1958.

Hemingway, Ernest. *A Moveable Feast*. New York: Scribners, 1964.

Ernest Hemingway: Selected Letters, 1917–1961, ed. Carlos Baker. New York: Scribners, 1981.

Koblas, John J. *F. Scott Fitzgerald in Minnesota: His Homes and Haunts*. St. Paul, Minn.: Minnesota Historical Society Press, 1978.

Latham, John Aaron. *Crazy Sundays: F. Scott Fitzgerald in Hollywood*. New York: Viking, 1971.

LeVot, André. *F. Scott Fitzgerald*. Paris: Julliard, 1979; Garden City, N.Y.: Doubleday, 1983; London: Allen Lane, 1984.

Mayfield, Sara. *Exiles from Paradise*. New York: Delacorte Press, 1971.

Principal Works about Fitzgerald

Mellow, James R. *Invented Lives*. Boston: Houghton Mifflin, 1984.

Milford, Nancy. *Zelda*. New York: Harper and Row, 1970.

Miller, Linda Patterson, ed. *Letters from the Lost Generation: Gerald and Sara Murphy and Friends*. New Brunswick, N.Y.: Rutgers University Press, 1991.

Mizener, Arthur. *The Far Side of Paradise*. Boston: Houghton Mifflin, 1951.

Ring, Frances Kroll. *Against the Current: As I Remember F. Scott Fitzgerald*. San Francisco: Ellis/Creative Arts, 1985.

Smith, Scottie Fitzgerald, Matthew J. Bruccoli, and Joan P. Kerr, eds. *The Romantic Egoists: A Pictorial Autobiography from the Scrapbooks and Albums of F. Scott and Zelda Fitzgerald*. New York: Scribners, 1974.

Tompkins, Calvin. *Living Well Is the Best Revenge*. New York: Viking, 1971.

Turnbull, Andrew. *Scott Fitzgerald*. New York: Scribners, 1962; London: Bodley Head, 1962.

Critical Studies

Allen, Joan. *Candles and Carnival Lights*. New York: New York University Press, 1978.

Bruccoli, Matthew J. *The Composition of Tender Is the Night*. Pittsburgh: University of Pittsburgh Press, 1963.

——. *'The Last of the Novelists': F. Scott Fitzgerald and The Last Tycoon*. Carbondale & Edwardsville: Southern Illinois University Press, 1977.

——, ed. *Apparatus for a Definitive Edition of Under the Red, White and Blue [The Great Gatsby]*. Columbia, S.C.: University of South Carolina Press, 1974.

Chambers, John B. *The Novels of F. Scott Fitzgerald*. London: Macmillan/New York: St Martin's Press, 1989.

Crosland, Andrew T. *A Concordance to F. Scott Fitzgerald's The Great Gatsby*. Detroit, Mich.: Bruccoli Clark/Gale Research, 1975.

Cross, K. G. W. *F. Scott Fitzgerald*. New York: Grove, 1964.

Eble, Kenneth. *F. Scott Fitzgerald*. New York: Twayne, 1963.

Goldhurst, William. *F. Scott Fitzgerald and His Contemporaries*. Cleveland and New York: world, 1963.

Higgins, John A. *F. Scott Fitzgerald: A Study of the Stories*. New York:

St. John's University Press, 1971.

Lehan, Richard D. *F. Scott Fitzgerald and the Craft of Fiction.* Carbondale: Southern Illinois University Press, 1966.

Long, Robert E. *The Achieving of The Great Gatsby.* Lewisburg, Pa.: Bucknell University Press, 1979.

Miller, James E., Jr. *F. Scott Fitzgerald: His Art and His Technique.* New York: New York University Press, 1964.

Piper, Henry Dan. *F. Scott Fitzgerald: A Critical Portrait.* New York: Holt, Rinehart & Winston, 1965.

Shain, Charles E. *F. Scott Fitzgerald.* Minneapolis: University of Minnesota Press, 1961.

Sklar, Robert. *F. Scott Fitzgerald: The Last Laocoön.* New York: Oxford University Press, 1967.

Way, Brian. *F. Scott Fitzgerald and the Art of Social Fiction.* London: Arnold, 1980.

Collections of Essays

Bloom, Harold, ed. *F. Scott Fitzgerald.* New York: Chelsea House, 1985.

Bloom, ed. *F. Scott Fitzgerald's The Great Gatsby.* New York: Chelsea House, 1986.

Bruccoli, Matthew J., ed. *Profile of F. Scott Fitzgerald.* Columbus, Ohio: Merrill, 1971.

Bruccoli, ed. *New Essays on The Great Gatsby.* Cambridge: Cambridge University Press, 1985.

Bryer, Jackson R., ed. *F. Scott Fitzgerald: The Critical Reception.* New York: Burt Franklin, 1978.

Bryer, ed. *The Short Stories of F. Scott Fitzgerald.* Madison: University of Wisconsin Press, 1982.

Cowley, Malcolm, and Robert Cowley, eds. *Fitzgerald and the Jazz Age.* New York: Scribners, 1966.

Donaldson, Scott, ed. *Critical Essays on F. Scott Fitzgerald's The Great Gatsby.* Boston: Hall, 1984.

Eble, Kenneth, ed. *F. Scott Fitzgerald: A Collection of Criticism.* New York: McGraw-Hill, 1973.

Hoffman, Frederick J., ed. *The Great Gatsby: A Study.* New York: Scribners, 1962.

Kazin, Alfred, ed. *F. Scott Fitzgerald: The Man and His Work.* Cleveland: World, 1951.

LaHood, Marvin J., ed. *Tender Is the Night: Essays in Criticism.* Bloomington: Indiana University Press, 1969.

Lee, A. Robert, ed. *Scott Fitzgerald: The Promises of Life.* London: Vision/New York: St Martin's, 1989.

Lockridge, Ernest, ed. *Twentieth Century Interpretations of The Great Gatsby.* Englewood Cliffs, N.J.: Prentice-Hall, 1968.

Mizener, Arthur, ed. *F. Scott Fitzgerald: A Collection of Critical Essays.* Englewood Cliffs, N.J.: Prentice-Hall, 1963.

Piper, Henry Dan, ed. *Fitzgerald's The Great Gatsby: The Novel, the Critics, the Background* . New York: Scribners, 1970.

Stern, Milton R., ed. *Critical Essays on F. Scott Fitzgerald's Tender Is the Night.* Boston: Hall, 1986.

Journals

Fitzgerald Newsletter (1958–1968). Washington: NCR Microcard Books, 1969.

Fitzgerald/Hemingway Annual. Washington: NCR Microcard Books, 1969–1973; Englewood, Col.: Information Handling Services, 1974–1976; Detroit: Gale Research, 1977–1979.

NOTES

Full publication information is provided in Appendix 3 for books cited here by title only.

The following short titles are used:

As Ever:	*As Ever, Scott Fitz—*
Scott/Max:	*Dear Scott/Dear Max*
Letters:	*The Letters of F. Scott Fitzgerald*
Correspondence:	*Correspondence of F. Scott Fitzgerald*
Ledger:	*F. Scott Fitzgerald's Ledger*

The letters PUL designate manuscript material in the Princeton University Library, but the several collections of Fitzgerald material have not been identified.

Preface to the First Edition (1981)

1. Undated letter to Henry Dan Piper, c. May 1947. Southern Illinois University Library.
2. Alden Whitman, *Come to Judgment* (New York: Viking, 1980), p. 36.

Taps at Reveille

1. *Beloved Infidel*, p. 329.
2. *Ibid.*
3. Spring 1919. PUL. *Correspondence*, p. 45.
4. Laura Guthrie Hearne diaries, PUL.

5. 'Scott Fitzgerald, Author, Dies at 44,' 23 December 1940, 19.
6. 'Notes and Comment,' XVI, 9.

Romantic Egotist

1. *St. Paul Pioneer Press* (12 April 1877), 7; (13 April), 7; (14 April), 7.
2. *Baltimore Sun* (13 February 1890), 1.
3. Scottie Fitzgerald Smith papers.
4. 'Author's House,' *Afternoon of an Author*, p. 184.
5. To Perkins, 20 February 1926. PUL. *Scott/Max*, p. 135.
6. 'Foreword,' Don Swann, *Colonial and Historic Homes of Maryland*, p. 9.
7. PUL, Chapter I, pp. 21–22.
8. *Ledger*, p. 158.
9. Edwin R. Benson, Sr., to MJB, 9 January 1982.
10. 18 July 1907. PUL. *Letters*, p. 449; *The Romantic Egoists*, p. 12.
11. *Ledger*, p. 162.
12. *All the Sad Young Men*, p. 131.
13. Michel Mok, 'The Other Side of Paradise,' *F. Scott Fitzgerald in His Own Time*, p. 296.
14. To Morton Kroll, 9 August 1939. PUL. *Letters*, p. 593.
15. June 1936. *Letters*, p. 535.
16. 18 July 1933. PUL. *Letters*, p. 503.
17. I, 4 (Easter 1909). The note is signed by Sam Kennedy.
18. *Taps at Reveille*, pp. 5–6.
19. ' "Wait Till You Have Children of Your Own!" ' *F. Scott Fitzgerald in His Own Time*, p. 199.
20. 30 July 1909. Scrapbook, PUL. *Correspondence*, p. 5.
21. 'The Romantic Egotist,' PUL, Chapter I, p. 21.
22. *The Apprentice Fiction of F. Scott Fitzgerald 1909–1917*, pp. 26–27.
23. 'Who's Who – and Why,' *Afternoon of an Author*, p. 83.
24. *Ledger*, p. 165.
25. *Thoughtbook of Francis Scott Key Fitzgerald* (facsimile), pp. XII–XIV.
26. *Ledger*, p. 164.
27. *Ledger*, p. 165.
28. *F. Scott Fitzgerald's St. Paul Plays 1911–1914*, p. 16.

29. P. 19.
30. *A Handbook of the Best Private Schools 1915* (Boston: Sargent, 1915), p. 53.
31. *F. Scott Fitzgerald in His Own Time*, pp. 3–4.
32. 'Author's House,' *Afternoon of an Author*, pp. 186–87.
33. *The Romantic Egoists*, p. 16.
34. 'My Lost City,' *The Crack-Up*, p. 23.
35. *Taps at Reveille*, pp. 101–02.
36. *The Romantic Egoists*, p. 16.
37. 'Pasting It Together,' *The Crack-Up*, p. 79.
38. *Notebooks*, #938.
39. *The Apprentice Fiction of F. Scott Fitzgerald 1909–1917*, p. 54.
40. *The Bride of the Lamb and Other Essays* (New York: Encyclopedia Press, 1922), p. 130.
41. P. 26.
42. P. 28.
43. Review of *The Oppidan, F. Scott Fitzgerald in His Own Time*, p. 134.
44. *Ledger*, May 1913, p. 167.
45. *The Romantic Egoists*, pp. 18–19.
46. *This Side of Paradise*, p. 27.

Spires & Gargoyles

1. *The Romantic Egoists*, p. 20.
2. *This Side of Paradise*, p. 40.
3. 'Princeton', *Afternoon of an Author*, p. 72.
4. 'Sleeping and Waking,' *The Crack-Up*, p. 66.
5. Scrapbook. PUL.
6. 'Princeton,' *Afternoon of an Author*, p. 75.
7. *Correspondence*, p. 322.
8. 'Princeton,' *Afternoon of an Author*, p. 75.
9. *Ibid.*, p. 76.
10. 'The Most Disgraceful Thing I Ever Did,' *F. Scott Fitzgerald in his Own Time*, p. 234.
11. P. 211.
12. Wilson, *A Prelude* (New York: Farrar, Strauss & Giroux, 1967), p. 67.
13. *F. Scott Fitzgerald in His Own Time*, pp. 7–8.
14. P. 57.
15. 3 August 1940. PUL. *Letters*, p. 88.

16. 'Pasting It Together,' *The Crack-Up*, p. 79.
17. *This Side of Paradise*, pp. 131–32.
18. 26 September 1917. Yale. *Letters*, p. 318.
19. To Hazel McCormack, n.d.; postmarked 26 June 1922. PUL. McCormack, a young woman in St. Louis, wrote Fitzgerald a fan letter in 1922, which initiated a sixteen-year correspondence.
20. *A Prelude*, p. 106.
21. P. 302.
22. *A Prelude*, p. 148.
23. Scrapbook. PUL.
24. Scrapbook. PUL.
25. (Cambridge, New York & c: Cambridge University Press, 1991), p. 116. All subsequent quotations from *The Great Gatsby* are taken from this edition.
26. *Notebooks*, #1378.
27. *Tender Is the Night*, p. 176.
28. *The Apprentice Fiction of F. Scott Fitzgerald 1909–1917*, pp. 77.
29. 6 November, 1915, 5.
30. *F. Scott Fitzgerald in His Own Time*, p. 39.
31. 'Pasting It Together,' *The Crack-Up*, p. 76.
32. 'The Crack-Up,' *The Crack-Up*, p. 69.
33. P. 114.
34. Gauss, 'Edmund Wilson: The Campus and the Nassau "Lit," ' *Princeton University Library Chronicle*, V (February 1944), 49.
35. 10 January 1918. Yale. *Letters*, p. 324.
36. *The Daily Princetonian* (28 October 1915), I; *F. Scott Fitzgerald in His Own Time*, p. 22.
37. Pp. 117–19.
38. Pp. 165–66.
39. 8 May 1916. Scrapbook. PUL. *The Romantic Egoists*, p. 29.
40. *Ibid.*
41. PUL. *Correspondence*, pp. 15–18.
42. PUL. Chapter I, pp. 11–12.
43. C. 5 July, 1937. PUL. *Letters*, p. 16.
44. PUL. Wilson M. Hudson, 'F. Scott Fitzgerald and a Princeton Preceptor.'
45. *F. Scott Fitzgerald in His Own Time*, p. 107.
46. *Ibid.*, pp. 45–46.
47. *The Apprentice Fiction of F. Scott Fitzgerald*, p. 98.
48. 18 April 1938. PUL. *Letters*, p. 28.

49. 'Thoughts on Being Bibliographed,' *Princeton University Library Chronicle*, V (February 1944), 54.
50. *The Apprentice Fiction of F. Scott Fitzgerald*, pp. 158–59.
51. *F. Scott Fitzgerald in His Own Time*, p. 62; *This Side of Paradise*, p. 168.
52. Wilson. *Letters on Literature and Politics 1912–1972* (New York: Farrar, Straus & Giroux, 1977), p. 30.
53. Undated. *Letters*, p. 101.
54. 3 August 1940. PUL. *Letters*, p. 88.
55. C. Spring 1938. PUL. *Letters*, p. 29.
56. Shane Leslie, 'Some Memories of Scott Fitzgerald,' *The Times Literary Supplement* (31 October 1958), 632.
57. P. 100.
58. PUL. *Correspondence*, pp. 19–21.
59. 'Some Recent Books,' *The Dublin Review*, CLXVII (October–December 1920), 290.
60. 26 September 1917, Yale. *Letters*, p. 318.
61. *F. Scott Fitzgerald in His Own Time*, p. 97.
62. *Ibid.*, p. 98.
63. Pp. 189, 246.

The Last of the Belles

1. 14 November 1917. PUL. *Letters*, pp. 451–52.
2. Pp. 173–74.
3. *The Far Side of Paradise*, p. 70. 23 April 1934. PUL. *Letters*, p. 385.
4. 'Who's Who – and Why,' *Afternoon of an Author*, p. 84.
5. PUL. Chapter I, pp. 18–19.
6. Bruccoli Collection. *Letters*, p. 371.
7. Dated 10 January 1917. Yale. *Letters*, p. 323.
8. PUL.
9. Alonzo Myers, 'Lieutenant F. Scott Fitzgerald, United States Army,' *Papers on English Language & Literature*, I (Spring 1965), 167–76.
10. New York: Scribners, 1932. Quotations from *Save Me the Waltz* are from the emended edition (Carbondale and Edwardsville: Southern Illinois University Press, 1967), p. 35.
11. Scrapbook. PUL. *The Romantic Egoists*, p. 34.

12. There are three typescripts for the preface: PUL, Harold Ober Associates, Bruccoli Collection.
13. Prangins, *Zelda*, p. 8.
14. Sara Mayfield, *Exiles from Paradise*, p. 23. See Fitzgerald to Marjorie Sayre Brinson, 1939. PUL.
15. *Save Me the Waltz*, p. 29.
16. *Ibid.*, p. 56.
17. *Ibid.*, p. 3.
18. Minnie Machen Sayre to Fitzgerald, 16 July 1930. PUL.
19. *The Great Gatsby*, p. 117.
20. PUL.
21. *Flappers and Philosophers*, p. 21.
22. James Drawbell, *The Sun Within Us* (London: Collins, 1963), p. 176.
23. 'Sleeping and Waking,' *The Crack-Up*, p. 67.
24. Fitzgerald claimed this experience twice: *Afternoon of an Author*, p. 179; 'My Generation,' *Esquire*, LXX (October 1968), 119 (reprinted in *Profile of F. Scott Fitzgerald*), p. 5.
25. *Letters*, p. 454.
26. Bruccoli Collection. *Letters*, p. 375.
27. Scrapbook. PUL. *The Romantic Egoists*, p. 48.
28. *Ibid.*
29. PUL. *Correspondence*, p. 43.
30. *Ibid.*, pp. 44–45. Fitzgerald used this graveyard description in *This Side of Paradise*, pp. 303–04.
31. Scrapbook. PUL. *The Romantic Egoists*, p. 48.
32. *This Side of Paradise*, p. 232.
33. 'My Lost City,' *The Crack-Up*, p. 25.
34. *Ibid.*, pp. 25–26.
35. Thomas A. Boyd. 'Literary Libels – Francis Scott Key Fitzgerald,' *St. Paul Daily News* (5, 12, 19 March 1922). *F. Scott Fitzgerald in His Own Time*, p. 251.
36. *The Twenties*, p. 52.
37. 'Pasting It Together,' *The Crack-Up*, p. 77.
38. PUL. *Scott/Max*, p. 17.
39. *Ibid.*, p. 20.
40. Berg, *Max Perkins: Editor of Genius*, p. 16.
41. PUL. *Scott/Max*, p. 21.
42. *Ibid.*
43. *The Crack-Up*, pp. 86, 89.

44. Edmund Wilson, *Letters on Literature and Politics 1912–1972*, p. 46.
45. PUL.
46. Enoch Pratt Free Library. *Correspondence*, p. 55.
47. *Invented Lives* (Boston: Houghton Mifflin, 1984), pp. 80-84.
48. 15 June 1940. PUL. *Letters*, p. 80.
49. PUL. *Scott/Max*, p. 22.
50. Bruccoli Collection.
51. PUL. *Scott/Max*, p. 28.
52. PUL. *Letters*, p. 140.
53. January 1920. PUL. *Scott/Max*, p. 24.
54. *Ibid.*, p. 25.
55. *Bits of Paradise*, p. 310.
56. *Flappers and Philosophers*, p. 48.
57. To Scottie Fitzgerald, 5 September 1940. PUL. *Letters*, p. 93.
58. To Harold Ober, c. December 1940. *As Ever*, p. 424.
59. C. February 1920. PUL. *Correspondence*, p. 50.
60. PUL. *Correspondence*, p. 51.
61. Bruccoli Collection, *Correspondence*, p. 53.

Early Success

1. Scrapbook. PUL.
2. 3 April 1920, 11. *F. Scott Fitzgerald: The Critical Reception*, p. 3.
3. August 1920, 140. *F. Scott Fitzgerald: The Critical Reception*, p. 28.
4. 11 April 1920, Section 7, p. 9. *F. Scott Fitzgerald: The Critical Reception*, p. 10.
5. 26 February 1921. *Letters*, p. 469.
6. *This Side of Paradise*, p. 279.
7. The review is signed R.V.A.S. 12 May 1920, 362. *F. Scott Fitzgerald: The Critical Reception*, p. 22.
8. *The Great Gatsby*, p. 119.
9. *Ibid.*, p. 2.
10. *Notebooks*, #316.
11. *The Liberal Imagination* (New York: Viking, 1950), p. 249.
12. Retyped, PUL. *Letters*, p. 101.
13. 'How to Waste Material: A Note on My Generation,' *F. Scott Fitzgerald in His Own Time*, p. 147.
14. PUL, p. 305.

15. 20 October 1936. PUL. *Letters*, p. 11.
16. *The Autobiography of Alice B. Toklas* (New York: Harcourt, Brace, 1933), p. 268.
17. *This Side of Paradise*, p. 209; *Tono-Bungay* (Boston: Houghton Mifflin [Riverside Edition], 1966), p. 306.
18. *This Side of Paradise*, p. 238.
19. PUL, p. 238.
20. *This Side of Paradise*, p. 265.
21. *Ibid.*, p. 272.
22. *Ibid.*, pp. 304–05.
23. Strater's career at Princeton is described in Michael Culver's 'A Model for Fitzgerald,' *Princeton Alumni Weekly*, LXXXV (19 June 1985), 9-11.
24. New York: Viking, 1945; p. vii.
25. *Notebooks*, #1021.
26. Dorothy B. Good, ' "Romance and a Reading List": The Literary References in *This Side of Paradise*,' Fitzgerald/Hemingway Annual 1976, pp. 35–64.
27. Scrapbook. PUL. *Correspondence*, pp. 58–59.
28. PUL. *Letters*, pp. 461–62.
29. 6, 14 July 1920.
30. 'Introduction,' *The Great Gatsby*, pp. l-liii.
31. *In the Company of Writers: A Life in Publishing* (New York: Scribners, 1991), p. 44.
32. Bruccoli, 'Getting It Right: The Publishing Process and the Correction of Factual Errors – With Reference to *The Great Gatsby*,' *The Library Chronicle of the University of Texas*, XXI, nos. 3-4 (1991).
33. Scrapbook. PUL. *Correspondence*, p. 56.
34. *Save Me the Waltz*, p. 42.
35. PUL.
36. 'Early Success,' *The Crack-Up*, p. 87.
37. *The Crack-Up*, p. 16.
38. 'Echoes of the Jazz Age,' *The Crack-Up*, p. 14.
39. 'My Generation,' *Profile of F. Scott Fitzgerald*, p. 6.
40. 'My Lost City,' *The Crack-Up*, pp. 28–29.
41. 4 November 1939. PUL. *Letters*, p. 63.
42. *Bits of Paradise*, p. 302.
43. *Letters on Literature and Politics*, p. 478.
44. *Ibid.*

45. Edmund Wilson, *The Twenties* (New York: Farrar, Straus & Giroux, 1975), pp. 222–23.
46. To Ludlow Fowler. PUL. *Zelda*, p. 74.
47. Correspondence, p. 424.
48. The circumstances behind this interview are unclear. Fitzgerald wrote it as a self interview, but when Heywood Broun printed it in his *New York Tribune* column on 7 May 1920 it was credited to Carleton R. Davis. *F. Scott Fitzgerald in His Own Time*, pp. 161–63.
49. *New York Tribune* (7 May 1920), 14.
50. *F. Scott Fitzgerald in His Own Time*, p. 164.
51. *Tales of the Jazz Age*, pp. 61–62.
52. P. 155.
53. *The Twenties*, p. 60.
54. PUL. *Letters*, p. 145.
55. To Perkins, 29 April 1920. PUL. *Scott/Max*, p. 30.
56. *Smart Set*, XLIII (December 1920), 140; *F. Scott Fitzgerald: The Critical Reception*, p. 48.
57. Enoch Pratt Free Library. Correspondence, p. 68.
58. New York Public Library. Correspondence, p. 69.
59. John Tebbel, *George Horace Lorimer and the Saturday Evening Post* (Garden City, N.Y.: Doubleday, 1948), p. 45.
60. C. February 1920. PUL. Correspondence, p. 52.
61. 9 February 1921. Scottie Fitzgerald Smith. Correspondence, p. 80.
62. C. Lawton Campbell, 'The Fitzgeralds Were My Friends,' *Fitzgerald/Hemingway Annual 1978*, pp. 48–49.
63. To Shane Leslie, 24 May 1921. *Letters*, p. 379.
64. C. May 1921. Yale. *Letters*, p. 326.
65. 23 June 1921, 402.
66. 27 May 1921, 5.
67. 19 April 1922. PUL. *Letters*, pp. 155–57.
68. C. Summer 1930. PUL. Correspondence, p. 241.
69. 14 June 1940. PUL. Correspondence, p. 600.
70. To Ober, 29 November 1921, *As Ever*, p. 31; to Wilson, postmarked 25 November 1921, *Letters*, p. 327.
71. Manuscript: Book II, Chapter 2, p. 1. *The Beautiful and Damned*, p. 191.
72. Manuscript: Book II, Chapter 3, pp. 338–39. *The Beautiful and Damned*, p. 276.

73. Manuscript: Book III, Chapter 3, pp. 93–94. *Metropolitan*, LV (March 1922), 113.
74. PUL. *Correspondence*, p. 89.
75. PUL. *Scott/Max*, pp. 45–47.
76. C. 16 December 1921. PUL. *Scott/Max*, p. 49.
77. PUL. *Scott/Max*, pp. 61–62.
78. Clipping, Scrapbook. PUL. *The Romantic Egoists*, p. 87.
79. 5 February 1922. Lilly Library. *As Ever*, p. 36.
80. 22 December 1921. PUL. *Zelda*, p. 85.
81. *The Romantic Egoists*, p. 88.
82. F. *Scott Fitzgerald in His Own Time*, pp. 131–32.
83. *Ibid.*, p. 140.
84. *Ibid.*, p. 123.
85. To Ober, before 1 December 1921. Lilly Library. *As Ever*, p. 32.
86. 24 January 1922. Lilly Library. *As Ever.* p. 34.
87. *Exiles from Paradise*, p. 80. Fitzgerald noted in his *Ledger* for March 1922: 'Zelda + her abortionist.' *Notebooks*, #1564: 'His son went down the toilet of the XXXX Hotel after Dr. X – Pills.'
88. 21 November 1930. PUL.
89. Vol. XLVII (April 1922), 140–41. *F. Scott Fitzgerald: The Critical Reception*, p. 107.
90. 5 March 1922, section 8, p. 1. *F. Scott Fitzgerald: The Critical Reception*, p. 74.
91. C. January 1922. Yale. *Letters*, p. 331.
92. LV (March 1922), 20–25. Wilson, *The Shores of Light* (New York: Farrar, Straus & Young, 1952), pp. 27–35.
93. 2 April 1922, Section 5, p. 11. *F. Scott Fitzgerald: The Critical Reception*, p. 111.
94. C. 21 February 1921. PUL. *Scott/Max*, p. 29.
95. Marguerite Mooers Marshall, 'F. Scott Fitzgerald, Novelist, Shocked by "Younger Marrieds" and Prohibition,' *New York Evening World* (1 April 1922), 3. *F. Scott Fitzgerald in His Own Time*, p. 258.
96. 'Literary Libels – Francis Scott Key Fitzgerald,' 5, 12, 19 March 1922. *F. Scott Fitzgerald In His Own Time*, p. 253.
97. Lilly Library. *As Ever*, p. 39.
98. 26 May 1922. PUL. *Letters on Literature and Politics 1912–1972*, p. 84.
99. Rejected scenes are included in the 1976 Scribners edition edited by Charles Scribner III.

100. PUL. *Scott/Max*, p. 61.
101. PUL. *Correspondence*, p. 112.
102. *Assembly* (New York: Random House, 1961), pp. 18–19.
103. *Tales of the Jazz Age*, p. viii.
104. Vol. XIX (November 1922), 24. *F. Scott Fitzgerald: The Critical Reception*, p. 52.
105. *All the Sad Young Men*, p. 90.
106. Minnesota Historical Society.
107. *The Best Times* (New York: New American Library, 1966), pp. 129–130.
108. To Xandra Kalman, Fall 1922. Minnesota Historical Society.
109. 'Ring,' *The Crack-Up*, p. 38.
110. *Ibid.*, p. 36.
111. Scrapbook. PUL. *The Romantic Egoists*, p. 104.
112. *Jersey City Evening Journal* (24 April 1923), 9. Syndicated by the North American Newspaper Alliance.
113. *What of It?* (New York: Scribners, 1925), p. 59.
114. *Ibid.*, pp. 115–16.
115. Jonathan Yardley, *Ring* (New York: Random House, 1977), following p. 274.
116. To MJB, 10 April 1982.
117. 4 May 1925. Enoch Pratt Free Library. *Letters*, p. 480.
118. C. January 1923. PUL. *Scott/Max*, p. 66.
119. To Hazel McCormack, n.d.; postmarked 20 March 1923. PUL.
120. PUL.
121. *The Price Was High*, p. 63.
122. *F. Scott Fitzgerald in His Own Time*, p. 144.
123. There are conflicting recollections of this encounter. See Llewelyn Powys, *The Verdict of Bridlegoose* (New York: Harcourt Brace, 1926), p. 131; *Sherwood Anderson's Memoirs* (New York: Harcourt Brace, 1942), pp. 336-37; and Harry Hansen, 'The First Reader,' *New York World-Telegram* (9 and 14 April 1942).
124. New York: Knopf, 1930, p. 239.
125. Henry Dan Piper to MJB, 22 April 1974. See Bruccoli, ' "How Are You and the Family Old Sport?" – Gerlach and Gatsby,' *Fitzgerald/Hemingway Annual 1975*, pp. 33–36.
126. The clipping is reproduced in *Fitzgerald/Hemingway Annual 1976*, p. 108.
127. *New York Herald Tribune* (22 December 1939), Late City Lift, p. 15.

128. *This Room This Gin and These Sandwiches* (New York: New Republic, 1937). Bruccoli Collection.
129. PUL.
130. Joseph Corso, 'One Not-Forgotten Summer Night: Sources for Fictional Symbols of American Character in *The Great Gatsby*,' *Fitzgerald/Hemingway Annual 1976*, pp. 8–33.
131. Minnesota Historical Society.
132. Bruccoli, ' "An Instance of Apparent Plagiarism": F. Scott Fitzgerald, Willa Cather, and the First *Gatsby* Manuscript,' *Princeton University Library Chronicle*, XXXIX (Spring 1978), 171–78.
133. P. 103.
134. Morris E. Chafetz, 'Alcoholism and Alcoholic Psychoses,' in Alfred M. Freedman et al., *Comprehensive Textbook of Psychiatry*, second edition (Baltimore: Williams & Wilkins, 1975), II, p. 1333.
135. 'Psychodynamics of Chronic Alcoholism,' *Journal of Neuroses and Mental Disease*, LXXXVI (1937), 538. Cited by Chafetz. See also Donald W. Goodwin, 'The Alcoholism of F. Scott Fitzgerald,' *Journal of the American Medical Association*, CCXII (6 April 1970), 86–90).
136. *Beloved Infidel*, p. 273, reports that Dr. Hoffman provided Sheilah Graham with this diagnosis; on p. 111 of *The Real F. Scott Fitzgerald* she states that Dr. Hoffmann 'told my *Beloved Infidel* collaborator, Gerold Frank, that Scott drank – both liquor and Cokes because he had the reverse of diabetes, an insufficiency of sugar in the blood.'
137. Dr. William Ober to MJB, 28 October 1979.
138. To Dr. Louis Hamman, n.d.; c. 1936. Possibly not sent. PUL.
139. PUL.
140. 4 May 1925. Enoch Pratt Free Library. *Letters*, p. 481.
141. *All the Sad Young Men*, pp. 237–38.
142. To Hazel McCormack, n.d.; postmarked 1 September 1924. PUL.
143. C. 10 April 1924. PUL. *Scott/Max*, p. 69.
144. To John Jamieson, 15 April 1934. PUL. *Letters*, p. 509.
145. *All the Sad Young Men*, p. 131.
146. *F. Scott Fitzgerald in His Own Time*, p. 188.
147. Bruccoli Collection.
148. *Afternoon of an Author*, p. 95.

149. Reported by Henry Dan Piper, *Zelda*, p. 380.
150. Hearne diary. PUL.
151. C. 10 April 1924. PUL. *Scott/Max*, pp. 69–70.
152. 16 April 1924. PUL *Scott/Max*, p. 71.
153. *The Romantic Egoists*, p. 115.
154. May 1924. PUL. *Correspondence*, p. 141.
155. Received 28 July 1924. Lilly Library. *As Ever*, p. 64.
156. *Exiles from Paradise*, p. 97.
157. *Notebooks*, #839.
158. *A Moveable Feast*, p. 172.
159. *Zelda*, p. 114.
160. PUL. *Correspondence*, p. 145.
161. P. 35.
162. 'Pasting It Together,' *The Crack-Up*, p. 79.
163. 6 June 1940. PUL. *Scott/Max*, p. 263.
164. C. 25 August 1924. PUL. *Scott/Max*, p. 76.
165. PUL. *Scott/Max*, p. 77.
166. 18 November 1924. PUL. *Scott/Max*, p. 82.
167. After 18 May 1925. PUL.
168. PUL. *Correspondence*, p. 146.
169. *What of It?*, p. 18.
170. PUL. *Correspondence*, p. 154.
171. To Hazel McCormack, n.d.; postmarked 1 September 1924. PUL.
172. Yeiser, 'Total Unrecall,' *Dimension: Cincinnati*, 1 (June 1963), 10–14.
173. C. 10 October 1924. PUL. *Scott/Max*, p. 78.
174. Received 23 January 1925. Lilly Library. *As Ever*, p. 73.
175. The article was posthumously published in *Interim*, #1, 2 (1954), 6–15.
176. C. April 1925. Retyped, PUL. *Letters*, p. 357.
177. *All the Sad Young Men*, pp. 189–90.
178. PUL. *Scott/Max*, pp. 82–84.
179. July 1925. PUL. *Scott/Max*, pp. 117–18.
180. PUL. *Scott/Max*, pp. 88–90.
181. C. 18 February 1925. PUL. *Scott/Max*, p. 94.
182. 24 January 1925. PUL. *Scott/Max*, p. 93.
183. Wheeler to Paul Revere Reynolds, 16 December 1924. *As Ever*, p. 70.
184. To Ober, received 26 January 1925. Lilly Library. *As Ever*, p. 74.

For the recollections of H.N. Swanson, editor of *College Humor*, see *Sprinkled with Ruby Dust* (New York: Warner, 1989).

185. Fitzgerald to MacKenzie, March 1924. University of Texas.
186. PUL.
187. PUL.
188. PUL. *Correspondence*, p. 153.
189. PUL.
190. PUL.
191. C. 24 April 1925. PUL. *Scott/Max*, p. 102.
192. Vol. LXXIX (August 1925), 162–64. *F. Scott Fitzgerald: The Critical Reception*, p. 239.
193. 31 December 1925. PUL. *The Crack-Up*, p. 310.
194. Collection of Daniel Siegel. *Correspondence*, p. 180.
195. *Baltimore Evening Sun* (2 May 1925), 9. *F. Scott Fitzgerald: The Critical Reception*, pp. 211–14.
196. 4 May 1925. Enoch Pratt Free Library. *Letters*, p. 480.
197. Spring 1925. Yale. *Letters*, pp. 341–42.
198. P. 9.
199. P. 34.
200. P. 51.
201. *Ibid.*
202. To Corey Ford, July 1937. PUL. *Letters*, p. 551.
203. 'The Swimmers,' *Bits of Paradise*, p. 210.
204. P. 30.
205. To Hazel McCormack, n.d.; postmarked 15 May 1925. PUL.

The Drunkard's Holiday

1. Chaplin to MJB, 26 November 1976.
2. P. ix.
3. *F. Scott Fitzgerald: Inscriptions* (Columbia, S.C.: Matthew J. Bruccoli, 1988), item 34.
4. *A Moveable Feast*, p. 176.
5. *Ibid.*, pp. 181, 183.
6. *Exiles from Paradise*, pp. 137, 141.
7. PUL.
8. PUL. *Fitzgerald/Hemingway Annual 1972*, pp. 86–87.
9. Bruccoli Collection.
10. Chanler to MJB, 4 August 1959. See 'What Really Happened at the Pavillon Colombe,' *Fitzgerald Newsletter*, pp. 25–26.

11. PUL. *Scott/Max*, p. 104.
12. Enoch Pratt Free Library. *Letters,* p. 481.
13. *All the Sad Young Men*, pp. 1–2.
14. Lilly Library. *As Ever*, p. 77.
15. C. March 1925. PUL. *Correspondence*, p. 152.
16. Fitzgerald to Ober, received 14 October 1925. Lilly Library. *As Ever*, p. 81. Fitzgerald to Fowler, 6 November 1925. PUL. *Correspondence*, p. 181. See James L. W. West III and J. Barclay Inge, 'F. Scott Fitzgerald's Revisions o "The Rich Boy," ' *Proof 5* (Columbia, S.C.: Faust, 1977), pp. 127–46.
17. 4 March 1938. Lilly Library. *As Ever*, p. 357.
18. *All the Sad Young Men*, p. 56.
19. 18 February 1926, 116.
20. Vol. IV (October 1926), 776.
21. Vol. LXIII (May 1926), 348–49. *F. Scott Fitzgerald: The Critical Reception*, p. 272.
22. *The Crack-Up*, p. 308.
23. 'They Who Came to Paris to Write,' *New York Times Book Review* (6 August 1950), 1, 25.
24. *Tender Is the Night*, p. 332.
25. Gilbert Seldes, 'Uneasy Chameleons,' *The Saturday Evening Post*, CXCIX (1 January 1927), 21.
26. *Taps at Reveille*, p. 338.
27. Shirer, *20th-Century Journey* (New York: Simon & Schuster, 1976), pp. 231–33. In 'Scott in Thorns' Thurber states that he did not meet Fitzgerald until 1934; see *Reporter*, IV (17 April 1951), 35–38 and *Credos and Curios* (New York: Harper & Row, 1962), 153–63.
28. Retyped, PUL. *Letters*, p. 359.
29. 'Echoes of the Jazz Age,' *The Crack-Up*, p. 19.
30. *Tender Is the Nigh*ᵗ, p. 44.
31. 19 September 1925. PUL. *Correspondence*, p. 178.
32. Bruccoli Collection.
33. PUL. *Scott/Max*, p. 120.
34. *Notebooks*, #884. The second and third sections mention Governor Franklin D. Roosevelt, so parts of the poem were written after 1928.
35. Swinnerton, *Figures in the Foreground* (Garden City, N.Y.: Doubleday, 1964), p. 158.
36. P. 75.

Notes

37. PUL.
38. New York: Scribners, 1926, p. 119.
39. Before 30 December 1925. PUL. *Correspondence*, p. 183.
40. C. 1 March 1926. PUL. *Scott/Max*, p. 135.
41. *F. Scott Fitzgerald in His Own Time*, p. 149.
42. Received 3 May 1926. Lilly Library. *As Ever*, p. 89.
43. Wescott, 'The Moral of F. Scott Fitzgerald,' *The Crack-Up*, pp. 324–25.
44. 'Pasting It Together,' *The Crack-Up*, p. 79.
45. Kennedy Library. *Correspondence*, pp. 193–96. See Charles Mann and Philip Young, 'Fitzgerald's *Sun Also Rises*: Notes and Comment,' *Fitzgerald/Hemingway Annual 1970*, pp. 1–9.
46. PUL.
47. *Exiles from Paradise*, p. 112.
48. *A Moveable Feast*, p. 186, and *Ernest Hemingway: Selected Letters* (New York: Scribners, 1981), p. 160.
49. Sotheby Parke Bernet Sale #3966 (29 March 1977), #117.
50. June 1926. PUL. *Correspondence*, pp. 196–97.
51. Transcription of Calvin Tompkins's taped interview with the Murphys.
52. *Living Well Is the Best Revenge*, p. 42.
53. 20 August 1935. PUL. *Correspondence*, p. 424.
54. Fall 1926. Kennedy Library. *Scott and Ernest*, p. 52.
55. 22 October 1926. PUL. *Scott and Ernest*, p. 54.
56. Finney, *Feet First* (New York: Crown, 1971), p. 65.
57. MJB interview with Braggiotti, 16 February 1978.
58. Harry Salpeter, 'Fitzgerald Spenglerian,' *New York World* (3 April 1927), 12M. *F. Scott Fitzgerald in His Own Time*, p. 276.
59. MJB interview with Lois Moran Young, 17 August 1978.
60. Johns Hopkins Hospital records.
61. PUL. 'Lipstick' is printed in the *Fitzgerald/Hemingway Annual 1978*, pp. 3–35.
62. PUL. 'The Last of the Novelists,' p. 16.
63. 'Show Mr. and Mrs. F to Number —,' *The Crack-Up*, p. 47.
64. Inscription in *Men Without Women*. Enoch Pratt Free Library. *Correspondence*, p. 210.
65. 18 April 1927. Kennedy Library. *Scott and Ernest*, p. 60.
66. 27 January 1928. Lilly Library. *As Ever*, pp. 107–08.
67. 'Princeton,' *Afternoon of an Author*, p. 79.
68. To Ober, late October 1927. Lilly Library. *As Ever*, p. 102.

69. 'Football & Fitzgerald,' *Princeton Alumni Weekly*, LVI (9 March 1956), 11–12; Donald A. Yates, 'Fitzgerald and Football,' *Michigan Alumnus Quarterly Review*, LXIV (7 December 1957), 75–80.
70. Lois Moran Young to MJB, 20 March 1980.
71. 31 October 1927.
72. Scottie Fitzgerald Smith papers. *Correspondence*, pp. 214–15.
73. *Correspondence*, pp. 212–13, 217.
74. 'Echoes of the Jazz Age,' *The Crack-Up*, p. 21.
75. *Basil and Josephine*, p. 185.
76. *Notebooks*, #1061.
77. Lilly Library. *As Ever*, p. 113.
78. C. 21 July 1928. PUL. *Scott/Max*, p. 152.
79. PUL. *Correspondence*, p. 218.
80. New York: Harcourt, Brace, 1959, pp. 116–17.
81. André Le Vot, 'Fitzgerald in Paris'; André Chamson, 'Remarks'; Herbert Gorman, 'Glimpses of F. Scott Fitzgerald'; *Fitzgerald/Hemingway Annual 1973*, pp. 49–68, 69–76, 113–18.
82. Bruccoli Collection. *Correspondence*, p. 219.
83. Chamson, 'Remarks,' *Fitzgerald/Hemingway Annual 1973*, p. 72.
84. Richard H. Goldstone, *Thornton Wilder: An Intimate Portrait* (New York: Saturday Review/Dutton, 1975), p. 64.
85. July 1928. PUL. *Scott/Max*, p. 151.
86. October/November 1928. PUL. *Correspondence*, p. 221.
87. PUL. *Scott/Max*, p. 154.
88. Kennedy Library.
89. *Taps at Reveille*, p. 274.
90. *Ladies' Home Journal* (February 1929), 107; (March), 41; (April), 85; (May), 43; (June), 71; (July), 29; (September), 41; (November), 39; (December), 29.
91. PUL.
92. Diary of Geneva Porter. Buffalo & Erie County Public Library.
93. Received 8 October 1929. Lilly Library. *As Ever*, p. 146.
94. 8 April 1930. Lilly Library. *As Ever*, p. 166.
95. Postmarked 30 March 1936. PUL. *Letters*, pp. 425–26.
96. *Bits of Paradise*, p. 252.
97. To Scottie, 12 June 1940. PUL. *Letters*, p. 78.
98. To Dr. Mildred T. Squires, 8 March 1932.
99. Kennedy Library. *Correspondence*, pp. 225–28.
100. Kennedy Library. Carlos Baker, *Ernest Hemingway Critiques of*

Four Major Novels (New York: Scribners, 1962), p. 75.
101. *A Farewell to Arms* (New York: Scribners, 1929), p. 267.
102. Kennedy Library
103. To Charles Poore, Charles Hamilton Auction Number 56 (1972), #146.
104. Gingrich, 'Scott, Ernest and Whoever,' *Esquire*, LXVI (December 1966), 188. Graham, *The Real F. Scott Fitzgerald*, p. 120.
105. P. 191.
106. C. Summer 1930. PUL. *Correspondence*, p. 241.
107. *Zelda*, p. 153. Milford cites no source.
108. *Notebooks*, #2054.
109. Note, PUL.
110. *Ledger*, p. 183.
111. *Taps at Reveille*, p. 241.
112. *Bits of Paradise*, pp. 209–10.
113. *That Summer in Paris*, p. 214.
114. To Arthur Mizener, 4 January 1951. University of Maryland. *Ernest Hemingway: Selected Letters*, pp. 716–18.
115. 4 September 1929. Kennedy Library.
116. PUL. *Scott/Max*, p. 156.
117. Lilly Library. *As Ever*, p. 144.
118. Kennedy Library. *Scott and Ernest*, pp. 96–97.
119. 13 September 1929. PUL. *Ernest Hemingway: Selected Letters*, pp. 306–07.
120. 24 September 1929. Lilly Library. *As Ever*, p. 147.
121. C. 15 November 1929. PUL. *Scott/Max*, p. 158.
122. *Save Me the Waltz*, p. 124.
123. October 1929. PUL. *Ernest Hemingway: Selected Letters*, pp. 309–11.
124. *That Summer in Paris*, p. 243.
125. *Notebooks*, #62.
126. C. 11 December 1929. PUL. *Ernest Hemingway: Selected Letters*, pp. 312–14.
127. 'Auction – Model 1934,' *The Crack-Up*, p. 62.
128. *Notebooks*, #1769.
129. 'Echoes of the Jazz Age,' *The Crack-Up*, p. 21.
130. *The Crack-Up*, p. 69.
131. 'Show Mr. and Mrs. F. to Number —,' *The Crack-Up*, p. 51.
132. PUL.

133. *The Stories of F. Scott Fitzgerald*, p. 275.
134. Received 13 May 1930. Lilly Library. *As Ever*, p. 168.
135. PUL.
136. 8 June 1930. PUL.
137. Johns Hopkins Hospital.
138. C. Summer 1930. PUL. *Correspondence*, pp. 239–41.
139. C. Summer–Fall 1930. PUL. *Correspondence*, pp. 245–51.
140. PUL.
141. PUL.
142. PUL. *Scott/Max*, pp. 166–67.
143. C. Summer 1931. PUL. *Correspondence*, p. 243.
144. 1 December 1930. PUL. *Correspondence*, p. 255.
145. *Afternoon of an Author*, p. 161.
146. *Taps at Reveille*, p. 406.
147. *Ibid.*
148. *The Letters of Thomas Wolfe*, ed. Elizabeth Nowell (New York: Scribners, 1956), p. 263.
149. *Notebooks of Thomas Wolfe*, ed. Richard S. Kennedy and Paschal Reeves (Chapel Hill: University of North Carolina Press, 1970), II, p. 511.
150. C. 1 September 1930. PUL. *Scott/Max*, p. 168.
151. Elizabeth Nowell, *Thomas Wolfe* (Garden City: Doubleday, 1960), p. 238.
152. *Bijou O'Conor Remembers F. Scott Fitzgerald* (London: Audio Arts, 1975).
153. 29 January 1931. PUL.
154. Bruccoli, 'Epilogue,' *Esquire*, XCI (30 January 1979), 67. In 1962 Mrs. Goldstein gave Princeton a collection of Fitzgerald manuscripts relating to his *Esquire* work.
155. *The Apprentice Fiction of F. Scott Fitzgerald*, p. 178.
156. P. 267.
157. MJB Interview with Helen Hayes, 30 April 1978.
158. Spring/Summer 1931. PUL. *Correspondence*, p. 265.
159. To Ober. Received 11 November 1930. Lilly Library. *As Ever*, p. 172.
160. 12 November 1930. PUL. *Scott/Max*, p. 170.
161. *The Crack-Up*, pp. 13, 22.
162. *The Price Was High*, p. 381.
163. 'Show Mr. and Mrs. F to Number —,' *The Crack-Up*, pp. 52–53.
164. After August 1931. PUL. *Correspondence*, p. 267.

The Long Way Out

1. Bruccoli, 'Zelda Fitzgerald's Lost Stories,' *Fitzgerald/Hemingway Annual 1979*, p. 123.
2. *Bits of Paradise*, p. 339.
3. *Notebooks*, # 902.
4. Scrapbook. PUL. *Correspondence*, p. 282.
5. November 1931. PUL. *Correspondence*, p. 271.
6. *Exiles from Paradise*, pp. 175, 178.
7. Dwight Taylor, *Joy Ride* (New York: Putnam, 1959), pp. 234–50
8. 8 February 1936. Lilly Library. *As Ever*, p. 250.
9. C. 15 January 1932. PUL. *Scott/Max*, p. 173.
10. 10 March 1932. PUL.
11. PUL.
12. Johns Hopkins Hospital.
13. PUL. *Correspondence*, p. 289.
14. March 1932. PUL. *Correspondence*, pp. 288–89.
15. PUL. *Correspondence*, p. 290.
16. PUL. *Correspondence*, p. 290.
17. April 1932. PUL. *Correspondence*, pp. 290–91.
18. C. 30 April 1932. PUL. *Scott/Max*, pp. 173–74.
19. C. 14 May 1932. PUL. *Scott/Max*, p. 176.
20. PUL.
21. See color inserts in *The Romantic Egoists*.
22. Received 23 April 1932. Lilly Library. *As Ever*, p. 191.
23. MJB interview with Dr. Benjamin Baker, 30 October 1979.
24. *Save Me the Waltz*, p. 68.
25. Pp. 138–39.
26. P. 47.
27. P. 99.
28. PUL.
29. *The Edward and Catherine O'Donnell Collection of Modern Literature* (Rochester: University of Rochester Library, 1979), p. 16.
30. *Selected Letters of John O'Hara*, ed. Bruccoli (New York: Random House, 1978), p. 402.
31. John F. Kelly, 'Memories of Scott and Zelda,' *Pittsburgh Press Roto* (6 February 1983), 16, 18.
32. Thurber, 'Scott in Thorns,' *The Reporter*, IV (17 April 1951),

35–38 and *Credos and Curios* (New York: Harper & Row, 1962), 153-63.

33. Turnbull, 'Scott Fitzgerald at La Paix,' *The New Yorker*, XXXII (7 April 1956), 98–109. 'Further Notes on Fitzgerald at La Paix' (17 November 1956), 153–65. Turnbull's biography *Scott Fitzgerald* provides the fullest account of Fitzgerald at this time.

34. Bruccoli Collection. *Correspondence*, p. 305.

35. C. March 1933. Yale.

36. 11 March 1935. PUL. *Scott/Max*, pp. 218–19.

37. 18 April 1933. PUL.

38. Spring 1933. PUL. *Correspondence*, p. 311.

39. 'Sequence.' PUL.

40. *Scandalabra*, Act III, p. 3.

41. 1932. PUL.

42. *The Crack-Up*, p. 14.

43. *Notebooks*, #395.

44. 19 January 1933. PUL. *Scott/Max*, p. 177.

45. C. March 1933. Yale. *Letters*, p. 345.

46. Postmarked 17 August 1934. PUL. *Letters*, p. 417.

47. 'Hopkins Liberal Club to Sponsor Anti-War Meeting. F. Scott Fitzgerald Will Speak At Rally To-morrow Night.' Clipping, PUL.

48. Johns Hopkins Hospital. The text of this document has been transcribed from a dim microfilm. Punctuation has been provided, but no words have been altered or supplied.

49. PUL.

50. *Zelda*, p. 278.

51. *Selected Letters of John O'Hara*, pp. 75–76.

52. *Afternoon of an Author*, p. 132.

53. *Notebooks*, #1072.

54. To Bertha Wood Cozzens, 22 December 1940. PUL.

55. *The Crack-Up*, p. 33.

56. Perkins to Fitzgerald, 18 October 1933. PUL.

57. June 1930. PUL. *Letters*, p. 496.

58. 4 August 1933. PUL. *Scott/Max*, p. 180.

59 *The Romantic Egoists*, p. 192.

60. *The Crack-Up*, pp. 38, 39–40.

61. October 1933. PUL. *Correspondence*, p. 318.

62. *Selected Letters of John O'Hara*, p. 79.

63. 6 October 1933. PUL. *Scott/Max*, p. 185.

64. PUL. *Scott/Max*, p. 183.
65. P. 176.
66. P. 390.
67. P. 391.
68. Postmarked 12 March 1934. Yale. *Letters*, p. 346.
69. Bruccoli Collection. *Correspondence*, p. 344.
70. *New York Herald Tribune Books* (7 October 1934), VII, 17. Bruccoli, *The O'Hara Concern* (New York: Random House, 1975), p. 111.
71. Fitzgerald's annotated copy of the catalogue is fascimiled in *The Romantic Egoists*, p. 195.
72. Vol. XXIII (9 April 1934), 42, 44.
73. PUL. *Correspondence*, p. 341.
74. *Notebooks*, #1362.
75. PUL. *Scott/Max*, p. 220.
76. *Selected Letters of John O'Hara*, p. 266.
77. PUL. *Correspondence*, pp. 333–34.
78. PUL.
79. P. 17. *F. Scott Fitzgerald: The Critical Reception*, pp. 294–96.
80. *New York Times Book Review*, 7. *F. Scott Fitzgerald: The Critical Reception*, p. 305.
81. P. 15. *F. Scott Fitzgerald: The Critical Reception*, p. 312.
82. Pp. 105–06. *F. Scott Fitzgerald: The Critical Reception*, pp. 323–25.
83. MJB interview, 9 April 1980.
84. July 1935, 115–17. *F. Scott Fitzgerald: The Critical Reception*, pp. 331–32.
85. 12 April 1934, 23. *F. Scott Fitzgerald: The Critical Reception*, pp. 292–93.
86. 27 September 1934, 652.
87. Vol. III (December 1934), 316–19.
88. University of Tulsa Library.
89. Enoch Pratt Free Library. *Letters*, p. 510.
90. 13 August 1936. PUL. *Letters*, pp. 540–41.
91. 24 December 1938. PUL. *Scott/Max*, pp. 250–51.
92. PUL.
93. Bruccoli Collection. *Correspondence*, p. 426.
94. Kennedy Library. *Letters*, p. 307.
95. 30 April 1934. PUL.
96. PUL. *Ernest Hemingway: Selected Letters*, pp. 407–09.
97. Kennedy Library. *Letters*, pp. 308–10.

Notes

98. C. 1934. PUL. *Correspondence*, p. 398.
99. 15 August 1935. PUL. *Letters*, pp. 423–24.
100. 31 December 1935. PUL. *Correspondence*, p. 425.
101. Scrapbook. PUL.
102. PUL. *Scott/Max*, pp. 219–20.
103. Scrapbook. PUL. *The Romantic Egoists*, p. 201. *Ernest Hemingway: Selected Letters*, p. 483.
104. Scrapbook. PUL. *The Romantic Egoists*, p. 200.
105. March 1934. Scrapbook PUL. *Correspondence*, p. 332.
106. PUL.
107. Charles Marquis Warren.
108. PUL.
109. 21 May 1934. PUL. *Correspondence*, p. 364.
110. 31 May 1934. *Letters*, p. 513.
111. MJB interview with Garry Moore, 20 October 1979.
112. 26 April 1934. PUL. *Correspondence*, p. 356.
113. After 9 June. PUL. *Correspondence*, p. 367.
114. 13 June 1934. PUL. *Correspondence*, p. 368.

In the Darkest Hour

1. *Notebooks*, #1034.
2. 4 January 1939. PUL. *Scott/Max*, p. 254.
3. PUL.
4. 'The Count of Darkness,' *Redbook* LXV (June 1935), 21.
5. TS, PUL. *The Crack-Up*, p. 46.
6. *The Crack-Up*, p. 60.
7. *The Crack-Up*, pp. 67, 68. See *Notebooks*, #857, for the full text of the poem.
8. PUL.
9. 7 and 26 September 1934. PUL. *Letters*, pp. 386–87.
10. 15 and 21 May 1934. PUL. *Scott/Max*, pp. 195–200.
11. 24 August 1934. PUL. *Scott/Max*, p. 207.
12. *F. Scott Fitzgerald in His Own Time*, p. 156.
13. *Ibid.*, p. 236.
14. PUL. *Scott/Max*, p. 210.
15. 5 December. Lilly Library. *As Ever*, pp. 206–07.
16. This previously unpublished statement was made available by Quill & Brush bookshop.
17. 27 March 1935, 19. *F. Scott Fitzgerald: The Critical Reception*, p. 340.

18. *Selected Letters of John O'Hara*, pp. 432–33.
19. *Notebooks*, #462.
20. *F. Scott Fitzgerald in His Own Time*, p. 73.
21. Fitzgerald's notes for the story are in his *Notebooks*, #928.
22. *Notebooks*, #447.
23. Courtesy of Dr. Benjamin Baker.
24. Laura Guthrie Hearne, 'A Summer with F. Scott Fitzgerald,' *Esquire*, LXII (December 1964), 160–65, 232, 236, 237, 240, 242, 246, 250, 252, 254–58, 260.
25. *Letters*, pp. 529–30. Unlocated.
26. C. June 1935. PUL. *Correspondence*, pp. 413–15.
27. Received 2 July 1935. Lilly Library. *As Ever*, p. 221.
28. The program was broadcast on 3 October 1935. The script seems to have been printed for distribution to listeners, but no copy has been found. A typescript of the play is at PUL.
29. 25 April 1936. Lilly Library. *As Ever*, pp. 265–67.
30. *Notebooks*, #1598.
31. *The Armchair Esquire* (New York: Putnam, 1958), p. 93.
32. *The Crack-Up*, pp. 69, 72.
33. 'Handle with Care,' *The Crack-Up*, p. 84.
34. *Ibid.*, p. 311.
35. PUL. *Ernest Hemingway: Selected Letters*, pp. 427–29.
36. Lilly Library. *As Ever*, p. 239.
37. *Fitzgerald/Hemingway Annual 1976*, pp. 2–7.
38. 8 February 1936. Lilly Library. *As Ever*, p. 248.
39. 21 May 1936. Lilly Library. *As Ever*, p. 271.
40. 25 March, 26 March, 2 April 1936. PUL. *Scott/Max*, pp. 227–30.
41. 26 June 1936. PUL. *Correspondence*, p. 436.
42. The Historical Society of Pennsylvania.
43. Sotheby Parke Bernet Sale Number 4335 (9 April 1980), #153.
44. 21 May 1936. Lilly Library. *As Ever*, p. 271.
45. 15 September 1936. PUL. *Letters*, p. 541.
46. *The Price Was High*, p. 739.
47. 20 October 1936. PUL. *Letters*, p. 11.
48. *Afternoon of an Author*, p. 185.
49. *Ibid.*, p. 178.
50. *Esquire*, VI (August 1936), p. 200.
51. Kennedy Library. *Letters*, p. 311.
52. 'Scott, Ernest and Whoever,' *Esquire*, LXVI (December 1966), 187. Hemingway's letter to Fitzgerald has not been found.

53. *Max Perkins*, p. 305.
54. PUL. *Letters*, pp. 542–43.
55. PUL. *Scott/Max*, p. 231.
56. *F. Scott Fitzgerald in His Own Time*, p. 299.
57. Received 5 October 1936. Lilly Library. *As Ever*, p. 282.
58. 28 September 1936. Kennedy Library. *Correspondence*, p. 454.
59. Carlos Baker, *Hemingway: A Life Story* (New York: Scribners, 1969), p. 295.
60. 'The Education of Dorothy Richardson,' *Fitzgerald/Hemingway Annual 1979*, pp. 227–28.
61. PUL.
62. PUL. *Scott/Max*, pp. 233–34.
63. To Perkins, 26 October 1936; *Selected Letters of Marjorie Kinnan Rawlings*, ed. Gordon E. Bigelow and Laura V. Monti (Gainesville: University Presses of Florida, 1983), pp. 125–28. Rawlings's typed memo, titled 'Scott,' is at the University of Florida Libraries.
64. Yale University Library. *Fitzgerald/Hemingway Annual 1972*, pp. 39–41.
65. *The Crack-Up*, pp. 87, 90.
66. *The Stories of F. Scott Fitzgerald*, p. 449.
67. Lilly Library. *As Ever*, p. 314.
68. *Ibid.*, pp. 308–09.
69. 2 July 1937. *Ibid.*, p. 324.

The Last of the Novelists

1. 'Cling to reality, for any departure from a high pitch of reality at which Jews live leads to farce in which Christians live. Hollywood is a Jewish holiday, a gentiles tragedy.' Notes for *The Last Tycoon*. PUL. *The Last of the Novelists*, p. 146.
2. 6 July 1937. Lilly Library. *As Ever*, p. 325.
3. PUL. *Letters*, pp. 16–17.
4. Hellman, *An Unfinished Woman* (Boston and Toronto: Little, Brown, 1969), pp. 67–69; 'Martha Gellhorn: On Apocryphism,' *The Paris Review*, LXXIX (Spring 1981), 286–87.
5. Kennedy Library. *Correspondence*, p. 475.
6. *Notebooks*, #1915.
7. C. 26 July 1937. Bruccoli Collection. *As Ever*, p. 330.
8. PUL.

9. PUL. See Alan Margolies, 'F. Scott Fitzgerald's Prison Play,' *Papers of the Bibliographical Society of America*, LXVI (First Quarter 1972), 61–64.
10. 29 July 1940. Bruccoli Collection. *Letters*, p. 603.
11. PUL. *Correspondence*, p. 477.
12. July 1937. *Letters*, p. 552.
13. 26 July 1937. PUL. *The Letters of Thomas Wolfe*, pp. 641, 643.
14. Powell, 'Hollywood Canteen,' *Fitzgerald/Hemingway Annual 1971*, p. 77.
15. 23 April 1938. PUL. *Correspondence*, p. 498.
16. P. 26.
17. Bruccoli, 'Afterword,' *F. Scott Fitzgerald's Screenplay for Erich Maria Remarque's Three Comrades*, p. 258.
18. PUL.
19. PUL. *Letters*, pp. 563–64. Mankiewicz has stated that he did not receive this letter.
20. Jacques Bontemps and Richard Overstreet, 'Measure for Measure: Interviews with Joseph Mankiewicz,' *Cahiers de Cinema in English*, XVIII (February 1967), 31.
21. Winter 1938. PUL. *Letters*, p. 565.
22. 11 March 1938. PUL. *Letters*, pp. 427–28.
23. 4 March 1938. PUL. *Scott/Max*, p. 242.
24. PUL. *Correspondence*, p. 500.
25. *Beloved Infidel*, front endpapers.
26. 7 July 1938. PUL. *Letters*, pp. 32–33.
27. 9 March 1938. PUL. *Scott/Max*, p. 243.
28. 23 April 1938. PUL. *Scott/Max*, p. 245.
29. 24 May 1938. PUL. *Scott/Max*, p. 246.
30. 4 January 1939. PUL. *Scott/Max*, pp. 253–54.
31. *Notebooks*, #1889.
32. PUL. *Letters*, pp. 37–38.
33. Frances Kroll Ring, *Against the Current: As I Remember F. Scott Fitzgerald* (San Francisco: Ellis/Creative Arts, 1985), pp. 42–43.
34. *College of One*, p. 204.
35. 'Lest We Forget (France by Big Shots).' PUL. *Beloved Infidel*, p. 313.
36. Scottie Fitzgerald Smith to MJB.
37. From Leila Cook Barber, 28 November 1938. PUL.
38. 31 October 1939. PUL. *Letters*, p. 62.
39. 5 October 1940. Retyped, PUL. *Letters*, p. 96.

40. MJB interview with Frances Goodrich Hackett and Albert Hackett, 9 July 1980.
41. 18 July 1940. PUL. *Letters*, p. 85.
42. 29 July 1940. PUL. *Letters*, pp. 86–87.
43. Retyped, PUL. *Letters*, p. 101.
44. 19 February 1940. PUL. *Correspondence*, p. 527.
45. *The Real F. Scott Fitzgerald*, pp. 236–75.
46. *Ibid.*, p. 142.
47. To Berg, Dozier, and Allen. 23 February 1940. PUL. *Correspondence*, p. 582.
48. *Last Tycoon* notes. PUL.
49. 20 May 1940. PUL. *Scott/Max*, p. 261.
50. PUL. *Fitzgerald/Hemingway Annual 1977*, pp. 3–8.
51. To Margaret Turnbull, 13 November 1941. PUL.
52. John D. Hess, 'Wanger Blends Abruptness with Charm in Personality,' *The Dartmouth* (11 February 1939). *Fitzgerald/Hemingway Annual 1979*, pp. 35–36.
53. *Beloved Infidel*, p. 273.
54. Winter 1939. PUL. *Letters*, p. 48.
55. *Beloved Infidel*, p. 281.
56. 6 May 1939. PUL. *Letters*, p. 105.
57. 22 May 1939. PUL. *Scott/Max*, pp. 256–57.
58. 29 May 1939. Lilly Library. *As Ever*, pp. 388–90.
59. 21 June 1939. Lilly Library. *As Ever*, pp. 393–94.
60. *Notebooks*, #885.
61. PUL. *Correspondence*, pp. 534–35.
62. Lilly Library. *As Ever*, p. 400.
63. 19 December 1939. PUL. *Scott/Max*, p. 160.
64. Lilly Library. *As Ever*, pp. 402–03.
65. *Ibid.*, p. 408.
66. July/August 1939. *Letters*, p. 588.
67. PUL. *Letters*, p. 59.
68. C. July 1939. PUL. *Letters*, p. 58.
69. 4 August 1939. PUL. *Letters*, p. 108.
70. PUL. *Correspondence*, pp. 545–50.
71. PUL. *Correspondence*, p. 615.
72. 19 September 1936. PUL. *Correspondence*, pp. 451–52.
73. PUL.
74. PUL. *Notebooks*, #2001.
75. *The Last Tycoon*, p. 20.

76. *The Last Tycoon* notes. PUL. *Last of the Novelists*, pp. 6–7.
77. 10 October 1939. PUL. *Correspondence*, p. 550.
78. To Littauer, 20 October 1939. PUL. *Last of the Novelists*, p. 34.
79. 20 October 1939. PUL. *Scott/Max*, p. 258.
80. *The Last Tycoon* notes. PUL.
81. 21 September 1939. Scottie Fitzgerald Smith papers. *As Ever*, p. 415.
82. PUL. *Correspondence*, p. 561.
83. 28 November 1938. NYPL. *Correspondence*, p. 562.
84. Typed draft. PUL. *Correspondence*, p. 562.
85. 7 February 1940. PUL. *Letters*, p. 599.
86. 18 May 1940. PUL. *Letters*, pp. 117–18.
87. *Notebooks*, #1765.
88. *The Stories of F. Scott Fitzgerald*, p. 472.
89. 6 May 1940. PUL. *Correspondence*, p. 595.
90. Gingrich, 'Introduction,' *The Pat Hobby Stories*, pp. ix–xxiii.
91. *Bits of Paradise*, p. 383.
92. Note on typescript. PUL.
93. To MJB, 20 February 1980.
94. PUL.
95. *The Last Tycoon* notes. PUL. *Last of the Novelists*, p. 89.
96. Pp. 77, 98.
97. *Selected Letters of John O'Hara*, p. 224.
98. *Ibid.*, pp. 428–29.
99. 'Certain Aspects,' *The New Republic*, CIV (3 March 1941), 311. *'An Artist Is His Own Fault,'* ed. Bruccoli (Carbondale and Edwardsville: Southern Illinois University Press, 1977), p. 137.
100. Her lecture is included in *College of One*, pp. 165–90. Wilkerson's editorial appeared on 21 November 1939, p. 1.
101. 'Introduction,' *The Portable F. Scott Fitzgerald*, p.x.
102. 6 October 1939. PUL. *Letters*, p. 110.
103. PUL. *Zelda*, p. 333.
104. PUL. *Correspondence*, pp. 558–59.
105. 6 April 1940. PUL.
106. PUL. *Scott/Max*, p. 261.
107. *Virginia Quarterly Review*, XIII (Winter 1937), 106–21.
108. 25 November 1940. Yale. *Letters*, p. 349.
109. 20 May 1940. PUL. *Scott/Max*, p. 261.
110. 1 February 1940. PUL. *Letters*, pp. 596–98.
111. PUL.

112. PUL.
113. PUL.
114. 12 July 1940. PUL. *Letters*, p. 84.
115. 2 November 1940. PUL. *Letters*, p. 97.
116. 12 June 1940. PUL. *Letters*, p. 79.
117. PUL.
118. Dr. William Ober to MJB, 7 June 1991.
119. PUL. *Letters*, pp. 126–31.
120. *Notebooks*, #2068.
121. Bruccoli Collection.
122. *Notebooks*, #2066.
123. PUL. *Letters*, p. 312.
124. Dr. William Ober to MJB, 7 June 1991.
125. *Letters*, p. 132.
126. The Publishers' Trade List Annual 1941 lists *Taps at Reveille*, *Tender Is the Night*, *All the Sad Young Men*, *The Great Gatsby*, *Tales of the Jazz Age*, *This Side of Paradise*, and *Flappers and Philosophers* as in print in August 1941; but *Paradise* was in fact out of print.
127. *Selected Letters of John O'Hara*, p. 279.
128. Lilly Library. *As Ever*, illustrations following p. 170.
129. 28 December 1940. PUL.
130. Biggs Papers.
131. Schulberg to MJB, 6 August 1980.
132. PUL.
133. 29 January 1941. PUL.
134. Wilson, 'Foreword,' *The Last Tycoon*, p. ix.
135. *Ibid.*, p. x.
136. *New York Times Book Review* (9 November 1941), 1. *F. Scott Fitzgerald: The Critical Reception*, p. 368.
137. *The New Republic*, CVI (9 February 1942), 211–12. *F. Scott Fitzgerald: The Critical Reception*, pp. 381–82.
138. 'A Note on Fitzgerald,' *The Crack-Up*, p. 343.
139. 15 November 1941. PUL. *Ernest Hemingway: Selected Letters*, pp. 527–29.
140. *Notebooks*, #2037.
141. *Saturday Review of Literature*, XXIV (6 December 1941), 10. *F. Scott Fitzgerald: The Critical Reception*, pp. 375–76.
142. *The Liberal Imagination*, p. 244.
143. 'Introduction,' p. xiv.
144. PUL. *Fitzgerald/Hemingway Annual 1974*, pp. 2–7.

ZELDA FITZGERALD'S TRIBUTE TO F. SCOTT FITZGERALD

This tribute was probably intended for the group of posthumous recollections and assessments of Fitzgerald published in *The New Republic* in 1941. It was not used, and first appeared in the *Fitzgerald/Hemingway Annual 1974*. Spelling and punctuation have been corrected.

During the last world war, many cosmic destinies were strung together on the tone of tragic gallantry and courage to the purpose of binding within tradition the dramatic and pictorial tempos to which the age had fallen heir. Habits of men at this time included shivering to death in boxcars over the lost frontiers of lonely foreign provinces, drowning in mud, and smothering in submarines. Many had learned too much of painful and even exotic ways to die so that life presented itself by contrast in less agonizing, if more immutable, terms than before the trouble in Europe.

This era assisted at the nursing of a badly shell-shocked logos back to some semblance of tenability on the dreary and dusty sun parlors of châteaux converted to convalescent hospitals and entered a failing social structure from personal necessities of survival.

A few facetious gestures: dancing with the dead at Cambrai, the painting of the Portughese leavened the four-year spectacle and diverted some of the spiritual casualties from despair to bitterness – perhaps the easiest to bear.

When nobody could think up any more mathematical formulas for destruction and no further ways for forwarding the plot, the war was declared to be a political inconvenience, and ended. Through the disorientations resultant from many distrusted and uncondoned experiences the soldiers looked toward home as the right of a long and hard-earned holiday. People that had been spared active participation in the gala debacle converted themselves into a grand pleasure chorus as effectively as possible and dedicated the decade to reconstituting the shattered illusions of those who had served in France with, perhaps, more verve and courage than judgment.

The United States greeted the returning young men with appropriate tragic and ecstatic pathos, and compensatory dramatics, but still the erstwhile doughboys languished, and weren't quite able to take up the thread on the same attenuate pitch as before.

It was past time for whatever had been scheduled to have happened and people were worn out with long abeyant attendance.

The prophet destined to elucidate and catalogue these pregnant and precarious circumstances was F. Scott Fitzgerald. The times exacted a dramatization compelling enough to save its protagonists from sleep-walking over the proscenium in the general doesn't-matter suasion of the letdown; and splendidly tragic enough to turn the barbarism of recent war experiences into drama. Fitzgerald was the first and always the most indicative of authors to persuade the desperate latent flare of these souls so tolerantly and self-abnegatively pursuing policies of *qui en-faire* to attitudes of a better-mastered Olympian regret. He endowed those years that might have been so garishly reckless with the dignity of his bright indicative scene, and buoyed the desperation of a bitter day with the spontaneity of his appreciation.

708

Fitzgerald's heroines were audacious and ingenuous and his heroes were fabulous strangers from lands of uncharted promise. His tragedies were hearts at bay to the inexorable exigence of a day whose formulas no longer worked and whose ritual had dwindled to less of drama than its guignol. His pathos was the pressure of inescapable necessities over the keeping of a faith. His poignancy was the perishing of lovely things and people on the jagged edges of truncate spiritual purpose. These were the themes that transcended the crassness and bitterness which so easily betrays the ironic pen and leads the conviction of tragedy too frequently astray in the briars of scathing invective.

Fitzgerald seized, from the nebulous necessities of an incubating civilization, the essence of a girl able to survive the new, and less forbearing, dramas and presented in poetic harmonies the tragically gallant stoicism so indispensable to traversing that troubled and turbulent epoch between world wars.

As the era is absorbed by its category and lost in its platonic sources, one remembers romantically the figure who so ingratiatingly reconciled his readers to the diminution of individuality and rendered more tangible those movements which he affectionately and indulgently humanized: 'youth movements, sufferage drives, temperance objectives,' and many no-matter-how-dearly-bought subscriptions to any dominant idea which carried the promise of salvation by rote.

As promissorily as the least tractable wellings of the soul are curbed to the poet's pentameter, as surely as the most unique of cadets is lost on the line of march, so does each generation yield to the thematic persuasions of the day. The meter being waltz time which moves nostalgic twilights to their rendezvous, the world believes again in sentiment and turns to fairy tale; whereas those years haunted by the more aggressive sadnesses of march time produce a more dynamic, tragic spiritual compensation. Thus the manners and aspirations that were not too long ago recut and polished in the staccato relevance of *This Side of Paradise* and *The Beautiful and Damned* have been able to defend themselves with a better-perfected hardihood and by means of a faith in *technique* from the heartbreak and subsequent ruthless purpose of the 1920s.

Fitzgerald's books were the first of their kind and the most indicative. If his people didn't have a good time, or things come out well at the end, the scene of their activity was always the arena of some new philosophic offensive, and what they did was allied with many salient projects of the era. The plush hush of the hotel lobby and the gala grandeur of the theater porte-chochère; fumes of orchidaceous elevators whirring to plaintive deaths the gilded aspirations of a valiant and protesting age, taxis slumberously afloat on deep summer nights –

Such Fitzgerald made into many tragic tales; sagas of people compelling life into some more commensurate and compassionate measure. His meter was bitter, and ironic and spectacular and inviting: so was life. There wasn't much other life during those times than to what his pen paid the tribute of poetic tragic glamour and offered the reconciliation of the familiarities of tragedy.

Rest in peace.

INDEX

711

Index

Eastman, Max, 278
"Echoes of the Jazz Age," 153, 368–369, 407
Edison, Thomas A., 526
"Editorial on Youth" (Fitzgerald), 304
"Ego Dominus Tuus," 435n
Egorova, Lubov, 280, 309, 317, 318, 335, 341, 355, 356, 358
Eisenhower, Dwight D., 96
"Elavo," 31
Eliot. T. S., 242, 256, 271n, 404
Elizabethan Dramatic Club, St. Paul, 34, 37, 44, 59
"Ellerslie" Delaware, 303, 308, 314, 317, 349, 354, 385
Ellingson, Dorothy, 281
Ellis, Walker, 53, 61, 281
"Emotional Bankruptcy," 342, 369
Encyclopaedia Britannica, 229, 298
"The End of Hate," 541, 574
Engalitcheff, Val, 246n, 352
Epstein, Julius J., 575
Epstein, Philip G., 575
Esquire (magazine), 7, 435, 503, 515, 557
  FSF's articles and stories published in, 457–459, 462, 464, 467n, 471, 476, 483, 485, 486, 492, 524, 544, 559, 561, 566
  FSF's unfinished screenplay published in, 517n
  Hemingway's contributions to, 436, 457, 486
Ethan Frome (Wharton), 178
Eton (school), 42
"Eulogy on the Flapper," 193
Evarts, Hal G., 126n
"The Eve of St. Agnes" (Keats), 82
Everything Happens at Night (movie), 577
The Evil Eye (Wilson), 65–66, 69, 72
Exeter (school), 50

Faber & Gwyer (later Faber & Faber), 271n
Fadiman, Clifton, 433
Fallon, Father Michael, 20
"Family Bus," 419
"Family in the Wind," 386, 387, 464
Famous Players-Lasky, 201, 209, 214, 288
Famous Story, 288
"Fantasy in Black," 387
A Farewell to Arms (Hemingway), 331, 405
  FSF's criticism of, 320–324, 444
The Far Side of Paradise (Mizener), 268n, 289n
"Fate in Her Hands," 467
Faulkner, William, 125, 127, 154, 217, 335, 434, 464, 502n
Fay, Father Cyril Sigourney Webster, 42, 58, 83, 97, 266, 325
  death of, 109–110
  during World War I, 75–77
  Monsignor Darcy based on, 40, 68, 143, 146
  poem for FSF, 93–94
"The Feather Fan" (screenplay), 532–533
Ferris, Walter, 505
Fie! Fie! Fi-Fi! (play), 53, 60, 61, 281
Fields, Lew, 204
Fields, W. C., 574
"The Fiend," 459, 464

Fiesta of San Fermin, Pamplona, 265, 294
The Fifth Column and the First Forty-Nine Stories (Hemingway), 488
"Fifty Grand" (Hemingway), 285
Film Guild, 208
"Financing Finnegan," 492, 543
Finch, Jack, 32, 34
Finch family, 32
Findley, Ruth, 351
Finnegan's Wake (Joyce), 311
Finney, Ben, 297–298, 395, 400
Finney, Eben, 404, 476, 490
Finney, Margaret (Peaches), 404, 475, 490, 525
Firestone, Harvey, 166, 352
First and Last (Lardner), 423
"First Blood," 341, 464
Fitzgerald, Annabel (FSF's sister), 24, 26, 29
  birth of, 18
  FSF's relationship with, 73–74, 177, 404
  instructions to improve her image and popularity, 73–74
  marriage, 404
Fitzgerald, Cecilia Ashton Scott (FSF's paternal grandmother), 12
Fitzgerald, Edward (FSF's father), 5, 7n, 32, 151, 199, 483, 583
  correspondence with FSF, 29
  death of, 365–366
  death of three children, 13, 18, 366
  drinking by, 215–219
  family history, 12–13, 44
  literary efforts, 25
  marriage, 13
  religion and, 19
  Scottie Fitzgerald and, 299
  unsuccessful career of, 13, 16, 20–21, 23, 24–25, 132, 177
  ZF and, 177
Fitzgerald, Frances Scott (Scottie, daughter)
  advice from FSF, 141, 142, 530–531
  articles by, 490
  at Ethel Walker School, 484, 492
  at Vassar, 526, 527, 529, 544–545, 556, 577, 584
  birth of, 6, 185, 352
  childhood and adolescence of, 187, 203, 204, 215, 229, 274, 299, 305, 346, 349, 365, 370, 382, 476
  correspondence with FSF, 54, 67, 78, 180, 307–308, 484, 500–501, 519–531 *passim*, 539, 544–545, 557, 577
  "How Would I grade my Knowledge at 40," 489
  on Keats, 81–82
  FSF's death and, 3, 4, 583, 583–584
  FSF's visits from Hollywood, 511, 517
  Gwen stories based on, 474
  in Hollywood, 509, 521, 525
  relationship with FSF, 274–275, 307–308, 362, 365, 366, 379, 387, 403, 404, 406, 456, 467, 475, 484, 488, 509, 519–531 *passim*, 577
  Sheila Graham and, 509, 519–520
  tea dance for, 490
  the Murphys and, 279

715

Index

Index

Index

722

Index

Index

726

Index

Index

Sabatini, Rafael, 256n
Safety First (Biggs and Bohmfalk), 76, 77
The Sailor's Return (Garnett), 437n–438n
St. John Evangelist Episcopal Church, St. Paul, 52
St. Mary's Church, Rockville, Maryland, 366, 583, 587
St. Nicholas Magazine, 20, 31
St. Paul Academy, 26–27, 29–30, 35, 50, 116
St. Paul Academy Now and Then, 27, 29–30, 32
St. Paul Daily Dirge, 187
St. Paul Daily News, 177, 187, 195, 211
St. Paul Seminary, 116
St. Paul Women's City Club, 177
St. Paul Y.W.C.A., 44, 59
Saint's Progress (Galsworthy), 178
Salies de Béarn (spa), France, 286, 354
Sallust, 105
Salt (Norris), 58, 189, 250
Salt, Waldo, 511
San Carlo Opera ballet, 331
San Francisco Chronicle, 435
Saturday Evening Post, 25n, 111n, 125, 171, 197, 244, 503, 518, 541
   FSF's articles for, 420
   FSF's stories published in
      from 1920–29, 124, 126, 127, 129–130, 132, 165–166, 185–186, 221–222, 224, 230, 245, 271, 283, 305–306, 310, 326–329, 334, 341, 343–344
      from 1930–37, 361–362, 369, 375–376, 386–387, 408, 419, 457, 459, 462, 471, 472, 474, 480–481, 486
      the last, 514
   FSF's stories rejected by, 271, 378, 467, 474, 492, 559
   serial rights to the *Last Tycoon* rejec, 557–558
   series stories in, 310n
   See also Lorimer, George Horace
Saturday Review of Literature, 256, 433
Satyricon (Petronius), 245
Saunders, John Monk, 449n, 505
Save Me the Waltz (Fitzgerald), 99, 103, 390–391, 482
   FSF's reaction to, 380–384, 386
   Jozan affair and, 232, 380
   Maxwell Perkins and, 379–384
   sales of, 389
   ZF's ballet training describ, 335–336, 380
Sayre, Anthony (ZF's brother), 104, 346
Sayre, Anthony D. (ZF's father), 102, 107, 151, 185, 280, 375, 390
   career of, 104–105
   death of, 377, 380
   nervous breakdown suffered by, 105, 346
   visit with Fitzgeralds, 168
   ZF's breakdown and, 361, 366
Sayre, Clothilde. *See* Palmer, Clothilde Sayre
Sayre, Daniel (ZF's grandfather), 105
Sayre, Marjorie. *See* Brinson, Marjorie Sayre
Sayre, Minnie Machen (ZF's mother), 102, 103, 107, 151, 185, 375, 390, 520, 522
   FSF's letter to, 506
   mother's death, 105, 346

   visit with the Fitzgeralds, 168
   ZF's mental problems and, 361, 366, 570, 571
   ZF's release from Highland clinic and, 570
Sayre, Musidora Morgan (ZF's grandmother), 105
Sayre, Rosalind. *See* Smith, Rosalind Sayre
Sayre, Zelda. *See* Fitzgerald, Zelda Sayre
Scandalabra (ZF), 407, 418
"The Scandal Detectives," 28, 310, 464
Scaramouche (movie), 333
Schopenhauer, Arthur, 87, 100
Schulberg, B.P., 454
Schulberg, Budd, 566, 575, 584
   at Dartmouth with FSF, 537
   collaborates with FSF on *Winter Carnival*, 537–538
Schulberg, Victoria, 575
Schurmeier, Gustave (Bobbie), 27, 73
Schwab's drugstore, Hollywood, 579
Scott, Walter, 21, 31
Scott family, 12, 26
Scottish Chiefs (Porter), 21
Screen Writers Guild, 508, 509n, 535
Scribner, Arthur, 179
Scribner, Charles, 118, 178, 499
   FSF's correspondence with, 169
   The Great Gatsby and, 247, 249
Scribner, Charles, Jr., 150, 540
Scribner's Magazine, 123, 128, 285, 314, 320, 359, 367, 375–376, 378, 401, 421, 426
Scribner's Sons, Charles, 20, 114, 123, 174, 289, 363, 480, 490, 540
   All the Sad Young Men and, 272
   donation of Fitzgerald Archives to Princeton, 588
   Flappers and Philosophers and, 170
   FSF's role in recommending authors for, 178, 207, 210–211, 243, 264, 285, 286, 302, 312, 330, 340
   loans to FSF, 158, 256, 305, 341, 389, 419, 421, 460, 462, 483, 484, 499, 500, 583
   posthumous sales of FSF's works by, 588
   Save Me the Waltz and, 381–382, 389
   Tales of the Jazz Age and, 198
   Tender Is the Night and, 402, 421, 427, 431, 439, 581
   The Beautiful and the Damned and, 188, 189–190, 193–194
   The Great Gatsby and, 236, 255–256, 581
   "The Romantic Egotist" submitted to, 94n, 96n, 97, 99–100
   The Vegetable and, 209
   This Side of Paradise and, 100, 117–119, 122, 123, 128, 130, 133, 137, 150
      out of print, 524
      publicity for, 161–162
      sales of, 137, 158–159
   See also Perkins, Maxwell E.
Scrutiny, 435
Sedgwick, Anne Douglas, 256n
Seldes, Gilbert, 237, 242, 256, 331, 353, 423, 435, 449, 480, 584, 585
Sélect café, Paris, 276
Selznick, David O., 197, 531

728

Index

Index

Index

731